TIM COOK

FIGHT TO THE FINISH

CANADIANS IN THE SECOND WORLD WAR 1944–1945

VOLUME TWO

ALLEN
LANE

ALLEN LANE

an imprint of Penguin Canada Books Inc., a Penguin Random House Company

Published by the Penguin Group

Penguin Canada Books Inc., 320 Front Street West, Suite 1400, Toronto, Ontario, Canada M5V 3B6

Penguin Group (USA) LLC, 375 Hudson Street, New York, New York 10014, U.S.A.

Penguin Books Ltd, 80 Strand, London WC2R 0RL, England

Penguin Ireland, 25 St Stephen's Green, Dublin 2, Ireland (a division of Penguin Books Ltd)

Penguin Group (Australia), 707 Collins Street, Melbourne, Victoria 3008, Australia
(a division of Pearson Australia Group Pty Ltd)

Penguin Books India Pvt Ltd, 11 Community Centre, Panchsheel Park, New Delhi – 110 017, India

Penguin Group (NZ), 67 Apollo Drive, Rosedale, Auckland 0632, New Zealand
(a division of Pearson New Zealand Ltd)

Penguin Books (South Africa) (Pty) Ltd, 24 Sturdee Avenue, Rosebank, Johannesburg 2196, South Africa

Penguin Books Ltd, Registered Offices: 80 Strand, London WC2R 0RL, England

First published 2015

1 2 3 4 5 6 7 8 9 10   (RRD)

Copyright © Tim Cook, 2015
Maps copyright © Penguin Random House Canada Ltd., 2015

Manufactured in the U.S.A.

Library and Archives Canada Cataloguing in Publication

Cook, Tim, 1971-, author
Fight to the finish : Canadians in the Second World War,
1944-1945 / Tim Cook.

Volume two. First volume has title: The necessary war.
Includes bibliographical references and index.
ISBN 978-0-670-06768-8 (bound)

1. World War, 1939-1945—Canada. 2. Canada. Canadian
Army—History—World War, 1939-1945. 3. World War, 1939-1945—Battlefields.
4. World War, 1939-1945—Campaigns. I. Title.

D768.15.C645 2015   940.54'1271   C2015-900956-1

eBook ISBN 978-0-14-319612-9

Visit the Penguin Canada website at **www.penguin.ca**

Special and corporate bulk purchase rates available;
please see **www.penguin.ca/corporatesales** or call 1-800-810-3104.

＊

For Flight-Lieutenant Gordon Francis Cook (1914–1974)
and Dr. Terry Gordon Cook (1947–2014)

CONTENTS

INTRODUCTION

At Bény-sur-Mer, in France, the Commonwealth War Graves Commission cemetery contains 2,048 gravestones. All but five are Canadians. The cemetery is at the top of a gentle rising hill with a view of Juno Beach, where the Canadians came ashore on June 6, 1944. Among the immaculate green Normandy lawns, row upon row of uniform, white gravestones lie throughout the tranquil space. The symmetrical lines of graves stretch out, creating an optical illusion of sorts, as they seem to shimmer and at times merge, to give the impression of a wall of stone. Above the sixteen sections of gravestones stands the Cross of Sacrifice, providing a focal point for the eye even as the trees cluster in places and provide a shroud from the sounds of the outside world. This is sacred land for Canada, and one of hundreds of Commonwealth cemeteries where more than 100,000 Canadian service personnel are interred.[1]

The fallen came from big cities like Montreal and Vancouver, as well as a host of counties, villages, and farming communities such as Yorkton, Owen Sound, Cordova Mines, and Arnprior. The surnames on the gravestones range from Smith, Macdonald, Roy, and Tremblay to Husak, Cohen, Radoy, and Kachor. This is Canada embodied thousands of kilometres from home.

There are no fewer than twelve pairs of brothers at Bény-sur-Mer. Six families had to suffer through the death of two sons on the same day of battle. The grief of such unthinkable losses still emanates like heat from the matching headstones. The Westlake family of Toronto lost one son on June 7, and then two more boys within the week. The official missives would have arrived one shattering blow after another. Another family, the Wagners of Teeterville, Ontario, had a son buried at Bény-sur-Mer, another on the road to Falaise fewer than 50 kilometres away, and a third in Groesbeek Canadian War Cemetery in the Netherlands.[2] It was the route of Canadian battles, soaked in blood and tears. And it did not stop with Northwest Europe. Families across Canada saw their sons buried in Sicily and Italy, in the jungles of Burma and the rocky ground of Hong Kong, next to the fiery remains of bombers along the route from Britain to Germany, and in the dark depths of the Atlantic.

As in all Commonwealth War Graves cemeteries, the Canadian headstones in Bény-sur-Mer display a maple leaf emblem, except for two, which also feature the Star of David, for the Jewish-Canadian soldiers buried there.[3] Almost all stones are inscribed with the regimental number (for non-commissioned officers and the rank

The Commonwealth War Graves Commission cemetery at Bény-sur-Mer in France, near Juno Beach, contains the graves of 2,043 Canadians who died during the Second World War.

and file) that was worn on an ID tag around the neck along with rank, name, unit, date of death, and, in most cases, age at death. Nineteen of the headstones are for the unknown—"A Soldier of the 1939–1945 War; A Canadian Regiment, Known Unto God." Standing before those headstones and contemplating the events of seventy years ago, one quietly shudders at the thought of bodies so badly burned or dismembered that there was no piece that could be used to identify the man.

The most powerful symbols of grief are the short epitaphs from parents, wives, and children etched on the stones. These mournful farewells draw from scripture, hymn, songs, literature, and raw sentiment.

To the world he was just another one. To us, he was our darling son.
Private Lawrence Burton Perkins, Stormont, Dundas and Glengarry Highlanders, 7.6.44 (age 26)

Nous l'avons donné a Dieu pour le salut de France. Son pére et sa mére. Canada.
(We gave him to God for the salvation of France. His father and mother. Canada.)
Private Leo Joseph Quevillon, Algonquin Regiment, 31.7.44 (age 21)

Life will never be the same now that we have lost you.
Ever lovingly remembered wife, son, mom and sister.
Rifleman Sidney Stephen Ryan, Queen's Own Rifles of Canada, 6.6.44 (age 27)

He died to save us all. In our hearts he'll always be.
Never forgotten by his wife and five children.
Private Soloman Kline, Canadian Scottish Regiment, 8.7.44 (age 38)

I have only your memory, Dear husband, to remember my whole life through.
Rifleman George Alexander, Royal Winnipeg Regiment, 16.7.44 (age 21)

Every stone and sentence is a forceful reminder of Canadians taken before their time. There would eventually be close to 45,000 of those headstones to mark Canadians who fought for freedom and liberty, to save the oppressed and occupied, and to defeat the evil of Fascism and Nazism. Canadian war hero Sydney Radley-Walters of the

Sherbrooke Fusilier wrote eloquently of his comrades and their families: "Many a home across the country had been darkened by these tragic losses and as time passes these losses suffered in WW 2 are little understood by those who have inherited the gift of peace. A quiet walk through the Cemetery at Bény-sur-Mer soon brings time to a halt and the words inscribed on the gravestones tells it all, and fills one with sorrow and painful recollections but also tremendous pride. Here is a tiny part of Canada where Canadians lie buried side by side regardless of rank, religion, or colour."[4] Notwithstanding what has been remembered or forgotten, those Canadian soldiers, sailors, airmen, nurses, and other service personnel who served during the Second World War understood that it was a war of necessity.

THE SECOND WORLD WAR was a war to prevent the total domination of Europe by Adolf Hitler and his Nazi Third Reich. The battles and campaigns fought by the Fascist, Communist, and democratic nations spanned the globe and unleashed ferocity, barbarism, and mass murder. German dictator Adolf Hitler had started the war to expand Germany's power, prestige, and geographic boundaries after the humiliating loss during the Great War of 1914 to 1918. War was also a means for Hitler, with his heinous Nazi ideology, to carry out his plan of subjugating the Slavic people of Eastern Europe and of removing and then annihilating the Jewish people of the same lands. The invasion of Poland on September 1, 1939, provoked the European war, although Hitler had already moved against his European neighbours before that, and Japan was engaged in a vicious struggle with China from 1937. Despite France and Britain having desperately tried to avoid war with Hitler in the late 1930s through appeasement and the sacrifice of democratic nations, actions that represented the will of most of their citizens, the move against Poland revealed that Hitler would never be satisfied and that he would continue to seek new campaigns to conquer and enslave millions.

Hitler's war dragged in almost all of Europe, and then much of the world; in the Pacific, Japan and the United States fought their own series of naval, aviation, and land campaigns from December 1941. In all theatres of war, clashing armies, navies, and air forces made targets of civilians, but it was only Nazi Germany that carefully crafted an official policy of genocide. With entire nations harnessed for prolonged war and their citizens indoctrinated into believing that only victory rather than negotiated settlement was a suitable outcome, the Second World War rapidly became a total war of domination, where defeat meant the destruction of one's society and way of life. The stakes were never higher and the nations of the world proved, in almost all cases, willing to accept millions of casualties and untold anguish in the pursuit of victory or the staving off of defeat.

Germany's victory over France in June 1940 shook Great Britain and the Commonwealth, and there was more misfortune when Fascist Italy, under the leadership of Benito Mussolini, joined its Nazi allies to pick through the spoils of war. The Battle of Britain in late summer and fall of 1940 inflicted the first reversal on the Germans in the war, and then the British people withstood the sustained bombardment of the Blitz that pummelled their cities until May 1941. Hitler had hoped that the British people would fold in the face of his bombers—which up to that point had unleashed the worst onslaughts of aerial bombing in human history—but they were made of stern stuff. Nonetheless, some 43,384 British people were killed and 52,370 seriously wounded and maimed.[5] "We can take it," was the rallying cry, and British citizens proved they could. Hitler would have kept ratcheting up the killing except that the Führer was distracted by his new war in the east against the Soviets in June 1941.

Predating the Blitz, and rising in intensity throughout 1940, the Battle of the Atlantic saw Hitler's U-boats seek to cut the lifeline from North America to Britain by sinking merchant ships during their ocean crossing. The Royal Canadian Navy's protection of the merchant ships carrying food, supplies, munitions, and all manner of war materiel meant living to fight another day. When Japan attacked the United States at Pearl Harbor on December 7, 1941, the American giant was dragged fully into the conflict, although Hitler's declaration of war on the United States a few days later allowed President Franklin Roosevelt to ensure that it would be a two-front war against Germany and Japan. The weak Allied positions in the Far East were rapidly overrun by the Japanese forces, who trounced the decrepit, myopic, and poorly led British and American defenders. Close to 2,000 Canadian soldiers were caught up in the Japanese assault, fighting in the hopeless defence of the British colony of Hong Kong. In seventeen days of battle, 290 Canadians were killed and 493 wounded before surrendering on Christmas Day 1941. The survivors faced unimaginable horrors in the Japanese prisoner-of-war camps. Over the next four years, 264 Canadians died in captivity through neglect, systemic malnutrition, and outright murder by their cruel Japanese overlords.

The German forces that invaded the Soviet Union in June 1941 had seemed destined for another rapid victory. Hitler had harboured a lifelong hatred of Communism and of the Slavic people of Eastern Europe, and he planned to crush the Soviet Union in an ambitious campaign. The first weeks and months of the German invasion staggered the Soviets and appeared to portend a rapid collapse, but they survived to keep fighting even as millions were killed and captured. Soviet dictator Joseph Stalin rallied his battered nation and his forces stopped the invading Wehrmacht at the gates of Moscow in December 1941. Thereafter, snow and ice ravaged the Germans, although most survived to fight into 1942. The Soviets were again hounded relentlessly and defeated at almost every turn. Yet like some battered fighter, the Soviet Union refused to go down, even as its people underwent unimaginable hardship.

For behind the waves of invaders, German special groups systematically exterminated Jews, Communists, and others whom Hitler and his high command, with the compliance of most of the armed forces, viewed as subhuman or a threat to their total dominance. The Einsatzgruppen, as they were known, executed hundreds of thousands by bullet, by asphyxiating victims in specially constructed vans, and by all means of cruel torture. But the process was not efficient enough for the Nazis. By early 1942, the Nazis planned for and carried out an even more efficient and wicked form of mass murder. The names Auschwitz, Sobibór, Dachau, Treblinka, and Bergen-Belsen will forever haunt history—the concentration camps where millions of Jews and others deemed undesirable were systematically annihilated in the Holocaust.

In the face of this terror, first on the battlefield and then in the depraved campaign against civilians, Stalin pleaded with his allies, American president Roosevelt and British prime minister Winston Churchill, to open up a second front to relieve pressure on his forces by siphoning off German strength. The Americans and British were too weak to do more than fight in peripheral theatres, and even then the

British campaigns in North Africa throughout much of 1941 and 1942 were a series of bloody tug-of-wars, with the British and German armies lurching back and forth in the desert achieving no knock-out blows.

Closer to the German centre of gravity, Allied raids along the west coast of France were mere pinpricks against the enemy, and even when these operations escalated in size and scope, such as at Dieppe in August 1942, they carried with them inherent dangers. The Dieppe raid, conceived with unwarranted optimism and plagued by shoddy planning, saw some 5,000 Canadians led to the slaughter. The 2nd Canadian Infantry Division fought with courage and skill, but it never stood a chance: 907 were killed, 586 wounded, and almost 2,000 taken prisoner. The raid revealed debilitating service rivalries, the inherent challenges of an amphibious landing, the many ways that coordinating operations on multiple landing sites could go wrong, and the effectiveness of German defenders in a fortified port. If Dieppe served any purpose, it was to highlight how difficult it would be for the Allies to carry out a full-scale invasion of France.

The Allied bombing campaign was a more prolonged means of striking back against the enemy. While prewar theorists had predicted that civilian morale would collapse in the face of massed aerial bombardment, the British people who withstood the Blitz had put paid to that notion. So too had the Germans, who were bombed with growing ferocity during the course of the war. With the need to open the Second Front, draw down German military strength and resources from the east, destroy war industry, and enact revenge for the Blitz, the Royal Air Force's Bomber Command took the war to the heart of the Fatherland. Joining the Brits were the thousands of new flyers from Canada's British Commonwealth Air Training Plan, which would eventually train over 131,500 airmen. The heroics of the Battle of Britain and the exhilaration of flight drew tens of thousands of Canadians to the air war, and by war's end nearly a third of Bomber Command consisted of Canadian airmen.[6]

Up to early 1943, the shortage of heavy four-engine bombers, effective guidance systems, and accurate bombsights, when combined with the resiliency of enemy industry and citizens, ensured that the bombers had little impact on the Nazis' ability to wage war. However, the Royal Canadian Air Force's No. 6 Group, which was established as a unique bomber group on January 1, 1943, added to the weight of the bombing force that had begun to crack the German defences through relentless assaults. The six bomber groups and a specialized pathfinder group from 1943 tipped the aerial assault in favour of the Allies, as the Lancasters and Halifaxes killed tens of thousands of civilians; forced the pull back of precious anti-aircraft guns, fighter planes, and hundreds of thousands of defenders from the fighting fronts; lowered the output of war materiel; and interfered with the movement of troops within occupied Europe. Bomber Command and its American counterpart formed the Second Front that Stalin demanded and that Hitler feared, and the bomber storm was a shrieking gale force wind of retribution by mid-1943.

The tide was also turning in the land war, with the Germans on the Eastern Front absorbing a stunning defeat at Stalingrad in January 1943. An entire army of a quarter of a million men was destroyed. A few months later, in May 1943, General Bernard Montgomery led his Eighth Army—with newly arrived American forces—to victory in the desert war in North Africa against General Erwin Rommel and the Afrika Korps. While the return to France remained the priority for the Allies—and the only way to overthrow Germany—the gathering of British, American, Canadian, Free French, and Polish forces was not yet strong enough to first pierce the German defences along the coast and then sustain the invasion against the massed enemy counterattack. And so, as the planning and preparation for amphibious attack continued, along with the naval war on the Atlantic and the bombing of German cities, in July 1943 the Allies invaded the German- and Italian-defended fortress of Sicily in the Mediterranean. The Allied armies were tested here, with the 1st Canadian Infantry Division and the 1st Canadian Armoured Brigade fighting in the vanguard. Major-General Guy Simonds led his untried Canadians in their first major campaign and they contributed mightily to the Allied victory.

While the Allied forces in Sicily under command of American general Dwight Eisenhower had stumbled at times, especially in corralling the three services—army, navy, and air force—to fight together and with one goal, the victory put the final nail in Italy's coffin. The Allies always struggled to work together in the life-and-death environment of campaigns, but their coalition was far more effective than that of the Axis Powers, which featured the Germans treating the Italians with open disdain and fighting separate wars from the Japanese. Italy surrendered to the Allies in early September 1943, and the Germans easily transitioned from scornful ally to cruel occupier. From that same month, the Canadians continued to fight with the British Eighth Army and clawed their way up the rough and hilly Italian terrain, with a series of battles culminating in the hard-pounding victory at Ortona throughout December 1943. But the Allies could not break through the German lines anywhere in Italy as both sides fought tenaciously. The body count rose with no end in sight.

From land, sea, and air to the home front, Canada had proved from 1939 to 1943 to be a committed and crucial ally to Britain. Its forces earned a fierce reputation at the cannon's mouth. While Britain was on the front lines of battle after the fall of France in June 1940, for a year and

A Canadian war poster exhorting the purchase of war bonds to support the war effort.

half before the Americans entered the war, Canada was Britain's ranking ally. The nation of fewer than twelve million had shaken off the lingering effects of the Depression and moved fully to a war footing. Its war industries produced thousands of tons of military weapons and equipment, and its farms fed the allied nations of the war. The air training plan was a major contribution. Fire, steel, fodder, and grain—this was the Canadian war effort. And flesh. Thousands of Canadian soldiers, sailors, airmen, and merchant mariners lost their lives in the great effort against totalitarianism from 1939 to 1943, and hundreds of thousands of Canadians grieved for their fallen loved ones, kin, and community folk. And all knew that the only path forward, towards final victory, was paved with sacrifice, sorrow, and more fighting.

THIS IS THE SECOND OF TWO VOLUMES, and it continues where the first left off. It can be read in isolation from the first, but there is much contextualizing information in the battles and campaigns of 1939 to 1943. While all three services fought in those years, the Battle of the Atlantic against the U-boats was the fundamental campaign if the Allies were to survive and then mount the invasion of Europe. The tide turned against the Kriegsmarine in May 1943, but the convoys across the Atlantic remained essential to the Allied cross-Channel invasion, even as the number of ships lost decreased. By the summer of 1943, when this book picks up the story, the aerial war against Germany had reached a frenzied pace, with hundreds of bombers flying nightly to pound cities. The war on land was also reaching a decisive point with the ongoing campaign in Italy and the coming D-Day invasion of June 1944. And while this book focuses more on the army and air force than the navy, as Canadian land forces fought in two major theatres of war, the Royal Canadian Navy continued its work in supporting the multiple Allied fighting formations on all fronts and in shepherding supplies across the Atlantic.

Victory over the Nazis in the worldwide war required moral compromise: from accepting and carrying out the strategy of starving nations of resources to mounting direct attacks against non-combatants with bombers. It also necessitated an alliance with Stalin—a mass murderer of millions of his own people. When dealing with Hitler, a dictator bent on conquering and carrying out genocide, only armed might could restore freedom to a doomed continent.

This total war involving millions fighting on continents and oceans spanning the world must be understood and reconstructed in its totality, with grand Allied strategy feeding down into national decision making and further down to wartime operations. Within this maelstrom are the tactics, weapon systems, logistics, and countless other factors that shaped warfighting capabilities. And often forgotten or pushed to the periphery in writing about the worldwide war is the role of combatants struggling for their lives. They made decisions to continue to fight, to go forward. Sometimes they were mowed down by scything machine-gun fire, or blown apart by flak, or sent to their graves in dark waters. Others succeeded, against the odds. This was the war of the infantry section, of the ship's crew, and of the Halifax bomber. It was a world made small, where the group banded together to carry on.

This book examines the Canadian fighting experience, from the challenges of command and control at the level of generals or admirals, to units in battle, and finally to the personal, terrifying, and at times exhilarating experience of servicemen in combat. Women in uniform played a part in the conflict, usually behind the lines, except for nurses who cared for the wounded within range of the guns. The book follows the fighting of Canadians on all three fronts—at sea, in the air, and on the ground—and tries to place the combat experience in the context of the Allied war effort without losing sight of the truth that battle is about individuals.

The war was a kaleidoscope of events and experiences. No one's war was the same, although there were commonalities. I have tried to draw these out, basing my research on seventy-five years of scholarship, newly uncovered archival documents, and published and unpublished Canadian eyewitness accounts and interviews. Rifleman J.L. Wagar of the Queen's Own Rifles stayed in touch with his former comrades in arms after the war, and found much in common with all veterans. Yet there were aspects of the war that only he had seen and felt. In those cases, he described such experiences as "my own private folklore of the war."[7] In this book, I aim to reveal the private and previously ignored, and to provide a narrative and collective biography for the more than one million Canadians who served in uniform. There is much here that should resonate with Canadians today, and in our own uncertain times. But history is also a foreign country. There are some things that should remain strange to us; there are some things the historian should not attempt to link to the present. The motivations for war and the ability of ordinary men to endure horrendous strain can be both grasped by and lost to the modern reader.

While the Second World War has rightly been called "the good war," insofar as it was fought against a regime of bestial evil, there were unwholesome elements to it. To beat an experienced and callous enemy, the Canadian soldiers, airmen, and sailors fought almost as ruthlessly. The killing of opponents in land battles and the bombing of cities, industries, and civilians were all elements of a "good" war that had to be won. We should not be surprised that when we send men into a violent environment they will likely be scarred by the actions they must carry out on behalf of their nation. Yet for much of the twentieth century, Canadians largely left veterans to deal with their own personal demons and were often not eager to hear from veterans. The story of veterans and the memory of the war are recounted here, as they are crucial for providing the capstone to the meaning of the Second World War.

And now, in the twenty-first century, the voices of veterans are becoming muted with time and age. This is the story of the survivors and the dead. It is about the war at the sharp end in all of its complexity. Canadians sacrificed much in the struggle. It is our duty to remember and to understand. This does not mean we must turn to hero worship. Surely that generation would recoil. It would be an even greater mistake, however, to misunderstand the past by judging it through the lens of present-day values. The two world wars shaped the modern twentieth century and forever changed Canada. Yet we need to understand war as an event within its own time and place. It was a time of brutality and desperate survival; those Canadians who enlisted had no idea how it would turn out, and for the first half of the war, from 1939 to 1943, there was the very real possibility that the odious Nazi regime would win, or at least force a draw and rule Europe. From 1944, there would be many battles to bring down Adolf Hitler and the Third Reich. Tens of thousands of Canadians never made it home in the fight to the finish.

CHAPTER 1

AIR WAR

"Each month brings heavier raids and heavier losses," recounted Royal Canadian Air Force (RCAF) Flight Lieutenant Leslie McCaig of No. 426 Squadron in his diary in late August 1943. "I can't help feeling that before many weeks a real push will begin on the continent. German morale must suffer from the relentless pounding the RAF is giving their cities."[1] The twenty-seven-year-old McCaig from Ormstown, Quebec, was a keen observer of the air war and the part he played in it, and he watched as Bomber Command added new planes and squadrons to its growing strike force. His squadron was a part of No. 6 Group, the Canadian-led bomber group that would eventually consist of fifteen RCAF bomber squadrons that were taking the war to German cities.

The first three years of bombing, from 1939 to 1942, had little impact on German wartime production or any measurable effect on civilian morale. Plans at the start of the war to target German industry and command centres with daytime bombing had quickly degenerated into a ghastly turkey shoot. The visible Royal Air Force (RAF) bombers were blown out of the skies by anti-aircraft guns and German fighters. The switch to night bombing saved some of the aircrews. It also complicated the task of finding blacked-out cities and then hitting targets. Yet the struggling British nation, losing on almost every front, had few other means of striking back at the Germans, and so it built up its bomber force. Yet by late 1942 Bomber Command consisted of only 11 percent of the entire RAF, with Fighter, Coastal, and Training Command engaged in multiple operations around the world.[2] The losses of the early years slowed the expansion of the bomber force, but throughout 1942 and 1943 the older two-engine bombers, such as the Hampden and Wellington, were phased out of service. The new four-engine heavies, especially the Halifax and Lancaster, allowed for a steady escalation of attacks, as they drove deeper into Germany and carried bigger bomb loads.

Continual study and appraisal, high hopes and harsh failures, hand-wringing and teeth-gnashing over the first half of the war revealed that despite all the improvements to technology, to doctrine and tactics, the bomber crews—dropping their loads from 18,000 feet in the dark and while under intense fire—rarely hit their targets. A well-documented series of decisions from the senior civilian high command, especially Winston Churchill, and through the air marshals, charted the gradual shift from the unpromising aim of bombing specific targets to plastering entire cities. While the air officer commanding-in-chief of Bomber Command, Sir Arthur Harris, claimed that the bombers could win the war single-handedly if he had the proper number of bombers available, his superiors, Chief of the Air Staff Sir Charles Portal, Chief of the Imperial General Staff Sir Alan Brooke, and even Churchill believed otherwise.[3] Harris was not deterred and he remained a fierce champion of the bombers; he eschewed talk of "dehousing" the enemy (destroying their houses but implying that civilians were not being killed) and other euphemisms, and urged on his flyers to "kill the Boche."[4]

The operations gathered in intensity each year, with 1943 seeing a large-scale expansion and a continuous targeting of German cities, civilians, and industry. The high-profile 1,000-bomber raid against Cologne of July 31, 1942, shook the Nazi high command, while the July 1943 Hamburg firestorm left all Germans trembling. For those beneath the bombs, rumours and speculation suggested an imminent apocalypse, to be delivered by the bombers. Hitler and his minister of armaments and war production, Albert Speer, had planned for a renewed push from German industry in early 1943, but the concentrated bomber operations had interfered severely with this plan. Steel production was curbed and flatlined, thereby slowing weapons production. At the same time, Hitler poured resources into aircraft research and manufacturing, almost entirely of fighters, largely to defend German cities against the Allied bomber campaign. This aircraft manufacturing reached an astonishing 41 percent of the German total war economy; by way of comparison, only 29 percent of the economy was devoted to producing ammunition and powder, 8 percent to naval vessels, and 6 percent to tank production.[5] Aircraft were also pulled back from the fighting fronts, especially in the east, where the land forces were increasingly left vulnerable. Finally, thousands of anti-aircraft guns, many of them doubling in an anti-tank role, were moved from the battle front to guard the cities, further leaving the German army susceptible to Allied armoured thrusts.[6] The bombing campaign of the Americans, British, and Canadians during the first half of 1943—known as the Combined Bomber Offensive—curtailed German war production and drew down on its already stretched military resources as Hitler scrambled to protect his cities. And it would only get worse.

A Canadian Lancaster bomber on a sortie over enemy territory.

THE BOMBERS HAMMERED CITIES, but they also continued to harass the bottled-up German navy and to target specific military sites. When intercepted coded messages revealed that the Germans were close to perfecting rockets carrying high explosives that would rain down upon Britain, the Anglo-American high command ordered a strike against the main research centre, Peenemünde, a rocket and research development station on the Baltic coast north of Berlin. Known as V-weapons (short for Vergeltungswaffen or "revenge weapons"), these missiles contained over a ton of high explosives and were one of Hitler's many "secret weapons" for winning the war by renewing the Blitz on the British people. A precision bomber attack on Peenemünde might delay the enemy's terror plans.

The crews selected for the August 18 sortie against Peenemünde were sequestered so as not to mistakenly reveal the target, and were even threatened with severe punishment should they talk to anyone. It was excessive security, but it impressed upon the flyers the importance of the mission. Led by Pathfinders, who would scout ahead of the main bomber force and drop flares to mark aiming points, and a master bomber who directed the bombers using a high-frequency wireless communication system to correct bomb drops in real-time—596 bombers flew in bright moonlight to the concrete-reinforced site. Canadian Pathfinder Johnnie Fauquier, who had already survived thirty sorties in his first tour of duty, was the tough and exacting commander of RCAF's No. 405 Squadron (part of the Pathfinding force). Acting as deputy master bomber, he made a shockingly dangerous seventeen passes over the enemy research facility, directing the bombers and assessing the damage. Against all odds, he survived and was awarded the Distinguished Service Order, one of four gallantry decorations he received during the course of the war.

The successful mission came at a cost. Ordered to fly at heights between 6,000 and 10,000 feet, the bomber force endured a nearly 7 percent loss, while RCAF's No. 6 Group, assigned to the end of the bomber stream and therefore flying into battle-ready defences, took an almost 20 percent loss rate with twelve of sixty-two bombers shot down.[7] Pilot Officer R.W. Charman, a navigator with No. 427 Squadron, recalled of the operation, "I had never seen such a night before. All over the sky, RAF [and RCAF] planes were going down."[8] Despite the withering losses, the mission was an outright success, killing enemy scientists and causing a two-month delay to the program. It was later calculated that the mission had reduced the number of rockets launched against British cities by 740.[9]

WITH THE TERRIBLE FIRESTORM of Hamburg in July 1943 and the Peenemünde raid a month later, Bomber Command's stock continued to rise in Churchill's eyes. Harris, with Churchill and Portal's blessings, ordered a new campaign against the greatest prize. Big City, as the airmen called Berlin, was the most hazardous target in Europe. Its distance from British bases of around 850 kilometres meant that the bomber stream had to pass through a gauntlet of several lines of night fighter defences, as well as taking fire from flak gun defenders that had been strengthened after the burning of Hamburg. Germany's capital was defended by over 100 batteries of 16 to 24 anti-aircraft guns each, and its enormous size of 200 square kilometres meant that it could absorb significant punishment. While Berlin accounted for about 8 percent of Germany's total industrial output, it symbolized the Nazi regime and strength.[10] Willing to throw everything against it, Harris boasted to Churchill that if the Americans agreed to a sustained air battle, "We can wreck Berlin from end to end.... it will cost between us 400–500 aircraft. It will cost Germany the war."[11]

Churchill and the other senior military and political leaders had heard these claims before. But now the bomber war reached new levels of effectiveness and destruction, and the British prime minister had long wanted to avenge the Blitz on London by bringing the war to Berlin. While Britain's senior political and military high command—save for Harris—had written off the claim that the bombers could win the war on their own, it was easy to put such beliefs aside in the hope that a relentless Anglo-American air assault might defeat Germany without having to unleash the armies building up in Britain. Unfortunately, the Americans were in no condition to send their bombers against Berlin. Following a series of high-level directives from earlier in the year to wear down the Luftwaffe, the Americans had been flying aggressively into German air space during daylight hours to better hit their targets and to draw the enemy fighters against them. It was thought that the American bombers, especially the heavily armed B-17 Flying Fortresses and B-24 Liberators, might be a match for the Luftwaffe's Me 109s and Fw 190s. It was not the case. German fighters were faster, and were battling over their homeland. The uneven combat led to terrible

American losses. In August 1943 alone, the German fighters claimed 250 Allied aircraft shot down, with most of these being American bombers.[12] These casualties culminated in a daylight raid against Schweinfurt on October 14, 1943, that saw 60 out of 291 American bombers sent flaming to the earth.[13] Licking their wounds and forced to rethink how to draw out the Luftwaffe on more favourable terms, the Americans would no longer fly deep into Germany without long-range fighter escorts. The blunt true-believer Sir Arthur Harris was undeterred. He would send his RAF and RCAF forces against Berlin alone.

The RAF and RCAF push against Berlin began on November 18, when a force of 440 Lancasters struck, including 29 bombers from Nos. 408 and 426 RCAF squadrons.

Lancasters of RCAF's No. 419 Squadron. The bomber in the foreground was shot down later that same evening during a raid over St. Ghislain.

Diversionary strikes were launched against other cities to draw away German fighters, and they succeeded. Thick clouds and freezing temperatures over Berlin also made it difficult for the Luftwaffe to locate the bombers, although this also meant that the striking of key targets was almost entirely impossible as high winds scattered the falling bombs and incendiaries. Still, only 9 of the 440 bombers were destroyed, and Harris was thrilled with the surprise attack, even if no industrial buildings or factories were hit. Harris launched a series of offensives throughout the month, and on the nights of November 22, 23, and 26, the Germans reported 8,701 buildings razed and 4,330 civilians killed. These attacks were painful stabs against the city, but not death blows.

As part of the November 22 attack involving 764 bombers, including 110 from No. 6 Group, the first Canadian-built Lancaster, *Ruhr Express*, took part in the raid, but it had to turn back when its Packard-built Merlin engines lost power.[14] The reporter and photographer sent to get the story demanded an "exclusive," and so the crew went through a fake debriefing, with the pilot, Flight Sergeant Harold Floren of Weyburn, Saskatchewan, told to act the hero. Many other bombers made it through. Those November raids pounded Berlin, and attesting to the broad swath of ruin, bombs fell over 180 square kilometres, hitting key manufacturing areas such as the Alkett tank factory that was damaged on the night of the 27th.[15] While precision targeting of known factories or warehouses remained nearly impossible, the widespread bombing terrorized much of the city.

Civilians were shaken on the ground, but morale also withered among the air crews. RCAF No. 6 Group's losses mounted, hitting 6 percent per sortie in December 1943 and 7.3 percent in January, far above the 5 percent per sortie that Bomber Command's senior staff had predicted was the critical level when squadrons would be permanently shattered. In the case of No. 6 Group's January casualty rate, a 7.3 percent loss rate per sortie meant that only 10 crews out of 100 would survive a 30-operation tour.[16] On December 21, 1943, Flight Lieutenant Leslie McCaig confided in his diary, after his best friend Tommy was killed during a sortie and two more crews were lost over Frankfurt a few nights later, "The laws of fate, skill and luck are constantly being defied but luck still seems to wear thin after a time."[17] Nearly at the end of his tour, McCaig's luck ran out too, and he never returned from over Berlin on January 20, 1944.

Flying during the winter of late 1943 and early 1944 led to other problems. Stormy conditions cancelled many sorties, and even when the bombers got into the air there was increased chance for mechanical failure from frozen instruments. The electronic navigational systems, such as Oboe, provided some assistance in getting to the targets, but the guiding electronic signals became fainter as the bombers flew farther into Germany. Yet the mounting casualties and increasingly poor weather did not deter Sir Arthur Harris. The offensive continued.

While Berlin, with its four million inhabitants, was so big that there was always something to strike, any approach had to be rammed through the waving arcs of

The bomber war laid waste to German cities. More than half of all German cities were destroyed by the end of the war.

searchlights and sustained fire. Some bombers decided it was wiser to avoid the concentrations of flak, and therefore rose high above the bomber stream or clung to its outer edges. They acquired the derisive name of "fringe merchants," with their bombs falling several kilometres off target. Flight Sergeant Vernon Hawkes, a twenty-seven-year-old pilot in RCAF's No. 419 Squadron, flew several operations against Berlin in late 1943 and recounted the tendency of some aircrews to drop their bombs short, either deliberately or unintentionally. These "drop shorts" were partially unavoidable, as the sea of fire on the ground obscured targets, but other crews, wise to the perils of the guns, deposited their bomb loads haphazardly to lift several thousand feet with lightened holds to avoid flak.[18] In some cases, the creep-back extended kilometres to the rear of the original target, as squadron after squadron dropped their bombs shorter than the one that came before it. Like so many of his comrades, Hawkes and his crew were shot down in the final stage of the campaign on January 21, 1944, and he survived almost a year and a half in the prisoner-of-war camp Stalag Luft III.

While Berlin was not the only goal for the Anglo-Canadian bomber offensive, it remained the focus of battle, and from November 18 to March 31, 1944, there were 35 major raids on German cities, 16 against Berlin. This equated into 11,113 individual plane sorties against Big City.[19] The casualty rate remained heavy for the bombers, with 157 aircraft lost.[20] When these casualties were added to those sustained earlier in the summer, it meant that more and more inexperienced aircrews were thrust into the front lines. Lancaster pilot Douglas Harvey of No. 408 Squadron, RCAF, observed of the frantic pace, "New crews arrived and went missing before you had the chance to know them."[21] It took time to learn how to survive in the air. RCAF Flying Officer Len Sumak noted, "We lost as much as fifty percent of our green crews when they went on their first trip."[22] He and his crew survived their first operation; many others did not, with sprog (new) crews disappearing in fire and flame.

The Berlin raids killed more than 9,000 citizens on the ground and made 812,000 people homeless.[23] These civilians were not collateral damage. They were deliberately targeted, at least insofar as the entire city and everything in it was a target. In turn, Bomber Command was nearly crippled, with more than 3,300 aircrew killed and

1,047 bombers lost—double the number Harris had predicted. The long Berlin run had proved that the four-engine Stirling was a death trap because of its inability to reach high altitudes, and those crews suffered a catastrophic average loss rate of 12.9 percent per sortie during the operations.[24] The Stirlings were removed from flying; so, too, were many of the Halifax IIs and Vs, which were replaced with the more resilient Halifax III. The Battle of Berlin did not knock Germany out of the war, as Harris had prophesized, and could not be considered a victory because of the high bomber losses, but it had shown that Germany's capital could be punished by the striking arm of the Allies. In the end, Harris's plan to destroy Berlin left him weakened in the eyes of his superiors, who were angered by his overly optimistic claims that the war could be won by the bombers. Perhaps most damaging, the losses were a blow to morale in Bomber Command.

THE BATTLE OF BERLIN tested all the flyers, coming as it did on the heels of years of grave losses to the Bomber Command crews. There were few missions where planes did not vanish in the night, and an unlucky operation could gut a squadron. "You never saw your friends actually die. They were just missing from the station the next day," remembered RCAF Flight Lieutenant John Zinkhan, a No. 6 Group navigator who flew in Halifaxes and Lancasters.[25] Norman Emmott of No. 433 Squadron, a prewar RCAF ground crew who re-enlisted as a navigator, echoed Zinkhan: "The airman practically never sees death at close quarters, never is required to advance over dead bodies, and seldom sees his comrades killed beside him."[26] After a sortie, lockers were emptied. Names came off the roster board. And the war went on. Of course, chums missed chums, but the distressing losses required a callousness for dealing with those who never returned from the night-time operations.

Airmen who were killed in flying accidents or were mortally wounded during a sortie were usually interred in a cemetery near their base. RCAF flyer D.J. Matthews was assigned the task of gathering and inventorying the personal effects of six crew members whose plane flew into a nearby hillside. It was a painful task. He also represented No. 547 Squadron at the burial of several of his British comrades. It rained throughout the service and Matthews spent much of the ceremony watching the mother of one of the slain airmen, a tiny woman with "pinched features." She had lost her first husband in the Great War, the second husband during this war, and now her son. "She seemed beyond tears."[27]

Though the dead were buried quickly, the notification of the next of kin in Canada was often mired in bureaucratic tangles. Multiple official letters were sent to families to update them about a slain son or father. Far worse was the fate of a missing airman over Europe. Most were killed when their planes exploded, but some parachuted safely and were captured on the run from the Gestapo, the Nazi paramilitary police force. Those at home agonized over the lack of definitive information.[28] As the months stretched out, hope flickered and faded.

Desperate families needed details to reconstruct the last moments of their loved ones in order to begin that process of healing. Possessions were usually sent back to Canada, along with a letter from the commanding officer, the padre, and maybe a few squadron comrades. With so many of the airmen listed as missing, grieving communities prayed for a miracle, with the uncertainty lasting for months and then years. While occasionally a flyer did turn up, having been protected by the French or Dutch resistance, more often the missing were gone: atomized into vapour, burned beyond recognition, or buried in graves by the German military or French civilians. It was not until after the war, when investigators could examine crash sites, talk to locals, exhume bodies, and exhaust all avenues, that they could declare an airman killed. RCAF airman James Baker recounted to his mother in a letter, after comforting a grieving friend whose fiancé had been shot down over Europe, "I certainly know now what tragedy and heart-aches lie behind that simple statement 'One of our bombers did not return.'"[29]

AIRMEN WERE GENERALLY not privy to the loss rates of their nightly missions, but they could look around their own mess and see who did not return. The empty chairs and beds were an indication of the cost of the bombing war. [30] The casualties disproportionately fell on the inexperienced crews. They succumbed to poor weather or made mistakes in the air that drew the attention of night fighters. They did not know when to turn back legitimately or when to break formation to find cover in a cloud. Moreover, RCAF Flight Sergeant B.G. McDonald observed during his thirty-one sorties, "Novice crews didn't get the good kites. They were reserved for the 'old-timers' who had developed the habit of returning them."[31] A large proportion of aircrews were shot down in their first couple of sorties; after some eighteen months of training and tens of thousands of dollars expended, many crews were killed before they even dropped a single bomb on an enemy target. RCAF flyer A.R. Sanderson and his crew sought to finish several operations in rapid succession after their first sortie because "We were all anxious to get to at least the ten op level," for it "was widely supposed that one would be lucky to survive past seven."[32] No one wanted to linger for long as a rookie crew. Yet even experienced crews went down in flames because of the solid walls of flak thrown up by defenders, or for any number of other reasons, from mechanical failure to unmerciful weather to the deadly night fighters. Experience saved lives, but luck eventually had to run out.

Good senior officers understood the strain that men faced. The commanding officer's willingness to fly on sorties against the enemy provided him with moral authority, and bomber crews could quickly turn on senior officers who exhorted sacrifice but did not share the danger. "The Commanding Officer of 427 Squadron was about the best kind of leader one could meet up with," believed RCAF navigator George Brown. "He was a friend to all the boys and did his share of the dirty work. He went on the toughest targets and did all he could to help the crews to safer flying. For social life he organized flight parties every fortnight, each flight taking turns, so that there was a feeling of comradeship that did not exist on many of the other squadrons."[33]

Despite the pressure, most airmen kept flying and found ways to cope night after night. Like their counterparts in the army and navy, they were young, fit, and determined. The desire to avenge the Blitz or their fallen comrades was a motivator. The airmen also saw themselves as an elite force, as a result of both education and training. The rest periods were long and generous in comparison to other service branches, and the food and drink were never scarce. But in the fight against the enemy, in the cold ethereality of the night sky, all of these advantages dribbled away quickly as Canadian airmen fought to survive and to keep their mates alive.

"Some aircrew, whose nerve ends may have become cauterized by the repetitive exposure to danger, flew on in an almost robotic state," reported one Canadian airman.[34] Flight Lieutenant Warren Duffy, a New Brunswicker in an RAF squadron and destined to be killed, wrote to his parents of his many friends lost over Europe, including one close chum, Mac: "It's amazing how one can make friends over here and good friends, too. Mac (my wireless operator) was killed last fall after I had finished ops.... He got it flying with another crew, pretty hard luck, but that's the way it goes."[35] That was indeed how it went, and airmen learned that too many of their comrades would go, as they casually remarked, "for a Burton"—a phrase whose origins apparently revolved around a type of beer, Burton Ale, and meant that the airman had gone for an extended drink and would not be returning. Lancaster bomber pilot Walter Thompson felt that "one had to learn to accept death and become used to the idea of it. One had to consider oneself as already dead."[36] That was the case for many airmen, although most also held the contradictory belief

Two Canadians in the cockpit of their Lancaster preparing to lift off for a sortie.

in their hearts that while death was an aspect of their everyday life, as one Canadian testified, "everybody was sure that the other fellow would 'go for the chop,' never themselves."[37]

Talismans and superstitions allowed some men to deal with the lack of control over the flak or the other nasty elements of flying. One pilot screamed obscenities at the Germans throughout the bombing run in an almost unconscious verbal shield. Jack Singer, a bomb aimer, observed somewhat apprehensively how his pilot, Doug Tweddle, coped with his fear. "He said that when things got really tough he would have an out of body experience. He would find himself out on the wing of the aircraft looking at a duplicate of himself flying the aircraft. He would offer words of encouragement to his duplicate, such as, 'just hold it steady, ride it out, it's going to be ok.' He always appeared to me to be very calm and in control, but I guess we all had our ways of achieving this outward calm."[38] There were countless other rituals, techniques, and prayers offered and embraced in hopes of passing unscathed through the storm of steel.

AIRMEN FLEW UNTIL it was "coffins or crackers."[39] Many believed the only way out of the service was through death or going mad, but that was untrue, for unlike the infantry and the seamen, airmen faced a finite number of sorties. For the first three years of the war, the service career of an airman was to be 200 operational hours, after which he was pulled from the front lines and made a trainer or staff officer. In August 1942, Harris set the figure at 30 sorties, whereupon the aircrews were "screened": pulled from flying into enemy territory, given a rest, offered a safer training job in Britain, and even sent back to Canada. In May 1943, Bomber Command headquarters codified the service of aircrews into two combat tours, one of 30 operations and the other of 20, with a break of staff duties or training in between of not less than six months. When an airman completed his first tour, he received his Operational Wings. They were a gold-plated, double-winged "O" (for "operations") and were attached on the centre panel of the left-breast tunic pocket. They were worn with pride; they had been earned the hard way.

Gallantry awards were one method of sustaining morale and encouraging airmen to keep flying. While few airmen were on the hunt for "gongs," as they irreverently called the medals, the decorations were a mark of service and survival. More than

9,200 gallantry awards were bestowed upon 8,300 individual Canadian airmen during the war, and most of these went to Canadians in Bomber Command.[40] Pilots and navigators received the most awards, with the rear gunners almost always passed over unless there was evidence of shooting down an enemy fighter, and ground crews, also eligible, almost never receiving special recognition. In late 1944, bomber pilot Walter Irwin felt that "Attrition was constantly wearing away at the squadron and at this point, we had lost 17 crews. Promotions came faster than usual as a result and I received a promotion to Squadron Leader." Having almost completed two tours, he was also awarded the Distinguished Flying Cross (DFC). "One thing that has always bothered me is that my crew members did not also receive decorations. After all, they had shared every hazardous moment with me and performed their jobs well.... Brave and dedicated as they were, it was difficult for a crew member to earn a decoration unless it was for an individual act of bravery."[41]

The low rates of survival for bomber crews merited some recognition, but the same might be assumed of the ground pounders, and they were far less likely to be rewarded with a gallantry award, while naval crew members were the least likely to receive medals. Though infantry soldiers at the front often sneered at the awarding of the Distinguished Service Order to senior officers who commanded for long durations, and not for specific acts of bravery, the issuing of the DFC to individual airmen was more acceptable in the air force, and was frequently given for surviving a tour of operations. The navy rarely received the same recognition, even though its members, too, had long and dangerous tours, but with much lower casualties. The distinction between the RCAF and RCN hinged on the number of deaths, which is perhaps correct. It is more difficult to justify awards for gallantry between the RCAF and the Army, except that the former had more officers and they were always recognized with a higher rate of awards than the non-commissioned rank and file. By the midpoint of the war, the airman's DFC seemed like a standard medal for surviving flying operations.

Notwithstanding the awards or recognition, all flyers were worn down by the unending stress. The exhaustion was etched on faces, although most flyers, in the words of one Canadian airman, protected themselves "in a veneer of denial."[42] But there was little chance of hiding the telltale signs of fatigue that the flyers irreverently called the "twitch" or "flak happiness." A table of flyers coming upon the end of their tour were often a seething mess, with involuntary leg jerks, stutters, and eye twitches. Worn-out airman hid their tremoring hands by holding their beer at an angle so as not to lose the contents. Many of these teenagers took on the appearance of old men, walking stooped from the constant pain in their shoulders and necks. Flight Lieutenant A.G. "Red" Sherwood, who flew a Lancaster and never broke his temperance promise, slowly succumbed to weariness, stress, and the "constant living in fear."[43] He weighed 150 pounds at the start of the war; by his fortieth sortie, he was a gaunt 120 pounds, all of the weight lost through sleepless nights and never-ending dread.

"The effects of a dozen operations, or a score, were discernible from time to time in various aircrew around the station," remarked Flying Officer Murray Peden. A chum, Mickey Claxton, had "nightmares in which he dreamed he was on operations and coming under fire. He would wake up in terror, often waking the rest of us in the process, and then try to compose himself again." Others sleepwalked or suffered daytime terrors. One experienced pilot grew so tense before flying that he could not talk, only gasping out responses in a hysterical voice. He wept frequently over the slightest inconvenience. Another respected member of his squadron, Jake Walters, vomited repeatedly before and after operations. Eventually the wing commander—the officer who commanded several squadrons—heard of Walters reaction and found him doubled over after a flight. He gently put his arm around him and remarked quietly, "I think you've had enough, Jake."[44] Not all senior officers were so understanding.

Every man used different motivations to survive, but it is revealing that less than 1 percent of the total number of flyers were diagnosed with combat stress so severe that they could no longer fly. Even fewer were categorized as "lacking moral fibre."[45] For those who showed cracks, station medical officers often gave them high doses of sodium barbital to knock them out for a day or longer. The forced sleep saved many men and, as was to be found in the Army, was an effective treatment.[46] Those who could not rest their imagination were a danger to themselves and their crews. Many pulled themselves from flying, and when they did, were labelled "Lack of Moral Fibre," a traumatic charge that registered with most airmen.

Lack of Moral Fibre (LMF) was a broad categorization for those aircrew who could not continue flying for what was deemed unjustifiable reasons. The bomber crews were all volunteers, but there was no volunteering out of Bomber Command. LMF was first employed as a term in September 1941, and it branded the condemned man as a coward. The relatively few cases of LMF suggest that most officers quietly removed troubled or broken airmen, reassigning them out of the squadron, but the impression remained among crews that LMF was an inhumane stigma. Like in the previous war with shell shock, LMF was applied out of fear that if humane treatment was given, the "disease" of cowardice might run rampant through the remaining flyers and destroy morale. In the words of RCAF pilot Douglas Harvey, the general perception among his squadron was that "Bomber Command reacted with ferocious cruelty against these unfortunates."[47] Another Canadian, John Harding, a navigator in No. 103 Squadron, shuddered after watching one of his comrades publicly humiliated for his mental breakdown: "I felt we were like cardboard pawns in the hands of these unfeeling, la-de-dah, upper-class Englishmen who seemed to run the RAF.... They would brook no battle fatigue, everything was blanketly labelled cowardice."[48]

The fear of LMF was a sufficient deterrent for some men. "There was no let-up in operational flying," noted Flight Sergeant John Patterson, an RCAF bomb aimer who flew in Lancasters. "We had a job to do and we were going to do it. What choice did we have? We could refuse to fly, but that would mean we would be classified LMF (lacking in moral fibre) and demoted, shunned by all our comrades, and probably returned to Canada in disgrace. So we carried on."[49] While LMF was a motivator for some, the label was widely despised by airmen, and the unfortunates were more objects of sympathy than of scorn. One 1942 RCAF report on morale observed, "The term now used ('lack of moral fibre') is universally disliked and should be dropped in favor of a more objective term such as 'Disciplinary demotion and loss of flying badge.'"[50] The label remained. David Chance, a bomber pilot with RCAF's No. 424 Squadron who completed thirty-three missions, believed that LMF was "a terrible label to put on anybody.... And I think that some of these guys that went LMF were quite brave, in a sense, in that they decided that they weren't going to do it. In a sense, they had a sort of bravery, the courage to admit they were scared. Of course, we were all scared at one time or another."[51] It took until 1944 for the RCAF to draft its own Canadian LMF policy that was more humane than the existing RAF one, and only applied when there was a "clear and willful evasion of operational responsibility."[52]

AIRMEN NONCHALANTLY OBSERVED that former comrades had "gotten the chop" or "gone for a Burton." Their chums were reduced to kit bags and chalk names in the operations room, to be gathered up in silence and erased from memory. The losses were particularly high in No. 6 Group. The group's commander, Air Vice-Marshal George Brookes, was a strong nationalist, but the uneven performance and high loss rates of the Canadians over the previous year was blamed on him. Brookes was not loved by his airmen, and his ouster in February 1944 was commented on by very few of the front-line flyers, although he remained an active champion of the RCAF after the war.

Air Vice-Marshal Clifford "Black Mike" McEwen took the helm. A Great War veteran, he acquired his name from his dark complexion and occasionally fierce tirades. McEwen was a stern disciplinarian—"a demon for standards and training"— who even demanded unpopularly that his airmen wear the wire in their cap to give it the formal stiff look of regulations and not the nonchalant appearance that the airmen projected.[53] McEwen backed up his discipline by accompanying crews on dangerous missions, where he earned their respect. Still, the casualties were terrible during the Battle of Berlin, and the loss rate of the Halifaxes of No. 6 Group in January 1944 was a staggering 9.8 percent, which, when extended out over a tour of thirty operations, meant that 95 out of 100 flyers would be killed or shot down.[54] Such casualty levels were unsustainable. Experience drained out of the squadron, morale was hammered, and sprog crews had no one from which to learn. Over the deadly winter of 1943 and into 1944, RCAF pilot Douglas Harvey saw more and more of his friends lost to combat. "I began to wonder if I would survive my tour." All flyers did the math and realized that the law of averages worked against them. "I watched as my chums disappeared into the night."[55]

CHAPTER 2

EVADERS AND PRISONERS

Almost every operation saw bombers disintegrate in fiery explosions, torn apart by night fighter cannons or ground-based flak guns. A doomed machine that did not immediately disintegrate in mid-air lost power and height as the pilot fought against the steady drop in altitude. If control could not be regained, the order went out to abandon the bird, often in a forced cheery quip: "Lads, time to hit the silk."

The rush out of the plane, which was likely on fire and shaking uncontrollably, possibly in a terminal spin, was not easy. As the stricken bombers went "down like a bomb," as one shot-down pilot remarked, the oxygen and the intercom soon cut out.[1] With no communication, the crew was isolated from the pilot and might not even know when he gave the order to jump. Some airmen waited too long and were not able to get out of the escape hatch; others dove out too quickly, and watched helplessly as they floated down to earth in their parachute, while the skipper and his chums righted the plane and headed home.

Though the Lancaster was a robust machine that could absorb terrible punishment, it had awkward escape hatches. The main wing spar ran across the body of the aircraft and it was a test to cross at the best of times when in full equipment, and far more difficult in a plummeting aircraft where the aircrew battled G forces. The Lanc crews were advised to go through the emergency hatch in the front nose, which was a long way for the tail and mid-upper gunner to travel. There was an escape hatch closer to the rear, but often the escapee, upon exiting the stricken plane, impacted with the horizontal tail surfaces and was killed or injured by the blow. Attesting to the challenge of slipping through the narrow hatches, only 11 percent of Lancaster crews survived being shot down, while 29 percent lived in the Halifax, although both statistics were damning in comparison to those of the American B-17 Flying Fortress and B-24 Liberator, which had about 50 percent of their crews survive a fatal blow to their plane.[2]

After the pilot gave the order to abandon the crippled bomber, he stayed in the cockpit, keeping the plane steady to provide his crew with extra minutes to escape. The pilots usually paid for their bravery with their lives, with statistics indicating that pilots and rear gunners had the lowest chance of escaping a plane in flight.[3] Sergeant Clifford C. Reichert of RCAF's No. 408 Squadron was one of the unlucky. In the early hours of June 22, 1943, his Halifax was hit by flak, causing the

Image of a Canadian bomber attack on Wangerooge Island, April 25, 1945.
Some 2,475 Canadian airmen were captured during the war.

dismemberment of two crewmen and nearly tearing the leg off G.F. Pridham, the bomb aimer. With the wind howling through the gaping holes in the fuselage, fire was soon sweeping down the plane. The skipper, Reichert, stayed at the controls to provide the time for his friends to bail out. Pridham, parachuting to the ground, saw the bomber explode in the skies above him. The injured bomb aimer survived his wounds and later wrote to Reichert's family that the pilot was the "bravest man I ever knew."[4] Reichert received a Mention in Dispatches award, and his self-sacrifice was not unique among the pilots.

As the doomed bombers plunged downward, the crew members tried to navigate against the centrifugal force that glued flyers to the inside of the fuselage. Crawling along the walls or ceiling to the escape hatch, they grabbed their parachutes. Wounded crew members had to be assisted with their parachute and thrown out first. In the confusion, and sometimes on fire, flyers panicked and tried to step through the hatch, which, at a velocity of 200 kilometres per hour, usually meant that their lower body went through but their upper body slammed against the metal siding. Those who kept their head knew to roll into a ball, with their backs to the slipstream.

Very few airmen had ever jumped with a parachute. They had been trained on what to do in case of an emergency, but in the frantic situation of a plane going down, we'll never know how many flyers lost their lives because they did not know how to jump, or pulled their cord too soon or too late, or suffered the many other mishaps that plagued scared men jumping out of hurling and usually burning machines at thousands of feet above the ground. One Halifax pilot, Stan Coldridge, asked for parachute training once, but his senior officer replied, "We have spent $20,000 to get you this far. There is no way we are going to endanger your lives."[5]

Descending in a freefall from anything above 10,000 feet meant that the airman was in an oxygen-deprived environment, disoriented and often unconscious.[6] Moreover, a descent in winter would likely lead to some form of frostbite, especially as the slipstream frequently sucked off boots, slippers, and socks. The parachute's ripcord was to be pulled at several thousand feet, but injured flyers were often in no condition to do this. Parachutes malfunctioned or caught fire. There were many factors working against an airman ever safely landing.

AIRMEN WHO DIDN'T GET CAUGHT up in a tree or some other structure, or who didn't land in water and drown, buried or hid the parachute and then moved away from the landing, and always in the opposite direction from the burning remains of the plane. "It's a dreadful feeling to find yourself on the ground in enemy territory," recounted Lieutenant-Commander R.E. Bartlett, born and raised in Fort Qu'Appelle, Saskatchewan, and shot down in 1941 while flying in RAF's No. 803 Squadron.[7] However, since most RAF and RCAF bomber raids were carried out at night, the hobbling airmen, known collectively as evaders, usually had a few hours of darkness during which they might put some distance between themselves and enemy search parties.

All flyers were equipped with kits that contained foreign money, greeting cards in several languages, and a silk map of Europe. Candy and chocolate supplied energy for the long run ahead. The escape kits also had purifying pills for potable water and Benzedrine tablets to keep men awake. Brass buttons had a secret compass in them, and the sheepskin-lined flying boots had a hidden pocket containing a file for cutting steel bars. But the most important tools for the evader were his feet and good sense. He had to run.

No one got out of Europe without the assistance of French, Belgian, or Dutch civilians, first farmers and then the Resistance—those groups fighting the German occupation. Both non-combatants and the Resistance fighters aided flyers at great risk to their own lives, as they were routinely tortured and executed when found out by the Gestapo. Canadian navigator Flying Officer Jo Foreman was shot down over France on July 25, 1944, with two of his crew slain in the initial night fighter attack and another dying during the crash. Foreman spent days roaming the French countryside, looking to connect with the Resistance. Most farmers fed him but were too scared to take him in. "As one farmer said," related Foreman, "if [I were] captured at his farm I would be a prisoner, but his entire family, including babies, would be killed on the spot."[8]

The Resistance groups operated in small cells to avoid the cascading effect of losing group after linked group to the Germans. But despite such precautions, some were exposed by spies and collaborators within the civilian population who sought to curry favour with the Nazi occupiers, and others were outed through bad luck, incompetence, or information extracted from torture. Airman Don Cheney of Ottawa, Ontario, remarked, "I owe a huge debt to the French people who sheltered me at risk of concentration camp, torture, and death of themselves and their families."[9]

The Resistance organized several escape routes, using a series of linked safe houses and groups, to ferry Allied flyers to the coast for a clandestine pickup by the Royal Navy, or to secluded aircraft landing sites, or even to neutral Spain. The most famous escape route, the Comet Line, was established by Andrée "Dédée" de Jongh, a Belgian teenager, living in Brussels. With her father, Frederic, and a small Resistance cell, they smuggled airmen from attics and cellars to the countryside, eventually making their way south to Spain. It was a race against time and the de Jonghs knew that they would likely be compromised at some point. The Gestapo eventually broke into the cell and in June 1943 they arrested Frederic. He was executed. On Andrée's thirty-third trip to Spain, she, too, was arrested and sent to a number of concentration camps, where she survived until her liberation in April 1945. However, the Comet Line lived on, with others taking the de Jonghs' place, and by war's end, some 800 Allied soldiers and airmen were ushered to freedom.[10]

Kenneth Woodhouse, a RCAF Spitfire pilot, crashed in France on March 16, 1944, after his Merlin engine died in midair. He went on the run and was aided by the French resistance. He witnessed first-hand the elaborate system used to avoid detection, when he was taken to a secret office where a studious Frenchman forged documents: "Here was everything for making up false identity cards or travel passes, restricted zone passes and so on. There were piles of blank ID cards, legal papers, lists of young men who lived in obscure places (whose identities we would assume), specimen signatures of village mayors and German authorities, rubber stamps and seals, various inks and papers, along with other materials."[11] Woodhouse, along with several other RCAF flyers, was eventually smuggled out of France, carried by rowboat to a motor torpedo boat off the coast, and returned to England. He had been "on the lam" for seven days; others spent months in the care of the French or Belgian underground.

Those who escaped German-occupied Europe were usually posted to a training formation and allowed time to recover from their ordeal. They were also inducted into the Caterpillar Club, receiving a badge and membership card. The little gold caterpillar—signifying the silk parachute—was worn on the left-hand tunic lapel or pocket. An even more select group became members of the Goldfish Club. Their badge was a winged goldfish, awarded to those who ditched their planes in water and lived to tell the tale.

Despite the harrowing tales of escape and the bravery on the part of the underground resistance, thousands of airmen did not find freedom. "For you, the war is over," came the sharp observation from German captors, as flashlights danced on the evader's faces and rough hands dragged them from hiding places. Yet the war was not over. A new war had to be fought: one in bleak conditions; of no longer being a combatant fighting for one's country but a prisoner behind barbed wire.

FLIGHT LIEUTENANT JOHN MAHONEY was shot down over Berlin in late August 1943 and seized almost as soon as he landed on the outskirts of the city that he had just bombed. As he was transported towards an interrogation centre, his mind raced: "What had happened to the rest of the crew? How would my wife take the news that I was missing?... and our little six-months-old boy—how old would he be when I next saw him."[12] The future was uncertain for all airmen in enemy hands, and some did not even survive the first encounters with German civilians.

While most parachuters did not drop into the smashed cities, they often landed among the rural population. Some of the Germans were surprisingly generous, providing drink and aid, while others wanted revenge. From the mid-part of the war, rumours circulated among the aircrews that caught airmen were burned alive—retribution for the fiery havoc they had wreaked on the cities.[13] There is little evidence of this type of murder, although summary executions were carried out by German civilians and military authorities. Condemned as *terrorfliegers*—terror flyers—the Allied airmen were cast by the German military, propaganda machine, and civilians as criminals.[14] German sources estimated that 350 Allied flyers were executed by vigilante civilians during the course of the war.[15]

All airmen recognized that their bombing missions involved killing civilians, but many took solace in never having to see those same civilians face to face. Pilot officer Robert Rogers, a tail gunner with RCAF's No. 419 Squadron, was shot down on December 29, 1944, near Essen. After flak ripped apart his bomber, he was blown clear of the turret into the fuselage of the plane. He awoke as flames licked along his body and face. Rogers stamped out the fire and then found his parachute amid the smell of burnt flesh. He managed to escape the doomed aircraft, but did not get far on the ground. Rogers was handed over to the police in the face of an angry mob that was shouting "Bastard baby killer" and surging forward to, he believed, tear him apart.[16] Rogers survived his ordeal, though he endured multiple interrogations while attempting to heal from his painful burn wounds.

Captives were prodded and baited for information.[17] Any sort of trick or leverage was used by the interrogators, including isolating prisoners in cells, applying heat and cold to break their will, and bombarding them with bright light and noise. Most airmen did not succumb, giving only name, rank, and service number, even as all feared Gestapo retribution and whether they might face a quiet execution that would leave their family forever wondering about their fate.[18] In the end, the flyer's knowledge was limited, and the interrogators rarely resorted to physical abuse.

Pilot Officer Earle White enlisted in 1940 after graduating from McGill with his B.A., and then served overseas as a navigator and bomb aimer with No. 58 Squadron, RAF. On June 20, 1942, while flying in his Halifax Mark II, the bomber was crippled by flak over Germany. White grabbed his parachute and strapped it on, only seconds before the Halifax exploded in midair. He had no memory of bailing out and could only surmise that he had been blown through the Perspex in the nose of the plane. Somehow he had pulled his chute cord before passing out. He landed with a fractured skull and many broken bones. Captured by Germans after scrambling 16 kilometres in a haze of blood and blackouts, he was the lone survivor of his crew. After a series of interrogations, he was transported through a number of cities and villages in an open car, where civilians spat at him in rage.[19] From there, he began almost three years of incarceration in POW camps.

Prisoners were put in boarded-up boxcar trains for the long trip eastward. It was a crowded and uncomfortable ride, and it took two or three days to travel to eastern Germany or Poland. The prisoners were given little food and water, and no place to deposit human waste except for an ever-filling bucket that slopped its vile contents over the floor and onto cringing prisoners. This was a period of self-doubt and open worry. One RCAF airman, Grant McRae, described it as the start of his "starvation vacation."[20]

IN THE FIRST THREE YEARS OF THE WAR, the limited number of Western prisoners was spread through a series of camps. By 1942, the German military authorities dealt with the growing number of Allied prisoners of war by ordering each of the armed services to be responsible for its own prisoners. The Wehrmacht processed all army prisoners in a Stalag, while the Luftwaffe incarcerated air force prisoners in a Stalag Luft. Naval prisoners were interned at Marlag und Milag Nord, in north-western Germany.[21]

Most of the camps were surrounded by a double fence about 2.5 metres high, with the 2 metre gap between the fences filled with barbed wire. Inside the main fence was a low wire, known as the warning wire, and anyone who passed over it was liable to be shot by armed guards in towers. The camp consisted of a series of low barrack buildings for the prisoners, with additional huts to store supplies and sports equipment, or even house small theatres. The prison grounds were usually sandy, and prisoners soon carved out space for football or other activities.[22] While all the camps were different, Flight Lieutenant John Taylor, an RCAF navigator shot down in late 1941 in Africa, wrote about the hard truth all men faced: "We were prisoners of war, which was a fate I had never foreseen for myself."[23] Warrior status was ripped away and a prisoner was forced to embrace a new, emasculated role in which all aspects of his life were governed by strict rules. A prisoner was now a "Kriegie," the shorthand for a prisoner of war, abbreviated from *Kriegsgefangenen*.

Newly arrived Kriegies were viewed suspiciously by the prisoners since the Germans often tried to insert their own spies and stooges into the camp. Subtle questions about Canada, hockey, or geographical places, quickly revealed a sweating and nervous prisoner to be the real thing. The new prisoners arrived with few possessions. The German authorities provided little, and it was the other prisoners who offered tooth brushes, clothing, and essentials. After a few weeks or months, the regular shipment of care packages from the Red Cross and loved ones augmented meagre supplies and replenished the group stock for future prisoners.

While the Germans treated the Western Allies relatively well, there were sadistic guards who took delight in taunting the men. As one Canadian prisoner remarked, "Our relationship with our captors was variable. As individuals some were quite decent and honourable within the constraints of their function and responsibility, others were utter 'bastards.' It was quite apparent that the decent ones had served in battle while the 'bastards' were substandard types who relished the authority they could never otherwise have attained."[24] No matter the guards, however, the rules of imprisonment included multiple daily role calls and control over mail and food, as well as restrictions over movement and action.

Prisoners had their own rules too. There was a hierarchy, and one of their own was elected to represent their needs and pass on their complaints to the German commandant running the camp. The "Man of Confidence" or "Senior British Officer," as the non-commissioned officers (NCOs) and officers called their separate leaders, held an unenviable job as the senior prisoner. He was usually held accountable for the actions of the entire group and was liable to face screams of rage over escape attempts or other perceived embarrassing events. The Germans nonetheless liked to deal with a prisoner representative, and these tough men defended the prisoners' rights and collective dignity.[25] The Allied prisoners also formed various committees, headed by long-service prisoners, to monitor actions in the camp but also to arrange for sports, education, and libraries, with the most secretive group coordinating escapes.

Information was rich currency for prisoners, and the new Kriegies were to share what they knew about the war effort, sports teams in Canada, and the latest popular songs. Occasionally, a German paper found its way into the camp, traded from a

Canadian airmen at Stalag Luft III. Note that they wear their uniforms.

guard or a civilian. A prisoner with language skills would translate it and his comrades could spend hours trying to decipher the propaganda and multi-layered messages. Hitler's forced guests were also adept at building contraband radios from scrap pieces collected or exchanged in the camps, often with the help of bribed guards. Every night the radios picked up the BBC broadcast. The news was taken down in rapid shorthand and then written out in fuller prose, to be distributed throughout the camp huts. When it arrived, lookouts watched for the guards while the prisoners huddled around an orator who read out the news; the best announcers made an art of it, using rhetoric, flourish, and some biting commentary on the Axis defeats. "Attempts were frequently made by the Germans to locate and confiscate the radio but they never succeeded," observed RCAF Flight Sergeant George Brown, a prisoner as of late August 1943.[26] Not all prisoners were so lucky or wily in hiding their radios. When the devices were discovered, the prisoners set to building new ones. Camp newspapers were also created, often by compiling information from the radio broadcasts and letters. The direction of the wider war effort brought the men together, providing optimism that the conflict might someday come to a close.

Upon an airman's failure to return to Britain, the military authorities sent letters to the next of kin on the status of the missing Canadian. No one knew—not the authorities nor the family—if the airman was dead, on the run, or in a prisoner-of-war camp. Often the German authorities withheld letter privileges from a prisoner for some time as a bargaining tool in the hope of extracting useable intelligence from him. And so it might take months for a family to learn that a loved one was alive.

Prisoners were allowed to write two letters and four postcards a month, which were sent through the Red Cross, and so there was the ability to get word home, albeit in sanitized form. Maimed prisoners—usually crippled with amputations or horrific burns—were also repatriated to England and brought news from behind barbed wire. Squadron Leader George Hill—who wore the DFC with two bars and had shot down fourteen enemy aircraft before he crashed in April 1944—had a repatriated friend write to his wife, "Don't name the baby until I get back!!"[27] His wife probably went ahead with the naming since it would be more than a year before he was reunited with his family.

BEFORE THE INVASION of Europe in June 1944, most Canadian prisoners were airmen, except for those who were captured during the failed Dieppe raid of August 19, 1942. Some 1,946 prisoners were marched into captivity. As they were moved east towards their new camps, word got around quickly that officers and NCOs, under the Geneva Convention, did not have to work, so most Canadians removed their rank from their uniform and provided their jailors with new ones, as corporals and sergeants. The Germans shook their heads, wondering how all the privates had been killed on the beaches! Many men kept their new rank for months, even years, and the Canadian government did not offer corrections.

The Dieppe prisoners faced a challenge unique from other Allied prisoners. After the operation, the Germans were furious to discover on the beaches the bodies of a few German prisoners with their hands tied.[28] The victors also seized orders stipulating that prisoners were to be tied to prevent their escape and the destruction of documents. This was not terribly nefarious, considering the nature of the raid that was planned as a hit-and-run affair in which prisoners would be dragged back onto the boats with the retreating forces. But the outraged Germans in early September ordered that, in retaliation, the Dieppe prisoners be manacled.

Canadian infantrymen captured during the Dieppe raid of August 19, 1942.
Some 1,946 Canadians were made prisoner.

An angry Churchill bristled against the punitive actions and, without consulting Ottawa, announced that German prisoners in Britain and Canada would in turn be shackled. The Canadian government was nervous about the tit-for-tat manoeuvre, but went along in the interest of unity. This led to a new round of binding the Dieppe prisoners, who were manacled during the day, from eight in the morning to eight at night. This manacling interfered with sports or leisure activities and was a humiliating action since many of the men could not properly defecate with their hands tied. After many prisoners' complaints, two medical orderlies per hut were allowed to keep their hands free to assist prisoners in pulling down their trousers and carrying out their bodily business.

The manacles were kept on for about two months and then replaced with hand-cuffs that allowed greater movement. The ingenious Canadians were always trying to pick the locks, and one of them discovered that the sardine cans in the Red Cross package had a key for opening the can that also unlocked the handcuffs. The prisoners took to their huts when they needed to, using the cover there to free their hands and rub down their wrists, though they rested the chains around their necks in case the guards burst in. Over time, the Germans became haphazard about policing the cuffs, even though the policy continued for nearly a year, from December 1942 to November 1943.

Many of the Dieppe prisoners, having been injured by shell fragments and small arms fire, were cared for in German hospitals, albeit with little compassion. Shortages of supplies, bandages, and pain medication meant that operations were often carried out without anaesthesia. When the prisoners were stabilized, they were usually shipped to the prisoner-of-war camps, where there was little medical treatment. It fell to the other prisoners to nurse their injured comrades back to health, both the soldiers and the airmen, who often arrived with weeping wounds. Canadian Andrew Cox, who flew with the RAF and had his Hampden bomber shot down on September 8, 1940, after more than forty sorties, wrote of the injured airmen in the camps. One of them had no eyelids and his nose and ears burned off. They occupied the same sleeping space. Cox watched his friend, who had other wounds and therefore had to be monitored at night, sleeping with no eyelids, so that only the whites of his eyeballs were visible. Another prisoner had much of his abdomen torn away by a shell blast. "He suffered great pain with the bandages sticking to the wound. A couple of enterprising prisoners were able to acquire through the German Luftwaffe some plexiglass from a crashed Junkers 88 aircraft and constructed a cover for his wound."[29] With this plastic shielding, the prisoner was able to avoid a life-ending infection and eventually recover. Countless lives were saved through medical ingenuity.

"FOOD WAS ALWAYS in just short enough supply to replace sex as the dominant preoccupation," observed Ray Silver, who was a prisoner from mid-1942.[30] Everyone was hungry, especially the young men whose bodies required a higher calorific intake for sustenance. In the morning, prisoners often received ersatz bitter coffee made of burnt barley, acorns, and chicory. Lunch and dinner was an assortment of turnips and potatoes. Some horsemeat might be thrown into the mix, and any other scraps that could be found. Pilot Officer Earle White described an incident of particular desperation: "Food was scarce and a wandering cat was killed with a well-aimed stone. As we tried to retrieve the frozen carcass from between the two wire fences, the Germans played a game of firing down the line whenever anyone leaned across. After three days they relented and allowed us to salvage the cat. It made a fine stew."[31] Even as prisoners became accustomed to horse and cat meat (although drew the line at the thousands of rats), the bread was particularly trying. It was a heavy, sour black loaf that seemed to consist primarily of sawdust. It probably did. Despite its unappealing taste and texture, there were fights over the bread crumbs, and any division of food took an excessively long period as each divided piece was weighed and studied by the ravenous prisoners.

"Food is the most important thing in a prisoner's life," believed RCAF navigator John Taylor. "It is for this reason that the Red Cross parcel is so important. Each prisoner receives one per week, and with this can supplement his ration to achieve a good diet."[32] Packages included treats and sweets, cigarettes and canned goods, and usually reading material and small games. If prisoners had been forced to subsist on the German food alone, they would have starved to death, like the poor Russian prisoners, who expired from starvation and disease by the millions. There were interruptions to the Red Cross deliveries, with White lamenting a trying period during the spring of 1943: "During the ten weeks we ate rotten potatoes and sawdust bread and ended up having to be counted in our beds, so many were too weak to stand outside. The hot meal was a weak soup or stew containing bits of turnip or cabbage or barley, and very rarely bits of meat. My meat portion one day consisted of a dog's paw with hair still on it."[33] RCAF gunner Sergeant Jim Finnie, who was captured when his bomber went down in France on July 4, 1944, remarked, "The Canadian Red Cross ... were very, very good, and a lot of thought had gone into preparing these food parcels." Without them, "you would have starved." Nonetheless, the incarceration, boredom, and lack of food, even with the Red Cross packages, meant that "When you went to bed at night you thought of food, when you wakened up in the morning you thought of food, it was always on your mind, that was the most important thing, food, food, food."[34]

A critical component of the Red Cross package was the cigarette ration. "Cigarettes were the medium of exchange in the camp," said George Brown, and they could be used to secure food, items, and almost anything.[35] A black market system emerged between the prisoners and guards, as well as with civilians outside the wire. There were even traders—prisoners who moved freely in the camps, securing material for one man, perhaps a chess set or a notebook, conducting the exchange, and making a commission (in cigarettes) for the transaction.[36] Those men with fierce nicotine habits faced difficult choices, and many traded their food or small pleasures as they smoked through the most recognizable source of currency in the camps. Sergeant Tom Crandell, a navigator with No. 419 Squadron who was shot down on April 20, 1943, wrote of his love for hockey and sports in the camps and his need to curtail his nicotine habit: "I smoke few cigarettes but they are money in this place."[37] Flight Sergeant Arnold Hanes was one of the smokers, a habit he had started at eleven years old. Even as he was "starving to death," he still dealt his hoarded scraps of food for cigarettes. In his mind, "A cigarette was more of a pacifier than a piece of bread."[38]

BY THE VERY END OF MARCH 1942, after less than half a year as a prisoner, RCAF Flight Sergeant Erle "Dusty" Miller of Renfrew, Ontario, wrote in his private diary, "Nothing new. Life so hellish boring. Getting used to this half-starved state."[39] All prisoners faced what they called "barbed wire disease."[40] This malaise was a combination of restlessness and depression, and prisoners counselled one another through the dark periods that came to every man at some point during the long months and years of incarceration. Within their confined grounds, and always under the watchful eyes of armed guards, prisoners walked in circles, sharing old stories and future dreams. Talk was vital, as were the stories and gossip that circulated through the camps on everything from food and mail to the eventual end of the war. "It's amazing the way men will repeat rumours that they know in their hearts are too good to be true," penned one Canadian prisoner in his diary. "There is no place on earth so full of wishful thinking as a P.O.W. camp. It's like drowning men grasping at straws, or like men repeating things as if the mere repetition could make them come true; make facts out of fancies."[41]

The YMCA eased the lives of thousands, and likely saved many too, through the donation of books, sporting equipment, and art supplies. Most of the leisure activities that prisoners engaged in to pass the time came through Canadian donations. Sports were popular with the young men. The various nations excelled at their own games, with the Aussies and English fighting it out on the cricket pitch, and baseball the obsession for Canadians and Americans. Everyone liked to kick the soccer ball around. Pathfinder Tom Lane of St. Boniface, Manitoba, who was shot down in the summer of 1943, described himself as a "Three Games a Day" man, willing to play anything with anyone in order to take his mind off his imprisonment.[42] Homesick Canucks during the winter months created ice rinks, although the cold might be sufficient to maintain ice for a few weeks at most. The desire for hockey would not be denied.

Most camps received musical instruments from Canada, and small orchestras were formed. "The quality of the music was excellent as we had some of the best musicians from the great orchestras of England and from Polish masters," felt Flight Sergeant George Brown.[43] After two years in an Italian prisoner-of-war camp, John Taylor was moved to Stalag Luft III at Sagan in Poland. He remembered fondly the rich theatre life there, with his comrades putting on a new play every week. They ranged from Noel Coward's *Design for Living* to Shakespeare's *Macbeth*, as well as original plays written by prisoners.[44] The troupe scrounged material for costumes and wigs, as well as the sets, which were often constructed from the sturdy Red Cross parcel boxes. By 1944, Stalag Luft III had a theatre that sat an audience of 360. Somewhat bizarrely, as one Canadian remarked, the German prison guards often asked to attend the show, and paid for admission: "A charge of one cigarette per person was made at the door and the proceeds were used to buy new costumes."[45]

Young men took the opportunity to better themselves in the camps, either to improve intellectually or prepare for a postwar career. Sixty thousand textbooks were supplied by the Canadian Legion, Red Cross, or in care packages to give prisoners an opportunity to study a new language, literature, or more practical skills, such as farming or mechanics.[46] Most camps had well-stocked libraries. Westerns and detective novels were gobbled up, while the racy bits of *Lady Chatterley's Lover* were read aloud and in secret. While some prisoners coped by living in the moment, others pondered a postwar future. Lists were kept of future jobs or travel spots. And when prisoners were fed up with studying or dreaming, some took solace in more potent spirits. Murry Bishop of New Minas, Nova Scotia, who was shot down over Germany

Prisoners fought the strain of imprisonment and boredom. These Kriegies are tending to a garden.

in March 1943, partook of the temporary pleasure of distilling booze from sugar, raisins, and yeast, which created a noxious alcohol to "break the boredom."[47]

The trials of imprisonment were warded off in other ways. Even though they had dull razors and little soap, prisoners tried to keep a clean face as per military regulation. Uniforms were stitched together and boots worn thin, but there was pride in appearance and a discipline of the body. Others passed the time by trying to order their most inner feelings. RCAF Flight Lieutenant John Mahoney served much of the war at Stalag Luft III. Like all POWs, he was thankful for the Red Cross packages, although his "most precious possession" was a small "war log" in which he detailed his experiences, providing him with the much needed opportunity to make sense of his trying wartime incarceration.[48]

DESPITE THE SPORTS, education, arts, and imaginings that sustained prisoners, many struggled with their gloomy existence. "Kriegy life meant sharing minimal living space under maximum stress conditions," witnessed downed navigator Ray Silver. "Day and night, in fair season and foul, we were thrust together in such close proximity that every skin blemish was counted."[49] Malnourishment led to fights over the division of food, while sick men with frayed tempers raged about minor slights and aggravations. Straw-filled mattresses were infested with fleas, and prisoners shared their already limited space with lice and rats. The daily inspections and parades by the Germans were trying, as well as periodic raids on prisoners' huts to locate contraband. Trooper Sam Dunn of Stalag IX C in Molsdorf recounted that the uncertainty of the wider war effort left him demoralized: "We thought we could be there five years. Could be ten years, or even fifteen. And that was what bothered me. Not the fact that we wouldn't get out, but when. You know, when they send you to jail, you even know that you're going to be there five years, or ten years. But we didn't know that. The uncertainty was the worst part. It was a real strain on you."[50]

The prisoners tended to band together, but not everyone was chummy. Like in all stressful environments, some men were unlikeable or did not pull their weight. While most of the officer camps saw cooperation among the prisoners, the enlisted men's camps were often divided. George Reid, a Seaforth Highlander captured in Italy, wrote of the Liverpool, Glasgow, and Irish gangs among the British population in several camps in which he was incarcerated. Beatings were not uncommon. Eventually, the Canadians banded together and sent a delegation to each of the three leaders. If any Canadian was hurt, they promised that the next victim would be the leader of the gang. At the latrine, in the chow line, or out in the yard—they would find him and kill him. "After that, we didn't have a problem with them."[51]

"POW life was a real mental shock," remembered Pilot Officer James Smith, a navigator with RCAF No. 432 Squadron who was imprisoned for almost two years. "The complete loss of freedom, anxiety about the future, thoughts about family and loved ones so far away, inadequate food and sheer boredom" all ate away at the prisoner. "Most managed to cope, but a few cracked up. It was called 'going around the bend.'"[52] Pilot Officer Earle White saw that "The grim situation was too much for some men." White testified that "suicide attempts were frequent but rarely successful for it took too long to bleed to death after cutting the wrist with a safety razor blade."[53] He observed one soldier who jumped from a second floor window and led with his head, while another demoralized airman, having made his decision, walked calmly to the inner wire fence and climbed it in front of guards who promptly shot him dead. Flight Lieutenant Al Aldridge observed that many of the men were "very despondent."[54]

Flight Lieutenant John Fry, a twenty-seven-year-old university-educated flyer from Jordan, Ontario, who was shot down in April 1943, described the static environment of the Kriegies after thirteen months of imprisonment: "It sometimes seems hard to realize that the rest of the world has gone on turning just the same since April last year."[55] While the home front support, care, and love sustained many men, Pilot Officer Harry Jay recounted how a number of fellow prisoners received "Dear John" letters from girlfriends and wives who would no longer wait for them. The men, in a show of masculine grit, often posted the painful letters on a message board, for all to see. Dark humour helped many prisoners deal with their painful conditions. Squadron Leader George Hill was imprisoned at Stalag Luft I at Barth, Germany, on the Baltic Sea, and he kept track of some of the pointed letters that circulated through the camps in a small scrapbook:

"... I'm living with a private, darling, but please don't stop my allotment because you make more money than he does!"

"I'm living with an artillery captain now—he's a swell chap, I know you'll like him...."[56]

Such painful realities may have brought some comfort to Hill, although there was no doubt deep unease in those sayings and cartoons, and in Hill's own need to write them in his secret notebook. Pilot Officer Harry Jay was shaken by one long-time British airman prisoner whose girl wrote to him that she had met an American, asserting meanly, "I'd rather marry a 1943 hero than a 1941 coward."[57] Prisoners carried many unspoken burdens.

"BECAUSE WE WERE BEHIND BARBED WIRE did not mean that we were out of the war," claimed Flight Sergeant George Brown. "Many of the boys spent most of their time planning ways to carry out sabotage, stealing coal, and anything else that was not under lock and key."[58] Prisoners felt it was their duty to disrupt work activities or to escape. The Germans accepted this attitude in the first half of the war, treating escape attempts almost like a game. However, by early 1944 the desperation and hardening effects of the losing war effort led to much stiffer penalties for attempted escapers, including execution.

Officers and NCOs were not required to work, but most prisoners took the opportunity a work detail gave to pass outside of the wire for a change of pace and scenery, and the chances it afforded for interacting with civilians, who often supplied illegal material for cigarettes. Many of the labour projects were in local factories, mines, or farms. Machinery was jammed, tools dulled, broken, or stolen, the work done haphazardly and with much inefficiency. Everything at the prisoners' disposal was put to use to slow or disrupt work done on behalf of the Nazi state.

Prisoners outside of the camps had opportunities to escape. But an individual Kriegie, in weakened physical condition and usually ill-equipped, needed assistance from the collective. And so it was made clear to all prisoners that any plan had first to be cleared by the escaping committee. These committees were set up in all the camps. If the decision was given to allow a prisoner to go, food was gathered, papers created, and maps issued. Flight Sergeant George Brown wrote that the "escape club ... had cameras, which were forbidden, and procured film on the black market from the Germans. They developed forged passports for those who tried to escape."[59] Civilian clothes were acquired, German money stashed away, and even train tickets manufactured. John Fry, a graduate of the University of Toronto who spoke Spanish, French, and German, gave language classes to his fellow prisoners at Stalag Luft III camp in the weeks before they planned their escape. Joseph Asselin, a flight lieutenant shot down in 1941 and imprisoned in eight camps over five years, made three failed escapes, and learned how to compromise his German guards by gaining illicit material through "stealing parties" and then blackmailing them to aid the escape.[60] An enormous amount of energy went into these plans, even though very few escapers got far, as they had to travel through thousands of kilometres of Germany and then through German-occupied Western Europe. Only 30 of the 10,000 British and Dominion air force personnel imprisoned in Germany found freedom.[61] Nonetheless, the planning kept the prisoners active, engaged, and obstinate in refusing to succumb to the malaise of their prison experience.

The most common method of escape for prisoners was the digging of tunnels. The tunnels took months to construct, and a constant cat-and-mouse game went on between the prisoners and their jailors. The guards, known as "goons," were generally middle-aged men, adolescents, or wounded veterans from the front. They took to their jobs with widely differing levels of engagement. The apathetic and bored guards were easy to deal with, and could be bribed with chocolate bars, according to Flying Officer John Anderson, who flew thirty-nine sorties with No. 405 Squadron before being shot down.[62] Not all guards were so compliant. Aggressive goons sought out the tunnels, inflicting night-time raids on the barracks to catch prisoners at their tunnelling work. Downed RCAF airman Andrew Cox worked on one underground passageway at Stalag Luft I. The prisoners burrowed a tunnel under the stove and floorboards. It was only half a metre high and wide, narrowing even further in parts. Reinforced with wooden bed-boards to shore up the roof, it was permeated by water during the spring thaw, yet still the prisoners pushed forward in the muck. At the entrance to the tunnel was an encouraging sign: "England, 350 miles this way."[63] Two French prisoners eventually informed on the men after half a year of work. Because of the length of time it took to dig the tunnels, most were eventually discovered: a mistaken tool left in the open or a slightly ajar cover to the pit, another prisoner attempting to curry favour or a spy within the ranks.

The German acceptance that it was the right of prisoners to attempt to escape changed in March 1944, when the Nazi high command passed their secret "Bullet Decree" (*Kugel-Erlass*). Those who were caught escaping would be transported to the Maulthausen concentration camp near Vienna, where they were either immediately executed or worked to death. This new directive was enforced after the "Great Escape" from Stalag Luft III in Sagan, Poland, in late March 1944. The tunnels at Stalag Luft III were engineering feats, as the prisoners—many of them Canadians, including Wally Flood, the "Tunnel King," who orchestrated many of the engineering feats—dug dozens of feet down through shifting sand, and then pushed out horizontally, seeking to go beyond the camp wire.[64] One of the tunnels, "Harry," was more than 100 metres long. Wooden beams prevented cave-ins, while a bellows machine

Diagram of "Harry," one of the three tunnels dug at Stalag Luft III, as part of the Great Escape on the night of March 24, 1944.

pumped oxygen into the claustrophobic tunnels as half-naked men scratched at the walls with home-made tools while lying on their stomachs. It was brutal work. Every night, diggers went down into the three tunnels through secret hatches in their huts that were covered by cement slabs in a kitchen, washroom, and under a stove. Sand and dirt was pulled out on trolleys and dumped stealthily throughout the camp, usu-ally in the cesspit under the latrine. An ingenious method of dropping dirt involved specially constructed bladders, held in the men's wide pants, with which the prison-ers, known as penguins for their stiff-legged waddling walk, released dirt throughout

Memorial poster of the fifty Allied prisoners of the Great Escape,
who were executed by the Germans. Six were Canadians.

the camp, scuffing it into the existing soil and sand to ensure the colour of the excavated dirt would not be noticed by the guards.

Despite the carefully camouflaged work, two of the three tunnels were discovered; the third allowed seventy-six airmen to slip free late on the night of March 24. All but three prisoners were recaptured. The Germans were livid, although the prisoners had seen this before. With the new order, however, fifty of the escapees were executed, including six Canadians. The ashes were eventually returned to Sagan camp, and the prisoners wore black armbands and created a cairn to mark their graves.[65]

The number of escape attempts decreased in 1944, partially because the Allies were clearly winning the war and also because fewer men wished to risk their lives. After the calamity of the Great Escape, naval pilot R.E. Bartlett, a prisoner since 1941, "lost a lot of the enthusiasm for escaping.... I decided to wait it out."[66] While modern films, television shows, and popular culture portray the prisoner-of-war experience as one long goon-baiting exercise or a relentless desire to escape, the true battle fought by all prisoners was against boredom and ennui, demoralization and disease, hunger and humiliation. Cecil Loughlin, an RCAF flyer who spent more than two years in Lamsdorf prison camp, during which time he dropped from 165 to 110 pounds, summed up the prisoners' ordeal: "To come out alive was our main objective."[67]

CHAPTER 3

THE HITLER LINE

The war in the Mediterranean theatre was fierce and costly, and it had ground to a halt in the winter of 1943–1944. Both the Allied and the Axis fighting forces were at near parity of strength on the ground, and although the Allies had overwhelming control of the air, they were hamstrung by a long logistical tail that stretched all the way back to North Africa. The Italians, Germany's weak ally in the Axis powers, had sued for peace in September 1943, hoping to avoid titanic campaigns on their soil, but the Germans refused to relinquish the ground, and moved easily from allies to occupiers. Humiliated repeatedly during the war, the Italians lost some 205,000 battlefield dead, and another 250,000 who would die in captivity or during the occupation and fighting over their territory.[1] Defeat was bad; defeat and German occupation worse; defeat, occupation, and witnessing the Allies and Axis armies rage up and down one's country for three years was a further reminder that the war one hopes for is never the war that is received.

On the east coast, the 1st Canadian Infantry Division, like all the divisions in the British Eighth Army, was recovering after the harsh fighting of 1943. During the Battle of Ortona in December of that year, the Canadians had suffered 2,339 casualties. Though over 2,400 reinforcements were sent forward to replenish the ranks, every platoon, company, and infantry battalion remained under-strength, as additional survivors were sent away on training and illness claimed even more men.[2] The new reinforcements arrived from Britain or were culled from rear-echelon formations. Twenty-one-year-old Jack Shepherd was one of them, arriving in December 1943 to shore up the Hastings and Prince Edward Regiment. As he marched to the front, he passed the bodies of about a dozen members of the Royal Canadian Regiment, wrapped in blood-stained tarps and awaiting burial. The complacency of training, with its make-believe battles, was left behind in that appalling moment, to be replaced, in his words, by "a dark blanket of dread."[3]

The new reinforcements, almost all of whom were infantrymen, were instructed by the long-service officers and NCOs on how to survive, but the experienced men viewed these green soldiers, who now outnumbered the veterans, with an unspoken wariness. "The old-timers, including me, wouldn't fraternize with them, but rather stayed within our own group, even though they would try to engage us in conversation, card games, and the like," recounted West Nova Scotia Regiment infantryman John O'Brien. "They didn't realize that we wanted no new friends to later grieve over ... we had been hurt inside far too many times in the past."[4] Over time, the new men were accepted, although the months following Ortona witnessed a test of morale. Fallen comrades were grieved, and an undercurrent of grumbling ran through the ranks about the divisional commander, Major-General Chris Vokes, who had commanded the 1st Canadian Infantry Division in relentless frontal attacks against the Gully, and then Ortona, throughout December. Aggressive and unimaginative, the red-headed and frequently swearing Vokes and his brigadiers had rightly relied on firepower to pound the enemy's lines, but had failed to prepare follow-on forces to support success. Some of Vokes's infantrymen had begun to call him "the butcher." However, the general's options had been limited in the battle, and it

Vickers machine-gunner of the Saskatoon Light Infantry (M.G.) laying down harassing fire north of Ortona, Italy, January 1944.

would not have been easy to bypass the defended city, as some suggested at the time and have ever since.[5] The open ground to the west of Ortona was held by the Germans in strength, with dense artillery formations positioned to punish those forces that advanced towards crossroads that snaked through the interior leading to Rome. And so Ortona had been reduced to an attritional slugging match, with both sides battering each other until the Germans withdrew their mauled divisions.[6] The debates over Vokes and Ortona would periodically flare up after the war, but in the early winter of 1944, all Canadian infantrymen were far more focused on survival in their slit trenches.

THE CANADIANS WERE ABOUT 2 KILOMETRES NORTH OF ORTONA, which was now an important winter headquarters and seaport for supply. They faced the enemy dug in along a series of ridges. There was an empty and blasted No Man's Land

The price of battle. Canadians sing a hymn at a mass burial
for their fallen comrades in Italy.

between the opposing sides, abandoned by day yet active at night. Robert Thexton of the West Nova Scotia Regiment, who returned to his battalion after recovering from a bullet to the chest, found that the "landscape was bleak and reminded me of pictures I had seen of the battlefields in World War I."[7] Shell-damaged, skeleton-like trees were shrouded in the dreary rain. Slit trenches for two men and more permanent trenches dissolved into a slurry of slush and mud. Unlike the Great War's Western Front trench system, the defensive lines north of Ortona were generally unconnected, based on weapons pits, with gaps protected by thin concentrations of barbed wire. Pestiferous sniper fire snapped back and forth, although only the foolhardy tempted fate by showing their heads above the fortifications. And it was cold. After a long night of sentry duty, woollen battle dress was often thick with frost until a man's body warmed it up, leaving it clammy and sodden. Rough army blankets draped over shoulders brought some relief, but were soon fouled and wet, and remained that way for weeks. Sentries scowled at the enemy lines; officers checked on them periodically, sometimes bringing body-warming rum. For the fought-out 1st Division, morale was tested over the coming months of battle that were marked by boredom, deprivation, and death.

The Allies were stopped well short of Rome. Attesting to the secondary nature of the front, Eighth Army commander General Bernard Montgomery and Supreme Commander Dwight Eisenhower had departed for Britain at the end of 1943 to lead the assault on Europe. Monty was much loved by the Canadians in the Eighth Army, and they lamented his loss. Farley Mowat of the Hastings and Prince Edward Regiment of the 1st Canadian Division, and no great friend of senior commanders, remarked of Montgomery, "There were those who hated him, but they were not amongst the fighting troops. There were a good many who were angered by him, but there were few men in the infantry who did not trust him, as they had never in the past, and would never in the future, trust another general officer."[8] With the best and most recognizable generals moved to Britain, it was evident to all that Italy was further pushed to the periphery, an unwanted drain on the main assault but still useful in holding down the enemy forces in battle so they could not be transferred to shore up the Western or Eastern fronts.

The new theatre commander, General Harold Alexander, inherited the stalemated battlefield. He was a decorated veteran of the Great War, who, as commander of the ground forces in Sicily and Italy, only lightly controlled his American and British generals. The cheerful British general was always overshadowed by George Patton, Mark Clark, and Bernard Montgomery, even though there is little evidence to suggest that a more dominating commander would have got more out of his subordinates. Alexander had spent much of the war as "mediator-in-chief," sorting out his quarrelsome generals, but he knew in early 1944 that his role was now to tie down the Germans in Italy and wear them out in combat.

Adolf Hitler played into the Allied strategy, ordering that the "Gustav Line, [south of Rome], must be held at all costs for the sake of political consequences."[9] Hitler sent more of his steadily dwindling formations to Italy, and by late 1943, Field Marshal Albert Kesselring had 400,000 troops—in 25 divisions (with additional support and logistical elements)—in Italy. Another 37 Axis divisions were situated throughout the Balkans and Southern France to protect against invasion.[10] While strength on the ground in Italy was about equal, the Allies had colossal advantages in the air since most of the German air force had been pulled back to defend the homeland against the Allied bombing campaign. Offsetting the Allied airpower, the enemy had all the benefits of fighting on land of his choosing, employing high ground or choking off narrow road networks.

Few expected a breakthrough in the difficult terrain that one American general dismissed as a "blind alley."[11] But while both sides committed resources and forces into the theatre of battle, it was the Nazis, hemorrhaging badly on the Eastern Front, who could ill afford the maelstrom in Italy.

OVER THE WINTER, with the Americans attempting an advance to Rome in a January offensive, it was up to the Eighth Army, with the Canadians as one of the key formations in the line, to probe the enemy positions, raiding and patrolling aggressively in order to prevent them from sending reinforcements to the main battle front. The Eighth Army was now commanded by General Oliver Leese, a tall, breezy former guardsman who had orchestrated several victories during the desert war in North Africa and had been commander in Sicily of XXX Corps, in which the 1st Canadian Division served.

In this aggressive trench warfare, the 1st Canadian Division was called on to harass the enemy, gather information, deplete his strength, and keep him focused on the front. Intelligence patrols were small and meant to avoid contact with the enemy; standing patrols and fighting patrols consisted of several dozen infantrymen who ambushed or crashed the enemy lines. Prisoners were prized, and often headquarters rewarded the fighting patrol with a bottle of whiskey if they came back with a Kraut.

The Canadians screwed up their courage for these butcher-and-bolt operations. Badges and unit identifiers were cut from uniforms, bulky equipment was left behind, and faces were blackened with burnt cork. The men of the dark were to move fast and quietly, past barbed wire and metal pickets. A full moon, new snow, or even frozen puddles around shell craters, could give away the raiders. Most nights there was little contact, but the engagements when Germans were encountered were bloody and costly affairs.

The survivors returned to a stiff shot of rum, while, as the Royal Canadian Regiment's Captain Strome Galloway noted, the "unlucky ones stayed out and their skeletons were recovered in the spring."[12] The spike of fear and danger made patrols and raids unpopular with most of the soldiers. Part of the frustration with the raids was that they were of questionable value to the front-line troops, with one Canadian sneering that "most of the patrolling was worthless, morale destroying and wasteful of manpower."[13] The high command, from battalion commanders to the corps head-quarters, thought differently. Lieutenant-Colonel Ronnie Waterman of the West Nova Scotia Regiment even remarked candidly that "he was well aware that the junior officers and the men hated his guts for ordering them out on night patrols, but there was no other way to obtain necessary information about the enemy and their plans."[14] The view from the front was different from that of the commanders in the rear.

PRIME MINISTER WILLIAM LYON MACKENZIE KING's government was anxious to send more Canadians to the Italian theatre of battle. During the late summer of 1943, the minister of national defence, J.L. Ralston, had convinced King to approve the transfer of I Canadian Corps headquarters and the 5th Canadian Armoured Division to Italy. The Canadian Army in England consisted of two infantry corps and supporting units totalling close to half a million men, but now Ottawa looked to split them up. The prime minister had enjoyed the positive media reports of the Canadians in the Sicily campaign, and he now hoped that Italy might also accrue additional coverage for his government, while avoiding costly disasters like Dieppe.[15] It was not much of a foundation for a strategic approach to the war, although neither Ralston nor King had mapped what such an approach might be—aside from setting the guiding principle that domestic political expediency was always to trump an overseas military strategy. King's primary motivation was to avoid casualties and restrict commitments to avoid another conscription crisis like the one that had torn the country apart in 1917. He was convinced that Italy would only consist of limited warfighting, while Ralston, urged on by senior army commanders, wished the army to forge a reputation in battle.

In direct opposition to Ralston, however, First Canadian Army Commander General Andrew McNaughton was dead set against splitting his army. The charismatic, nationalist McNaughton, the face of the Canadian Army since he had led the 1st Canadian Infantry Division overseas in late 1939, oversaw the overseas army's growth into the largest force ever fielded by Canada. Yet it was an army in waiting, and it was broken up in 1943 when the 1st Infantry Division and 1st Canadian Army Tank Brigade were sent to fight in Sicily. Such reckless action, McNaughton argued, diluted the Dominion war effort, but Ralston felt he needed the short-term objective of the Canadians fighting alongside their allies.[16] McNaughton's fury was redoubled in late 1943 when Ralston asked to send another armoured division and a corps headquarters to Italy. The row permanently damaged their already shaky relationship. With the British having lost faith in McNaughton after several failed training exercises and his fierce objections to breaking up his army, the chief of the imperial general staff, General Alan Brooke, conspired against the Canadian general.[17] The Canadian Army commander was edged out of command in late 1943, and the 5th Canadian Armoured Division and a corps headquarters were committed to the Italian theatre.

General Alexander did not need another operational headquarters, and an inexperienced one at that. He complained to London. Alexander was ignored, as political motivations trumped military necessity, but in the end, to avoid the dangers of shipping hundreds of tanks that could be sunk by U-boats, the newly arriving Canadians took over the machines from the outgoing 7th Armoured Division that was moved to Europe. That made sense, but it meant that the 5th Canadian Armoured Division inherited worn-out trucks and tanks that were described, in one official report, as being "for the most part desert veterans and they looked it."[18] Mechanics and engineers were forced to work day and night to keep the clapped-out vehicles running.

The new Canadians arrived at the front throughout December and January, with the Canadian Corps taking over the Adriatic sector on January 31. The corps commander was Lieutenant-General Harry Crerar, who had advised the government on military matters as chief of the general staff in Canada during the first three years of the war. He was known to Canadians but had gained limited command experience during his three decades of service, having held divisional and corps commands only briefly in Britain. General Alexander was distrustful of anyone who had not come up through the Eighth Army, and even more so of a desk commander, and he much preferred Major-General Guy Simonds, who had led the Canadians through Sicily. Crerar was astute enough to tread warily among the British. He was not by nature a glory seeker, but the new Eighth Army commander, General Leese, was as dismissive of Crerar as Alexander, and he whined that he would have to "teach" the Canadians.[19]

The fifty-three-year-old Crerar was intelligent and dedicated, but also shy and uninspiring in bearing and speech. Lacking the easy ways of McNaughton, he fell back on being a stickler for discipline and rules. Even among his own close staff, he rarely used Christian names. His dour professionalism rubbed many of the 43,500 or so Canadians under his command the wrong way, especially when he tightened up dress rules and ordered that the informal names painted on tanks and trucks (much like the bombers' nose art) be removed.[20] The Eighth Army had a rather jaunty approach to these matters, which suited the Canadians, who had, during the South African War and the Great War, embraced the notion of colonial warriors: rough and ready for the fight but disdainful of discipline. Even 1st Division commander Major-General Chris Vokes was unhappy with the new Canadian Corps headquarters that appeared more intent on fighting a paper war than the shooting one. "Life became a sort of administrative hell on earth," he fumed with characteristic ill grace. Reports and chits were demanded from every unit, and in Vokes's eyes, Crerar "stood for shining buttons and all that chicken-shit."[21] It took time for the men of the Red Patch, who had served in Monty's Eighth Army at the height of its worldwide fame, to adapt to being in I Canadian Corps, which contained the 1st Canadian Infantry Division and 5th Canadian Armoured Division, and had dedicated logistical, medical, and artillery assets. As in the Great War, the Canadian Corps would fight together and not be divisible by the British army command. This semi-permanent structure reinforced national pride and fighting cohesion but angered the imperials, who railed that it made the Canadian divisions less flexible. That was the case, but I Canadian Corps was now a national formation and the British would have to deal with these challenges.

"THE INTENTION IS TO 'BREAK US IN EASILY,'" wrote one staff officer in the 5th Canadian Armoured Division. "We shall soon see whether it is 'easy' or not."[22] Major-General E.L.M. Burns commanded the division and it consisted of the 11th Canadian Infantry Brigade, formed by the Perth Regiment, the Irish Regiment, and the Cape Breton Highlanders, and the 5th Canadian Armoured Brigade of three Sherman tank regiments: Lord Strathcona's Horse, the 8th New Brunswick Hussars, and the British Columbia Dragoons. The reconnaissance regiment was the Governor General's Horse Guards. Another motorized infantry battalion was attached, the Westminster Regiment, and it was equipped with half-tracks—lightly armoured personnel carriers. In January 1944, the division was fed into the line to gain experience. In an effort to focus their attention on the east coast while General Mark Clark's Fifth Army launched an attack south of Rome, the 11th Infantry Brigade under the command of Brigadier George Kitching—a British professional soldier who sported a handlebar moustache and had come to Canada in the late 1930s—was to assault a German position about 2 kilometres north of Ortona on January 17.

The Perth Regiment, recruited from Western Ontario, and the Cape Breton Highlanders, drawing from the hardscrabble regions of the east coast, sought to prove their own aggressiveness and to distinguish themselves from the veteran 1st Division. "We'll show you Red Patch bastards how it's done," remarked one cocky member of the division.[23] Private Stanley Scislowski of the Perth Regiment, who had grown up in Windsor, Ontario, observed, "I don't think there were many that looked to the fact that men died, often in droves, and in the most brutal and gruesome ways. And very few of us dwelled on the possibility of our own death in battle."[24]

The regiments prepared for the coming fight with two nights of patrols to locate mines and map out the terrain. Several of these stealth operations failed to achieve their missions, as the Canadians' old nemesis—the German 1st Parachute Division—had their own patrols in No Man's Land, and were on a steep ridge overlooking the wide-open Arielli valley and river. Brigadier Kitching hoped that the support of sixteen artillery regiments might even the odds for the two battalions who would soon advance over open ground, although he unwisely ordered a staggered attack, with the two battalions advancing hours apart.[25]

In a misty rain, the pre-battle artillery bombardment—consisting of more than 14,000 rounds—had little effect on the enemy, except to alert them to a likely operation. After a pre-dawn breakfast at 3:30 A.M., the Perths moved forward an hour later and were ready for the assault at 5:30 A.M. on January 17. Optimism melted away rapidly as the lead units of the Perths crossed the stream at the bottom of the valley only to be plastered with mortar fire and forced to go to ground. Mortars remained a simple yet deadly weapon that lobbed explosives into the Canadian lines, or, in this case, at troops as they were spread out along the valley floor. The German 81mm mortars fired a 3.5 kilogram bomb that could kill with its high explosive blast and by hurling shards of steel over a wide radius. Experienced crews could saturate an area with twenty bombs per minute.

The attack became unglued from the start and the Perths were in danger of being wiped out, with added fire from a fortified house from which a German machine-gun team raked the front. Junior officers tried to rally the men. Yet anyone moving beyond their cover, as limited as it was, soon became targets for the machine-gunners and snipers who ringed half of the valley. At one point, Lieutenant A.J. Clements led a small party from Able Company to assault the house, but it was cut to pieces. A second desperate attempt by Major Robert MacDougall of Charlie Company gathered a group of six riflemen and another officer, and they also charged the Spandau machine gun in the house. It was a doomed drive, and all of the Canadians were gunned down before they made 20 metres. "The attack died at this point," said one of the Perths. "It was impossible for anyone to move through the killing ground without meeting a like fate."[26] Snipers targeted men carrying wireless radios to further add to the chaos.[27] With the Perths exposed to snapping fire in open daylight, the rearward gunners attempted to mask their positions with smoke.[28] It offered only limited reprise from the German snipers. The Perths tried to extricate themselves from the trap, with machine-gun fire from the Brens, the PIATs (Projector, Infantry, Anti-Tank weapons), and even the 75mm guns of the Three Rivers Regiment Shermans directed towards the enemy, but the vulnerable Canadians still took a grievous pounding.

Despite the Perths being stopped cold, the Cape Breton Highlanders were ordered into the battle about a kilometre downstream on the right, in broad daylight, at 12:45 P.M. While it was initially planned that they would support the Perths digging in on the ridge, now the goal was to draw off some fire—which they did. However, the operation was long past the point of being salvaged. The "Boys from the Bay" advanced across a river stream, with the Germans holding their fire until

Mortar teams from the Princess Louise Fusiliers firing at night.

the Cape Bretoners were on flat ground with little cover. Then they opened up. Some of the Germans, it was later found, were firing from below ground, simply sweeping the Canadians by using periscopes to guide machine-gun fire and never even putting their head above the slit trench.[29] Sergeant Fred Cederberg, a lanky twenty-one-year-old high school dropout from Cape Breton, witnessed how, "All afternoon, unnerved and numbed, the remnants of the two assault companies clung to the soggy ground, pounded relentlessly by German mortars that churned the mud and water into great spouts."[30] There was very little aid from the Three Rivers' Shermans, and Major Herbert Fulleston, a forty-year-old company commander, complained after the battle, "[We] did not see the tanks until we were withdrawn."[31] The tanks were there, but their blasting guns were lost in the roar of German fire.

By the end of the day, the two bloodied regiments had suffered 157 casualties and another 28 men were taken prisoner.[32] Some of the wounded, like Private Toasty MacIntyre of the Cape Breton Highlanders lay out injured and delirious for four days, praying to God that someone might find him.[33] He was eventually rescued, although gangrene and the severe nature of his wounds meant that one leg had to be amputated. He figured he got off easy, as he lay in the hospital while his comrades lay rotting on the battlefield.

It took some time for the 11th Brigade to live down the drubbing from the veterans of the 1st Division, who cruelly taunted them for their earlier bravado. Along with the shallow graves and bruised egos, the Germans were so unimpressed by their floundering opponents that the enemy high command moved the elite 1st Parachute Division to the American front, situating the troops in the Benedictine abbey atop Monte Cassino, where they would fight tenaciously for another five months.[34]

THE STATIC WAR continued throughout the winter, with Canadian units cycled through the front lines to rear areas. For the infantry, the war was reduced to sitting in a wet hole, scanning empty ground where the "square heads" were sitting in their own wet holes. Other minor operations were carried out, both failures and successes, but most of the time, at the front, soldiers stamped their cold feet, scratched at their boils and lice, and kept constant watch. Even the hard-bitten faces of combat veterans sagged under the weight of fatigue. The food was awful, and living conditions worse. Officers knew morale was low when the usual banter and singing were muted or absent, even though the rank and file still had enough piss and vinegar to grunt to one another, "Come to Sunny Italy for your holidays."[35] The losses from sniper and mortar fire ate away: between February 1 and March 7, 120 Canadians were killed and 585 wounded. The deaths were in ones and twos and occasional unlucky bunches. The Perths' Baker Company, while lining up for meals on February 5, was hit by a stray single mortar bomb. Thirty-seven men were flung across the ground. Stanley Scislowski, who rushed to assist the wounded, described the scene: "Bodies were scattered all over the muddy floor of the wooded ravine. Many of these were almost completely dismembered. Others were twisted so that they looked unreal."[36] The horror of that moment was etched into Scislowski's mind. And the war went on and on. Illness removed some 3,466 from the line.[37] For the survivors of this trench warfare, one infantryman summed up the stress of the static front, noting that he and his comrades did not "know what it was like to relax and draw in a few easy breaths."[38]

Soldiers looked out for one another. They shared food, they passed on good news from home to their mates, and there was always a card game to kill time. "Those men were your real true friends," remembered infantryman Jack Currie. "The friendships you make in battle are different from any other kind of friendships…. Perhaps it's just that you both faced death together and during that time a special bond was welded."[39]

Some of the more adventurous and innovative of the "poor bloody infantry" learned to distill alcohol in forward or rear areas, bribing and buying off senior NCOs and officers to look the other way, and finding some pleasure in the rotgut known as "steam." The occasional scrawny chicken or pail of milk liberated from Italians also lessened the burden. Hunting for loot was the favourite pastime for most soldiers. War trophies were lifted from German prisoners or corpses, with Iron Cross decorations and Luger pistols among the most prized. The search for souvenirs and artifacts could extend to looting abandoned Italian mansions and villas, although there were strict rules against this.

Letters and care packages brought joy and relief. Lieutenant Sydney Frost of the Princess Patricia's Canadian Light Infantry (PPCLI) scoffed, "If Hitler had realized how much these parcels boosted morale, he would have intensified his efforts to intercept them."[40] The parcels followed the soldiers in the field, moving through the rear and logistical lines in an efficient snaking to the front. The occasional withdrawal to the rear rest areas also brought a much-needed respite. Private Bruce Walker, who served as an infantryman in the 48th Highlanders of Canada and a dispatch rider with an anti-tank regiment, yearned for those breaks in service. At the same time, he also feared going on leave and returning to find who had gone missing in his absence: "We lost an awful lot. You'd go back, and say, 'Hey! Where's old Joe? Oh, Christ, he got killed two weeks ago. And where's Sandy? Oh, he got killed.' It was an awful low."[41]

AS THE EIGHTH ARMY stewed on the right flank along the eastern, Adriatic coast, General Mark Clark oversaw an amphibious landing up the western Italian coast at Anzio, a series of holiday ports 50 kilometres south of Rome. The American Clark was gangly and vainglorious, demanding, for instance, that he only be photographed on his good side. He had been an indifferent commander to date, and he would soon prove to be a liability. The audacious Anzio operation of January 22, 1944, surprised Kesselring; unfortunately, timid leadership on the part of American generals at the front left the forces in a shallow beachhead, before the enemy sealed it off and seized the high ground around it. The Germans were so perplexed at the American inability to exploit their weakness that they believed the Anzio landing had to be a diversionary attack meant to hold down their forces. It was not. Churchill remarked uncharitably, "I had hoped that we were hurling a wildcat onto the shore, but all we had got was a stranded whale."[42] In fact, the Anzio operation looked a lot like the failed Gallipoli landings that Churchill had championed in 1915 during the war against Turkey. At Anzio, the Germans had the advantage of the high ground, while the Allies could unleash punishing naval gunnery and heavy bomber strikes. The corpses piled up.

On the other American front, south of Rome, a unique group of Canadians was involved in taking the war to the enemy and knocking out his outer defences before the primary attack through the Liri Valley. The Canadian and American 1st Special Service Force (SSF), known as the Devil's Brigade, had been formed in 1942 from the northern dominion and the southern republic to conduct operations in alpine regions. Its soldiers were recognized by their distinctive shoulder badge illustrating a devil and a red spearhead imprinted with the words USA-CANADA. The officers had selected 2,500 fit recruits and trained them aggressively in the art of fighting, mountain climbing, skiing, and parachuting.[43]

The 1st SSF was thrown into a number of battles after its arrival in Italy in November 1943. In the December 3 operation against Monte la Difensa, a snow-capped mountain, the Devil's Brigade carried out a difficult six-hour climb up the rocky face to the top, where they hauled their American weapons, supplies, and water, before engaging the enemy. The battles were fought above the clouds, with ghostly soldiers firing into the gloom and killing each other in driving sleet, rain, and billowing mists. "They threw everything they had at us," said Lieutenant-Colonel Tom Gilday.[44] Over seven days—all the while exposed to howling winds, freezing

The mixed Canadian-American 1st Special Service Force was known as the Devil's Brigade and fought in Italy from late 1943. This image captures members of the unit, with darkened faces, about to set out on a patrol.

rains, and with little shelter—the Canadians and Americans captured la Difensa, owning the mountain on December 9, and later Monte Rementanea. During these intense engagements, the unit suffered 511 casualties.[45]

The Devil's Brigade continued to be used in mountain-clearing operations into early 1944, especially in preparation for Clark's drive to Rome, and they acquired an elite reputation. One of the most famous of these irregular soldiers was twenty-eight-year-old Sergeant Tommy Prince, a former lumberjack turned scout. He was fearless on the battlefield and eventually earned the Military Medal and the United States Silver Star. There were others like him in the elite formation, although soon their numbers were much diminished by combat. The 1st SSF was so badly cut up in fighting that it was disbanded later that year. It lived on in reunions and was later immortalized in a 1968 film, *The Devil's Brigade*, in which the Canadians were portrayed as sticklers for drill and discipline and the Americans as loose-cannon cowboys. A few miffed Canadian veterans remembered their role differently.

GENERAL MARK CLARK'S U.S. Fifth Army, consisting of American and Commonwealth units, launched three attacks from January to March 1944, each time attempting to advance northward to Rome by breaking into the Liri Valley. Clark had little success. The mountain fortress of Monte Cassino and fierce German resistance shattered the American, Indian, and New Zealand–led offensives.[46] With the forces at Anzio up the west coast contained in what the Germans sneered was the "largest self-sustaining prisoner of war camp in the world," General Alexander considered a new operation through the Liri Valley, hoping that it would relieve the Anzio beachhead and secure the prize of Rome.[47] More importantly, Alexander was under orders from London and Washington to turn the screws against the German forces in Italy to ensure that the enemy high command could not siphon off divisions to protect against the Allied D-Day landings, which were then planned for May 1944. Alexander's forces were to hold down the enemy on the cheap. The vast bulk of new equipment and war supplies was earmarked for the invasion of Europe. The Allied forces in Italy were also constrained in fighting since the reinforcement tap had dribbled off, again to favour the D-Day invasion. As Alexander acknowledged in early 1944, "We cannot afford heavy casualties."[48] And so Alexander was forced to fight with the few advantages that he had. Airpower and firepower would even the odds, and Alexander planned an intensive, artillery-centric battle to slowly grind down enemy forces.

The most direct route to Rome was through the Liri Valley in the centre of Italy, bordered by the Abruzzi Mountains in the northeast and the Aurunci Mountains in the west. While the valley was narrow at only 6 to 10 kilometres wide and 20 kilometres long, and cut with four significant rivers—Rapido, Liri, Gari, and Garigliano—this gateway allowed for a direct thrust along the main Naples-to-Rome road. It was far from an easy strike. The valley was dominated by heights on each flank, including the mountain fortress of Cassino on the Allies' right, which had been pounded by bombers and reduced to rubble but remained defended fiercely by the 1st Parachute Division. Blocking the Allied advance lay two German barriers: the Gustav Line along the fast-flowing Garigliano, which defended the entrance to the Liri Valley, and then the kilometre-deep Hitler Line, which was a switchback position about 8 kilometres to the rear, and anchored on the villages of Aquino in the north and Pontecorvo in the south. Concrete pillboxes, reinforced redoubts, barbed wire, minefields, and all manner of anti-tank guns and machine guns made both trench systems formidable.

General Alexander ordered the Eighth Army to transfer to the west, cross the narrow spine of Italy, and then assault northward against the German Tenth Army. With luck, they would break through to Rome. If they failed, they might hold the enemy in place long enough for the Anzio forces to break out, punch southeast through the eight divisions of the German Fourteenth Army that surrounded the beachhead, and destroy the ten divisions of the Tenth Army from the rear. With the Germans aware of a likely operation through the Liri Valley, the Allies tried to deceive Kesselring that another amphibious landing was in the cards through purposefully leaked radio chatter and other counter-intelligence tricks. Overwhelming Allied airpower—4,000 or so aircraft against the 700 of the Axis—made it difficult for the Germans to use their interior lines (to shift forces along shorter internal roadways to meet threats or even reinforce sectors in a timely manner), but there was no way for Alexander's forces to dislodge the enemy from its main defensive trenches except through the mailed fist of infantry, artillery, and armour.[49]

OVER THE WINTER, Generals Crerar and Simonds returned to England to prepare for the Allied invasion of France. I Canadian Corps was taken over by Lieutenant-General E.L.M. Burns, another Great War veteran and professional soldier. In the chronically underfunded prewar army, Burns had remained one of the bright lights, having written about armoured warfare in the pages of the professional journal *Canadian Defence Quarterly*. Though Burns exhibited a keen mind, he had little charisma, saying little and inspiring few. One senior Canadian professional officer who never advanced as far up the rank as Burns sniped that he was "one of those clever fellows who writes articles and passes examinations with 90–100% but is not fit to command two men and a boy."[50] Burns was a complex man, a better academic soldier than fighting general, but not a bumbling fool. He understood industrialized

Lieutenant-General E.L.M. Burns, I Canadian Corps commander in Italy. Burns was an intelligent senior officer, but he had little charisma and was never accepted by his British military superiors.

warfare. And he was no cardboard character. His meteoric wartime career had almost been derailed when, as a married brigadier, he had unwisely shared military secrets with his mistress. The affair could be forgiven, but the disclosure of secrets was a national crime. Disgraced, his career seemed to be over, but he excelled in several command positions, returned to England, and was soon commanding an armoured brigade and later a division.

As Burns found his footing in Italy, the collective Canadian outlook improved as the weather warmed in March and rumours of a forthcoming offensive circulated. General Vokes of the 1st Division felt that the extended period of trench warfare had left the division "morally and physically soft."[51] Incompetent officers and NCOs were to be weeded out. Several weeks of intense training from late April toughened up Vokes's division, with emphasis on long marches and mountain climbing as well as combined infantry and tank operations.

The 5th Canadian Armoured Division also had a new commander. The dynamic Major-General Bert Hoffmeister, who had risen through the officer ranks in the Seaforth Highlanders of Canada and then as an infantry brigadier, now had to learn how to wield an armoured division, with its infantry, tanks, and artillery working in conjunction. How to coordinate tanks and infantry in battle was still a work in progress, and experienced soldiers knew that tanks provided much-needed firepower but that they also drew fire, and so it was not wise to stay too close to them. The relationship of the two arms was not as harmonious as one would expect, and the infantry and tanks had little opportunity to train together in England or in the campaign theatre, although the 1st Division had learned the value of tanks in Sicily and at Ortona. Hoffmeister, who often fearlessly led from the front, knew that his untried formations would have a steep learning curve as they faced their first divisional battle.

IN EARLY MAY, a massed force of French, American, Polish, Canadian, and British armies were set to drive north through the Gustav Line. Kesselring remained off balance and looking over his shoulder at a phantom amphibious landing, although there was no masking the buildup to the south of the Liri Valley. The Germans were ready for the frontal assault.[52]

At 11 P.M. on May 11, an Allied 2,000-gun bombardment and counter-battery program opened up to reduce the enemy lines and especially the Monte Cassino defence. The 8th Indian Division and 4th British Division in the centre, the French Expeditionary Force on the left flank, and the Polish Corps on the right advanced into the enemy fortress. Most of I Canadian Corps was in reserve, although the 1st Canadian Armoured Brigade, an independent unit not under Burns's command, supported the Indian division in its perilous crossing of the Gari, an 18-metre-wide and 2-metre-deep rapid-flowing river.

The guns from both Canadian divisions supported the Allies at the front by working over the German lines in a drumfire bombardment, destroying strongpoints, and blanketing the arterial roads with fire. The workhorse of the Royal Canadian Artillery was the 25-pounder, a better gun than the Great War's primary field piece, the 18-pounder. The crew worked as a team, methodically feeding the gun. One gunner laid the shell in the breech while another used a wooden rammer to jam it in. A third gunner put the cartridge containing the propellant into the breech, and then closed it. Finally, a gunner, responding to a senior NCO or an officer's gun-laying (aiming) instructions, pulled the firing lever. Canadian gunnery sergeant Alan Troy recounted that the 25-pounder was a "magnificent piece of artillery." An experienced crew was supposed to fire five rounds per minute, but Troy's experience was that "with a good layer and a bit of fiddling with the return valve, the oil field run up system, you could manage nine rounds."[53] The 5.5-inch medium guns delivered an even more devastating punch, and each time the gun fired, those in the vicinity could feel their teeth rattle and their bones vibrate. It was far worse to be on the receiving end of the 82-pound shell filled with high explosive.

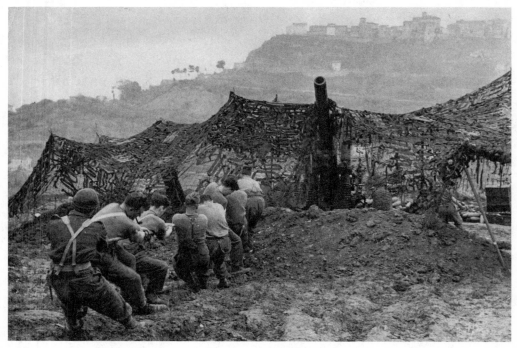

Canadian artillery gun team hauling a howitzer into position in preparation for a bombardment of the enemy lines. Note the camouflage netting.

The Indian division followed its creeping barrage to the Gari and, under enemy fire, prepared a difficult river crossing in assault boats. By dawn on the 12th, the Indians had established a bridgehead, but it was shallow and under fire. Nonetheless, it allowed sappers to begin the process of rushing forward tank-bearing bridges that would allow tanks and vehicles to cross the watery obstacle. But the Germans smashed the narrow bridgehead with shell and mortar fire, forcing engineers and infantry to dig for cover. The situation was bad. A few hours later, Canadian engineers came up with an innovative plan. A Sherman from the 14th Canadian Armoured Regiment, better known as the Calgary Regiment, was driven forward into the water, with the crew jumping out as it submerged.[54] With the turret removed, the Sherman had a 24-metre Bailey bridge firmly secured to its body, and the bridge remained above water. It was a model of ingenuity, and Shermans from the Calgary and Ontario regiments backed the Indians, knocking out artillery and machine-gun positions. The Indian advance continued.

On the left, a robust and over-strength Corps expéditionnaire français, consisting of Free French forces, broke through the Gustav Line, forcing Kesselring to throw in one of his few Panzer divisions, the 90th, to blunt the assault. It slowed the French, although they continued to make progress. On the right flank, however, the Poles were turned away from the German bastion at Cassino. With that anchor, the paratroopers were able to mount an aggressive defence, even as Allied bombers pounded known positions behind the lines and isolated the Cassino garrison from reinforcements.

The Gustav Line was broken, but the Allies could only inch forward along the pulverized road system. Traffic jams slowed the advance to a crawl. The 1st Canadian Division was thrown into the line to relieve the Indian division, and in the early hours of the 16th, it set about closing the eight kilometres to the Hitler Line.

With the ground opening up, the 17th saw Vokes order a two-brigade advance. Behind a light barrage at 6:30 A.M., three regiments overran a series of enemy strongpoints, employing aggressive platoon-level manoeuvres, in which the Canadians pinned the enemy down with machine-gun and rifle fire and dashed forward on the flanks to winkle out Jerry with grenades, guns, and bombs. One trooper remarked of the Quebec-raised Royal 22e Regiment infantrymen in the advance: "It was a real thrill to see the battle-wise [R22e] march straight forward, spread out and half crouching."[55]

The West Nova Scotia Regiment passed through the Van Doos, as the 22e were widely known, at around 10:30 A.M., and with tank support they closed with the enemy, according to one historical report, "like wildcats."[56] The Nova Scotians fought for much of the day, with the Carleton and York Regiment leapfrogging them and driving forward through the night, all the while under the fall of "nerve-shattering" artillery fire.[57]

On the left, the 1st Canadian Infantry Brigade surged over broken ground, streams, wooded areas, and gullies. One of the infantrymen from the 48th Highlanders of Canada breezily recalled that it was "like grouse hunting; we flushed [Germans] now and then and everyone let fly at him."[58] Of course, it was an exercise where the "hunted" could fire too, and the 190th Panzer Reconnaissance Battalion launched several counterattacks against the Canadians. By the end of the 17th, the 1st Brigade, with the 48th Highlanders in the lead, had crossed the Forme d'Aquino, a rapid-running stream about 5 kilometres from the Hitler Line. The Canadians sent more than 300 prisoners to cages and more than 400 Germans to their graves or to hospitals.[59]

WHEN THE SHATTERED MONASTERY FORTRESS at Monte Cassino finally fell on the 18th, the Germans retreated to the Hitler Line. General Leese ordered the British 36th Infantry Brigade to attack the enemy trenches, with the aim of bouncing it before the defenders could solidify their positions. The Canadian 3rd Infantry Brigade, with the Carleton and Yorks and Royal 22e Regiment in the lead, were to broaden the front, draw fire onto themselves, and perhaps find a way through the enemy defences. The operation had little chance of success, as Vokes put only two battalions into the attack and offered limited artillery support.

The two Canadian regiments advanced at 6:30 A.M. on the 19th into the enemy's prepared defences, with anti-tank guns savaging the supporting British tanks. On the Canadian front, the Germans stacked five battalions, one of them composed of elite paratroopers.[60] Snipers were particularly deadly. With no regard for the rules of war, the snipers even fired on stretcher-bearers attempting to pick up the wounded.[61] When it became clear the enemy was holding the front in strength, the Carleton and Yorks were ordered off the hopeless attack. The Van Doos pressed on, ultimately losing fifty-seven men in the fruitless operation. Their commanding officer, Lieutenant-Colonel Jean Allard, was furious at being sent off without adequate intelligence or artillery support, complaining, "I felt that my regiment had been the victim of recklessness of the High Command."[62] It had been the Van Doos's unpleasant role to act as bait for the German forces, although this was clearly not well explained to Allard. Neither the Canadian nor British attack succeeded.

With the Hitler Line reached, General Leese ordered a pause to arrange for a new set-piece battle. Kittyhawk and Hurricane fighter-bombers harassed the enemy, and at least one Canadian infantryman wrote that "it was heartening to know that our air forces controlled the skies over the battlefield."[63] The Luftwaffe still had a presence, however, and its fighters and bombers often flew under the cover of darkness. They found easy targets in the thousands of vehicles crammed on the roads or the large ammunition and fuel dumps behind the lines. Gwilym Jones, a trooper in the Three Rivers Regiment, described one aerial attack while standing near a petrol dump: "There is no more terrifying sound than a Stuka dive bomber coming straight down on you with its sirens blaring, firing phosphorus shells. As these shells landed, they bounced, like rubber balls, with glowing white lights. We scattered in a hurry."[64]

*The 48th Highlanders of Canada knocked out this
German Mark IV tank near Pontecorvo on May 19, 1944.*

There was no rest on either side of No Man's Land. Canadian infantry and engineering field companies tried to mask the buildup of war materiel for the new assault, while reconnoitring, clearing mines, and cutting paths through the barbed wire.[65] All was done under the Germans' noses. Soldiers died by shot and shell, a few at a time, but everyone knew a new round of mass slaughter was in store in a few days. As Vokes grumbled, "The Krauts we were facing were very determined."[66]

THE EIGHTH ARMY'S OPERATION was to be launched by half a million soldiers from ten national forces on May 23. Rain brought misery and mud as the Canadians prepared for their largest set-piece battle of the war to date, in Operation Chesterfield. Opposite the Canadians were the 90th Panzer Grenadier Division and the 1st Parachute Division, the defenders of Ortona, now ravaged by the last year of fighting. These once elite divisions were reduced to a motley collection of shot-up units and new reinforcements, but they were dug-in and fortified behind an effective trench system. The 1st Canadian Division's intelligence estimated that between the towns of Aquino and Pontecorvo the Germans had several thousand defenders and nine Panther turrets with 75mm guns—on concrete bases, with living quarters below—each protected by two to three towed 50mm anti-tank guns, as well as machine-gun pillboxes and conventional trenches.[67]

As befitting the Great War set-piece battle that Chesterfield was shaping up to be, the Canadians would advance behind a complicated creeping barrage laid down by 288 guns, while another 522 guns were tasked with counter-battery fire and the destruction of dozens of rearward strongpoints and crossroads. The Allied guns—which were in quantity almost on par with the number of artillery pieces backstopping the Canadian Corps during its historic battle at Vimy Ridge in April 1917—outnumbered the Germans by at least four to one. With the moving wall of shellfire pounding the way forward 90 metres every five minutes (and later every three), the infantry and armour advance was tied to it, with timed lifts and smokescreens. "We do not expect to kill many enemy in a prepared position even with a dense barrage," warned one artillery document. "It does, however, numb their senses for a time."[68] Even with the massive weight of shellfire, the infantry would have to stick close to their barrage and follow it through the enemy lines to overcome the stunned enemy before they recovered.

Canadian Corps commander Lieutenant-General Burns ordered the infantry of the 1st Division to hack open the line, and the 5th Armoured Division to punch through it. As Burns was later to write of control in battle, "When he orders an attack against an enemy in position, a general knows that some of the men he sends forward are going to be killed, and more will be wounded.... It would be idle to deny that professional training and temperament has given most successful generals a capacity to shut their mind to the inevitable 'butcher's bill.'"[69] While Burns suppressed his anxiety over the coming battle, he also ensured that the plan was sound and that he had done all that he could to contribute to the victory. It was out of his hands now.

In the early hours of the 23rd, the front-line forces snatched a few hours of fitful sleep and then munched on cold food and sipped tepid tea cut with rum. Weapons were checked and rechecked. Most men stared wide-eyed into the darkness, mouthing silent prayers, running through the next few hours in their head. A few cheeky infantrymen took bets on how long it would take to crack the enemy line. Most soldiers realized the serious nature of what was in store and did not partake in such bravado. Would they march across the smoking, desolate battlefield, or would the Germans, entrenched in their concrete bunkers, be ready for them?

AT 5 A.M. ON THE 23RD, the guns opened up in the first Canadian corps-level operation of the war. The opening phase saw a two-brigade attack of three infantry regiments: the PPCLI, the Seaforth Highlanders of Canada, and the Carleton and Yorks, with three more battalions in close support. Vokes should have put a stronger force into the sharp end (and had been forced by Burns and Leese to change his plan from a single brigade attack to a double), especially since his division was not responsible for the exploitation—breakout—phase of the battle. At the same time, even though the general believed that the artillery hammer would smash the enemy defences without the need to throw more flesh against fire, he had failed to sort out the boundary issue with the British 78th Division on the right. The British had not accounted for the town of Aquino in their sector, and its many defenders were able to shoot into the Canadian front with little impediment.[70]

For the infantry at the front, the air was filled with the howling, banshee wails of various calibres of shells, while the hurricane bombardment shook the ground. Field

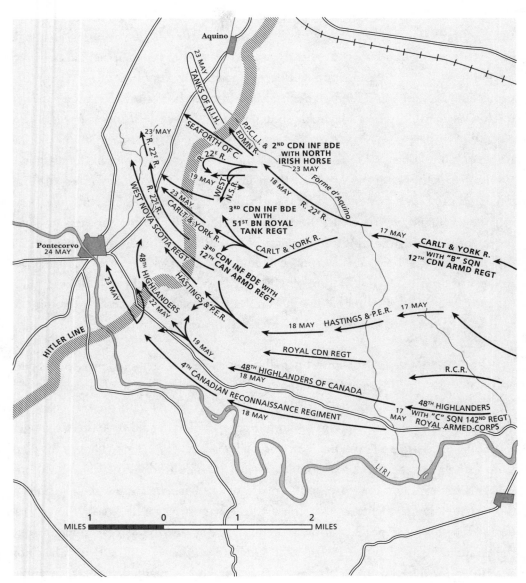

BREAKING OF THE HITLER LINE, MAY 11–23, 1944

historian Captain W.E.C. Harrison, while driving behind the lines, found the "noise so appalling" that he was forced to steer his jeep with his elbows, with both hands covering his ears.[71] An hour later, at 6 A.M., the creeping barrage was unleashed, and the front-line infantry formations, aided by two British tank regiments, went into the dust-shrouded abyss.

The torn and twisted front between the Forme d'Aquino waterway (which formed the boundary with the 78th Division on the right) and Pontecorvo, revealed the full power of the gunners. During the previous three days, since the 20th, each Canadian 25-pounder artillery gun had fired around 725 shells, with medium and heavier guns also adding to the bombardment.[72] An aggressive counter-battery bombardment by the Canadian artillery batteries had knocked out 10 guns before the battle and pummelled another 46 on the 23rd, so that when the infantry and tanks went forward at zero hour, it took more than two hours before the rearward German guns fired their first shot in retaliation.[73] The Desert Air Force also contributed to the

maelstrom. Squadrons from 239 Wing reacted to calls from forward infantry and RCAF observers—employing the "Rover David" system, whereby planes circling the battlefield were contacted on wireless to hit targets—harassed a strongpoint at Pontecorvo in the southeastern edge of the town.[74]

Amid the destruction, the enemy held on in his concrete and steel-reinforced positions that were largely impervious to shells. The Canadian advancing infantry were caught in the crossfire of bullets, shells, and mortars from these units, even as the German guns further to the rear were silenced. Explosive blasts ruptured internal organs or rent the air with shell fragments.

Canadians under fire, May 22, 1944.

Further away from the explosions, bodies involuntarily spasmed, muscles jerked, and men soiled themselves. Added to the horror, the rockets of the terrifying multi-barrelled launchers, called Nebelwerfers but known more commonly as "Moaning Minnies," crashed down in a scream of explosives that was, according to one Canadian, "undiluted terror."[75]

Barbed wire 6 metres deep in places, minefields that blew off feet and legs, and a string of craters 5 to 9 metres wide, provided a deep barrier that the Canadians had to cross. Interlocking machine guns, panzerfaust teams, and the feared panzerturms—the low-profile turrets of Panzer Vs with their 75mm gun encased in concrete—were a formidable defence. And still the Canadians pressed on, with one describing the day as consisting of "a thousand wild, breathless, brawling, cursing, tiny battles erupted, like spontaneous fires exploding in a rags factory. And as fast as one flickered out, another began."[76]

The first waves of the PPCLI, attacking on the far right, made some inroads towards their objective 1,400 metres away, but encountered a wooded area that made the barrage difficult to follow. Oak trees were reduced to splinters and the infantry hung back or were tripped up in the broken ground. At the same time, the British forces on their right, from the 78th Division, were held up by fire, as the Allied bombardment on this front had left most of the defenders unscathed in Aquino. When the PPCLI emerged from the debris of woods about 550 metres from the start line, they were cut down by machine guns. Junior officers gathered up the survivors and tried to lead them forward. Around 7:10 A.M., the wireless contact was lost on the PPCLI front. The commanding officer, Lieutenant-Colonel Cameron Ware, roamed the battlefield, seeking his men, rallied them, and pushed forward. "He bore a charmed life," recounted one of the Patricias, "again and again men were struck down around him."[77] The PPCLI inched their way forward.

On the brigade's left flank, the Seaforths had pushed into the tangle of interlocking machine-gun positions. When British Churchill tanks of the North Irish Horse Regiment rumbled into their sector, at least five of the 40-ton beasts were holed by a single, mounted 75mm turret gun. The Highlanders snaked past their British comrades, shuddering at the burning funeral pyres, and after the battle the Canadians asked the Iron Horse to carry a small maple leaf on their remaining tanks as a sign of the Canadians' gratitude.

Within this devastation, training and instinct took over for most soldiers. Advance, find cover, shoot, and advance again. One group, perhaps only a handful of men, fired on the enemy, while another half section raced forward. Then they fired, and another section rushed the enemy.[78] One of the Highlanders, Private Charles Johnson, an American who had served with the regiment since 1940, recalled the fighting: "My mind had but one thought; to get through the barrage.... No one except the wounded or the dead stopped.... Over to the left a German jumped up and seemed to be raising his hands when he was killed by one of our fellows. Directly ahead and about fifty yards away a Jerry stood up and held his machine-gun in his arms. A long burst tore into 8 Platoon to my right. I fired two rounds from the hip at the same time that others must have fired. The Jerry folded up and fell. I stepped on his bloody head as I passed over the position a few seconds later."[79]

The Seaforth Highlanders continued to drive forward, with one wireless report noting that the commanding officer of Baker Company had, by 8:40 A.M., picked up the remnants of all four companies, a mere 100 strong, and was pushing on through the defences.[80] Lieutenant-Colonel S.W. Thomson of the Seaforths noted, "There was only one possibility of succeeding and that was for each individual to fight forward until he dropped or obtained his objectives. Each man did just this and the line was broken. Certainly, it was a battalion success, not [one gained] by overwhelming artillery support silencing the enemy for this did not happen ... [nor by] brilliant infantry-cum-tank tactics for the infantry had to go on and break the line without tanks. But [the objective was gained] by bravery and sheer guts."[81] This was an infantryman's battle for survival, and at one point the Seaforths faced an enemy tank counterattack with only their Bren guns and a handful of PIATs. It was a massacre, with the tanks grinding over the terrified soldiers in shallow slit trenches.[82] Throughout the day, the 2nd Infantry Brigade was hit hard with over 500 casualties.[83]

On the left flank, the Carleton and Yorks and two squadrons of British tanks from the 51st Royal Tank Regiment made good initial advances, even as "the ground was boiling," according to Private Ernest Maller, a twenty-two-year-old from Shippagan in northeastern New Brunswick. He would be shot in both legs during the battle.[84] Soon the British tanks were knocked about in close-quarters combat. Captain R.T. Currelly reported that a single enemy 88mm anti-tank gun, protected by concrete, had accounted for thirteen Churchills before it was destroyed.[85] The tanks lay like great dead beasts. Others blew up in spectacular metal bonfires as the tanks' ammunition caught fire, flipping the machines over, sending the turrets flying through the air like up-ended spoons, and shrouding the battlefield in black, oily smoke. The charred remains of the tank crews lay in and out of their machines, some having made it halfway out of their turrets before succumbing to the terrible heat and fire. Tanks were reduced to twisted steel and flesh rendered into ash.

"Field Marshal Fickle Finger of Fate," was how PPCLI lieutenant Sydney Frost described the personal element of luck on the battlefield, as well as the all-encompassing confusion of the fog of war.[86] Within the blistering fire zone, the Canadians continued the advance against the enemy: some men shielded themselves with the knowledge that they would survive, no matter the cost, while others wrote off their lives so that they could continue to do their duty. "Many times during the fighting in Italy," recalled Lieutenant Robert Crozier of the Irish Regiment of Canada, "I considered my life as lost. You knew absolutely that you could not continue to go into battle engagements where you were constantly exposed to artillery fire, machine guns, snipers, mortars, schu-mines, tanks, or booby traps, without eventually catching a packet. And death had become a familiar occurrence, among your serving comrades, and in the forward areas where German soldiers lay stiff and cold after every battle. You knew it was only a matter of time until your own number came up."[87] Crozier survived the war, although he ended it in a prisoner camp.

A wounded stretcher-bearer caring for an injured infantryman from the West Nova Scotia Regiment.

The second wave, the Loyal Edmonton Regiment on the right flank, who pushed through the PPCLI but could not breach the Hitler Line, and the West Novas on the left, faced a still not yet broken defensive grid in depth. In the afternoon, the Germans mounted an armoured and infantry counterattack against the 2nd Infantry Brigade. The Canadians held off the enemy tanks with their anti-tank guns, and the Shermans of the Three Rivers Regiment chewed up the Germans. Around 10 A.M., the surviving Churchill tanks of the 51st Royal Tank Regiment and the Carleton and Yorks fought their way into the Hitler Line. Within the enemy's defences, they were safer from sweeping machine-gun fire, except that now they took the full force of artillery and mortar fire that the Germans levelled on them to contain the assault. Vokes worried about the New Brunswickers in the Carleton and Yorks getting too far ahead of 2nd Brigade, but later in the day he took advantage of the hole they had burrowed in the line by shifting over the Three Rivers Sherman tanks and the Van Doos, who along with the West Nova Scotia Regiment crashed through the gap.

While Vokes would have saved lives by better masking the German defenders on the British front, the Canadians at the spear thrust had fought with unbelievable courage in breaching the Hitler Line. "There were dead Germans everywhere; many prisoners were taken, completely demoralized by the speed of the attack," indicated one historical report.[88] Hundreds of enemy soldiers were killed and 540 were captured. The cost to the Canadians on the 23rd, and in repelling counterattacks in the early hours of the 24th, was 879 killed and wounded.[89] The strain was tremendous for all survivors, and Lieutenant-Colonel Cameron Ware, the commanding officer of the PPCLI, was one whose health was broken. Captain Howard Mitchell of the Saskatoon Light Infantry, a machine-gun and mortar unit, witnessed Ware as he was ordered to the rear for a rest, his eyes reddened with tears, clutching dozens of identity discs from killed soldiers. "Those were fine boys. They're gone. I haven't anybody left. They are all gone."[90] Roy Durnford, chaplain of the Seaforth Highlanders, remarked of May 23, "I can't begin to tell all I have seen, but it has been our best and our worst day."[91]

THE ATTACK AGAINST THE HITLER LINE shattered one of the most formidable enemy positions in Italy. That same day, on the morning of the 23rd, the Americans launched their Anzio beachhead breakout. The pressure from the British front left the Germans vulnerable to being enveloped, although American General Mark Clark was unimpressed with the speed of the Eighth Army. After a meeting with Sir Oliver Leese on the 21st, the ungenerous Clark had sneered in his diary, "All their actions are always dictated by their desire to save manpower and let someone else do it."[92] He felt the British and Canadians were too cautious, which was a strange sentiment since he had overseen the floundered Anzio landings that had wilted under fire and then been stalemated for months. The tension between the principal allies remained significant. It also revealed the British and Canadian way of war that remained predicated on the set-piece battle of careful planning and application of firepower, with an emphasis on protecting the infantry's lives. Not only was there a shortage of reinforcements in the Eighth Army, but both the Canadians and British wore the scars of the Great War deeper than the Americans. Perhaps most important, there was no other credible method of breaking enemy positions in frontal assaults than through the heavy application of shellfire. The challenge was in transitioning from the sledge-hammer break-in to the exploitation phase, and few British or American victories of that sort had yet been achieved in the war.

With the 1st Canadian Infantry Division having clawed open a hole in the Hitler Line by the end of May 23, Major-General Bert Hoffmeister's 5th Canadian Armoured Division—nicknamed Hoffy's Mighty Maroon

Troopers on a Sherman tank.

Machine because of its coloured shoulder patches—was ready for the armoured thrust. A prewar Vancouver militia-man who had proven his mettle as a company, battalion, and brigade commander, the charismatic Hoffmeister nonetheless had an inexperienced headquarters staff. Even as Hoffmeister was trying to get his division through the break, the attack was slow in forming as the lead units shifted left to better hit the hole in the line. It took time, and rain slowed all movement on the "third rate roads," so that the attack was delayed about twelve hours.[93] Brigadier G.A. McCarter, a senior staff officer at corps headquarters, penned in his diary, "It is a hopeless task to try to get any information out of HQ 5 Cdn Division. They are behaving like complete amateurs in every way."[94] It was an ungenerous statement, but it was accurate insofar as 5th Division's headquarters was in chaos.

The next morning, on the 24th, lead elements of the 5th Armoured Brigade were ordered into the line to cross the Melfa River—a broad, shallow, slow-moving stream with steep, 6 metre banks, about 7 kilometres from the Hitler Line. Two battle-groups consisting of infantry and armour were to turn the break into a rout. Speed was of the essence.

At 8:30 A.M., the Canadians drove on to the Melfa, which ran from north to south across the battlefield. The first of the armoured and infantry formations, consisting of the British Columbia Dragoons and the Irish Regiment of Canada, pushed for-ward, about halfway beyond the Hitler Line to the Melfa, to act as a forward base. The area was teeming with the enemy moving away from the Hitler Line. Many sought to surrender, while others still had fight left in them. The orchards and vine-yards contained concealed guns and mines, and the roads were reduced to mud through overuse and rain. Areas of resistance were hammered by Allied artillery. One of the troopers remarked that the bombardment left German soldiers reeling: "They wandered about, neither surrendering nor fighting effectively. Most were machine gunned, but a few were taken prisoner."[95]

Further to the south, the second battlegroup, consisting of Lord Strathcona's Horse (LdSH) and the Westminster Regiment (Motor), had an equally difficult time as they raced to the Melfa. On the 24th, the reconnaissance unit of the LdSH—lightly armoured Honey tanks armed with .50 Browning machine guns—crossed the river first, with the Westminsters' scout cars close behind them. While being in an armoured car in the middle of a tank battle felt like bringing a knife to a shootout, "Our job was to get to the river and get there fast," recounted Major John Mahony, commander of A Company of the Westminster Regiment and a former newspaper reporter from New Westminster, British Columbia.[96]

Though the Westminsters lost a few of their armoured cars to enemy fire, they reached the Melfa after passing by burning Shermans from the Strathconas who were battling it out with enemy forces on the west side of the river. In a whirling melee amid dust and burning vehicles, the Strathconas eventually lost seventeen of their Shermans but destroyed five German Panthers, two Mk IV tanks, eight self-propelled guns, three more field guns, thirteen Nebelwerfers, and fifteen additional vehicles.[97] The Shermans, one of the Strathcona's officers noted, had a tendency to "'brew up' quite quickly."[98] Often one shell from the German guns pierced through the tank's armour, setting their gasoline stores on fire. Yet despite the grim tally, the Shermans were not useless in battle and could fight it out with the best of the German tanks and self-propelled guns in Italy.

On the other side of the Melfa, from about 3:30 P.M. on the 24th, the LdSH recce tanks—led by Lieutenant Edward Perkins—were hull down, with their vulnerable tracks and wheels buried in the earth, and exchanging fire with the enemy. Their .50 calibre machine guns were outmatched by enemy cannon fire, but the bullets could still make a mess of a man. One soldier, in comparing the .303 rifle round to a .50 calibre, remarked, "Both bullets enter cleanly. But the heavier round on exit takes about a foot of material with it."[99] When the Westminsters' cars arrived, they aided the reconnaissance tanks. The Germans, aware of the threat, threw an armoured force, strengthened by self-propelled guns, against the vulnerable Canadians. Out-numbered, outgunned, and surrounded on three sides, the Westies, under command of Major John Mahony (described by Peter Stursberg of the CBC as "a nice guy, mild mannered, soft-spoken"), threw back two German counterattacks, destroying three enemy self-propelled guns and a tank.[100] As part of the lopsided battle, a German Panther turned towards the overextended force. One of the Westminsters, Private John Culling, a farm boy from Swift Current, Saskatchewan, skulked forward. When the German tank commander opened his turret to survey the battlefield, Culling sprang from a nearby hiding spot and tossed a grenade that landed on the tank, shredding the officer. "The Gods of War were smiling on Culling that afternoon," remembered Mahony, as Culling lobbed another grenade into the turret, exploding inside the tank.[101] The Panther was forever silenced and Culling was awarded the Military Medal for his bravery.

The gods of war were also smiling on Perkins and Mahony, the latter of whom was thrice wounded in the battle but refused to rest. With the company reduced to sixty men and all officers but one wounded, Mahony led the fight, determined to hold the position, even as he bled freely from his many wounds. His riflemen exhibited astonishing tenacity as they held out against tanks. At one point, with Panthers massing for another attack, Perkins, who led the steadily dwindling numbers of Strathconas, swore that "We fired everything we had from point fives to tommy-guns."[102] The Canadians bluffed the enemy with their frenzied fire and the Germans retreated.

"No one can really know himself until he has felt the all-searing heat of the crucible of terror," wrote one Canadian padre.[103] Mahony, Perkins, and their men had faced that terror, and they had not been found wanting. Mahony was awarded the Victoria Cross for his gallant leadership, and Perkins received the Distinguished Service Order, an award rarely given to junior officers.[104] The Canadians had survived five hours of ruinous fire and armoured assaults but had carved out the bridgehead that allowed follow-on forces to keep driving into the enemy's vulnerable rear. With the shallow bridgehead across the Melfa, lead elements of the Strathconas and the Irish Regiment also crossed at several points late on the 24th.

Canadian forces funnelled through the bridgehead, passing cratered meadows speckled with red poppies. Within this apocalyptic landscape, "bloated carcasses of cattle and horses, lay in the fields, their legs pointing skyward," witnessed Robert Sawdon, a twenty-one-year-old who followed two brothers into the service, one of whom would not make it home. "Nearby was a German pillbox, mounted with an 88mm gun. The remains of three Germans soldiers were inside." Others were buried under a few inches of soil. "I noticed, with a sickening feeling, the earth moving in an undulating manner, due to the action of maggots performing their life function."[105] Around the dead Germans were four burned-out British tanks. On the broken battlefield, with its sickening stench of rotting flesh, buzz of millions of flies, shattered concrete, and gutted farmhouses, there was ample evidence of the warriors' way: kill or be killed, and kill and be killed.

AT THE FRONT, the 11th Canadian Infantry Brigade continued to elbow its way through the bridgehead, but running battles with pockets of resistance from trapped German soldiers to the east of Melfa slowed the exploitation phase. If the enemy could be hounded backwards, the slow-moving artillery, headquarters units, and mountainous supply dumps might be captured. This would break the Germans' fighting spirit, even if their infantry and armour would likely escape destruction. But in the battlefield of less than 65 square kilometres, an astonishing 20,000 Allied vehicles were trying to make their way to the front, or from front to rear.[106] Matters were made far worse when General Leese pushed the 6th Armoured Division through the Canadian sector to avoid attacking Aquino, which was now held by only 200 exhausted paratroopers. This was a bizarre misreading of the tactical environment, and instead of capturing the town, which would have opened up new routes, the British bungled up the roads in a misguided attempt to manoeuvre around Aquino.[107] Those tanks and infantrymen simply joined the back of a very large parking lot.

Burns should have refused the order, but he was intimidated in his first battle, especially in the face of the experienced Leese, who was a veteran of the desert war. Unfortunately, Leese proved grossly incompetent here, and while he remained a charismatic commander, he and his staff were chronic mishandlers of the road system.[108] Gasoline shortages, mines, and rollovers left trucks, jeeps, armoured cars, and tanks immobilized, adding to the congestion. If the Germans had not been reeling from their losses or if they had held an air force ready to put into the skies over the battlefield, they would have easily punished the clumsy Allied advance. Frantic British and Canadian headquarters tried to sort out the mess: blitzkrieg was replaced by a self-imposed traffic jam.

It was not until the 26th, a blisteringly hot day, that the 11th Canadian Infantry Brigade pushed its way through the bottleneck and gagging petrol fumes. The next day, the Irish Regiment, supported by the Cape Breton Highlanders, the Perths, and tanks of the 8th New Brunswick Hussars, seized Ceprano. They had advanced through mortar and machine-gun fire, and withstood Moaning Minnies and high explosive shells. This was no easy march against a broken enemy, as the official regimental records make abundantly clear.[109] At every step, men were shot down or blown apart. Private Stanley Scislowski of the Perth Regiment watched one of the unit's popular sergeants step on a Teller mine, the type that could blow the tracks off a 32-ton Sherman. "The blast from fourteen pounds of TNT threw Bob's body high in the air.... Bob's legs and arms were mangled and twisted in such a grotesque way that they reminded me of a discarded rag doll."[110]

At Hoffmeister's divisional headquarters, confusion reigned, and it was unclear if the lead units were held up by poor traffic control, enemy fire, or hesitancy. The general sensed the disorder even as he understood the inherent friction of the advance. Urged on by Burns and Leese, Hoffmeister ordered his brigades forward, and even demanded night marches to make up for the slow crawl during the day. The 5th Division had to close the distance with the enemy. One optimistic Canadian, Captain G.E. Broomhall at corps headquarters, wrote to his wife that after the determined push, "It certainly begins to look as tho we have had the honor of striking the first blow in 'the beginning of the end.'"[111] The German defenders had been battered, but this was not the end, as the enemy regrouped and was fighting a coherent rearguard action. The 5th Division's armoured formations were gradually removed from the fighting front by the 30th, as British units took over, and the Canadians slipped into reserve on June 3. The 5th Division's spearhead role in breaking out of the Hitler Line was over.

With the German Tenth Army opposite Leese's Eighth Army withdrawing and vulnerable, it might have been destroyed—or at least savaged—by the Anzio force that had escaped the confines of the bridgehead. But the Allies could not close the pincer movement, and much of the German army fled to fight another day. The culprit of this failure was American General Mark Clark. He had long been obsessed with the glory of liberating Rome, to the point where he had threatened General Alexander that if the Eighth Army attempted to beat him there he would order his troops to fire on them.[112] Now, on the 25th, as his forces were preparing to savage the Germans by cutting through their line of retreat, he redirected his Fifth Corps to capture Rome. Instead of hounding the enemy, Clark pursued publicity. The Americans garnered the glory of liberating Rome on June 4, but Clark's manoeuvre allowed most of the Germans to escape. Clark's reputation was made in newspapers and magazines across the Western world; in reality, he should have been tried by court martial for gross dereliction of duty. His actions in late May would result in the deaths of thousands of Allied troops later in the campaign.

THE CANADIANS RECUPERATED from the battle and cared for the dead. Captain R.T. Currelly observed how "The burial parties deal with our own dead first, and then the bloated, fly-blown bodies of German soldiers have become an everyday sight. One gets so used to seeing them that one forgets the horror and tragedy and thinks of it primarily as a sanitation problem."[113] The regimental padre, usually with a few men, gathered the fallen for burial, collecting their personal effects, such as paybooks, photographs, and letters, and passed them on to the regimental head-quarters. As one officer observed, "We had to make sure that nothing incriminating was sent back, such as a photograph of an extra girl friend or love letters that were not appropriate. All personal effects were returned but care had to be taken to make sure feelings, already saddened by the death of a loved one, were not unnecessarily hurt."[114] Rough crosses were erected, and the details of the buried men—name and regimental number—were placed in tins at the foot of the cross, often under a steel helmet. Warrant Officer Vic Bulger recalled the sad story of one fellow gunner, who had heard that his nineteen-year-old brother had arrived as a reinforcement to the 48th Highlanders of Canada. "As if drawn by a hidden fear, he inspected several of the new graves and found to his shock and sorrow, that his younger brother's 'ID' Tag was nailed to a makeshift cross."[115] He barely had time to process the discovery before his unit moved out.

The crashing of the Hitler Line cost the Canadians almost 800 killed, 2,500 wounded, and another 4,000 listed as sick, with at least 400 of those diagnosed as battle exhausted. Lieutenant Ken Smith of the Hastings and Prince Edward Regiment served at the front for 144 days. At the Hitler Line in May 1944, he recounted how the regiment was preparing: "Lance-Corporal Jim Gillan had often said to me that his main ambition was to get safely home to a Manitoba farm and behind a plough. That afternoon he died instantly right behind me as a long burst from a heavy machine gun cut us down together."[116] Smith survived with an agonizing leg wound. For every Canadian lost, and there were thousands by mid-1944, grief washed over immediate families—parents, wives, siblings, and children—but also friends and community members in church, local businesses, schools, and factories. At the same time, those deaths galvanized Canadians towards victory in a war that had to be won. Too much had been sacrificed to give up. Hitler's regime was on its back foot by late May 1944, reeling from defeats on land, in the air, and on the oceans. But it fought on. Tens of thousands of additional families across the Dominion of Canada would face unimaginable loss before the war of necessity was ended.

During the course of the battle, Alexander's forces suffered 42,000 casualties, with the Germans losing about 30,000.[117] Perhaps the Canadians and their comrades were lucky to get away with those losses since the Allies attacked into the teeth of a defence-in-depth bristling with guns. Yet hard on the heels of the Hitler Line victory came scapegoating and accusations: why was the victory not more decisive? Somewhat surprisingly, General Leese was disappointed with the performance of the Canadian Corps, and even tried to have Burns fired and the corps command given to a British general.[118] Burns thought he had soothed matters over with Leese by sacking some of his most senior staff officers—the corps' brigadier general staff and the chief engineer—but the British general had it in his head that the Canadian had to go. Leese's complaints were especially capricious considering the success of the Canadians. While some of the 5th Division's poorly coordinated actions had revealed inexperience, most of these issues were endemic throughout the Eighth Army, and a good portion of the logistical breakdown could be attributed to Leese's headquarters. In England, Canadian authorities supported Burns and he survived as corps commander, but he was a marked man.

Despite the Allies' failure to annihilate the Germans, the Liri Valley campaign was a triumph, in breaking the enemy lines, freeing the trapped Anzio forces, liberating Rome, and destroying Kesselring's strategic reserve. Driving the Germans back was another blow in the global war against Hitler. One advantageous knock-on effect was the ability now of the Anglo-American bombers to hit the Ploesti oilfields in Romania, destroying precious supplies and siphoning off additional flak batteries from the Eastern Front and German cities to protect this crucial oil asset.

The breaking of the Hitler Line was overshadowed by the liberation of Rome, although both victories were almost immediately forgotten in the aftermath of the

D-Day landings on June 6, 1944. On that day, as momentous events were happening in France, Captain Strome Galloway, then in the Royal Canadian Regiment headquarters, heard about the landing of the 3rd Canadian Infantry Division in Normandy. He repeated the information, absent-mindedly, to one of the clerks, who, without missing a beat, looked up wickedly and remarked, "It's time those bastards did *something*, Sir."[119]

CHAPTER 4

PLANNING THE INVASION

On D-Day, June 6, 1944, all three military arms of the Canadian forces—the navy, air force, and army—came together as the Allies prepared to claw their way back to France. The long shadow of Dieppe shrouded the complex invasion known as Overlord, and many of the Allied planners wore brave faces but worried in their hearts that the cross-Channel attack might be repulsed. Several successful Allied amphibious operations had been carried out since Dieppe—in North Africa, Sicily, the southern toe of Italy, Salerno, and Anzio, as well as American campaigns in the Pacific—but the spectre of the Dieppe slaughter haunted the high command. Almost all of the victories of the previous two years were achieved against weak enemy defenders. Now, for the return to France, all expected the fight to be a ferocious struggle from the first minutes of battle.

Stalin had demanded a second front almost from the start of his war with Hitler, to siphon off the German forces that were marauding through his country. The bombing campaign was an important marker in meeting Stalin's increasingly desperate pleas. Yet the Soviet dictator wanted more: a full-scale invasion of Europe. Up to 1944, Churchill had played a skilful shell game in keeping both the anxious Russians and the naively optimistic Americans at bay, waving the Mediterranean theatre operations as a red flag. He had rightly claimed that any invasion of France would only end in ruin if the Allies did not first win the Battle of the Atlantic and then gather a sufficient number of warships, landing craft, and bombers.

The planning for the invasion had begun seriously a year earlier, in March 1943, but had stalled because of a lack of oversight and a supreme commander. In early

1944, with the appointment of American general Dwight Eisenhower, the planning took on a new urgency. Eisenhower had risen meteorically throughout the war, with his agile mind and congenial manners soothing many of the tempestuous generals, admirals, and air marshals under his command. He was a careful leader who had stumbled in his first large-scale engagement in Tunisia when his American divisions were roughly handled by the combat-hardened Germans in early 1943. The general had also been timid in corralling the necessary forces to cut off the retreating German garrison from Sicily in August 1943. Since then, however, his triumphs had outweighed his defeats. Commanding millions in a battle for the survival of democracy brought unimaginable strain, but Eisenhower had tremendous endurance and inner strength, both of which he would need to call upon in the following year of non-stop warfare.

While there was a significant degree of mistrust in the senior echelon of the Anglo-American high command, Eisenhower's Supreme Headquarters Allied Expeditionary Force (SHAEF) began to hammer out the complicated plan that he would label the "Great Crusade."[1] The timing of the operation shifted, as the planners sought low

The Allied high command, including Supreme Allied Commander Dwight Eisenhower in the centre, seated, and speaking to British General Bernard Montgomery.

tides for the landings and a full moon for the airborne division drop behind enemy lines. They eventually settled on June 5, with the next suitable window not being until the period of the 17th to the 21st of that same month.

Though the American general had to lead the operation because of his nation's massive contributions to the war effort (and for the purposes of home front consumption), the land armies would be commanded by the British hero of the war in North Africa, General Bernard Montgomery, until a sufficient beachhead was established to allow for Eisenhower and SHAEF to cross the Channel. Monty would also command the 21st Army Group, consisting of British, Canadian, Polish, Free French, and other national formations. Eisenhower was esteemed and genuinely liked by almost everyone, and he in turn respected Montgomery's talents, but he was wary of the British general's abrasive personality and absurd hubris. "Damn it," spoke Eisenhower once, "Montgomery is the only man in either army I can't get along with."[2] Eisenhower would suffer over the coming months from Montgomery's chronic acts of insubordination and arrogance, but he understood the importance of maintaining the Anglo-American alliance, and he had that rare ability to swallow his pride for the greater good of the coalition.

Hitler's forces had fortified the French coast for four years with thousands of defensive installations, from concrete bunkers to hundreds of machine-gun and artillery encasements, and some 4.2 million mines. When General Erwin Rommel was defeated in North Africa, he moved to France, and by December 1943 he was strengthening the defensive wall. Rommel commanded Army Group B, consisting of the Seventh and Fifteenth armies, and he reported to Field Marshal Gerd von Rundstedt at *Oberbefehlshaber West*, or OB West. The Germans' Atlantic Wall, as the 4,500 kilometres of French coastline was called, was defended by sixty infantry divisions; however, many were burned-out husks that had endured churning battle on the Eastern Front.[3] The German garrison divisions had also been stripped of many of their trucks and armoured vehicles to shore up the remaining Eastern Front divisions, which numbered 239 in June of 1944. Nonetheless, Field Marshal von Rundstedt assumed that the logistical challenge of supporting Allied invading armies would require a major port to offload supplies, and so static divisions with little mechanized transport could be dug-in behind concrete defences and still fight effectively.

Von Rundstedt spread his divisions along the Atlantic Wall in a perimeter defence, with a strong crust facing the Allies and with a concentration of counterattack formations grouped in the north around the Pas-de-Calais. This was the narrowest point from Britain to the continent, a mere 30 kilometres. An invasion there, under maximum air cover, would give the Allied armies a nearly direct route into Germany. The nineteen divisions of the Fifteenth Army were situated here and set to repel the invasion, along with an elite reserve of ten motorized and panzer divisions in Panzer Group West, further to the south, which could be rushed forward to drive any invaders into the sea.

A fierce debate smouldered within the German high command, especially between Rommel and von Rundstedt, over how to employ the panzer divisions in reserve. Von Rundstedt believed that even if the Allies gained a foothold on the beaches, the mobile reserves could be formed up into an armoured counterattacking force within days. He was backed by the commander of Panzer Group West, General Geyr von Schweppenburg, who also felt that a counterstrike could be unleashed after a few days as the vulnerable Allies left the beaches and moved away from the devastating firepower of the warships waiting off the coast. Rommel thought differently, and in keeping with his aggressive nature, he wanted a strong defence along the coast and a hard and fast strike by units close to the front. Rommel was willing to risk the losses from naval gunfire because he feared that Allied airpower would never allow the panzer divisions to form up for a massed assault several days after the invasion. Better to stop the landings on the beaches or attack swiftly to decapitate the Allies at the earliest opportunity. The generals received little assistance from Hitler, who was exhausted, drug-addicted, and despondent from the avalanche of bad news. He found most military decisions challenging, especially major ones like this. The Führer characteristically waffled and then decided to split the reserve into three parts: Rommel and Schweppenburg would control three divisions each, and OKW (*Oberkommando der Wehrmacht*), Hitler's headquarters, would retain control over four divisions. To the generals, this was the worst of all possible decisions—it diluted the impact of the panzers and made any concentration of force more difficult.

Eisenhower and his staff were aware of the German indecision through their Ultra decryptions, which provided top-secret intelligence of enemy communications. Still, few were certain that the invasion formations could overrun the German defenders on the beaches. Eisenhower shuddered at putting a handful of divisions on the continent where they, largely alone, might face the full might of the panzers.

To forestall this epic battle, an elaborate Allied deception plan, Operation Fortitude, was conceived, involving turned German spies in Britain supplying false facts back to their handlers. To reinforce the misinformation, dead bodies washed ashore on the continent with fake plans. The Allies even created a phantom army under George Patton's command, as the Germans had profound respect for the hard-thrusting American general and assumed he would lead any assault. Finally, deliberately sloppy wireless communications indicated that the First Canadian Army was preparing to invade Calais, and the Germans were wary of the Canadians because of their reputation as shock troops in the Italian theatre. All of this subterfuge kept the German high command fixated on the north of England, across from Calais.[4] The true landing site was to the south in the Normandy region, specifically the Cotentin-Caen sector.

The Normandy coast around Caen had no deepwater port, but it had long beaches with good exit routes for moving men and material to the interior. The area was more lightly guarded, too, although the Calvados coast of Normandy was a peninsula that could be sealed off by the enemy. However, to give the invasion force a fighting chance, the soldiers at the front needed mountains of ammunition. Each division required about 500 tons a day of supplies, and to feed the machine, hundreds of merchant ships would run materiel to the beachhead daily. SHAEF also eventually decided to build its own "Mulberry" harbours, using pre-made constructions consisting of multi-thousand-ton concrete caissons linked together. This critical supply chain was contingent on the Allies having command of the air.

THE FAILURE OF SIR ARTHUR HARRIS'S bomber offensive against Berlin in early 1944 had left a frustrated Churchill again questioning his confidence in Harris, who argued incessantly that bombing could win the war on its own. It could not, and the carnage above the German capital raised the challenging question of how the bombers should be deployed for maximum effect. Throughout the war, the three services clashed over targets, with the navy asking for bombers to assist in holding off the U-boats, the army interested in softening up enemy tactical defences, and Bomber Command seeking to destroy German infrastructure and morale. In the preparation for the Normandy landings, Eisenhower wielded his power to bring the bombers under control of SHAEF so that his staff would now select the targets.[5] The bomber barons complained indignantly, but there was tempered steel behind

Eisenhower's genial smile, and he got his way in March 1944. Under Eisenhower's unified command, the bomber offensive shifted from Germany to France, and the bombers were given orders to target railways, bridges, road networks, and canals in what became known as the "transportation plan." The bomber crews had no say in the matter, although the closer targets offered a much-needed reprieve from the pitiless losses of the previous months and the casualty rates to aircrews dropped significantly.[6]

In early 1944, the German war industry had dispersed as the bombing campaign grew in ferocity. Through the relocation of factories to rural regions or to the outskirts of towns, industry had often survived the blanket bombardment of the cities. While those dispersed industries were harder to target, the transportation networks—especially the rail and road lines that carried the war supplies—were immovable. The Allied bombing campaign slowly destroyed many of the

General Dwight Eisenhower, Supreme Allied Commander in Europe, took control of the bomber squadrons before D-Day. He redirected them away from city bombing towards targeting German fortifications and French logistics to degrade the enemy's ability to strike back at the Allied invasion force.

French railways, bridges, and roads, thereby stranding war materiel while also slowing any German military response to the invasion. Ultra intelligence kept the Allies informed of the enemy's growing panic. Crushing the German economy by aerial bombardment was impossible, but choking off the Nazis' resources—especially coal and steel—and crippling transportation severely damaged the enemy's ability to effectively wage war.[7]

The German Luftwaffe defences were on the verge of collapse. The U.S. Air Force had suffered crippling casualties throughout the fall of 1943, but they had also chewed up precious enemy planes in the air battles. By early 1944, the Americans took the fight more forcefully to the Luftwaffe. Though the bombers were protected by their own guns—which occasionally took down enemy machines—the long-range P-51 Mustang was their saviour. The British had initially flown the Mustang as a tactical reconnaissance plane, but with the addition of a more robust engine, the Rolls-Royce Merlin 61, and armed with six .50 calibre M2 Browning machine guns, the Mustang was transformed into a formidable weapon. When the P-51 was equipped with additional drop fuel tanks, it could range deep into enemy territory, pushing beyond Berlin by March 1944. The P-51 was faster than the Focke-Wulf 190 and Messerschmitt 109 at high altitudes and could turn tightly like the Spitfire.[8] Hitler poured enormous treasure and effort into superweapons—jets, guided bombs, and snorkelling U-boats—but the P-51 proved to be the only truly super weapon of the war.

The Americans targeted Luftwaffe airfields and factories manufacturing ball-bearings—crucial in most machines and vehicles—from early 1944. To protect these sites, the Luftwaffe fighters were dragged into unfavourable battles in the skies against the P-51s, as well as P-47 Thunderbolts and P-38 Lightnings, and, to a lesser extent, the RAF and RCAF's Spitfires and Hurricanes. The German first-line defenders, the two-seater Me 110s and Junkers 88s, were no match for the faster American fighters that acted as both shield and sword. In February 1944, the Luftwaffe lost one third of its planes and a fifth of its crew. In March, half its remaining aircraft were shot down; and over the next three months, almost the entire complement of fighter pilots was killed or wounded.[9] "Wherever our fighters appeared, the Americans hurled themselves at them," reported one German. "Nowhere were we safe from them;

we had to skulk on our own bases. During takeoff, assembling, climbing, approaching the bombers, once in contact with the bombers, on our way back, during landing, and even after that the American fighters attacked with an overwhelming superiority."[10] The Luftwaffe was so badly ravaged that Hitler pulled experienced aces from the Eastern Front and Italy, with 80 percent of the German fighters eventually serving on the Western Front. The first half of 1944 broke the Luftwaffe, and by May 1944 it had only 498 serviceable aircraft against more than 9,000 Allied planes, including 5,000 fighters.[11] This turning point in the aerial war ranks with the defensive victory of the RAF during the Battle of Britain, although it had not been without its costs: the Allies lost 2,000 aircraft downed and 12,000 aircrew killed in the first six months of 1944.[12]

THE AIR WAR WAS CRITICAL to the success of D-Day, but the sea lanes also had to be cleared or the Allied troop ships would be sunk before they ever reached land. Royal Navy Admiral Bertram Ramsay oversaw naval planning for Operation Neptune, the supporting naval component to Overlord. Operation Neptune would

Ship's company of H.M.C.S. Athabaskan. *RCN Tribal class destroyers* Haida, Huron, Iroquois, *and* Athabaskan *were involved in a series of battles in the Channel before the D-Day invasion.*

be the largest armada ever assembled in human history, with some 6,900 vessels, including 1,213 warships ranging from battleships to torpedo boats. One hundred and twenty-six Canadian warships and vessels of all types, with no fewer than 10,000 Royal Canadian Navy officers and seamen, played a part.[13]

Airpower from land-based bombers and aircraft carriers, when combined with specialized hunter groups, chased the U-boats and enemy surface raiders. The Germans had been defeated in the Battle of the Atlantic in May 1943, but they had regrouped for a new offensive a few months later. Launching U-boats from the Bay of Biscay, they hoped to sink the Allied merchant ships closer to British waters. But the U-boat crews had a misplaced faith in their ability to fight off the swarming Allied warships and Coastal Command's land-based aircraft. RAF and RCAF

squadrons in Coastal Command had laid mines, patrolled against subs, and had been shooting up shipping since 1940, but now, from mid-1943, with Allied intelligence providing information on the general location of U-boats, and with Coastal Command's bombers and sea planes further able to pinpoint targets with new radar and high-powered searchlights, they attacked relentlessly. In just three months, from June to the end of August 1943, aircraft revealed their impact on the naval war, sinking eighteen U-boats in the Bay of Biscay, along with thirty-two of thirty-nine additional boats that the Germans lost during this period.[14] This was another crippling blow to the Kriegsmarine. And the German introduction of new weapons— such as the feared glider bomb, a

Coastal Command's squadrons, including several from the Royal Canadian Air Force, harassed the Kriegsmarine in preparation for the invasion of Europe.

remote-controlled missile packed with high explosives launched and directed from aircraft, or an acoustic torpedo that sought out ships through the sound of their engines—could not turn the tide.

The primary battlefield had shifted from the mid- and western Atlantic to the waters around Britain and along the French coast. Yet convoys still sailed in an unyielding tide. With the Royal Navy focused on preparing for Operation Neptune, it gradually handed over all convoy duties—the escorting and protection of civilian merchant supply ships against U-boats—to the Royal Canadian Navy, until by June 1944 the entire system was under Canadian escort.[15] The "sheep dog navy" that had tried to run circles around the merchant ships to keep the wolves at bay in the first four years of the war was now delivering the supply ships on time and with almost no losses. It was an incredible contribution from a navy that had boasted a mere handful of ships in 1939 and now numbered over 200, and was, with new builds, on its way to growing to 400 warships. Under the command of Rear-Admiral George Jones, the chief of the naval staff, and Rear-Admiral Leonard Murray, commander-in-chief Canadian Northwest Atlantic, who coordinated war ships and air power off the east coast, and who was the only Canadian theatre commander of the war, the RCN made a significant contribution to the grand logistics that were necessary for any invasion of France to succeed.

The Allies were winning the war decisively at sea, but they needed an absolute victory for the invasion to succeed. The fear of the Kriegsmarine running amok among troop ships was intensified when nine enemy torpedo boats pierced naval defences in late April 1944 during an American exercise at Slapton Sands, a stretch of beach along the south coast of England. Two troop ships were sunk and close to 750 soldiers and sailors killed. To minimize the damage of the raid to morale, the dead were buried in mass graves and their deaths attributed to events later in the D-Day campaign. There could be no more Slapton Sands. The Allied navies were going to take the war to the German surface fleet and U-boats.

The Allies had become far more efficient in destroying subs since the dark days of 1941 and 1942. New technology, tactics, radar, and weapons left the U-boats hounded at every turn. While the U-boats still ranged all the way to Canadian waters, Rear-Admiral Murray was persuaded that the best way to help the Allied cause was to send his best warships to the eastern Atlantic to be involved in the submarine hunt. Royal Canadian Navy support groups and elite submarine-killing groups, involving teams of warships that worked together to hone tactics, took the war to the U-boats. From late 1943 to early 1944, the Canadian C Groups and EG Groups, making up about 40 percent of the Royal Navy's sub hunters, sank seven of the thirty-one U-boats that met their end during that time.[16]

Long, relentless pursuits marked many of the battles, and RCN commander Charles Nixon was involved in one of the longest U-boat clashes of the war over the course of March 5 and 6, 1944, about 650 kilometres west of Ireland. The Canadian submarine-killing group C.2, which consisted of the Canadian warships *Chaudière*, *Gatineau*, *St. Catharines*, and *St. Fennel*, as well as the Royal Navy's HMS *Icarus*, located *U-744* with an asdic (underwater radar detection) sweep. With the warships sweeping in for the kill, the U-boat captain dodged and evaded the depth charges in hour after hour of frantic underwater manoeuvres. The Canadians and British sailors were no less obstinate. Depth charge attacks, patterned grid searches, and systematic pursuit kept the U-boat submerged. Contact was lost and then regained by the five warships seeking the enemy. After thirty hours, the sailors were exhausted and only managed to remain at their posts since they knew that the U-boat crew below was in an even more desperate situation. Commander Nixon of HMCS *Chaudière* described how the Canadians eventually got their prey: "We used our new technique of creeping attacks, of one ship guiding another over the contact so that the sonar would remain in contact while the

The Royal Canadian Navy engaged in an extensive campaign against the German U-boats in the summer of 1944. Here, a depth charge is being fired.

depth-charges were being dropped, instead of having to lose contact when she ran over the target and dropped her own charges." The relentless dropping of depth charges—metal canisters filled with 300 pounds of TNT or amatol—shook the Canadian warships, but wrought havoc on the submarine, which suffered small leaks, electrical shortages, and fires. Finally, after the gruelling battering, the U-boat surfaced. It was met with a hail of gunfire and soon surrendered. "The U-boat surrounded by five stopped ships presented a strange sight," Nixon recounted, "rather like a wild animal at bay."[17]

IN THE CHANNEL OPERATIONS OF EARLY 1944, RCN Tribal class destroyers *Haida*, *Huron*, *Iroquois*, and *Athabaskan* were involved in a series of battles along the French coast. The Tribals were larger than the River-class destroyers, the first having been commissioned in November 1942. Equipped with six 4.7-inch guns in three double turrets, two 4-inch guns, and four 21-inch torpedo tubes, the Tribals could unleash formidable firepower. Although they had some birthing pains, they were extremely fast, at 36 knots, and equipped with modern radar for locating vessels on the surface or underwater. RCN commander Harry DeWolf commented that the Tribals were "a fighting destroyer."[18]

The Channel operations were welcomed by the Canadians warships. *Athabaskan* had returned after suffering glider bomb damage the previous year—when a "Chase me Charlie," as the gliders were known, had struck and passed through it, luckily without exploding—and several Canadian destroyers had recently finished their tour serving on the frigid Murmansk convoys to deliver crucial supplies to Russia. That convoy run—six to eight days along 3,000 kilometres—was the "most hazardous and horrible place for naval operations," wrote one officer. The danger from U-boats and the German surface fleet that were concentrated in Norwegian waters, the inhospitable harbours and bases, the long periods of darkness, and the nearly instant death for anyone who went into the icy waters made it unpopular with all sailors.[19] Lieutenant P.D. Budge, the first lieutenant on HMCS *Huron*, described the conditions:

> It seemed that gales were forever sweeping over the dark, clouded sea. The dim red ball of the sun barely reaching the horizon as the ship pitched and tossed, the musty smell of damp clothes in which we lived, the bitter cold, the long

frequent watches that seemed to last forever. This on a diet of stale bread, pow-
dered eggs and red lead [stewed tomatoes] and bacon. The relief to get below
for some sleep into that blessed haven—the comforting embrace of a well-slung
hammock. There was no respite on watch for gun, torpedo or depth-charge
crews as every fifteen minutes would come the cry, "For exercise all guns train
and elevate through the full limits"—this to keep them free of ice.... The watch
below would be called on deck to clear the ship of ice.... Each trip out and back
seemed to last an eternity with nothing to look forward to at either end except
that perhaps mail would be awaiting us at Scapa Flow.[20]

One of the few redeeming features of the Murmansk run, according to Able Seaman
Gordon Dunlop, who had enlisted at age eighteen in 1943, was the chance for HMCS
Sioux's hockey team to play against various Russian teams.[21]

The Canadian Tribals had moved south in January 1944 to more fulfilling action
in the Channel as part of the 10th Destroyer Flotilla. Based at Portsmouth, the flotilla guarded the western approaches to the English Channel. While Allied fighters
and bombers harassed and sank enemy vessels during daylight hours, the battle at
night was far from won. The Germans had a formidable force of torpedo boats and
destroyers that laid minefields or struck Allied shipping under the cover of darkness.
Since February 1944, the 10th Destroyer Flotilla had been engaged in Operation
Tunnel, anti-shipping sweeps, which, in print, the Canadian sailors described as "fooling around the French coast"—a sanitized version of their common reference to it as
"fucking" around the French coast. The operations initially met little success, with one
embarrassing "battle" seeing the heavily armoured destroyers pounding an enemy vessel located by surface radar, only to find that it was a group of small islands.[22]

After about twenty operations, the 10th Flotilla finally found their enemy in the
early hours of April 26, when they intercepted three German torpedo boats near
St. Malo. In a running gun battle, the Tribals—Huron, Haida, and Athabaskan—
illuminated the sea with starshells while the Germans laid smokescreens to escape. It
was not a fair fight. The German ships were outclassed and at a disadvantage as they
were not equipped with flashless cordite, so that each round fired gave away their
position anew. The German boats let loose their torpedoes, forcing the destroyers to

turn away, but *Haida* and *Athabaskan* quickly regained radar contact. As they closed the distance, starshells lit the sky and soon a salvo of shells pummelled the enemy vessel, *T-29*. After a fierce hammering, the German ship was ablaze and the crew eventually scuttled it. The other enemy vessels barely survived their full-tilt flight from destruction. The victory was a much-needed boost to morale, and *T-29* was the RCN's first enemy surface vessel sunk.

Three nights later, in the early hours of April 29, the 10th Flotilla's *Haida* and *Athabaskan* caught scent of the German warships *T-24* and *T-27*. There was another fierce clash. The enemy fired torpedoes and the Tribals blasted away with their guns. A German torpedo found its way to *Athabaskan* at 4:17 A.M. and the destroyer suffered catastrophic damage, with 10 metre flames and ammunition exploding below deck. *Haida* laid a smokescreen to cover the wounded *Athabaskan* and continued to pursue the enemy, punishing *T-27* with accurate gunfire until she was run aground by her crew. With the other German T-boat fleeing, *Haida* returned to assist *Athabaskan*. However, within ten minutes of the first torpedo strike, *Athabaskan*'s magazine exploded, shooting 200-metre-high flames that were witnessed from over 40 kilometres away. For many years, conspiratorial accusations circulated that a British motor torpedo boat had mistakenly torpedoed the lame *Athabaskan*, but the case of friendly fire has been proven conclusively to be wrong.[23] Nonetheless, the second explosion was fatal to *Athabaskan*, and the ship took on water and settled by the stern.

After the second explosion, André Audet, who served on B gun, reacted to the order to abandon ship. With the fire out of control, and fearing additional explosions below deck, Audet jumped in the water, but not before putting on his coat, an oilskin, and a life jacket over top. Even then, the water was freezing. As the ship went down, darkness shrouded the last resting place of the destroyer, with only the red blinking lights on the life jackets providing some indication of the sailors' location in the water. Audet later recounted, "We swam and swam and swam. It was cold like hell. Holy Jesus Christ. And we could see the coast of France."[24] Dozens of crew members died in the burning oil that polluted the surface water or succumbed to the freezing cold. Leading Seaman Jim L'Esperance was in the sludgy surf holding a friend who was burned and paralyzed from damage to his back—"The skin was hanging from his face."[25] He prayed for rescue as his comrade succumbed to hypothermia.

When *Haida* finished off *T-27*, it steamed to *Athabaskan* even though the destroyer was vulnerable, as U-boats were likely converging on the conflagration to sink rescue ships. *Athabaskan*'s captain, Commander John Stubbs, the victor of the August 6, 1942, battle with *U-210*, was even heard giving the courageous cry of "Get away, *Haida*! Get clear." *Haida*'s crew tried to gather survivors by lowering life rafts and scramble nets, but dawn was breaking and it would soon be even more exposed to stalking enemy ships. The captain, Harry DeWolf, gave the agonizing order to sail at first light. *Haida* steamed away with only 42 men from her sister ship, including Audet and L'Esperance. When the survivors were counted, it was found that 129 were lost with *Athabaskan*, including her captain, Stubbs, while 83 were picked up by German boats and sent to prisoner-of-war camps.[26] The Canadian Tribal destroyers grieved the loss of *Athabaskan*, even as they continued to play a key role in clearing the Channel for the coming invasion.

GENERAL HARRY CRERAR prepared the Canadian forces for the seaborne assault, although he had no role in the strategic planning of the operation. The First Canadian Army had been formed in April 1942 and it was the largest land formation ever fielded in Canadian military history. It had been commanded by General Andrew McNaughton, but he had worn out his welcome with both the British and his political master, Minister of National Defence J.L. Ralston, with whom he warred openly. His replacement, Crerar, had openly campaigned for the job and actively undermined his commander. He took over the army in early 1944 even though he had only the most limited command experience in Italy. Yet Crerar was a survivor, who had somehow escaped unscathed from the debacles of Hong Kong and Dieppe, with which he was intimately involved. He had noteworthy strengths, including a keen mind, an agreeable attitude, and relationships stretching back to the Great War with many British senior officers, particularly Chief of the Imperial General Staff Sir Alan Brooke.

His friendships over four decades of service did not extend to 21st Army Group commander General Bernard Montgomery. The forceful British general, who would command ten infantry and five armoured divisions when his army group was at full strength, made it clear that he did not want untested commanders, and he was unhappy with Crerar leading one of his two armies. In the months leading up to the invasion, Montgomery had weeded out generals he saw as unfit, replacing them with his Eighth Army veterans. In his cheery words, "The Gentlemen are out and the Players are in."[27] With every single corps and divisional commander having earned more experience in battle than Crerar, the Canadian general seemed little more than a desk soldier. However, Crerar was cautious and competent, eschewing dash and daring but also rarely making an error. Also, as a national army commander, he had military and political responsibilities, the latter to the Canadian government. At any time he could, technically, refuse the use of his divisions in an operation that he felt might be against national interests. Canada was an ally, not a colony—even though Montgomery refused to acknowledge such constitutional evolutions.

The First Canadian Army remained a Canadian army only in name, with about half the divisions made up of Polish and British formations. McNaughton's earlier warning that the splitting of the Canadian Army would weaken it for the invasion of France had come true, with I Canadian Corps stuck in Italy despite requests from Ottawa to bring it back to England. The British, having other worries, roundly ignored the pleas until early in 1945. Crerar commanded the 2nd, 3rd, and 4th Canadian Divisions, of which Major-General Rod Keller's 3rd Division—about 18,500 strong— would be in the vanguard of the assault on D-Day. It was to be supported by the 2nd Canadian Armoured Brigade. While the forty-four-year-old Keller was a hard-living, slightly pudgy soldier's soldier, no one mistook him for a brilliant commander. In England, he had proved himself a fine trainer of men, and had focused enormous time on the amphibious operation, to the point that he described his division as "web-footed," but he, like his infantrymen, was without combat experience and no one knew what to expect after the beaches.[28]

Most of the Canadian infantrymen were chomping at the bit for battle. They had trained for years and now they would finally take part in the liberation of Western Europe. The riflemen were, as a group, very young. Two thirds were between eighteen and twenty-five years old, and junior officers were not much older. The officers were better educated than the enlisted men, with most of them having a high school diploma, while about two thirds of the rankers, children of the Depression, had left school before grade seven.[29] All were fit, muscular, and healthy after years of training.

As the invading force was placed in quarantined camps in preparation for the assault, they were issued new kit. The Canadians wore the 1937 British-type battledress, but the colour was distinguished by its olive-green tint. Live ammunition and grenades were handed over carefully, to be stored, before battle, in the various pouches on the webbing, with its braces, straps, attachable canteens and mess kits, and a place for the 1908 pattern-entrenching tool. French francs, maps, chocolate bars, and cigarettes were stuffed into battledress pockets. New assault helmets, covered in fishnet and able to hold a wound dressing, were studied with interest, as the Mark III was deeper than previous models. It soon acquired the nickname "tortoise." In the weeks and months to come, the helmet was the sign of a D-Day veteran, as newly arriving reinforcements were issued the flatter, Mark II helmet. On their backs, the infantrymen had a small pack jammed with a personal hygiene and toilet kit (in a "hold all"), a camouflage/anti-gas cape, spare socks, and perhaps a few sheets of paper for writing home.[30] Closer to the chest, inside the jacket, men stowed their

Some of the Canadians spent four years in England training for battle.
The infantryman on the left carries a Bren machine gun while the man in the centre
holds a Sten gun. The two on the right are armed with the Lee Enfield rifle.

paybook and wallet, along with lighter, matches, and cigarettes. Their identification discs were worn against the skin on a chain around the neck and provided critical information in case of death. Even the non-religious soldiers often carried a small Bible. As Farley Mowat wrote, "Innumerable tales have been told in every nominally Christian army about men whose lives were saved because the Bibles they carried in their breast pockets stopped what otherwise would have been fatal bullets."[31] Who were mere soldiers to argue with such widely held beliefs? Mowat had his life saved not by a Bible but by a can of bully beef that stopped a bullet.

Riflemen were equipped with the dependable bolt-action Lee Enfield rifle and a bayonet. Many of the infantry were also issued a wicked-looking knife, strapped to the leg, which inculcated the fighting spirit, although most hoped not to be reduced to hand-to-hand combat. Each infantry section of ten infantrymen had two specialists equipped with a Sten and Bren machine gun. The former was a dodgy sub-machine that looked like it was made by a blind welder. It had a hairpin trigger and a poor safety mechanism. Soldiers found it was liable to go off at any time. But it offered automatic fire and it was usually used by the section commander. The Bren, a larger and more robust weapon, consumed ammunition at a rapid rate, but the Canadians had faith in its high rate of fire and all infantrymen carried their share of 30-round Bren magazines for the machine-gunner.[32] The PIAT (Projector, Infantry, Anti-Tank weapon) was unwieldy and inaccurate beyond 100 metres, but the Normandy soldiers would find, like their cousins in Italy, that the bazooka-like weapon could knock out an enemy tank at close range, even if it felt like a pea-shooter against those metal monsters. Though infantrymen were used to being laden down like Christmas trees, before the assault they would have to hump even more grenades, ammunition, anti-tank mines, wire cutters, wireless sets, and long cylindrical Bangalore torpedoes to cut wire. Only years of training and built-up core strength, mixed with controlled fear and a surge of adrenaline, would push the infantry to run when they hit the landing beaches.

While most infantrymen felt an affinity to the brigade and division, it was the battalion that defined a soldier's identity. In the 3rd Canadian Infantry Division, there were nine infantry battalions—usually known, confusingly, as regiments—in three brigades. The 7th Canadian Infantry Brigade, commanded by permanent force officer Brigadier Harry Foster, was formed from three western battalions, the Canadian Scottish Regiment, the Royal Winnipeg Rifles, and the Regina Rifles. Brigadier Ken Blackadder, a militia officer from Montreal, commanded the 8th Canadian Infantry Brigade, which consisted of the Queen's Own Rifles, the North Shore (New Brunswick) Regiment, and Le Régiment de la Chaudière, the only French-speaking battalion in the 3rd Division. The 9th Canadian Infantry Brigade, led by Brigadier D.G. Cunningham, held the Highland Light Infantry of Canada from Waterloo County, Ontario; the North Nova Scotia Highlanders; and the Stormont, Dundas and Glengarry Highlanders, which had initially recruited from and been formed by communities around Cornwall, Ontario. The infantry numbered fewer than 8,000 in the 18,500-strong division, but they comprised the sharp end of the spear. Three field artillery regiments and an anti-tank regiment consisted of another 2,400 artillery officers and gunners. There was also an attached heavy machine-gun and mortar battalion that used the Vickers machine gun and the 4.2-inch mortar. This increased firepower—in the case of the 3rd Division, from the Cameron Highlanders of Ottawa—could be grouped with the battalion's own support company, who were equipped with mortars and anti-tank guns, to concentrate fire when needed.

An infantry battalion consisted of 40 officers and 812 other ranks, although after any time in the field these numbers were reduced by casualties, illness, and postings. The fighting strength came from the four rifle companies—A, B, C, and D, or Able, Baker, Charlie, and Dog—each composed of 5 officers and 122 other ranks, and commanded by a major. The companies had three platoons, which, at full strength, consisted of 37 men: three sections of 10, each led by a corporal; as well as a platoon headquarters, commanded by a lieutenant and supported by a sergeant, three mortar men, and two runners. There was also a support company of 7 officers and 185 other ranks that operated mortars, universal carriers, and anti-tank weapons, and engaged in pioneer work. The added firepower from the six 3-inch mortars and the six carrier-towed 6-pounder anti-tank guns could stop massed infantry and armoured attacks, with the 6-pounders boasting a range of 2,500 metres and the ability to kill enemy tanks at 800 metres. These large weapons were still out-gunned by German tanks, but they ensured that, if used closely with the riflemen, a battalion had a fighting chance against an armoured thrust. Thirteen universal carriers, also known as Bren

Gun Carriers, provided important mobility for the battalion. The five companies were commanded by a lieutenant-colonel, and his battalion staff interacted closely with the company headquarters below him and the brigade headquarters above.

The 3rd Canadian Infantry Division had no tanks—unlike the 4th Canadian Armoured Division, which consisted of an infantry brigade and a tank brigade—but it would be supported in battle by the 2nd Canadian Armoured Brigade. Commanded by Brigadier R.A. Wyman, who was brought back from Italy to supply combat experience, the brigade consisted of three regiments: the Fort Garry Horse, the 1st Hussars, and the Sherbrooke Fusilier. Though the infantry and tanks had rarely trained together in England, the Shermans and the up-gunned Fireflys—Shermans equipped with a more powerful 17-pounder gun—provided crucial fire support to the infantry. The Canadian infantry ordered to land on the beaches were going to need all the help they could get.

A SHORTAGE OF LANDING CRAFT constrained how many divisions could be put ashore on D-Day, but eventually six Allied divisions were ordered into the assault on an 80 kilometre front of five discontinuous beaches. While most of the German radar stations had been knocked out by the bombers to mask the invasion, it was not easy to obscure thousands of ships carrying tens of thousands of sailors and soldiers. The lead assault force would be transported to their beaches in a dizzying array of landing craft, and each division required a mixture of about 45 of these: the mammoth Landing Ship, Tank (LST), which could carry twenty tanks; the Landing Craft, Infantry (LCI), which transported 200 men; and the smaller Landing Craft, Assault (LCA), which would run in about 25 men for the beach assaults. The American 4th, 1st, and 29th Divisions would land at Utah and Omaha beaches, while the British 50th Division was in the centre at Gold Beach, with the British 3rd Division on the far left flank, storming Sword Beach. In between the two British divisions, the 3rd Canadian Infantry Division would land at Juno Beach. On the flanks, the Allies would drop in three British and American airborne divisions, including the 1st Canadian Parachute Battalion. No one liked the prospect of lightly armed paratroopers holding off a panzer counterattack, but few other options were available for guarding the British and American beach landings' open flanks.

In the Canadian sector, the 7th Canadian Infantry Brigade would land on the right, with the 8th Brigade on the left, and the 9th Brigade in reserve. However, for the two forward brigades, the beach area allowed for only five battalions, and generally only two companies from each in the lead. And so on June 6, the first wave consisted of nine infantry companies from the five infantry battalions, supported by two armoured regiments, with two more infantry battalions and an armoured regiment in reserve. There was also a substantial force of engineers, machine-gun formations, and medical personnel. Significant naval and artillery guns would hopefully even the odds. With the planners worried about a sustained German counterattack, the number of artillery field regiments was doubled for the 3rd Division, and consisted of six regiments of 144 guns, a regiment of medium 4.5-inch guns, and two self-propelled Royal Marine regiments firing 95mm howitzers. In fact, the number of gunners in the Canadian division had tripled to 8,000, with the addition of many British light, medium, and anti-tank guns, for a total of nearly 200 artillery pieces.[33] All of this was in preparation for holding the beachhead against the feared enemy attacks that were expected to land most heavily on the 3rd British and 3rd Canadian divisional fronts, as they were closest to Caen. The Canadians would serve with I British Corps until II Canadian Corps became operational, although this would not be for several weeks and would depend on the extent of the Allied advance.

By the end of June 6, it was planned that more than 21,000 Canadians would be ashore, with over 2,000 vehicles. They would join another 130,000 Allied soldiers. It was critical for the Allied divisions to drive inwards, off the beaches, to allow for follow-on forces to land and push forward into the space behind the initial strike, and to link up with the paratroopers. The final Canadian objective on D-Day was the Carpiquet airfield on the outskirts of the major city of Caen, about 14 kilometres from the beaches. Canadian Rifleman J.L. Wagar spoke for many when he pondered the momentous battle, "Invasion Day was going to be a test of things: a test of me; the test of a Division; the test of an Army; and the test of an invasion of Nazi Europe; and I was silenced by the whole tremendous thing, and scared."[34]

CHAPTER 5

D-DAY

"I thought about the things that meant a lot to me—my home," recalled Major Fred Baldwin of the Sherbrooke Fusilier Regiment, in the final hours before the assault. "The shroud of Dieppe creeped into my idling thoughts once in a while."[1] On board the ships, officers briefed their men with aerial photographs. Padres gave sermons to calm nerves. The wait before battle was always the hardest time for combatants. Soldiers reflected on the traces of black ink on their finger tips, evidence that the army expected some men to be destroyed beyond recognition save for their finger-prints. Despite the palpable tension on D-Day, June 6, 1944, several of the ships witnessed impromptu singalongs, with songs ranging from the maudlin to the raunchy. On another vessel, one of the padres organized, somewhat peculiarly, a quiz contest over the broadcast system.[2] A few of the regiments took a more warlike approach, with infantry officers urging their men to shave their heads or adopt mohawks; one unit called these "assault haircuts."[3]

Most of the Canadians had been sequestered for several days (some since June 1) and seasickness was taking its toll on the young men, especially with the violent weather rocking the ships on June 5. Some of the 3rd Division men were also react-ing badly to the booster doses of typhus vaccine and other inoculations that had been jabbed into their shoulders with dull needles. The storm on the 5th left all the Allied planners agonizing over whether to launch the operation, as a rough sea would likely result in landing craft coming ashore at different times. But cancelling and postponing the invasion would be a blow to morale. Eisenhower was forced to make the gut-churning decision to go ahead, after being guided by one of the most important weather forecasts in history. To gain some leeway, he pushed the invasion to the 6th, hoping to ride out the storm. The soldiers knew none of this, intent as they were on their own final preparations: chain-smoking, poker and dice (playing for the French francs that most men were issued), and all the while scratching at raw skin beneath their new battledress uniforms that were impregnated with chemicals to counter gas attacks. Foldable bikes were secured with a sneer, as officers explained with little enthusiasm that they were meant for a rapid exploitation. Bikes against Panther tanks: even the most naive private knew that was a bad joke.

Canadian infantrymen Privates Art Robertson and Ken Mardon,
aboard a landing craft before the assault on Juno Beach. Nineteen-year-old Mardon
was mortally wounded on July 8, 1944, and died two days later.

The infantry were roused from their fitful sleep around 3 A.M. on June 6. Final preparations were made. Lieutenant John D. McLean, a platoon commander in the Queen's Own Rifles, met with his sergeant and a corporal to make a list of all the men in his platoon, with names and home addresses, so he could write to their next of kin if they were killed. He created three copies, with the hope that between himself and his two subordinates at least one of them would survive. As it turned out, McLean was the only one of the three to be alive at the end of D-Day. He was shot through the shoulder and during his recovery he made the effort to write the eighteen letters to the parents of those lads in his platoon who were killed.[4]

Most Canadians were like Private Dutch Ramsay of the Canadian Scottish, who wrote, "We knew some of us were going to die but we didn't know who."[5] Others were so shaken by the enormity of the coming events that they foresaw their own deaths. Private Ben Mackereth of the North Shore Regiment observed one distressed comrade who had a premonition of his certain demise: "I can feel it in my bones. It's going to happen and there is nothing I can do about it."[6] A concerned Mackereth had few words of comfort, as uneasy as he was too about the coming events, and the man was indeed killed on Juno Beach. So were dozens, perhaps hundreds, of others who had told themselves over and over again that they would survive.

Lieutenant-Commander D.W. Piers, commanding officer of Algonquin, *promised to fire his destroyer's guns in support of the invasion to the bitter end, and even to run his warship up on the beach.*

ON JUNE 6, Canadian warships supported the invasion force in the largest naval operation in the history of warfare. Destroyers such as *Algonquin* and *Sioux* would bombard German fortifications along the coast, while RCN corvettes protected the landing craft that ran the troops in to the beaches. Lieutenant-Commander D.W. Piers, commanding officer of *Algonquin*, had ordered his crew to man the destroyer's 4.7-inch guns no matter the cost. "If our ship gets hit near the shore we will run the ship right up on the shore and keep firing our guns, until the last shell is gone."[7]

The Allied armada overwhelmed the Kriegsmarine's small fleet of U-boats and surface raiders, most of whom refused the suicidal battle, but there was fear among the Admiralty that the enemy might try some desperate runs to wreak havoc among the troop-carrying ships. While the Royal Navy had prepared itself for this type of chaotic fighting, the Germans proved unwilling to snap the cyanide. More dangerous was the mine-infested water that might disrupt the choreographed assault. And so 247 Allied minesweepers were engaged in clearing 10 approach lanes across the English Channel to the Normandy coast, including 16 Bangor-class RCN minesweepers. Torpedoman E.A. Rudall of HMCS *Blairmore* was briefed that the flotilla could expect 75 percent casualties.[8] The room went silent.

In the dark hours of June 6, the minesweepers moved forward like a fleet of Zambonis on ice, catching and cutting the mine tethers in their path, and allowing them to rise up and be destroyed by gunfire. One officer in HMCS *Georgian* remembered, "We were to hold our course, no matter what was ahead—there must be no holes in our sweeping as ships loaded with troops would be following on us, and would be depending on us."[9] Most of the Canadian ships were assigned to sweep the American Omaha and Utah beaches, which disappointed some of the sailors, who wanted to assist their countrymen assaulting Juno Beach.

As the minesweepers went about their dangerous business of clearing lanes to the ten-fathoms-from-shore line, the Channel filled up with thousands of ships, moving toward the rendezvous point. RCAF mid-upper gunner Gordon Cross, whose RCAF No. 433 Squadron Halifax III was returning from a bombing mission, looked down at warships and vessels through the broken clouds: "Row after row of them in neat lines all headed to the Normandy coast. It was an unbelievable sight, the largest armada ever assembled, and we were getting a special panoramic view of it."[10]

Despite the overwhelming force, Eisenhower and his staff remained worried that the landings would be turned back. No one was sure if, despite their years of training, the lack of real combat experience would leave the Allied infantry too soft to face the enemy soldiers hardened in battle. The German high command, aware that an invasion was possible due to favourable tides, was confident of victory, with most generals echoing Rommel's claim to his wife that "In the West: I believe we'll be able to beat off the assault."[11] Hitler, too, welcomed the invasion: if it was broken on the Atlantic Wall, the Western Allies might withdraw from the war or at least lick their wounds for months, allowing him time to deal with the Soviets in the east. The Allied high command knew there were many things that could derail the operation: poor weather might disrupt combined service work, the likelihood of surprise could easily be lost, and the inherent complexities of landing more than a hundred thousand men on beaches while under fire would result in unexpected challenges. Even if the Allies clawed their way onto the beaches, one American general calculated that the chances of holding the shallow beachhead against counterattack were "only fifty-fifty."[12]

ABOUT 10 KILOMETRES OFF SHORE, the assaulting infantry scrambled down the nets hanging on the sides of the large troop transports to their waiting LCAs (Landing Craft Assaults). There were five for each infantry company, and anywhere between twenty-five and thirty-five men per craft. Choppy water caused delays, leaving NCOs barking orders in a weird half-whisper as the infantry tried to hold the wet, clammy ropes in the dark, while carrying what felt like a fridgeful of equipment on their shoulders. One wrong footstep and the man would be crushed between the hulls of the vessels and sink to the depths.

Canadians on a landing craft closing in on Juno Beach.

The pale gloom was taking on an eerie, pre-dawn, green hue. Over 2,000 landing craft of multiple sizes set off to carry the infantry, support weapons, artillery, and tanks towards the beaches. The lack of shooting from the enemy seemed to confirm the rumours that this might be another training operation, although even in the dark the mass of ships could be glimpsed. Slowly, for each man, the truth was revealed: jaws were clenched, a silence overtook the boats, and men stared straight ahead.

With the hope of landing at 7:45 A.M. on the 7th Brigade's front and ten minutes later on the 8th Brigade's (the staggered times were due to the different depth of the beaches and the incoming tides), the landing craft surged for shore through the rough seas. The ungainly craft pitched wildly, with the blunt ramp bows scooping into the onrushing swell, dropping and rising again, much like the soldiers' unwell stomachs. "We were tossed about like a tiny cork," remembered Corporal Cecil Lelonde of the Royal Winnipeg Rifles, "and most of the group were sick."[13] During the eighty- to ninety-minute run-in, water sloshed over the steel sides of the landing craft, drenching men; some wrapped their rifles in their ground sheets to keep them dry.

Around 5:30 A.M., the first of the naval guns opened up in an ear-shattering bombardment along the French coast. Two hours later, HMCS *Algonquin* hurled forty shells at a German 75mm battery east of Saint-Aubin-sur-Mer, obliterating the enemy gun team. On Juno Beach, where the Canadians were assaulting, the 2nd Battalion, 736th Grenadier Regiment of the 716 Infantry Division, took the brunt of the battering, while the German 441st Ost Battalion all but fled the naval shellfire. Two British cruisers and eleven destroyers smothered the enemy front in fire, although the Canadian beach received less naval gunfire than any other sector.[14]

Amid this sonic and physical assault, the Canadian infantry instinctively ducked low in their landing crafts, but one of the North Shore Regiment officers told Private Ben Mackereth, "Stand up and look around. If you live you'll never forget this sight."[15] While the weight of shells suggested that all the defenders would be obliterated, naval fire plans had long acknowledged that most of the bunkers—many with 2-metre-thick concrete ceilings—could not be knocked out with shellfire. The bombardment was meant to neutralize rather than destroy.[16] The infantry would face the enemy guns in a headlong assault across the open beaches.

"WE HAD NEVER felt so alone in our lives," recounted Queen's Own Rifles Company Sergeant Major Charlie Martin as his landing craft headed for shore.[17] On the Canadian sector, a port and two small French villages overlooked the expanse of

CANADIAN ASSAULTS ON D-DAY

sand: Courseulles-sur-Mer, the fortified port, on the right, Bernières-sur-Mer in the centre, and Saint-Aubin-sur-Mer on the left. "You're a phoney if you're not afraid," recalled Rifleman E.R. Butler of the Queen's Own Rifles. In his mind, almost all the men were more worried about "letting the other fellows down."[18] Vomit rolled in the pitching landing crafts. Foam-flecked geysers erupted from the water as enemy shelling crashed down. Bullets pinged off the steel hulls, causing an eerily musical sound. Not all defenders were dead.

Above the Canadian beaches, RCAF Typhoon fighter-bombers from Nos. 438, 439, and 440 Squadrons dove on enemy objectives, dropping their 500-pound bombs. Spitfires and Mustangs also blasted away at targets with their machine guns and cannons. Although the Luftwaffe wisely refused to engage in battles where the German fighters were outnumbered by at least fifteen to one, a few of the low-flying Allied planes were hit in midair by rocket salvos or shell fire. They disintegrated, spewing flaming wreckage over Juno. The fighter-bombers did little damage against the dug-in enemy forces, but added to the cacophony of destruction.

Though the minesweepers had cleared their approach paths of mines, the German defences closer to the beaches could not be removed. The LCAs had to navigate past layers of wooden stakes and welded iron pyramids of jutting steel known as "tetra-hydras."[19] Many of these stakes were hung with mines that exploded on contact. Eyewitnesses gave chilling accounts of landing craft blown out of the water, body parts floating in the red bilge. Those who survived the blast were often drowned, as they were weighed down with more than sixty pounds of equipment. The survivors of the daring run-in crashed ashore at different times, and all late. They did so as gunners and rocket-launchers fired over open sights from some landing craft, while the naval guns to the rear continued their dance of death. One of the riflemen at the water's edge remarked that he was struck by how the buildings in front of him appeared to be "blowing up in slow motion."[20]

ON THE RIGHT SECTOR, against Courseulles-sur-Mer, two lead companies of the Royal Winnipeg Rifles, with a company of the Canadian Scottish Regiment, ran up on the packed sand at about 7:50 A.M. Tanks of the 1st Hussars were delayed. The waterproofed M4A3 Shermans, nineteen in total, had to "swim" into shore, except for five that were landed directly on the beach. The 29-ton beasts churned through the water, their crews filled with the anxiety that their DD (duplex drive) flotation devices—an inflatable canvas bladder around the tank and a screen that extended up far beyond the turret, along with two propellers—would fail. Several of the Hussars' tanks were sunk by shellfire, but most made it ashore without being swamped, albeit proceeding at a crawl of 4 knots per hour and landing about twenty minutes after the "Little Black Devils," as the Royal Winnipeg Rifles had been known since 1885.

Courseulles-sur-Mer was a port, although a small one, and the Germans fortified it more strongly than other waterfront urban areas. Five concrete gun positions straddled the harbour, and these could be focused on the beach. The infantry hoped that they had already been put out of action by naval gunfire. They were not. "The bombardment having failed to kill a single German soldier or silence one weapon," wrote the war diarist for Royal Winnipeg Rifles, "these companies had to storm their positions cold and did so without hesitation.... Not a man flinched from his task."[21] The two lead companies of Rifles—Baker and Dog—faced at least fifteen MG-42 machine guns, each firing more than five hundred bullets per minute, as well as riflemen, mortars, and 75mm and 50mm anti-tank guns.[22]

Baker Company ran into a bristling arsenal. The infantry were ordered to clear the beach as quickly as possible, but many of the Winnipegers never had a chance to set foot on dry soil. They were gunned down as the landing craft doors dropped, and bloodied rags that were once men were hurled back into the open chasm. Others took a few strides onto the sand before a bullet found them. Rifleman Neil McQuarrie of Baker Company remarked of the frantic assault, "I'd never seen a dead man before that day ... and all of a sudden there were a lot of them around."[23]

Sweeping German machine-gun fire raked the open ground, and while soldiers knew it was safer to move forward than to stay where they were, they had to draw upon reserves of courage to overcome the natural terror of running into the fire. Some went to ground and dug; others crawled through the sticky sand, holding their breath against the fear that a bullet might tear through flesh at any moment. Most allowed their training to take over, muscle memory overriding the brain, firing and throwing grenades, as they looked for gaps in the barbed wire that was up to 10 metres deep in places.

The five Hussars tanks that landed on the beaches were effective in crawling up and down the sandy expanse, firing their twin .30 calibre machine guns and 75mm main gun to blast enemy positions.[24] Supported by the tanks, the infantrymen surged forward, overcoming the German resistance. The last of the enemy were snuffed out around 10:30 A.M., by which time most of the Winnipeg Rifles lead and follow-on formations, Able and Charlie, along with the Canadian Scottish on the far right, had fought their way into the interior villages of Sainte-Croix, Banville, and Colombiers. Baker Company of the Winnipeg Rifles was reduced to a single officer and twenty-six men, while Dog Company was not much stronger.[25]

TO THE LEFT OF THE BLACK DEVILS, the Regina Rifles landed around 8 A.M. against the eastern part of Courseulles-sur-Mer. During the run-in, two LCAs carrying twenty-five men each struck mines and were blown apart. The beach was swept by ten enemy machine guns in a concrete bunker with 1-metre-thick walls, as well as by mortar fire and riflemen positioned in dunes. "[It was] a gruesome landing for my

A German machine gun emplacement along the Atlantic Wall set to repel the Allied invasion.

platoon," remembered Bill Grayson of the Reginas. "A couple of my buddies were lying dead and wounded in front of me—some of our men were still moving, but not too many. That made me realize we were playing for keeps."[26]

A hail of bullets clipped the open area, but the "Johns"—as the Reginas were known—wormed forward, with Able and Baker Company shooting and advancing. Some sacrificed their lives to draw fire so that others could continue closing the distance with the enemy. Major Ronald Shawcross of Able Company led only four out of twenty-five men across the beach, with the rest shot down as they exited the landing craft. His small band followed him closely, and Shawcross covered the ground by running and dropping to the sand on a "1, 2, 3, 4" count, synchronizing the advance with the machine-gunners' reloading, and trying to scramble over the 350 metres of open ground to get to the sand dunes. "There were two kinds of people on the beach, the already dead and those that will be killed there," he would write after the battle. "It was better to press on and get away from the predetermined gun, and mortar fire, also machine guns."[27]

The Reginas made it off the beach after about thirty-five minutes of fierce fighting, although Able Company encountered more guns as they pushed into the streets of Courseulles-sur-Mer. Both companies were ably supported by the tanks of the 1st Hussars, who methodically shelled enemy strongpoints until there was nothing left but mangled defenders and broken concrete.[28] The Reginas continued forward, clearing the town; it was, in the words of one of the riflemen, "grim going."[29]

ON THE 3RD DIVISION'S centre and left flank, the 8th Brigade's Queen's Own Rifles of Canada faced Bernières-sur-Mer, with its church steeple rising over the battlefield, while the North Shore Regiment crashed onto the beaches in front of Saint-Aubin-sur-Mer. The Queen's Own Rifles went in after a delay of thirty minutes, circling far from shore, in the hope that their tanks would catch up to them. The Shermans of the Fort Garry Horse arrived late because of the rough water, and so the Rifles faced the fire alone. "Had we been able to hit the beach on time, we could have taken out all the machine guns that were firing at them," reflected Bob Grant of the Fort Garry Horse. "We would have saved dozens and dozens of lives. But we were late and those poor guys in the Queen's Own were beat to hell."[30]

The Rifles landed under fire at 8:12 P.M. A 4.5 metre wall faced the invading force, with the entire beach—a mere 275 metres wide and 180 metres deep from water to wall—swept by interlocking fields of fire. A German 88mm anti-tank gun was camouflaged and it survived the bombardment; its fearsome shells smashed Able Company, to the west, causing horrendous casualties. The 3rd Division's soldiers learned quickly what their comrades in Italy had already experienced: that the 88s were the most feared weapon in the German arsenal. Yet the Germans also had the Pak 38 (which fired a 50mm shell) and the Pak 40 (which fired a 75mm shell), both of which could knock out tanks at close range. The cost to the Queen's Own was terrible until brave riflemen scrambled forward and destroyed the guns.

Baker Company had been blown off course during the run-in and several of the LCAs landed in front of enemy machine-gun positions that had survived the bombardment unscathed. Despite what looked to be a slaughter, the Queen's Own charged forward. "We were the best trained troops," recounted Rifleman Bill Bettridge, "but there was one thing they didn't teach us—it strikes me very strongly—they didn't teach us how to react when someone suddenly becomes a lot of pieces in front of you."[31]

Infantrymen of the North Shore Regiment hit the beach under fire.

Undulating sand dunes provided some cover for the advancing Rifles, but it was death to go to ground and stay there for long in the fire-swept zone, especially as many German machine guns were firing enfilade along the beach rather than sweeping forward, side-to-side. Riflemen were hit and sprawled lifeless, or lay stunned from the violence of steel tearing through their bodies, the pain more numbing than excruciating. Shrapnel, bullets, and all manner of whirling metal created an almost surreal level of violence, but many soldiers never forgot the sight of Rifleman George Grout being set alight when the phosphorous bombs he was carrying were ignited by a bullet. He burned at the water's edge, his screams rising above the explosions until someone pushed him back into the ocean. Somehow Grout survived, although he faced years of recovery and many skin grafts.

Uncut barbed wire and mine fields channelled the Canadians into a killing ground, which was soon revealed as the bodies of soldiers accumulated at certain spots on the beach. Bill Bettridge watched three of his comrades running with a ladder. The middle man stepped on a mine and was transformed into "a piece of raw meat; I could hear him screaming for several minutes afterwards; it took him such an awful long time to die."[32] The survivors, scratching for concealment in the sand or held up by barbed wire, knew that they had to reach the sea wall. "That first rush—racing across the beach, scaling the wall, crossing the open railway line that ran parallel to the beach, all under heavy MG fire—claimed a lot of us in the first minute or two," testified Charlie Martin, who made it off the beach only to have a bullet strike his helmet.[33] He was left dazed but not dead.

Sergeant John Missons (considered "pretty old" by his mates at age twenty-two) survived the massacre in a landing craft that had dropped its door in front of a German machine-gun bunker. Only 6 of the 27 men on the craft staggered out, and Missons believed that about 85 percent of the 127 Queen's Own casualties on D-Day happened in the first fifteen minutes.[34] Running and firing, the infantrymen crossed the murder zone and cleared the enemy pillboxes by throwing grenades through apertures and then spraying the interiors with Sten and Bren gun fire. About twenty minutes later, the reserve companies landed, and all four companies pushed into the southern outskirts of Bernières-sur-Mer.

On the far left, the North Shore Regiment faced a 90-metre-wide beach in front of Saint-Aubin-sur-Mer. It had a vast concrete bunker housing a hundred-man garrison that had survived the naval and aerial bombardment. With bullets striking the steel landing craft from hundreds of metres out, few of the North Shore riflemen assumed the beach would be anything other than an abattoir. The soldiers found their courage as they exited the landing craft, with platoons and sections rushing forward in sprints before dropping to the coarse sand that felt like salt. In the lead waves was Private Ben Mackereth, who was "expecting every moment to be hit"; it was so terrible that, in his words, I felt my "belly drawn into my backbone" in terror. As a sniper got the bead on him, he had to make the difficult decision to use a dead comrade's body as a shield.[35] Enemy slugs thudded into and through the corpse as he lay vulnerable until a sliver of mortar shell tore into his shoulder. Dazed yet aware that the beach was a lethal trap, he crawled forward in a sideways crab movement, passing through the mines and barbed wire that gallant men in front of him had cleared with their bodies or Bangalore torpedoes.

"Into the jaws of death," described Chaplain Honorary Captain R. Myles Hickey. "The beach was sprayed from all angles by the enemy machine guns and now their mortars and heavy guns began hitting us.... The noise was deafening. You couldn't hear our huge tanks that had already landed and were crunching their way through the sand. Some men, unable to hear them, were run over and crushed to death.... When a shell came over, you dug into the sand and held your breath ... waited for the blast and shower of stones and debris that followed. Then, when it had cleared a little, right next to you, perhaps someone talking to you half an hour before, lay dead."[36]

The North Shore soldiers drove forward, aided by Sherman tanks of the Fort Garry Horse that overran several German positions. But even after the enemy surrendered to the North Shores, rifle fire continued to fell officers and men. "Soon the sniping," recalled Lieutenant C.F. Richardson, "became the most demoralizing aspect of the day as we began to lose one man after another."[37] The New Brunswickers sent out patrols to search for the hidden enemy, only to discover a vast underground network linking much of the defensive site. "There were more guns and well concealed defences inland than were expected," noted one chronicler.[38] Lieutenant "Bones" McCann remembered that enemy snipers popped up and "appeared at unexpected places" to fire and then move back through the underground tunnel. A clearing party of the New Brunswickers entered the subterranean maze, bombing, bayoneting, and shooting their way forward. After two hours of claustrophobic battle, seventy-nine Germans were made prisoner, with about twenty-five corpses left in the labyrinth.

THE CANADIANS EXITED the beaches by around 10:30 A.M., but the day was not yet over. Behind the dunes lay the built-up French towns that were occupied by the

Germans. They had to be cleared in slow and vicious fighting. Throughout the towns, enemy soldiers fired from upper-floor windows of French houses. A few shells from the Shermans usually silenced the snipers, although some defenders held out until a bullet or a well-placed grenade ended their stand. Captain Bill Harvey of the North Shore Regiment attested to the fierce resistance at one road junction that held up the advance until infantrymen skilfully flanked it. "Jerry began flying white flags but as the assault moved in, they opened fire again, causing more casualties. But the boys drove in and the tanks did their stuff. White flags went up again but the North Shore had had enough of that trickery and went in with bombs, cold steel and shooting."[39] All along Juno Beach, the two reserve companies for most of the five Canadian battalions (with two more battalions coming in on their heels) spearheaded the attack inland. No fewer than 1,500 men faced the German defenders of roughly half that number.

There was no single experience of combat on D-Day. Every man faced death; some were claimed, while others survived by chance or skill, and often the combination of both. Infantrymen recalled only a few flashes of banality or horror, although others ran through every second, like a looping film, forever burned into their minds. The fast clatter of the MG42 and the deliberate chug of the Bren that rose and fell under the multiple explosions of high-calibre shellfire and crumping mortars were never forgotten. The beachhead battle and the push into the villages created for most men a profound dreamlike unreality. Regimental Quartermaster James Sutherland of the Canadian Scottish later described D-Day as a nightmare: "I was scared thoughtless as I saw nothing but death and destruction."[40]

Tanks rumbled along the beach, trying to avoid the wounded, but some were ground out of existence by the nearly blind troopers who were essentially driving a small house by looking out through the mail slot. Those injured soldiers who could pull themselves to the safety of the seawall were treated there by medical personnel. Captain Darius Albert, the medical officer of Le Régiment de la Chaudière, one of the reserve battalions to come ashore around a half hour after the first wave, spoke of the ruined combatants he encountered: "It was awful. I'd never seen so many wounded men. In the first two hours, I must have attended at least 200 of them. They didn't scream or swear or shout. They just moaned."[41] Some of the wounded smoked calmly, while others stared off with morphine-glazed eyes; many were slumped over, unconscious, bleeding out, or dead. A number of hurt Canadians lying along the water's edge were dragged out to sea, too weak to fight against the tide.

Blood stained the water red, and Canadians floated lazily face down in the swill. The dead lay curled up and spread out. Some seemed to have died without a mark on them, while others were little more than eviscerated meat. The bodies of tank crews were often burned so badly when their Shermans exploded that the corpses could not be moved without their blackened skin sloughing off and legs and arms separating from the torso. After the battle, the medical personnel poured a hot, gluey pitch over them that hardened and allowed for the grisly task of movement and burial. Charlie Martin took mental stock of the firestorm through which he had passed, and where he had left so many comrades: "Four years of training and living together, a common purpose, friends who became brothers, only to lose more than half of us.... What could we do? Carry on and do the best we could, that's what."[42]

Beach masters from the RCN directed traffic and tried to ease congestion, hurrying the thousands of men and vehicles off the beaches that continued to be under shellfire.[43] "Monster was the first thing that went through my mind," said one Canadian infantryman when he saw a Flail tank—equipped with chains that beat the ground for mines.[44] The Flails were joined by the flame-throwing Crocodile tanks and armoured bulldozers.[45] The Americans eschewed these specialty vehicles—known as "Funnies"—and paid the price on their beaches.[46]

The stench of cordite continued to lay heavy on the beach, while the buzzing black flies, drawn to the blood and body parts, descended in shimmering flights. War correspondent Ross Munro, who had scooped the world with his story of the Canadian invasion of Sicily eleven months earlier, now did the same at Juno. As one of nine Canadian correspondents, Munro waded through the water around 10 A.M with his precious typewriter held overhead.[47] Moving past the dead and wounded on the beach, he settled down to write in Bernières village, amid a rush of Canadian vehicles and with French civilians crying in joy and thanking their liberators. Nearby, the self-propelled guns of the 13th Field Regiment were banging away, lifting the "typewriter off my knees" with every shot fired.[48] No stranger to writing under pressure, Munro got the story back to the beach, after which it was carried by a sympathetic naval officer to London. It was another worldwide scoop.

Munro's missive was joined by iconic footage from the Canadian Army Film and Photo Unit, established in 1942 to send photographers and cameramen into the field to shoot the war on film. None of the soldiers armed with cameras were killed at Juno, although some would fall later in the campaign. Amid the chaos, the Canadians sent their film back to Britain, where it was soon developed and sent around the English-speaking world. It was the best footage secured from any of the five beaches.[49] More would follow, but the surviving footage is intensely moving, documenting the Canadian landing on Juno, and offering us a glimpse into the face of battle.

HAVING BROKEN THROUGH THE DEFENCES, the Canadians pushed inward, linking up with units beside them and continuing the slow grinding sweep of clearing pockets of resistance. The ground was thick with mines, and many soldiers had feet and

Canadian medical officers and stretcher-bearers care for the wounded on the beach. Note how the injured have been pulled near to the seawall to shelter them from mortar fire and remove them from the path of tanks and vehicles.

legs blown off. Surviving officers and NCOs studied maps and recollected the aerial photographs that they had burned into their brains; then they gathered whoever was still standing and set off to their objectives. Lieutenant Stan Biggs, commander of the carrier platoon for the Queen's Own Rifles, had been ordered to take ten men, meet up with two tanks, and knock out an observation post several kilometres inland. Biggs completed his mission, although on the way he encountered two Germans, one unarmed and looking to surrender and the other with an automatic weapon. In an instant, Biggs fired his Sten light machine gun, dropping the armed German. His instinct had taken over: "In the stress of the excitement when there's no time to think, the necessary action has to be automatic. Kill or be killed."[50] Despite the harrowing experience and the cruel nature of combat, the thirty-one-year-old Biggs felt odd about taking another man's life at fewer than 3 metres, and he never forgot that dead German, even as he was wounded at the end of August and returned to Canada to make a life for himself, have four children, and practise law for sixty years in Toronto.

As the Canadians fanned out from the beaches, they faced frightened French civilians, for whom D-Day was the 1,453rd day of German occupation. It was also the last. The French Canadians in Le Régiment de la Chaudière greeted the civilians in their own language, one of the few delights for the French men, women, and children who witnessed their small villages become a battleground. Most understood that this destruction was the price of liberation, and Captain Hector Belton of the Sherbrooke Fusilier later remarked, "It's rather amazing to see people whose homes you have just blasted to bits coming out with tears in their eyes to welcome you."[51] A few of the brave civilians celebrated their new freedom by handing out wine or flying previously hidden flags, but most French families wisely scurried for cellars, as German snipers continued to pick off Canadians or anyone who moved in the open.

New headquarters were established past the beaches, with company commanders—or whoever was left—rallying troops, organizing a forward defence, and even, when their radio sets worked, calling down naval gunfire to knock out enemy positions. Because of the range and angle of fire, the naval guns were more effective now, and salvos of shells made mincemeat of a few enemy counterattacking forces. More Canadian units went forward, passing dirty, dishevelled, and scared German prisoners of war who were marching, hands raised and without weapons, to the beach. Some of the prisoners lost their lives there from their own shells. Most found protection where they could and waited to be directed. The Allies had other priorities.

The 8th Brigade's reserve, Le Régiment de la Chaudière, took the lead on the left, punching forward to secure Bény-sur-Mer, a few kilometres inland, by mid-afternoon. The Germans gave up the village easily, although three German 88s west of Tailleville, more than 2,000 metres away, knocked out three of the 14th Field Regiment's self-propelled 105mm M7 Priests in less than a minute. As the field guns burned, their newly formed ammunition dump caught fire, setting off a tremendous explosion, with shells cooking off in all directions for over an hour.[52] The "Chauds" inched their way towards the enemy guns, with officers eventually able to contact HMCS *Algonquin*. Lieutenant-Commander Piers and his crew were pummelling the Germans all morning with their 4.7-inch guns, from a distance of 4 kilometres. As they bracketed the enemy gunners, with each shell corrected by a British artillery forward observer, the Germans knew that doom was upon them. They were obliterated by the naval gunfire.

THE CANADIANS WERE ORDERED to push on to their objective of Carpiquet airfield 6 kilometres west of Caen and 14 kilometres from Juno, even as the 21st Panzer Division surged in the opposite direction in an armoured drive to the 3rd British Division's beaches on the afternoon of the 6th. The panzers were handed a crushing defeat, stopped cold by airpower and a robust British defence of tanks, infantry, and anti-tank guns. Losing 70 of the 124 tanks, 21st Panzer was thrown back on its heels. The survivors dug in to hold Caen, denying the Allies the vast plain to the south that could be used for air bases.[53] Even as Caen was steadily reduced to rubble by artillery fire over the coming weeks, it remained the rock of the German defence. The defenders there soon drew in other infantry and armoured forces from which to launch attacks against the British and Canadian lines.

By the end of the day, the Canadians had advanced farther inland than any other Allied formation—to a depth of 11 kilometres—and the 9th Brigade's North Nova Scotia Highlanders fought until after 8 P.M. At that point, they were ordered by corps commander Lieutenant-General Miles Dempsey to halt on the intermediate objectives and dig in to protect against additional German counterattacks from

21st Panzer.[54] Pre-battle assessments had identified that the German counterstrike would likely fall on the British and Canadian divisions, and Dempsey now feared having his forces rolled up by a determined attack hitting the divisional seams.

All Allied divisions made it ashore, although two American divisions were needed on Omaha Beach, where they suffered about 40 percent of the total 7,500 Allied casualties on June 6. The British lost fewer men, but the veteran 3rd British Division was unable to take its objective on the far flank, Caen, while the Canadians did not reach Carpiquet airfield. The Americans also failed to reach their final objectives, meaning that all of this terrain would be fought over for another month. Nonetheless, some 150,000 Allied soldiers had breached the Atlantic Wall and were ashore by the end of D-Day, along with 900 tanks and another 5,000 guns and vehicles. While there was pride in the accomplishment, no one was naive enough to believe that the war was over. The next few days would be critical, with Eisenhower's command hoping that the concentration of the German reserves remained around the Pas-de-Calais waiting for the phantom invasion that would never come.[55] Yet even with the Germans focused on the north, they had or were massing three of their best divisions—21st Panzer, 12th SS, and Panzer Lehr—around Caen, and these would soon hurl themselves against the Canadians and the British. The goal for the Allies over the coming days was simply not to lose.

At Juno Beach, the aerial bombardment and rocket fire, when combined with the naval bombardment, had done little to destroy or even suppress the enemy defences. The Canadians had clawed their way forward, sacrificing their lives on the beaches and fighting skilfully to overcome the fortified defenders. They paid for their bravery and endurance on June 6, with 359 soldiers killed and 715 wounded, although that was about half of what was predicted by the operation's planning officers.[56] Such figures were of little consolation to the survivors, many of whom reflected on the sad irony of training with comrades for four years only to have them knocked out in the first minutes or hours of combat. Nor were the lighter-than-expected losses any consolation to hundreds of families who would soon be receiving the telegrams that informed of the death of a loved one.

CHAPTER 6

A BATTLE FOR SURVIVAL

"There was that beach, and us, and nothing in between," wrote tank officer Frederick Baldwin.[1] All along the tenuous front, the Allies waited for the enemy counterattacks, aware that if they were driven back their fate was assured annihilation at the water's edge. But few looked over their shoulder. The Queen's Own Rifles' Doug Hester wanted revenge for his dead and wounded comrades and, in his words, he became "a killer with a single purpose."[2] Other men felt the same, although their anger was cut with grief. Lieutenant Clifford Chadderton had witnessed many of his friends in the Royal Winnipeg Rifles die on Juno Beach. A distraught Chadderton had a chance to return to the wreckage-strewn landing site to pay homage to his close friend, Corporal Lawrence Scaife.[3] In a symbolic act, he exchanged helmets with his fallen chum, carrying his memory and the burden of his death through the fighting in Normandy.

The night of the 6th reminded all the planners that even though the Luftwaffe was vastly outnumbered, just a few fighters and bombers, flying in darkness, had a target-rich environment. The Luftwaffe paid for these operations, however, and RCAF's No. 401 Squadron intercepted a dozen Junkers Ju 88s heading for the beaches and shot down six of the twin-engine light bombers, while forcing the rest to break off.[4] But other brave Germans made it through the aerial screen. It took a lot of ordnance and firepower to kill a man on the battlefield, but there were always chance deaths, singularly and by groups. Reinforcements from the Cameron Highlanders of Ottawa coming off the beach on June 7 were hit by a bomb dropped in the dark. Amid the mulch of bodies, three officers, two sergeants, and nine other ranks were killed, while another fourteen were wounded.[5] Such was the chanciness of war.

Closer to the front, the infantry regiments lay low in their slit trenches and drove off several probing enemy assaults. "Every night dig deep," was the warning given to the infantry, "it may be your grave."[6] The memorable road signs, "Maple Leaf Up," pointed in the direction of the front, although the lack of fixed lines meant that trucks manned by the Royal Canadian Army Service Corps (RCASC), running forward ammunition and supplies, blundered into ambushes. The enemy did the same, and a truckload of Germans drove into the Canadian lines near Anguerny. All were taken prisoner.

With the enemy lurking somewhere in the dark, infantrymen were edgy and trigger-happy. "What a bastard of a night—no time for sleep; no time to eat; no time for anything but looking into the dark and wondering what is ahead," worried Sergeant T.C. Reid of the Sherbrooke Fusilier, whose Sherman tanks were slightly behind the front lines but ready to spring into action.[7] Just before midnight on the 6th, Lieutenant James Doohan from Vancouver, British Columbia, went forward to find the guns of the 13th Field Regiment, only to be shot six times by a nervous

A Canadian Bren gunner is dug-in to a slit trench and ready for an enemy attack.

sentry. Doohan survived his wounds to become an actor, best known as "Scotty," the chief engineer on the starship *Enterprise* in the original *Star Trek* TV series.

"IF ANYTHING SHOULD HAPPEN TO ME, do not feel sad or burdened by it, but take the attitude of 'He served his country to his utmost.'"[8] Such was the last letter of Private Leslie Neufeld from Nipawin, Saskatchewan, who jumped into Normandy on D-Day with the 1st Canadian Parachute Battalion. His parents never saw him again. Many others were lost in the jump into enemy territory. Battered by the weather and blown off course by the wind, the parachutists landed throughout the drop zone. Some were shot as they floated to earth; others were tangled in trees; some drowned in water, their eighty pounds of kit dragging them down. Lance-Corporal H.R. Holloway described how those who survived the drop were scattered "all over hell's half acre."[9]

The paratroopers were vastly outgunned, with almost no heavy weapons such as artillery, but they had been bred tough. They moved through the enemy rear area shooting up sentries and detonating bridges. The paratroopers' confused the German high command, who knew that almost 25,000 enemy troops might be behind their lines but could not pinpoint their exact location. After a night of skirmishing, the 1st Canadian Parachute Battalion gained its objectives of capturing a German gun position and garrison at Varaville and bringing down bridges over the Dives and Divette Rivers to delay enemy counterattack forces. Then they dug in and held the crossroads at Le Mesnil, high ground between the Dives and Orne Rivers and almost within sight of the beaches. The Canadians paid a steep price for their daring actions. Of the 541 who jumped from the C-47 Dakotas, 116 were killed, wounded, or taken prisoner. The survivors joined up with the units moving off the beaches and into the interior.

LEAD ELEMENTS OF THE 3RD CANADIAN INFANTRY DIVISION marched forward at first light on the day after D-Day, known as D+1. On the Anglo-Canadian front, a gap had appeared on the left flank between the Canadians and the 3rd British Division, which had been unable to seize Caen, a significant city of around 55,000 inhabitants. But there was no time to wait and consolidate. General Montgomery, in his baggy, unpressed corduroys, turtleneck, and black tanker's beret, urged the Anglo-Canadian force to continue biting off German-held terrain before the enemy responded in strength.

While Montgomery's headquarters dealt with the confusion inherent in coordinating more than 150,000 soldiers on enemy soil, the Germans reeled from the invasion. Having believed that the inclement weather of early June would spoil any operation, many in the German high command had taken brief holidays or attended war games at Rennes. Closer to the front, von Rundstedt—the commander of the German armies in the west—surveyed the sporadic intelligence filtering into his headquarters. He had deployed most of his best formations, including six mobilized infantry divisions and two panzer divisions, in the northern Calais region, and now he only had three static divisions, two mobile infantry divisions, and one armoured division, the 21st Panzer Division, in Normandy. But two more elite armoured divisions, Panzer Lehr and the 12th SS, were on the march to Normandy, with the latter having units already in place to strike by June 7.

On D+1, the Canadians were spread out to the northwest of Caen. The plan was simple: advance to contact with the enemy. On the Canadian right flank, furthest away from Caen, the 7th Infantry Brigade (the Winnipeg Royal Rifles, Regina Rifles of Canada, and Canadian Scottish) was to occupy a number of small villages, including Putot, Bretteville, and Norrey, and set up a loose defensive line. They were in a race against the coiling attack that they knew was coming, and they had to be dug-in on ground of their choosing before the storm swept over them. On the left, the 9th Infantry Brigade continued to drive south towards Carpiquet, 6 kilometres from Caen. This was a bad situation, with the Canadians' left flank open since the British, wary of another 21st Panzer Division strike, were moving cautiously and were unable to keep up to provide a solid defensive shoulder.

And so, early on June 7, on the 9th Brigade's front, the North Nova Scotia Highlanders and Sherbrooke Fusilier tank regiment pushed on to Carpiquet. To get to the important airfield, the battlegroup would first have to clear the villages of Les Buissons, Buron, and Authie. Stumbling forward, the blind leading the blind, Charlie Company of the North Novas drove the German defenders from 21st Panzer Division out of Buron in the late morning and then pushed on a kilometre south to

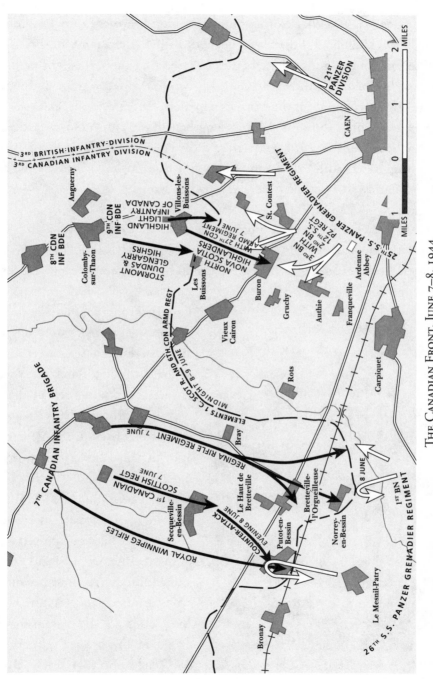

THE CANADIAN FRONT, JUNE 7–8, 1944

Authie, which was cleared, according to Major Don Learment, "under intense mortar fire."[10] The Highlanders destroyed pockets of enemy resistance in small farms, as well as several 88mm guns. These battles revealed that the Canadians' training had paid off, as they skilfully drove the Germans before them, using fire and movement tactics to engage elements of the panzer grenadiers, flank positions, and reduce them with grenades. But as the day's shadows lengthened, the North Novas readied themselves for the full onslaught, having spotted the enemy massing at about 1 P.M. The infantry dug like mad for cover and Shermans tried to find some shelter. Around 2 P.M., a fanatical force rolled over the Canadian front.

IN NORMANDY, the Canadians fought a personal battle with the 12th SS Panzer Division Hitlerjugend. Wearing camouflaged smocks, the 12th SS Hitler Youth were commanded by a cadre of hardened NCOs and junior officers from 1st SS Hitler Division who had served on the Eastern Front. In that savage fight to the finish, prisoners were rarely taken and, as a result, almost everyone fought to the last bullet. Rarely has such ruthlessness been witnessed in the history of warfare. The survivors brought these experiences back to the Western Front and, in the 12th SS, they led totally indoctrinated Nazi youth. Teenagers who had been inundated with the Nazi mythos of the master race and racial purity since childhood proved willing to throw themselves into battle heedlessly and endure horrendous casualties. The SS stormtroopers (Schutzstaffel, or "protection squad," a term that had its origin in the prewar military link to SS Reichsfuhrer Henrich Himmler's

Youthful members of the 12th SS Hitlerjugend.

Brown Shirts) revelled in sacrificing for the Führer. The division was close to full strength with 17,000 ranks and 202 tanks (94 Mark IVs, 67 Panthers, and 41 tank destroyers), and anxious for combat.[11]

Much of the German high command hesitated in committing its reserves to Normandy, for fear of another Allied landing in Calais, but Major-General Fritz Witt, commander of the 12th SS, recognized the perilous nature of the invasion and within a few hours of the beach landings, his first units had set off for Caen. Led by thirty-four-year-old Colonel Kurt Meyer's 25th Panzer Grenadier Regiment, a three-battalion formation of mechanized infantry, they arrived in Caen early on June 7. From the outskirts of Caen, atop an observation tower at the Abbaye d'Ardenne, a 12-century monastery surrounded by thick stone walls, Meyer could see the activity

on the beaches in the British sector, and he studied the Canadians in Authie and Buron a mere 2 kilometres away. Meyer, a Nazi veteran of Eastern Front fighting who had broken out of Soviet encirclement three times, had orders to wait and consolidate with forces from 21st Panzer Division. But "Fast Meyer," as he was known, spied the advance and threw two of his three infantry battalions, as well as about fifty Mk IV tanks, against the overstretched Canadians. "Little fish!" gloated Meyer. "We'll throw them back into the sea."[12]

German tanks, divided into two groups, attacked shortly after 2 P.M., with the 12th SS infantry in support. The Canadians faced the Mark IV and Panther (Mark V) tanks in Normandy, both of which had formidable armour

German 12th SS Colonel Kurt Meyer.
An Eastern Front veteran, Meyer was aggressive and bloodthirsty. His forces tried to drive the Canadians back to the beaches during the first days of Normandy. They failed.

and high-velocity 75mm main guns. "It can be stated definitely that we are out-gunned both by the long 75mm and the 88mm," wrote one Canadian officer.[13] The Allies' Sherman tank was on par with the Mark IV, but the Panthers far surpassed it. When the German tanks were situated in a hull-down position (with their forward-sloped armour facing the enemy), they were nearly impervious to Canadian fire. The only way to kill a Panther was to hit its mantlet, below the main gun, or from the side and rear where the steel plating was thinner. Even when Shermans closed to spitting range—500 metres—their armour-piercing shells, each as thick as a man's arm, often bounced off the enemy's steel plating. However, the Shermans were not completely hopeless, as is sometimes portrayed in history books. They could defeat enemy tanks in duels, especially when the German tanks were on the move.

A Canadian M4A4 Sherman in Normandy. The Shermans were on par with the German Mk IV tanks, but outgunned and outperformed by the enemy's Panthers and Tigers. Nonetheless, the Sherman 75mm gun could unleash crucial firepower in support of an infantry attack.

Though the North Novas were prepared for an attack, the ferocity of the assault shocked them. They were also severely outnumbered by the 12th SS infantry, the fifty tanks, and the fifty or so German artillery pieces.[14] Canadian outposts near Carpiquet airfield were quickly overrun by twenty panzers. The Sherbrookes' fifty tanks engaged in fierce battles, and soon they were fighting for their lives. "I spotted seven or eight enemy tanks at 1,000 yards on my left," reported Lieutenant Norman Davies. "I halted, stopped two of them with the 17 [pounder gun], advanced, halted and fired again scoring another hit. Then all hell broke loose."[15] Tracers danced over the wheat fields, followed by scything machine-gun fire. Enemy 75mm shells tore through armour, igniting the Shermans. Major Sydney Radley-Walters, known as "Rad" and destined to become a Canadian tank ace with eighteen destroyed tanks to his credit, testified to the baptism of fire: "As a youngster going into action for the first time, the thing that hits us all apparently, was that tremendous surprise. All of a sudden there's a rain of fire coming down, tanks started getting knocked out, and communications and the command and control started to break down."[16]

Battlefield studies later revealed what all Canadian soldiers and troopers already knew: that the Shermans, with their higher profile and lighter armour, and with high-octane fuel running through rear fuel cells, were dangerously vulnerable to all calibres of enemy anti-tank shells. Sixty percent of the Shermans in Normandy were wiped out by a single shot from a 75mm or 88mm shell.[17] Moreover, two thirds of all the tanks "brewed up" when hit. Bursting into flames was so common that the Shermans earned the ironic nickname of "Ronsons," after a brand of cigarette lighter with the memorable slogan "lights first every time." Many crews burned alive before they could bail out of the tank, usually through the top turret, although there were two smaller escape hatches lower down in the hull for the driver and co-driver. Trooper Ray Lane of the 1st Hussars remarked, "On average, half the crew never got out." Most troopers estimated they had thirty seconds at best to get out of the tank before the 250 gallons of high-octane fuel ignited.[18] The smell of roasted humans permeated the air.

At Authie, the North Novas' infantry were attacked by a large force, about six times that of the defenders. As the Hitlerjugend came overland at them, and were further supported by shellfire from the 21st Panzer Division, the Canadians laid down a punishing fire from Lee Enfields and Bren guns. The SS troops were cut down in sickening numbers. Major V.O. Walsh of the Sherbrookes, one of the regiment's few officers to land on D-Day and to go through the entire war, described the Canadian defence: "They used everything—machine guns; they threw grenades; as well as firing all other guns. That finally stopped them."[19]

While the infantry's light weapons found flesh, the Canadians' artillery, the 14th Field Regiment, equipped with 105mm self-propelled guns, was trapped in the lines of communication far to the rear and unable to advance through road congestion and German mortar fire. When they arrived closer to the front, a number of the forward artillery observers were killed or wounded, making it difficult for the guns to target the enemy. Most of the Canadian and British anti-tank guns, especially the effective 17-pounder, had also not yet made it off the boats or the beaches to strike

The 12th SS Hitlerjugend in action.

deep inland. With no field or anti-tank artillery, and with communications cut to the offshore warships, a renewed enemy attack, overwhelming in numbers and ferociousness, pressed the Highlanders back. Confusion reigned, as sections of the North Novas were cut off and destroyed while others held off the assault. Reflecting on his combat experience in Normandy, one Canadian noted, "In addition to the overpowering sense of sinister menace lying over the front, all soldiers in a battle zone must learn to live in a dense fog of mystery."[20] Highlanders were surrounded and close to being wiped out in Authie, but the Sherbrookes came back through hell to rescue some of their comrades on foot, charging into the pitched melee with their Shermans' guns blasting away at the enemy. Despite the heroics, few of the North Novas from Authie made it back through the tall grain fields to the burning village of Buron, which was also under heavy attack. By the time Authie fell, around 5:30 P.M., the Canadian gunners had come forward within firing range and were directed from a forward observation post by Major N.B. "Ike" Buchanan, who called in crushing defensive fire. The Germans were thrown back. Buchanan barely survived several near-death bombardments and was awarded a second bar to his Military Cross for his bravery.

By the end of the day, the Canadian survivors of Buron, waiting for another counterattack, were pulled back to Les Buissons, where the Highland Light Infantry and the Stormont, Dundas and Glengarry Highlanders had organized a robust defence. The day of battle cost the Sherbrookes 21 tanks, although the Germans lost 17 tanks.[21] The North Novas were mauled badly, suffering more than 200 men killed, wounded, or missing, including 37 Canadian prisoners murdered after the guns fell silent.[22] The 12th SS paid for their reckless assault with over 300 casualties.[23] Historians have often depicted the Authie and Buron battles as a clear-cut German victory, but with the 12th SS outgunning the Canadians, and in view of the Germans' considerable losses, it was a draw at best. Brigadier Meyer had found that the "little fish" had sharp teeth.[24]

WITH THE GERMANS AND CANADIANS bloodying themselves on the outskirts of Caen, the 7th Canadian Infantry Brigade, on the right flank, had significant warning of an impending attack. The Winnipeggers, Reginas, and Canadian Scottish, along with Shermans from the 1st Hussars, had made a fortress of the small villages of Bretteville, Norrey, and Putot by D+1, and had the full day to prepare their defences. Though the infantry were steeled for the coming battle, there was no continuous line of trenches. Brigadier Harry Foster, a no-nonsense professional soldier who would eventually command a division, worried about the holes in his broad sector, and how to plug them. The 7th Brigade was far better supported by British and Canadian artillery and anti-tank guns than the overextended 9th Brigade, but having thrust into enemy territory, as one of the Reginas, J.G. Baird, observed worriedly, "We were out on a limb if the enemy could organize his forces for an attack."[25]

Farthest from Caen, the Winnipeg Rifles held Putot, a nondescript French village, with houses and farms built of Caen stone. It was the site of a whirling battle early on the 8th, when the 2nd and 3rd Battalions of the 26th SS Panzer Grenadier Regiment hit the Canadians hard. The Winnipeggers were unlucky to be on the far right of the brigade, the far right of the 3rd Division, and the far right of I British Corps, with the British on their right not yet having advanced to close the gap.

Canadian infantry hold ground.

Wilhelm Mohnke, the sociopathethic, morphine-addicted Nazi brigadier, ordered the first assault around 3:00 A.M., but the Hitlerjugend were taken apart in the open fields by the Winnipeggers' rifle fire and backing artillery. Then came a second, even more determined thrust, around 1:00 P.M., behind air-bursting shells from two battalions of artillery, including the feared 88s. The Winnipeggers, who had lost close to 130 men on D-Day, had dug slit trenches in front of Putot as opposed to within the target-rich village, but they were nonetheless dazed by the ferocity of the bombardment. Firing up to twenty shells per minute, the 88 was anti-tank and anti-aircraft; indeed, as one Canadian officer moaned, it was "anti-everything."[26] Striking from all directions, the Germans enveloped and cut off three of the Winnipeggers' forward companies by early afternoon. Attesting to the ferocity of the battle, at one point the Germans used Canadian prisoners as human shields, driving them forward into positions held by the remaining Winnipeg Rifles.[27] The Rifles did not surrender, even as their pocket collapsed under the weight of the enemy's attack.

A Canadian artillery gun team feeds a 25-pounder.

Foster ordered a reinforced battlegroup of the Canadian Scottish, with eleven Shermans from the 1st Hussars and supporting machine-gun teams, to relieve the Winnipeg Rifles. The Scottish had little time to prepare for the operation and they found their wireless sets jammed by the Germans, who played music to drown out dialogue with headquarters. The Scottish set off at 8:30 P.M. with the sun dipping low. Nerves were taut. They marched rapidly forward through wheat fields and orchards behind a creeping barrage and a smoke screen from five field artillery regiments. Private Harry Roberts of the Scottish had enlisted at sixteen and now, at age twenty, felt nearly paralyzed with fear. As he closed in on Putot, he stumbled across several Winnipeggers who had been executed by the enemy—hands tied and shot in the back of the head. His resolve was stiffened by the horrible sight and now, in his mind, "it was a case of fighting to the last round and the last man."[28]

After three hours of fierce conflict, the Germans were driven back a little before midnight, although, according to Lieutenant-Colonel F.N. Cabeldu, commander of the Scottish, "at a terrible cost."[29] Many of the Scottish infanteers remembered witnessing a figure of Christ on the Cross in the village square, bullet-riddled and shrapnel-scarred, as Canadians and Germans fought over the contested terrain. Captain R.M. Caldwell, the regimental medical officer for the Winnipeg Rifles, remarked sadly after the war, "It was a battle of youth versus youth, for the average age of the Riflemen was about 19."[30]

The survivors of the Winnipeg Rifles emerged from the cellars and slit trenches that they had held at great cost. Most were down to their last rounds of ammunition, and this after having rifled through the pouches of killed comrades for ammo clips. That night, according to Tony Foulds, who served in the British 62nd Anti-Tank Regiment that backed the Canadians with 17-pounder M-10s (mobile armoured guns), they "sorted out the wounded from the dead, both Canadian and German."[31] The Scottish lost 125 men killed and wounded in storming Putot, while the Winnipeg Rifles lost nearly full three companies, 298 casualties—making the total for the battalion nearly 450 casualties since D-Day three days earlier. The Germans reported 40 killed and 58 wounded, although those numbers appear too low considering the ferocity of the battle.[32] The 12th SS had sought to knife through the Canadians to the coast, but had barely pierced the crust of their defensive lines before being thrown back.

FURTHER TO THE EAST, the Regina Rifles faced four fierce attacks throughout the night of the 8th and the early hours of the 9th, as they held the villages of Norrey and Bretteville. At Bretteville, the Reginas created a series of strongpoints around a handful of Normandy farms, their thick stone walls largely impervious to shellfire. They defended against twenty-two enemy tanks from the 12th SS Panzer Regiment's 2nd Battalion, and supporting Grenadiers, who closed in on Bretteville around 10:00 P.M. on June 8. With no tanks and few anti-tank guns, the Reginas were outgunned, but they held on as dusk faded to darkness, with sharpshooters picking off German officers, machine-gunners breaking up the enemy advance, and 3-inch mortar fire scattering concentrations of 12th SS troops. Living on a steady diet of the stimulant Benzedrine, the Reginas fought through the night. The PIAT teams snaked forward to engage the Panthers in uneven actions. The Canadian bravery paid off. Two Panther tanks were destroyed around midnight in close-quarters combat, with Rifleman Joe LaPointe stalking a Panther on his own and killing it with a shot from his PIAT. As one of the Reginas observed, "The dreaded Panther tank was not invincible and could be knocked out by infantry who knew how to use their weapons."[33]

The Germans learned to fear the PIAT, even though the bombs often failed to penetrate the tanks' armour and the brave teams of PIAT gunners were annihilated after exposing themselves when they fired.[34] The Reginas turned to laying necklaces of No. 75 grenades along the roads to break the enemy tank tracks and achieve a "mobility kill." Six Panthers were eventually wrecked in the mad melee, including three killed by the 6-pounders of the 3rd Canadian Anti-Tank Regiment, who were holed up with the Reginas and firing new armour-piercing shells. The ground was also covered with

Rifleman Daniel Corturient of the Regina Rifles takes cover behind a stone wall in the defence against the 12th SS attacks on June 8–10, 1944.

dozens of slain 12th SS troops. "During this test of real war," declared Lieutenant Frank Proctor, "we suffered many casualties and lost several Bren gun carriers, but we had held against a powerful enemy attack, and had inflicted a heavy toll against the enemy infantry."[35]

The fighting also raged at Norrey, less than a kilometre south of Bretteville and therefore jutting into the enemy lines. Burning farms and magnesium flares lit the sky, while tracer fire and muzzle flashes illuminated the gloom. The shadows of soldiers darted across the battlefield, scrambling from cover to cover. The war diarist for the regiment wrote that the riflemen of the forward companies "are beginning to resemble the earth they live in and are feeling the strain."[36] Panzers rumbled forward, firing as they moved; and when they were unable to break into the houses and the stone walls, they prowled outside for victims. Some of the Reginas were in slit trenches outside the mansions, and the panzers took their revenge, grinding through the fields looking for the trenches, whereupon they crushed to death or buried alive those men in the ground. The screams of the doomed—especially those caught by the tanks as they spun on one tread—left the survivors within the stone walls shaken by the sheer brutality of facing tanks. But even when the 12th SS attacked in waves, the Reginas never faltered as they fought for their lives and for one another. There was no breakthrough.

The cost of war.

Though the Germans proved dogged fighters, they struck piecemeal throughout the battle, with their infantry often separated from the tanks. Brigadier Harry Foster later characterized the swarming but clumsy assault as being "launched without any semblance of tactical sense.... The enemy flung himself straight against the strongest p[oin]ts and utterly failed to exploit the undoubted weakness of his opponents' position."[37] Hubert Meyer, a 12th SS divisional staff officer and historian of the division, later said of the Canadians, "The enemy was especially strong in the defence and could not be taken by surprise. He fought with determination and courage."[38] After several hours of combat, the 12th SS retreated, leaving behind many of their dead. Frustrated and angry, the Germans switched tactics, and throughout June 9 and 10, according to one of the Reginas' officers, the Canadians were "shelled 23 hours a day."[39] The Reginas' defence was one of the finest Canadian holding actions of the entire war, and it drove a stake through the German plans of driving the Canadians back to Juno Beach. It came at a high cost. Gordon Brown, commander of D Company, wrote candidly that "Most of the soldiers were in their late teens or early 20s, but they were aging rapidly as the horror of what they had seen began to sink in."[40]

IN THE FIRST DAYS of the Normandy campaign, the Canadian infantry found that the Lee-Enfield bolt-action rifle, the Bren gun, and the 3-inch mortar were the most effective weapons for laying down fire against the enemy. The mortar, with a range of 2,500 metres, provided close fire support. The Sten gun remained dangerous to everyone—user, victim, and bystanders—because of its poorly designed safety catch and its tendency to fire at unwanted times. German snipers also learned to look for soldiers carrying them, as the guns were almost always wielded by NCOs and platoon officers. The 2-inch mortar was not a key weapon for the infantry, and only one was issued for the platoon headquarters section. The crew of two could easily carry the light mortar and its 2-pound bombs; yet with a rate of fire of eight bombs per minute it was difficult to carry enough bombs to fire for any length of time. Captain Donald Findlay, a Canadian serving with a British regiment, one of 623 Canadian infantry officers to do so as part of the Canloan program, also observed that the mortar tended to draw fire "because of revealing flash and sound at close range."[41] While the Great War infantryman had found great value in having, by 1918, about a fourth of the platoon issued a rifle that fired a grenade to a range of 100 metres, the same did not occur in Normandy, where the 2-inch and 3-inch mortar took the grenade rifle's place on the battlefield. That said, grenades remained an essential infantry weapon, with all soldiers carrying them, and while there were many types, the No. 36 fragmentation grenade, with its four-second fuse, was useful in clearing the enemy from their defences. Its explosion had a range of about 18 metres. Infantrymen learned to throw it from cover so they did not have to expose themselves to either enemy fire or the grenade's wide and lethal blast radius. The No. 77 phosphorous smoke grenade was useful for obscuring troops from enemy eyes and fire, but it was scary to wield as there were a few cases of grenades exploding in the thrower's hands and causing, according to one Canadian officer, "very severe phosphorous burns."[42] The initially unpopular PIAT had proven essential in the early Normandy battles, and would continue to be one of the few infantry weapons that could be used against tanks, while also, in the words of one officer, proving useful in "housebreaking."[43]

Even though the Canadians took heavy losses, they unlocked the secret to the German tactical doctrine. The Germans were fierce in the attack: indoctrinated, ideologically driven, and willing to absorb high casualties as they hurled themselves at their opponents. However, they launched these offensives with the aim of shocking the Canadians, and they often did so without proper planning or coordination with other arms. These immediate counterattacks were sometimes very effective, and always unnerving for those on the receiving end. When the defenders were driven back, they usually bore significant casualties—men killed in combat, the wounded splayed on the ground, and large numbers captured. These losses often overshadowed the German's own casualties, which were, in comparison to their overrun opponents, fewer in number. But when the defenders stood resolute against the assault, the Germans absorbed heavy losses. The German doctrine was a gamble—when the attacks worked, they paid off big, but when they failed, there were grave casualties. It was unsustainable over time. Moreover, the fighting arms of the 3rd Canadian Division had begun to plan more methodically for both the initial operation and the holding of positions. The Allies turned increasingly to firepower to stop the enemy counterattacks. In the first days of Normandy, the Canadians proved not only that they could take a punch but that they could, in turn, stagger their opponent. As one

Canadian artillery officer sneered, "The Germans thought we were fucking Russians. They did stupid things, and we killed those bastards in large numbers."[44]

THE PANTHER TANKS surged forward again in the early morning of the 9th, seeking to drive the Reginas out of Norrey. The Reginas were exhausted, but they had been reinforced by Sherman tanks from the 1st Hussars that had rolled forward to strengthen the line. Several of the tanks were the newly issued Fireflys equipped with the 17-pounder gun, which fired an armour-piercing Sabot shot. The round consisted of a tungsten dart embedded in a full-bore shoe that was discarded as the round sped downfield. At 90 metres-per-second muzzle velocity, it had double the power of a standard 75mm Sherman gun.[45] When the dart penetrated through the tank's steel, it ricocheted in the interior, causing terrible damage to all inside. The Fireflys had only been delivered to the armoured regiments in May, and the troopers were still working on tactics, doctrine, and how they should fight with the 75mm Shermans—eventually

One of the German Panther tanks destroyed by the Canadians at Bretteville, France.

settling on having one Firefly with three Shermans in a four-tank troop—but they evened up the odds when facing German tanks. As twelve Panthers charged over open ground and in broad daylight, they encountered fire from Canadian 6-pounder anti-tank guns, and they turned away to find easier targets. In doing so, the Panthers opened up their flanks to twelve Shermans and Fireflys from the 1st Hussars and Fort Garry Horse waiting in ambush. At 900 metres, the Canadians pounded the Panthers, destroying seven of them in a matter of minutes.[46] "After a muffled bang and a swaying, as if a track had been ripped off, the vehicle came to a stop," one SS sergeant recalled. "When I looked to the left, I happened to see the turret being torn off the panzer driving on the left flank. At the same moment, after another minor explosion, my vehicle began to burn.... To my left, other burning panzers."[47] The surviving German tanks retreated from the shooting gallery.

A Sherman Firefly. The Fireflys were equipped with the 17-pounder gun that gave them twice the striking power of a Sherman tank's 75mm gun.

Another day of fighting left the 12th SS holding a wide front and unable to dislodge the Canadians. With half a dozen Panther and Grenadier attacks thrown back, and another 300 casualties to the Hitler Youth, the Canadians resumed their push, with the Queen's Own Rifles, supported by the 2nd Armoured Brigade, closing on Le Mesnil-Patry on June 11. The Rifles were ordered to seize high ground a few kilometres south of Putot, passing through scores of Winnipeg Rifles and 12th SS bodies that still lay in the field. The Queen's Own and 1st Hussars had initially planned to advance on June 12, but the operation was moved back a day to coincide with a British attack on the flank. And so the front-line officers had little time to reconnoitre the position and they had no access to aerial photographs. Nor was any artillery available. As one of the company commanders muttered, the plan was "conceived in sin and born in iniquity."[48]

On the warm and sunny afternoon, the attack went in at 2:30, with the Canadians crossing 1,100 metres of level ground, and Dog Company of the Queen's Own Rifles riding on the Shermans' tank decks. From intercepted radio traffic, the Pioneer Battalion of the 26th Panzer Grenadier Regiment, backed by tanks and artillery, knew the Canadians were coming. They let the Shermans roll into the trap before they opened up with artillery, catching the Canadians to the northeast of Le Mesnil-Patry. The 75mm Pak 40 anti-tank guns rifled shells into the Hussars. Within a few minutes, six Shermans were on fire. Trooper Larry Allen of the 1st Hussars had his Sherman knocked out. Allen remarked of some of his unfortunate comrades, "What a mess they were in! [Many of the troopers were] burned beyond recognition ... their flesh hanging in shreds from their faces and hands."[49] Another of the Hussars, Sergeant Leo Gariepy, shuddered at the horror of informal funeral pyres within the blackened Shermans: "In some cases the bodies were indistinguishable from one another, simply a mass of cooked flesh welded together in the great heat."[50]

When the firing started, the Queen's Own infantrymen jumped off the tanks into the wheat, moving rapidly on knees and elbows from the tanks that invited enemy fire. "The drivers," recounted one infantryman, "couldn't see the ground directly ahead or under them, so a soldier on the ground had almost as much to fear from his own raging tanks—twisting, speeding up, retreating, flames everywhere—as from enemy fire."[51] The Queen's Own officers tried to rally their men and to coordinate a defence, but there was mass confusion. As the firefight thickened, mortar shells ignited some of the hay, with flame and thick smoke adding to the chaos. Major J. Neil Gordon, Queen's Own D Company commander, observed, "We didn't know where the firing was coming from. The Germans were all nicely dug in those fields and they were just sitting there potting us off."[52] Gordon was shot through the mouth, although he later returned to the front and commanded the North Shore (New Brunswick) Regiment. Seven more of the Hussars' tanks were blown up by a single German tank, and the Shermans raced back and forth firing at the enemy. This in turn separated them from the infantry who were protecting them and it made it easier for the panzergrenadiers to kill the Shermans with anti-tank weapons.

The order went out for the Queen's Own and Hussars to retire. As the battlegroup tried to pull back, the Germans broke into the wireless network and put a call in to bring down Canadian artillery fire on the vulnerable infantry. For twenty minutes, the guns shelled their own men until the trick was recognized. As the Canadians withdrew, the SS troops continued to fire into the wheat and then sent out patrols to shoot the wounded. Beating the bush, listening for the cries and moans, many of the Queen's Own were found and executed on the spot, while others were led to the rear and murdered after interrogation.

The battle for Le Mesnil-Patry cost the Hussars 38 tanks, all but gutting the regiment. The Queen's Own suffered 103 casualties—killed, wounded, and prisoners—and the battle was thereafter known to some as "Mess in the Pantry."[53] Others found it too painful to talk about. A few more engagements like that would wipe out the battalion. The surviving officers instigated the Great War practice—eventually adopted by all units—of preparing an LOB list: a core of 10 to 15 percent of the men who were to be Left Out of Battle in order to rebuild the unit should it be badly shattered. Such precautions were a reflection of the harsh realities at the front.

COMBAT IS VICIOUS AND DEHUMANIZING, and some have dismissed it as sanctioned murder. But it is sanctioned within a defined set of rules. While the 12th SS was known informally as the "milk bottle division" because of the young age of its soldiers, many of these adolescents were wilful executioners. At Authie, twenty-seven of the thirty-three Canadian prisoners were murdered after the battle. At the Abbaye d'Ardenne, nineteen Canadians were killed in cold blood. Neither of these mass executions was a case of soldiers being cut down in the confusion and fury of combat, in which some unarmed men were trying to negotiate surrender while others were still fighting. These cases were the premeditated murder of Canadians who had surrendered: their hands were bound and they were shot in the head or bayoneted to death. Many of the dead were thrown in the street and run over by tanks until the bodies were ground into the mud. Nor was this an isolated incident perpetrated by rogue officers. Both Nazi brigadiers, Kurt Meyer and Wilhelm Mohnke, interrogated a number of prisoners and then, hours later, ordered their execution. From June 6 to 11, 156 Canadian prisoners were murdered by the 12th SS, including 66 soldiers from the Royal Winnipeg Rifles.[54] One out of seven Canadians killed during this time were victims of post-battle execution.

Many of the Canadians realized that the Hitlerjugend had never had a chance to develop their own belief system outside of the crazed Nazi regime that had indoctrinated them at a young age. Of course, the Canadian infantrymen were often not much older: eighteen-year-old boys from the Prairies were killing and being killed by sixteen-year-olds from Munich. Though the Canadian high command sent out an order to avoid "retaliation in kind," the 12th SS executions of Canadians led to reprisal killings.[55] The fanatical German resistance only added to the savagery, as there were numerous accounts of Nazis pretending to surrender and then throwing a grenade, or setting up an ambush with a white flag to draw out the Canadians and working with other comrades to gun them down in the open.[56] The Canadians promised no mercy. Yet there were many like Charlie Martin, who witnessed his comrades executed and promised the same revenge on the enemy, but found, when he had helpless prisoners in his hands, that he "couldn't follow through with that kind of revenge."[57] It was no easy thing to execute a man when staring into his cringing face and while he held up pictures of his family. Others hardened their hearts. Sergeant John Missons of the Queen's Own Rifles testified, "We didn't take SS prisoners till we were ordered to do so."[58] While the Canadians still accepted hundreds, and then thousands, of prisoners from all the units they faced, there were clearly unwritten rules among the Canadians facing the Hitlerjugend.[59] Little quarter was asked or given.

AFTER SURVIVING THE GERMAN COUNTERATTACKS in the days following D-Day, the Canadians were strung out in an arc northwest of Caen. The 12th SS, stronger and better equipped than the 3rd Canadian Infantry Division, had been not only stopped in their attempt to drive the Canadians back, but delivered a resounding rebuke. There were no bloodless victories, however. By June 11, the Canadians had lost 2,831 killed or wounded. The 3rd Division was in need of a rest, and a short pause developed at the front.[60] While the Canadians were shelled and mortared by the enemy, the hinge of Allied fighting shifted to the British front, where new formations came into the line to press the battle against the entrenched Waffen SS forces in and around Caen.

Not all was well in the Allied high command. The air marshals were furious with Montgomery's slow progress in pushing his armies deep into France. The struggle around Caen meant that few new airfields could be constructed for squadrons, and, at the moment, the long flight from Britain consumed so much fuel that the Spitfires were left with little time over the battlefield. Montgomery urged on his army, but it was slow progress as the Germans converged on Caen. Having survived the first week of Normandy, Montgomery organized a new three-division thrust—Operation Epsom—employing Lieutenant-General Richard O'Connor's British VIII Corps to the west of Caen. He told Eisenhower it would be a "showdown" with the Germans, and implied through bold talk that the Germans would be driven back.[61] But in reality Montgomery planned a fairly safe, methodical battle.

The Canadians, on the right of British I Corps, were to patrol aggressively to prevent the Germans from shifting reserves to block O'Connor's main thrust. The operation was set for June 18, by which time the Allies had put twenty-one divisions in Normandy to face eighteen German divisions. However, a wicked storm hit the next day, on the 19th, forcing the delay of Epsom for a week. The storm severely disrupted the naval logistical line from Britain for five days, as gale-force winds whipped the supply vessels that snapped at their anchorage like frenzied dogs. One of the Mulberries—the giant artificial harbours off the D-Day beaches—was destroyed, greatly hindering the unloading of supplies from the daily run of 150 to 200 ships that crossed the Channel. The effects of the unusually bad weather slowed the already creaky Allied offensive on the ground, with supplies temporarily cut off and the Axis able to move reserves forward without weather-grounded aircraft reporting on their disposition.

The Germans, aware of the buildup opposite them, rushed anti-tank guns to the now revealed Epsom front. Some of the best German divisions—Panzer Lehr and the 12th SS, backed by elements of the 1st SS, 9th SS, and 10th SS—were defending the battle space, and O'Connor's divisions did not advance very far when the offensive was finally launched on June 25. The rolling hills and plateaus were turned into a kill zone. The slaughter was appalling, forcing Montgomery to shut down the offensive on June 28, although several days of additional skirmishes ensued. Montgomery's enemies at Eisenhower's headquarters criticized him, arguing far from the front that he should have pushed longer and harder. His forces could not. Montgomery knew that no breakthrough was possible but that the Germans were being sucked more deeply into the Anglo-Canadian front, which would allow the Americans to pursue a breakout. While the British casualties exceeded 5,000, the German high command was demoralized and panzer commander Geyr von Schweppenburg wrote to Hitler that he could not hold out much longer.[62] He was removed from command.

The battles ground up the infantry and armoured divisions on both sides. The Anglo-Canadian forces found that the vast majority of casualties fell on front-line fighting units. For example, the Regina Rifles lost 17 officers and 360 other ranks from D-Day to June 22, a casualty rate of 44 percent.[63] New men filled the ranks of chums who had been like brothers and now lay broken in hospitals or buried in shallow graves. But the regiments showed an incredible resiliency in rebuilding themselves, and even a few core leaders—usually NCOs and junior officers—could shape the new reinforcements, instill morale, and lead by example. They had to, as there was no end in sight.

Almost all of the tank regiments had taken grievous losses too, although many of the Shermans were reclaimed by the squadron fitters and motor mechanics who repaired them in the field. The mechanics of the Royal Canadian Electrical and Mechanical Engineers, known affectionately as "Reme," slipped onto the battlefield at night, using armoured recovery vehicles to pull the broken tanks back to safety. Behind the lines the tanks were rebuilt using parts cannibalized from other tanks, and by late June about 40 percent of vehicles were returned to service.[64] Later in the fighting, by the end of July, they also modified tanks to assist them to survive at the front. Engineers welded old tank tracks to the armour to provide additional protection. The tracks did not stop an enemy shell, but they were found, on occasion, to deflect them. And when the Shermans were nothing more than a scorched lump of steel, they were replaced by new tanks that came in on the never-ending ships ferrying war equipment from Britain to the slowly expanding front.

THROUGHOUT LATE JUNE, the 3rd Canadian Division remained exposed in the farmers' fields, holed up in and around the small villages whose names would become part of the pantheon of the nation's military history. The stone houses, while beckoning with comfort, were too visible a target for German artillery, so it was back into the ground like moles. Soldiers learned not to dig their slit trenches under trees, for although the shade was welcomed, the trees were also aiming markers for enemy gunners.

Dig for your life. Every day and night, Canadian soldiers at the front dug their slit trenches to protect against mortar splinters and bullets.

The Canadian battalions were echeloned in depth, as were companies and platoons. The tanks tended to stay to the rear, and every night they "harboured" in a stronghold, digging an all-around defence where they refuelled, rearmed, and recharged batteries. Like the infantry, the troopers dug their slit trenches, and usually under the steel tank to protect against shell splinters. Every day witnessed mortar and artillery shells smashing into the fields, but most never found flesh. The Queen's Own Rifles reported on June 23 that some 2,000 mortar bombs fell in the battalion's area, causing one killed and nine wounded.[65]

Infantry platoon commanders situated two sections forward, about 140 metres apart, with a third to the rear and the commander's small headquarters and mortar team in the middle. They were backed by the hammer of the artillery. Forward artillery observers were linked to the rear through wireless radio and able to call down fire on grid references. The rearward gunners, whose accuracy was improved by survey units, meteorological teams, and sound-ranging and flash-spotting technology, were a formidable force.

The sunburnt Canadians did not feel much like conquering heroes. Lice had begun to multiply in the filthy conditions, with the dirty insects burrowing into the skin, causing men to itch and scratch as the little vampires drew blood. Burton Harper, a northern New Brunswicker who served as a Canloan officer in a British regiment, complained, "we were living in the same uniform, the same socks, the same underwear, which is dried on the body, usually sweaty and dirty and grubby, and after a number of days of that, you feel that every part of your body is dirty."[66] Filth-spattered uniforms still wore the grime from D-Day. Shortages of water precluded much cleaning, and so men used the powerful chemical DDT to powder themselves to disinfect their uniforms. Mosquitoes tormented day and night. By late summer, special anti-mosquito cream was sent forward with the rations. More than a few men mistook it for margarine or a new paste, and a few commented that it tasted better than most of the packaged food.

Behind the sparsely defended front, the division's logistical units pulled forward food, water, ammunition, and fuel. The First Canadian Army would eventually operate 14,000 American-made jeeps, as well as thousands of trucks, including the CMP (Canadian Military Pattern) vehicles.[67] For those in the front lines, hot tea and the occasional stew were a luxury; most men nibbled on the hard biscuits, learning the sideways chew of grinding molars. Canned meat—the dreaded "M and V"— and the occasional mush that was supposed to be porridge offered something a little more substantial. Soldiers complained, as was their right, but few expected any better until the precarious front was sorted out and the Germans driven back. Adventurous soldiers hunted for potatoes and cabbage on abandoned farms and gnawed them raw. Single-use cans of soup that heated upon pulling a tab were popular, and cigarettes remained a staple, although men learned to smoke close to the ground, covering the red embers at night to avoid a hoarse chewing out from their officers or a sniper's bullet. Liberated French wine or the apple brandy Calvados of the region was often shared clandestinely among mates. Captain H.S. MacDonald of the North Shore Regiment wrote of the Calvados, "It didn't steady the nerves, it deadened them."[68]

In this static phase of battle, infantrymen were cycled to the rear for a rest. Behind the lines, the Canadians occupied barns or French houses. With the bridgehead so shallow, there was no safe area, and the larger divisional kitchens and bakeries had not yet crossed the Channel. But away from the front, the company cooks prepared better food and men could stretch and walk freely. The many cows that meandered over the fields were milked, while chickens were caught and cooked. Rabbits occasionally enlivened a stew, although men ate carefully, using their teeth and tongues to separate out pieces of metal.

After a day or so in the rear areas, the soldiers lost some of their haggard looks. Each regiment had a medical officer to provide care and to engage in preventative medicine that kept men healthy in the field. The front-line doctors found that many of the Canadians had small wounds from shell splinters, and some serious cases of infection were discovered among the tough infanteers who had not complained when they were first injured. The medical officers, often attached to roving field hygiene units, also ensured that water was purified to reduce the opportunities for infectious diseases. French wine took on new value when the officially issued water tasted like a modern-day swimming pool. Seemingly mundane matters such as latrines required detailed attention, as poor hygiene discipline could invite disease. Nonetheless, the difficult

Canadians resting with their universal carrier in France. Note the camouflage on the helmets of several infantrymen.

living conditions, not to mention the stress of being killed at any moment, led to sickness, and in June alone some 451 Canadians contracted an illness (although not all were evacuated from the front), with the numbers growing toward the end of the month as fatigue deepened.[69] In addition to the serious cases, most soldiers suffered from the "Normandy Glide," a mild form of dysentery that saw men afflicted with explosive diarrhea. This only added to the nightmare of living in ditches, especially when some soldiers were forced by snipers or shellfire to deposit their own bodily waste there. Others refused to endure such indignities. Men squatted over shovels or helmets collected from dead Germans and then threw the ugly mess away from their slit trench. It went against all sanitary regulations, but it was better than chancing a sniper's bullet or bunking down in one's own filth.

During the quiet moments, footsloggers penned letters for those who waited at home. While some men kept up a methodical correspondence, those to whom writing did not come naturally struggled to find the words to express their emotions or experiences. Some asked mates to write a few lines. Most soldiers had someone writing to them, and the receiving of letters was a boost for morale. Corporal Tom Didmon felt that "between writing her [Jean, his wife] daily and receiving mail from her frequently, (generally in batches), it was the only thing that kept me sane!"[70] Canadian officer Burton Harper remembered that "quite often chaps would get their letters ... and read and re-read [them] till the next one came."[71] Lieutenant Paul McCann of the North Shore Regiment recounted one care package, lovingly assembled by his family. The treats were consumed, and McCann and a chum joked about how among the goodies there were two pairs of flannelette pyjamas. For warriors who barely took off their boots, let alone changed clothes, this provided "a good laugh." Later that night, as McCann held the pyjamas in his filthy hands, he was riven with "pangs of nostalgia." More than fifty years later, that deep yearning was still raw and he believed it "will be with me to my dying day."[72]

With rest and recuperation, the idle chat and rumours started again, as well as the bad jokes, manly ribbing, and dirty songs. No one at the front knew much of what was happening elsewhere, and as one official report noted, "'What's new?' is a query heard a hundred times a day."[73] Musical instruments were smuggled forward or located in ruined French houses and they added to the revelry. Captain Harold MacDonald observed of his batman Dickie Knowles, "He's a comical cuss and good for morale."[74] There were many men like Knowles who uplifted the spirits of their comrades.

Sergeant Tom Carney of the Canadian Scottish Regiment enjoyed the "battalion paper called *The Tommy Cooker* and every once in a while one of the boys will come out with a poem that is very good indeed."[75] A series of regimental papers were published in the summer months—the North Nova's *Fish Billie Express*, the Queen's Own Rifles' *Big 2 Bugle*, the Royal Hamilton Light Infantry's *Section Post*—containing news from the front, humorous accounts, and even odes to fallen comrades. One combat veteran wrote that "a few digs were taken at anything and anyone."[76] The papers were popular and good for morale, although they faded from the scene as editors were killed and wounded, and after *The Maple Leaf*—first made popular in Italy—began publication at the end of July.[77]

In those first two months, however, men with deft pens found an outlet for their poetry. Jock McAuger of the Can Scots penned "C'est La Guerre," capturing the exhaustion and fatigue of the poor bloody infantry, and even employing the popular phrase from the Great War, which was meant as an ironic quip.

> Cheer up boys, when the war is won
> We can talk of all the things we've done
> Of weather, folks and "compo stew"
> That miracle food for me and you.
> When the mortars fall
> And bullets whiz around,
> Just dig in, boys
> And hold your ground
> C'est la guerre.[78]

McAuger's poem was no cry of despair; it was a humorous, if fatalistic, view into the soldiers' hard world, but one infused with the hope that they would survive to someday look back on it. The now hardened campaigners faced the coming battles with a grin and a grimace, and there would be no stopping until the job was done.

CHAPTER *7*

FIGHTING ON ALL FRONTS

The Anglo-Canadian ground forces survived the first month of battle, and now prepared for their own offensive. General Montgomery had two goals: first take Caen and push south to Falaise, and then draw in enemy reserves to give the U.S. First and Third Armies the opportunity to break out into Brittany and crush the German armies in a massive envelopment. Hitler's armies, in turn, continued to defend the Normandy bridgehead and wait for what they thought was the main assault to fall farther north at Pas-de-Calais. While the Germans were masters of the rapid strike, their command structure remained split over how to respond in Normandy, with Hitler determined to contain the bridgehead but not releasing all of the armoured divisions. German generals at the front were increasingly frantic about using their mobile reserves, especially those in the north, to destroy the Normandy beachhead. With each day, the Allies grew stronger—reaching 500,000 boots on the ground within the first two weeks—and Hitler's generals' pleas to release the reserves were ignored.[1] The Führer's strategic oversight had been largely reduced to a fierce determination to give no ground, which became a straightjacket for his generals, who could no longer manoeuvre to trade ground for space or time. They were left with the choice of charging into the Allies' guns or waiting on the defensive and reacting to the Anglo-American-Canadian attacks. Neither side could drive the other from the field, although it was the Germans who could not make good the losses.

The Allied air forces wore down the fortified Germans. The 3rd Canadian Infantry Division was supported by the Second Tactical Air Force, which had squadrons based in Normandy a few days after D-Day. Somewhat strangely, most of the RCAF's sixteen Spitfire and Hurricane squadrons served in 83 Group, making up about half of its strength, but this group was assigned to the Second British Army. While the RCAF was given the option of holding back and waiting for the First Canadian Army to be activated in late July, the senior RCAF officers did not want to squander the chance of facing the Luftwaffe as early as possible.[2] And so Canada's army and air force would not serve together for most of the campaign; this was a missed occasion to create a more recognizable Canadian presence in Northwest Europe. Only a supreme Canadian commander could have insisted on such a joint operation, and none existed. The army commander General Harry Crerar had no control over the RCAF. The defence minister, J.L. Ralston, had the authority, but by June 1944 the Canadian government had few channels with British politicians or senior military officers, having long ago surrendered any influence over the formulation of strategy.

Train-busting and flying escort for bombers were all part of the RCAF's duties. By the fall of 1943, the Spitfire Vs had their .303-inch machine guns augmented with the deadlier 20mm cannon, thus making them more effective in ground interdiction. The .303 was the same round fired by a rifle, while the 20mm round was as long as a man's index finger, and caused significantly more damage, especially against

An RCAF Spitfire Mk 5b from No. 401 Squadron.

soft-skinned vehicles such as trucks and cars.[3] Al Harley of the RCAF's No. 401 Squadron observed the combined firepower of his Spitfire's 20mm Hispano cannons and four .303 Browning machine guns when he turned "all guns" on a convoy of ten trucks carrying supplies and troops: "The results were devastating. Parts of the trucks flew in all directions as drivers and troops dove for the ditches. Several of the trucks blew up as we hit the gas tanks. Although we made only one pass at the truck convoy, we left a sorry mess behind."[4]

But dogfights with enemy airplanes were the raison d'être of most of the RCAF squadrons. The once-feared German air arm, which had done so much to contribute to early Nazi victories, was all but destroyed by the summer of 1944. Forced to rely on poorly trained reinforcements, the German pilots were outclassed in aerial combat.[5] Even veteran Luftwaffe aces were suffering from exhaustion. The results were a spectacular slaughter. The Spitfires and Mustangs flew in search of their prey, shooting up ground targets behind enemy lines and seeking to draw out enemy planes. In June, RCAF pilots claimed more than a hundred German aircraft shot down. The claim was likely exaggerated, as all kills were, largely because it was hard to keep track of a downed enemy fighter in the middle of an air battle, but the RCAF was doing its part in the Allied air effort to bleed the Luftwaffe. By the end of the Normandy campaign, the grand total of Canadian shot down enemy planes had risen to 239, with No. 401 Squadron scoring the most kills at 43.5 (the half being a plane shared with another squadron). In turn, 58 RCAF Spitfire pilots were killed or captured, 21 downed by flak, 17 lost to enemy fighters, 12 crashed due to mechanical error, and the other 8 lost to undetermined causes.[6]

The Allied planes not only harassed enemy ground forces but also disrupted the movement of supplies and provided photographic reconnaissance. There was a widely circulating joke among the Germans: "If it's white, it's American, if it's black, it's British, if you can't see it, it's the Luftwaffe."[7] Moreover, as the enemy's forward radar and air control positions were slowly seized as the armies moved into Normandy, the Luftwaffe's response to Allied aerial patrols was increasingly ragged and uncoordinated. New Allied gyro gunsights also improved accuracy of shooting and led to days like June 28, when the RCAF bagged twenty-six enemy aircraft against the loss of only three Spitfires.

The Allied air forces also played a role in suppressing German V-1 rockets, the first of which was launched in the early hours of June 13, 1944, from Pas-de-Calais. The inaccurate unmanned missiles contained a ton of high explosives and rained down on London, and wherever else they landed in Britain. While the bombers saturated identified V-1 sites, the Allied fighters were also tasked to shoot down the rockets—known as buzzbombs or doodlebugs—even though they reached speeds in excess of 600 kilometres per hour. Aircraft that dove from a height on the missiles' reddish-orange exhausts could time their descent to blast the rockets, and many pilots took on the challenge, with varying results. RCAF's No. 418 Squadron downed eighty-two of the buzzbombs, and a few daredevils even used their wings to tip the rockets off course and send them into the Channel.[8] Several thousand V-1s would be fired over the summer, and they remained a terror weapon feared by the British civilian population, but the RCAF and other flyers helped to reduce their numbers.

WHILE ALLIED FIGHTERS maintained air superiority against their enemy counterparts in the air and targeted vehicles on the ground, fighter-bombers sought out land targets exclusively. Three fighter-bomber Typhoon squadrons arrived in mid-June: No. 438 (City of Montreal "Wildcats"), No. 439 (City of Westmount "Sabre-Toothed Tigers"), and 440 (City of Ottawa "Beavers"), comprising RCAF's 143 Wing, part of No. 83 Group. They were operational by mid-June and soon engaged in a tactical support role. While the Typhoon had been disappointing in air-to-air combat, and much surpassed by the Mustang or Spitfire IX, it found a new role as a form of flying artillery.

At seven tons and with a 24-cylinder Napier engine, the Typhoon was a monster of an aircraft. Its screaming engine, five times as noisy as the elegant Spitfire, suited the machine, especially as it dove from several thousand feet, picking up searing speed as it brought death to ground forces. There were two types of Typhoons—rocket firing and bomb carrying. The bombers were typically armed with two 500-pound bombs under their wings and unleashed a storm of fire from four 20mm cannons that could hurl 760 shells per minute. The other variant was equipped with eight rockets with 60 pounds of high explosives in the warhead, as well as cannons.

Most of the Typhoons, or "Tiffies," as they were affectionately known, flew at

8,000 to 10,000 feet before swooping down on a target. As one Typhoon pilot remarked, "You scrunch yourself over the stick, to hold it for a vertical dive and watching through your gunsights and at the same time watching your altimeter and, if I may add, also watching your comrades to see when they let go."[9] Some airmen screamed themselves hoarse in the dive, with the G-force pushing a man back into his seat. At about 4,000 feet, as flak exploded upwards, they released their bombs and pulled out, climbing back to normal height in about thirty seconds. "All of us pilots on Typhoons were hit many times," said John Friedlander, a McGill University graduate. The planes generally survived, and the Typhoon, in his experienced opinion, "was a fearsome beast."[10]

Typhoon fighter-bomber unleashing rockets at ground targets in France, summer 1944.

The screaming Tiffies, firing rockets or dropping high explosives, raised morale for the Canadian infantry. While the army was frustrated by not having control of air assets, and this often led to delays, communication between air and ground forces had improved considerably since North Africa and Italy. The "cab rank" system allowed Typhoons and Spitfires to circle the battlefield and be ready to pounce on the enemy when contacted by radio from ground forces.[11]

Spitfire pilot Bill McRae wrote of the Typhoon fighter-bombers providing "excellent close support to the Army and their efforts were noticed and appreciated. Unfortunately, we Spitfire-types were usually engaged far behind enemy lines where our contribution was not obvious to the troops. Consequently, when we occasionally went into a cafe and were approached by Army personnel asking what we flew, we always answered 'Typhoons' and the drinks were on the Army!"[12] The ground-pounders appreciated the flying artillery above them, but later operational studies revealed that Typhoons had little chance of hitting targets from 4,000 feet, although accuracy increased with a steeper dive.[13] So did flak. While the Typhoons were not like snipers, they were murderous against groups of soft-skinned vehicles, to the

Typhoon fighter-bomber from RCAF No. 439 Squadron taking off for a sortie.

point where they could cripple a large formation in transit. While it is difficult to quantify the Allies' command of the air, the Typhoons and other aircraft were a significant deterrent for the gathering of Wehrmacht forces, who always had to make a calculation that trucks, artillery pieces, and sometimes tanks would be lost if they were moved from camouflaged sites.[14] Canadian artillery officers also reported that when the Allied fighters and Typhoons were in the air, many enemy guns stopped firing so as not to give away their positions. The eyes in the sky were "an essential adjunct to modern art[iller]y."[15]

Airpower was not as effective as either the Allies or Germans believed, but the infantry loved the flyboys. "If I ever run into Typhoon pilots," claimed one Canadian infantry officer to his wife, "I shall go down on my knees before them. They've given us an awful lot of support and saved us from some bad attacks."[16] And on the receiving end of the bombs, shells, and rockets, one German *frontsoldaten* lamented, "Unless a man has been through these fighter-bomber attacks he cannot know. You lie there, helpless, ... pressed into the ground, your face in the dirt—and then it comes toward you roaring.... Then the bird is gone. But it comes back. Twice. Three times. Not until they've wiped out everything do they leave. Until then you are helpless. Like a man facing a firing-squad. Even if you survive it is no more than a temporary reprieve. Ten such attacks in succession are a real foretaste of hell."[17]

THERE WAS NO SHORTAGE OF BRUTALITY, savagery, or renditions of hell in France. While the tactical fighters and fighter-bombers ranged over the front, the blunt hammer of the bombers continued to pound the roads and rail lines. Since the blitzkrieg of 1940 and the fall of France, the Nazis had occupied Western Europe and incorporated its factories, farms, and arms into the German war machine. From 1942 onwards, the Allied bombers regularly struck military and civilian industrial areas in Belgium and France to disrupt the Axis Powers. Were they legitimate targets in a total war? The Allies certainly thought so, but there was a heavy price to be paid.

During the lead-up to the Normandy landings, the number of French civilian casualties rose substantially. For example, Bomber Command struck over 100 railroads, coastal installations, and airfields in France and the Low Countries between April 17 and D-Day. Churchill pleaded with his air marshals to avoid civilian casualties, and fretted over the "cold-blooded butchering" of enslaved civilians, but he also consulted Charles de Gaulle, leader of the Free French, who said that his countrymen would have to bear the blows of liberation.[18] On D-Day, the Allies struck the German defences along the coast and in fourteen French towns. The targets in the urban centres were bridges and rail lines, which were to be destroyed in order to slow the German counterattacking forces, but thousands of French civilians were also killed. Later in the campaign, French cities—such as Caen on the British and Canadian front—were also bombed when the Germans organized their defences in them. The Allies often dropped leaflets urging French civilians to evacuate the cities, and thereby put their own bomber crews in danger by alerting the enemy to their intentions, but an estimated 60,000 French civilians were killed nonetheless.[19]

Though the aerial attacks on the canals, railway yards, and trains killed civilians, they also profoundly damaged the Nazi war machine, as well as curtailing much of the fighting forces' ability to move large concentrations of troops or armour without losses. Transport remained a vulnerable link for the Germans, and one American postwar report came to the conclusion that the bombing campaign against units on the move "was a decisive factor in the breakdown of the German army."[20] Any movement of troops led to casualties, although it is important to note that the Germans were rarely unable to shift their divisions—albeit sometimes in piecemeal formations—to their desired positions.

NAVAL GUNFIRE CONTINUED to pulverize the German lines, even as the Anglo-Canadian ground forces slowly pushed forward and out of the range of the smaller ships' guns. The huge naval guns could deliver a devastating weight of fire from a 30 kilometre distance, with the salvos of shells falling like freight train cars and leaving craters several metres wide and deep. One bombardment killed the commander of the 12th SS, General Fritz Witt, on June 14. With orders to give no ground, the Germans were forced to dig in within the range of naval guns, and they continued to lose men every day.

On the Canadian front, the 12th SS, now commanded by Kurt Meyer, had situated a forward line of defences along a large east–west ridge, a few kilometres south of Caen. This geographical formation allowed German forces on the reverse slope (the back side) to avoid much of the shellfire, which sailed overhead, while machine-gun teams along the crest or on the forward slope could sweep the ground to the north and northwest. The German lines encompassed Caen, Authie, and Buron, with the Waffen SS dug in around the hangars, bunkers, and control buildings of Carpiquet airfield. Backed by 88mm anti-tank guns and hull-down tanks, the enemy held a fortress.

After the stalemate of Operation Epsom, General Montgomery planned a new offensive to capture Caen in early July. At SHAEF headquarters, Eisenhower was urging him onwards. Air Marshal Arthur Coningham, a New Zealand air veteran of the Mediterranean and commander of the 2nd Tactical Air Force, was a vocal critic of Montgomery, especially of his failure to advance beyond Caen, which in turn had constrained his squadrons from getting established in Normandy. Montgomery shrugged off his opponents and assured Eisenhower that he was making progress. He even boldly claimed that the stalemate around Caen was part of his plan—that he was drawing the German strength to his front to allow the Americans to break out of the Cotentin Peninsula. Even though memories were short, most of Montgomery's detractors well remembered his other promises that he would make much deeper inroads into Normandy before pulling the German forces towards his divisions in the field.[21] Montgomery's questionable claims made him look petty to the eye-rolling SHAEF staff, and he ordered new campaigns to avoid what was beginning to look like a First World War Western-Front-type stalemate. In the words of one German general, the coming battle would be nothing less than "a monstrous bloodbath."[22]

THROUGHOUT LATE JUNE, Canadian infantry probed the outskirts of Carpiquet in nighttime patrols, looking for weaknesses in the enemy lines. In the dark, one Canadian remarked, "You learned to live like an animal: by instincts, by sense, smell and everything else."[23] Rank body odour could be detected on a light summer breeze, along with the German tobacco and food. When flares went up, the stealthy warriors froze under the eerie whitish glow, as any movement might be detected by enemy snipers. "Unless one has led night patrols in a weird and utterly strange no man's land," recounted Lieutenant C.F. Richardson of the North Shore Regiment, "the feelings are hard to describe."[24] No Man's Land was a place where mistakes cost lives, and Charlie Martin of the Queen's Own Rifles observed laconically, "Patrols are not for the faint-hearted."[25] Slowly, the German strongpoints and guns were mapped out from the ground and with aerial photography, and information was collated at battalion, brigade, and divisional headquarters. The targets were then given to the artillery to reduce with shellfire. At the same time, the Germans, aware that the increased activity on the Carpiquet front likely portended a large-scale operation, were increasingly at the ready.

In order to destabilize the German defence of Caen, Montgomery ordered the Canadians to seize the village of Carpiquet and the surrounding airfield, which held a commanding view of the countryside.[26] Operation Windsor was to kick off on July 4, four days in advance of the main Anglo-Canadian operation against Caen, and the day when the one millionth Allied soldier landed on the Normandy beaches.

The terrain and defences favoured the enemy, and the Canadians predicted Operation Windsor would be a tough "show." Major-General Rod Keller organized the largest set-piece battle to date in the Normandy campaign. All three of the 8th Infantry Brigade battalions were ordered into the attack, and they were supported by the Shermans and Fireflys of the Fort Garry Horse. To the south, a fourth battalion, the Royal Winnipeg Rifles, was to secure three hangars. The Canadians would have to cross 2 kilometres of open farmers' fields, although they were to be backed by 21 artillery regiments of 760 British and Canadian guns, and further supported by the punishing naval guns of HMS *Rodney*, *Roberts*, and *Belfast*.[27] This would be a set-piece firepower-driven battle not dissimilar to those fought by the Canadian Corps during the latter part of the Great War, and the concentration of artillery was far heavier than, for example, the Canadian offensive at Vimy Ridge in April 1917. On this narrow front, the artillery would saturate enemy positions with fire and lay down a creeping barrage roughly 1,750 metres wide and 300 metres deep and lifting 100 metres every three minutes, while the naval guns, mortar teams, and machine guns targeted other front and rear areas. Despite this ferocity, the barrage was meant only to stun the enemy because dug-in troops were rarely killed, even by tremendous curtains of shellfire.[28]

The plan to capture Carpiquet village called for the North Shore Regiment to advance on the left and Le Régiment de la Chaudière on the right, with the Queen's

Own Rifles in reserve, and to pass through the two lead battalions in the second phase. Each battalion had two companies up and two back, and these companies were also echeloned, with the two platoons up and another back. There were about 1,000 men in the forward thrust from the two forward battalions.

"The whole horizon in a semi-circle behind us became a blaze when the artillery opened up," said one Canadian. The infantry battalions crossed the start line at 5 A.M.[29] The shells screamed overhead and the ground buckled. The infantry moved forward cautiously, many shielding their eyes from the terror churning up the fields in front of them, stepping around small fires in the grain and the black, smoking craters. Almost immediately the Canadians were met by a counter-barrage by the 12th SS defenders. The Hitlerjugend had spent weeks plotting out every sector of the front—as

Canadian infantry attacking Carpiquet airfield, July 4, 1944.

evidenced by remaining lengths of white tape—thereby allowing their mortars and gun teams to fire indirectly from map coordinates adjusted by forward observers. One official Canadian report noted that the enemy use of mortars was highly efficient, with the bombs aimed to land behind the creeping barrage where the infantry were advancing.[30] Some of the Chaudières believed, for example, that they were being shelled by their own guns, while other Canadians hugged their own barrage too closely to escape the bombs and therefore were torn up by their own shells.[31] As Private Abraham Feldman of the Chauds later remarked of the shelling that seemed to come from every direction, "all Hell broke loose."[32]

Captain Bernard-Georg Meitzell, a German staff officer with 12th SS Panzer Division, later wrote, "I watched the fighting and movements of the British [sic, Canadian] and German tanks from our Divisional Observation Post and was impressed by the close co-operation of Canadian tanks, British fighter bombers and artillery."[33] By noon the main Canadian force had cleared the enemy—numbering about 150 troops—from the village, the bunkers, and the airport control buildings that were reduced to twisted metal. It was less promising to the south. There, the Winnipeggers faced a tenacious enemy around three hangars, including five Panzer Mk IVs. Far fewer Allied guns were devoted to the Winnipeggers' front, and the 12th SS soldiers, backed by MG42s, 88s, and Panthers, as well as by artillery south of the Odon River, held up the advance with withering fire. "They look like babies," remembered one Canadian corporal of their youthful opponents in their oversized coal-scuttle helmets and field-grey uniforms, but "they die like mad bastards."[34]

The Little Black Devils from Winnipeg took refuge in the metre-high wheat and were forced to retreat, but they were ordered back into the battle in the afternoon. The Hitler Youth was blasted with shells and bullets but continued to hold out. After the outer enemy positions were cleared, it looked like the tide was turning, but a German counterattacking force of Mark IVs and Panther tanks drove the Canadians out. During the day of fierce fighting, the Winnipeggers suffered some 40 killed and 132 wounded.[35]

Carpiquet was an anchor on the German front, and with it under Canadian control they would outflank the German-held Authie and Buron and encircle a good portion of Caen. It did not take long for the Waffen troops from 1st SS Panzer Division, positioned to the north, to launch a counterstrike, which washed over the Canadians from dusk to midnight on the 4th. Keller was prepared for it and had rushed forward Vickers machine guns from the Cameron Highlanders of Canada. "We sucked wave after wave of enemy infantry into the hollow where the withering crossfire of the Camerons cut off any hope of escape," recalled Lieutenant Paul McCann of the North Shore Regiment.[36] The infantry added to the storm of bullets, and the enemy soldiers were, according to Major Bill Harvey, "cut to pieces."[37] The SS troops were supported by Panthers and Mark IV tanks, but these too were knocked out by the Canadians' anti-tank guns firing at a range of 500 metres. The considerable artillery support from the 3rd Division's rearward batteries also shattered the enemy formations with Mike and Uncle calls, in which, respectively, either the twenty-four guns of the artillery brigade or the division's entire seventy-two guns were brought to bear on limited targets. The results were devastating.

With several enemy counterattacks broken between the 4th and the 6th, the Germans turned to their artillery, mortars, and Nebelwerfers. Captain T.J. Bell witnessed that the rocket fire was "shattering to nerves and morale but did not cause many casualties."[38] However, as the Germans had observers in the high points of Caen directing fire, Carpiquet was pulverized, and the flatness of the airfield made it difficult for the Canadians to find cover. "I don't know if we ever got shelled worse than at Carpiquet airport," recounted Rifleman Bill Bettridge.[39] Another Canadian infantryman remembered, "We were in a world of shell fire at Carpiquet with shelters being smashed in and nobody safe."[40] Dozens of Canadians were buried alive, and it fell to their comrades to excavate them from their tombs before they ran out of oxygen.

American studies of Normandy soldiers revealed that about 20 percent admitted to losing control of their bowels during drumfire bombardments, so alien was the experience that assaulted them sonically, physically, and emotionally.[41] Experienced veterans of battle warned new reinforcements to plug their ears and open their mouths so their eardrums would not burst as the high explosives rained down. For many men, there was no avoiding the concussions from these multiple blasts—especially from the Moaning Minnies—but the Canadians managed to pull themselves together each time, blood oozing from noses and ears, to defend against the SS troops over the next three days. The dead fouled the ground, while countless flies blanketed their decomposing corpses. A burned-out tank lay as a blackened memorial to the failed German attacks, its gun barrel pointing to the sky like a grave marker. But the shelling never let up, and the Canadian casualties mounted. The wounded came out on stretchers and the replacements went in. "Often there would be a dozen [men] arrive at a company in the evening," said one infantryman of the North Shore Regiment, "and before morning half that dozen would be casualties."[42] The Canadians held on and would not be driven from the airfield, even as the battle cost 377 casualties, with most of the infantry battalions losing about one in five men from their forward rifle companies.[43]

Canadian 3-inch mortar team supporting an attack. Note the slit trenches behind the mortar.

While the Canadians cleared much of Carpiquet, they could not dislodge the resolute defenders in the southern hangars, who held on until July 8, when they withdrew on their own. Despite the victory, British Second Army commander General Miles Dempsey complained to Montgomery that Keller had lost his grip on the division and should be removed.[44] Though Keller was a lacklustre commander who had turned to the bottle, it is hard to see how he could have fought a better battle. It is not clear what Dempsey assumed Keller might have done differently during the five days, as throwing a larger force at Carpiquet would only have crammed more soldiers into the artillery and mortar-fire kill zone. Moreover, the rest of Keller's division was preparing to attack Caen on the 8th, and it made no sense to dilute that force. The problem, in fact, was that Crocker had ordered a rather limited attack, which had put the Canadians into a salient that was heavily shelled by the Germans. As in Italy, the British continued to have little faith in Canadian commanders, and even in triumph they assumed that more could be accomplished. Montgomery barely knew Keller and readily accepted Dempsey's assessment, but he delayed action since he wanted a Canadian to deliver the coup de grâce. He also had more pressing matters: Eisenhower and Churchill were desperately urging him onwards.[45]

AS THE 8TH CANADIAN INFANTRY BRIGADE fought a bite-and-hold battle over the airfield, the rest of the division was preparing for Operation Charnwood. This was Montgomery's plan to capture Caen and the bridges over the Orne River. The main assault was to be carried out by the British 3rd and 59th Divisions, with Keller's Canadians anchoring the right flank and maintaining pressure on the enemy from their sector. The 9th Canadian Infantry Brigade would return to the villages of Buron and Authie, from which it had been ejected a month earlier, and then the 7th Canadian Infantry Brigade would secure Cussy and the fortified Abbaye d'Ardenne.

The Allies had hoped to occupy Caen on June 6, needing the large city for headquarters, hospitals, and the movement of supplies, but the enemy had held it against several attacks and systematically turned it into a fortress. Frustrated by the German defence, Montgomery called for a thundering artillery and aerial bombardment to level the city. While most of the French citizens of Caen had wisely fled by this point, several thousand remained. On the night of July 7, hundreds of aircraft

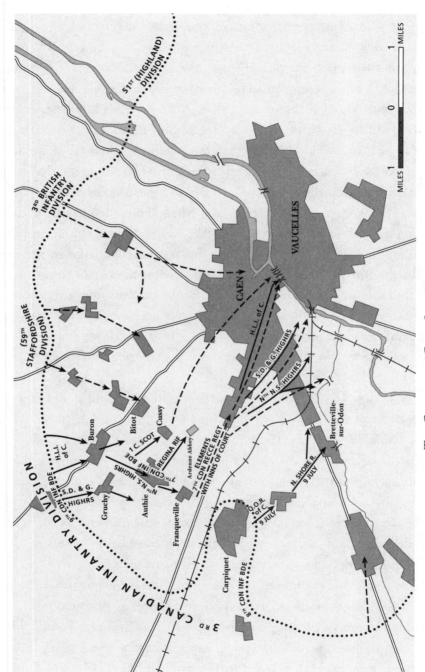

THE CAPTURE OF CAEN, JULY 8–9, 1944

Map labels:

51ST (HIGHLAND) DIVISION

3RD BRITISH INFANTRY DIVISION

(59TH STAFFORDSHIRE) DIVISION

VAUCELLES

CAEN

H.L.I. of C.

S.D. & G. HIGHRS

N TH N.S. HIGHRS

N. SHORE R.
9 JULY

Bretteville-
sur-Odon

Cussy

Bitot

Buron

C. SCOT
L.

REGINA RIF

Ardenne Abbey

Gruchy

S.D. & G.
HIGHRS

N TH N.S. HIGHRS

7 TH CDN INF BDE

Authie

Franqueville

H.L.I. of C.

9 TH CDN INF BDE

ELEMENTS
CDN RECCE REGT
WITH INNS OF COURT

Q.O.R.
of C.
9 JULY

8 TH CDN INF BDE

Carpiquet

3RD CANADIAN INFANTRY DIVISION

MILES
0   1

MILES
1   1

dropped 2,570 tons of bombs. "We had never seen such a display of airpower," remarked an awestruck J.G. Baird of the Regina Rifles.[46] Despite this aerial havoc, which turned the sky over Caen a sinister red from the fires and dust, the 12th SS on the Canadian front received few bombs, due to the Allies' fear of their aircraft dropping explosives on the Canadian positions.

With the British attacking behind 656 artillery pieces and Typhoon fire, the British 59th and Canadian 3rd Divisions faced their old foes, the 12th SS, backed by tanks and artillery. The Canadian assault at 7:30 A.M. was to follow the British one that went in a few hours earlier, but while the 59th Division, with its two lead battalions, had made progress, the Hitlerjugend remained in its many strongpoints.

The Highland Light Infantry faced Buron. The company, platoon, and section commanders were well briefed and the bombardment accurate, but the German reputation for doggedness and resiliency left the Highlanders expecting a struggle. They got it. About 200 of the 12th SS were in shallow slit trenches. Camouflaged in the grain, they were difficult to spot until the riflemen and machine-gunners opened up. Anti-tank ditches, barbed wire, and anti-personnel mines blocked off sections of the front and hampered movement. Striking off at 7:30 A.M., the Highlanders fought their way towards Buron through the German positions, supported by self-propelled guns and tanks from the Sherbrooke Regiment. They left behind a trail of bodies. The tanks and the infantry were still learning to fight together, and if the armour got ahead of the infantry it tended to be knocked out by anti-tank guns; at the same time, the infantry needed the mobile gun platforms of the tanks but struggled to keep up with the faster vehicles.[47] With almost no way to communicate, confusion prevailed, and a coordinated infantry and tank attack under fire was no easy thing. Of course,

Crew of a self-propelled artillery in the 14th Field Regiment, RCA.

the tanks were useful on their own—raking the enemy lines with machine-gun and cannon fire, and grinding out slit trenches with their tracks. Flail tanks using whipping chains thrashed the ground to set off mines, and some of the flail tanks went after Germans in their slit trenches, pounding the earth, caving the ground in on the terrified occupants, and tearing flesh from limbs. Even the most hardened Canadian soldiers were shaken by the site of the dead defenders, who looked like they had been fed through a wood chipper.

The Highlanders cleared a series of German positions in ditches—"My platoon had a field day," wrote Lieutenant Donald Todd. "They just mowed 'em down"—and then moved through the village tossing grenades and rooting out the enemy.[48] Though the Highlanders had suffered dozens of killed and wounded, with its two lead companies losing half their strength in the initial attack, they knew to prepare for the counterattack that was preceded by a mortar bombardment.[49] A battlegroup

Sherman tank of the 1st Hussars, June 28, 1944.

of tanks struck back at the Canadians, but the German counterstrike was blunted by anti-tank fire from a British artillery regiment that had expertly situated their self-propelled M10 17-pounders. Much credit and fear was given to the enemy's 88mm anti-tank guns, but the Allies' 17-pounders were just as effective, especially when armour advanced in the open. Throughout the late afternoon, fierce fighting saw thirteen panzers left on the smoking battlefield, with eleven Shermans destroyed in turn.[50]

As the tanks and artillery hammered each other, the greatest killer of the infantry remained mortar fire. German mortar teams were usually situated about 900 metres behind the lines.[51] Operational research conducted by the 21st Army Group would later conclude that a shocking 70 percent of all casualties in the first seven weeks of the war were caused by mortars, although the number of fatalities from mortar fire was lower than that from small arms.[52] If one could not find cover, a mortar bomb exploding in all directions was particularly deadly. Padre John "Jock" Anderson recounted with anger that "many of the wounded were killed by the mortar fire as they lay out in the field."[53] The Highlanders held Buron but lost 262 men, including the commanding officer. The 12th SS lost even more men, with 272 casualties and another 46 prisoners.[54]

It was a little easier on the right flank, where the Stormont, Dundas and Glengarry Highlanders, along with B Squadron of the Sherbrookes, charged Gruchy, which was in sight of Buron. The Glens overran much of the enemy defences in two hours of fighting, but they were held up in places by stubborn pockets of resistance. At one point in the battle, the division's reconnaissance regiment, the 17th Duke of York's Royal Canadian Hussars, rushed forward fifteen universal carriers. Crashing through the enemy lines, with Brens firing until they were red hot, the Canadians saw the Hitlerjugend collapse. Less than a kilometre to the south, Authie fell to the North Nova Scotia Regiment, which had passed through the Highland Light Infantry to capture the village around 9:45 A.M. It was a bittersweet victory for the North Novas, who returned to the site where, a month earlier, they had been overrun and forced to leave dozens of comrades behind who had been executed in cold blood.

With the 9th Infantry Brigade clearing the outlying fortified villages, the 7th Infantry Brigade punched through the newly won terrain as the sun was setting low on one of the Canadians' most costly days of combat. The Canadian Scottish drove the Germans from Cussy, while the Reginas marched on the Abbaye d'Ardenne around 6:30 P.M. Regimental medical officer Captain W.S. Huckvale remembered the nervous tension before the battle, although not all men were worried. Huckvale watched as one of the Reginas attempted to entice a French woman into a last-minute sexual rendezvous.[55] She declined his not-so-subtle gestures, even as the artillery shells screamed down.

Captain Gordon Brown of the Reginas observed, "The advance was awfully slow because of the relentless machine gun and rifle fire. The two forward platoons began to use fire and movement effectively, but it was heavy going. We had already lost several men and were forced to crawl and run in short bursts to avoid heavier losses.... We had heard First World War veterans describe the infantry as 'cannon fodder.' Now we were realizing what an apt description it was!"[56] Brown and his men

Canadians clearing Caen of the German defenders in bitter house-to-house battles on July 10, 1944.

fought for superiority throughout the night and the early hours of the 9th, advancing in short rushes, often through smoke from their 2-inch mortars, and eventually making the 12th SS position untenable.

As dawn broke on the 9th, lead elements of the Glens and the Sherbrookes pushed tentatively into western Caen. Scarcely a building was undamaged by the bomber attack and artillery bombardment. From under the rubble, civilians could be heard crying out for rescue. The smell of the rotting dead—estimated at about 2,000—was already overpowering. Lieutenant-Colonel C.D. Stewart Leef of the 15th Canadian Field Ambulance would recall that the "stink in Caen could be almost tasted."[57] The British push from the north was driving the Germans before it, and the Glens, supported by the North Novas, eventually infiltrated to the centre of the city, where a Canadian flag was erected. Emerging from the rubble, the liberated French brought out flowers and wine for the grimy and dust-covered Canadians. One padre lamented the losses of civilians caught in the crossfire and bombing—"It made my heart bleed to see little children injured"—but with the Germans turning the French cities into battlegrounds, there were few other viable options.[58] Captain Harold MacDonald, a newly arrived officer of the North Shore Regiment, summed up his thoughts about the enemy's use of civilians as shields in a letter to his wife: "The Germans—all bastards, rotten, sneaking, back-shooting, double-crossing devils. Only one thing good for them."[59]

The Canadian dead were gathered, their possessions sorted, dog tags collected, and last rites given by the padres. The battle for Carpiquet and Caen was over. It cost the Canadians 330 killed and 864 wounded, losses

Exhausted but victorious.
A Canadian infantryman surveys the destruction of Caen, July 10, 1944.

comparable to those on D-Day.[60] Bodies were wrapped in blankets, until there were no more blankets. Then the remains were carried by hand to dark holes in the ground: a stark indication of the cost of liberating Europe.

THE CAPTURE OF CAEN allowed for follow-on divisions and air force squadrons to be unleashed against the enemy. But each yard advanced took the ground forces farther out of the range of the Allied warships that laid down shellfire.

With their fire support role diminished, the Allied warships turned to defeating the Kriegsmarine. They also had to keep the sea lanes open, as thousands of tons of supplies flowed daily into the Normandy beaches and mulberries. If the Germans could prevent this materiel from reaching land, they would not have to face it in battle. This meant the warships were constantly sweeping for mines and acting as armed protectors of the convoys.[61]

"The invasion fleet is to be attacked with complete recklessness," demanded Admiral Karl Dönitz, commander of the U-boat arm, on June 11.[62] One estimate from the Royal Navy Admiralty warned that if the entire U-boat fleet was set against the vessels ferrying supplies across the Channel, the Allies could lose a crippling 240 ships per week.[63] But the German U-boats could not pierce the thick naval defences assisted by the bombers and fighters of Coastal and Fighter Command, and in the weeks following June 6, twenty-eight U-boats were sunk for the loss of just ten ships. This was another shattering defeat. Thereafter, U-boats were forced to hide on the periphery, hoping to shoot and run before the British, American, and Canadian warships destroyed them.

The Allied naval forces sought out the enemy. Two Canadian flotillas of motor torpedo boats patrolled the Channel. The 29th MTB Flotilla operated 71½-foot motor torpedo boats that ripped across the water at a maximum speed of 41 knots and had as their main armaments two 18-inch torpedoes, a number of machine guns, and 20mm Oerlikon cannons on the stern.[64] The 65th MTB Flotilla was equipped with swift boats, 115 feet in length and armed with a 6-pounder, six heavy machine guns, and 18-inch torpedoes. The motor torpedo boats, with a crew of about twenty-five to thirty, were an aggressive force, violently clashing with the Germans in the darkness. Malcolm Knox, a native of Pointe Claire, Quebec, and commander of one of

HMCS Algonquin's *Bofors 40mm anti-aircraft gun crew at action stations.*

the motor torpedo boats, remarked on the nature of battle: "Your first purpose was to get in and strike them, and then get away safely to live another day."[65]

Lieutenant-Commander C.A. Law, commander of the 29th Flotilla, described one attack against an enemy shipping convoy in the early hours of May 23. Eight of the torpedo boats swept along the coast looking for trouble. They found it, around 2:30 A.M., and closed on the enemy. "Through my binoculars I could see four of the low flak barges. The torpedo boats roared through the water ... heavy 88-mm [anti-]personnel shells burst above our heads and left angry puffs of black smoke. Others exploded nearby, sending up gigantic needle-shaped columns of water. Green and red tracers, brilliant and terrifying missiles of death, flew through the air in graceful hose-pipe arcs towards our vulnerable wooden vessels. They danced over the water, then hit with a sharp resounding crackle."[66] Amid the clamour of battle and the strong smell of cordite, the two forces fired at each other and then quickly broke off. The motor boats were useful against weaker armed vessels, especially barrage boats that fired at aircraft over the Channel, but they had to be careful about engaging in a fight that they could not win. The Canadian boats added another threat to disrupting German coastal vessels, although many met a tragic end when a fire from spilled fuel on February 14, 1945, engulfed the 29th Flotilla's eight vessels docked in Ostend, Belgium, destroying five of them and killing twenty-six Canadian sailors.

Canada's larger destroyers, the Tribals, were also in on the hunt. In the early hours of June 9, a number of British warships, along with *Huron* and *Haida*—the latter commanded by Harry DeWolf, known as "Hard-over-Harry" and the RCN's finest warrior-captain—established contact with the enemy. The Germans turned to flee, after letting loose torpedoes, but the British and Canadians bore down on the enemy. *Haida* made radar contact with *Z-32*, a Narvik-class destroyer, which was larger and better armed than the Canadian Tribal, and led the attack. The destroyers steamed after the Narvik, which was laying down a smokescreen, making it difficult to track and hit with long-range gunfire. Nonetheless, good gunnery delivered several hits on *Z-32*, even as it kept running. The Canadian and British warships, four in number, continued to pursue, skilfully manoeuvring in order to close with the fleeing enemy ships. The 10th Flotilla sank one German ship, *ZH1*, an ex-Dutch destroyer, but it looked like the German warships would escape. *Haida* and *Huron* continued their dogged pursuit and caught *Z-32* again at a killing range of 6,400 metres at 4:45 A.M. They opened fire.[67] The German warship fired off its torpedoes, but it was caught square in a crossfire, and the Tribals' armour-piercing 50-pound shells raked it. Fifteen minutes of fire left the Narvik's port engine out of action, and it was now almost dead in the water, with much of the upper deck engulfed in flames. With no hope of escape, the German captain drove *Z-32* aground on the rocky shore of Île de Batz. It was another significant victory for the Canadian Tribals, reinforcing DeWolf's already stellar reputation as an elite captain.

The Tribals were also on the lookout for U-boats, and they destroyed *U-971* on June 24. While the convoys continued to be protected by warships, there were now escort groups that patrolled on their own, seeking to kill U-boats. Ten escort groups operated in the Channel, including four of the best RCN formations, which consisted of destroyers, frigates, and upgraded corvettes. Airpower from Coastal Command bombers added to the Allies' arsenal.

The best Canadian submarine killer, James "Chummy" Prentice, was a forty-five-year-old RN veteran who had held key training and command positions during the war in the attempt to sharpen the RCN's ability to track and sink submarines. Prentice often wore his cap tipped over in a rakish style and, somewhat strangely, sported a monocle. This left him a fascinating oddity. He was known to flip his head back, shoot his monocle up in the air, and catch it neatly again in his eye.[68] Despite these affectations, as one officer remarked, "he was a captain to respect."[69]

Prentice led EG-11, an escort group designated as an "A/S Killer Group"

Commander James "Chummy" Prentice, Canada's expert sub-killer.

after D-Day, against the new snorkel-equipped U-boats. These boats ran fast under-water, up to 20 knots, recharged batteries while submerged, and were adept at hiding in the wreck-strewn Channel waters. They were a tough opponent. However, by the summer of 1944, the Allied anti-submarine warships were assisted in attacking the U-boats by more effective underwater radar such as the 144 asdic, and new weapons like the Hedgehog. The Hedgehog was a variation on the depth charge that fired ahead of a ship. The cone of missiles, which numbered 24 in a full set, were projected about 180 metres, and only exploded on contact with a sub's hull. While this removed the chance of the depth charge detonating at a depth that might damage a U-boat, it also meant that the asdic radar was not thrown off by multiple explosions and gasses in the water. The Hedgehog allowed for more con-sistent contact with the U-boat. The evolving sub-killing tactics dictated that when a warship located a submerged U-boat, it kept its prey in its sonar, directing other vessels onto the echo, which then dropped their depth charges or projected their Hedgehog bombs. The two or more surface ships alternated their attacks, with one always trying to keep the U-boat from slipping away and the others saturating the depths with explosives.

The tide turned against the German U-boats from the summer of 1943. In this photograph, another submarine dies at the hands of the Allies.

There were also more mundane patrols to find U-boats lurking on the bottom of the Channel. EG-11 became very effective in the disciplined tactic of mapping the wrecks, where the U-boats rested in silence, waiting for the war-ships to pass overhead before rising to launch torpedoes into supply ships. With the U-boats hiding among the many sunken ships, "it boiled down to us literally having to assume that any contact we made was a bottomed sub-marine," noted one Canadian sailor.[70] Each contact with sonar was investi-gated, usually by plastering it with depth charges or systematically checking with a grappling hook on a wire. A depth charge was slid down the wire to detonate and ensure the wrecks were dead ships and not lurking U-boats.[71] In EG-11 this was known as "tin opening," and it was an effective if unglamorous method of hunting the U-boats and occasionally killing them.

Prentice and his warships destroyed *U-678* on July 7 after a long hunt and sent *U-621* to a watery grave in the Bay of Biscay on August 19. On the return trip to England, *Ottawa II*, *Chaudière*, and *Kootenay* discovered *U-984* and sank it with depth charges. The U-boat battles were not entirely lopsided, and the new Type XXI submarine continued to claim victims, including the RCN corvettes *Alberni* and *Regina*, both lost in August. On August 8, the Flower-class corvette, HMCS *Regina*, stopped to pick up survivors from an American merchant ship, *Ezra Weston*, which had struck a mine. In the gathering twilight, the lurking *U-667* unleashed a torpedo at *Regina* and it went down in less than a minute. One of the crew, Thomas "Spud" Malone, had acted on his own initiative and set the on-board depth charges to safe; if he had not, the explosions would have killed the men in the water. Malone was one who did not survive.

Doug Tope was on the starboard bridge when *Regina* was hit. He was blown over the rail and dropped onto the gun deck. The corvette was already going down, and the dazed Tope barely had time to kick off his weighty sea boots before going into the drink. He survived but was forever haunted by those sailors who could not exit the ship's interior before it filled with water. Stoker Don McIntosh remembered the explosion of the torpedo: He was hurled into the water, but fortunately he always wore his life vest because he could not swim. Bunker oil soon smothered him, as it did his comrades, to the point where they could not recognize each other in the tarry sludge, and only later did he learn that he had lacerations to his face and head. In the fouled water, men gave up the struggle and sank beneath the waves. Others struggled on, even those with broken limbs or puncture wounds, gulping in thick oil, throwing up, and struggling to find something to cling to as waves smashed against them. "Those remaining," wrote Surgeon-Lieutenant G.A. Gould, the ship's medical officer who was also in the water, "clung to life with that grim tenacity known only to those who have had to fight against the hungry sea."[72] Some sixty sailors were eventually rescued; twenty-eight men were lost.

Despite these successful U-boat attacks in the Channel and along Canada's east coast, the tide had turned forever against the Germans at sea. All the U-boats, many captained by inexperienced officers and tired crews, were under constant threat by the submarine killer groups and Coastal Command bombers and fighters, including RCAF's Nos. 404, 407, 415, 422, and 423 squadrons. Rocket-firing Bristol Beaufighters from RCAF No. 404 Squadron shot up German merchant ships and sank two destroyers, while Wellingtons, Short Sunderland flying boats, Liberators, and other bombers accounted for almost half of all U-boat kills during the course of the war.

In port and at sea, the German vessels were hounded, and while the warships and U-boats could throw up thick anti-aircraft fire, they were at a disadvantage in any contest. On June 24, 1944, for example, Flight-Lieutenant David Hornell of the RCAF's No. 162 Squadron, a former Sunday school teacher, sighted a U-boat while in his Canso flying boat at the end of a twelve-hour patrol. *U-1225* was on the surface about 150 kilometres north of the Shetland Islands, and the Germans fired bursts of shells as Hornell tried to position the unwieldy Canso for a bombing run. The starboard engine caught fire and soon the fabric of the wing was burning, leaving nothing but the exposed wing. The plane jerked violently, but Hornell continued the attack run on the sub, eventually dropping four depth charges. The U-boat was hit and sunk, and Hornell brought the flaming plane down in the water, skipping along a series of waves, bucking violently skyward, until it finally came to a rest. The eight-man crew evacuated the plane and crammed into a small dinghy built for two, with several of the airmen taking turns holding on to the side. They were spotted after five hours, but the sea was too violent for a rescue. The exposed crew had to wait sixteen more hours for a ship to find them in the rough and cold water, by which time two airmen perished from hypothermia and Hornell slipped into a coma. He never awoke from it.[73] Hornell was awarded posthumously the Victoria Cross, one of only two for RCAF members during the Second World War.

The U-boats were pushed back on all fronts and, in September 1944, as the Allied armies drove through France, the submarines were forced to abandon their bases on the Bay of Biscay. It was a severe blow to their ability to interdict Allied shipping. While the U-boat threat could not be ignored, never again would the Germans threaten the crucial lifeline from North America. The RCN continued to provide about a quarter of the escort ships for convoys transporting goods from Britain across the Channel through the newly liberated ports and harbours along the coast. And convoys from North America sailed throughout the war, although with few losses in comparison to the first four years of the war.

The minesweeper HMCS *Esquimalt*, lost on April 16, 1945, was the last Canadian warship sunk in the war. Louis Audette, who rose to the level of commander in the Royal Canadian Navy Volunteer Reserve during the course of the war, wrote of sailors and ships and the tremendous loss felt by the men for their vessels: "Those who have never beheld the dread moment of the death of a ship can hardly imagine the enormous drama of such an occasion, doubled of course for those who served in her.... I never witnessed such a spectacle without deep emotion.... Few non-seagoing men will ever understand the strange bond of love for a ship on the part of men who served in her or even a ship in which they have not served."[74]

THE BATTLE OF THE ATLANTIC—the longest-running campaign of the entire war— ended on May 5, 1945, when the U-boats were recalled to their ports. The advanced Type XXI U-boat was another of Hitler's super weapons that came too late to affect the outcome of the war. It was also staggeringly expensive, with one estimate indicating that the research and production of the XXIs amounted to 10 percent of all German war production in 1943 and 1944.[75]

The U-boats had suffered crippling casualties during the course of the war, with approximately 30,000 submariners killed out of 40,000 in the service; 749 U-boats were lost at sea. This was the highest casualty rate of any army on any front during the war.[76] Airpower had threatened the submarines, often guided by Ultra intelligence reports, but it had taken several years to bring its full force to bear. By war's end the RCAF had destroyed twenty-one submarines, almost as many as the entire RCN, at thirty-three.[77]

But it was the navy that bore the brunt of the U-boat war. From a prewar navy of about 3,000 permanent and reserve sailors, the RCN had grown to 96,000. The navy's primary job was to protect the merchant vessels carrying war supplies. And they succeeded. The RCN and RN were a story of success: 25,343 merchant ships carrying

164,783,921 tons of cargo were escorted across the Atlantic. Between September 1942 and May 1945, 99.4 percent of merchant ships reached their destinations intact.[78] The battle cost 1,990 RCN personnel killed, while another 1,629 Canadian and Newfoundland merchant mariners lost their lives.[79]

"The war," observed Lieutenant John Kilpatrick of the Royal Canadian Naval Volunteer Reserve, was "won by youngsters. Many of whom aged very quickly."[80] Canadian Frank Curry characterized the battle at sea as one of "survival of ship and crew. The strength to go on, hour after hour, day and night, until we reached a port, a safe haven for ship and sailor alike. These were the experiences to test and try us to the limits of our young lives."[81] The survivors of the North Atlantic carried a significant burden, but by any assessment, the seamen of the RCN and the merchant marine helped to win the Battle of the Atlantic, the war at sea, and the worldwide war.

CHAPTER 8

OPERATION SPRING

"I cannot tell you much about what is going on over here," wrote Private Arthur Wilkinson of the Black Watch (Royal Highland Regiment) of Canada, to his mother on July 10, 1944. "I can say this much though: it is a gigantic business and we are fighting a tough enemy."[1] Private Wilkinson would be killed eight days later, as the Canadians renewed the push against the Germans.

With Caen in Allied hands, the 2nd Canadian Infantry Division was sent across the Channel in early July to join Lieutenant-General Guy Simonds's newly established II Canadian Corps. The battles of June and early July were fought by the 3rd Canadian Infantry Division and supporting tank regiments, and Simonds had been aching to exert control over the ground war. Simonds was Canada's most experienced commander, having cut his teeth during the Sicily campaign during the summer of 1943. A professional soldier who had studied war intensely, he was confident, cold, and calculating. His analytical mind impressed officers, and his chief of staff, Brigadier N.E. Rodger, believed, "He reduced problems in a flash to basic facts and variables, picked out those that mattered, ignored those that were side issues and made up his mind and got on with it."[2] He had a shrewd eye for good and poor officers, and fired the latter freely during the war. Well liked by Montgomery for his experience and precise manner, the corps commander was also detached, at times arrogant, and not a great communicator with the average soldier. Simonds was never loved by his own troops, who found him both physically and emotionally remote from the front lines. And despite his agile mind that sought new ways to aid his soldiers, he also had an ungenerous tendency to blame his junior officers for not implementing his complex operations. Nonetheless, Simonds would emerge as Canada's best general of the war.

The reinforcing 2nd Division took its place in the line, relieving the 3rd Division. It was not easy to acclimatize to the front. Private Alexander Molnar of the Essex Scottish revealed his anxiety: "In the back of my mind a gnawing question—will I be able to meet the challenge and not let my comrades down?"[3] Molnar stood the test of battle, if briefly, for he was captured in his first engagement and spent a year as a prisoner of war. But Molnar was not alone in his worries, and every man wondered how he would fare when he faced combat. David Havard, a signaller with the 5th Field Regiment, remembered feeling confident after years of training in non-lethal environments. "We were lined up in convoy and moving along beside our infantry and one of the fellows that I had been in training with was just across from me. I was talking to him and all of a sudden, a shell dropped and a piece of shrapnel killed him instantly. And I suddenly became aware that I was no longer invincible."[4] Shellfire and mortar bombs claimed lives indiscriminately. So did mistakes. Corporal Tom Didmon of the Royal Hamilton Light Infantry recounted that the first regimental comrade he saw killed was a Dieppe veteran. Well liked and a good soldier, the sergeant was checking in on his platoon, which was situated in a number of slit trenches at the front. Creeping around in the dark, he was confronted by his own men for the nightly code word.[5] The sergeant did not hear the demand and a trigger-happy sentry gunned him down. It was a bad way to die. But there would be far worse over the coming months.

Lieutenant-General Guy Simonds inspects Canadian soldiers.

The 3rd Division was worn out and cut up. Grey with exhaustion, the front-line soldiers in their late teens and early twenties looked like old men. The world had diminished to immediate survival. Almost everyone who had fought through that month of battle had endured numerous exposures to death: shells that landed nearby but killed others in the vicinity, bullet holes through uniforms and kit, shrapnel deflected by helmets. The veterans developed acute survival skills, an almost sixth sense of knowing when to drop to the ground and when to run like hell. Yet this hyper awareness was matched by the bone-deep exhaustion that left men more susceptible to a mental breakdown. Constant exposure to stress often led to reckless behaviour. There was both a sharpening and a dulling effect that occurred among the battle-tested.

"SLOWLY, WE MOVED FORWARD," recounted infantryman Charles Forbes of Le Régiment de Maisonneuve, "with casualties beyond imagination."[6] In the first month of combat, the infantry, making up less than half of a division's strength, had suffered some 70 percent of the total losses.[7] The swing of the scythe was arbitrary and cruel. Trained men were killed in freak accidents, the good died badly, and the brave were felled. While experienced soldiers found ways to survive longer than reinforcements, luck, chance, and fate ruled the battlefield.

Yet despite the losses in June and July, morale remained high among the Canadians. An analysis of the letters of over 2,000 wounded men revealed that most were eager to rejoin their comrades in the field and end the war.[8] How was this high morale achieved, especially with the heavy

This was the war of the infantryman. At the front, a soldier spent most of his time in a slit trench.

casualties? At a basic level, the Canadian ground troops believed in their cause. They knew that the Nazi occupying forces had to be driven out of Western Europe. It was also evident that notwithstanding the high cost, victory was within reach. One Canadian rifleman admitted in a letter that the combat to date had been "damned grim"; but at the same time, he "wouldn't have missed it for the world."[9]

For those who study combat motivation, it is an axiom that men in battle fight for those beside them. The warriors' bond is strongest at the smallest level—the section and platoon—where soldiers have known, trained, and lived next to their buddy humping a Lee-Enfield or Bren gun for years, and where they rely on one another for survival. As J.F. Swayze of the Lincoln and Welland Regiment noted, "All ranks are held together by the fear of having their peers realize that they too are afraid.... What is a soldier? He's thinking not so much of himself but of the unit to which he belongs. At some stage, you're with this platoon or section and you're going to keep on because you're part of that section."[10] However, while the Canadian soldiers fought for the men in their primary group, those chums and comrades with whom they had trained for years, this cohesion, as the military sometimes calls it, was blown apart in fighting.[11] All of the infantry battalions were destroyed several times over by the end of the war and had to be continually rebuilt with replacements.[12]

If a battalion was soon composed of men who barely knew half of their mates' names, how did it continue to fight coherently? One must conclude that the training in England had welded together an effective system.[13] Battle drill gave the soldiers the common skills, training, and tools to engage in combat. Though some historians have condemned the training in England for what it did not teach—especially infantry and armour cooperation—battle drill provided a foundation for all soldiers. Many veterans of the front nonetheless complained that the new infantrymen were hesitant and unsure of themselves and their weapons, although this is not surprising as no amount of training fully prepared a man for combat. The reinforcements, both officers and rankers, "were not hard physically," griped Lieutenant Thomas McCoy of the Essex Scottish. "They did not know the tremendous capabilities of the human body."[14] But they soon toughened up, if they survived. This cycle of replacements gave the battalion a resilience to rejuvenate itself after near-fatal losses, much the same way that the Germans could amalgamate destroyed units and keep fighting. In the latter stages of Normandy, and throughout the rest of the long war, it was common for two or three depleted Canadian platoons, or even companies, to serve together under one junior officer during a battle, and to remain an effective unit.

A crucial factor in allowing battalions to rebuild effectiveness was the vibrant regimental tradition among British and Canadian formations. Loyalty to the regiment was complex and profound. Replacement soldiers were instructed in these sustaining bonds. The colonel embodied the regiment, and the Canadians were lucky to have forceful and magnetic personalities in command in almost all their battalions. Many of these senior officers had risen through the ranks and understood the pulse of their troops. But this did not make them the soldiers' friends. Good officers were firm and fair, and the rank and file understood that they were to follow orders without question. This type of iron discipline—backed up by punishment—provided a structure for men in times of terrible strain. Edward Borland, an American serving in a Canadian armoured regiment, felt that with so much carnage, "you had to be treated that way or you would go right stark raving mad."[15]

The senior regimental officers, supported by junior officers and NCOs, exerted control through discipline, rewards, and charisma. Captain Harold MacDonald of the North Shore Regiment wrote to his wife after several costly battles in July 1944: "Checking the posts [during the night] and trying to boost morale after casualties, that's part of our job—can't think of our own hides when our boys are getting it."[16] That kind of selfless action, of officers caring for their men, fostered and sustained morale. Yet it exacted a price. Major Ronald Shawcross of the Regina Rifles landed on D-Day in top shape, weighing 220 pounds; four months later, when he was wounded, he had lost fifty-five pounds through unending strain, constant attention to his men, and daily brushes with horror.[17] Not all officers thought of their men first, acted honourably, or even had the necessary skills to lead, but most of the poor leaders had been weeded out of the Canadian army during its long training period in Britain. The high loss rate among the officers, higher than that of their own men, proved that they led their soldiers into battle, and usually from the front.[18]

Soldiers had to find ways to cope with death. They had to protect themselves from seeing comrades killed by shells, sniper bullets, or freak accidents. One unlucky member of the Stormont, Dundas and Glengarry Highlanders was stung to death in

July when enemy shelling enraged several hives of bees.[19] But there was no shortage of ways to die at the front. The artillery barrages were, according to Sergeant Lloyd Pauli, "the hardest part of the whole war."[20] At the same time, studied nonchalance and an acquired toughness allowed soldiers to cope with the strain. The war diarist for the Royal Hamilton Light Infantry witnessed one occasion during the constant shelling at the front: "Two D Co[mpany] lads were sitting in their slit trench when an 88mm shell passed between them. Neither one spoke for a second then one of the lads calmly pulled himself to his feet and said 'I think I'll write a letter' and walked off."[21]

Men necessarily became callous, and this extended to the soldiers' slang. Sergeant Louis Trenton of the Royal Regiment of Canada claimed, "We never used the term 'he was killed' or 'died of wounds' and no elaboration. If one was sure his buddy was killed, he would say: 'He bought it' or 'He went west' and drop the subject and never speak of him again."[22] Such defence mechanisms were required in a world where death claimed friend and foe. Soldiers found new and interesting ways of expressing their discomfort and displeasure through vulgarity and profanity. Other than the padres, around whom language was usually toned down, few cared what came out of the soldiers' mouths.

Rum, letters, cigarettes, and the occasional leave were minor rewards that lightened the mental load. Though some men were motivated by the prospect of medals, most recipients seemed positively bashful about being awarded them. Almost all award-winners knew that they had succeeded in battle usually through the assistance and sacrifice of others. Captain Joseph Greenblatt, a medical officer in the Royal Canadian Army Medical Corps, told his beloved Fran, after surviving several close calls with death, "Haven't won any medals, but then you don't get any medals for doing your job. Actually, the only medal I'm interested in is the Victory medal, as long as I am there to receive it personally."[23] Survival was reward enough. Lance-Corporal Bill Saunders, who served with his brother in the Irish Regiment (who was later killed), was awarded the Distinguished Conduct Medal for carrying five wounded soldiers off the battlefield and then leading a small contingent back into the fight. He was unfazed by the award since, he noted, "I didn't even know what a DCM was!"[24]

The high command knew that an award system, according to one official report, had "a most advantageous effect on the morale of the army." But the awards also had

The infantry had to find ways to cope and endure.
These cheery Canadians, posing in a staged shot, enjoy letters from home.

to go to those who deserved them. General principles of allotment in the First Canadian Army followed 21st Army Group regulations, with at least one decoration provided for every 250 men during each six-month period.[25] The prolonged fighting in Normandy and later in the Scheldt, and the incredible bravery of soldiers on the battlefield, resulted in the Canadians exceeding the normal six-month quota, although the lull in intense combat from November 1944 to February 1945 helped to restore the balance. For the entire campaign, the First Canadian Army awarded to personnel under its command 3,636 Commonwealth decorations and medals, as well as 6,422 Mentioned-in-Dispatches and 1,060 foreign awards. At headquarters, there was an understanding that some units received more awards than others, as they were more fully committed to combat, but "sustained efforts were made throughout the campaign to ensure that inequalities which arose were straightened out."[26] Also, it was not surprising that the infantry arm consisted of 25 percent of the total strength in the army yet received 38 percent of the decorations. It also sustained 73 percent of the casualties.

Religion remained a central method of providing some calmness in the chaos. "There are no battlefield atheists," remarked Lieutenant Eric Marion of the Cameron Highlanders of Canada.[27] And even those who did not trust in God or organized religion often found solace in the sympathetic regimental padres. The padres provided spiritual guidance, acted as a conduit between the men and their officers, and even penned comforting letters to loved ones.[28] The battalion's padre, believed one major, was "a tower of strength to all the troops."[29] Jewish-born Lieutenant Barney Danson, a future Canadian cabinet minister, recalled, "I once canvassed my platoon to see who wanted a Bible, [and] I found that every single man carried his army-issue Bible in his top left pocket, over his heart, me included." A belief in a higher power, for Danson and his men, was "a lifeline to sanity amidst the insanity of war."[30]

There were other forms of belief that guided and protected soldiers. Stanley Scislowski wrote about his experiences during the Italian campaign, but they were equally applicable to Normandy. He scoffed at all the talk about angels, magic charms, and ritualistic mantras that his comrades embraced, especially when "so many of our guys were getting killed or maimed." Yet after one particularly harrowing battle, reflecting on the barrage of bullets that cut the air but somehow spared him, he "became a convert, a believer in the angel that must have been running alongside of me as I sprinted and flopped my way towards the promised land. She did one hell of a job, let me tell you. By all rights I should have been dead."[31] Having emerged from the gauntlet of fire unscathed, he could only attribute his survival to some kind of higher power. Another private in the Cape Breton Highlanders, in one suicidal charge, with bullets "going between my legs and around me," concluded that he survived because "There just had to be someone up above looking after me."[32] A third soldier—although there were more—offered his views: Sergeant Charles Kipp of the Lincoln and Welland Regiment, who also had numerous brushes with death in Normandy, twice heard a spectral voice instructing him at dangerous moments on how to escape his fate. In his mind, a supernatural presence "was looking after me."[33]

"I never thought I'd survive," remembered Private Elmer Allard, who was wounded in Normandy but returned to serve in October with the Algonquin Regiment and was later captured.[34] Another Canadian, Burton Harper, a Canloan officer in a British regiment, recalled, "I knew the law of averages was going to work out, and I couldn't see any end to it except by becoming a casualty because there was no end to the war." After several months of combat, and aware that all the other Canloan officers in his regiment had been killed or wounded (with the 623 Canloan infantry officers suffering a 75 percent casualty rate from D-Day to the end of the war), Harper could not stop pondering his own likely death. "I began to take risks that weren't logical," even as he knew he was courting danger.[35] He was wearing down, was easily irritated, and was constantly haunted in his sleep by the sights of dismembered bodies. Soon Harper envisioned himself torn apart by a shell burst or sniper fire. Harper survived six months at the front before a mortar bomb shredded his face, but vast numbers of others only found a final resting place in France.

AFTER CAEN WAS WRESTED from the enemy during the second week of July, the German high command worried that the front opposite the Anglo-Canadian armies might collapse entirely without the city as an anchor for the overall defence. Moreover, German casualties had surpassed 100,000, and only a trickle of 9,000 reinforcements had been sent from the central reserve.[36] Attesting to the severity of the wide-ranging battles and the constant air attacks, 9 generals and 137 commanding officers had been killed or seriously wounded. Yet even with these losses, Hitler remained fixated on a second landing in the Pas-de-Calais, even as his generals on the Normandy front gnashed their teeth in frustration. But slowly the German reserves were shifting south, and in a desire to reinvigorate the Normandy front, Hitler fired his commander-in-chief, Field Marshal von Rundstedt, and replaced him with Field Marshal Günther von Kluge. But even the optimistic Field Marshal Rommel warned, on July 15, of a coming crisis.

In preparation for a new offensive round, Simonds's II Corps shuffled eastwards, with its front lines running through the southern part of Caen and curling up to the northeast of the city. Directly south of Caen was the critical Caen–Falaise road, and it was here that the Germans were struggling hardest against British attempts to push south across the Odon River. The Germans, adapting to the Allies' huge advantage of naval guns, bombers, and artillery, echeloned their defence in depth to diffuse the number of defenders holding the front. A forward buffer zone of machine-gun nests and isolated, patchwork defences was meant to slow any assault, while another zone, usually 900 metres deep, was stacked with mortars, Nebelwerfers, and anti-tank guns. Given the Allies' command of the air, the Germans were forced to fight in smaller groups, reducing their knock-out power. These disadvantages were offset by the open, rolling French fields that allowed the anti-tank guns to make mincemeat of any armoured thrust.

On the Eastern Front, a renewed Soviet offensive, Operation Bagration, was launched on June 22, and it tore a hole through the 800,000-strong central German army group. More than 1.7 million troops, supported by over 4,000 tanks, crashed against each other, and by mid-August the Soviets had advanced some 300 kilometres and killed or captured 300,000 Germans. Hitler's forces survived the onslaught only by relying on sacrificial rearguard divisions that allowed the rest of the armies to retreat and because the Soviets outran their logistical system.[37] The Red Army's victory was chilling evidence to the Western Allies that Stalin's soldiers had improved immeasurably and would likely be unstoppable in battle. Even as the Allies in Normandy needed the Soviets to keep the Eastern Front open, there was a growing wariness towards Stalin. The Allied generals were increasingly told by their political masters to move more rapidly, with the goal of racing to Berlin and holding it fast against the Communists.

ON THE WESTERN FRONT, the Canadians, as part of Lieutenant-General Miles Dempsey's Second British Army (the First Canadian Army would not be activated until July 23), had the unenviable task of continuing to hold down the bulk of the German reserves, especially the elite panzer divisions, with the Americans facing far weaker forces. To keep up the pressure, Montgomery ordered an armoured assault southeast of Caen, codenamed Operation Goodwood, with the goal of driving on to Falaise. As he had with Epsom in late June, Montgomery sold the plan to Eisenhower as a battle that would break the enemy's willpower. The operation was to kick off on July 18 and coordinate with the Americans, who were to launch their offensive, known as Cobra, around the same time, although poor weather eventually delayed the American attack near St. Lô by a week.

The Canadian component of Goodwood, known as Atlantic, would entail Simonds's two divisions attacking through Caen southwards to protect the British right flank. Simonds urged his forces forward, telling senior officers that the enemy was "close to cracking."[38] While the epicentre of German strength was opposite the British to the east, where the wide flatlands there were considered good tank country, the Canadian front was defended by several enemy battlegroups and a battalion of the most feared tanks in the world, Tigers. The massive 55-ton Tigers, with their thick armour and 88mm gun, could kill a Sherman at 2,300 metres, and were nearly invulnerable to long-range fire. As Private Bill Hennessy of the Stormont, Dundas and Glengarry Highlanders remarked of his first encounter with the Tigers, they "looked so terrifying you were scared to death."[39]

Goodwood, with its armour-infantry-artillery fist, was aided by over a thousand bombers that pounded the German lines and rear areas, as well as by hundreds of guns hurling a quarter of a million shells into the enemy positions. Though these bombardments obliterated large parts of the front, troops that were dug in often survived even the most earth-shattering of explosions. Within the smoke and dust, German Tigers and 88s emerged from the destruction to wreak havoc on the advancing British forces. The age of tanks blasting forward to victory in a blitzkrieg-like romp was long dead.

Amid the landscape of brewed-up Shermans and blackened armoured vehicles, the only saving grace for the Allies was that many of the Shermans could be repaired by tank fitters. The crews generally survived, taking only a 7 percent casualty rate (in comparison to over 70 percent for the infantry).[40] At the same time, the wounded tankers suffered unique injuries. Surgeon J.B. Hillsman wrote that "tank wounds were horrible things to treat. They are always accompanied by more or less severe burns and are multiple in nature. The wounds are not usually from shell fragments but one digs out pieces of armour plate and large lumps of hard rubber and nuts and bolts."[41]

Goodwood achieved little ground and the British armoured divisions lost over 320 tanks in the fighting, but the offensive had drawn in more German reserves, achieving its strategic objective even as it made future tactical success on the ground more difficult.[42] Eisenhower and his senior officers at SHAEF were, however, unimpressed with the limited gains, and senior generals, air marshals, and staff officers were disgusted with Montgomery's self-satisfied reports to the war journalists. Yet even Montgomery's critics could see how Goodwood had begun to suck in the German reserves and free up the Americans to the west, who faced far weaker forces and were preparing their major breakout battle.

ON THE CANADIAN FRONT, on July 18, the experienced 3rd Division pushed southward through an industrial, built-up area, dotted with factories, buildings, and slag heaps. While the German defenders were outnumbered by the 8th Canadian Infantry Brigade's advance, they held the main roads and villages. The Canadians would blast their way forward. Captain T.J. Bell of the 12th Field Regiment recalled that the hours before Operation Atlantic were a time to "Praise the Lord and pass the ammunition."[43] Thousands of shells were manhandled into place near the guns and fired. Though shellfire stunned and suppressed the enemy, it allowed for no surprise, since the first round telegraphed the forthcoming battle. Still, it was terrifying to be on the receiving end of a battering assault. One German private, writing to his parents of the barrage, described the punishment: "We hear the whole long day nothing but artillery fire of all calibres.... Whoever succeeds in passing through this hell without being killed can really be thankful to God."[44] The soldier, intelligence records revealed, was killed the next day.

The Queen's Own Rifles, on the left and in touch with the British 11th Armoured

Division, pushed along the Orne River and into the outskirts of the steel-mill town of Colombelles, and then on to Giberville and Faubourg de Vaucelles. Meanwhile, Le Régiment de la Chaudière cleared the German positions in Colombelles. According to one Canadian infantryman, Colombelles was "just masses of twisted iron and concrete rubble, white dust everywhere and men all look like ghosts."[45] Artillery and mortar fire further smashed the machinery and masonry; the French Canadians crawled through the ruins, killing with grenades, rifles, and Bren guns, and methodically clearing pockets of resistance that held out throughout the day. The Queen's Own found themselves fired on from the town and from their front, but they eventually prevailed. Some 200 German corpses were found in the area and another 600 prisoners taken.[46]

With the battle raging in Colombelles, Major-General Rod Keller sent the 9th Canadian Infantry Brigade on a flanking attack, bypassing much of the opposition, which allowed for the North Novas and the Highland Light Infantry of Canada to meet up with the Regina Rifles, Royal Winnipeg Rifles, and Canadian Scottish to capture Vaucelles and the surrounding region. The imaginative operation, which emphasized speed and manoeuvre over firepower, isolated the German resistance opposite the Chaudières, and this combined weight and pressure ensured that its sector of the enemy line was soon broken. The total cost for the 3rd Division was 386 casualties, of which 89 were fatal. The Canadians had cracked through the Germans' outer defences, although several kilometres to the south lay the enemy strength around the Verrières and Bourguébus Ridges.

Major-General Charles Foulkes's 2nd Canadian Division was confronted by fewer Germans than the 3rd Division, but it was carrying out its first major action since Dieppe. Foulkes, a dour prewar professional who had held staff positions and commanded the 3rd Canadian Infantry Brigade in Italy, was not particularly imaginative or inspiring. He had risen to the top through his friendship with Crerar and by being a "yes" man who rarely pushed back against his seniors. He ordered a pincer attack from the right flank, which was to join up with the 3rd Division at Vaucelles. The primary obstacle on the 2nd Division's front was the Orne River, which snaked through Caen and then southwards. The Royal Regiment of Canada, which had been destroyed at the Puys beach at Dieppe, fought their way into Louvigny, north of the

ATTACK SOUTH OF CAEN, JULY 18–21, 1944

Orne, on the 18th, in a fierce battle that lasted into the next day. On the other side of the Orne, Le Régiment de Maisonneuve and a squadron of Shermans burst out of Caen, running southward along the Orne in a smart manoeuvre that took the Germans by surprise. The Maisonneuves were hit by their own artillery fire but reorganized and pressed forward into Fleury-sur-Orne on the 19th; this put them behind the German defenders across the Orne at Louvigny. The tanks of the Sherbrooke Fusilier, a Quebec unit, offered fire support. Sergeant John Taylor, who less than a month later was wounded and invalided home, wrote in his diary, "Going was tough—killed several Germans."[47]

The 2nd Division had performed well in its first day of sustained battle in Normandy, and by the end of the 19th, the Black Watch (Royal Highland Regiment) of Canada occupied the town of Ifs, about 1.5 kilometres southeast of Fleury. Another push by the Calgary Highlanders was stopped by concentrated mortar fire coming from camouflaged enemy slit trenches along Verrières Ridge, combined with an armoured counterattack from 1st SS Panzer Division. With Verrières Ridge directly in the path of the 2nd Division, the Canadians paused on the 19th, warily eying an enemy line that was bristling with guns.

SIMONDS TEED UP A NEW PUSH. This move was at odds with his mission of providing a protective flank for the British in Operation Goodwood, since the British were now winding down the fighting on that front, having made little progress. But Simonds wished to hound the Germans from the villages of Verrières, St. André, and St. Martin along Verrières ridge. St. André and St. Martin were situated on a wide-open ridge, with a gentle 75-metre rise covered in ripening wheat to the crest, and Verrières on the reverse slope below the crest. On the other side of the ridge's natural barrier, the Germans situated many of their tanks and counterattacking forces, making them relatively safe from Allied shellfire. Despite this strength, Major-General Foulkes, commander of the 2nd Division, reported to Simonds on the 20th that "the enemy forward [defences] appeared softening up."[48] This was nonsense. The general was repeating what he knew Simonds wanted to hear, with Foulkes having the unfortunate tendency to ingratiate himself to those in higher command positions. Simonds had told his senior officers only a fortnight earlier that it was "fatal to stop" and that he was willing to accept up to 70 percent casualties to achieve his objectives.[49]

The Canadians would now engage in a new drive forward to achieve Simonds's objectives, even as the British offensive on the left flank was drawing to a close. This would allow the Germans to shift artillery to the Canadian front. Simonds ached to show that his green corps could deliver in battle and elevate Verrières Ridge into the history books.

Brigadier Hugh Young's three battalions of the 6th Infantry Brigade would assault across the Verrières Ridge front, with the Cameron Highlanders of Canada attacking St. André-sur-Orne, while the South Saskatchewan Regiment (in the centre) advanced on the ridge southeast of St. André, and Les Fusiliers Mont-Royal (FMRs) aimed to punch through Beauvoir and Troteval Farms on the left flank, before mopping up the village of Verrières. The reserve battalion, the Essex Scottish, attached from the 4th Infantry Brigade, was to leapfrog the South Sasks over the crest of the ridge and ram home the victory. The Sherbrooke Fusilier's and 1st Hussars' Sherman tanks were ready for battle, but they were held back to protect them from anti-tank guns and to be thrown into the line to shore up weakness. This proved to be a poor idea, and the infantry needed their support closer to the action during the break-in phase. With little room to manoeuvre and no chance to surprise the enemy that looked down on them, Brigadier Young ordered an intense barrage. Yet even with this gun power, the Canadian operation was too light given the enemy strength in the region, and it was an oversight that Simonds's headquarters did not arrange for air power to assist in blasting the enemy positions behind the ridge.[50]

The Canadian guns opened up at 3 P.M on July 20. Following the barrage laid down by 25-pounders and heavier guns into St. André, the Camerons cleared it in hard fighting. They knew they were not finished and they prepared for the enemy reaction that was unleashed later in the day. Several additional attacks followed and were destroyed by the combined guns of the Camerons and Able Squadron of the Sherbrooke Fusilier, commanded by Major Radley-Walters.

On the far left of the line, sweeping southward, the FMRs ran into concentrated fire from Beauvoir and Troteval Farms, where elements from the 1st SS Panzer Division had established themselves behind the thick stone walls. The Fusiliers bounded forward, moving and firing. Those who were hit appeared to have been jerked backward by a rope, their bloodied bodies flailing in mid-air. When the enemy was eventually broken, the Canadians pushed on. Unbeknownst to the FMRs, however, a contingent of Germans survived in the farm-house cellars, emerging after the storm had swept through and taking the FMRs from behind. With the Fusiliers caught in the open, and under fire from several directions, they were forced into a chaotic retreat to the north of Troteval, leaving behind corpses, holed anti-tank guns, and burning Shermans, some with flames shooting out of the hatch like a blowtorch.

In the centre, the South Saskatchewan Regiment was handled even more roughly. Through waist-high wheat, the Johns advanced on the enemy, although they felt naked without tanks. Exhibiting the firm fire discipline the Canadians had witnessed over the last six weeks, the German defenders of the 2nd Panzer Division waited until the prairie soldiers were in the open. The South Sasks' 6-pounder anti-tank guns and the Royal Canadian Artillery's larger 17-pounders had to be unhitched from their towing vehicles before they could be brought into action. Catching the Canadians on the move, the enemy's tanks and gunners massacred them. As the infantry and gunners took cover, the creeping barrage moved off without them, leaving them exposed, overextended, and unsupported. An enemy tank attack around 5 P.M. broke the already savaged infantry, who had lost their commanding officer and two company commanders in the crushed and blackened wheat. Major John Edmondson recalled, "One tank came right into my left forward platoon driving right over top of people it didn't shoot. I was hollering at the platoon sergeant when the tank fired a HE [high explosive shell] which struck him in the back, and he disintegrated into pieces before my eyes."[51] The demoralized Sasks retreated rapidly from the front to a reverse-slope position. They were later accused of a rout, but it was more controlled than that, although only barely.

The reserve battalion, the Essex Scottish—wet, tired, and hungry because their rations had not come up—provided support for their Saskatchewan comrades. They had moved forward and dug in around 6:20 P.M., but the Scottish were shaken when the Sasks streamed back through their lines. Shortly thereafter, a number of enemy tanks ground through the Essex position. Without anti-tank guns or tanks, which should have been organized by 6th Brigade headquarters, two companies of Essex Scots retreated in haste from their precarious position.[52] The official report observed, "It is difficult to tell the exact details of what happened to these coys [companies] because of the great number of missing personnel, particularly from C coy."[53] It was a bloodbath.

The Germans were not done, and they rolled forward with armour on June 21, overrunning the new front-line positions of the Essex Scottish, who had reformed at the foot of the ridge. The situation was ugly, although a renewed drive by the Black Watch later in the day, at 6 P.M., regained much of the ground. The infantrymen from Montreal were aided by Sherman tanks and Canadian gunners. One gun team from the 2nd Anti-Tank Regiment, firing a 17-pounder—the Canadian equivalent to the powerful German 88mm gun—systematically traded blows with four German Panther tanks. The Canadian gunners had expertly situated and camouflaged their gun next to a burned-out Sherman, and the Germans were confused as to where the shells were coming from. They thought it was the dead Sherman, which they pounded relentlessly with shells. Firing every ten to twenty seconds in a mad race against time, the gunners methodically knocked out the increasingly desperate tanks, eventually destroying all four. Most of the gunners were wounded, and the 17-pounder was scarred and holed by shrapnel, but they were the only survivors on that part of the battlefield.[54]

The Canadians hung on to their minor gains, but they were still at the foot of Verrières Ridge. Foulkes later blamed his troops for their failure to advance farther, claiming "when we bumped into battle-experienced German troops we were no match for them." In reality, few formations—battle-hardened or green—would have been able to punch through the enemy gun screens and defences in depth.[55] And somewhat shockingly, the Canadian commanders, from Simonds on down, had not insisted that tanks accompany the infantry, and little planning had gone into how to withstand a German armoured counterattack.[56] There was simply no easy way forward, and it was a long way back if the Germans struck hard, as they did. Operation Atlantic, the Canadian arm of Montgomery's Goodwood campaign, officially ended on September 21, and cost 1,614 casualties; these losses were added to the 8,500 Canadians killed, wounded, and made prisoner since D-Day.[57] The removal of a few battalion commanders and the scapegoating of the Essex Scottish colonel were little more than a panacea to a lost tactical situation.

MONTGOMERY WAS DISAPPOINTED with Operation Goodwood, which had made little progress at the cost of 6,168 casualties.[58] The armoured thrust had failed to deliver a high-profile victory, and Eisenhower's headquarters continued to hound him to punch through the enemy lines. Monty also needed to tie down the Germans on his front to ensure reserves were not moved to block General Omar Bradley's U.S. First Army (and later the 12th U.S. Army Group, which would eventually command four U.S. armies), which was to break out in the west, in what was dubbed Operation Cobra. To date, the Americans and the Anglo-Canadian forces had fought completely different campaigns with little coordination. On the American front, the GIs had finally pushed through the bocage—a series of lush apple orchards surrounded by tall, thick hedgerows consisting of a tangle of trees, vines, and brush that created a series of fortresses—and were now ready for their breakout battle into Brittany. While Montgomery would have preferred to have had the opportunity for glory, his shifting strategy had settled on the British and Canadian divisions holding the enemy around Caen. The disparity of the German strength on the two fronts was staggering: Montgomery's 21st Army Group were opposed by the 21st, 2nd, and 116th Panzer Divisions, as well as the 1st, 9th, 10th, and 12th SS Divisions, while the Americans stood against only two of the elite armoured units. In all, the British and Canadians faced 14 divisions and 600 tanks, while the Americans confronted 9 divisions and roughly 110 tanks.[59]

Despite this inequality of strength, Eisenhower was increasingly unsatisfied with Montgomery, who was commanding the ground war on his behalf. The American general was anxious to cross the Channel and take control. There was a worry among some of the American generals and at SHAEF headquarters that Montgomery talked a good game but was too cautious to give free rein to his forces in a breakthrough engagement. Montgomery was indeed wedded to a "tidy battlefield," where infantry and armour were protected by heavy firepower, but he ordered operations like this to save British and Canadian lives. He did not want to oversee an attritional, Somme-like campaign, and there were far too few reinforcements in the shallow ranks behind the front-line units.[60] Eisenhower had no burning desire to send soldiers into the meat-grinder either, but he needed progress, with London and Washington urging him to make greater advances in Normandy, especially as the Red Army was crushing the Germans in the east. Nonetheless, for the sake of unity and to avoid the friction that had damaged relations in Sicily and Italy, Eisenhower withstood demands from American papers, his own senior staff, and Churchill to harass or remove Montgomery because of his perceived reticence in pulling the trigger on a big offensive. An impotent Eisenhower was reduced to smoking four packs of cigarettes a day and aging visibly before the eyes of his concerned staff. Montgomery, in turn, not liking the rapping on his knuckles, exhorted his generals to renew the battle. From every direction came the need to attack.

The Germans had furiously built up their defences in the region south of Caen, incorporating anti-tank guns, machine-gun pits, and mortar teams into the naturally

A German mortar team preparing to fire. Mortars were the primary killers of infantrymen in Normandy, with 70 percent of casualties attributed to their bombs.

defensive landscape. Verrières Ridge was no mountain, but its long slope and ridge line provided an uninterrupted view of the surrounding countryside. The Germans could see that it was the exact place where the Canadians would form up to launch the next phase of the offensive, known as Operation Spring. The Canadian attack was set for July 25, to be followed three days later by a new push by British XII Corps. Montgomery's orders to Simonds and his other generals emphasized caution, and despite the growing agitation from SHAEF, he knew there were few opportunities for a breakthrough.

Simonds's Canadians had fewer than three days from the end of Atlantic to plan for Spring. The objective was a series of strongpoints on and behind Verrières Ridge. On July 23, Canadian intelligence reported that the enemy front was held in strength. This could not have come as a surprise, but Simonds did not let the appreciation change his plan of attack, except to widen the front to 6 kilometres to allow two divisions into the battle.[61] In fact, the new German commander in the west, Field Marshal von Kluge, believed that the Anglo-Canadian front was the centre of the Allied offensive (when in fact it was the American Cobra breakout set for July 25), and so he crammed five Waffen SS panzer divisions, three army divisions, and three Tiger tank battalions into the battle space.[62] Simonds was the only Canadian general in France with the killer instinct, but sometimes this left him failing to sniff out the enemy's intentions in his pursuit of victory.

The operation took the form of a typical Anglo-Canadian phased attack, in which the first waves would push forward at 3:30 A.M. on the 25th, while secondary forces, including the 7th British Armoured Division and 2nd Canadian Armoured Brigade, exploited gains through the shattered front.[63] On the 3rd Division's left flank, as it looked south, the 9th Infantry Brigade's North Nova Scotia Highlanders marched from Bourguébus, crossing about a kilometre of open wheat fields to close on Tilly-la-Campagne. The two dozen stone houses were about 1.5 kilometres from Verrières village, which was on the reverse slope of the ridge, a little below the crest. The cluster of houses at Tilly were held by a reinforced company of 1st SS Panzer Division, backed by well-situated anti-tank guns and Mk IV tanks, with fallback positions around stone houses and protective cellars. The North Novas set off at 3:30 A.M., advancing under a ceiling of Allied shells made all the more otherworldly by the

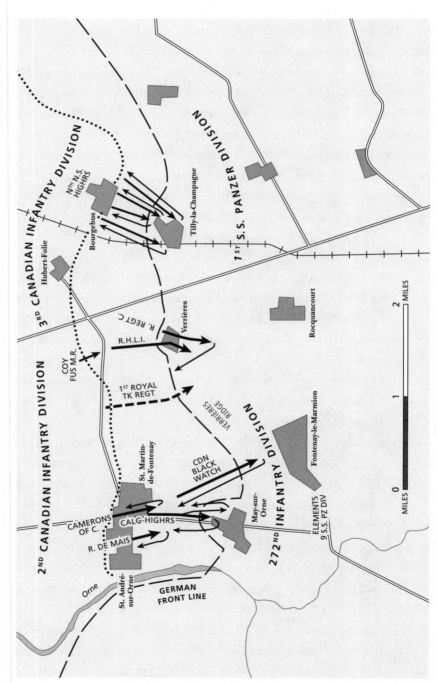

VERRIÈRES RIDGE, JULY 25, 1944

3RD CANADIAN INFANTRY DIVISION

N TH N.S. HIGHRS

Bourgebus

Hubert-Folie

Tilly-la-Champagne

1ST S.S. PANZER DIVISION

Rocquancourt

2ND CANADIAN INFANTRY DIVISION

COY FUS M.R.

R.H.L.I.

R. REGT C.

Verrières

1ST ROYAL TK REGT

VERRIÈRES RIDGE

St. Martin-de-Fontenay

CDN BLACK WATCH

CAMERONS OF C.

CALG·HIGHRS

R. DE MAIS

May-sur-Orne

272ND INFANTRY DIVISION

Fontenay-le-Marmion

ELEMENTS 9 S.S. PZ DIV

Orne

St. André-sur-Orne

GERMAN FRONT LINE

0   1   2

MILES   MILES

deliberate bouncing of searchlights off low clouds to create a ghostly, artificial light. Unfortunately, while the light provided the troops with better vision, breaking the shroud of darkness allowed the Waffen SS troops to open fire on the silhouetted Canadians.[64] Surviving section, platoon, and company commanders rallied their men, and they set off again across the battlefield. The North Novas snuffed out the grenadiers in the forward slit trenches but found themselves raked by concealed guns, and were unable to advance into Tilly. Radio contact was lost, and the commanding officer, Lieutenant-Colonel Charles Petch, was cut off from his forces. He felt he had little choice but to send forward the reserve company, which was also soon forced to ground. The situation went from bad to worse as the Fort Garry Horse rolled into battle and became easy pickings for the Germans' anti-tank guns. Eleven of the sixteen Shermans were left burning in the nightmarish scene.[65]

The North Novas held the outer edges of Tilly around 5:25 A.M., but they were eventually driven back from the village. The vulnerable wounded were spread over the wheat fields. As stretcher-bearers tried to drag them to safety, snipers took no pity and killed those who stumbled to the rear in delirium or revealed themselves as they thrashed about in agony. When Brigadier D.G. Cunningham of the 9th Brigade ordered another attack for late in the afternoon, both of the regimental commanding officers, Lieutenant-Colonels Charles Petch of the North Novas and G.H. Christiansen of the Stormont, Dundas and Glengarry Highlanders (which had been rushed up to reinforce the precarious front), refused to make the daylight assault.[66] The war diary for the Highlanders noted frankly, "We are ordered to be on notice to move to assist the NNS. This is indeed a mental blow and is felt by all ranks. We need a rest and refit."[67] The 9th Brigade stayed put, avoiding another horrific slaughter that would have achieved nothing.

To the right of the North Novas, the Royal Hamilton Light Infantry had the unenviable task of capturing the village of Verrières. They would traverse much of the same terrain as the South Sasks four days earlier. The veterans of Dieppe knew about killing grounds, and few went forward with confidence. Yet still they went. The Rileys passed through the FMRs, who were tasked to clear German defenders at Troteval Farm, and they succeeded in doing so by throwing almost every rifleman into the battle, including cooks and officers' batmen. Major Jacques "Mad Jimmy"

Dextraze, a future chief of the defence staff, led the FMRs and secured the farm for the Rileys.

The advance parties of the Rileys pushed forward past Troteval but ran into a number of Panthers. A fierce battle ensued, with the Rileys making good use of the ground and their PIATs to blast the enemy tanks. "There wasn't the slightest reason in the world why I wasn't killed three or four times," wrote Tom Didmon, a clerk who was pulled from the headquarters company and thrown into the offensive.[68] He and a comrade, scared out of their wits, faced a German tank and knocked it out with a PIAT, a weapon neither one of them had faith in. Biting back their fear, Didmon and his comrades continued to move forward.

The new colonel, John Rockingham, who had replaced the much-respected and recently wounded Denis Whitaker, worried about the German strength in front of him if the enemy was using Panthers so recklessly, but the attack went forward a little after 4 A.M. Three companies of Rileys swept up the ridge through the firestorm from at least four German machine-gun teams. The surviving Rileys methodically cleared out the slit trench defences and then occupied Verrières, before holding off several counter-attacks of grenadiers and panzers.[69] Throughout the day, Rockingham ordered forward British anti-tank guns, Shermans from the 1st Hussars and the 1st Royal Tank Regiment, and even rocket-firing Typhoons. A Canadian infantryman eyewitness remembered, "One Sherman burst into flame.... The hatch flew open, emitting clouds of black smoke.... One man came out backwards, catching his knee on the edge of the hatch, and hung there for a moment, blazing like a torch, before he fell to the ground."[70]

With most of the regimental officers down, Rockingham advanced into Verrières to see the situation first-hand and reorganize the wobbly defence. Tom Didmon, who had a view from a slit trench, commented on Rockingham's fearless walk through town, even as bullets and shells were striking all around: "He was either very brave and cool or completely nuts."[71] "Rocky" was awarded the first of his two Distinguished Service Orders for his leadership during the battle.[72] The Rileys held the village, spraying the enemy forces that came overland at them. The men from Hamilton had made a remarkable attack and defence, but with the Germans committing reserves, the follow-on unit, the Royal Regiment of Canada, had little chance of pushing on to Rocquancourt, about 1.5 kilometres down the ridge.

On the right flank, the Cameron Highlanders of Canada had to pass through St. André and St. Martin, neither of which were secure at the time of their 1 kilometre march southwards. With German defenders in the two villages, the Camerons brawled through farms, sunken roads, buildings, and cellars. A patch of mud or a stone wall was fought over as though it were Paris or Berlin. Grenades were the weapon of choice in the close-quarters fighting. As one officer said of battle: once contact with the enemy was made, "you lose control so damned fast."[73] The Canadians, surging forward in section-level attacks, smoked out the SS troops in the area several times, only to find the persistent Nazis emerging from subterranean hideouts and slit trenches to begin shooting again.

The Germans were finally cleared and the Calgary Highlanders pushed on to the small village of May-sur-Orne. The Highlanders struggled to keep formation in the dark, as German sniper teams harassed them. As dawn broke, the Calgarys were short of May-sur-Orne. The tactical situation was very unclear, and the brigadier, W.J. Megill, had little concrete intelligence because so many of the Highlanders' officers had been killed and wounded. The exploitation battalion, the Black Watch (Royal Highland Regiment) of Canada, were ready to go, but Megill feared sending them into the unknown.

No one knew what was happening at the front, but Simonds wanted to smash the enemy again. Though the Canadian general was receiving updates in his Staghound armoured car, he remained overly optimistic about the hold his soldiers had on the ridge, which was in fact very precarious. The most challenging situation was that the Calgarys had failed to secure May-sur-Orne and the Camerons of Canada had not entirely cleared the village of St. Martin. Both positions were held by enemy troops and machine-gun teams. The Black Watch, whose forward companies were already advancing into the fight, was to thread the needle between the positions.

The Black Watch soldiers had left their rear trenches at 3:30 A.M., and the men came under fire as they weaved forward over the next two hours. They kept up the advance through enemy machine-gun fire, mortars, and snipers from St. Martin and May-sur-Orne. Soon most of the company and regimental officers were down. Sergeant Benson, of the scout platoon for the Black Watch, was part of the attack and he later testified that the mass of enemy MG42s was "extraordinarily well sited for cross-fire."[74]

The operation to capture the summit of Verrières Ridge and then push into Fontenay-le-Marmion, held by elements of the German 272nd Division, seemed destined to fail. Into the breach stepped twenty-four-year-old Major Philip Griffin, a former scholar who had enlisted having almost finished his Ph.D. He was described by a fellow officer as a "brilliant officer of outstanding courage and ability." The Black Watch, strung out along a lengthy front, faced heavy fire; Griffin nonetheless rallied his men and corralled tank support.[75] The nasty situation could hardly have been worse, but Griffin was under pressure from Brigadier Megill and those higher up the chain of command to push on to the objective of Fontenay. Griffin ordered a new artillery barrage to adjust for delays at the front, although May-sur-Orne was still held by the Germans, who were sticking like a thorn into the Black Watch's flank. Around 6:30 A.M., not unaware of the grim situation, Griffin sent a patrol to investigate. It found that the Calgarys had been unable to clear May-sur-Orne and that there was an enemy machine gun there. Griffin sent a larger force to destroy it, but that too failed.

At that point, with machine-gun positions still active in May-sur-Orne and St. Martin, Griffin should have called off the advance, but he felt he needed to snatch some sort of victory. Griffin planned to continue the operation, even when Brigadier Megill came forward to discuss the degenerating situation. Megill knew the difficulties of pushing forward through a crossfire, but he did not douse the ardour of Griffin. Megill might have gathered additional artillery resources or delayed the attack until the front settled, but Griffin must have assumed that the Germans would be off balance now, although there was no evidence of such a circumstance since the enemy had been fighting non-stop for days. Megill, for his part, testified years later that Simonds pressed him onwards even though the situation "was almost hopeless."[76]

The Black Watch went forward shortly after 9 A.M., with the 1st Hussars' Shermans covering the right flank, which was open to the Germans at May-sur-Orne. "We headed for the ridge with bayonets fixed," recalled Sergeant MacGregor Roulston, who was shot in the thigh and taken prisoner. "Cruel 88 airbursts began to rain down on us with their deadly load of shrapnel."[77] Taking casualties even before they reached the start line, the Black Watch found that their own barrage failed to suppress the German fire, and most of the survivors thought that there had been no bombardment at all.[78] A more perfect killing ground could not have been devised, as the Black Watch—two companies up and two behind—moved up the gentle rise, with enemy machine guns on the ridge and on the flanks, and German forward artillery observers calling down accurate fire in broad daylight. The Black Watch did not panic, even as men were torn apart, thrown back, and taken down. As one of the German 272nd Division officers on the ridge swore, "This was a most unreal sight.... [It was] sheer butchery."[79]

About sixty of the Black Watch, including Major Griffin, made it to the top of the ridge, but then they found themselves surrounded by a dozen Panthers and Jagdpanzer IVs, a mobile anti-tank gun, as well as hordes of enemy infantrymen. They did not stand a chance. The 1st Hussars rushed forward to aid the infantry, but the hull-down Panthers on the ridge, almost impervious to shellfire, took them apart. The brave troopers died with their infantry comrades. Only fifteen infantrymen made it back to the start line, and Griffins was not one of them. Griffin was later criticized for leading the Black Watch into the killing fields, although surely the blame must also fall on Brigadier Megill and General Simonds. Much of battle is a gamble, with decisions based on unclear intelligence and the necessity of rapid choices, but Simonds encouraged aggressiveness and never fired senior commanders for thrusting forward.

JULY 25 WAS REMEMBERED for the slaughter of the Black Watch, which suffered 123 dead, 101 wounded, and 83 prisoners of war, but all the infantry and armoured units were harshly handled, sustaining around 1,500 casualties.[80] This day of battle was second only to Dieppe in terms of worst single-day losses for Canadians in the war. Simonds's men had tried to bite off the ridge and had got their teeth broken in the process.

Lieutenant-General Simonds proved himself to be particularly intransigent and inflexible in overseeing Operation Spring, refusing to modify the plan when intelligence revealed German strength and failing to increase the available firepower. A fuming Simonds, who was largely out of touch on the 25th, could only order his men forward in futile attacks, stewing afterwards in the broth of the failed battle. Much to his discredit, Simonds fired Lieutenant-Colonels Petch and Christiansen, who had saved their soldiers further losses by refusing to order a new advance in the suicidal assault on Tilly; the brigadier, D.G. Cunningham, who had already been criticized by senior British generals for his supposed caution in seeking out the enemy, was also sent packing, and replaced by the very successful and charismatic Rockingham of the Royal Hamilton Light Infantry.[81] The divisional commander, Keller, was almost fired, and the British had already lost faith in him, but Simonds held off, worried that such a move would further damage the low morale in the division.[82] Simonds also wanted to oust Foulkes, who had proven useless and dangerous, but he was talked out of it after surveying the brigadiers and finding no better replacement. Simonds's fury extended further downwards too. He heaped blame on his junior officers, which was, to the say the least, ungenerous, and it revealed his misunderstanding of the cold realities of the battlefield.[83] Simonds was hell-bent on showing his own bellicosity. However, throwing away soldiers' lives in fruitless battles made him appear careless to British army commander Dempsey and to Montgomery, who had previously cautioned Simonds about charging blindly into the enemy's strength.[84]

A handful of successful Canadian actions surfaced from the sea of defeat during Operation Spring—particularly the Royal Hamilton Light Infantry's defence against repeated enemy counterattacks. The limited gains also allowed for the unlocking of German positions in future battles. At Verrières Ridge, in the cauldron of combat, no force—American, British, Polish—could have done better. And no force should have been ordered to do what the Canadians did.

CHAPTER 9

WAR AND MEDICINE

Battlefield surgeon John Burwell Hillsman recalled the mayhem of combat medicine in Normandy, under the fall of shells, in tents close to the front:

> We saw the tragic sights from which we were never to be free for ten long months. Men with heads shattered and grey, dirty brains oozing out from the jagged margins of skull bones. Youngsters with holes in their chests fighting for air and breathing with a ghastly sucking noise. Soldiers with intestines draining feces into their belly walls and with their guts churned into a mess by high explosives. Legs that were dead and stinking—but still wore a muddy shoe. Operating floors that had to be scrubbed with Lysol to rid the Theatre of the stench of dead flesh. Red blood that flowed and spilled over while life held on by the slender thread of time. Boys who came to you with a smile and died on the operating table. Boys who lived long enough for you to learn their name and then were carried away in trucks piled high with the dead.

Hillsman's depiction of the maimed and dying provides stark insight into the horror and destruction of combat. Shrapnel, bullets, mortar bombs, and shell splinters broke bone and tore the flesh. Those who cared for the battered Canadian soldiers "became the possessors of bitter knowledge that no man has ever been able to describe. Only by going through it do you possess it."[1]

All modern armies require medical systems. Without an efficient method of clearing the battlefield and providing forward care, a soldier loses faith in his superiors and the army for failing to uphold their unspoken end of the bargain: we will fight and possibly be hurt, but you must care for us. There has always been military medicine in Canada, with surgeons attached to units while on campaign. As civilian medicine evolved, along with a greater understanding of germ theory, military medicine also improved. On August 1, 1901, the Canadian Army Nursing Service was established, and after the South African War, the Canadian Army Medical Corps (CAMC) came into existence. Then the Great War changed everything. The mobilization of resources and manpower over a period of more than four years eventually saw upwards of half of all Canadian doctors serving overseas.[2] Within that war, medical personnel encountered traumatic wounds, infectious diseases, and chemical agents. New techniques were developed in the field for cleaning the gaping holes in bodies to slow the life-threatening secondary infections prevalent in the age before antibiotics; to treat compound fractures of legs and difficult brain and abdominal injuries; and even to carry out blood transfusions. Behind the lines, clearing stations and hospitals cared for the masses of wounded. In recognition of the critical work of doctors, nurses, and orderlies, "Royal" was added to the title of the CAMC in 1919.

During the Second World War, the Royal Canadian Army Medical Corps (RCAMC) was based on a structure similar to that established during the Great War. The medical element of the division remained intimately tied to the fighting forces, with each 18,500-strong division served by three field ambulances, a main dressing station, an advanced dressing station, and casualty clearing stations. Closer to the front, each battalion had a regimental medical officer, who, with his team of stretcher-bearers, was responsible for front-line care and preventative medicine. Further to the rear were hospitals.

Physicians had learned lessons in Italy, and brought them to bear in caring for the wounded in Normandy. Despite the improvement in surgical techniques and drugs, abdominal injuries were still fatal more than 50 percent of the time, with death resulting from both the initial wounding and the subsequent infection.[3] And there remained the ongoing challenge of transporting casualties to the rear medical formations, with delays from fighting, lack of vehicles, poor roads, or overwhelmed stretcher-bearers. One of the solutions was to move critical care closer to the front, and field surgical units tried to remain 3 to 5 kilometres behind the forward lines.

With about three times as many soldiers hurt as killed, the thinly stretched medical system showed the strain.

WOUNDED MEN WERE BOWLED OVER IN BATTLE. Some described the effects of being hit by a bullet as akin to being bashed with a sledge hammer. Agony did not come first; most felt only numbness. For those soldiers not killed outright, and still conscious, the surprise of being struck down was soon replaced by dread regarding where they were injured. Men patted down their groin area to ensure, as one wounded Canadian put it, that they had not been reduced to a "eunuch."[4] If an artery was hit, a soldier could bleed out in less than a minute; there was no hope of survival. More often bullets and shell fragments tore through muscle and shattered bone, but did not deliver an immediate fatal blow. The entry wounds were often quite small, but the internal damage was extensive, and exit wounds could be as large as a clenched fist. For those who escaped a rapid death, there was a race against time to obtain medical care before they slipped into shock from loss of blood. When that happened, the final destination was likely death.

Stretcher-bearers, remarked one experienced Canadian infantryman, were the "unsung heroes of battle. In the midst of shrapnel and bullets, they went about aiding and patching up the wounded, evacuating them to safety on their stretchers. During every action, day or night, under any and all circumstances the cry 'stretcher-bearer!' brought them running. It took a special kind of man to do this kind of mercy work."[5] The stretcher-bearers, known as "medics" in the American army, exposed themselves to fire when racing across the battlefield to offer front-line care. When they found a downed man, they rifled through his pouches to find his dressing, administering their own morphine and a sip of water or rum (if there was no stomach injury). The gashes and contusions were sprinkled with sulpha powder, which reduced the chance of infection.

"The men expected us to look after them," believed Private Gerry Campbell of the Stormont, Dundas and Glengarry Highlanders, who was awarded the Military Medal for rescuing his comrades under fire.[6] The wounded were left behind as the troops pushed forward. The stretcher-bearers tried to cover the broad terrain, but in Normandy, finding the casualties in the wheat fields was no easy task. A crushed and blood-soaked trail might reveal an unconscious man, but in the chaos of battle a fallen soldier might be lost for some time. The greatest danger to the wounded came when an offensive was driven back in a counterattack. Fighting formations would move across the same battlefield where the injured lay vulnerable and where the back lines became the front lines; and then, even worse, the Germans might surge past them. These see-saw engagements were rare, but in the defeats of Operation Spring in late July, the wounded were often left behind if they could not be dragged to the rear.

The stretcher-bearers were non-combatants, but no one was safe from shelling. Corporal Norman Selby of the Queen's Own Rifles testified that on D-Day the stretcher-bearers were equipped with armbands and white helmets bearing the

Stretcher-bearers with Red Cross armbands bandage up a wounded Canadian. Rapid care for injured men was often the difference between survival and death.

Red Cross. Nonetheless, many of the medics thought, rightly or wrongly, that they were being targeted by malicious enemy snipers. Like the officers who soon learned to remove all distinguishing marks to avoid the attention of marksmen, the stretcher-bearers also sometimes removed their Red Crosses and tried to blend in with their comrades.[7] Shooting stretcher-bearers left more wounded at the front, contributed to the chaos there, and required units to either divert riflemen into caregivers or leave the casualties to slowly die in the forward zone. While some of the front-line caregivers were involved in emergency surgery—often tying off severed arteries—most sought to stabilize the wounded, offer some pain relief, and, if possible, organize parties to carry the injured to the rear. Prisoners were a source of raw labour, and while it may have felt odd to put a comrade in the hands of the same men who had been trying to kill him only minutes earlier, most prisoners were anxious to assist because it made them useful on the battlefield. As unarmed prisoners moved to the rear through smoke and fire, many were cut down by oncoming waves of advancing Canadians—who in the confusion, and with adrenaline pumping, shot first and rarely asked questions. Prisoners carrying the wounded were clearly distinguished from combatants and, at the same time, were an unmistakable asset. The destination for the wounded, no matter how they got there, was usually the battalion's medical officer.

The medical officer, a trained doctor, tried to stabilize the wounded and prepare them for evacuation to the rear. Mangled bodies, fractured skulls, and crushed legs were bound and splinted to reduce pain, but battlefield amputations were rare, and patients had a greater chance of survival if such work was done in surgical formations to the rear. The screams, moans, and cries rose and fell in the make-shift medical areas that could be anything from old barns to a protected reverse-slope dugout. It was common, remarked Private George Couture of the Royal Winnipeg Rifles, for men to wail for their mothers.[8] Private Ben Mackereth of the North Shore Regiment was shot in the leg and hit in the shoulder with shrapnel on D-Day. Left in a collection area and largely abandoned because the medical services were overwhelmed, Mackereth recalled, "Two of our small group died in the early afternoon. It was a relief to the rest of us when one of them passed away. His moans and groans were getting on our nerves."[9] Mackereth's callous observation rings with authenticity. It took all day for the wounded to be cleared, and by then several other men were close to death. As Mackereth was taken into a tent to be operated on, he wondered why some of the more grievously injured were not cared for first. A stretcher-bearer replied, "They're set aside because the doctor reckons they're past saving. They'll probably all be dead by morning."[10] Mackereth survived his ordeal and even returned to battle in August, as a stretcher-bearer. He understood that harsh choices had to be made in managing the avalanche of bloodied men.

THE PROCESS OF EVACUATING injured soldiers to the rear usually involved a jeep ambulance, although trucks and universal carriers were also used. The robust jeeps had been used profitably in Italy to transport the wounded, and were later modified to allow for stretchers to be placed on the roof. But this design was found to leave already weakened men too exposed to the hot sun or driving rain, so an extended canvas-covered rear area was added. Whatever the vehicle, the pitted and shell-pocked roads left patients in agony from the constant jarring of broken bones and internal injuries. Along the way were casualty clearing posts, where the stretcher-bound patients might sometimes be deposited to allow the larger field ambulances to transport more patients to the next link in the medical chain.

Field surgical units were the sites of desperate battles for life, and few days passed without a steady trickle of the wounded. During sustained firefights, long lines of bloodied soldiers formed outside the medical tents. Doctors, orderlies, and nurses studied the casualties, and their rough notes were usually written on a wound tag. They were ranked according to priority of treatment, with most of the pale-faced bleeding cases receiving plasma or blood transfusions. Official reports noted that most patients required an immediate two to three pints of blood to keep from slipping into shock.[11]

Patients often suffered from multiple bleeding wounds that looked as if someone had taken a meat cleaver to their flesh. Traumatic amputation from whirling metal or high explosives required immediate surgery. Arms, legs, hands, and feet were often blown away or remained attached by only a few strands of muscle. In other cases, the blast from high explosives could injure a man without leaving a scratch, as internal organs collapsed when struck by a wall of compressed air moving at several times the speed of a tornado. Canadian nurse Nora Cook, from Lindsay, Ontario—one of 2,263 nurses serving overseas—described the flood of patients: "It was so tragic, all these boys with arms and legs blown off. You can't explain what it's like to try and deal with all these casualties. They were filled with shrapnel and had every imaginable injury."[12] One study of 1,688 casualties in Normandy found that 15 percent of the casualties had wounds to the head, 8.5 percent to the chest, 5 percent to the abdomen, 31 to the upper extremities, 28 to the lower extremities, and a mere 2.7 percent to the back.[13] Captain W.W Middleton, a battlefield surgeon from Bruce County in southwestern Ontario who served in a Canadian field hospital throughout Normandy, noted of the men's injuries, "Every man seems to have at least three, and what wounds they are! Great masses of muscle and flesh torn to bits. One wonders how the human frame can stand so much."[14]

Caked in gore and mud, with pants often filled with their own feces, patients slipped in and out of consciousness, alternating between nightmare-filled delusions and their new horror-filled reality. Dirty uniforms were cut off. Anaesthetists offered some relief from the pain. Surgeons opened up men with precise cuts, searching in body cavities to find steel fragments as lives drained away. The ground was soon littered with bandages and gauze, remnants of patients past and present. Thousands of black flies, drawn to the gore and excrement, swarmed the area.

By the time of the Normandy battles, experience had revealed that wounds should be excised freely, with dead skin cut away and the area cleared of pulped muscle to reduce the chance of infection. The Thomas splint, developed during the Great War, was useful in reducing fatalities as it immobilized high breaks on the femur. Abdominal and chest injuries were operated on as soon as possible, for wounds became infected the longer

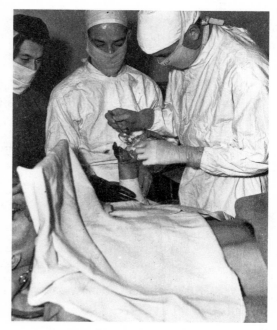

*Canadian surgeons operate on
a wounded Canadian.*

they went untreated, and even the new antibiotics could not kill all the bacteria in festering cavities.

For patients on the table, lacerated openly or bleeding internally, plasma and blood transfusions were essential and saved countless lives. The technique of transfusion was pioneered in the later part of the Great War and honed by Canada's Dr. Norman Bethune in the 1930s in Spain and China. Blood transfusions saved the lives of many exsanguinating patients at the field surgical units. Plasma—a dried blood compound that looked like cornflakes before it was mixed up—was less effective than whole blood, but it could be stored for longer and it reduced the risk of passing on infections such as syphilis or malaria. Life flooded back into the cadaver-like patients; the wounded described how they shivered as the refrigerated blood coursed through their veins. Nursing Sister Margaret Carruthers, who served at multiple clearing stations and hospitals, remarked, "When you give blood to an unconscious patient and you can't get their pulse and can't get their breathing, and you wonder if you're wasting this precious blood, and half an hour later they sit up and say, 'When do we eat?' That's the most rewarding work you ever, ever do!"[15]

Penicillin, which was first introduced on the battlefield in Italy in January 1944, was a new super-drug. Jagged pieces of metal or bullets dragged filthy bits of uniform into the body, and many wounds became infected. Throughout the war, anti-gas gangrene serum, tetanus toxoid, and sulfanilamide were used to combat the spread of infection, but penicillin, which consisted of cultured mould, was a significant step forward in saving lives. At the start of the war it had initially been so rare that patients in hospitals given the drug had their urine collected to extract the penicillin for reuse; now, in Normandy, it was more readily available and thousands were saved. The dark, viscous serum, injected with large needles into the backside of a patient, smelled like manure and caused considerable pain to recipients. As battlefield nurse Betty Dimock remembered, the patients "just screamed."[16] The skewering was hard on the patients and the nurses, but penicillin saved lives.

The RCAMC treated 84,000 patients, achieving a 93 percent survival rate for wounds and 99.91 percent for victims of disease.[17] As in previous wars, many soldiers hemorrhaged to death before reaching medical care, but if they made it to the operating table they had a high chance of survival. Infantryman Irving Penny reflected appreciatively on the critical role played by the doctors and nurses, noting, "They gave life and a future back to the gravely injured men."[18]

ALMOST ALL OF THE SURGEONS AND DOCTORS carried out their work plagued by exhaustion, and during the big rushes anyone who had ever held a scalpel operated on the wounded. Medical officer Stephen Maley was no surgeon, but he soon qualified for certain procedures and he worked on all who came across his table, often in "18 to 20 hours shifts."[19] At the height of the Normandy battle, Major Gerald Petty of No. 33 Field Dressing Station had only just sat down after three days of non-stop surgery and care for the injured when a shell arrived in the midst of the tents. He staggered to his feet and tried to kick awake his senior medical orderly, but the man slept like he was in a coma. Walking like a drunk man because of the fatigue, Petty moved towards the dust from the nearby shell explosion that had landed square on a truck, later recalling, "I saw six bodies without heads, and scattered everywhere like a mad dentist's surgery there were bits of jaw with teeth attached, curved bits of skull bone, bits of brain, with blood and hair attached to bits of scalp."[20] He steadied himself and set to work on the survivors.

Field surgeon Angus Campbell Derby was part of the first Canadian advanced surgical unit to land in Normandy, and he witnessed the rush of casualties in the late July and early August battles. As the tents were filled to capacity, patients waited in the hot sun, forming a checkerboard of stained stretchers. Derby noted candidly, "It was impossible for our staff to deal with this large group of wounded. Casualties died from lack of care—from bleeding to death from lack of a tourniquet, from respiratory failure for need of a needle in their chest, from profound shock from lack of resuscitative fluids. These were devastating experiences—ones I shall never forget."[21]

With the doctors and surgeons so hard pressed, recovering patients were not always monitored with vigilance, and some men succumbed to their wounds because of shortages in medical personnel. Those losses were slowed with the arrival of the dedicated nurses who assisted in surgery and cared for patients in post-op. Changing bandages and watching for complications, they also administered morphine when it was available. For the injured who were stabilized, the nurses offered a smile, a kind word, or a cigarette. Such generosity profoundly affected the wounded, afraid and far from home. Many of the nurses took on the task of writing to families, informing them of a man's injuries and, sometimes, his last words. It was heart-rending work, and it couldn't have been more important. Sydney Frost, an Italian campaign veteran who was in the hospital for malaria and later wounded in battle, felt that the nurses were "a secret morale builder.... Not enough can be said about these angels of mercy. Many a soldier survived the war due to their care and devotion, above and beyond the call of duty."[22]

"SOME OF THE FELLOWS I know that have been on the wrong end of a terrific shelling are now as jumpy as cats even at our own guns firing," wrote Cape Breton Highlander Lieutenant Reg Roy. "It is only natural that a soldier is one hell of a lot more nervous when he comes out of a shelling than when he went into it."[23] Physical

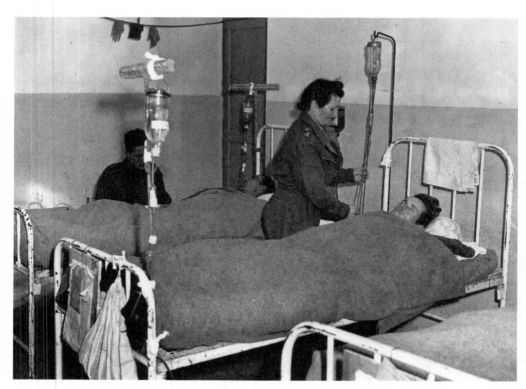

A nurse cares for Canadian patients at No. 1 Field Surgical Unit.

wounds were of immediate concern for the medical services, but the doctors and nurses also treated psychologically traumatized patients. Each soldier had his breaking point. The medical literature from the Great War, the interwar period, and the early part of the Second World War tried to pinpoint mental inferiority or emotional defects in those who succumbed to shell shock or battle stress. It was eventually recognized that even the most ardent warriors could break down under the unnatural strain of harsh living, constant stress, poor food, lack of sleep, and appalling carnage.[24] "Each time a man goes through an ordeal," reported one medical officer in Italy, "though he overcomes fear and does his job, the memory or the effect of the ordeal is pushed into his subconscious and the gate is barred and guarded by will. But the day comes when there are too many ordeals; the will breaks and the gates fly open and fear and torment come swirling through."[25] Canadian medical officer J.W.B. Barr claimed that the experience of battle was a "form of extreme bodily and emotional stress" that had to be treated early with "physical rest, adequate diet, and ample clean drinking water."[26] Yet even with this better understanding of the strain at the front and its impact on soldiers, it was not easy to pull exhausted men from the line when everyone was in the same state. Nonetheless, good leaders and officers watched out for those on the verge of collapse and tried to cycle them to the rear. One study of American combatants revealed that large numbers of men in infantry battalions—perhaps a quarter of the total strength—were unable to return to active service but were not reported in casualty lists.[27] They did other less stressful jobs behind the lines and out of the forward rifle companies. At the same time, cycling out exhausted but experienced officers, NCOs, and other ranks was a recipe for future disaster, as these were often the most effective warriors at the front.

Over time, battle exhaustion diminished the fighting efficiency of Canadian units. During the Italian campaign, 5,020 casualties were labelled as "neuropsychiatric," amounting to 16.9 percent of the total casualties.[28] In Normandy, the psychological casualties accumulated from June 6, with two front-line doctors reporting that "a few days of heavy shelling and loss of comrades brought home the grim reality of combat, and in many cases brought on shakiness under fire."[29] A soldier's limited reserves of endurance began to seep out of him like sweat, and it was increasingly difficult to restore, with each new incident further wearing him down. By late July, 17 officers and 506 men from the 3rd Division, which had been in battle since June 6, had been diagnosed with battle exhaustion. No. 1 Canadian Exhaustion Unit was overrun with patients, especially during the supposed "down time" after the major engagements, when survivors had time to reflect on the accumulated mental trauma. One of every four non-fatal casualties in Normandy was attributed to battle exhaustion.[30]

Mild cases of battle stress were largely the result of sleep deprivation; however, more intense cases included concussions to the brain or severe psychic damage. Jack Leddy, a medical officer in a casualty clearing station, was an eyewitness to the behaviour of psychologically traumatized men: "Some of them had seen their buddies blown to smithereens. They would be picked up wandering around on a road or huddled by some tree. They were brought into the station, where we had set up a special ward for them. They would be crying hysterically or just sitting and staring into space. There were those who trembled and shook uncontrollably. They were in shock but with no visible wounds."[31]

An injured Canadian is evacuated back to England. Note the wound tag on him, providing his medical information.

While "shell shock," "battle stress," and "cracking up," all served as shorthand for the condition of succumbing to the stress of sustained combat, the military and medical command settled on "battle exhaustion" as the official term. It relieved the need for a soldier to prove whether he had a legitimate injury, and it suggested that soldiers might be returned to the front after some rest. Sleep was a chief component of healing the bodies and spirits of the warriors. Sedatives such as sodium amytal could knock a man out for 24 hours or longer. Lessons from earlier in the war had revealed that patients kept close to the front—within earshot of the explosions—recovered more rapidly than those sent far to the rear. The soldier could regain strength and return to his unit; far to the rear, the sacred link with the unit was broken, and there was less incentive for men to recover. The medical officers and padres offered therapeutic talks to the worn-out soldiers, in order, as one Canadian officer remarked, to "restore courage to go back and take part in a dangerous and deadly existence."[32] There were some malingerers—men avoiding their duty and the danger—but most patients were genuinely depleted. Yet even when battle exhaustion was identified and treated, it was not easy to overcome. Statistics shifted between theatres of war and intensity of fighting, but only about 40 percent of the soldiers returned to full duty.[33] Those who could not regain their mental health, or who had received a shock to the brain, were sent to the rear, usually in the Canadian Army to No. 1 Neurological and Neurosurgical Hospital, also known as "No. 1 Nuts."

As in the Great War, both the stick and the carrot were used to restore men. The military, with its hierarchical system based on obedience, was inclined to threaten and punish those who could not function. As the number of battle stress casualties rose, the RCAMC was criticized by the army command, and especially by Crerar and Simonds, for being too lenient with the men. The generals wanted the soldiers sent back into the line, particularly since the Normandy fighting was so costly among the infantry battalions and there was now a shortage of trained riflemen. Many of the doctors resisted the orders and evacuated hundreds of men they judged unable to return to combat. There are no records available on how many soldiers were returned to their units, only to break down again. As one eight-month veteran of the Italian campaign testified after being sent back to his regiment, "I just never could be responsible in a tight place again and I know it."[34] He was not alone. A tension remained—at times expressed in open disputes—between the medical services and the high command, as many medical officers saw the soldiers' responses to death or maiming as entirely rational.

"WE ARE NOT CONCERNED with the ultimate reconstruction of the patient," said one Canadian front-line surgeon. "We are only concerned with getting the kid out of here alive enough for someone else to reconstruct him."[35] Men with severe wounds were sent back to Britain by air lift or by hospital ship. Nurse Harriet Sloan, who served in France with No. 8 Canadian General Hospital, recounted the devastating sights, with some of the worst being maxillofacial injuries. "These were dreadful wounds to the face. They would have a part of their jaw shot away. They wouldn't have a tongue. They'd, perhaps, be very badly burned in a tank."[36] Soldiers with trauma to their bodies often required multiple surgeries, needed time for bones to heal, and ran the risk of secondary infections.

By March 1944, there were 10,000 Canadian hospital beds in England in a series of stationary hospitals along the coast, in towns on railways lines, and in rural areas. There were also long-term convalescent homes. The goal of the military was to return the men to health, and then to their units. Some, of course, would never fight again, and would face a new battle in rehabilitation. William Newell of London, Ontario, a mere nineteen years old when he was wounded in Normandy, reflected on his time in hospital: "A young lad was in the bed beside me. He was seventeen. He had his right leg off. The fellow on my other side had both hands off. Those were the kind of things you ran into in the hospital. The young lads with shock in their eyes."[37]

Nursing Sister Mary Bray was shaken by the broken boys she cared for, describing many as "like young children." She hated the dawning awareness "that even with surgery some wounds were too horrific to ever heal. It was hard to accept what war can do."[38] Kay Poulton, a twenty-three-year-old nurse from Moose Jaw, Saskatchewan, who aided the recovering Canadians, recalled, "It was rather earth-shattering for me. There were these young boys with the arms and legs off and all sorts of other horrible injuries.... Despite this, we had few deaths in our hospital, and we were proud of the record. We had a group of dedicated doctors and nurses who worked like dogs and of course by this time, we had the new wonder drug penicillin."[39] In the Great War, even minor wounds often became infected, and therefore soldiers were lost to their units for lengthy periods. Now, with penicillin staving off most infections, the wounded men were more rapidly returned to the front.[40]

Comrades in the field wrote letters to the injured. When Queen's Own Rifles infantryman Stan Biggs was shot through the leg at the end of August 1944 and recovering in hospital, one of his decorated mates told him that he should not hurry back: "You've got a wife and two kids to think about. You've done your bit for the infantry. If you did get back to the unit you wouldn't recognize anyone. Most of the comrades we knew are either dead or wounded or promoted higher."[41] Biggs's injuries were serious enough that he never returned to the firing line, but thousands of other Canadians did, to support their mates, to follow orders, or to finish the war.

THE GUINEA PIG CLUB was an organization of which no one wished to be a member. It consisted of burned servicemen of the Commonwealth air forces and some tank crews, and the name came from the multiple operations that members underwent to graft new skin over their burns. In July 1941, as reported by a doctor, one of the burned patients, "who'd had ten operations and perhaps was feeling a bit down, said they were nothing but a plastic surgeon's guinea pigs."[42] The name stuck and the Guinea Pig Club was formed, eventually claiming 590 members, including 170 Canadians.

The colossal advances in medicine and care ensured that many men survived what before the war would likely have been fatal wounds. In the Great War, burned soldiers often succumbed to infection and gangrene. Now, new treatment and drugs kept many alive, and the challenge was to remake faces and bodies out of the melted-wax-like

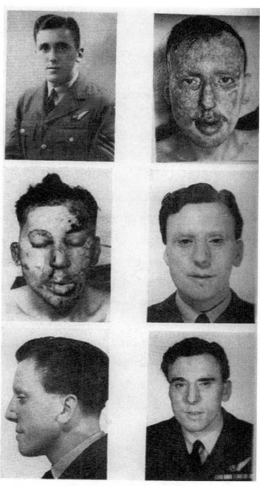

A member of the Guinea Pig Club, as pictured through several restorative surgeries.

skin and fire-scorched extremities. Tannic acid assisted in the immediate recovery process, with burned men spreading the jelly on their skin that soon hardened to a cement-like substance; it lessened the opportunity for infection and offered some relief from the pain. Yet many of the airmen and tankers, the two groups of warriors most likely to receive burns, had little skin left that had not been burned off. Trooper Al LaRose of the Sherbrooke Fusilier recalled with horror the fighting in Normandy and his attempts to pull comrades from burning Shermans: as men cooked alive and he tried to wrench them out of the turret, the burnt skin pulled off upraised arms like plastic wrap.[43]

Most of those who survived their ghastly wounds were treated at Queen Victoria Hospital, East Grinstead, south of London, where reconstructive surgery attempted to give them back some semblance of normality. Sir Archibald McIndoe, a driven and short-tempered New Zealander, was a leader in the field, pioneering plastic surgery and skin grafts for men who had lost large patches of their hair, ears, eyebrows, lips, and skin.[44] The cutting-edge facility at East Grinstead also had a fifty-bed Canadian section run by Wing Commander Albert Ross Tilley, another expert in rebuilding burned bodies, and a medical magician in rehabilitating claw-like burned hands. Tilley was recognized with an Order of the British Empire in 1944, and after the war he set up a practice in Kingston, Ontario, and taught the first plastic surgery course at Queen's University. "Restoring faces and hands took as much as five years," wrote Tilley. "Five to 40 operations were required."[45]

The airmen's and troopers' burns were often catastrophic, reducing the skin to a rubbery texture as the fire melted hair follicles, sweat glands, and nerve endings. Often eyelids had burned away. Scarred and disfigured, and often in terrible pain, warm saline solution baths reduced some of the agony and assisted in skin regrowth. Undamaged skin from parts of the body were also grafted to burned areas. In this way, noses were created from the skin of the forehead or the buttocks. One of the strangest-looking techniques used the tube-like pedicle, made from a patient's own grafted skin, which allowed healthy blood to rejuvenate burned areas and those with new grafts. After several weeks, the pedicle was cut away and the damaged area was much improved. However, it took months, sometimes years, to reconstruct the shiny skin, gnarled hands, and scarred faces. Many, of course, never recovered.

LANCE-BOMBARDIER LESLIE JAMES was badly injured in Italy while driving a truck that set off a Tellermine, blowing the vehicle into a roadside ditch. The truck's fuel tanks ignited and James was pinned in the cab. He was finally rescued but was close to death. Another gunner, John Matheson, found himself in the same hospital as James after a shell exploded over him and steel fragments tore through his helmet and into his skull. Matheson sought out James to offer him some comfort. Despite his own terrible wounds, including paralysis from the waist down and with a right-sided hemiplegia (paralysis of the right arm and leg), Matheson was always badly shaken by visiting the man he remembered as virile and athletic. "With no nose, no hair, no ears—his eyes and mouth were slits—he was terribly hard to look at. His hands were mere stumps."[46] These were not easy visits. Following his thirty-ninth surgery, James died of his grievous burns and secondary complications. Matheson partially recovered from his serious injury, although he wore steel leg braces his whole life. Returning to Canada, he practised law and served as a Liberal member of Parliament from 1962 to 1968, a position that allowed him to play a critical role in the adoption of the Canadian flag. James was cruelly cut down in his prime; Matheson helped shape Canada. That was their war.

CHAPTER 10

THE DRIVE TO FALAISE

"Our own operations are rendered extraordinarily difficult and in part impossible to carry out [owing to] the exceptionally strong and, in some respects overwhelming, superiority of the enemy air force," Field Marshal Erwin Rommel reported in a cable to Berlin early in the Normandy invasion.[1] Though Allied fighters and fighter-bombers had a difficult time destroying fortified German units, they were deadly when deployed against transport vehicles and troops in the open. Canadian Spitfire pilot Al McFadden observed that the fighters were most effective against soft-skinned trucks on the roads: "When you come down to strafe a vehicle like that, you are a one-man execution squad. There is no escaping."[2]

Spitfires went in search of trouble, but often did not find it as the Luftwaffe was all but shattered, and so they spent most of their flight time, along with the fighter-bomber Typhoons, seeking ground targets. German flak guns sent up a stream of shellfire. Even a single hit on the fragile fighters was usually enough to send it into a death spiral. Lieutenant Ed McKay, who survived ninety-five sorties in Spitfires and Typhoons over France, recalled, "Our casualties were extremely high. More than ninety percent of our losses were due to flak. We would go to a target to dive-bomb it. We'd approach it at about ten thousand feet, in line astern, or echelon right, to the right of the leader. The leader would, once we'd identified the target, he would say, 'Going down.' He'd roll over on his back and we'd all follow, one after the other, and dive on the target, and pull out at about three thousand feet. But the minute we rolled over, the flak would open up. Many times we had a hard time seeing the target, the flak was so thick. We'd go through layer after layer of flak."[3] The flak fire got its victims, but the Spitfires and Typhoons continued their aerial assault against the ground forces.

And the Allied air forces had spectacular triumphs against the Germans throughout the Normandy campaign. On June 10, General Geyr von Schweppenburg, commander of Panzer Group West, was wounded, and seventeen of his senior staff knocked out, when Ultra intercepts identified his location and his headquarters was bombed by seventy-one bombers and Typhoons. The decapitation strike disrupted command and control, especially in the British and Canadian sector, leaving enemy armoured reserves uncoordinated for a number of days. Other German senior officers, including the commanders of the 12th SS, 77th Division, and 243rd Division, were killed by aerial bombs.

Arming up a Typhoon fighter-bomber. Note the .50-calibre shells being fed into the machine guns and the rockets underneath the wing.

Typhoon fighter-bomber taking off and looking for trouble in France.

Even more significant was the July 17 patrol by Charley Fox, a twice-decorated Canadian Spitfire pilot, who flew with RCAF's No. 412 Squadron. As he circled the French countryside looking for targets, he spotted a black German Horch staff car travelling at high speed along the road below: "I maintained steady, level flight until the vehicle passed us at 9 o'clock. I then began a curving, diving attack to my left, with my number two following to watch my tail. The other two aircraft maintained their height, keeping an eye out for enemy activity. I started firing at approximately 300 yards, and hit the staff car, causing it to crash. At the time, I had no idea who it was ... just a large black open car ... gleaming in the sun without any camouflage, which was unusual."[4] The next day, it was reported that Field Marshal Erwin Rommel was strafed by a Spitfire and severely wounded. It happened at, of all places, Ste. Foy de Montgommery—the namesake of his arch enemy. The loss of Rommel, whose skull was cracked in four places, was a severe setback to the enemy high command, and although other fighter pilots claimed to have shot Rommel, Fox was in the right

The Allies won command of the air before the D-Day invasion. These Germans are doing what most did in Normandy: scanning the sky anxiously for Allied planes.

place at the right time. Rommel never recovered from his wounds and he committed suicide on October 14, 1944. The field marshal wanted to avoid a show trial and death sentence after he was implicated in the July 20 plot to assassinate Hitler.

Command of the air gave the Allies an enormous advantage, and while the vast majority of sorties did not lead to the shooting of German generals, every damaged train and blasted truck demoralized the enemy. "The fighters were good," observed Lieutenant Ronald Shawcross. "We loved to see them coming in over us."[5] The Typhoons and Spitfires buoyed the morale of the Canadians on the ground, who cheered wildly as they witnessed enemy positions strafed with fire or blown skyward by high explosive bombs or rockets. Such attacks, one officer wrote with genuine feeling, were "a beautiful sight."[6]

Airpower did not win the battle in Normandy, but in combination with the other arms it eroded German combat effectiveness. John Fitzgerald, a decorated RCAF gunner who flew in a Lancaster in No. 166 Squadron, RAF, apologized in an August 17, 1944, letter home for not having written more over the preceding months, but claimed it had "been absolutely impossible to write [since] we have been operating steadily with no time in between flights except to sleep. We are on now but there is a time between take off so I can dash off this letter.... We have been doing a few battle front trips and it was really a pleasure to do them." Fitzgerald and his crew were killed before the end of the month, but he was right in noting to his parents that they had been "knocking the living daylights out of Jerry."[7]

A French train destroyed by Allied airpower.

"AT TIMES IT SEEMED that the Normandy battle would never end," felt a weary John Gray, an intelligence officer at II Canadian Corps.[8] The horror show at Verrières Ridge revealed that the enemy was far from breaking. Following orders from Hitler not to give an inch of ground, the German forces in Normandy prepared for the renewed Allied onslaught. Too weak to drive Montgomery's armies back, and unable to give up terrain to gain advantage of time or space, the Germans seemed doomed. But dislodging them would entail a bashing, especially on the Anglo-Canadian front, where most of the best German divisions were situated. Matters were made worse for the Germans when the long-delayed American Operation Cobra was finally launched on July 25 against weak opposition. After a week of fighting, on July 31, Bradley's U.S. First Army captured the important town of Avranches, through which ran many crucial roads. General George Patton's newly activated Third Army, on the western flank of the Normandy battlefield, kept the momentum going. The long-awaited breakout was fast becoming a breakthrough, and the Germans were in danger of being enveloped.

To meet that threat, the German commander in the west, Field Marshal von Kluge, sought to retreat to more secure positions, but Hitler denied his request. Instead, the Führer ordered his generals to shift forces from the Anglo-Canadian front to shore up the crumbling defence against the Americans. In early August, von Kluge moved several of his elite panzer divisions to form a six-division corps to stop Patton. However, Ultra intercepts and aerial intelligence revealed the manoeuvre, and the Americans hammered the Germans from the air as they were forming their armoured fist. When the Germans finally attacked on August 7, there was no panic among the GIs. The Germans were butchered and broken at Mortain and other battlegrounds. Patton galloped off again, his army eating up kilometres of terrain in the big push to encircle the remaining Germans.

With Patton sweeping south and eastward and the Anglo-Canadian divisions poised to advance southward, the two major Allied pincers were closing in on the Germans. The German armies—the Seventh and the Fifth Panzer—had to retreat, but by this point in the war the generals were thoroughly cowed by Hitler, who, after the failed July 20 assassination plot by his own officers, had blood in his eyes. Those senior staff who spoke of retreat were considered defeatist at best and traitorous at worst. Some generals half-heartedly applied Hitler's insane demand that not only should the German forces fight to the last bullet and last man; they should even attack into the bulge that was forming in the Allied lines.

As the Americans were pressing into Brittany and St. Lô, Montgomery ordered a multi-division Second British Army offensive on July 30, known as Operation Bluecoat. Six infantry and two armoured divisions were cobbled together to blast their way to Falaise in the hope of catching the Germans when they were off balance and moving troops to the American front. But the British attacked on too narrow an axis, and the armour did not make it far before lead units were devastated by anti-tank fire. The infantry, now largely unsupported, did not thrust very hard past the burning tanks. The thousands of resulting British casualties revealed that the German guns and terrain favoured the defenders, even though they were spread thin.[9] While Montgomery's army were unable to hack through the weakened enemy lines south of Caen, the general felt he had the tiger by the tail, and on August 4 he advised the First Canadian Army to prepare a new thrust down the main Caen-to-Falaise high-way. If the Canadians could break open the enemy lines, their hammer would smash

The Germans fought tenaciously in the defence, although they were slowly driven back in prolonged fighting.

down against the American anvil, catching and destroying the two German armies caught between them.[10] Yet the Canadians would have no more formations available than the British had for Bluecoat, and they would be fighting against a far more desperate enemy that was facing annihilation.

THE FIRST CANADIAN ARMY was ready to strike on August 8. General Harry Crerar's army headquarters was finally activated on July 23, nearly a month after this had been planned, as Montgomery had actively delayed Crerar's crossing over to France, hoping that somehow Simonds would be given the army command.[11] He was not, and now Crerar commanded three Canadian divisions, with additional British and Polish divisions. Crerar had an uneasy relationship with his Canadian corps commander, Guy Simonds. The two had clashed in Italy, and Simonds wore lightly his ambitions to rise to army commander. Crerar had no better relationship with his British I Corps commander, Lieutenant-General J.T. Crocker. Taking his lead from Montgomery, who openly disrespected Crerar as an inexperienced desk soldier, Crocker refused a direct command from Crerar on his first day as army commander. Crerar, who was trying to find his own feet in France while suffering from illnesses contracted during his time in Italy, condemned Crocker's action in writing.[12] The usually politically smart Crerar might have found a more diplomatic way to deal with his difficult subordinate, but few army commanders would have tolerated such insubordination. Nonetheless, Montgomery's opinion and treatment of Crerar were not improved by the incident. Indeed, as one of Montgomery's staff officers observed on a more general level, "I feel Monty was astonishing in his relationship with all the Dominion troops. He ordered them around like British troops, ignoring the devolution of the British Empire ... he was completely out of date."[13] It was Crerar who had to manage Monty's difficult manners and ways, and he did, although it was a bruising task and there would be other challenges as the war progressed.[14] In the end, Monty felt that Crerar was to blame for Crocker's insubordination—surely

General Harry Crerar, commander of the First Canadian Army. Crerar had little battlefield experience when he arrived in France to command in late July, but he was an able manager of his generals and a key lynchpin between the Canadian authorities in England and his troops on the ground.

an odd reading of the situation—but he told the two generals to get along. They did.

In early August, Simonds's II Canadian Corps planned the operation to strike southward. Confident in his well-honed abilities, Simonds gathered intelligence documents and appraisals from his staff officers and subordinates and retreated to his private caravan to forge the plan. Operation Totalize was audacious and aggressive, much like the general who conceived it. It would manifest as a deep armoured thrust through the guts of the Germans. The drive from Caen to Falaise would take the Allies through rolling farm land, winding roads, and small villages, all protected by German guns and tanks.[15] The Canadians were trained by the British to engage in a planned set-piece battle, often on a limited front that emphasized firepower over manoeuvre, but in response to the debacle of Operation Spring, Simonds shuffled the tactical cards and looked for a better hand.

Simonds planned for a surprise night attack. But this was no engagement of surgical cuts. The Canadian general ordered bomber blows against enemy defences, and a continuous pounding during each phase of the action. While Bomber Command was wary about conducting any sort of tactical bombing, Crerar's headquarters convinced the RAF to assist in softening up the enemy lines and cordoning off the battlefield with bombs.[16] When Simonds explained the plan to his senior staff, especially the nighttime armoured thrust, they sat in stunned silence. One of them finally remarked that this had never been done before; to that, Simonds sharply replied, "That's why I'm doing it."[17]

An attack through darkness might initially surprise the enemy, but Crerar and Simonds still struggled with how to get their ground forces through the enemy defence-in-depth that was protected by multiple gun screens. To assist in closing the distance with the enemy rapidly, Simonds arranged that improvised armoured personnel carriers would transport the infantry into battle. First Canadian Army's Royal Canadian Electrical and Mechanical Engineers converted seventy-six Priests—the M7 self-propelled 105mm howitzers—into armoured personnel carriers that carried a ten-man infantry section. With the gun removed and an armour plate put across the aperture, the carriers were known slyly as "defrocked" Priests or "Holy Rollers," and later as Kangaroos (suggesting empouched infantry). A comparison of casualties sustained by infantry regiments riding in the Kangaroos and by those that travelled

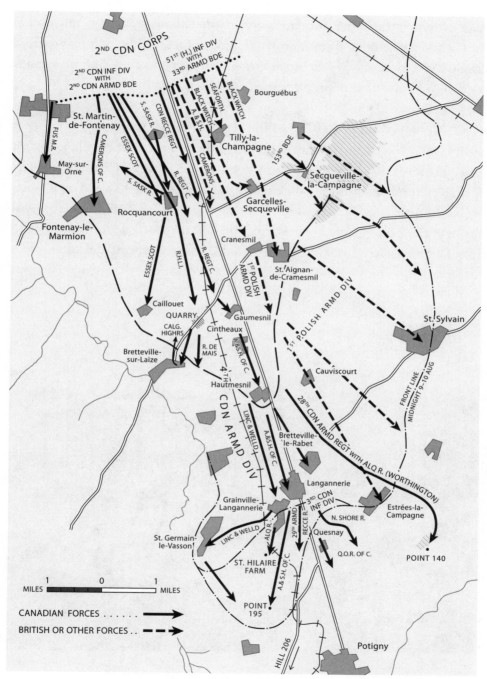

2ND CDN CORPS

51ST (H.) INF DIV
WITH
33RD ARMD BDE

2ND CDN INF DIV
WITH
2ND CDN ARMD BDE

FUS M.R.

St. Martin-
de-Fontenay

May-sur-
Orne

Fontenay-le-
Marmion

S. SASK R.

CAMERONS OF C.

ESSEX SCOT

CDN RECCE REGT

S. SASK R.

R. REGT C.

BLACK WATCH

SEAFORTH

BLACK WATCH
& S.H.

CAMERONS

Bourguébus

Tilly-la-
Champagne

Rocquancourt

ESSEX SCOT

R.H.L.I.

R. REGT C.

Garcelles-
Secqueville

Cranesmil

1ST POLISH
ARMD DIV

St. Aignan-
de-Cramesmil

153RD BDE

Secqueville-
la-Campagne

St. Sylvain

Caillouet
QUARRY

CALG.
HIGHRS.

Cintheaux

R. DE
MAIS

Bretteville-
sur-Laize

Gaumesnil

A. & S.H. OF C.

Hautmesnil

4TH

CDN ARMD DIV

LINC & WELLD.

A. & S.H. OF C.

1ST POLISH ARMD DIV

Cauviscourt

FRONT LINE
MIDNIGHT 9–10 AUG

28TH CDN ARMD REGT WITH ALQ R. (WORTHINGTON)

Bretteville-
le-Rabet

Langannerie

Estrées-la-
Campagne

POINT 140

Grainville-
Langannerie

St. Germain-
le-Vasson

LINC & WELLD

ALQ R.

29TH ARMD

RECCE R.

3RD CDN
INF DIV

N. SHORE R.

Quesnay

Q.O.R. OF C.

ST. HILAIRE
FARM

A. & S.H. OF C.

POINT
195

HILL 206

Potigny

1   0   1
MILES   MILES

CANADIAN FORCES . . . . →

BRITISH OR OTHER FORCES . . ⇢

OPERATION TOTALIZE, AUGUST 7–10, 1944

outside without steel protection later revealed that those marching suffered much higher losses.[18] Simonds's innovation saved lives, but he also thought that speed and aggression would be the key to victory; there would be "no holding back, and ... every division must press on, regardless of casualties."[19]

SIMONDS'S PLAN CALLED FOR A THREE-PHASED OPERATION, beginning with a nighttime foray by the 2nd Canadian Infantry Division and 51st Highland Division, who would break through the forward crust of the enemy defences on Verrières Ridge. The second phase, during the daylight hours of August 9, would see a renewed effort by the 4th Canadian Armoured Division and 3rd Canadian Infantry Division to the next ridge line situated on Hautmesnil, and then a final effort further south. Simonds worried about his forces being stranded in the Germans' defensive grid and so he ordered a second bomber strike for the 9th, to shock the enemy. Finally, the

Canadian Kangaroos filled with infantrymen before Operation Totalize, August 7, 1944.

third phase would see the 1st Polish Armoured Division finish the thrust to Falaise. It was an ambitious and complicated plan that involved five divisions plus auxiliary forces and committed over 100,000 troops to a narrow battlefield.

In early August, and in preparation for the full offensive, Major-General George Kitching's 4th Armoured Division, which consisted of armoured and infantry formations like its sister 5th Armoured Division in Italy, captured a number of small villages to prepare for the attack. Kitching had only limited command experience, having flubbed a small raid in Italy in January 1944 before being sent to England to

Two Vickers machine gunners of the Cameron Highlanders of Canada fire at the enemy.

take over the division. He was lucky, however, to inherit some experienced officers from Italy, who helped to calm the raw troops before their first battle. Nonetheless, many were shaken as the units formed up in the apocalyptic remains of blackened and twisted tanks and vehicles, and near the shallow graves of their comrades-in-arms—all reminders of Operation Spring.

Totalize was set for midnight on August 7. Stockpiles of more than 150,000 gallons of gasoline and 200,000 shells were stacked in mountains.[20] The 51st Highland Division and 2nd Canadian Infantry Division were set to attack along the Caen-Falaise highway, driving to a distance of 7 kilometres before the second phase commenced. Opposite the Canadians was the 89th German Infantry Division, which had recently arrived from Norway and consisted of eight battalions, largely of non-German troops (and therefore seen as less reliable). Yet it was backed by the usual assortment of mortars, artillery, multi-barrelled Nebelwerfers, and about sixty 88mm anti-tank guns.[21] This "ring of steel," noted Major D.W. Grant of the Toronto Scottish Regiment, would be exceedingly hard to break through.[22] Equally troubling, the 1st and 12th SS Divisions, both formidable forces despite the 12th SS being down 85 percent strength to some 2,000 fighting men—although supported by 76.tanks and assault guns—were close enough to rush in reinforcements behind the 89th.[23] Simonds was aware of the strong German defences, and he hoped that the several planned bombing runs would "destroy or neutralize enemy tanks, anti-tank guns, and mortars," while a rapid advance would close the distance with the enemy guns and allow for the breakthrough.[24]

Because of the limited number of roads, Simonds's corps would advance like a steamroller, in six columns (four Canadian and two British), with about 200 vehicles and tanks in each formation. Nose to tail, and only about 15 metres wide to accommodate four vehicles abreast, the columns looked like gargantuan metal centipedes. "As far as the eye could see were armoured vehicles stretching for two miles towards the slopes behind Verrières," observed one officer of the Fort Garry Horse.[25] The snaking lines were an enemy gunner's dream target, although with the thousands of motorized vehicles churning up the earth, the entire front was covered in a gargantuan dust cloud.

As the last rays of the long summer day faded, engines started in an unholy clatter, and the columns set off around 9 P.M. towards the start line, about 1.5 kilometres away. Above them a roar filled the night sky as 1,019 Lancaster and Halifax bombers passed over the battlefield, dropping the high explosive bombs on forward and flank targets that were lit up by the Pathfinders. Around 11 P.M., the ground rumbled from the impact, and dust was thrown hundreds of metres into the air; however, as with all bombing, more trees died than enemy personnel.[26] In the aftermath of the aerial hammering, the Allied guns opened up in a complex barrage at 11:43 P.M., allowing the Allies to push on to Rocquancourt, Fontenay, and Cintheaux on the right side of the dividing road to Falaise, and to Garcelles-Secqueville and Lorguichon on the left.

The gloom of darkness, dust, and defensive smokescreens was cut by searchlights and tracer fire. Into this destruction went the columns, almost blind, with no idea if the enemy had survived and, if so, where he was located. Each column had flail tanks at the front beating the ground with their chains in search of mines. The procession moved in lurching starts and stops in the lowest gear, trying to keep up with the creeping barrage that marched off at 100 metres a minute towards objectives more than 6,000 metres away. Some shells fell short into the columns, due to faults in the rounds or worn-down gun barrels, leaving burning vehicles jamming up the columns until they were rammed off the road. Other vehicles that were pushed out of the line or that drove off mistakenly in the wrong direction were sometimes fired on by the column, which mistook them for enemy tanks. Chaos ruled. All of the Allied soldiers were used to friendly fire, as demoralizing as it was, and later operational reports found that at least 7 percent of identifiable shell fragments removed from British and Canadian casualties had come from Allied ordnance.[27] Private Elmer Allard of the Algonquin Regiment, who was hit with shrapnel in the shoulder a few days later, recounted that "it was just like the end of the world."[28]

The three lead infantry battalions of 4th Canadian Infantry Brigade of the 2nd Division—the Royal Regiment of Canada, the Royal Hamilton Light Infantry, and the Essex Scottish Regiment—were borne forward in the armoured Kangaroos. Men sat sweating, fingering their weapons, staring in silence or praying. While riding in the armoured vehicles was safer than being outside, the infantry had no control over their destiny, could see nothing, and could only wait in dread for each lurching stop, at which point they hoped the Kangaroo was not being sized up by an enemy gunner. It was the stuff of bleeding ulcers.

"We had fought our way through the night under incredible conditions," remembered Corporal Bruce Evans of the 1st Hussars. "Tanks were on fire; smoke and dust from the fields clouded our vision."[29] Delays were inevitable as commanders were knocked out, wireless radios were rendered useless with maddening frequency, and formations were scattered in the firefights. But the armoured thrust continued through the wreckage until dawn at about 5 A.M. The 4th Brigade had secured its objectives with few casualties.

On the 6th Canadian Infantry Brigade's sector, the enemy put up a stiffer defence, and the winding and cratered roads were difficult to navigate. Enemy anti-tank guns fired into the column and forced a mad scramble and dismounting of the infantry. With little time to organize the attack, the South Saskatchewan Regiment was shot onto the target by Canadian gunners, and the Regina Rifles swept through the village of Rocquancourt. Elements of the German 89th Division, fortified on Verrières Ridge, especially in strongpoints on the reverse slopes, escaped the worst of the artillery bombardment. Les Fusiliers Mont-Royal (FMRs) and the Cameron Highlanders of Canada were forced to clear May-sur-Orne and Fontenay-le-Marmion in fierce fighting. Battles over the same villages that had eluded the Canadians' grasp during Spring were now won. With the Canadians blasting forward, Lieutenant-Colonel Mel Gordon, commander of the Sherbrooke Fusilier Regiment, wrote after the war that the road to Falaise looked open "and we had more Germans behind us than we had in front of us."[30]

THE FIRST PHASE of Totalize was a success, with much of the German front lines broken by 6:30 A.M. on the 8th, including the previously impregnable Verrières Ridge. Hundreds of prisoners trickled back to the rear, and more than 2,000 from the 89th Division were in Canadian hands by the next day.[31] The armoured formations saw daylight and looked to roll down the Falaise highway, but traffic congestion slowed everything and eliminated the chance for a hell-for-leather charge. Simonds's second phase, the armoured thrust, was set for about six hours after the completed first stage, and was to follow another bomber operation a little after noon. The pause was too long. While Simonds had felt it necessary to build in time for potential delays, as well as to clear the road for the new Polish and Canadian armoured divisions passing through the 2nd Canadian Infantry Division, the Allies now had no means of exploiting the situation without advancing down the road and being hit by the bombers. It was also too late to call off the aerial strike. The exploitation phase, based on set-in-stone plans, prevented Simonds's forces from capitalizing on the initial shock, and one Canadian armoured officer described the delay as akin to "stopping to water the horses in the middle of a cavalry charge."[32]

The delay gave precious time to the Canadians' old nemesis, the 12th SS Panzer Division. The Hitlerjugend had been decimated in fighting since June, but it remained an elite force, equipped with over a dozen self-propelled guns, a brigade of Luftwaffe 88mm flak guns, and more than fifty tanks, including ten formidable Tigers. Even as fuel shortages plagued the panzer divisions by late July—a testament to the effectiveness of the Allied bombers in damaging trains, roadways, and bridges—the Germans gathered what they had for short counterattacks.[33] Moreover, much of the artillery from the shredded 89th Division survived and was now at the disposal of 12th SS commander Kurt Meyer, who set about shifting units on the morning of the 8th to block the advance southward.[34]

The Germans' feared Tiger tank. Larger and more powerful than anything the Allies could put into the field, the Tigers were relatively few in number but fierce in battle.

By 12:30 P.M., battlegroups had already begun to throw themselves at the Allied drive to slow it down, with German tank ace Major Michael Wittmann—one of the most celebrated tank commanders of the war, with 143 kills—leading seven Tiger tanks against the Canadians. The Tigers and supporting Mk IVs were a terrible threat, but Major Radley-Walters of the Sherbrooke Fusilier had organized a number of camouflaged tanks to lie in wait for the advancing Tigers, each one locked and loaded with an armour-piercing round "up the spout." Tension mounted as the Sherbrooke Fusilier and Northamptonshire Yeomanry tanks, their commanders' vision limited and their ambush site potentially jumped by other German tanks moving through their positions, finally opened fire at 500 metres. The terror of the Western Front, the Tigers, were caught in a crossfire, their superior guns and armour negated by the skilful British and Canadian tactics. Wittmann, wearer of the Knights Cross, was killed during the clash, likely by a Canadian shell, and four other Tiger tanks were destroyed. It was a crippling blow.[35]

Tank battles raged up and down the Anglo-Canadian sector, and not all were as successful as the Radley-Walters ambush. Battle is fickle, and victory on one front can occur while another group suffers defeat. For instance, a handful of Panther tanks got into the midst of Bren-gun carriers of the Royal Regiment. The Canadians suffered heavily and retreated, but an artillery forward observer with the Royals, Captain William Waddell, guided a number of Sherbrooke Fusilier Shermans back to the enemy and orchestrated the Panthers' destruction. Though these German attacks had little chance of reversing the advance, they slowed the Canadians, forced them to dig in, and bought time for Meyer to form a new line of defence.

When the lead Canadian and Polish armoured divisions moved out again in the early afternoon, they faced a prepared enemy. Any chance of surprise was lost, but Simonds hoped the second phase of the aerial bombardment, coming in waves from 12:30 P.M. to 1:35 P.M., would again soften up the enemy. Three of the four groups of bombers hit their targets, but the fourth one, composed of American B-17 bombers, dropped their loads short, right into the Canadian and Polish lines. Twisted and blackened vehicles were strewn about the landscape. Dismembered bodies lay unidentified. Among the post-bomber craters, a soldier, on fire, was seen by many stunned survivors, running through the area.[36] More than 350 Canadian and Polish troops were killed or wounded, including divisional commander Rod Keller. Rumours inflating these numbers and the impact of the bombing circulated throughout the Canadian Corps.[37] There were even stories that the Germans had hijacked the bombers. "I've seen blood and death on the battlefields but not as concentrated as that day," wrote Captain Harold Macdonald to his wife after tallying the thirty-seven killed and seventy-eight wounded in his North Shore Regiment. "When we got up you could reach out anywhere and pick up limbs. It was frightful and I know our men would have killed those pilots if they had been available.... However that is just another of those bad dreams we go through and forget."[38]

This was a poor start for the Allies, and especially the raw 4th Armoured Division, which had taken over after chainsawing through the enemy at Cintheaux, Gaumesnil, and Hautmesnil. Advancing into the enemy lines, the division engaged in skirmishes throughout the day. Black smoke rose from burning vehicles shrouding the sky and infantry and grenadiers fought to the death in the wheat fields. Canadian tanks charged to cover, either in undulations in the ground or small forests. Herbert Danter, a gunner with the 23rd Field Regiment, employing self-propelled guns, recalled the "mad dash chasing the remnants of the German army (and they were powerful remnants)," as well as the "oppressive heat, the choking, blinding dust, and especially the stench of rotting bodies."[39] While the sharp-end forces were awash in violence, the traffic again snarled behind the lines; Bruce Hunt, another Canadian gunner, admitted that the parking lot of vehicles created a "curious apathetic" situation among the huge line of tail units that could not see what the teeth was biting. "There is no special feeling of a surge to victory, no sense of impending triumph."[40]

The melee was confusing as the fog of battle descended over those farmers' fields. Commanders in the rear barked over the wireless, exhorting the tanks to crash forward, but that meant rolling into minefields and the anti-tank guns, which, as one Canadian trooper remarked, "filled everyone with dread."[41] By the end of the 8th, the Polish division was held up on the left flank by anti-tank fire from St. Sylvain, which had wrecked more than forty tanks, and the Canadians—the Argyll and Sutherland Highlanders assisted by the South Alberta Regiment—pushed to north of Hautmesnil. The Canadians had not reached their final objectives, which included Bretteville, Quesnay, Point 195, and Potigny.

UNSATISFIED WITH THE DAY'S PROGRESS, and aware that the Germans were rushing reinforcements to the front, the hard-thrusting Simonds ordered his friend, Major-General George Kitching, to attack through the night until Bretteville on the left side of the Caen-Falaise road was in his hands, and then to press further on

5 kilometres to Point 195, a high point overlooking the town of Potigny. It was the right call by Simonds, who knew the lead elements were tired but had to press on to give the next day's operation some chance of success. Two battlegroups set off, with Halpenny Force, consisting of the Lake Superior Regiment and the Grenadier Guards' tanks, capturing Bretteville by dawn. The second formation, Worthington Force, was commanded by Lieutenant-Colonel Don Worthington, commander of the British Columbia Regiment, whose Shermans, along with two companies of infantry from the Algonquin Regiment, set out for Point 195.

Worthington Force pushed off in the dark, with few landmarks to guide its way and with a heightened fear of running into an enemy ambush. Long-range fire occasionally raked their line of tanks and trucks. They moved quickly toward their objective and turned east to avoid German guns in Bretteville, which was being cleared by Halpenny. But in the confusion, the column lost its way and mistook one dirt road for another, sending Worthington east of Point 195 to Hill 140, about 3 kilometres beyond the Caen-Falaise road. Without the benefit of aerial observation, Worthington and his officers had no way to correct themselves in the gloom. The armoured and infantry force dug in on Hill 140, in a rectangular laager, weapons pointing outward on the high ground, a little before 7 A.M. The contingent was lost—about 6 kilometres from their objective at Point 195—and, even worse, they had penetrated the front line of the 12th SS.

Meyer reacted to the news of a large Canadian tank force in his lines by immediately ordering a sustained attack backed by every available gun and mortar. The Canadians had set up a slit trench defence in the 90-by-275-metre rectangular field, and had tried to get the Shermans hull-down to present less visible targets, but they had no artillery. Throughout the morning of the 9th, the German guns hurled high explosives and shrapnel at the isolated position. Outgunned, Worthington called in artillery fire, but it was directed against non-existent targets at Point 195, because that was where both the gunners and Worthington thought he was located. Later in the morning, while he continued to take heavy fire, Worthington's communication was severed, leaving him further isolated.[42]

The Canadians held on, even as they were hammered with shells from three sides. They defeated several counterattacks by Panther tanks and grenadiers, but took heavy losses. German staff officer Captain Bernard-Georg Meitzell observed, "One Canadian tank after another was knocked out and ended in smoke and flames."[43] By about 10:30 A.M., half of the Canadian Shermans were burning and the entire hilltop was scored with shell craters and blackened grass. With Worthington's force bottled up, the enemy artillery fire simply smashed back and forth. Even slit trenches offered little protection. Twenty-four-year-old Private John Patterson of the Algonquin Regiment, a former CPR clerk in Fort McNicoll, Ontario, described the tanks burning around him: "It was a horrible thing to see. Once they were hit they would brew up, and you could see the guys trying to crawl out of them, and a lot of them were on fire."[44] The smell of burning flesh wafted over the front. Morphine for the wounded was soon used up; and then the water was drained too. The infantry clawed deeper, shrapnel bursting above their heads, hedges and trees exploding around them. Patterson and his chum Larry O'Callaghan, a string-bean of a man, were hugging the earth in the same slit trench: "One minute he was there," wrote Patterson of O'Callaghan, "and the next I looked over and he was lying dead."[45]

Worthington Force endured the blitz throughout the day, fending off Panthers and then Tiger tanks. Never had a unit faced such armoured strength on such a limited sector. To add to the misery, two roaming Typhoons were attracted to the conflagration and fired on the Canadians, unsure of what was happening in the chaos and smoke below. Worthington's officers were eventually able to call them off with identifying smoke, but the Typhoons, who returned throughout the day to fire at the Germans, did surprisingly little damage to the enemy. Moreover, with the Germans bunched up in a target-rich area, the failure of cross-service communication is clear in that more fighter-bombers were not sent against the enemy position.

By late afternoon on the 9th, most of the Canadian tanks were in ruins, with shells cooking off in a deadly display of fireworks. Worthington sent the last eight Shermans to retreat and run the gauntlet to safer ground. It was clear the softer-skinned vehicles had little chance, as a few hours earlier half tracks displaying Red Crosses and carrying the wounded had been fired upon and several destroyed.[46] The garrison defenders slowly used up their ammunition and rooted among the dead and wounded for anything that could be used in the Alamo-like last stand. Worthington was killed around 5:30 P.M. by a mortar bomb, and a final push by the Germans at last light overran the ragged Canadian force. Small groups of Algonquins snuck away in the twilight carrying wounded comrades. For the dozens more who surrendered to the 12th SS, it must have been a terrifying prospect, considering the take-no-prisoners history of the Nazi youth, but there were no recorded cases of post-battle executions. The final casualty figures are stark evidence of the relentless battering the Canadians endured: 47 tanks wrecked, 112 casualties sustained by the British Columbia Regiment, and 128 Algonquins killed, wounded, or taken prisoner.[47]

It was not until late on the 9th that Kitching realized that Worthington was fighting his own separate and now lost battle, and that the reinforcements he had ordered to support them were now in the vanguard to seize Point 195. It would be wrong to blame Kitching for losing his soldiers, but more bad luck followed, and the Governor General's Foot Guards that Kitching had sent forward were held up by snipers and then also got lost in the Normandy countryside. With Point 195 needing to fall to remove German observers directing their guns from the surrounding area, the Argyll and Sutherland Highlanders, drawn largely from Hamilton, Ontario, crept onward in the early hours of the 10th without a backstopping barrage. The battalion commanding officer, Lieutenant-Colonel Dave Stewart, personally led his men up the hill, surprising and defeating a small German garrison. As Stewart recalled later, "You can't win battles being behind."[48] It helped that Worthington Force, during its fated stand, had siphoned off enemy strength and artillery power.[49] The Argylls' capture of Point 195, which was occupied and fortified during the 10th, also revealed that not all operations required the artillery hammer. Innovation and drive still counted for something in the killing fields of Normandy, although the Argylls relied on their guns—from the battalion's support weapons, the Governor Generals' tanks, and artillery—to hold off several enemy excursions during the rest of the day.

"Everything in war is very simple," goes the old maxim, "but the simplest thing is difficult." Such was the case with Simonds's plan for Totalize. The destruction of Worthington Force exposed the profound confusion of battle and the danger inherent in confronting the 12th SS, but other Canadian units continued to gain ground on the 10th. However, by the next day, German defences stiffened and all hope for surprise was lost. Any attack would now be more costly in terms of lives expended.

In Totalize, the Canadians advanced some 13 kilometres until Simonds called the operation off on the morning of the 11th. The battle saw some 600 Canadians killed, but it was estimated the enemy lost more than 3,000 men.[50]

Simonds was frustrated by the inability of his divisions to achieve a breakthrough. He studied and attended to his maps, calculating and measuring the Germans' ability to hold out, almost willing victory into being. He felt let down by his soldiers. Yet it was the plan that was too complicated. Perhaps an all-out blitz southward, with no stop or pause for rigidly timed phases, might have allowed the Canadians, British, and Polish to take advantage of the momentary confusion in the German lines. But that type of armoured spearhead might also have met its doom in other ways had it been held up in the German defensive grid, especially if the Canadian infantry had been left behind. Simonds hoped to give the troops at the front a better chance than those who had been mangled in Spring. While the friendly-fire bomber attacks slowed the full potential for exploitation, Totalize also achieved one of the deepest penetrations of German lines in Normandy to that point.

PATTON'S ARMY WAS MAKING good progress as it swarmed southeastward towards Argentan. It was coming around the southern flank of the Germans, which were increasingly trapped in a pocket on three sides, shaped like a squashed letter "C" tilted upwards, with the Canadians and British exerting pressure from the top. If the fourth side could be closed by the Canadian, British, and Polish divisions driving south to Falaise, two German armies of twenty-one divisions would be encircled and destroyed. Reacting to Hitler's demented order that his two armies stand their ground and not retreat, Montgomery urged the ground forces onward. Generals Crerar and Simonds planned another operation, this one known as Tractable, which would see the Canadians steamroll to Falaise through the Laison River valley, a depression that had some rough, wooded areas but was generally open ground and suitable for an armoured thrust. Infantry carried in Kangaroos would support the 2nd and 4th Armoured Brigades that were formed into two large 150-tank squares, which were to lurch forward on August 14.

Even with the Germans in a desperate situation, the Allied inter-army rivalry reared its ugly head. General Omar Bradley, commander of the U.S. 12th Army Group, harboured a fierce mistrust of Montgomery, with bad feelings over the old slights from the British general during the Sicily campaign and, more recently, believing that the egotistical commander had not pulled his weight in the Normandy fighting. Even though Patton's army was crashing ahead from August 10 to 12, on the night of the 12th, Bradley ordered Patton to halt his advance at Argentan, the boundary separating the American and Commonwealth forces.[51] Bradley might have finished off the Germans if Patton had continued his drive, but he chose to be careful, perhaps spiteful, and not a little bit stupid. Montgomery, too, was unsure of his own mind and seemed little interested in what Bradley was doing. At this stage, he expected many of the German divisions to escape, and he aimed to destroy them further north when they were caught against the Seine River. Montgomery did not provide Crerar with any additional British formations—not even the 7th Armoured Division, which was within range to strike—to close the gap.[52] While all of this muddling about was going on, the flow of information back to Eisenhower was too slow for him to keep a tighter rein on his warring generals, who had lost sight of the goal of the campaign in their mistrust of one another. In the end, it fell to the Canadians to capture Falaise and the surrounding region to fully envelop the two German armies.

In the lead-up to Operation Tractable, the Canadians scrambled to move into the line and shore up shattered units, but they were ready at zero hour, a little before noon on the 14th. Simonds had held a stormy pre-battle meeting, at which he demanded that his armoured commanders be more aggressive. Betraying his tendency to blame his troops, the general suggested that tank squadrons in Totalize had been too cautious.[53] The harsh rebuke from Simonds did not go over well with the armoured officers, who well remembered the smouldering Shermans and the fire-shrivelled corpses of their comrades.

The Canadians continued to vastly outnumber the German 89th Division opposite them, which was supported by the remnants of the 12th SS, with the 85th and 1st SS divisions in the vicinity. At the spearpoint were two Canadian armoured brigades, the 2nd and 4th, followed by waves of infantry and self-propelled guns. The rear-echelon formations would be cycled through to press home the attack, but success at the front was needed first. The previous four days, from August 11 to 14, had witnessed battalion-level skirmishes across the Canadian sector, as elements of the 2nd Canadian Infantry Division cleared a number of enemy positions that jutted into the start lines and could have caused holdups by laying down enfilading fire.

Simonds ordered another heavy bomber operation on the enemy lines, and at 11:42 A.M. on the 14th, the Allied artillery guns opened up. The ground rumbled and some 300 tanks leapt forward in a tight series of columns to overwhelm the enemy gun screen before it could stop the assault. The artillery bombardment was a sonic stabbing, and soon dust blanketed everything, with the bright noonday sun reduced to a quivering red globe in the murk. The Canadians advanced en masse in a steel charge. The German 88mm and 75mm guns took out a number of tanks, but the weight and speed of the thrust soon overran the enemy lines. The Canadians also used the feared Wasp, a flame-thrower mounted on a universal carrier. The Wasp was especially useful for clearing defenders from fortifications, and it caused widespread terror.[54] Behind the armour, the infantry pushed head-long, foot to pedal, but were forced repeatedly throughout the battle to dismount from their armoured carriers to snuff out areas of resistance that were bypassed by the lead formations.

The Canadians pushed on to the Laison River, but intelligence officers had mini-mized the body of water as an obstacle, and the tanks soon found its steep banks impossible to climb. Elements of the German 85th Division, a combat-hardened unit formed around a nucleus of Eastern Front veterans, alongside 1st SS Panzer Corps, were dug-in deeply. Many of their defenders and anti-tank guns were overrun north of the Laison River, but now the Canadian tanks milled about looking for ways across the obstacle. The Fort Garry Horse found a crossing but lost eleven of its nineteen tanks in the running battle.[55] Follow-on tanks, armoured vehicles, and self-propelled guns became bogged down, forced to trade fire with the enemy's anti-tank guns across the river.

The northern river bank became a tank graveyard. At the same time, a traffic jam extended back from the Laison. The situation was made worse when the 4th Armoured Brigade's Brigadier Eric Booth was killed by shellfire, and confusion reigned after his death. All across the front, officers were knocked out, adding to the tumult over where the armoured formations should engage, which was further exacerbated by poor inter-unit communication.

After the disaster of Totalize's short-bombing, a new system was put in place that called on ground forces to alert the bombers with smoke. But in a cringe-worthy mistake, the Pathfinders leading the bomber stream were not informed of the army's use of yellow smoke to warn off the bombers, and their own target markers were yellow. A little after 3:00 P.M., at 15,000 feet, the bombers could not distinguish one from the other, and seventy-seven Halifaxes and Lancasters, including forty-four RCAF bombers from No. 6 Group, dropped their payloads short.[56]

Nineteen-year-old Corporal Jack Martin of the Queen's Own Rifles watched the bombers fly towards them, and then, to his horror, saw the bomb doors open. Thousands of men dove for cover, finding ditches and holes, or digging into the ground with bleeding fingernails. As the terrible seconds ticked off, those who remembered their training opened their mouths so their eardrums did not burst when the bombs detonated. As the bombs struck, the ground for kilometres around the zone buckled and the oxygen was temporarily sucked out of the entire area. Groups of soldiers and vehicles were wiped out of existence. A regimental aid post near one of the bomb blasts was buried by a mushroom-cloud of debris: "There were legs, and arms all over the place," recounted Corporal Martin.[57] Dazed soldiers stumbled among the dismembered bodies. Other soldiers were killed with barely a scratch on them as the explosion ruptured internal organs. A number of soldiers had their lungs collapse; in one medical unit, sixteen of the twenty soldiers died as they slowly asphyxiated from what the doctors called "blast lungs."[58] Around 150 Canadian and Polish soldiers were massacred by the aerial fratricide, and another 241 were wounded.[59] Captain T.J. Bell of the 12th Field Artillery, who received the Military Cross for bravery, reflected on the disaster that killed 21 of his comrades and injured another 46: "It is difficult to write coherently about the catastrophe as only those who have seen from a thousand feet bomb bays open and bombs head straight for them, can appreciate the fear with which most of us cowered in our trenches."[60]

The Laison bombing was not an isolated event, although it scarred almost all those who survived, leaving many soldiers "bomb-happy" and unable to function.[61] A First Canadian Army report issued in the aftermath listed 52 cases of friendly fire by RAF, RCAF, and American air forces between August 16 and 18, which resulted in 72 men killed, 191 wounded, and numerous vehicles demolished.[62] The bombing enraged the ground soldiers, but it also provided some indication of the effectiveness of the bomb loads against the Germans when they were caught in the open.[63]

DESPITE THE BOMBING INCIDENT and the struggle at the Laison, the Canadian advance southward continued on the 15th. The Shermans of the Grenadier Guards and the British Columbia Regiment almost made it to the prize of the long ridge to the north of Falaise, but they were driven back in combat. To the west, the 3rd Canadian Infantry Division's infantry regiments surged forward, also closing on Falaise, metre by metre.

The German high command knew the Allies were slowly pinching their forces out. With Patton's divisions set to encircle them from the south and the British, Canadian, and Polish army driving southward to Falaise, Field Marshal von Kluge was frantically trying to pull back the remnants of the Seventh and Fifth Armies. Yet the Führer continued to refuse to hear any talk of retreat for the 100,000 or so Germans in the Falaise Gap. Questioning Kluge's commitment to finding a way to deliver a victory, Hitler sent one of his most trusted commanders, Field Marshal Walter Model—known as the "Fire Man" because he raced from one compromised sector to another—to stiffen the defence. Kluge committed suicide as the debacle played itself out, and the fierce Nazi Model soon confirmed what all the other generals knew. He ordered a retreat from the slow-forming trap, and on the 15th, the Germans began their race to avoid annihilation.

As Model's armies finally started to run, Montgomery did nothing to urge on the Americans in the south to close the trap. Nor did he commit his three divisions—the 11th Armoured and the 59th and 53rd Infantry Divisions—all within striking distance, as were other American and French divisions, to support Crerar. Exhibiting a grand failure of vision, Montgomery did not grasp that tightening the noose on the Germans was possible. Matters were not helped by Montgomery remaining out of touch with Crerar, whom he had largely ignored throughout the campaign and whom he had consistently condemned in reports to his seniors as not "fit for command." While Crerar was not privy to Monty's damning assessment, he noticed the cold shoulder. To his credit, Crerar took the snubs without complaining to his political masters, who might have intervened and further bothered the already worn-down British general. The Canadian army commander was also wise not to interject himself deeply into the battle unfolding, and he continued to allow Simonds, who had a very good grip on things, to plan and execute the operation. With Crerar's agreement, Simonds ordered a renewed attack, pushing Foulkes's 2nd Canadian Infantry Division to take Falaise, and Kitching's 4th Canadian Armoured Division to the east to catch those Germans who were fleeing the city and surrounding region.[64] Even farther eastward, in a widening half circle, the 3rd Canadian Infantry Division punched forward, with the 1st Polish Division on the far left flank, to capture Trun.

The town of Falaise was defended by a garrison of 200 Waffen SS Grenadier troops from the 12th SS, along with anti-tank guns and two Tiger tanks. They were to hold on until death. As one Canadian official report noted of the 12th SS troops, "The Pte [private] soldiers were fanatics, and had been convinced by their Offrs [officers] that if caught they would be shot. They neither ran nor surrendered."[65] Bombers had already pulverized the town, but the Nazi survivors simply dug deeper into the rubble. The Canadians closed on them in the late afternoon of the 16th, with the South Saskatchewan Regiment and Queen's Own Cameron Highlanders fighting through the suburbs and capturing key bridges to allow the tanks of the Sherbrooke Fusilier to bring essential fire to bear. Throughout the night and into the 17th, the Canadians cleared house after house. But it was not until the 18th that the FMRs, in a final grinding battle, broke the last resistance of the Waffen SS troops who had holed up in a girls' school in the southern part of town. The 12th SS fought almost to the finish. Only two soldiers emerged. The taking of Falaise on August 18 opened up the road to cut off Germans to the south—troops that were propping open the corners of the closing trap against Anglo and American forces. Field Marshal Model realized that the clock was ticking for his overextended twenty-one German divisions in the pocket, which was now only 56 kilometres deep and 20 wide.

WITH 100,000 ENEMY SOLDIERS trapped in a confined space, Allied fighters and bombers made mincemeat of the retreating Germans, raking the jammed roads with rockets, cannon-fire, and high explosives. From August 18 onward, hundreds of Spitfires, Mustangs, and Typhoons flew operations over the battlefield, firing off all their ammunition before heading back to their airfields, where they refuelled and rearmed for another round of shooting fish in a barrel. The RAF claimed to destroy or damage 112 enemy tanks and 3,057 transport vehicles in the third week of August.[66] Though many of these vehicles survived the shellfire and bomb blasts, the carnage on the roads was terrible. In the Falaise Gap, by battle's end, the Allies located 7,576 smashed or abandoned enemy vehicles and innumerable horse-drawn carts along the funeral-pyre roads.[67] While there were only 150 abandoned tanks and anti-tank guns, and few appeared knocked out from the air, the wreckage of the soft-skinned vehicles had clogged roads and shattered morale. This was how armies died.

The August sun baked the dead and wounded, and the stench wafted for kilometres. The only escape route for the Germans was along the valley leading to the opening between Trun, St. Lambert-sur-Dives, and Chambois. It was here that the Canadian 4th Armoured Division tried to close the gap. The German forces, fighting for their very lives, were not going to go down without a battle. For those who faltered, the discipline of the revolver was a means by which to stiffen resolve, and Waffen SS troops murdered hundreds of demoralized and deserting regular army soldiers. As German turned on German (and on the other conscripts from occupied nations who were press-ganged into the ranks), the now desiccated 12th SS continued to block the Canadian and

German wreckage on the roads leading out of the Falaise Gap. These trucks were caught by Allied airpower.

Polish advance, giving their lives to purchase time for the exodus.[68] Notwithstanding their fanaticism, one of the 12th SS staff officers recalled, "Nobody doubted any longer that we were doomed to be killed or captured one of these days."[69]

Montgomery, Crerar, and Simonds would have liked to have seen a more rapid advance by the Canadian and Polish forces, but those at the sharp end faced a tremendously complicated and dangerous environment. The Germans had few coherent units in the direct Canadian path, but pockets of resistance, from machine-gun nests to snipers, claimed lives. Sergeant Doug Conklin of the Stormont, Dundas and Glengarry Highlanders remembered sacrificial snipers who tied themselves up in trees to "hold us up," and who required time-consuming stalking before they were eliminated. After the war, Major V.O. Walsh of the Sherbrooke Fusilier observed, "We were slow—no question. The men were tired then and the infantry needed reinforcements."[70] But slowness—if such a thing can be measured—saved lives. By August 15, the Canadian infantry battalions, never numbering more than about 7,500 in a division, were short 2,644 men.[71] Paul Fussell, an American soldier in Normandy and a postwar academic, quoted one Canadian during the war, who said, "Who the hell dies for King and Country any more? That crap went out in the first world war."[72] In the face of the step-by-step costly engagements, the front-line soldiers and tank crews, in regiments that were decimated and exhausted, quite rightly made their own decisions on how willing they were to risk their lives to quicken the pace.[73] There were no mutinies, but caution was the watchword.

Trun fell to the Canadians on the 18th, and the next day Polish and American divisions joined hands at Chambois, closing the gap on the Germans while the Canadians were nearing their final objectives. Though it might have appeared on the maps at the various national army headquarters as if the bag was closed, on the ground only the lightest membrane of Canadians and Poles blocked the fleeing Germans. Over the next three days, the Canadians, caught in the avalanche of desperate humanity, captured and killed thousands of panicked Germans who flooded over their lines.

Some of the most intense combat occurred at St. Lambert, around 3 kilometres southeast of Trun and a main escape route for the Germans, with two roads leading to bridges over the Dives River. A battlegroup of the South Alberta Regiment, led by

Major David Currie, and a company of the Argyll and Sutherland Highlanders of Canada seized the town on the 19th. "There were thousands of Germans in various stages of organization and disorganization struggling to get through," wrote Private Arthur Bridge of the Argylls, "and we were right in their way."[74] Clinging to key crossroads and buildings, Currie's men led a heroic blocking action against enemy forces that dwarfed them in size and strength.[75] As the town burned, German bodies piled up through and around the town. Major Currie was in the forefront of the battle, directing the defence, situating machine-gun teams, and even using his Sherman tank to lay down fire on the exposed enemy. In describing Currie's fearless leadership, one of the Canadians noted, "We knew at one stage it was going to be a fight to the finish, but he was so cool about it."[76]

Two additional Canadian companies from the Lincoln and Welland Regiment and the Argyll and Sutherland Highlanders of Canada filtered in on the 19th to withstand against the enemy horde. Currie narrowly avoided death several times, and

The outnumbered and outgunned Canadians fought a brilliant backing action in St. Lambert. This is a burning Sherman, likely from the South Alberta Regiment.

even took on and killed a feared Tiger tank. When Currie and his small force were finally relieved on the 21st, they had fought for three days and nights straight. "Tired and hungry, we left behind a scene of death and destruction that is hard to imagine," recalled Arthur Bridge, who would continue to fight with the Argylls along with his older brother Ralph. Both survived the war.[77] As Canadian trooper Ray Lane testified, "It is hard to get a clear, intelligent picture in my mind of the events.... I can't get it all in proper sequence. It was such a blur of burning tanks, dead bodies, wounded being carried off on stretchers, desperate faces of Germans wanting to surrender, angry faces of SS soldiers trying to prevent it—shooting their own countrymen. For our own safety, there was no time to be selective. We had no choice but to shoot everything that came at us. There was killing and being killed at an unprecedented rate. The enemy, however, was the big loser."[78] Major Currie, lean, tall, and haggard, never let up. His battlegroup captured and killed some 2,000 Germans, and Currie was awarded the Victoria Cross.[79]

Major David Currie, on the left holding the revolver, led the Canadian battlegroup in St. Lambert that killed, wounded, and captured some 2,000 fleeing Germans. For his inspired leadership, Currie was awarded the Victoria Cross.

German units coordinated attacks from outside the Falaise trap in a breakback operation to cut through the Polish sector and allow thousands of troops to escape on the 19th, but by the 21st the cauldron was reinforced and the will of the enemy to fight had been smashed. After seventy-seven days, the Battle of Normandy was over.

CLOSE TO 8,000 DESTROYED, damaged, or abandoned German tanks, trucks, and guns lay in the Falaise Pocket. There were also about 10,000 dead Germans. General Dwight Eisenhower visited the battlefield, and while he had seen much death in his life, he was shaken: "It was literally possible to walk for hundreds of yards at a time, stepping on nothing but dead and decaying flesh."[80] It would take teams, largely composed of prisoners of war, weeks to bury the thousands of dead. Some of the disgusted soldiers in the area took to wearing their gas masks to deaden the stench.

The Canadians' hated adversary, the 12th SS—known even among German troops as the "murder division"—was wiped out, reduced to ten tanks and a few hundred men. Meyer escaped, but he was taken prisoner in early September and would later be convicted of the execution of Canadian prisoners, for which he received a commuted death sentence.[81] Two German armies were written off, with only about 40,000 Germans escaping the pocket, although about a quarter million more were left in Northwest Europe.

The Allies suffered about 206,000 casualties from the D-Day landing to the end of the Normandy campaign, about equal to the Germans. The enemy lost another 200,000 as prisoners.[82] In total, some 11 panzer divisions and panzer grenadier divisions along with 36 infantry divisions were

The Germans were defeated in Normandy on August 21, 1944, after seventy-seven days of combat. It was a brutal attrition campaign, but resulted in a decisive victory for the Allies.

destroyed, badly mauled, or isolated in coastal garrisons.[83] The Canadians took 18,444 casualties, including 5,021 killed. Operational research teams in the 21st Army Group determined that the 2nd and 3rd Canadian Infantry Divisions were in more "intense combat days" than any other British division, and suffered higher casualties as a result—the most (9,263) and second most (8,211) of any of Montgomery's divisions.[84] The casualties also fell disproportionately on the infantry battalions.[85] Although the Allied infantry made up fewer than 8,000 of an 18,500-strong division, they absorbed about 70 percent of the total casualties and 76 percent of those in the Canadian forces.[86] Such crippling losses could not continue without serious repercussions to the Allied divisions' fighting efficiency.

Much vitriol raged among the Allied high commands over the failure of various national armies to break through the Germans more rapidly in Normandy. The Canadians, in the vanguard of battle, bore some of that blame, with Montgomery accusing them of being "badly handled and very slow."[87] Montgomery was not happy with the Canadians, but the British and Polish divisions, both armoured and infantry, had also been predictable and ponderous in their many failed operations. The finger pointing was no surprise, but perhaps the focus should have been less on who had failed and for what reasons, and more on acknowledging the difficulties of piercing the defences-in-depth. No army had found a way to break the fortified trench systems and defenders until they were worn down in attritional combat.

Accusations of Canadian slowness would have enraged those who faced the enemy for the better part of three months. The Canadian units bore the scars of relentless battles. They were the ones who overcame the enemy opposite them—an enemy who were on the best tactical ground and who employed all the advantages of their substantial arsenal. The Allies were just as resilient when fighting on the defence in their slit trenches protected by hull-down tanks and guns, as revealed through the costly German assaults in June following D-Day or the German's failed attempts to smash the Americans during Cobra. Most operations needed, according to the military doctrine of the time, a three-to-one ratio of attackers to defenders to succeed. The Canadians usually achieved this throughout July and August, with their advantage in firepower but not in manpower. In fact, in many of the disastrous battles, such as Spring, the force ratios were often even, meaning that an equal number of

Canadians fought an equal number of Germans. This story is usually lost in the popular memory of Normandy, where success has repeatedly been attributed to the "brute force" of the Allied firepower and airpower overwhelming the enemy.[88]

The Anglo-Canadian approach to battle was also shaped by an appreciation from the start of the campaign that few reinforcements would be on hand for the forward units.[89] The Germans, who faced their own shortages of soldiers, remained wedded to a reckless counterattack doctrine that demanded infantry and armour be hurled into battle to hit the overextended force, now turned defenders, when they were most vulnerable. This flair and drama have caught the attention of soldiers and historians, who are drawn to seize-the-initiative offensive action, but it ultimately led to much damage being inflicted on the Germans as the Allies learned to prepare and repel such shock tactics. A soldier must be willing to die for his country, said Patton, but it is better to make the other fellow die for his. The Canadians at times were cautious on the battlefield, but they much preferred to let the other fellow, careless and at times fanatical, die for his country.

Throughout Normandy, the experienced 3rd Canadian Infantry Division had fought well, even with dwindling numbers of infantry, while the 2nd Division had been uneven in battle and the 4th Division had shown aggression but could not put together a series of sustained operations. Of course, no one could, with the British and Americans facing their own cascade of failures when confronting the resilient enemy. Nonetheless, necks were on the chopping block. Simonds fired his friend George Kitching, commander of the 4th Armoured Division, who had been a fine staff officer but had failed to inspire as a commander, and he replaced the 3rd Division commander, Rod Keller, who had been injured but likely would have been removed from command in any case, for perceived failures in the capture of Carpiquet. He also looked to dump Charles Foulkes, a lacklustre commander who was disliked by his staff but was protected by Crerar. Down the chain of command, six of nine brigadiers and fourteen of twenty-four battalion commanders were gone. Some of these had been killed, wounded, or worn down, but Simonds also engaged in a major housecleaning.

Simonds, too, might have been sent home for the failure of Spring, and for the setbacks in Totalize and Tractable that resulted from the rigid battle-by-timetable, although his methodical approach to fighting the enemy was in line with British doctrine, and, furthermore, he was a favourite of Montgomery. It was not all failure, of course. Simonds's plans were innovative and aggressive. His use of armoured personnel carriers was brilliant and saved lives. But after surveying the Canadian general's operational career from Sicily to Normandy, one must conclude that he was not nearly as effective a general as historians have given him credit for: he did not understand what soldiers can and cannot be asked to do in battle; he blamed subordinates for the failure of his overly complex plans; he fired senior officers too quickly; and he showed in Sicily and Normandy that he often did not have an innate grasp of the enemy's potential reaction to his plans or of enemy strength concentrations. Simonds's battlefield accomplishments in the summer of 1944 revealed an agile mind—albeit one that too easily overreached tactical realities—but he would continue to learn and improve in the coming months. And he was one of those rare senior officers who got better with each level of command he assumed, reaching his peak of efficacy as temporary army commander in October 1944.[90] While Simonds made mistakes, it is also clear that every other senior Canadian commander (save for Major-General Bert Hoffmeister) was decidedly average, and no one was even remotely suitable as his replacement. The lion-like Canadian soldiers at the front deserved better.

The Canadian-Anglo method of battle was condemned by the Germans—who ironically were defeated by it—and then by generations of historians. The Canadians marshalled men and resources before attacking behind artillery bombardments and airpower. They did this, quite simply, because they could. Some of the soldiers' initiative was sapped in the multi-phased, planned battles, but supporting fire suppressed the German defenders, saturating their positions with shellfire and bombs, and helped to ration Canadian lives. Even with the gift of hindsight and decades of study, not to mention a good deal of conjecture and outright fantasy, few viable suggestions have been offered as to how the battles could have been fought differently against a dug-in enemy on ground of his choosing and backed by defensive firepower.

In seventy-seven days, the Allies destroyed two armies and inflicted some 400,000 casualties on the Germans, who had had nearly five years to prepare for the campaign. If the Allies were blamed for lacking speed and dash, certainly such a criticism would not have come from their surviving fathers and uncles, the Great War veterans who had fought at a crawl's pace at the Somme and Passchendaele. In assessing the Canadian performance in the battle to close the Falaise Gap, it might be best to leave the final word to gunner George Blackburn: "Armchair strategists writing of those days—whether British, American, or Canadian—have all spent too much time wondering why we were so slow getting down past Falaise to meet up with the Americans. They should have spent more time wondering how men ever summoned up the necessary moral courage and physical stamina to get there at all."[91]

CHAPTER 11

THE GOTHIC LINE

In the summer of 1944, the eyes of the world were focused on the intense fighting throughout Normandy. While the multiple campaigns in the Mediterranean had allowed the Allies to strike back at the Axis Powers—by chipping away at the periphery in North Africa, then Sicily, and finally south of Rome in Italy—it was, after the D-Day invasion, cast as a stagnant battleground. With all effort directed towards Normandy, Allied commanders in Italy were starved of resources, troops, and airpower, yet still tasked with holding down the enemy and grinding him out in attritional warfare.

The liberation of Rome and the mauling of the German Tenth and Fourteenth Armies in May 1944 had been a clear-cut victory for the Allies, but they had suffered about 42,000 casualties. The Germans suffered about 30,000 losses, half of whom were prisoners. Nevertheless, as General Harold Alexander, commander of the Allied armies in Italy, noted wistfully, the triumph was "not as complete as it might have been."[1] Because of inter-Allied conflict and American general Mark Clark's prideful insistence on capturing Rome at the expense of letting most of the German forces escape in early June, there would be further battles. Unless they were put down decisively, the Nazi forces revealed their remarkable ability to reorganize mangled formations and fight again.

Ortona and the Hitler Line were titanic affairs for Burns's warriors, who spearheaded the Eighth Army in major operations. The Dominion commanders had made mistakes, but no more than their British counterparts, and now I Canadian Corps was a combat-forged machine. Despite the victory at the Hitler Line, Lieutenant-General E.L.M. Burns was severely criticized by Eighth Army headquarters for his corps' slow exploitation through the choked roads beyond the broken enemy defences. The congestion was due more to the crowding caused by Eighth Army commander General Sir Oliver Leese's own headquarters that had put too many divisions through a limited road network, and the questioning of Burns's competency seemed little more than an attempt to make him the scapegoat.

The Canadian general was an intelligent student of war who sought to innovate and study previous failures to improve upon the fighting capacities of his Canadians. At the same time, Burns lacked charisma, was cold and diffident, and failed to motivate his troops. He was also excluded from the tight group of British senior commanders, who were all known to each other and who respected above all else their shared experience with Montgomery through the North African desert war. In the aftermath of the battle, Burns survived Leese's attempt to have him removed, receiving the full backing of senior Canadian commanders in Britain who refused to throw him to the wolves, but he was never accepted by the senior Eighth Army commanders.[2] There would be further friction between the British and Canadian senior leaders in Italy.

Canadian infantrymen laden down with kit and passing through the village of Pancrazio, Italy.

The Canadian Corps emerged battered but victorious after the Hitler Line campaign. While some of the Canadians smarted at being kept from the prize of Rome, which was deemed out of bounds to them but not the Americans, they started the slow process of rebuilding regiments, promoting promising NCOs to officers to fill the casualties at that level, and replacing worn-out kit. The corps had passed through a bloodletting, with 789 killed and 2,463 wounded before and during the battle, and there were few replacements in the reinforcement system.[3]

As part of the process of rebuilding, Burns hunted for answers to tactical problems, ordering all units to conduct investigations into successes and failures.[4] This analysis extended up to his corps headquarters and even to Eighth Army. Leese took the criticism badly, even if it was implicit rather than explicit, and the study of events at the Hitler Line appears to have further soured him on Burns.[5] The Canadians continued to learn and evolve, using their lessons as a stepping stone towards greater professionalism. Their lives depended on it, for everyone knew there would be more battles in Italy before the enemy admitted defeat.

AS THE GERMANS RETREATED NORTHWARD, the Allies nipped at their heels but were unable to bring them to battle before they fortified along what became known as the Gothic Line. This was the last trench system before the Alps, and the defensive line bristling with guns was anchored between two mountain ranges, across the Po River valley and along the Adriatic coast. It was here that the Allies would attack in August against the reconstituted Tenth and Fourteenth Armies, backed by new panzer divisions.

The Canadians spent much of the summer out of the line in a valley of the Volturno River, about 150 kilometres southeast of Rome, though the 1st Canadian Armoured Brigade fought some costly tank battles, especially around Lake Trasimeno. These armoured engagements reminded the Allies that while the Germans had been defeated at the Hitler Line, they still had fight left in them. Lessons of the Liri Valley campaign continued to be processed. The British and Canadians had found after study that their armoured divisions were too light in terms of infantry, with only a single brigade of three battalions, and so another brigade was added to the 5th Canadian Armoured Division. But attesting to the pinched-off reinforcements, Burns was instructed from

London to find the necessary troops from those in theatre.[6] To augment his numbers and provide a reinforced striking arm, Burns tried to bring the orphaned 1st Canadian Armoured Brigade back into the corps, but the semi-independent brigade had no desire to serve under I Canadian Corps, due to clashes between commanders and the 1st Brigade's success in fighting throughout the Eighth Army. Leese blocked the transfer, wishing to keep the brigade a more mobile unit. He also observed of the Canadian troopers, "They are acknowledged by all as the best brigade out here and every division asks for them."[7] And so, the creation of the 12th Canadian Infantry Brigade was done within the corps, draining the already shallow reinforcement pools and cannibalizing the armoured cars of the Westminster Regiment and the division's reconnaissance unit, the 4th Princess Louise Dragoon Guards, as well as two light anti-aircraft batteries, who had nothing to shoot at.[8] There was little time to transform the reconnaissance forces and gunners into infantry, but the new units, such as the Lanark and Renfrew Scottish (formed from the anti-aircraft gunners and showing their displeasure by calling themselves, informally, the "slaughterhouse battalion"), would prove themselves on the battlefield.[9]

While reforms kept the officers busy, the soldiers had time to relax. There was increased leave to a number of cities, primarily to the sanctioned Canadian rest camps at Bari and Salerno, where soldiers could enjoy wine and beaches. Entertainers also came into the field. Artilleryman Gordie Bannerman, who for months after the Hitler Line battle had nightmares about friends killed, remarked that morale was raised when No. 1 Canadian Entertainment Company, consisting of male and female dancers, singers, and musicians, visited the area. Though some of the performers had become physically sick while travelling through the devastation of the battlefield, with its gagging

Watching and waiting for the enemy.

summer stench of shallow-buried bodies, they put on a great show. For Bannerman and his mates, "They were a touch from home. WE LOVED THEM."[10] Some 25,000 Canadians would eventually see the rollicking performances.[11] Throughout the Italian campaign, the soldiers' spirits were also buoyed by their own in-house productions, which involved the ever-popular cross-dressing, lewd humour, ridiculous songs, topical jokes, and even outrageous skits that, according to Stanley Scislowski of the Perth Regiment, provided "the only time a private could unload on officers and not be put on charge."[12]

Another pleasant distraction was the army newspaper, *The Maple Leaf*, which had published its first issue on January 14, 1944. It was filled with stories from Canada about politics, war-related work, and, most popular with the men, sports. The paper highlighted Allied victories and Canadian deeds of valour, and it became a mainstay with the troops. But it also offered frank accounts of combat, interviewed survivors who spoke of their near-death experiences, and even addressed the challenge of battle exhaustion.[13] While the paper could have become a voice-piece for the army, its editor, Canadian journalist Brigadier Richard Malone, refused to allow it to be reduced to a source of pablum or propaganda. He knew this would never be accepted by the soldiers in the field. Malone, who was a friend of Minister Ralston and a future publisher of *The Globe and Mail*, used his authority as commander of No. 1 Public Relations Group—which was responsible for the army press and public relations—to shield the newspaper from political or military interference. This was no easy task, but Malone succeeded, partially because *The Maple Leaf* was such a hit with the soldiers and no officer dared to interfere too deeply with the editorial direction.[14]

"The life and soul of the paper," noted one Canadian, was Sergeant Bing Coughlin's *Herbie* cartoon.[15] Its intellectual origin was in Bruce Bairnsfather's popular Great War cartoon, *Old Bill*, whose anti-hero displayed fear, anger, and petulance towards the absurdity of war. Herbie's great appeal was that he represented the common soldier, battling the elements, the enemy, and his own generals. The sad-sack soldier, according to one admiring Canadian officer, was "the little guy" in the army, dismissive of discipline and courageous acts.[16] Regimental Sergeant Major Harry Fox believed that "Humour was, and is, essential to survival in the Army and especially in combat."[17]

Soldiers found many ways to cope with the strain of service, and their embracing of *The Maple Leaf* in Italy resulted in editions appearing by war's end in other theatres, including England, France, Belgium, Germany, and the Netherlands.

Away from the shells, the soldiers banded together to play soccer and baseball games. Sports offered leisure breaks, kept the men fit, and integrated the new reinforcements into the squadrons and platoons. Canadian mobile baths moved into the field, and records revealed, in that chit-counting army way, that from May to July, 60,458 soldiers benefited from the waters.[18] There were demonstrations on how to clear minefields and instruction in cliff climbing. Small-unit tactics were practised, especially sections firing and advancing together, as well as moving forward within stimulated artillery barrages to close the distance on enemy positions. The blade was being honed for another battle.

« *Jeez!... Even the kitchen sink!!!* »

« *A tank? — I don't think so, Sir, but I'll take another look.* »

THE GERMAN WAR EFFORT WAS IN A SHAMBLES. Cities in the Fatherland were being steadily reduced as the bombers carried out relentless missions. In the summer of 1944, the Eastern Front collapsed in the face of a series of Soviet offensives, and by mid-August the clash in Normandy was almost lost. Eisenhower also opened a new front on August 15, when the Allies invaded southern France. The Germans retreated from this new threat, but lost tens of thousands of soldiers captured or killed in the process. The Dragoon landings, as they were code-named, liberated key Mediterranean ports at Toulon and Marseilles to partially alleviate the Allies' logistical problems. And now, in Italy, the Germans faced another colossal blow, although the Allied force there was much reduced from the Dragoon operation that had siphoned off seven American and French divisions and more than half of the Allied airpower. Only the most optimistic planners in the Eighth Army believed a breakthrough was possible through the German lines and further into the Alps towards Vienna. But success would be defined as destroying and drawing down the strength of the German defenders.

Playing into the Allies' hands, Hitler rushed a dozen additional divisions to the Italian front during the summer of 1944, despite their being critically needed in the eastern and western theatres. While the Allies still had an enormous advantage in the air, the ground forces were approaching parity.[19] A deep Allied thrust under such conditions—and through the rocky terrain and natural barriers—seemed unlikely, but the goal was battle not breakthrough.

The German commander-in-chief in Italy, Field Marshal Albert Kesselring, was prepared for another Allied offensive but remained unsure about where it would fall. He was wary of deception plans, having been caught off guard by the Anzio landings earlier in the year. With probing attacks all along the line siphoning off his reserves and sucking in forces, he instructed his intelligence officer not to be distracted by such operations and instead to focus on a number of elite formations that he assumed would spearhead any assault. One of these was the experienced Canadian Corps.[20] After the Canadians' summer of rest, and in the wake of their victory at the Hitler Line, if they were moved to a front, Kesselring felt sure that would be the place where the Allies would attack.

GENERALS ALEXANDER AND LEESE prepared for the upcoming offensive in late summer, but they remained wary of working closely with the American commander, General Clark, for whom they had built up a healthy distaste. To break through the enemy lines and take advantage of the Allies' armoured strength, Alexander and Leese sought a less hilly and mountainous battlefield. They found it along the Adriatic coast, which was relatively flat, although criss-crossed with rivers and defended by the Gothic Line. Leese convinced Alexander to give him the lead role in the offensive, and to let Clark follow up in the second phase through the mountains north of Florence when Kesselring had used up his reserves or shifted them to block the British advance. Clark accepted the secondary role, partially because it appeared that any attack on the Gothic Line would be difficult and costly, and largely because, after the Dragoon landings, he no longer had the forces to deliver anything but a flanking attack.

Despite the strong German defences in the Gothic Line, which were even more daunting than those in the Hitler Line, Leese devised an ambitious plan that required an initial rapid advance through the outer crust, followed by a sustained armoured drive. The grand goal was to push on to the River Po and, should the enemy break, to thrust into the key industrialized sectors of northern Italy. The Germans, it was hoped, would be hurled back to the Alps. But given the force ratios at play, the operation was unlikely to succeed in such an ambitious manner. That said, generals are meant to drive their forces on, and most of them like to dangle red flags in front of their charging-bull armies.

Opposite the Eighth Army's British, Polish, and Canadian forces in the Gothic Line was the Tenth German Army, along the north bank of the Foglia River. Although only four German divisions held the trench system (with more divisions further to the rear), Allied aerial photographs revealed that these formations, assisted by slave labour, were fortifying the positions daily. There was a rush to attack before the Germans made any more progress, and the Allied operation with nine divisions had to go ahead sometime in August, for late September would bring rain and reduce the roads to a quagmire. Yet even with the earth baked hard by the sun and with their significant superiority in ground forces, this was no easy battlefield for the Allies. The Germans had a 15-kilometre defence-in-depth in front of the main line—between the Metauro and Foglia Rivers—in which to engage in a delaying fight before the Allies arrived at the 4-kilometre-thick main Gothic Line bristling with guns and anchored on concrete dugouts. And behind that was the Rimini coastal plain, cut by several dried-up rivers and streams that would hinder the armoured breakout and allow defenders, backed by anti-tank guns, to smash armoured units.

The Tenth Army had two corps consisting of 81 battalions of varying strength: about a third were considered effective with over 400 riflemen, a third were under-strength with between 300 and 400, and another third were exhausted and with fewer than 200 men. While the infantry regiments were between a half and a quarter the size of Allied battalions, the defenders were protected by 566 guns of all calibres, from howitzers to anti-tank pieces.[21] The ground also favoured the Germans, as the Allies moved along a northwest and then western axis that followed the Adriatic coastline but saw the plains narrow and the flat land become foothills. With mountains to the north, and the towns of San Marino, Cesne, Forli, Ravenna, and Faenza along the road system, this was ideal territory to defend.

A steel and concrete 75mm fixed artillery gun on the Gothic Line. With a low profile and a high striking power, these guns were devastating against advancing armour and difficult to destroy with artillery fire.

Against this fortress, Leese's Eighth Army consisted of three corps along a 35 kilometre front: the Polish II Corps of two tired divisions that had been fighting since June; the Canadian Corps of two divisions and the 21st British Tank Brigade; and V Corps, an over-sized British formation of five divisions and two tank brigades, including the very good 1st Armoured Division. British V Corps, as befitted its size, was to have the central position, where the terrain was flattest and where the enemy's defences were best able to be broken by its armoured divisions. The Poles were to their right, along the coast, and the Canadians were given the rough terrain on the far left to guard the flank. The Canadians had acquired a reputation as a hard-pounding force. As one wit observed of them, "if 'fuck' and 'frontal' were removed from the military vocabulary, the Canadian army would have been both speechless and unable to attack."[22]

In early August, Polish senior officers warned Eighth Army headquarters that they would likely face stiff opposition, and that a swift advance was likely out of the question. Leese pondered the dilemma and settled on a bizarre change of plan. Instead of assisting the beleaguered Poles on the right, Leese shifted his gaze to the left flank and moved the Canadians to the centre, in a spearhead role against the best-defended part of the Gothic Line.[23] Leese professed to have little faith in Burns, but he paradoxically now gave him the most important battleground, and placed V Corps into rougher terrain on the far left. Far worse, Leese did nothing to bolster the Canadian Corps in the centre. Leese left little evidence of why he made the odd decision, and he should have, at a bare minimum, shifted a division or two from V Corps to Burns. And so the Canadians were given the key role in the battle but with only two divisions to carry it out.

With the plan worked out, as flawed as it was, Burns's headquarters turned to the monumental task of moving troops to the front. The Canadian engineers cut a 150-kilometre road through the Appenine mountains to provide a route for the tanks and vehicles. Under an umbrella of air cover from the Desert Air Force and the U.S. Fifteenth Air Force, the rest of the Canadians, with other components of the Eighth Army, used rough roads to move 11,000 wheeled vehicles, 650 tanks, 1 million shells, and 50 million litres of fuel.[24] It was a dust-choked, frustrating voyage that required constant improvisation and consummate professionalism when trucks and carriers broke down, ran out of gas, or rolled down culverts. R.T. Currelly, historical officer for the 5th Armoured Division, wrote of the journey, "In all this filth, fatigue and bodily discomfort the same old time-worn humour and perpetual good nature persist. Someone's truck slips on a soft shoulder and rolls over. The driver is sitting dejectedly in the burning dust waiting, perhaps hours, for a Recovery Lorry. Nearly everyone who passes has something to shout, such as 'Wotcha thinkin'

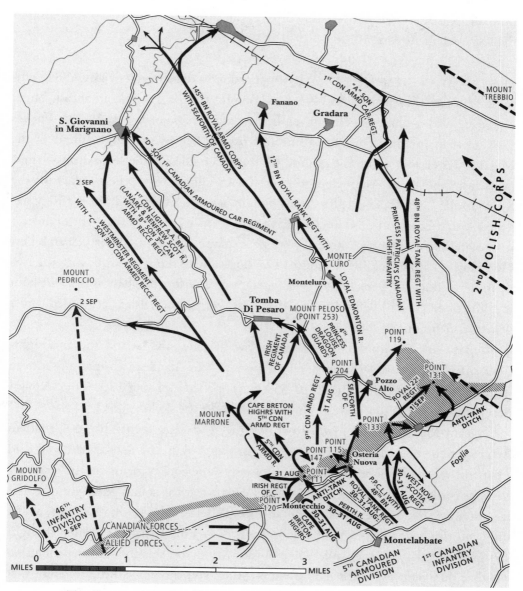

THE BREAKING OF THE GOTHIC LINE, AUGUST 30–SEPTEMBER 3, 1944

about Jock?,' or 'That's a stoo-ped place to park!'"[25] The Canadians delivered on the difficult logistical task, and Burns's corps was in position for the set-piece battle in the last week of August.

THE CANADIAN INFANTRY BATTALIONS were up to a full strength of around 845 officers and men. They would need every last one for the long campaign ahead. Burns organized a four-phase operation: the first would see Major-General Chris Vokes's 1st Canadian Infantry Division stealthily cross the bed of sand and shingle of the Metauro River and secure the ground on the other side. In the second phase, new units from the 1st Division were to close the 15 kilometres to the outskirts of the main Gothic Line. The third phase, the dogfight, was more flexible. If the 4-kilometre-deep Gothic Line could be breached, Vokes's warriors were to blast through it; if it was held too strongly, there would be a pause to allow Major-General Bert Hoffmeister's 5th Canadian Armoured Division time to move forward, with the two divisions striking in a major set-piece operation. The fourth phase was a breakout into the open ground behind the Gothic Line, with Hoffmeister's armoured forces driving to Rimini.

The 1st Canadian Infantry Division sent two brigades, the 1st and 2nd, in a night-time assault across the Metauro on August 25–26. The lead formations moved silently, 90 minutes before the corps' 350 guns opened up along a series of German-occupied ridge lines to the west. The sheet of fire lit the skyline, at 11:59 P.M.

Sergeant-Major Gordie Bannerman of the 17th Regiment, Royal Canadian Artillery, remembered, "The flashes of the guns lighted up the sky so you could read a paper it was that bright. What a relief to send some back as being on the receiving end was getting a bit nerve wracking. You never forget the sound and sight of a barrage of a few hundred guns all firing at once. Whether you think so or not, at the time you still have to think of the poor devils that you are shelling. I often thought just give up and go home while you still can. Mind you this thought depended on whether they had just killed one of yours—then you thought a little differently."[26] The 1st Division's senior gunner, Brigadier William Ziegler, confused the enemy about the direction of the attack by laying down pulverising fire far from the advancing Canadians. The German doctrine was to follow such barrages with their own counter-bombardments, and to rush reserves to that section of the front in preparation for battle. The tricky bombardment worked and there was little fire directed towards the lead Canadian units. Vokes's infantry pushed northwestward through the night and carved out a 3,000-metre salient from which to launch additional attacks.

The operations on the next day, in the crippling heat of late summer, were more difficult. The German 71st Division stiffened along the series of outposts in what they called the Red Line, and reinforcements were raced into the breach. Eighth Army intelligence had anticipated that the Red Line would not be held in force, but the Germans intended to fight a delaying action there, for up to seven days, in order to better garrison the Gothic Line to the rear. Throughout the 26th, the Canadians encountered growing resistance, but they continued to drive forward, backed by artillery. The guns hammered enemy machine-gun outposts, many of which were on hills and ridges. As there were only dirt roads to travel on, which soon dissolved under the weight of armour and thousands of army boots, the engineers cut new roads, particularly for the tanks. A city of soldiers had to be moved under fire, but as Brigadier T.G. Gibson, commander of the 2nd Canadian Infantry Brigade, observed proudly, "the men covered the ground very quickly."[27]

The Canadians battered their way across the parched earth, passing vineyards and olive groves. Rear-guard German units fought to purchase time for their retreating comrades, while combat engineers blew bridges and blocked the roads with debris from toppled buildings. German gun teams waited for infantrymen or tanks to be channelled into kill grounds through the road network or narrowing terrain. Every shell or sniper disrupted the Canadian charge, as the sections, platoons, and companies went to ground, searching for the enemy's camouflaged positions to direct their fire.

There was confusion on both sides. With unclear intelligence coming from the front, Kesselring was not sure if the Canadian operation was a diversion or the main attack, since the Eighth Army had planted information about an amphibious landing northward along the Adriatic coast. But Kesselring felt he had time, with his troops holding the Red Line, so he demanded that a prisoner be taken, to interrogate him. He pointedly told his subordinates that if "they really are Canadians ... then it will be a true operation."[28] When they captured a Canadian a day later, Kesselring firmed up his belief that the Gothic Line was the true objective. Kesselring ordered two of his elite formations, the 26th Panzer and 29th Panzer Grenadier Divisions, to the Gothic Line, although it would take at least two days for them to arrive. The field marshal was not worried, since his experience with the Eighth Army told him that its commanders preferred, as per Montgomery's teachings, a slow-forming set-piece battle based on heavy firepower rather than a hell-for-leather charge.

In the meantime, the Canadians drove through the Red Line and on to the Gothic Line. With the German defenders fighting stubbornly, it looked as though the third phase of the operation would require both the 1st and 5th Canadian Divisions, and so Burns ordered Hoffmeister to prepare for combat on the night of the 26th. The Canadians continued to tangle with German defenders, while also pushing forward relentlessly, marching day and night. In one audacious move, Able Company of the Loyal Edmonton Regiment seized the hilltop of the Monteciccardo-Ginestreto ridge

Infantrymen of the 48th Highlanders of Canada carrying a stretcher under fire at Gothic Line, near River Foglia, August 28, 1944.

during the night of the 26th and the early hours of the 27th. German reinforcements arrived just as the Canadians set up a crossfire of Bren guns, and about seventy Germans were cut down.[29] Stunned at the depth of the Canadians' penetration, the enemy counterattacked with elements from their elite 1st Parachute Division, supported by armoured mobile guns. Able Company was thrown back, resulting in some forty Canadian casualties. The other companies of the Loyal Eddies converged on their exposed comrades the next day, eventually driving the Germans from the ridge with the assistance of British Churchill tanks and Royal Canadian Artillery M10 self-propelled anti-tank guns. Another thirty-four Eddies were killed, but an important position overlooking the Canadian advance had fallen. There was no rest, and the 1st Division continued to march forward, with the 5th Armoured Division mounting up.

Burns's men rubbed up against the Gothic Line on the morning of the 29th. The Germans were on the other side of the Foglia valley—known as the Green Line to the Germans and the Gothic Line to the Allies—behind which was a series of fortified towns and ridges. The enemy's defences consisted of some 3,604 dugouts, 2,375 machine guns, and 479 anti-tank guns, all of which were protected by 72,127 mines, 117,370 metres of barbed wire, and 8,944 metres of anti-tank ditches.[30] Major Howard Mitchell, who commanded a company of machine-gunners with the Saskatoon Light Infantry, studied the objective and shivered at the prospect of confronting the fortress: "This could only be a stupid slaughter."[31]

THE VALLEY FLOOR was a daunting 900 metres of open ground overlooked by sharply rising hills. To create a killing ground, the Germans had cut down every tree, razed every house, and used Italian slave labour to fill in many ditches and depressions that might be used for cover. As an official Canadian report noted, the enemy had "excellent f[iel]ds of fire."[32] A 4-metre-wide anti-tank ditch blocked much of the valley and the area was strewn with mines and tangles of barbed wire. On Hoffmeister's front, to the left of Vokes's division, aggressive patrols by the Perth Regiment and the Cape Breton Highlanders revealed that the Germans had not yet fully manned the position, although intelligence had pinpointed that two German divisions, the 98th Infantry and the 26th Panzer, were moving toward the Canadian sector. Leese had planned for a pause until September 2 to bring the guns forward, but now the Canadians were aching to gate-crash the line.

As more intelligence filtered in during the early hours of the 30th, the Canadians pleaded with Leese's headquarters to be allowed to attack. After some soul-searching, Leese gave the order. The 5th Division commander, Hoffmeister, had already acted on his own; and the 11th Brigade was preparing for battle. Brigadier Ian Johnston, the former commanding officer of the 48th Highlanders of Canada, a prewar Toronto lawyer and a director of Maple Leaf Gardens, told his 11th Brigade battalion commanders to crack the line. All of this took time, but by late on August 30, the Cape Breton Highlanders and the Perth Regiment had reconnoitred in strength on the far left flank. On the right, the 1st Division's Princess Patricia's Canadian Light Infantry and West Nova Scotia Regiment had already let loose a company each to cross the open valley to exploit the seemingly unmanned enemy positions along the far hills that gradually sloped upwards to a great height. As speed was of the essence, no barrage was deployed, although the Canadian gunners were ready to lay down counter-battery fire if enemy guns opened up. The plan was hurried and, as Burns was later to observe, "From this point on, it may be said that the battle to get through the Gothic Line and to seize the commanding high ground about two and a half miles beyond it ... was mainly a battalion and regimental commander's battle."[33]

The valley floor was festooned with mines, so the Desert Air Force was called in to drop bomb loads across the terrain to detonate them. Many of the German mines were destroyed, but not all of them. The schu-mines, in their deceptively miniature wooden boxes, carried a seven-ounce explosive. This was powerful enough to blow off a man's feet, fracture legs, hips, and pelvis bones, drive bones and metal fragments up into the groin, and reduce the genitals to mush. As one stretcher-bearer wrote, "the blast from these tiny wooden mines would tear off the foot but seemed to sear the blood vessels."[34] Most victims lived but were crippled for life. These mines were tremendously frightening devices, maiming rather than killing.

The four lead battalions pushed forward: from right to left, the West Nova Scotia Regiment, the PPCLI, the Perth Regiment, and the Cape Breton Highlanders. Around 4 P.M. on August 30, the West Novas sent Baker Company across the valley floor, while Charlie and Able established a secure position from which to lay down fire. There was no sniping from the enemy. The Maritime veterans of battle searched the hill uneasily. Something was wrong.

Baker Company advanced until they set off the schu-mines, as well as the S-mines (Schrapnellminen), which sprang several feet into the air before spraying ball-bearings in all directions like a shot-gun blast. As the first of these mines exploded, German paratroopers emerged from concealment and opened fire, sending the North Novas diving off the narrow roads into ditches and folds in the land. Chaplain Laurence Wilmot was close enough to the front to witness the massacre: "As soon as the mines started going off, the enemy opened up with machine-gun fire from the adjoining hills on both flanks, accompanied by a barrage of shells and mortars.... It was agonizing to hear the cries of the wounded."[35] These ditches and depressions were mined by the Germans, and a number of Maritimers were blown apart, their torsos, legs, and arms scattered in all directions. In the carnage, most of the radio men were knocked out, as were the two company commanders, both of whom had their legs ripped off. Pinned down by fire, unable to move for fear of mines, and with their leadership wiped out, the West Novas were at the mercy of the Germans for several long hours. The butchery was only relieved by the fall of darkness.

As the news filtered back to battalion headquarters, Lieutenant-Colonel Ronnie Waterman, the experienced commander of the West Novas, became unhinged. Stunned by news of the losses at the front, he ordered a renewed advance. Even though there was an opportunity to coordinate an artillery and tank attack to provide crucial aid, Waterman blustered at an emergency briefing that his infantrymen could overcome the enemy on their own. Chaplain Wilmot, who was present, recounted being "shocked" at the reckless claim by the commanding officer. Why not wait for tanks to provide support? Waterman refused to be deterred. "I feared disaster and felt helpless to do anything to prevent it," wrote a shaken Wilmot.[36] The padre went to the regimental aid post where he knew he would soon be needed.

Waterman ordered two more companies forward to extricate Baker Company, but they too got sucked into the battle as they crossed the minefield and were forced to go to ground in the face of enemy fire. With most of his battalion cut up, Waterman became even more unbalanced. Furious and thinking unclearly, he sent his remaining forces into the trap, rejecting the pleas of his officers who cautioned a withdrawal. The West Novas fought into the 31st but were eventually forced to retreat, leaving behind twenty of their dead comrades. Another fifty-six were wounded, many with feet blown off or legs mangled.[37] It was a bad day for the regiment, and Waterman was soon removed from command. He had been a good soldier, but the strain of long service and the sharp reversal had left him a broken man. His Maritimers paid for his breakdown.

Though the West Novas' thwarted attack was a low point for the Canadians, next to them in the line, on the left flank, the PPCLI snaked forward in an aggressive and successful drive by first passing through minefields and then stalking into the enemy lines. "Colin McDougall's company went through a mine field 600 yards deep with a mine every two feet," recounted one official report. "The pioneer Platoon raised 25 box mines within 100 yards, in addition to Teller and 'schu' mines."[38] The Patricias lost only three men. When they encountered firmer resistance in the small hours of the 31st, the Patricias mauled the tough paratroopers opposite them and grabbed the high ground known as Point 204. Major Edward Cutbill, who commanded a company in his first battle and would be awarded the Distinguished Service Order, cleared a number of hilltop positions, including at least one through a bayonet charge. He reported, "In the initial stage, we took 42 prisoners including two officers; after beating off local counterattacks, we captured 53 more, making a total of 95. In addition, some 20 Germans were killed."[39] The PPCLI eventually curled around to seize Point 133 on a spur jutting into the Canadian lines, from which much of the fire had been directed against the West Novas. Skilled junior leaders had delivered a significant victory against a tough opponent.

ON THE FAR LEFT, the Perth Regiment and the Cape Breton Highlanders also ran into concentrated machine-gun fire on the 30th, but they found ways to push forward, flanking positions and snuffing them out. Two strongpoints manned by elements from the 26th Panzer Division held out: Point 111 and, 1,000 metres to its left, Point 120. The Cape Breton Highlanders called in artillery fire and smoke to smother the opposition and provide some cover, and they almost made it to the objective, albeit at the cost of sixty-five casualties.[40] Overstretched and vulnerable to attack, the Highlanders pulled back but prepared a new assault on the 31st.

Next to the Highlanders, a company of the Perths advanced on Point 111 during the night of the 30th, close to a kilometre in front of the small town of Montecchio. A number of infantrymen were lost to mines and an entire company was pinned down by fire, but Dog Company briefly found its way clear and charged up the ridge around 8:30 P.M. Private Stan Scislowski recalled the confusion:

Someone off to my left closer to the road had gone up on a mine. It wasn't an ear-ringing bang like the Teller mines made, so I knew it could only be one of the small anti-personnel Schumines. A few more paces and two more men went up, the lower extremity of their legs mangled by the searing blasts. We stopped dead, afraid to go on. We were trapped smack in the middle of a mine field, there was no getting away from it. Then I heard Blackie Rowe's stentorian voice hollering from behind, "Get your goddamn asses moving! Come on! Move! Move! Move! Haul your asses!" I turned to Gord and said, "Holy shit! The crazy sonofabitch is determined to get us all killed!" We resumed the advance, but with cold fear in our hearts. Again I turned to Gord, "I can't see us getting out of here alive." He didn't even have time to agree with me when bang, down he went. My first instinct was to stop and help him somehow, but Blackie kept barking at us to keep moving, so I moved on.[41]

Scislowski and his surviving comrades cleared the minefield and continued into the enemy line. Such attacks took unbelievable courage, determination, and drive.

Supported by the 75mm guns of the 8th New Brunswick Hussar's Shermans and their raking coaxial machine guns, the Perths fought their way forward for about ninety minutes and gathered themselves for the final assault around 10 P.M. The infantry surged up Point 111 in a blood-curdling bayonet charge, driving the shaken Germans through with cold steel. [42] Only thirty prisoners survived. Those Germans who retreated, remembered Lieutenant Hunter Dunn of the 8th New Brunswick Hussars, were "machine-gunned ... until they surrendered."[43] The Gothic Line was pierced, with the Perths jutting into the German defences. Up to this point, the battle on the right had revealed no victory, or in the case of the West Novas, grave defeat, but the thrust by the Perths changed the outcome, attesting to how the aggression and sacrifice of small groups of men can shift momentum in combat.

The Perths sent in two more companies to widen the breach, but it was a precarious hold. Confusion was widespread along the front, where all the Canadians were involved in fierce engagements, with some units thrown back while others held their ground. Hoffmeister's headquarters struggled to make sense of the shifting front. But the same situation was plaguing the Germans, who rushed forward reinforcements only to find them fired upon by the Perths, who were, in effect, behind their lines on Point 111.

In this gunfight, the Canadians were faster on the draw. The Irish Regiment and the 8th New Brunswick Hussars pushed past the Perths propping open the gap, and around noon on the 31st, they curled to the left and attacked the enemy at Point 120 on Montecchio hill. The Irish passed over the dead Cape Bretoners who

A camouflage Sherman tank kicking up dust.

had gone up the ridge and been driven off the day before. Artillery, tank, and mortar fire kept the Germans down in their trenches, and the Irish climbed the hill. Sergeant F.J. Johnston, commanding one of the platoons, knocked out several machine guns on his own, leading from the front even as he was wounded. He was awarded the Military Medal, and his bravery may have tipped the balance in favour of the Canadians. Dozens of Germans were killed and another 121 captured at the cost of 18 Irish killed and 32 wounded.[44] The superb Canadian fieldcraft had evicted the enemy from their prepared positions, where they had enjoyed all the advantages.

THE GAP IN THE GOTHIC LINE widened as the Canadians unspooled their attack. Sensing that the enemy defences might be wavering, Hoffmeister—who had proven as a company, battalion, brigadier, and division commander that he had an innate sense of battle—ordered the 5th Armoured Brigade into the line under command of the 11th Infantry Brigade and the trusted Brigadier Ian Johnston. The infantry and armoured force, which numbered seven units, was to overcome three prominent hills, including the primary objectives, spurs known as Point 204 and Point 253 (Mount Peloso), about 5 kilometres deep into the Gothic Line. The enemy was far from broken and this new attack would require jamming an armoured blade into the German innards.

The 30-ton Shermans of the British Columbia Dragoons put spurs to flanks a little after 9:30 A.M. on August 31. Tank commanders tried to coordinate their four-tank troops, but although the rudimentary wireless system allowed for communication, it was easily and frequently knocked out of action. Nonetheless, the Canadians pushed the pace on the Germans and continued to widen the breach in the enemy lines.

Canada's best fighting divisional commander, Major-General Bert Hoffmeister.

The British Columbia Dragoons crashed forward with two squadrons of tanks through the rolling, treeless countryside, wiping out at least one platoon of terrified Germans caught in their path. Using streams and sunken roads to hide from the screen of German anti-tank guns, the Dragoons ran the gauntlet of fire.[45] Only twelve Shermans arrived at Point 204 at 12:30 P.M., many with hulls scarred and blackened. The commanding officer, Lieutenant-Colonel Fred Vokes (brother of 1st Division commander Chris Vokes), led some reinforcements to the advance guard later in the afternoon but was killed shortly thereafter by mortar fire.[46]

The Dragoons had made an impressive assault, but now their heads were deep in the enemy noose. Without Canadian infantry, the troopers were vulnerable to Germans who skulked around with panzerfausts—the hand-held anti-tank launchers. In a show of aggression, and refusing to let down their comrades, a number of the Canadian tank crews that had jumped free of their burned-out Shermans raced forward armed with Thompson machine guns to assist in holding the hill. As the Canadians blazed away at the enemy, many of the tank commanders were forced to open their hatches to survey the front. A few were sniped through the head by sharpshooters and one crew was blown apart when a German soldier threw a grenade into the open hatch. But even with the losses mounting, the Dragoons held off the enemy, raking the areas of advance.

Around 8:45 P.M., some fifty tanks of the Strathconas passed through shellfire and obscuring smoke, arriving in time to defeat a counterattack in the early hours of September 1. Three companies of the Perths also closed the distance after having been pinned down by severe shelling; they now fought on the Dragoons' perimeter, retreating slowly back into the protection of the Shermans' guns. It was a skilful defence. Dozens of Germans were killed and wounded and thirty taken prisoner.[47] Canadian PIAT teams were especially effective in harassing several German field guns that were being dragged forward, some by Italian tractors. To the rear, 25-pounder guns manned by the 17th Field Regiment dropped their shells outside of the brittle Canadian perimeter as the beleaguered garrison coordinated with the rear gunners. The Canadians held.

ON SEPTEMBER 1, with the Gothic Line pierced, Hoffmeister's 5th Armoured Division and Vokes's 1st Division drove deeper. The 1st Division's Van Doos and

Carleton and Yorks flexed their muscles and snatched a few key points, but the main objective was the twin towers of Mount Peloso and Monteluro, which would all but unhinge the German defences. The operation against Mount Peloso, also known as Point 253, would be carried out by the 5th Division's recently formed 4th Princess Louise Dragoon Guards, supported by Shermans from Lord Strathcona's Horse. They girded themselves for a frontal assault.

Advancing behind a heavy barrage at 1 P.M. on September 1, the Dragoon Guards engaged the enemy in classic fire and movement tactics: two companies of infantry moving forward in leaps and bounds, directing small-arms fire to keep the enemy's head low. Through grit and tactical skill, the Guards took Peloso, although the commanding officer, Lieutenant-Colonel Bill Darling, reached the objective with a mere 15 infantrymen left from the nearly 200 who had started at zero hour. Darling was awarded the Distinguished Service Order for his leadership in battle, and the citation read: "Ignoring the continual shelling, machine-gun and sniper fire, [Darling] visited each company in turn, urging his men on, and by sheer gallantry and personal example led them towards the objective."[48] Flanking advances by the Loyal Edmonton Regiment forced the Germans to abandon the 285-metre-high Monteluro without much of a fight, and other ridges to the east fell to the Van Doos and the Seaforth Highlanders.

By late on September 1, the Gothic Line was broken. General Leese crowed about the Canadians, writing officially that much of the credit went to the "leading divisions that by active and aggressive patrolling and by the quick follow-up of these patrols ... 'gate-crashed' the enemy."[49] The German Tenth Army commander had expected the Canadians to lumber forward, stopping to wait for their guns to catch up, but instead they had raced through his lines, engaging in close-quarters combat and boldly driving through the confusion that plagued both sides.

HOFFMEISTER'S AND VOKES'S DIVISIONS were in a position to thrust to the next German line of defence. Twenty kilometres away lay Rimini on the Adriatic, boasting historic sites that included a Roman arch dating to 27 B.C. Anchored on Rimini, running in a southwestern direction, was another major defensive system. While these positions were now firmly defended, an intense naval bombardment by Allied warships along the coast shelled them continuously and kept Kesselring on edge, renewing his fears of an amphibious attack up the coast. The seaborne pressure forced the Germans to rush reserves to the crumbling front, and these formations were harassed, fired upon, and bombed by the Allied air force, which made life miserable for those wearing the field grey uniforms.

Even as they were beaten at the Gothic Line, the Germans recovered quickly. A rainstorm over the night of September 1 slowed the Allied advance, and the two Canadian divisions were close to exhaustion. British V Corps on the left, with its mass of divisions, remained largely out of the battle, caught up in the rough terrain and the spider web of German defenders. The strongest position on the British front was the 6-kilometre-long Coriano Ridge, held by the 29th Panzer Grenadier Division, which stopped V Corps cold with massed fire.

Kesselring ordered four divisions to the now shattered front, as well as eighty artillery batteries. Rimini, on the Allies' far-right flank, looked like Ortona, so stacked was it with defenders and guns. It was to be held at all costs. The new front beyond the Gothic Line was a coastal plain cut by several rivers and interrupted by occupied ridges allowing the Germans a clear view of any advance. The enemy artillery, according to Lieutenant Zeke Ferley of the British Columbia Dragoons, had prepared a ruthless "killing ground."[50] The Canadian infantry, caught in a withering fire of artillery shells and mortar bombs, scrambled to carve out slit trenches in the sun-packed earth. The plunging mortar fire was particularly deadly, and one Canadian medical report calculated that 66 percent of all casualties from August 25 to September 30 were caused by it.[51] As the Germans gathered in strength, the Canadians prepared for the onslaught. There were enemy infantry assaults day and night, and an enemy armoured counterattack on September 3 was destroyed by the 5th Canadian Armoured Regiment, with eight Panthers left in ruins and not a single Sherman lost in return.[52] Further German actions on September 4 convinced Burns, who had flown over the battlefield to survey the enemy position, to order a pause until British V Corps could catch up.

There was no break in the air war. The Desert Air Force (DAF) struck the enemy repeatedly. At least 50 percent of the DAF attacks by medium bombers and fighter-bombers were directed against "gun positions," as one official report noted, because "the enemy had concentrated an unusually larger number of guns on our front." The

RCAF's No. 417 Squadron, flying Spitfires, took part in the operations. Equipped with 500-pound bombs, they flew multiple sorties every day against strongpoints while shooting up targets of opportunity to the rear, especially vulnerable trucks carrying supplies and ammunition. Despite the bombing, the Germans clung to their trenches like ticks. Prisoners testified that, in their opinion, although the bombers and fighters slowed the movement of supplies to the front, "they caused very few casualties to troops actually in position in the forward areas, and seemed to regard their effect as negligible in comparison with that of artillery and mortars."[53]

As of September 4, the Canadians were forced to entrench on the left flank, facing Coriano Ridge, while the right flank continued to probe in the direction of Rimini. The ridge was about a kilometre away, a position that, according to one Canadian, "bulged out of the rolling land like an elongated groundhog, dominating vineyards and bristling with the guns of the 29th Panzers."[54] Any movement on the Canadian front required, as one official report observed, "running the gauntlet of his guns."[55] Hoffmeister appealed through Burns to Leese to let him attack Coriano from the flank and rear, but the British general refused the order, hoping that V Corps could dislodge the enemy. However, momentum was now lost and the British made little headway, especially when rain fell on the 6th and continued for several days, reducing the already poor roads to gluey mud.

After days of bombardment, Leese was finally ready for another assault on the ridge. At 11 P.M. on September 12, V Corps swept forward from the south and the Canadians surged from the east two hours later. Through darkness, clouds of dust, and enemy fire, the 11th Canadian Infantry Brigade's Cape Breton Highlanders, Perth Regiment, and Irish Regiment followed a creeping barrage from almost 900 guns into the enemy lines. Two squadrons of Sherman tanks from the 8th New Brunswick Hussars further assisted.

In the course of the confusing night attack, during which the fragile wireless sets broke down, the lead formations tried to keep pace with the barrage, but the effects of the explosions and dust, combined with enemy fire, made the assault a ragged one. It seemed to work in favour of the Canadians, as they crept about in small sections, flushing out the surviving enemy troops. Lieutenant Robert Crozier of the Irish Regiment passed through the German and Canadian artillery and mortar fire.

"We kept going, never looking back ... there were dead Germans by a stone fence, caught in our artillery barrage, sprawled in strange poses, figures in a wax museum."[56] Through an eerie mist, the Cape Breton Highlanders and Perths rushed up the ridge, leaving behind wounded soldiers crying for help and stunned prisoners scuttling to the rear. By dawn Hoffmeister's men were on the ridge, along with British troops from the south, and the Hussars' tanks and the Irish Regiment soon thereafter cleared the "sniper-infested town" of Coriano.[57]

In the battle's aftermath, the survivors contemplated their fate. Private Ted Patrick of the Irish Regiment, who survived thirty-six hours of mortar and shellfire, recalled, "I was dehydrated and emotionally and physically exhausted."[58] Lieutenant Crozier wrote, "I have been through just about the works now—heavy shelling, mortaring, mine fields, German Tiger tanks, Spandau machine gun nests, snipers in the fields and buildings, street fighting and house clearing—and even aerial strafing (our own planes). While you are in it, you are so keyed up and busy ducking, dodging, digging, running across open gaps, that you don't have much time to worry, except occasionally you have to fight the jitters. Only when it's over do you think: 'My God! How bloody dangerous!'"[59]

"IT WAS A HARD FIGHT," Sir Oliver Leese said of Coriano, "and a decisive action in the battle." The Germans had been driven back and the 29th Panzer Grenadier Division reported "considerable losses in men and materiel."[60] The 5th Canadian Armoured Division needed a rest. It was pulled from front-line service after having lost 320 of its tanks (although many were repairable). One German corps-level report observed, "Enemy armoured formations, particularly Canadian tanks, are no longer sensitive to artillery fire, but carry on even under heaviest fire concentrations."[61]

Three weeks of grinding combat had left the Canadians in a bad way, but the Germans were even worse off. The offensive continued as Burns's I Canadian Corps, now strengthened with the 4th British and 2nd New Zealand Divisions and a Greek brigade, joined the much-reduced 1st Canadian Division. Leese, seemingly won over by Burns's rupturing of the Gothic Line, recommended him for a Distinguished Service Order, which he received.

Major-General Chris Vokes was still grieving the death of his younger brother, Fred (who was killed while leading the British Columbia Dragoons against Point 204), when he drew up the 1st Division's operational plan for September 14. The 1st Canadian Infantry Brigade, on the right, was ordered to snatch Rimini airfield, and the 3rd Canadian Infantry Brigade, on the left, was to capture San Martino Ridge, with the ultimate goal of pushing on to San Fortunato, an anchor town on the major defensive system known as the Rimini Line.

The attack went in on September 14 and was the start of a week of headlong battle. On the right, the 1st Brigade's Royal Canadian Regiment and 48th Highlanders of Canada clawed their way south of the airfield but were denied its capture by a hail of mortar fire. On the left, the 3rd Brigade had to advance 6 kilometres to the 1,500-metre-long San Martino Ridge, which ran south to north, with the fortified villages of San Lorenzo in the south and San Martino on a northern spur. The Van Doos and the West Novas drove forward in the early hours of the 14th, overcoming numerous machine-gun nests, but they were hit hard by enemy counterattacks and raking long-range fire. The next morning, the Van Doos tried three times to cross the heat-baked fields to reach San Martino; each drive was shot to pieces, and the French Canadians suffered twenty-nine killed and sixty-one wounded in their most costly day of the war.[62] The Novas had an equally ghastly time in reaching the southern village with its stone church. As one of the regiment's chroniclers noted, "It was a murderous place in the broad

Private Stanley Rodgers of the 48th Highlanders of Canada, with a PIAT anti-tank weapon. He has seen the face of battle.

afternoon despite the dust and smoke."[63] The West Novas were outgunned by the Germans and were forced to dig in below the ridge.

On the 15th, the Canadians, Greeks, and New Zealanders, with the British 1st Armoured and 46th and 56th Infantry Divisions on the left flank, cranked the vice a little tighter along the front, capturing key bridges over several rivers. That day, the Van Doos finally overran San Martino, with its balustraded 700-room Palazzo des Vergers, while the West Novas evicted the Germans from the dusty village of San Lorenzo. It was their fourth attack in forty hours, and it only succeeded when the West Novas dragged forward their own 6-pounder guns at a crucial moment to blast enemy trench systems at point-blank range. Nearly every Nova Scotian soldier was thrown into the line, and skilful support was given by a battle-scarred squadron of 12th Royal Tanks that took on and defeated a German Tiger tank and other lesser beasts. The 2nd Canadian Infantry Brigade was now on a ridgeline and secure against German counterblows, save for those enemy guns at the Rimini airfield, which was now behind them. The brigade prepared to make the final push to San Fortunato, about 5 kilometres to the northwest.

Though pockets of German resistance were encountered along the San Martino Ridge, and some held out for hours, the Canadians prepared a secure jumping-off point. But problems arose when, during the early hours of the 16th, the Seaforth Highlanders set out to relieve the 22nd Regiment. Under fire, the two battalions became mixed up, the handover was botched, and a number of Canadian machine-gun positions and strongpoints were left empty. The Germans were too skilled to let the opportunity pass, and about fifty soldiers infiltrated back into the inadvertently abandoned San Martino. The enemy force cleverly set up interlocking fields of fire amid the rubble of the dozen or so houses, and forward artillery officers could now call down painfully accurate fire. The Seaforths moved into the village unaware early on the 16th, only to be ambushed. Two days of patrols and three set-piece battles later, they still had not driven out the enemy, who was defended by dozens of guns on the Rimini Line.[64] The Seaforths lost ninety men and San Martino remained in German hands.

By the afternoon of the 17th, the Canadian advance had ground to a halt. The British on the flanks, near the border of the small Republic of San Marino, were also stalled. With the Germans still jutting into the Canadian line at San Martino, Vokes could do little to situate his artillery for a new offensive. The Loyal Edmonton Regiment was drawn into the battle for San Martino early on the 18th, but the Loyal Eddies found the Germans were there to stay. Several attacks were turned back sharply. The PPCLI, hoping to snake forward through the vineyards and fields as the Edmonton Regiment kept the Germans busy at San Martino, were hit in a cross-fire from all directions, which blew up half of their tanks. "How anyone survived the enemy fire directed from San Martino behind us and San Fortunato ahead is a miracle," marvelled Lieutenant Syd Frost.[65] The Carleton and Yorks had some marginal success along the line, pushing northwestward and eventually forcing the Germans out of San Martino, but the fight felt like a replay of Ortona the previous December, with battalion after battalion fed into the maelstrom.

THE CANADIANS WERE SHOT THROUGH for their final attack on San Fortunato Ridge, a promontory running along much of the front and more imposing than either the Coriano or San Lorenzo ridges. It was also protected by the Ausa River, a shallow obstacle running from Rimini through the Canadian front. Vokes put almost everything he had in the shop window. It would be a two brigade assault, with the 3rd Brigade to engage in an unenviable frontal battering while the 2nd Brigade cut off the garrison over the Marecchia River, thereby flanking Rimini.

The Canadian ground pounders received good support: the guns from the Eighth Army were methodically working over the defenders at San Fortunato and the Desert Air Force bombers flew hundreds of sorties against them. As part of the 1st Division's operation at 5 A.M. on the 18th, twenty-two sites were selected for aerial bombardment, and these were hit by 80 fighter bombers dropping 128 tons over the next couple of hours.[66] At this point in the campaign, the DAF and the U.S. Fifteenth Air Force outnumbered the Luftwaffe by at least ten to one, but it was never easy to deposit bombs on their targets, especially while harassed by flak.[67] When the ground troops moved forward, interdiction artillery fire was directed against enemy rear positions containing mortars and guns, and this was thickened up by devastating naval shellfire from warships in the blue waters of the Adriatic.

The Canadians and British crossed the flat plain on the 18th in a series of costly battles, but the formations remained short of the Ausa River. The grind continued.

Through widespread skirmishes during the early hours of the 19th, the German defences were broken in several places amid a haze of yellow dust thrown up by the incessant bombardments. The Van Doos were ordered back into the line, having been badly mauled over previous days but ready to storm ahead at last light. Hoping to catch the enemy off guard after a long day of killing, the French Canadians drove up the slopes of San Fortunato Ridge, which rose to 143 metres and had a large reinforced villa on its crest. The two assault companies of Van Doos pushed hard and fast, aware that they were in a race against an enemy that was recovering and saturating the front blindly with mortar and machine-gun fire. The Van Doos won the sprint. Fifty Germans were killed and 200 captured, against the loss of only a handful of men.

Mounting a well-coordinated attack, the Loyal Edmonton Regiment, the Seaforth Highlanders of Canada, and the West Novas were on the Van Doos's heels, charging to the right of them to the summit in the early hours of the 20th. The combined force took the final parts of the ridge before the Germans could react, and enemy reinforcements were ambushed as they marched forward to the already pierced line. "The enemy were completely disorganized and our troops were behind and among them," recounted Brigadier T.G. Gibson. "There was plenty of hand to hand fighting.... One of the LER coys [companies] saw an enemy tank followed by infantry coming towards them. They let the tank go by and copped the sheep behind. The tank came back to look for its flock. This had been anticipated, so a string of 77 grenades had been strung along the ground and the tank blew its tracks. Finito was put to it by a Sgt with a PIAT."[68]

The German position was fatally compromised. While local enemy commanders bravely pulled together a ragged force to launch a few desultory counterattacks during the hot day, the Canadians now held the key terrain, and artillery fire broke up the assaults. Later in the day, Kesselring—upon being informed by Tenth Army commander Heinrich von Vietinghoff that "something unpleasant has happened"— ordered his troops to fall back across the Marecchia River. Vokes, anticipating the German withdrawal, had already sent the PPCLI to cross it. Rimini was now cut off, and the Germans abandoned it on the 21st. The city had been ruined by fire missions, aerial bombs, and demolitions, with 75 percent of its buildings destroyed, although the 2,000-year-old Roman arch had somehow survived. The Allies and the Germans had fought each other into the ground, but the enemy had finally been broken and the battle closed down on September 22.

The twenty-six-day fight through the Gothic Line and beyond was the most difficult for the Canadians in the entire Italian campaign. Of the Eighth Army's 14,000 casualties, I Canadian Corps claimed close to 3,900, including 1,016 killed.[69] With the Canadians having shattered the Gothic Line, captured 8,000 prisoners, and killed several thousand additional defenders, one would think they would have been feted for their spearhead role. But General Leese was still not convinced that Lieutenant-General E.L.M. Burns was suitable corps commander material. While the intelligent Canadian general had prepared his corps for the intense operation and then ably handled the difficult breakthrough, he remained an uninspiring figure. Vokes, who was a mediocre divisional commander but a fiery leader, believed that Burns was an "introvert" with little "presence."[70] He was right, yet surely the measure of Burns should be his two major victories. Burns is always compared unfavourably to Guy Simonds, his counterpart in Northwest Europe. The comparison is unfair, as Simonds had access to countless additional resources, from troops to guns to bombers, and any assessment of Burns must acknowledge how the resource-poor I Canadian Corps scrambled successfully to find advantages against a determined enemy. The campaign for the Gothic Line remains one of the most audacious and skilful operations carried out by the Canadian army in all its military history.

THROUGHOUT OCTOBER, the Allies continued their advance on the Germans. The terrain and weather were the enemy's best defences, with one Canadian report lamenting how the incessant rain "turned the ground into a quagmire of mud."[71] Writing in late 1944, one of the Hastings and Prince Edward Regiment's infantrymen fumed, "So help me, it's so Goddamned wet out here that even our hair is rusting."[72] Burns's headquarters now commanded the 2nd New Zealand Division and the 5th Canadian Armoured Division and the two formations faced a terrain criss-crossed by rivers, irrigation canals, and dykes, with all bridges blown and most positions covered by mortar fire. The Allied trek northward slunk forward amid mud and carnage.

The late fall and early winter stalemate was hard for everyone to take, and the constant shelling by both sides accounted for hundreds of lives. Morale plummeted. Crime rates rose in all Allied armies, as British, American, and Canadians deserted in high numbers; more than 5,000 British troops were serving sentences in brutal military prisons during 1944 alone.[73] The dispirited soldiers voted with their feet and weren't willing to die in a now meaningless campaign. These desertions only further hurt units that were already critically under-strength. Chaplain Laurence Wilmot, who served eleven months with his beloved West Nova Scotia Regiment, wrote after the Gothic Line, "The Regiment was not in good shape. So many of the old hands were done in and weary and in need of a thorough rest and reconditioning. New men coming in under those conditions became infected with their spirit."[74] By late 1944, the Italian front appeared perilously similar to the Western Front of the Great War—but unfortunately with all the horror and none of the poetry.

General Burns was finally done in by the British, though it was his own divisional commanders who pulled the trigger on him. On October 8, Burns ordered an attack

Canadian infantrymen in wet and muddy Northern Italy.

across the rain-swollen and mud-slick Fiumicino River, and both Hoffmeister and the New Zealand divisional commander objected to the plan. A miffed Burns, who was often accused of not being forceful enough, demanded that his generals comply but they refused again. This led to an unseemly row, with Hoffmeister insisting on being paraded before the new Eighth Army commander, Sir Richard McCreery, who had replaced Leese on October 1 after he was transferred to the Pacific theatre.[75] Hoffmeister was right in his objection to the plan, but he handled it badly. He knew that Burns's career was hanging by a thread. McCreery had no more sympathy for Burns than Leese, and now, with discontent voiced publicly by an experienced divisional commander, the wheels were set in motion to relieve Burns of his command. Burns was victorious on the battlefield, but McCreery declared, "... he does not lead.... His manner is depressing, diffident and unenthusiastic and he must completely fail to inspire his subordinate officers."[76] With the British looking to rid themselves of Burns, the Canadian high command in London and Ottawa—situated far from the backwater theatre, and now fully engaged in Northwest Europe—refused to expend much energy on his behalf. Burns took his dismissal with resentment, rightly noting, "We went farther and faster than any other corps."[77]

Burns's career seemed over, but he reinvented himself, remaining an active figure in postwar Canada as a senior civil servant, historian, and, at the end of his career, returning to the military. Could such a successful commander be truly as inarticulate and uninspiring as many have claimed over the years? Whatever the case, he, like so many generals, has been forgotten by Canadians, although modern papers occasionally acknowledge his role in establishing the roots of peacekeeping, in which Canadians take justifiable pride.

THE DRAGOON INVASION of southern France in mid-August all but put a bullet into the emaciated body that was the Italian campaign. While Churchill ordered that the Italian campaign should continue—with the goal of seizing Italy's northern industrial region, which was still feeding the Nazi war machine—the Americans were no longer willing to play along, especially with the Normandy campaign won and the Germans in Western Europe on the verge of collapse. The Americans were now calling the shots, but an obstinate Churchill demanded that General Alexander find ways to limp on. And so the offensive continued in Italy throughout the cold, rainy season of November and December, with the Allies driving the Germans back. Both sides had about twenty divisions to call upon, but since all of the units were depleted and short of men as a result of the constant wastage, sickness, and desertions, the term "division"—especially for the wiped-out Germans—is not terribly accurate. Nonetheless, there still remained hundreds of thousands of Germans and Allied troops in theatre. With the front all but stalemated, Allied airpower and firepower took a steady toll on the enemy, but Kesselring's forces continued to use all the advantages of battling on the defence. The fighting season closed down in early January because of the harsh weather, and both sides knew that the war would never be decided in Italy.

The Canadian government's decision to send I Canadian Corps to Italy divided the Canadian army and ultimately weakened Dominion influence in the primary campaign theatre, Northwest Europe. However, the Canadians gained valuable experience and proved they were able not to only match, but to consistently surpass, the efficiency of their comrades in the vaunted British Eighth Army. The Canadian success at Sicily, Ortona, the Hitler Line, and the Gothic Line contributed to victory in the poorcousin theatre of war. And the Canadians, as judged by German intelligence, were widely regarded as shock troops: masters of all-arms warfare and hard in the attack.

Both the Allies and the Axis were drawn into the prison of the Italian campaign, but that cage was of the Allies' making. Hitler's plan from 1942 to hold Tunisia, Sicily, and then Italy robbed him of forces to be used on the Eastern and Western fronts. The Italian campaign also allowed Churchill to forestall the invasion of Europe until the invaders were ready, and even then success was a near-run thing. Commentators at the time, and those since, have found it difficult to evaluate the achievements of the Allies in Italy, with the conflict between the senior Allied generals further muddying the water. But there were important strategic goals in the campaign, and the Allied forces achieved them. The Germans were defeated at the tactical and operational level, which ultimately led to a strategic victory. The supreme Allied command, both civilian and military, kept the Mediterranean theatre active to ensure that the German armies there—totalling twenty-two divisions in August 1944—could not be withdrawn and transferred to shore up Germany's borders.[78] The maintenance of pressure through battle also forced Hitler to deploy significant divisions in the Balkans, for fear of an amphibious landing from Allied troops in the Mediterranean. The Allied strategy in Italy was interwoven with that in Western Europe, and Italy was the long right flank in the global war. In April 1945, the Germans, 599,514 strong, faced 616,642 Allied soldiers in the Fifth and Eighth Armies, albeit with an additional million or so in the long logistical tail that wound hundreds of kilometres south through Italy and into North Africa.[79] While it might appear that the Germans were holding down the Allies, it was the Allies who could better afford the draw and strain on manpower, although one can't be sure how the dispersal of these forces would have shifted the balance of fighting in Europe. If Hitler had deployed some of his German Mediterranean formations in France at a time when the Allied divisions were most vulnerable—after the invasion landings—he might easily have tipped the balance in his favour. Such are the "what ifs?" of history. But it is also certain that the Mediterranean Allied forces could not have been immediately thrown into the clash along the French coast, because there was not enough shipping to transport them across the Channel. These divisions would simply have stewed in Britain, as German divisions fought for the beachhead. For the Allied high command, it was a far stronger strategic case to stretch out the Germans and force them to defend Italy, southern France, Greece, and the Balkans, which ultimately tied down fifty-five German divisions that could have been used on other fronts.[80]

The casualty figures bear out the attritional nature of the Allied victory. The Fifth Army suffered 188,746 casualties, while the Eighth Army lost another 123,254, for a total of 312,000. The German losses were even higher, at 434,646, which included 48,067 killed, 172,531 wounded, and 214,048 missing (captured or killed and with no known graves).[81] Of the 92,757 Canadians who served in Italy, 5,399 were killed, 19,486 were wounded, and 1,004 were taken prisoner.

There are few Canadian memorials to this day in the Sicilian or Italian theatres of war. Unlike in France or the Netherlands, where the liberated people still joyfully remember the Allied soldiers who gave their lives to free their occupied countries, the Italians were enemies first and then haplessly faced occupation. Much of their country was destroyed in the Allies' defeat of the Germans. One should not be surprised that the few Canadian memorials are rather shabby and ill cared for, save for those in the Commonwealth War Graves cemeteries.

Italy may have been a forgotten theatre of war, during and after the fighting, but Canadians serving there turned their sideshow status into a bleak badge of honour. One of their popular songs was "The Ballad of the D-Day Dodgers," sung to the tune of "Lili Marlene" and composed in direct response to a thoughtless comment by Lady Astor (the first woman to sit as an MP in the British House of Commons), who besmirched the reputation of all in the Mediterranean theatre by suggesting they had dodged their duty by not fighting in Normandy.

> We're the D-Day Dodgers out in Italy—
> Always on the vino, always on the spree.
> Eighth Army scroungers and their tanks
> We live in Rome—among the Yanks.
> We are the D-Day Dodgers, over here in Italy.
>
> We landed at Salerno, a holiday with pay,
> Jerry brought the band down to cheer us on our way.
> Showed us the sights and gave us tea
> We all sang songs, the beer was free.
> We are the D-Day Dodgers, way out in Italy....
>
> When you look 'round the mountains, through the mud and rain
> You'll find the crosses, some which bear no name.
> Heartbreak, and toil and suffering gone
> The boys beneath them slumber on.
> They were the D-Day Dodgers, who'll stay in Italy.
>
> So listen all you people, over land and foam
> Even though we've parted, our hearts are close to home.
> When we return we hope you'll say
> You did your little bit, though far away.
> All of the D-Day Dodgers, way out there in Italy.

CHAPTER 12

THE LONG LEFT FLANK

On August 25, a few days after the Falaise Gap was closed and two enemy armies were destroyed, Field Marshal Alan Brooke noted in his diary, "News of German decay on all fronts continues to be almost unbelievable."[1] The sense of impending victory from field marshals down to privates, was electric. General Harry Crerar's army chief of staff, Major-General C.C. Mann, recounted that "many people felt that the war might be won in a matter of weeks."[2] With the Nazi economy in ruins, its cities pounded by the bombers, and the Russians advancing in the east, Ultra intelligence based on tens of thousands of decrypted messages suggested that the German people could not keep on fighting into the new year. The terrible war seemed to be coming to an end.

General Bernard Montgomery remained the cocksure commander of the Allied ground forces even though his reputation had been tarnished (at least among the Americans) during the Normandy campaign. He would remain the senior general for another week before Eisenhower crossed over the Channel to set up his head-quarters. Following SHAEF's pre-D-Day strategy, Montgomery ordered his Anglo-American-Canadian armies to advance northward on a broad front, hounding the Germans before them. The Allied formations outnumbered the Germans by a factor of at least two to one, with 2,168,307 men and 49 divisions on the continent.[3] They sought to annihilate the fleeing Germans before they could re-establish themselves in new defensive positions to the north of the Seine River, but the Germans were running faster than the Allies could follow.

The First Canadian Army, on the far left of the Allied northern drive and closest to the Channel, was to cross the Seine and then clear the Channel ports of Le Havre, Dieppe,

Boulogne, Calais, and Dunkirk. Theirs was very much an unglamorous role as the British and American armies went charging off in all directions towards liberating Paris and taking the war to German soil. But the Canadian left flank was crucial for opening up the constricted logistical funnel from the Normandy beachheads. Liberated ports would relieve the pressure on the Commonwealth's 21st Army Group and the American's 12th Army Group, consisting of the U.S. First and Third Armies (and later the Ninth and Fifteenth), which consumed more and more oil, fuel, and ammunition with each step they took into France.

From August 22 to 30, Crerar's First Canadian Army—consisting of I British Corps and II Canadian Corps—advanced northeastward, with the British hugging the coast and Canada's 2nd, 3rd, and 4th Divisions surging ahead to close the 60 kilometres to Rouen and the Seine River. Running and gunning, the Anglo-Canadian divisions found that rather than German defenders it was the shortage of fuel, the poor quality of roads, and the crowding and confusion on them that slowed the pursuit. Reginald Dixon, intelligence officer for the Stormont, Dundas and Glengarry Highlanders, observed that one infantry brigade took up 27 kilo-metres of road space, while a full division was strung out along 135 kilometres.[4] The stop-and-start advance was annoying for all, but there were no grinding battles like the attritional struggle in Normandy.

Above the snaking armies, air observers in their Austers scouted ahead, while on the ground lead units like II Canadian Corps' armoured car regiment, the 12th Manitoba Dragoons, rushed forward in a ranger role, sending back intelligence to commanders and guarding bridges across the waterways. Behind the reconnaissance formations came the main body, moving in "advance to contact" readiness, with troops shaking out into combat positions at the first sign of enemy fire. Major Doug McIntyre of the Essex Scottish said that although "not even the most duty-bound infantry sol-diers relished the idea of acting as 'bait' stuck out in front of a divisional column on strange terrain and unknown countryside to draw enemy fire," the men followed their orders.[5] Moving in the opposite direction were thousands of despondent Germans who gave themselves up to the first Canadian they could find, often fear-fully clutching Allied pamphlets that promised safe passage, along with pictures of their parents or children to soften the hearts of their captors. Almost all the prisoners kept their lives; just as many lost their wristwatches and wallets to light-fingered victors.

Despite making giant bounds forward, the Canucks were reminded on August 25 that they were far from the campaign's centre of gravity, as Paris was liberated to worldwide celebration. That was the same day that a large German force ambushed a group of Black Watch and Royal Canadian Army Service Corps soldiers, who had to fight off a determined attack. All along the wide front, skirmishes and shoot-outs continued. "The Germans fought in several different ways," wrote Sergeant Charles Kipp of the Lincoln and Welland Regiment. "Maybe they would leave an 88 sitting on a corner or out in a field. When we would come down the road, they would knock out one of our tanks and everyone would have to stop. Sometimes, it would be several hours before we could move again.... The Germans would retreat up the road a ways and do it all over again; or maybe they would leave a platoon of infantry or just a machine gun."[6] The enemy still had the ability to turn and strike.

The next day, on the 26th, the scout platoons of the Lincoln and Welland Regiment, one of the advance formations on the right flank from the 4th Canadian Armoured Division, closed to the Seine and, encountering no opposition, crossed the 80 metres of water using boats and shovels as paddles. The 60-kilometre advance had cost hundreds of casualties due to enemy mines, shells, and bullets, but the operation was a cakewalk compared to Normandy. While most of the Germans had already fled across the Seine in their headlong retreat, even combat-hardened Allied soldiers could not help but allow themselves to think, as the wild rumours predicted, that the campaign might be winding down. But not all were optimistic. Reginald Dixon warned in his diary, "We have to curb the tendency to feel too much like liberating heroes. The war was not over."[7]

WHILE THE 3RD AND 4TH CANADIAN DIVISIONS cleared enemy stragglers on their fronts—which intelligence described as "confused and disorganized"—and provided fire cover for engineers to build Bailey bridges across the water at Elbeuf for follow-on forces, the 2nd Division ran up against two German battlegroups. The 2nd SS Panzer Division and the 85th Division defended the high ground within the Forêt de la Londe. Expecting a routed enemy, the 4th and 6th Canadian Infantry Brigades walked into a large-scale ambush in the early hours of August 27.[8] Within the 4-kilometre-wide forest, the Germans were cleverly hidden, having fortified a series of ridges that allowed them to rain down fire on the few roads that wound through the dense trees.

When the front-line battalions—Les Fusiliers Mont-Royal and the Royal Hamilton Light Infantry—were fired upon, they wisely went to ground and retreated. The divisional commander, Major-General Charles Foulkes, urged on by an impatient Lieutenant-General Guy Simonds, demanded another operation on the 27th. It failed, as did new attacks on the 28th. Bullheaded and bloodthirsty orders continued from the high command. The Canadians could easily have waited out the Germans, who had no capacity to storm out of the woods, and Simonds's insistence for action came from a general looking to the horizon instead of paying attention to the losses mounting in the forest. He was also urged on by Montgomery, who characterized the Canadians as too slow "and prone to bellyaching."[9]

The wooded terrain hampered movement and coordination. When tanks were thrown into the mix, they were diverted along open roads and cleared spaces, where they were minced by anti-tank guns. Corporal Richard Bryant of the Sherbrooke Fusilier remembered, "The brass kept sending us in every day against the same thing. We could have bypassed right around them." Bryant's Sherman took four hits from 88 shells, two of which sliced through the steel armour from front to back of the tank and miraculously did not kill the crew. The situation was, in his mind, "unreal. Every time we moved, we were getting it."[10] Gunners tried to assist their beleaguered comrades, but inaccurate maps made it difficult to pinpoint enemy positions, and the forest provided cover from the prying eyes of forward artillery observers. Even as the commanders of the Royal Hamilton Light Infantry and the Royal Regiment of Canada objected to the renewed attack, arguing "that this task was beyond the powers of a battalion composed largely of reinforcements personnel with little training," Foulkes ordered a renewed push.[11] The Rileys from Hamilton were carved up again, and more Canadian units were thrown into the cauldron, with territory won and lost in confusing see-saw encounters. The Calgary Highlanders' war diarist for August 29 recounted frankly, "Today has been a nightmare. We were subjected to constant fire and had little protection."[12] Three days of fierce fighting saw six battalions take 577 casualties.[13] Late on the 29th, when the Germans were in danger of being overwhelmed on the flanks, they retreated safely across the Seine. The Canadians were badly outfought.

Was the stiff resistance in the Forêt de la Londe an anomaly? The Canadian high command hoped it was, and that this outer crust of defenders could be swept aside and the rotten core of the German army pierced. But if the enemy had proved masters of anything, on battlefronts from North Africa to Italy to the Russian steppes, it was of a phoenix-like ability to rise from the ashes. And now, in late August, as they enjoyed some breathing room between Allied attacks, the German high command combed out new troops, young, old, and decrepit, from home defence units and conscripted civilians, with slave labour increased to fill the gaps in work and production. In early September, the Germans could have been routed, but with every step away from the Normandy beaches the Allied lines of communication were stretched a little longer to reach the forces at the front. The enemy was getting away, although Allied fighters and bombers exacted a fearful toll in lives. The German retreat was chaotic, with little water or medical care available for their suffering soldiers, but a beaten army that is not ready to surrender can go a long time on starvation and panic, especially when its soldiers are threatened with execution should they try to surrender. This was the discipline of the revolver mixed with fanaticism and fear. The Germans still had fight in them.

WITH FRANCE WELL ON ITS WAY to being liberated, Eisenhower, who was preparing to take over command of the ground forces from Montgomery on September 1, was encouraged by the headlong German retreat from Normandy. Eisenhower's plan, known as the "broad front" strategy, ordered the Allied armies to advance on a wide front, with thrusts to the north and northeast that would take them into the industrialized Ruhr area of Germany, and to the south to overrun the resource-rich Saar region. The broad front was a steamroller that was safe and methodical, and had been the pre-invasion plan. However, in early September, with the Germans on the run, the enemy appeared ripe for a knock-out. Montgomery believed now was the time to strike more aggressively.

The normally cautious Montgomery had proposed a new plan on August 23: a narrower and more focused northern drive using his 21st Army Group, along with elements of General Bradley's 12th Army Group. A sharpened stab to the northeast across the Rhine River would take the Anglo-American armies into the industrial heartland of the Ruhr more rapidly. Like a needle puncturing a balloon, a thrust like this would compel the Nazis—especially the relatively untouched Fifteenth Army in the Scheldt area—to pull back to cover the Fatherland, thereby leaving themselves open to destruction from the mass of airpower. It was an audacious plan. For it to work, Montgomery required colossal amounts of ammunition and fuel, both of which were in short supply. It also required difficult choices. This single thrust would starve the American southern advance—especially Patton's Third Army—of resources, even though his formations now appeared to have the greatest opportunity of breaking into Germany proper.

Montgomery had formulated his "narrow thrust" plan in the final days of the Normandy campaign. At a meeting of Eisenhower and Montgomery on August 23, the two wilful commanders, encumbered by their past unease over the perception that the British general had been too cautious in Normandy, did not see eye to eye. Many of the SHAEF senior commanders briefing Eisenhower thought that Montgomery's new plan was unworkable due to logistical stretch. There was also a widely held feeling at SHAEF that the much-disliked British general was simply trying to feather his own nest by commanding this new Anglo-American lunge, despite the fact that the number of American troops outnumbered British and Commonwealth ones by a ratio of three to one. Moreover, a single thrust, no matter how concentrated, could be more easily stopped than a broader and more methodical advance north and south of the Ardennes. While SHAEF was uneasy with Monty's new plan, Eisenhower was willing to consider it if only to keep the Anglo-American alliance intact. He was also pleased to see Montgomery go for the jugular instead of following his usual inclination to deliver body blows. Eisenhower was inclined to back Montgomery, but he knew that the Allied advance would break down if supplies had to be rushed along the roads from the Normandy beaches, as each division needed about 500 tons of material a day. And so he demanded that Montgomery devote and divert significant forces towards liberating the Belgian inland harbour of Antwerp.[14] Antwerp's 50 kilometres of docks and established railway facilities, and its discharge capacity of 100,000 tons a day, would allow for the feeding of the Allied armies and would support either the narrow thrust or the broad front advance.

Antwerp was fundamental to the Allied war effort in Europe. The city was at the mouth of the Scheldt River, some 70 kilometres inland from the sea. Chalking up a significant victory, British armoured units from XXX Corps had thrust hard to capture Antwerp on September 4. It was such a stunningly quick advance that the city fell almost without a fight and with the docks largely intact, although the Belgian resistance had paid a heavy price in stopping the retreating Germans from demolishing key structures and emplacements. With the enemy ousted, it looked as though the German Fifteenth Army might be destroyed if the British kept pushing northward. Yet XXX Corps had sprinted to the finish and then stopped on the line. With the British exhausted, fought-out, and low in fuel, the Germans, driven out of Antwerp, realized that there was no longer pressure against them and simply dug in on the outskirts of the city, north of the Albert Canal. Their position proved, once the bridges were blown, to be a perfect anti-tank ditch. While Antwerp was in Allied hands, the port remained closed because the long estuary leading to the sea was still held by German gun batteries along the South Beveland Peninsula and Walcheren Island, and to the south along the enclave of Breskens. Antwerp was useless until the Scheldt estuary was cleared of enemy forces.

Even with the deepening logistical crisis, Montgomery was focused on his audacious narrow thrust to cross the Neder Rhine at Arnhem, in the Netherlands, and he barely paid attention to Antwerp. He ordered Crerar's First Canadian Army, all but abandoned on the far left flank, to begin the process of clearing the coastal fortresses of Le Havre, Boulogne, Dieppe, and Calais, but continued to ignore the need to open the Scheldt.[15] This was a significant oversight for Montgomery, who prided himself in his careful planning. After the slow sludge of Normandy, Montgomery was going for broke.

Montgomery allowed General Crerar to plan and execute the coastal battles to clear the Channel ports. These fortresses were built around hardened positions of concrete and steel, and defended by seaward naval guns as part of Hitler's Atlantic

Wall. The multiple concrete gun bunkers were designed to repel an amphibious invasion, so the German defenders had frantically been laying minefields and digging anti-tank defences to protect against a push from the landward south or east. These ramparts were not yet complete, but nor were they soft positions.

Crerar ordered I British Corps to liberate the coastal sector of the Le Havre peninsula, while Simonds's three divisions of II Canadian Corps advanced to objectives up the coast. Simonds faced a challenge in that two of his three divisional commanders were new—with Harry Foster having replaced George Kitching after his firing and Dan Spry taking over from Keller when he was wounded—and he did not feel that the third, Foulkes, could do his job. Nor could he keep close watch over them. The three Canadian divisions would soon be spread out over a battlefield that ranged for more than 100 kilometres. On the far right, Foster's 4th Armoured Division raced towards the Somme region, south of the Scheldt, covering the right flank, while the central thrust, Spry's veteran 3rd Division, was directed towards Boulogne and Calais. Foulkes's 2nd Division was to have its revenge by liberating Dieppe and then moving on to Dunkirk. When the Channel ports were cleared, the First Canadian Army would converge on the Germans in the Scheldt to open up the approaches to Antwerp.

THE SEPULCHRE OF DIEPPE BECKONED. The disaster of August 1942 was forgotten by no one in the 2nd Canadian Infantry Division, even after the fighting in Normandy had wiped out many of the veterans of that earlier, ill-fated raid. The advance to Dieppe on the coast saw the Canadians pass through innumerable small towns and hamlets. Wild cheering greeted the liberators, and many Tricolors and Union Jacks were waved. Long-hidden bottles of wine were uncorked. Songs of stilted English were sung with gusto, including "The Maple Leaf Forever," Canada's unofficial national anthem. "Occasionally a village, where the Boche makes a stand, has to be blown to bits before we can get on," shrugged a Canadian gunner, "but in general it is lovely."[16] Jeeps, universal carriers, and even Sherman tanks soon resembled parade floats with flowers and flags draping them. "Mothers held their children high to catch a glimpse of the heroes from Canada," wrote Major D.W. Grant of the Toronto Scottish Regiment.[17]

The celebration came to an end on September 1, as the Canadians girded themselves for battle. Lead reconnaissance units closed on the port, but instead of encountering ambushes, they were greeted by more indebted crowds thronging the roads. The German garrison troops had bugged out. It was a race against time to cancel the Bomber Command operation that was set to flatten the defences around Dieppe, and many French civilians in the process. In the end, the bombers were called off with twenty minutes to spare.[18] During the celebration over the next couple of days, the liberators were further feted, although more than a few Canadians were uncomfortable at witnessing the rough justice that was meted out as the French freedom fighters caught and punished collaborators. A few such traitors were hung from lamp posts, and many more were dealt with in the shadows.

"Canadians, Dieppe is Yours," read one large sign from the grateful citizens. On September 3, the Canadians held a ceremony to honour the memory of their fallen comrades from August 19, 1942. It was an opportunity to bury painful memories. General Crerar rightly thought it was important for him to attend, and he took the salute from the entire division marching by in columns. However, recently promoted Field Marshal Montgomery had ordered Crerar to a crucial meeting on the 3rd at Second Army's headquarters. Crerar replied tactfully but firmly that, as Canadian army commander, his duty was at Dieppe, unless the matter was urgent. With no reply from Montgomery, he continued with the ceremony. But communications were slow, and when the field marshal—still smarting from having recently handed command of all ground forces to

The liberating Canadians are greeted with celebrations.

Eisenhower, which some muck-raking journalists had erroneously reported as a demotion—subsequently insisted that Crerar attend, it was not possible for the Canadian general to make the trip in time. Montgomery saw this as the wilful disobedience and overreacted. He had never liked having Crerar as an army commander, feeling that he was little more than a political appointee and that he had not driven his army hard enough in Normandy.[19] The field marshal intimated darkly that Crerar might be removed from command for his disobedience. The Canadian

The Canadians return to Dieppe as victors. The 2nd Canadian Infantry Division marches past General Harry Crerar, September 3, 1944.

had been the target of Monty's slings and arrows in the past, and might have reacted with more anger at his renewed mean and misdirected ire, but he kept his head. Crerar would not be bullied. While Monty could do how he saw fit, he warned his superior that he would, of course, report the situation to Ottawa. Crerar was a subordinate general to Montgomery, but he was also a national battlefield commander and could, at any time, invoke his dual roles. Montgomery did not need another fight with politicians, and he retreated in haste from his threats. Crerar was the bigger man, and his patience with hotheads, be it superiors like Montgomery or subordinates like Simonds, was a strength not often seen by others. The ugly incident also revealed that the uncharismatic Canadian general, with his thirty years of military experience, could twist the blade with the best of them.

British engineers had immediately begun to restore the port installations at Dieppe. By September 7 the first vessel docked, and by the end of the month the port's daily capacity of moving supplies rose to some 7,000 tons.[20] Canadians would forever remember Dieppe for August 1942, but the town would play a far more central role in the Allied war effort as a supply port.

THE 4TH CANADIAN ARMOURED DIVISION faced the weakest German opposition in their advance northward. As the armoured regiments made deep gains, the French underground resistance provided valuable intelligence on the retreating enemy. The armoured cars, vehicles, and tanks raced northward to the Belgian border, and on September 2 passed the Somme battlefields where thousands of Canadian soldiers from the last war lay buried. They reached the southern outskirts of Bruges on September 7. Throughout the advance, there were few stand-up battles, but nighttime remained dangerous as German stragglers moved from their hiding spots and set out again on the long march back to their lines. The lost enemy troops blundered into Canadian formations, and though many surrendered, some of the more fanatical ones fought to the death. At the same time, one of the welcome results of the northern drive was the freeing of dozens of downed airmen who emerged from French farms and attics after weeks and months of being on the run from the Gestapo.

Four hundred years earlier, in August and September 1544, Henry VIII had besieged Boulogne and captured it after eight weeks. The Canadians of 1944 did not have that

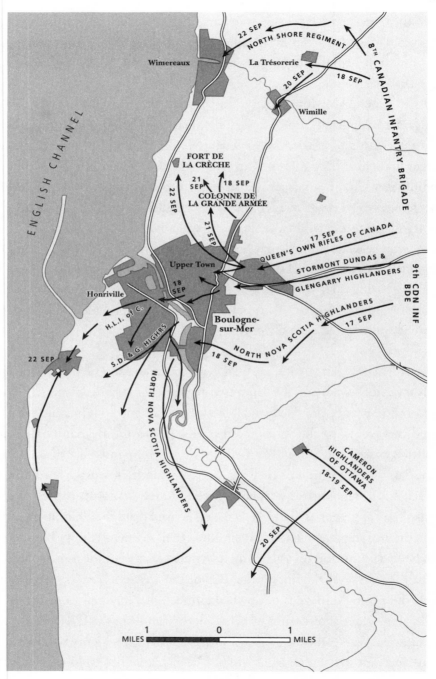

CAPTURE OF BOULOGNE, SEPTEMBER 17–22, 1944

long to wait, although theirs would have to be a similar, methodical siege. Operation Wellhit would see Major-General Dan Spry's 3rd Division snuff outposts along a series of high hills that ringed the landward advances, before the attackers closed on the town itself. Even though the fort's main armaments were directed out towards the sea, the German hind-end defences bristled with guns—ninety pieces of at least 75mm calibre or higher—and were sheltered by concrete and steel, able to resist all but direct artillery shell strikes.[21] "The 25-pounder shells would bounce off those fortifications like peas off a tin pan," lamented the Commander Royal Artillery (CRA) of the 3rd Canadian Infantry Division, Brigadier Stanley Todd.[22] These formidable positions would have to be reduced by artillery, bomber, and rocket fire, as well as careful counter-battery fire based on gathered intelligence, but much of the Canadian Corps medium and heavy artillery was assisting the British 51st Division's siege of Le Havre, the second largest port in France and about 240 kilometres away on the coast. Any assault on Boulogne and its 10,000-man garrison would have to wait for these siege guns. In the meantime, the guns commenced their softening up of the enemy positions outside the concrete emplacements, even as the gunners suffered ammunition shortages.[23]

Major-General Dan Spry, an Italian campaign veteran, at age thirty-one was the youngest general in the Allied forces. He had a feel for battle and was aware of the weak morale among the enemy garrison troops, but there was no easy way to bring the fortress to surrender. A direct charge would be costly for his troops, and Spry hoped that a punishing bombardment, combined with terror weapons such as flame-throwers, would lead to surrender for the trapped defenders.

The Wasps—universal carriers fitted out with flame-throwers—spouted a napalm-like liquid fire that burned through flesh and bone. The Germans were terrified of flame-throwers, and always called down artillery or mortar fire to knock them out. Corporal Horace Tudhope of the Algonquin Regiment was torn between the act of killing with flame and the need to end the war as soon as possible. Tudhope embraced the Wasp, and even manned one for a time, but he still believed, after seeing the carbonized remains of the enemy, that using napalm "was a terrible thing."[24]

Throughout the week starting on the 5th, hundreds of demoralized German prisoners sneaked from their lines to surrender to the besieging Canadians. And in a humane move in an inhumane war, the Canadians worked with their German counterparts to allow French civilians to pass through their lines, with some 8,000 fleeing between September 11 and 13.[25] With most of the civilians cleared, and siege guns now brought forward after the fall of Le Havre on September 12, Spry planned for the infantry assault. There was little intelligence on the enemy fortifications and few reliable maps, and even the obliging civilian occupants of the city were of limited value. The Canadians had lost some of their edge, too, as the last two weeks had consisted of more liberation than battle. Many of the vehicles still contained flowers thrown by jubilant citizens. A bomber strike might induce a hasty surrender, but with all of the ground commanders spread along the hundreds of kilometres of front anxious for the limited aerial support, the Canadian request for such an attack was turned down. General Simonds took matters into his own hands and flew to England to convince the air marshals he needed bombers. They were given.

The artillery bombardment thickened from the 12th onward, and a steady series of aerial photographs provided a number of targets for the gunners. New sites were also added daily by infantry patrols and prisoners who provided a fuller picture into the enemy defences. As the 8th and 9th Canadian Infantry Brigades prepared for the assault on the early morning of September 17, aware they were facing a dug-in force that outnumbered them considerably, 762 bombers dropped more than 3,232 tons of high explosives on enemy positions starting at 8:25 A.M.[26] One Canadian infantry-man remarked, "The explosions of bombs were very great and quite unlike artillery-fire. The latter crack and pound with individual reports. Bombs make a deep, raging and roaring sound, as if some vast thing in the distance were shaking a vast piece of tin; sort of a rushing noise.... Though the bombs probably fell in succession, the percussions came in one heavy roar.... You could feel the noise on your eyeballs."[27]

With the dust still swirling, the infantry advanced over the cratered roads and fields. Behind them, 328 artillery pieces laid down crushing fire. In a clever man-oeuvre, another wave of bombers passed over Boulogne as the Canadians started their advance, driving the German defenders back into their bunkers to escape the fall of the non-existent bombs. Hugging the artillery barrage closely, the Fort Garry Horse Shermans and Fireflys blasted away at any sign of life. Behind the armoured thrust came the infantry riding into battle in Kangaroos and half-tracks.[28] Lieutenant

The bombers hit the German defences around Boulogne before the infantry assault.

Reginald Dixon of the Glens described the scene: "one big bunker turned on its side, and the huge craters which had been made. Also, there were great blocks of concrete planted by the Germans across and beside the road to prevent movement of our tanks and Bren carrier. They had been tossed around like toy building blocks."[29]

When the minefields and bomb craters—some of which were 15 metres across and 6 metres deep—stopped the Kangaroos, the infantry dismounted and pushed forward on foot. The North Shore Regiment advancing to the north at La Trésorerie were held up by a series of thick concrete fortifications, bunkers, and gun positions, but they stabbed their way through the Germans, capturing three artillery batteries by the early hours of September 18. PIATs blew the enemy out of strongpoints, and phosphorus bombs burned out the die-hards. One Canadian officer commented, almost in tears, "It was inspiring and awe-inspiring to watch the attacking companies, like ants, moving up the slope under heavy fire and over mines. With every puff of smoke and dirt you wondered what fellow had got it."[30]

Canadian medium artillery guns firing against the
German positions to soften them up before the attack.

Further to the south, Le Régiment de la Chaudière, the Queen's Own Rifles of Canada, the Stormont, Dundas and Glengarry Highlanders, and the North Nova Scotia Highlanders ground their way into the town, with the Novas having to pass through at least twenty minefields. The outer defences were cleared, but the Germans were holed up in the ancient limestone citadel overlooking the port. The Canadians might have been forgiven for feeling like crusaders of old. The Glens surveyed the battlements and, coordinating with tanks, raked the walls with machine-gun fire and high explosives. The enemy refused to surrender. Castles can be taken in many ways, however. Major J.G. Stothart, aided by a sympathetic civilian, led a platoon through an underground tunnel. Emerging within the garrison, Stothart's Highlanders gunned down the surprised German defenders as artillery blew in the portcullis. Some 200 German prisoners were taken.

Scrambling through the city, the Highland Light Infantry of Canada and the Glens drove the rest of the way through Boulogne on the 18th, curling southward. The last German defenders in Boulogne surrendered on the 20th, and a garrison to the north at Wimereux—where Great War Canadian poet John McCrae is buried—finally succumbed on the 22nd. When the last Germans ran up the white flag, 634 Canadians had been killed or wounded. In return, the two brigades had bagged 9,517 prisoners, about the same number as the British had taken at Le Havre.[31]

Boulogne provided another port for the Allies, but their own bombardment and German demolitions had ruined much of the harbour, and even with an urgent rebuilding effort, ships did not begin unloading cargo until mid-October. The port's capture did not alleviate the Allies' logistical challenge, and the continuing desperation

Private F.J. Coakley of the North Shore Regiment sitting on a captured German coastal artillery gun, Boulogne, France, September 21, 1944.

drove the 3rd Canadian Infantry Division onward, moving up the coast. Behind shell-heavy attacks, the 7th Canadian Infantry Brigade, which was held back from the Boulogne fighting, burned and blasted their way forward in a series of battles against coastal batteries from the 16th to the 18th, and then confronted the fortress at Calais. The guns there had spent much of the war hurling 2,000-pound shells across the English Channel, and now the Canadians sought to put an end to that harassment.

Allied intelligence estimates severely underestimated the strength of the Calais garrison, which was nearly as large as that at Boulogne. It would never fall to a single infantry brigade supported by limited artillery. The Canadians dug in and waited for high-calibre guns to arrive, while the smaller ones, the 25-pounders, as one gunner put it, "hammered happily away."[32] A series of bomber sorties started on the 25th and resulted in more than 6,000 tons of high explosives being dropped on the enemy-held area, but it did little to force a capitulation. The enemy could not be dislodged, even as German defenders and French civilians alike were blown apart or buried alive.

In preparation for a climactic battle, 224 artillery guns engaged in destructive and counter-battery shoots to destroy the enemy defences, but it was a slow way to demolish thousands of tons of concrete. The Canadian infantry fought their way forward, metre by metre. The huge siege guns at Cap Gris Nez, halfway between Boulogne and Calais, and garrisoned by some 1,500 Germans, were netted by the 9th Canadian Infantry Brigade on the 29th.[33] The next day, the Canadians clawed their way into Calais's inner sanctum. German resistance collapsed. The victory was achieved, as Rifleman Stan Creaser recalled, by "stepping over dead comrades."[34] The Calais garrison formally capitulated on October 1, and 7,500 Germans trudged to the barbed wire prisoner camps. Another damaged port fell into Allied hands, but it was not enough to feed the voracious Allied armies.[35]

WITH ANTWERP IN ALLIED HANDS, but not the approaches along the Scheldt, and with the Canadians steadily reducing the Channel fortresses, Field Marshal Montgomery pounced. Even though he had a reputation for being careful, even ponderous, in planning battles—remarking to journalists only a year before, "You must never attack until you are absolutely ready"—Montgomery decided on September 4 that it was time to drive hard to Germany.[36] Montgomery and his senior generals knew that Antwerp was crucial to the war effort, but instead of allocating resources to clearing the Scheldt in order to open the crucial port, the field marshal was hell-bent on crossing the Rhine into the industrial centres of the Ruhr.[37] It was a risky operation but not reckless, as some hindsight historians have painted it, and if the German lines had been pierced, as it appeared they might be in the ashes of Normandy, then the war might have been ended in 1944. Millions of lives would have been saved. Yet the Master, as Montgomery was known to his staff, never fully weighed the danger of failing to take Antwerp in a timely manner. He became a fierce champion of his narrow thrust, which he code-named Market Garden.

His superior, Eisenhower, had long grown tired of the British field marshal, and when the two met on September 10, they clashed again over the grand strategy. Eisenhower, who had now crossed over into Europe to exercise overall command of all forces, did not want to diverge from his broad front strategy, but the British terrier refused to let go of the morsel that was so firmly lodged in his jaws. The two departed the meeting intensely unhappy with one another, and the future Allied ground campaign seemed very much uncertain, but Eisenhower eventually relented and cabled a few days later to give Montgomery the green light for Market Garden.

Another possibility was open to the Allies. The British army could have pushed north of Antwerp about 30 kilometres, which would likely have cut off three German corps of the Fifteenth Army that were west of the city and south of the Scheldt, collapsing the front on some 90,000 Germans, 600 guns, and 6,200 vehicles, and creating the conditions for another aerial slaughter like at the Falaise Gap. Some historians have criticized Montgomery for failing to follow through with this manoeuvre, but a major campaign to the north, against an enemy whose defences had already congealed into a more coherent position, would have likely resulted in a long and costly battle.[38] Nonetheless, because of Montgomery's fixation on Market Garden, the German Fifteenth Army was able to move most of its troops out of danger and into the Scheldt— where the First Canadian Army would have to fight them in a few weeks.

Despite the supply famine, Montgomery planned to drive to the Lower Rhine at Arnhem, which was about 150 kilometres northeast into the Netherlands and protected by several canals and rivers. It would be a killing blow. However, since Lieutenant-General Brian Horrocks's XXX Corps—consisting of some 20,000 vehicles—would have to travel along a narrow road and cross several bridges, the Germans would demolish the crossings long before the armoured cars and tanks could reach them. So Montgomery planned a daring airborne drop to seize each of the bridges. Horrocks's armoured thrust would crash forward to relieve the paratroopers and the bridges, one after another.[39]

Montgomery planned to employ the American 101st and 82nd Airborne Divisions to seize several rivers and crossings between Eindhoven and Nijmegen, while the 1st British Airborne Division, supported by the 1st Polish Airborne Brigade, was to occupy the last, most northerly bridge over the Rhine. The advantage of using airborne troops was that they could be dropped behind enemy lines to sow confusion and disrupt the exposed lines of communication. But being lightly armed, they were vulnerable to counterattack, especially from tanks. The operation was a gamble, no doubt, but it might catch the demoralized Germans off guard long enough for the Allies to bore a hole through their line.

Montgomery's plan was formulated in early September as German divisions were falling back in confusion or holed up in fortresses, but now, ten days later, the enemy had regained his balance. Intelligence officers warned that enemy armoured forces, particularly the 9th and 10th SS Panzer Divisions, had moved to the area around the British drop zone, the furthest one from Horrocks's advancing tanks and infantry. But Montgomery and his staff allowed uncritical thinking to influence the decision of going for what has become known as "a bridge too far."[40] Everything had to fall into place for Market Garden to work. Yet the Germans could read a map as easily as the British—and they were aided by a full set of plans when an American officer, disobeying orders, carried them with him to his death in a glider crash. The Germans knew exactly what Montgomery hoped to achieve with his audacious plan.

As 5,000 aircraft and gliders dropped the airborne troops on the night of September 17, the masters of the delaying action worked their craft. German resistance slowed Horrocks's armoured thrust northward, which shifted from a rapier-thin stab to a slow, bashing rumble. Fighting against the enemy, time, and geography, the armoured convoy linked up with the 101st Airborne on the 18th, but was delayed in taking the second bridge held by the 82nd Division until the 20th. They were behind schedule. Advancing the 150 kilometres without heavy concentrations of artillery went against the British attack doctrine, and it was not surprising that they found it hard going against the measured German retreat. All the while, the 1st British Airborne Division and a Polish brigade were battling for their lives at the furthest bridge. With German Tiger tanks converging on the exposed positions, and artillery pounding them, the British and Polish paratroopers were ground down in fighting over nine days, and all but annihilated, suffering 7,400 casualties. The remnants of the 1st Airborne and the Polish brigade—about 1,700 strong—were withdrawn on the night of the 25th, in an assault boat crossing of the Neder Rhine, where two field companies of the Royal Canadian Engineers—the 20th and 23rd—served with British engineers to run the gauntlet of mortar and shellfire. They saved hundreds of paratroopers from death or imprisonment. Montgomery's force had been guillotined.

The failure at Arnhem had a profound impact on the Allied strategy for late 1944, and it ensured the war would continue into 1945. Montgomery suffered another blow as he had bet heavily on Market Garden and now wore the failure, much to the delight of his many detractors. But Monty remained the Allies' ablest and most dynamic general, save for perhaps Patton, who was fighting in the south and frustrated by shortages of fuel. After devoting enormous resources to Market Garden, Eisenhower tried to reinstate the shattered broad front plan, but southern, central, and northern armies were now converging on Germany in widening and diverging arcs, each lurching forward at a different speed due to enemy resistance and chronic shortages of ammunition and POL (petrol, oil, and lubricants). Armies, corps, and divisions were spread over France and Belgium, and the logistical nightmare mounted, especially with all the rail lines devastated by the effective Allied bombing campaign. Again Eisenhower ordered Montgomery—even more emphatically—to open Antwerp as a critical objective for the continued Allied advance. But now the German Fifteenth Army was ready for a long campaign. Tens of thousands of German defenders had retreated to Walcheren Island, South Beveland, and the Breskens Pocket. It was the First Canadian Army, neglected on the left flank and now much weakened after having lost three divisions to Market Garden, that had the decisive role of clearing the enemy from behind daunting natural and military defences. The battle for the Scheldt would become one of the most important campaigns of the war.

CHAPTER 13

BATTLE OF THE SCHELDT

The Canadians emerged from the coastal campaign bruised and scarred. Denied the glory of liberating Paris or thrusting for Germany, the First Canadian Army was, as one journalist called it, the "Cinderella allied army."[1] The thankless campaign was made even worse as the Germans fought hard for Boulogne, Calais, and their other coastal fortresses. Dieppe was liberated without a shot fired, but the 2nd Division, lulled into a false sense of security, had run up against another 10,000 defenders at Dunkirk. There, the 5th Canadian Infantry Brigade was outnumbered by the German garrison troops and entirely outgunned by the fort's artillery. It led to a miserable siege from September 6 to 14. During that time, the Dunkirk defenders blasted the Canadians, forcing them to dig into the muck. The 5th Brigade's war diary showed the frustration of the troops: "This 'sitting-and-looking-at-the-enemy-game' NOT being what we are used to, particularly when we have to sit and be shelled by his big guns ... a somewhat depressing business."[2] When the front was handed over to British troops on September 14, the Allied command decided wisely to simply starve out the garrison.

While the masking of Dunkirk with a siege force saved lives by avoiding a fruitless blind battering, it meant that the port facilities were denied to the Allies, with the Germans occupying them until May 9, 1945. Operations continued up the coast, past the Franco-Belgian border. As the Canadian and British troops pressed north, they overran flying-bomb sites housing the feared V-1 bombs that had been raining terror down on London for three months. Destroying the V-1s was an Allied strategic objective. Churchill had instructed the air marshals to send their bombers to terminate the sites, known as Crossbow targets, from which some 10,492 rockets would be launched by the war's end. Harris had objected strenuously to these missions because of the difficulty of hitting such positions, especially the mobile launchers, and because they diverted resources away from city bombing. Calculations would later reveal that the bombing resources used to strike these targets amounted to 73,000 tons of bombs, the equivalent of eight Eiffel Towers' worth of stacked explosives.[3] And so the First Canadian Army's overrunning of these positions was welcomed throughout military and political high commands. With some 6,000 Londoners having been killed and another 18,000 injured in the rocket bombardments, Lieutenant-Colonel J.A. Roberts, commander of the 12th Manitoba Dragoons and a former ice cream salesman, remarked, "We felt especially happy to have contributed to the easing of the load carried by the long-suffering and gallant British civilians."[4]

The battles throughout September were long and costly, but the First Canadian Army had captured over 46,000 prisoners and killed countless thousands of Germans.[5] Lieutenant-General Simonds was temporarily in command of the army as of September 27, after General Crerar was felled by illness. Having reached the pinnacle of the command structure, Simonds took over an army that had proved adaptive in its fighting methods, having shifted from the slow grind of early to mid-August to close the Falaise Gap to the open warfare of late August, and then, in September, to its engagement in three weeks of siege. Yet while the stalemate of Normandy had been left behind, the attritional combat remained front and centre. After a pause to regroup and integrate reinforcements into the depleted ranks of the infantry battalions, whose companies were down by almost half strength, the Canadians were ordered to clear the Scheldt estuary to open up Antwerp.

The Breskens Pocket, the South Beveland Peninsula, and Walcheren Island—all interconnected and with German gun batteries able to fire throughout the defensive triangle—would have to fall before Antwerp could receive shipments. General Simonds found himself on the horns of a vexing dilemma: he had to fight on three wide battlefields, extending some 75 kilometres, with only three tired divisions. And with Montgomery still pulling British formations, including all of I British Corps, towards the failed Market Garden front to achieve some sort of victory there, and

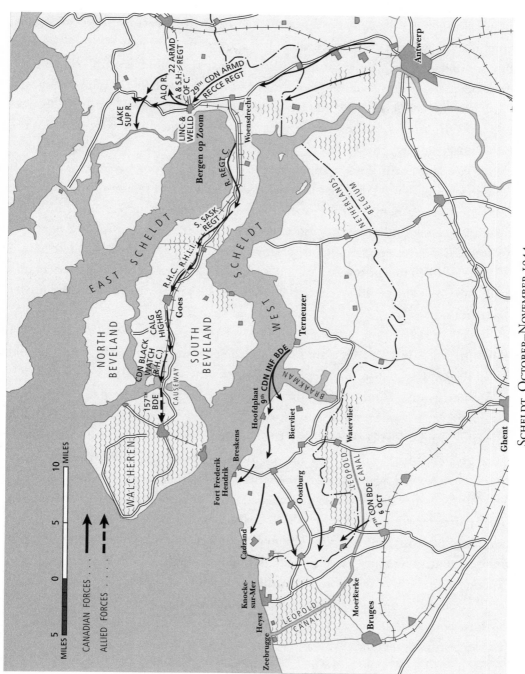

SCHELDT, OCTOBER–NOVEMBER 1944

still unwilling to make Antwerp a priority despite Eisenhower's express instructions, Simonds was left with not nearly enough men or guns to rapidly clear the Scheldt. But Simonds was no whiner; nor did he want to appear timid as army commander. And so he set to his task and ordered the 3rd Canadian Infantry Division to clear the south bank of the West Scheldt, known as the Breskens Pocket, while the 2nd Canadian Infantry Division would drive north from Antwerp and then push westward into the Beveland Peninsula. The 4th Canadian Armoured Division, on the far right, was to charge east and north across Leopold Canal and offer a protective screen. Simonds would rather have used the 4th Division to support the 2nd Division, which faced a concentration of enemy forces, but he did not have enough troops under his command. Once the 2nd Division cleared its objectives, it was to turn to the west and assist British naval commandos in clearing the final objective, Walcheren Island, which controlled the most westward entrance to the Scheldt estuary. On every battlefield, the Germans could wait for the attacking Canadians to come at them over open ground.

THE BRESKENS POCKET consisted of flooded farmland bounded by the Leopold Canal to the west and south, the West Scheldt to the northeast, and the North Sea to the northwest. Within this 35-by-15-kilometre rectangle, the flat polder landscape was cut by innumerable canals, ditches, and dykes, and was swamped with anywhere from a few centimetres to 1.5 metres of water. To close with the enemy, every artillery piece and vehicle, not to mention the tens of thousands of shells, would have to be dragged through the muck. The Germans called it Fortress South Scheldt; Lieutenant O.A. Robertson of the North Shore Regiment described it as a "devil's dream of mud, dykes, and rain."[6] The occasional town and a few villages, groupings of farms, and church towers offered enclaves for the 14,000-strong battle-tested 64th German Division. Their morale was high, they had good leaders—experienced men who had fought on the Eastern Front—and, as one soldier later testified, they had orders to "fight to the last man."[7]

The swampy ground created natural obstacles that made it difficult for armoured vehicles to make much headway, and the 4th Canadian Armoured Division's infantry regiments had been repulsed in several costly reversals north of the Leopold Canal in

September. And so the difficult assault fell to General Dan Spry's 3rd Canadian Infantry Division, even though his brigades were worn out from the siege along the coast. Spry planned a two-pronged attack that would include the main crossing of the Leopold starting on October 6, and a second amphibious landing a few days later to the east. At the Leopold Canal, the frontal assault fell to Brigadier J.G. Spragge's 7th Infantry Brigade, whose intelligence officers had only two days to prepare. The eastern half of the pocket was flooded, creating a formidable barrier, so the Canadians focused on the area to the west, a narrow strip of dry land near the village of Eede.

The operation, code-named Switchback, began at 5:30 A.M. on October 6 with no accompanying barrage, despite the presence of one of the largest concentrations of Allied guns along a divisional front, with 327 barrels ranging from 25-pounders to the super-heavy tractor-drawn 240mm howitzers that fired 360-pound shells. Though the guns had harassed known enemy positions before zero hour, it was left to twenty-seven flame-throwing Wasps to drench the enemy-held canal banks, cutting the darkness with a terrifying display of flames and jellied fuel.[8] Most of the Germans fled the onslaught or were burned alive, but handfuls of them survived.

The Scheldt campaign's flooded polder fields through which the Canadians fought the Germans.

Two companies from the Canadian Scottish Regiment and one from each of the Regina Rifles and the Royal Montreal Regiment ferried across the water in assault boats manned by the North Shore Regiment. At least one of the boats was ripped apart in a crossfire of enemy machine-gun fire, but the rest of the Canadians scrambled ashore.

The gunners waited expectantly, ready to open fire at the first signs of enemy resistance. On the right, the Scottish surged forward a few hundred metres, but the Reginas, who were further to the west, almost immediately ran into fire. Using PIATS, the Johns hammered a pillbox and continued their scramble up the slick canal banks and then into the sodden ground. While there were countless acts of bravery, the actions of Corporal Sammy Letendre, a Métis rifleman, became the stuff of regimental lore. Letendre had joined the Reginas after D-Day, and Major Gordon Brown remarked that "he was completely fearless in combat and rapidly gained a reputation for bravery."[9] At the Leopold, he defended against several enemy counterattacks, to the point that he picked up unexploded German potato masher stick

Canadian flame-throwing Wasps at the Leopold Canal battle.

grenades and threw them back at the enemy. Letendre was recommended for the Victoria Cross but was awarded the Distinguished Conduct Medal, the only one received by the Reginas during the course of the war.

The Germans responded rapidly to the incursion, with the divisional commander throwing at least three battalions against the threat.[10] As one Canadian artillery war diarist recorded laconically, "Apparently the Germans have a lot more stuff over there than we had thought. He has concealed his strength very cleverly."[11] With a determined enemy ringing the beachhead, the thin khaki line was pressured nonstop and in places the Canadians were only 50 metres deep from the canal. But the vulnerable infantry were supported by the rearward artillery that now opened up in crushing defensive fire from two large groupings on the flanks. Using sound ranging and flash spotting techniques, whereby sophisticated listening devices and observers triangulated the enemy's gun blasts and muzzle flashes to locate the guns, enemy positions were smothered in shells. With only two dry approaches to the battlefield, the enemy lost fearful numbers of men as Canadian guns fired airbursts of shrapnel over these roads.

The Royal Winnipeg Rifles, the follow-on force, pushed through those on the other side of the canal on the morning of the 7th, eventually closing the gap between the Reginas and the Scottish on the 9th, but they made little further headway. "Enemy parties were frequently encountered," noted one Canadian report, "and violent skirmishes ensued."[12] But Spry's assault force, supported by their guns and by Typhoon fighters that flew hundreds of sorties against the enemy, could not be dislodged. As one Canadian observed of the enemy's counterattack doctrine, "At least [the Germans] are out in the open and it is always easier to kill a rat out of his hole than in it."[13]

Under constant small-arms and shellfire, the Canadians spent every day digging into the ground, their slit trenches filling up with water before they had dug even a metre into the mulch. Officers and NCOs slithered through the mud to visit their men spread out in the flooded area, and the steady pounding of guns threw up geysers of filth. Hot meals from the rear were a thing of the past, although experienced infantrymen used candles and rags to heat the tinned meat that came their way by re-supply men who, on improvised sleds, pulled forward food, ammunition, and, if a platoon was lucky, rum.

"Heavy casualties were suffered by both sides," wrote the war diarist for the Royal Winnipeg Rifles, "and the ground was littered with both German and Royal Winnipeg dead."[14] The fighting dragged on for days, and the Regina's official war diary for the 12th described the battle with candour: "Medical Officer advises us there have been between 250 and 300 casualties go through regimental aid post since 6 Oct, which is a grim reminder that this operation has been no push-over. It is the opinion that the past few days have seen some of the fiercest fighting since 'D' Day."[15] After a week of combat, the Canadians had driven only 1.5 kilometres to the northwest, in the direction of the small village of Eede on the border of the Netherlands and Belgium. The 64th Division's committed battalions had been chewed up, and one captured German colonel remarked under interrogation that his troops stood firm despite the casualties from artillery fire and that he "attributed the stiffer resistance to the fact that the hour was critical for Germany."[16] It was, but he also credited the Canadians who had withstood his multiple attacks. The deadlock was eventually broken by the 9th Infantry Brigade's advances to the German rear, which threatened their positions by October 13. On the southern Leopold Canal front, the week of fighting cost the 7th Brigade 533 casualties, of which 111 were fatal.[17] Another 150 men were suffering from battle exhaustion.[18]

WITH THE LEOPOLD CANAL operation checked from the start but drawing in crucial German formations, the 9th Canadian Infantry Brigade at Terneuzen, some 60 kilometres to the east, planned to crash through the back door. Simonds ordered a waterborne attack, with Buffalos—tracked amphibious troop carriers, the larger version of which were able to transport thirty men—carrying the infantry to land along the northern edge of Breskens, near Hoofdplaat.

Moving in daylight on October 7, the Canadians were shocked to hear the loud noise of the Buffalos' aircraft engines that powered the vehicles along at a sitting-duck three knots per hour.[19] Jock Anderson, the chaplain of the Highland Light Infantry of Canada, recounted his experience of chugging up a canal in one such carrier while "the Dutch were out doing their Saturday afternoon shopping."[20] Many young boys followed the waterborne convoy on their bikes, shouting out encouragements. Anderson and his comrades could only wonder, "Good Heavens, this is a surprise attack?" It got worse. Challenges in navigating the lock system around the Terneuzen Canal delayed the operation for the better part of two days. Somehow secrecy was kept.

The plan was remounted for October 9, and ninety-seven Buffalos transported the lead elements of two battalions—the North Nova Scotia Highlanders and the Highland Light Infantry of Canada—onto the beaches near Hoofdplaat and at the mouth of the Braakman inlet. The landing took the enemy by surprise and cut off an escape to Walcheren across the Scheldt Estuary to the north, but soon the 64th Division was unleashed against the bridgehead.[21] The Canadians were ready and made the Germans pay with concentrated fire. Each side shelled the other relentlessly. Donald Pearce of the North Nova Scotia Highlanders described one terrible pounding: "I felt with needle-keenness that my life was hanging by a thread.... I was reduced to impotence or, worse still, to insignificance, and that there were no special virtue about me which in any way made me more likely to survive this target than anybody else."[22] Pearce survived, along with most of his companions, as the muddy terrain absorbed most of the shells that exploded in the ground. But not all men were

Buffalo amphibious vehicles carrying troops across the Scheldt River to Hoofdplaat.

so lucky. Lieutenant Hugh B. Hall, wearer of the Military Cross and a signals officer with the Glens, was present at the landings and within a few metres of a friend who was cut down. He was left to wonder, "He had a wife and kids and I asked myself many times: 'why him, why not me?'"[23]

The Buffalos gathered more reinforcements—the Stormont, Dundas and Glengarry Highlanders and the Cameron Highlanders of Ottawa, and then other units—and gunners across the southern Leopold Canal laid down tens of thousands of shells. The Glens took the lead on Hoofdplaat, a small village on the Scheldt, where the Germans had two large bunkers. Deadly accurate artillery fire, directed by Royal Canadian Artillery forward observers who were fewer than 200 metres from the enemy, plastered the position and it fell on the 10th.

Brigadier John Rockingham, a superb and brave officer, tough and willing to engage the enemy, took control of the defence. Over the next couple of days, with "Rocky" at the helm, the Canadians defeated several German attacks, thus breaking the enemy's back. The Germans pressed again on the 12th but could not penetrate the Canadian lines. When they retreated, they left behind dozens of their dead.[24] The next day, 530 Germans surrendered in the face of new assaults, persuading divisional intelligence that the enemy's morale was cracking.[25]

Major-General Knut Eberding, commander of the 64th Division, was surprised by the audacious landing and he was never able to recover the initiative. But there were no bloodless victories. The Germans regained their balance and Eberding even invoked the "kith or kin" law—a directive from Hitler that any soldier who surrendered would find his family prosecuted by the Gestapo in Germany, as punishment for the soldier's lack of willpower.[26] As the 64th Division was hounded, Eberding's forces rallied around camouflaged concrete pillboxes painted to simulate small houses, to the point of including fake bricks, doors, and curtained windows, as well as fake trees from which forward observers spied on the Canadians and directed fire.[27] Machine-gun teams were hidden in hay stacks, which the Canadians soon learned to set alight with burning tracer fire from their own machine guns. The Germans were also experts at directing their 20mm high explosive anti-aircraft shells into the trees that lined the dykes. "This had the effect," one report noted, "of extremely accurate air-bursts, for fragmentation occurred directly over the slit trenches dug into the bank."[28] Reginald Dixon, the intelligence officer for the Stormont, Dundas and Glengarry Regiment, was handed an artillery map showing that "every road in the whole area had been registered and numbered as a German artillery target. It was not comforting to look at it."[29]

Simonds reported that the 64th Division had the advantage of "fighting a bitter defensive battle from interior lines," and that it "made the most of the flooded and difficult country … and was able to render our advance both slow and costly."[30] Closer to the front, Company Sergeant Major Charlie Martin of the Queen's Own Rifles described how farm after farm was seized through methodical attacks. All were surrounded by open fields and dykes. "Deep water had collected at the sides of the dykes and it took courage for the men to move along them. There was no cover. It was what we called a section job. Each section—a corporal and a few riflemen usually—would leapfrog forward.... We'd do this five or six times a day—tense, stressful manoeuvres."[31] All the while, the enemy sharpshooters tried to bag the Canadians moving from

The Scheldt campaign, with its water and mud, made fighting, logistics, and simple survival all the more difficult.

their cover. More devastating were the mines, which the Germans had buried in and along the dykes where the infantry scrambled for cover. The devices exploded upwards, shredding flesh and shattering bone. Men feared most for their genitals and their eyes, usually in that order. Dead Germans and livestock fouled the water. "As the fight has been from polder to polder and from dyke to dyke, all the homes, barns, villages, and towns have been pretty badly shot up," witnessed Donald Pearce. "The people are not sure whether to cheer us or curse us."[32]

Rockingham's fought-out forces were relieved somewhat by the 4th Canadian Armoured Division's thrust from south of the Leopold Canal northward on October 14, which pressured the German defenders, especially those in the southeast who were all but cut off. With the Canadians assaulting from three directions, the artillery regiments were particularly effective as many were situated on the enemy's flanks, allowing them to drop shells behind German lines.[33] While the shellfire was much appreciated by the Canadian infantry, victory came down to the sharp end.[34] Lieutenant O.A. Robertson of the North Shore Regiment described the attack on the 16th, in which he was wounded: "About 60 fanatical Jerries charged us but were beaten off leaving half their number in the mud. Twice more they tried it, like mad-men, and each time our guns simply cut them to pieces."[35] The price was high for both sides. Captain Harold MacDonald remembered the combat experience as one of being "pinned down & having men die in your arms or screaming from mor-phine, to lie doggo, unable to do anything but pray & say words of encouragement to a shell-shocked case, or reorganize a platoon of men numbering 6 to 8 out of 35 or so who started out an hr. before." One could talk bravely of taking the battle to the Hun, MacDonald told his wife, and make exhortations of "for God's sake kill those bastards," but when "one is in the midst of the enemy with one chance in 100 of getting out alive, things are slightly different—words can't be wasted & aren't necessary. A pat on the back, a grin, and that's all. The old saying still holds good, we who have seen a bit of the real thing, dislike & refuse to talk about it."[36]

ABOVE THE BATTLEFIELD, the fighters and fighter-bombers of 84 Group prowled almost with impunity. While most of the RCAF squadrons were in 83 Group work-ing with the Second British Army, 84 Group consisted of a multi-national force of

British, Polish, Norwegian, Czechoslovakian, New Zealand, Belgian, and French squadrons. Poor weather limited flying to about every second day, but the Spitfires and Typhoons still managed at least 1,600 sorties in support of Canadian ground forces in the pocket.[37] An officer in the Queen's Own Rifles—whose regiment had crossed over into the Switchback battle on October 12—wrote that "According to PWs [prisoners of war] they [Typhoons] are a great morale breaker as well as doing a lot of damage."[38] The enemy learned to avoid moving in the open during daylight hours.

The development of a workable doctrine that unified the land armies and air forces was years in the making. Each campaign taught lessons. Through improvements in communication equipment, the response time from target identification to aerial engagement was reduced to as little as fifteen minutes.[39] When wireless radios failed, junior officers or men, seeing friendly Typhoons or Spitfires circling overhead, waved their arms, got the pilots' attention, and, through exaggerated hand signals, tried to point out the enemy strong-points. It was dangerous for those on the ground to expose themselves to German snipers in this way, but there was much satisfaction when a Typhoon wagged its wings in acknowledgment and then rained rockets or bombs on the enemy. It was terrifying to be on the receiving end of high explosives, and the lack of vegetation in the waterscape worked against the defenders, whose positions were laid out to the hawks above. General Eberding testified after his capture, in an interrogation report, that Allied "air support had caused him some casualties but that its greatest effect was to prevent movement by day and limited the activity of his artillery."[40] Eberding's opponent,

Typhoon rocket attack on German defences in the Scheldt.

Major-General Dan Spry, believed that the effect of the Spitfires and Typhoons was "of NO greater importance than the encouragement given to our own troops."[41]

THE GERMANS WERE slowly pushed back towards the sea in the west, with positions slammed by artillery shells, infantry fire, and rocket-firing Typhoons. However, there were few tank attacks, as the ground was too soggy for the weighty armour to make any headway. A few of the troopers learned about the dangers of sodden earth the hard way. At night most of the crews had taken to sleeping under their Shermans for protection from shellfire, but at the Scheldt, recounted Trooper Bill Cullum of the Sherbrooke Fusilier, "some of the guys got under their tanks and the next morning, the tank had sunk on top of them."[42] Frantic digging saved some, but not all, of the suffocating men.

The Canadian infantry continued to swarm forward, and were supported, as of October 18, by the British 52nd Division. The British soldiers that had trained as mountain specialists for an invasion of Norway now found themselves fighting below sea level. Along the coast, the port town of Breskens fell on October 21, and four days later Fort Frederik Hendrik, an ancient stronghold, was cleared. To the south, in the interior, Oostburg was overrun by the Queen's Own Rifles and the Chaudières in house-to-house skirmishes on October 26. The Canadians fought among frightened civilians, who crouched in cellars, ditches, or drains as the liberating force swept over them. At one point in the fight, the Queen's Own fixed swords and routed a number of defenders who never expected a bayonet charge. About 200 prisoners were taken.[43]

The Germans finally surrendered on November 3 and Operation Switchback ended in victory. The fighting had been exceedingly difficult and the Germans resolute, despite their isolated position. The 3rd Canadian Infantry Division lost 2,077 men, including at least 314 killed and another 231 "missing"—almost all of whom were dead, with their bodies lost to the bog. An official report stated that 18 percent of total casualties were due to battle exhaustion, noting, "The extremely trying conditions and the number of repeat cases were contributing factors to this high figure. Attempts must be made to spot likely battle exhaustion cases early and to find employment for these men in the rear areas. True battle exhaustion cases will undoubtedly break down again and, therefore, steps should be taken to keep such personnel from returning to the fwd areas."[44] Despite the Canadians' significant losses, their victory was total. The 64th Division was annihilated and the Canadians took more than 12,700 prisoners.[45] The clearing of the Breskens Pocket became a proud battle honour for the 3rd Canadian Infantry Division, but most combatants would have echoed the nameless officer at divisional headquarters, who upon being informed that the battle was over, wrote in the operations log, "Thank God!"[46]

AS THE 3RD DIVISION bled through the Breskens Pocket, the 2nd Canadian Infantry Division was fighting to the east. Though Antwerp had fallen to the Allies on September 4, the Germans were dug in on the northern outskirts of the city. For two weeks in mid-September, the 5th and 6th Canadian Infantry Brigades were part of the Allied force that probed the enemy lines in what was dubbed the "streetcar war." The unconventional battle saw Canadians and British troops enjoying the bars and brothels in the city and then moving into the forward lines before returning again to the rear areas, often riding streetcars. The 5th Brigade finally turned the enemy position in a daring flanking movement across the 30-metre-wide Albert Canal during the early hours of September 22, but fighting by Allied troops continued until the end of the month. On October 2, the Canadians set off northward towards the eastern end of the Beveland isthmus, beginning the 25-kilometre advance to the village of Woensdrecht, which sits astride the peninsula to South Beveland. It had to fall before the Canadians could turn westward towards Walcheren Island.

The 2nd Division slowly floundered towards the enemy. The stretch of land had been reclaimed from the sea, but the Germans had deliberately flooded it. As on the other Scheldt battlefields, the farmland was criss-crossed by 4-metre-high dykes—raised roads—that were the only way across the fields. "Movement along the dykes was almost suicidal," recounted one infantryman.[47] And when the Canadians advanced along the low, drenched farmland, its flatness afforded few places to hide.

Near Woensdrecht, the Germans had all areas under observation and could bring down fire on the approaching Canadians. They had also rushed forward an ad hoc force of defenders, known as Battle Group Chill, which consisted of about 1,500 young, indoctrinated, and fanatical parachutists, whom one intelligence officer described as the "cream of the crop ... fine physical specimens, keen to fight and with excellent morale."[48] Given the water-soaked condition of the fields, the only way to close the distance was to slither forward, mostly at night.

On the morning of October 7, the Calgary Highlanders and Le Régiment de Maisonneuve led the division into the forward defences south of Woensdrecht. Aerial photographs and Dutch civilians warned them of a German force gathering for an attack the next day, and this was stopped cold by the Canadians when the paratroopers advanced recklessly with little artillery support. Ferocity could not defeat firepower, and the Germans suffered an estimated 580 casualties.[49] The German commander admitted, "The Canadians—I say that as a German—fought brilliantly. To the rank of brigadier, the officers stood side by side with their men on the front lines."[50]

Delaying actions and ambushes by the Germans slowed the Canadians, but they closed steadily on the enemy along Woensdrecht Ridge, as well as in the surrounding towns. The Black Watch (Royal Highland Regiment) of Canada led the assault on the 13th, behind a shellfire barrage from three Royal Canadian Artillery regiments, machine guns and mortars from the Toronto Scottish Regiment, and Spitfires and Typhoons from 84 Group.

Infantrymen of the Calgary Highlanders advance in battle, October 1944.

The Black Watch drove across beet fields in broad daylight, but it was a ragged advance, with one of the lead formations, Charlie Company, caught up in a firefight before even reaching their start line. As at Verrières Ridge, most of the Black Watch did not falter or flag, but nor did they get far. One of the surviving officers, Lieutenant W.J. Shea, blamed the failure on three factors: the German position on the dykes, which were 6 metres high and acted as nearly impassable walls; the effective enemy defence; and poor recent reinforcements. With all four of the company commanders hit early, the new reinforcements, many of them remustered service corps men, were not ready for the rigours. Shea witnessed several of them dive for cover in craters or hide in haystacks and not emerge until after the shooting stopped.[51] The officers knew they could not count on these men and therefore had to expose themselves more often, resulting in casualties. As Shea observed, "Against tough, seasoned, enemy paratroopers, these reinforcements were more of a liability than an asset."[52] The attack failed and the Black Watch went over the top again later that day in what became known in the regiment as "Black Friday." By the end of the 13th, the regiment had lost fifty-six killed, twenty-seven captured, and sixty-two wounded, and had advanced the line only a little.[53]

Three days of fighting saw the Canadians drive the Germans back, but it was not until the 16th that the Royal Hamilton Light Infantry seized Woensdrecht. Lieutenant-Colonel Denis Whitaker, the decorated veteran of Dieppe and former Canadian Football League star, had returned after recuperating from a wound in Normandy. Aggressive patrols gathered intelligence on the enemy, and Whitaker found too many strongpoints for his liking. But the position had to fall. The Rileys went up in the dark and behind a massive barrage supplied by five artillery regiments. Even then, sending a single battalion into battle was risky, but the decision was unavoidable for the weakened Canadians. Whitaker's men, along with reinforcements, seized the village and held it against several assaults over the coming days.

Captain W.D. Stevenson, the forward observer for the 4th Field Regiment, was at the front and was nearly killed by counterattacking German troops. He held his ground and called in shells onto the Riley's coordinates. "The fire caught the enemy in the open, whereas our men were deep in slit trenches having been warned," the commanding officer reported. "Our troops cheered; the slaughter was terrific."[54] Stevenson survived four direct shellfire strikes on his observation post and received the Military Cross for his bravery.[55] The Rileys held the ground but suffered 21 killed and 146 wounded.

By the 21st, the German blocking action was defeated, and the 2nd Division, much reduced in strength, set off two days later to plunge westward into Walcheren Island. On the division's right and northern flank, the 4th Canadian Armoured Division was engaging the enemy and offering some protection for the 2nd Division, but Major-General Charles Foulkes's soldiers had fought non-stop for nearly three weeks and were in desperate need for a rest. One 5th Infantry Brigade officer had lamented in the official pages of the war diary, "Cannot understand why they do not put more troops in the area and finish the job once and for all instead of playing about shifting first one battalion and then another."[56]

AS THE 2ND DIVISION turned westward for more fighting, the 4th Canadian Armoured Division on the right flank continued to clear a number of Belgian towns, the largest being Esschen. It then pushed north into the Netherlands to liberate Bergen-op-Zoom on October 24. The cost of these battles is starkly evident in two large Commonwealth War Graves cemeteries 3 kilometres east of the city, one of which, Bergen-op-Zoom Canadian War Cemetery, contains 1,087 dead, most of whom are Canadian. The inscription on a monument in the cemetery reveals the sentiment of the people in the region: "*Aan onze Canadeesche bevrijders*—To our Canadian liberators." While the 4th Division left behind a trail of bodies, there was also a sea of Belgian and Dutch flags that flew for the first time since 1940.[57]

The Canadians were dead-eyed and worn down. Since D-Day, the infantry battalions had been entirely gutted, some with over 100 percent casualty rates. This did not mean that every man from June 6 onwards had been killed or wounded, since many of the subsequent waves of reinforcements were rendered casualties, but there was a steady loss of experienced men. As officers and NCOs were knocked out, promotion also came from the ranks, with experienced men rising to take the challenge. And although this brought the battle-tested into command positions where they were desperately needed, often these soldiers were sent away on courses to be trained, denuding the battalion of experienced warriors for several months. The four French-speaking regiments, the Maisonneuves, the Chaudières, the Van Doos, and the Fusiliers Mont Royal, were out of replacements and had already turned to unilingual, English officers to fill the gaping holes.

The reinforcement crisis would only get worse, especially as the last of the trained infantry in England were now being drip-fed into units. Battalions reduced from 800 to 400 riflemen could not achieve the same results or be as effective on the battlefield, and ordering under-strength companies, platoons, and sections into the combat led to more strain, stalled attacks, and higher casualties. One method of filling the ranks was by combing out some of the rear echelon formations, making fighters out of clerks, cooks, or remustered artillery and transport men. But often these soldiers were in rear positions for a reason: they were not as robust as the riflemen and were likely to have outdated training. The front was especially bewildering for these men. As one Canadian veteran of battle opined, "If you stay alive a week, you're learning all the time and you've got a chance of staying alive."[58] Many experienced soldiers believed that the new recruits stood little chance of survival; Major John D. McLean of the Queen's Own Rifles shared the view that these remustered soldiers "were just bodies ... and I felt sorry for them."[59]

Within this bleak environment, made all the worse by the wet and cold weather of late October, there was a dawning realization among those in the field that the declarations of an impending death for the German army were grossly exaggerated. It all led to a deepening exhaustion among Allied soldiers who knew they had to continue on with no end in sight. Stretcher-bearer David Gordon recalled, "There were many soldiers who could not handle the stress after weeks, or maybe even a few days of combat." The dread deepened to debilitating levels. "You have no control over yourself but you fight to keep control. Your stomach is tight and does not want to accept food. You are in a constant state of anxiety and your mind races with all sorts of crazy thoughts, 'Should I dig my slit trench here or over there?'... It used to give you a safe feeling to be in any old slit trench until the guy next to yours caught one."[60]

Major Robert Gregory, the 3rd Division's field psychiatrist, reported that during the long battle for the Scheldt the number of exhaustion cases had risen dramatically. Hundreds of soldiers were removed from the lines for breaking down mentally, although an undisclosed number of soldiers were sheltered by sympathetic regimental officers who discreetly rested tired comrades in rear positions. Gregory recorded that most of the patients he treated were plagued with a sense of "futility" and a "lack of volition to carry on.... The men claimed that there was nothing to which to look forward to—no rest, no leave, no enjoyment, no normal life and no escape. The only way one could get out of battle was death, wounds, self-inflicted wounds and going 'nuts.'"[61]

Around this time, Queen's Own Rifles officer John D. McLean rejoined his regiment, having taken a bullet in the shoulder on D-Day. He found himself a stranger, noting bleakly that almost all the officers with whom he had trained for five years had been killed or wounded. Those who were left were haggard, pale, and drawn; most had lost more than twenty pounds from stress, poor eating, and being pushed to the mental brink.[62] One Canadian observed of the officers and men in the field—they all wore "grey masks of exhaustion and shock."[63] Their senses were dulled; they stumbled around in a stupor. Others slept with their eyes open or so deeply that their comrades feared they had stopped breathing. And when groups of soldiers slumbered, lying in strange contortions, the snoring was interrupted by weird moans, gibberish talk, and even shouts, as they fought private battles in the recesses of their subconscious.

Everyone in the firezone had frequent brushes with death. Captain Joseph Greenblatt, a doctor with the Royal Canadian Army Medical Corps, said to his wife on October 12, 1944, "The last five days ... have been absolute hell on earth, and I do not think I have ever had such a harrowing and nerve-wracking experience before in this war. I can honestly say that I have never been more scared in my life.... Perhaps in a couple of week's time I'll tell you all about it, but in the meantime I'll lock it in securely."[64] Like most soldiers, Greenblatt buried his worry, but over time the vaults of the mind could not hold back the flood of experiences.

Crerar and Simonds worried about the high levels of casualties to their fighting forces since Normandy, which were far beyond the projected rates. Most worrisome to Crerar was the number of battle exhaustion cases. This affliction was an uncontrollable bogeyman. Crerar was uncertain if soldiers breaking down because of combat were truly ill or if they were faking it. These types of casualties were a significant drain on manpower strength, with about one in four wounds during July being attributed to mental stress.[65]

As early as July 15, Crerar had written to Simonds of his fear. The general believed that many of these men were malingerers rather than truly wounded, and he ordered that the "processes of diciplinary [sic] action should be tightened up and speeded up. Secondly, punishment should be as severe as the circumstance permit. Thirdly, by 'education,' all ranks should be brought increasingly to the view that 'escapism' is a shameful thing." While he acknowledged that some soldiers were afflicted with "real nervous breakdowns," he thought, most certainly erroneously, that most of the exhaustion cases were being faked by men with previously defective personalities or who were of "unstable mental character."[66] Crerar's beliefs would not be out of character for a blimpish Great War colonel, and they revealed both ignorance and fear. Simonds was no better informed, and he took Crerar's message to heart, writing to his divisional commanders in late August that there was a noticeable and growing problem of battle exhaustion that "requires the close attention of commanders to see that malingering is not only discouraged, but made a disgraceful offence and disciplinary action to counter it."[67] Simonds warned that the situation would likely only get worse among the troops as the unkind living conditions of the fall and winter months wore away on the men. He made no reference to the continued fighting also draining soldiers, not to mention the unending casualties and low rates of long-term survival, all of which were more important factors in declining morale.

Most of the infantry at the front calculated their chances in the life lottery. Regardless of his level of combat experience, every man assumed that in the end a shell, bomb, or bullet with his name on it was going to get him one way or the other. This type of fatalism—a not uncommon belief that bomber crews embraced as they too endured brutally high casualties—allowed infantrymen to face the storm with some serenity. But even as they continued in their duties, many soldiers embraced minor wounds that would take them out of the line. In the last war, these had been known as Blighty wounds. "Blighty" was the nickname for England, and an injury that evacuated one there was to be welcomed, even if it meant losing a hand or facing intense pain. The term "Blighty wound" had faded from use by 1944, but men knew the concept and it was a measure of the difficult fighting in the Scheldt that many had begun to hope for one.

Some desperate soldiers weighed the poor odds of surviving the battle, or the war, and realized the only escape was to run away. Desertion meant abandoning one's comrades. New recruits who had not fit into the ranks, or dispirited ones who had witnessed most of their chums killed or wounded, were less tied to the primary group and more susceptible to desertion. But anyone could flee if he hit the point of no return. Captain W.S. Huckvale, the regimental medical officer for the Regina Rifles who served many months until he was blinded in one eye by a bullet, remembered how "Some men who seemed imperturbable on the parade square, broke down under shellfire. Some who seemed weak and insecure came through in a pinch."[68] By late 1944, II Canadian Corps headquarters tracked desertion numbers. One report noted that in the infantry and armoured brigades, as well as among other divisional troops, there were 870 deserters. The same report showed 571 English and 299 French deserters, a far higher proportion of French personnel in comparison to their overall numbers in the ranks.[69] The report offered no clues as to why French-Canadian soldiers were deserting at higher rates.

Sergeant Charles Kipp, a long-service veteran, was on the verge of a breakdown during the Scheldt. "My nerves were nearly shot from stress and too much war. Most men who prayed just prayed to stay alive.... I prayed to be killed and get it over with. I would say, 'God, make it today.' I was not afraid of dying.... It was the uncertainty of not knowing when or how, and preparing for death every day, that was more than people could stand."[70] Some soldiers took matters into their own hands. Medical officer J.W.B. Barr observed after the Leopold Canal that morale dropped visibly among the survivors, with distressing results: "The lack of progress and the stressful climatic conditions affected the morale of some of the troops, and the incidence of self-inflicted injuries increased slightly."[71] At this time, the medical services, acting on the First Army's orders, compiled statistics on the number of Canadian soldiers with self-inflicted wounds (SIWs) and found some 166 suspected cases from D-Day to the week of October 6, although some were later ruled out as legitimate after investigation.[72] Previous reports had warned that SIWs were "difficult to diagnose."[73] They ranged from a gunshot wound to the foot or hand, to stabbing oneself in a fleshy area, to having a vehicle run over one's legs, to ingesting poisonous liquids. And all in an attempt to escape the front.

While the loss of hundreds of battalion mates could be treated callously, even with little thought, not all deaths were considered equal. The demise of a close comrade or a respected officer could shatter a soldier who was hanging on by his fingertips. Suicides particularly traumatized surviving soldiers, not only because they lamented the waste of life but also because most long-service men mulled over their own death, in its multiple forms, including by their own hand. Sergeant John Missons recounted one scene that troubled him for his entire life. A young private received a "Dear John" letter from his girl, who sent him a piece of wedding cake and told him she could no longer wait for him. The distraught private put his Bren gun in his mouth "and pulled the trigger with his foot and blew his whole face off."[74]

WALCHEREN GUARDED THE ENTRANCE to the Scheldt estuary. Eleven gigantic gun batteries watched for any ship foolish enough to sail to Antwerp. The saucer-like island with a rim of 18-metre dykes had been reclaimed from the sea and it sat below sea level. It was only accessible by passing over a 1.2-kilometre-long and 40-metre-wide causeway that ran over salt marshes and mud flats. Even the hardened veterans of the 2nd Canadian Infantry Division blanched at crossing that shooting gallery, which was sighted by enemy artillery, anti-tank guns, and mortars.

Long before the 2nd Division came to face the causeway, Lieutenant-General Guy Simonds had studied the problem of capturing Walcheren and knew it would be difficult. Simonds's plan was to bomb the dykes and flood the island before sending in a seaborne assault by British commando and infantry units. The swamp would restrict German movement and force them to group defenders on dry land that would be vulnerable to additional bomber strikes. He had coordinated and negotiated with the navy and the air force to attack jointly, while holding off Dutch representatives who petitioned him to avoid the catastrophe the flooding would inflict on the 30,000 or so civilians still on the island.[75] In early October, Montgomery supported Simonds, more fully willing now to do anything to open up Antwerp. The request for permission to breach the dykes went all the way up to Eisenhower and then to Churchill, who ordered the bombers to back the First Canadian Army. After leaflets were dropped, warning the Dutch to evacuate the island, 247 Lancasters blew a 75-metre hole in the western dyke on October 3. The inrushing seawater submerged much of the island.

The allocation for using bombers on this mission did not mark a change in attitude on the part of Harris and his senior staff, who continued to see city smashing as the most effective means of wielding the bombers against Germany. Additional requests by Simonds to destroy a number of bunker-protected gun batteries were ignored, or the gun positions only half-heartedly attacked. Air Marshal Arthur Tedder, deputy supreme commander at SHAEF and a former commander of the Allied air forces in the Mediterranean, encapsulated the air forces' attitude towards aiding the infantry in his comment, "The Army having been drugged with bombs, it is going to be a difficult process to cure the drug addicts."[76] It was an ungenerous assessment to say the least. Lacking additional bombers, Simonds planned an amphibious assault to avoid the strongest German fortresses, working closely with the Royal Navy and Admiral Sir Bertram Ramsay, Eisenhower's naval chief. The Royal Navy understood the importance of defeating the Germans on Walcheren to open up Antwerp, and it supplied the warships and Royal Marine commandos to do the job. But Simonds had no success in convincing airborne commanders to land troops along the western end of the causeway. It looked too much like another Market Garden disaster, with the Canadians unable to cross the causeway, the amphibious operation denied, and paratroopers likely drowning in the flooded polders.

As Walcheren lay largely submerged, Simonds spent the rest of the month waiting for his divisions to complete their operations throughout the Scheldt to allow him to better position this final battle. While the 3rd Canadian Infantry Division was in the final stages of clearing out the Breskens Pocket in Switchback, Simonds ordered the 2nd Division to cross the causeway to distract the Germans from the amphibious landings to the south at Flushing and to the west at Westkapelle on November 1.

The 1,200-metre-long causeway was a death trap. The Germans had blocked both ends with concrete bunkers protected by barbed wire. All of the German mortars and artillery guns in the area were focused on the narrow bridge. The Black Watch drew the short straw and was ordered across on October 31. Even the normally stoic brigade and divisional headquarters were not pleased with an operation uncomfortably similar to the Charge of the Light Brigade, but with less chance of victory.

Seeking a solution to the likely slaughter, the Calgary Highlanders tried to sail across the flats under the bridge but found there was not enough water. On the causeway, the Black Watch advanced with three companies around 10:30 A.M. on October 31. It was no surprise that they ran into sheets of machine-gun, small-arms, and mortar fire. They did not get far.

That night, on All Hallow's Eve, the Calgary Highlanders attempted to bounce the causeway behind a bombardment that opened up twenty minutes before midnight. The Germans were aware that the Canadians were likely to turn to their guns to shoot the infantry across the bridge, and so they moved their front-line defenders forward onto the causeway and laid down murderous fire. "The heavy shells were the worst," recounted Signaller Frank Holm. "The explosions would send a shock through you that would reach the very depths of your nervous system and put in doubt your ability to take it.... I swore that if I ever got out of this hellish place alive I wouldn't mind eating dirt for the rest of my life."[77]

The Highlanders retreated but were sent back across the causeway a few hours later, on November 1, for a pre-dawn storming behind a creeping barrage that lifted 50 metres every two minutes. With shells tearing through the enemy defenders, the Highlanders sprinted into the fire-shrouded darkness. An official report observed that the enemy mortar fire was devastating, while "an 88mm gun firing directly along the Causeway, also caused numerous casualties."[78] With incredible bravery, the Highlanders made it across and spread out on the western side, where they were hammered by enemy fire and burned with flame throwers. The position was untenable and the Canadians were forced to pull back late in the day. However, elsewhere on the island, British commandos and infantrymen were landing at Flushing and Westkapelle, and overcoming the static German defences.

One final drive was made in the cold rain early on November 2, with Le Régiment de Maisonneuve ordered to pass through the Calgary Highlanders, who were still clinging to their battered positions. A seventy-two-gun barrage opened up, rendering the causeway, according to Lieutenant Charles Forbes, "like a steel beam being pushed into a hot furnace."[79] Heavy cloud cover, obscuring rain, and poor intelligence caused much of the bombardment, delivered by the guns of the 52nd British Division, to come crashing down on the unlucky Calgary Highlanders. Some of the Highlanders withdrew through the barrage, but in the smoke, dust, and fire they looked like attacking German troops, and some of the Maisonneuves cut down their own brothers in arms.

Around the perimeter of Walcheren, the commandos converged on the Germans, while the British 52nd Division, taking over from the 2nd Canadian Infantry Division, found some hardened trails across the mud flats and outflanked the Germans to the south of the causeway on the night of November 2. The futile frontal assault on the causeway was bait to attract the Germans away from the amphibious operation, but the plan was flawed from its conception since the Germans' lack of mobility meant that they were largely incapable of transferring troops over the wet ground. The attack on the causeway was little more than a senseless diversion. Simonds's marshalling of resources to bomb the island and to organize the commando raids was top-shelf, but his order sending the Canadians to their doom showed a wasteful heartlessness.

By November 8, Walcheren fell to the British commandos and infantry, aided by Canadian gunners. Four days before the German surrender, Allied minesweepers had already begun clearing the West Scheldt. Three weeks later, on November 28, the first convoys carrying war supplies entered Antwerp. Finally, thanks to the First Canadian Army, Eisenhower's armies began to receive supplies in sufficient quantities to prepare for the final offensive into Germany.

The battle for the Scheldt ended in total victory for the Canadians but at a terrible cost in lives.

FROM THE FIRST COSTLY DAYS of the Normandy battles, where the casualties from the Germans' frenzied attacks and the Canadians gritty defence had bled both sides white, infantry companies were rarely up to strength. Major Ronald Shawcross of the Regina Rifles described how, by the end of campaign, combat had worn down his 120-strong company; the NCOs "got thinner by the day and their faces got gaunt and looked strained, they started to tremble whenever a shot went off or a gun boomed.... People came and went like flies, some wounded recovered and came back but we never got above 65 men."[80] Army reports revealed that by the end of August, the 800-man infantry battalions in the

2nd Canadian Infantry Division were short, on average, about 200 infantrymen.[81]

The RCAF bomber airmen received a break after their thirty-operation tour, but the infantry had to keep fighting until they were maimed or killed. It was not until September 1944 that the army brought in the "tri-wounded" program, a six-month tour to Canada for long-service veterans with multiple wounds. But soldier shortages limited this reward to a paltry three men per battalion per month.[82] There were simply not enough riflemen to do anything else, even though tens of thousands of other army non-combatants were behind the lines or in England. The air force had even begun to demobilize some of its surplus flyers.

The reinforcement crisis was a failure of the army command in England, who had misread the potential destruction of their units in the unending violence of Normandy. In battle periods, the normal attrition rates were planned at 48 percent for the infantry, 15 percent for armoured units, and 14 percent for artillery. In reality, Normandy was far more vicious in terms of casualties and the intensity of combat had gone on for much longer than anticipated, with attrition rates for the infantry at 76 percent, while armour and artillery had lost 7 and 8 percent of their unit strength.[83]

Despite the desperate need for men at the front, about 120,000 National Resources Mobilization Act (NRMA) conscripts were kept in Canada for home defence, and about another 90,000 non-infantry remained in Britain.[84] Canada had brought in the NRMA in June 1940 after the fall of France, and it led to limited conscription for service in Canada. But King had promised these soldiers and the nation that they would not have to serve beyond the Dominion's borders. In the divisive April 1942 plebiscite, Canadians had released King from his promise of not conscripting NRMA soldiers for overseas service, but the prime minister was shaken by the unrest in Quebec over the question that French Canadians had overwhelmingly voted against. Minister of Defence J.L. Ralston demanded that King bring in overseas conscription; King resisted, believing it was not necessary at the time. And he was right. Nonetheless, the NRMA soldiers were shamed, bullied, and even physically abused. Very few went "active."[85] Even as rumours of infantry shortages circulated in the summer of 1944 and following, King refused to force the NRMA soldiers into overseas service. In his mind, his duty was to ensure unity on the domestic front, and bringing in conscription—even if limited to the NRMA solders—would split the country as Borden had during the Great War. It was important to avoid such a schism, but King showed far less concern for his countrymen overseas who were more likely to be killed because of shortages of trained infantrymen.

Canadians had suffered very little at home. While European citizens were put to the sword and the British faced aerial bombardment and tens of thousands of fatalities, Canadians, at most, had to deal with shortages of tires, rationing of sugar or liquor, and frozen wages (offset by stabilized prices of goods). Almost every Canadian was wealthier than in the previous, depressing, decade.[86] The conscription debates had raised passions, but very few men had been affected to date, and none had been sent overseas. The burden of the war effort had fallen to those serving in uniform, and now they needed assistance.

In mid-September, when rumours of infantry shortages turned to outright revelations in the nation's papers, the conscientious defence minister, James Ralston, a former battalion commander and a long-time supporter of veterans, went overseas to investigate. He first visited the Italian front and interviewed soldiers about the crashing of the Gothic Line and the chronic shortages of supplies and reinforcements. He was badly shaken, as every infantry battalion he visited was under-strength. Ralston next flew to Northwest Europe, where investigations again revealed the dire situation. Canadians were dying for want of comrades in the line, with the burden of fighting, sentry duty, patrolling, and all the other tasks falling heavily on the survivors. He was told how ill-trained reinforcements were put in the line and often killed or wounded before the end of the first day at the front.

Ralston returned to Ottawa on October 18 and informed Prime Minister King that now was the time for conscription. King was horrified. He had spent the entire war trying to rein in the conscriptionists in his cabinet and across the country. To bring in conscription now, with the war all but won, was madness. King characterized it as a great betrayal of French Canadians. Moreover, it was clear to him after some digging that it was the army high command who had failed to properly plan for the casualties and allocate enough replacements to fill the ranks. This was true, but it did not alleviate King's responsibilities to the overseas soldiers.

In late October, the King government faced its greatest crisis. The prime minister tried to appease the persistent Ralston, but day after day of negotiations proved fruitless. The cabinet was tearing itself apart, trying to squeeze the necessary 16,000 army reinforcements from the 120,000 NRMA men in Canada and the 90,000 or so uniformed Canadians in Britain. To King and his ministers' fury, they were informed that most of these soldiers were not suitable for the infantry, being medically unfit or untrained. King raged at the army's failure and considered resigning, but the political survivor found it ingrained in him to first push others onto their swords. During the 1942 plebiscite, a frustrated Ralston had tendered his resignation. King had talked his minister down but had kept the letter. On November 1, as Canadians were dying overseas in the attack across the causeway in the Scheldt, King fired Ralston, using the pretext of the earlier resignation letter. King won the political battle, but the army still needed reinforcements.

After Ralston's removal, the newspapers condemned the government relentlessly, especially after King's new defence minister, former army commander General Andrew McNaughton, was unable to convince the NRMA soldiers to enlist voluntarily. They were known as "Zombies," for their apparent lack of soul. The government was called worse: murderers, complicit in the killing of overseas soldiers. King finally seemed out of luck. But on November 22, the prime minister flip-flopped in the House of Commons—after having told his caucus only hours earlier that he would never waver—and ordered that 16,000 NRMA soldiers be sent overseas against their will.[87] McNaughton was thrown to the wolves. The enraged opposition shredded his reputation as he was forced to defend King's sudden change of policy. The slippery King largely escaped censure, as he had done countless times over his uniquely long political career.

At the front, the infantry were dismayed by the delays. Major Joe Pigott recalled, "We had only feelings of disgust, of contempt for the prime minister and the politicians who were not facing the realities of the crisis, and most of all, we felt anger. The feeling was becoming very deep-seated in all the troops that they were being used and being sacrificed by their government in order not to face public opinion."[88] Another infantryman, Elmer Bell, wrote to his parents in late October, of his comrades bearing the brunt of the fighting: "It makes me mad every time I think of those fellows here who go on and on and on without a weeks rest even and 75,000 Zombies in Canada. It is building up a hatred that wont be erased in a generation. It is criminal to keep those reinforcements at home." Who could blame angry soldiers like Pigott, Bell, and their mates for feeling betrayed by the nation and government for which they fought?

THE DIVISIVE CONSCRIPTION DEBATE raged through October and November, but by the time King made his decision, the Canadian Army was pulled from the line. The immediate crisis had been averted. The Canadians suffered 6,367 casualties in the Battle of the Scheldt, and an equal number of British soldiers serving in the First Canadian Army were killed and wounded.[89] In their complete defeat, the Germans lost more, as the 64th Division was annihilated and other divisions were thrashed. Some 24,000 became prisoners, and unknown thousands of additional Germans were buried.[90] One First Canadian Army document observed that the campaign was "as bitterly contested as any operations have ever been."[91] Yet Simonds's army had opened up Antwerp, and in few other periods in all of Canada's rich history did its military force play such a crucial role in coalition warfare. Even though Montgomery had made a self-admitted error in shorting the First Canadian Army of divisions and resources, and in giving them too much of a job to do, the Canadians had delivered victory.[92]

CHAPTER 14

BATTERING GERMANY

The German fronts were collapsing in the east and west, but the centre continued to hold. And so it was battered by the Allied bombing campaign. Though General Dwight Eisenhower had exerted control over the aerial armada in preparation for D-Day and, by shattering the rail and road lines, had slowed the enemy's ability to shift forces to shore up defensive positions, Sir Arthur Harris (and his American counterpart) re-exerted control over their bomber groups before the Battle of the Scheldt was won. Harris reinstated his policy of city busting, believing that his bombers could best degrade the German capacity to wage war by destroying factories and urban centres, although this idea remained contested even within the RAF senior command. Harris's superior, Sir Charles Portal, had issued orders to focus attacks on the petroleum industry, but Harris pushed back and used the bombers as he saw fit. Petroleum was far down the list of targets.[1] The oil factories were dispersed, and Harris knew that his aircrews could not hit them with any degree of accuracy. Even with the evolution in tactics and technology, sorties against targets in rural areas or on the periphery of cities left too many bombs landing on empty farmland. But Harris was not nearly as headstrong or disloyal as some historians have suggested, for about 15 percent of the missions were directed against oil, which was not inconsiderable given the wide range of targets available, from tactical objectives that would support the land formations to transportation hubs and cities.[2]

By the late fall of 1944, enemy ground defences were severely degraded, much of the Luftwaffe had been shot down, and large sectors of its radar installations had been overrun. The skies swarmed with Allied fighters and bombers. The last of

Hitler's superweapons, the Messerschmitt Me 262, the world's first jet fighter, proved not to be the game changer that the dictator had hoped it would be. The pilots were too inexperienced, and not enough of the jets were produced to reverse the inevitable Luftwaffe defeat. The Me 262 was a technological wonder, but it was too little, too late.

The Allied air forces became even more effective as the armies liberated France. Airfields were built, and Gee and Oboe stations were established in Europe to provide more accurate navigational guidance to the bombers. With a steady increase in the quantity of aircraft available, crewed by airmen emerging from the various air training programs, the number of tons of dropped bombs increased significantly in the last year of the war. In rough figures, the RAF dropped 13,000 tons on Germany in 1940, 32,000 in 1941, 48,000 in 1942, 200,000 in 1943, and, with the added weight of the Americans, nearly 1 million tons in 1944. In the first three months of 1945,

The Allied bomber offensive battered German cities in relentless sorties night after night. By late 1944, Germany's economy was in ruins, its cities reduced to rubble, and its citizens killed by the hundreds of thousands.

despite poor flying conditions, Bomber Command alone dropped 200,000 tons of high explosives and incendiaries.[3] During the last full year of the war, the Allied ordnance also became more effective, as aluminum powder was introduced into the high explosive bombs, making the blast effect up to ten times more powerful than that of conventional explosives.[4] As a consequence of these Allied advantages, large portions of the German cities were reduced to rubble, and rubble was pounded to dust. "It seems our job at the moment is to pulverize the Ruhr so the army can move in," observed Flight Lieutenant Millar Brittain on November 8, 1944, who would survive thirty-four sorties, be awarded the Distinguished Flying Cross, and later became an official war artist. "There is only little left of either Cologne or Duisburg after our visit. But I regret to say they in turn have accounted for some of my friends."[5] From the air, the German cities looked like gutted animals, their blackened and broken innards jutting up like desiccated rib cages.

A gutted German city after prolonged Allied bomber raids.

At this stage in the narrative, before returning to the final land war campaign into Germany, it is worthwhile to reflect upon the bombers' contribution. Perhaps the most heated debate during the war and to the present day has been about the effectiveness of the bombers against the Nazi war machine. Critics of the campaign argue that the cost to the Allies of using the bombers was too high in terms of both airmen's lives lost and resources wasted. This accusation is false on both counts. The casualties to the aircrews were frightful, but they were far fewer, in the case of the Canadians and British, than those expended in the ground battles. Moreover, throughout the war, Bomber Command never absorbed more than 10 percent of Britain's war effort: about 7 percent from 1939 to 1943, and rising to 12 percent in 1944–1945.[6] And while some of these bombers would have been better used by Coastal Command in its war against the U-boats in the Atlantic, especially during the desperate year of 1942, it was Churchill who ordered that the Halifaxes and Lancasters remain in Bomber Command to strike back against Germany and keep open the Second Front. This was a decision he made, and with the knowledge that the heavy bombers were the only means by which he could hurt Hitler.

German production rose until early 1943 despite the bombing, but this increase was more a result of ingenuity and of wringing blood from the stone of industry. The economy was far more robust and resilient than the Allies had anticipated, and the Nazi military dictatorship's shift to using slave labour, which offset some of the damage and losses wrought by the bombing campaign, had not been foreseen.[7] Mitigating the most crushing effects of the aerial attacks, the Germans learned to save key parts of their cities. Firefighter crews were instructed to direct their attention to factories and plants, and to let the residential areas burn. The Germans also dispersed their factories to the periphery of their cities or to more rural areas to reduce the effects of area bombing. Despite these preventive measures, recent studies suggest that German industry was irreparably damaged by the bombing campaign, with manufacturing curtailed in mid-1943 when steel production flatlined.[8]

The Halifaxes and Lancasters opened and maintained the Second Front against the German war machine, which Stalin had pleaded with Churchill and Roosevelt to do since 1941. Throughout the war, the bombers succeeded in reducing pressure on the Soviet armies that were bearing the brunt of the Wehrmacht. In January 1944, for example, 68 percent of Germany's fighter aircraft were committed to the Western Front and to defending the targeted cities, leaving just 17 percent of the remaining force to face the Soviets.[9] Moreover, the best field gun in the German army was also the most effective anti-aircraft gun, the 88mm flak gun, and some 19,713 88mm and 128mm dual purpose flak/anti-tank artillery pieces were pulled back from the fighting to defend the Reich against the bombers, along with 25,000 20mm and 30mm guns.[10] Manning these weapons were 900,000 defenders. Even though many were teenagers or overage soldiers, by the end of the war these Germans would have been pushed into front-line service; instead, they were tied down defending against the bombers. Tens of thousands of Allied soldiers' lives were saved by their not having to confront the 88s. Even a few dozen guns on a divisional sector could inflict carnage on advancing forces, as had been discovered in Normandy, on the Russian steppes, and in Italy. Further, the air war had other less tangible knock-on effects, not the least of which was the diversion of German resources to the building of fighters and anti-aircraft guns, thus preventing their use in producing tanks or munitions.[11] For all of these reasons, the Second Front represented a significant contribution of Bomber Command to the Allied victory.

The bombers' blows also had a profound effect on civilians, who suffered the full terror of the aerial onslaught night after night, month after month. The war was brought home in the shattered cities. Wartime surveys revealed that the bombing campaign, more than anything else, showed the German people in no uncertain terms that they were losing the war.[12] We can never know how many more shells, planes, and tanks the Nazi economy might have produced without the aerial campaign's disruptive effects, but the bombers unequivocally hurt enemy production and morale while meeting several key Allied strategic objectives.

ABOVE THE BLACKENED CITIES, the bomber crews continued to face the strain of flying, and although the Luftwaffe fighter threat was all but gone, the flak guns still claimed their victims. But the numbers lost were far fewer than during the bloodbath over Berlin in late 1943. In just one week in October 1944, for instance, the RCAF's No. 6 Group sortied four times against Wilhelmshaven and Stuttgart, and twice against Duisburg; 677 aircraft were involved in the operations, resulting in the destruction of only eight machines.[13] While aircrew fatalities crept up from the low rates prior to D-Day, they never returned to the nearly crippling figures from 1940 to early 1944. In this new environment, the nighttime stab was increasingly replaced by the day-light run. From August 1944 to the end of the war, the RAF and RCAF carried out 153 daylight raids.[14] These raids brought different challenges to the air forces, as targets could be better located but ground flak guns could also see the planes without radar. Walter Irwin, a bomber pilot who was on the verge of completing his second tour in February 1945, remarked, "It was an eerie experience, flying in daylight, when all our previous missions had been flown at night. We felt completely exposed, as though we were naked."[15]

In No. 6 Group, the losses continued at manageable levels, and by the end of the war they were the lowest of all the groups in Bomber Command. Much of the credit went to Air Vice-Marshal Clifford "Black Mike" McEwen, whose inspired leadership and willingness to share the dangers with his crews raised morale.[16] More robust aircraft helped too. By war's end, ten squadrons in No. 6 Group were equipped with Lancasters, which were far more resilient than the two-engine planes the Canadians had started with in January 1943. Flight Lieutenant John Patterson, on his second tour of operations, observed on July 19, 1944, "The losses in RAF have not been as heavy as had been expected, which is a sign that we have gradually obtained mastery of the sky."[17] A few months later, Patterson allowed himself to express the fleeting hope: "I felt that I might survive the war."[18]

Of course, the war was not over, and while Patterson did survive, many of his comrades did not. The first months of 1945 saw the heaviest tonnage of bombs up to that point in the war fall on German cities. In fact, it was Churchill, furious about the ongoing V-2 rocket attacks against British civilians, who pushed for a renewed focus on the saturation bombing of enemy cities. He wrote to his secretary of state for air on January 26, 1945, wondering forcefully whether "Berlin and no doubt other cities in eastern Germany should not now be considered especially attractive."[19] Churchill had also toyed with the idea of incorporating chemical weapons into the bombers' arsenal in response to the use of V-weapons, but he was dissuaded by the chief of the general staff, Field Marshal Alan Brooke, and others because of the difficulty in delivering the chemical agents from a great height and because it would be condemned in the future as another step towards the precipice of unparalleled barbarity. Eisenhower was right to note, "I will not be a party to so-called retaliation or use of gas. Let's for God's sake keep our eye on the ball and use our sense."[20] Churchill backed down, but he wanted blood.

The Anglo-American-Canadian bomber offensive did not need to turn to chemical weapons to carry out its task of punishing Germany, and the last five months of the war saw enemy cities saturated with high explosives and incendiaries. Many old, majestic towns such as Hildesheim and Nordhausen, with limited war production facilities, were gutted and burned. More than 50 percent of the urban areas in Germany were destroyed—not damaged, but destroyed.[21] The aerial assault was relentless, and Germany at this point in the war had no chance of winning, with the Luftwaffe on its last legs, the Russians closing in from the east and recapturing the breadbasket of the Ukraine (and the raw materials of other occupied nations), and the Allies on the Western Front driving towards Germany. Yet Hitler and his band of criminals were unwilling to surrender, knowing full well that most of them would face a death sentence for their crimes against humanity. And so the Nazi leaders demanded that the German soldiers, and the civilians who supported them, fight to the end. And they did.

THE MOST INFAMOUS BOMBER MISSION of the war came late on the night of February 13, 1945, against Dresden, a picturesque baroque city that was also a site of wartime production. With Soviet armies nearing the Elbe, the Germans were using Dresden as a jumping-off position to send reinforcements to shore up the crumbling front. The Russians asked that the city be struck.[22] Seven hundred and ninety-six bombers, including sixty-seven from RCAF's No. 6 Group, drove hard to the city, smothering it with a mix of high explosives and incendiaries. Another firestorm erupted, as at Hamburg two years earlier. As the flames swept through the devastated buildings and houses, many of the refugees who had flocked to the previously unhit city had no access to the bomb-proof shelters or did not know where they were located. Thousands died in the initial conflagration and in two American bomber assaults over the following days. In reports to neutral countries, German propagandists inflated the losses to highlight the horror, and each generation returned to sifting through the ashes to recount the dead. The number of civilians killed was likely around

35,000, although it has been quoted as high as 120,000.[23] The whispers of "Coventry" and "Blitz"—of Dresden being revenge for these early bombings against Britain—lost some of their ability to persuade in the face of such an Armageddon.

Yet Dresden was just another mission for the airmen involved, and it would not become a symbol of the unfettered obliteration of Germany until long into the postwar.[24] Six weeks later, at the end of March, the always warlike and frequently vengeful Churchill retreated from his aggressive stance on targeting urban centres and wrote to the chiefs of staff that the "moment has come when the question of bombing German cities simply for the sake of increasing the terror, although under other pretexts, should be reviewed.... the destruction of Dresden remains a serious query against the conduct of the allied Bombing."[25] Churchill, as war leader, could change the bombing policy at any time, either because city-blasting was no longer needed or because he was aware of the need for postwar re-industrialization of Germany, or because of his ever-watchful eye on history, but his use of the term "terror" was an unfortunate one that rankled the RAF senior command. Even though he later withdrew it, the term has since been used by later generations looking back on the war and knowing how it ended, to question and even condemn the bomber offensive.[26]

We now know that the Nazi war machine was only months away from collapsing but the view at the time was far less clear. The First Canadian Army, for example, was still battling in the Rhineland by the time Dresden was hit, and it would endure two and a half gruelling months of combat, often against fanatical resistance and at the cost of 5,000 more Canadian dead. Those at the sharp end certainly did not see a defeated enemy, and for them it would have been unthinkable to stop bombing the cities and enemy fortifications. And of course the issue went beyond the fighting armies. The Jews continued to be gassed to death in sickening numbers, the Dutch continued to starve, and the horrible list of atrocities and madness went on and on. None of these factors can be separated from the final bombing campaign against Germany that might, with hindsight, have seemed punitive. It was not. And so RCAF's No. 6 Group continued to fly until April 25, 1945, while the last RAF Bomber Command attack was carried out against Kiel on May 2. In total, No. 6 Group flew 40,822 sorties during the war, dropping a total of 126,122 tons of bombs and losing 814 aircraft.[27]

THE BOMBERS WERE the only means by which to strike back at the enemy for much of the war. Germany had unleashed its aerial bombardment against Britain first, and would have continued to do so until it brought that island kingdom to its knees. Hitler's decision to turn his attention to the east in his long-standing desire for territory and war against the Communists had bought time for Britain. But having been forced into retreat from Europe, and after Japan entered the war, the British faced another string of humiliating defeats. When these catastrophes were considered along with the Battle of the Atlantic, which at several crucial points was in danger of being lost, and the war along with it, it was clear that the bombers were the only means of harassing the Germans. And it was but mere harassment from 1940 to 1942. In 1943, however, the increased numbers of four-engine aircraft, carrying heavier bomb loads, took the war to Germany and never stopped. It was not realistic to curtail the bomber offensive—nor was this suggested by any influential politicians or military men (save for a few in the clergy) until the final months of the war.[28] Moreover, Allied planners well remembered the Great War, when Germany was beaten on the battlefield and strangled of food by the naval blockade, but its cities were left untouched. In the years following that war, uninformed citizens were too willing to accept the propagation of the "stab in the back" theory, and the idea that the German nation had been undermined by Jews and saboteurs, not by fighting and blockade. Throughout the Second World War, German propagandists continued to claim victory, but in the shattered cities there could be few other than the demented or delusional who believed such lies. It was Bomber Command, not the navy or the land forces, that was delivering that hard truth.

It is necessary, nonetheless, to determine the cost of the aerial campaign. Bomber Command consisted of 125,000 airmen, and of those flyers 55,573 were killed. The 12,330 aircraft that were shot down account for many of these, but 8,305 airmen were killed in training accidents or in other non-operational environments.[29] Next to Britain, Canada was the largest contributor to Bomber Command, and nearly 40,000 Canadian airmen made up almost a third of the force's strength. Canada's creation and administration of the British Commonwealth Air Training Plan meant that more Canadians were drawn into the flying services, and the total casualties reflect this fact, with 9,919 losing their lives in Bomber Command. Another 4,000 Canadians were killed in all the other RCAF commands or were lost as prisoners of war, and an equal number died in training accidents or from other causes, for a total of 17,101 killed.[30] Only 1,555 airmen were wounded, which is a far lower number than the army casualty figures, which usually reveal a four-to-one ratio of wounded to killed. The comparatively small number of wounded attests to the all-or-nothing nature of the air war, in which most crews died together in fiery crashes. But some got out. Hundreds of evaders made it back to England, although 2,475 became prisoners of war.[31] The prisoners had to fight their own battles that will never be codified in statistics. The weight of losses fell most heavily on the bomber crews as opposed to those in the fighters, but also on those who flew during the crippling years of 1942 to 1944. Aircrews who served later in the war benefited from improved bombers that could fly at higher altitudes, and from better technology, fighter escorts, and sorties against weakened German defences. Such evolutions of technology and tactics never made it easy to fly a Lancaster or Halifax into enemy territory, but the losses were far less severe in the final full year of the war. While the total number of casualties inflicted on air crews was a far cry from those accrued in the worldwide land campaigns, Bomber Command suffered, proportionately, worse than any other military arm save for the German U-boat fleet and the Allied merchant mariners.

The price paid in civilian lives was even more terrible. In Great Britain, some 60,000 civilians were killed during the Blitz and by the V-rockets. They were the markers held by Bomber Command as they carried out their vengeance against German cities. Even seventy years later, no one is certain of the total number of dead. Because of the years of bombing, there were large numbers of transitory refugees' bodies who were uncounted in the twisted metal and charred remains of the urban areas. Others were slaughtered by Russian armies sweeping in from the east. Adding to this fog of war, German propagandists inflated or deflated the number of slain depending on their message or agenda. However, best estimates suggest that 593,000 Germans were killed on the ground and 675,000 were wounded, with the majority being women, children, and the elderly, since almost all available men of military age were in uniform.[32] This was indeed the cruel hand of war.

AFTER THE BATTLE FOR THE SCHELDT in November 1944, the First Canadian Army was put into reserve. Over that winter, most of the weary Canadians were given a rest, although the front was never quiet, with patrols and large-scale raids remaining constant. "The combination of danger, monotony and poor living conditions during less active periods," warned one report, "can have a deleterious effect on fighting spirit." Once soldiers were out of the line, measures were taken to restore morale. The first day, they were left alone, to write letters, sort out kit, clean up, and "have a really good sleep." The daily routine was reintroduced, with tightened-up discipline and saluting on the second day, and then over the coming days a "general smartening up and physical training."[33] In these ways, the high command made a conscious effort to cultivate and restore morale among the fighting units that had absorbed heavy casualties over the previous half year.

In what the soldiers dubbed the "winter war," Canadian troops were stationed along the Nijmegen sector, the area fought over during Operation Market Garden in September. The forward trenches were held rather loosely, with the bulk of the infantry, armour, and artillery men living in houses, sheds, and barns behind the lines, and often billeted with Belgian and Dutch families who welcomed them with baths and fresh linen. The Canadians, in turn, shared their rations or care packages, and often partook in leisure activities. The cold weather allowed ice skating, reminding homesick Canadian boys of their own frozen ponds back across the Atlantic. There were forty-eight-hour leave passes to local towns and occasional week-long furloughs to

Throughout the winter of 1944–1945, the First Canadian Army was dug in along the stalemated front at Nijmegen, Netherlands. In this image, a camouflaged Queen's Own Rifles sniper waits for his target.

Brussels or England, but almost no one was sent to Canada. The "48s" were extremely popular, and soldiers going on leave received their banked pay, pooled souvenirs from mates to sell to rear-echelon types for extra cash, and went in search of "R and R"— Rest and Relaxation—or "I and I"—Intercourse and Intoxication.

During this supposedly quiet period, between November 9 and December 31, 1944, 68 officers and 1,171 other ranks from the First Canadian Army were killed or wounded.[34] The Germans across from the Canadians suffered even heavier losses. Many demoralized enemy soldiers voted with their feet, with the "line-dashers" sneaking into the Allied trenches clutching leaflets promising safe passage.[35] This they were given, although they were interrogated, too, to determine what was triggering the surrenders. Many of the prisoners claimed that their units were hanging together only because hard-core Nazi officers and NCOs threatened the men with execution. But prisoners eager to please new masters are not usually trustworthy sources of information, and the Canadians found little rot in the enemy lines.

In late December, Hitler ordered a last-ditch offensive in the Ardennes, known as the Battle of the Bulge. The Germans were always at their deadliest when they seemed beaten, and they revealed an amazing ability to reform new formations from the shattered pieces of old ones. Yet even with a reconstituted force, Hitler deluded himself in thinking another miracle blitzkrieg could be unleashed by thirty or so depleted divisions, with his forces crashing through to Antwerp and forcing the Western Allies to the negotiating table. The logistical challenges of piercing the Allied lines on a narrow front meant that the breakthrough would not likely get far, even if his divisions ransacked Allied supply dumps. Nonetheless, Eisenhower's command had long surmised that the German army in the west was near death. The Allies' sense of surprise at the operation, when it was launched on December 16, was akin to that of a group of doctors watching a terminal patient have his life support shut down and then lurch out of bed. In this case, the patient even took a few wild swings. But a shortage of Axis fuel, a resilient American defence around Bastogne, Allied airpower, and a rapid shift by Patton's Third Army put paid to the last-ditch offensive. Hitler's final gamble on the Western Front only resulted in eating up his remaining reserves of armoured formations and leading to the death of 12,652 and the wounding of 38,600, with another 30,000 listed as missing.[36] However, the Wehrmacht's strike, which cost the Americans about 70,000 casualties and prisoners, caused Eisenhower and his planners concern about the beast that refused to die.

AS THE WINTER LENGTHENED, the Allies planned their drive into Germany. The battle for the Rhineland aimed to clear enemy defenders west of the Rhine and east of the Maas, and to allow for the invasion into the heart of Germany. Montgomery ordered Crerar's First Canadian Army to attack from Nijmegen, pushing southeast along the Rhine River to meet a southern pincer moving northwestward from the U.S. Ninth Army. This area, the German Siegfried Line, consisted of a series of anti-tank positions and minefields protected by flooded fields and wide swaths of forest, particularly the Reichswald and the Hochwald. A few good roads ran through towns such as Goch and Cleve, both of which had been transformed into fortresses. The Allies had hoped the ground would still be frozen, but the thaw came in late January and the front was reduced to a morass of mud.

With the Luftwaffe unable to put up many planes, it was not until February 6, two days before the operation, that the Germans became aware of the buildup

A Canadian artillery gun team fires its 25-pounder.

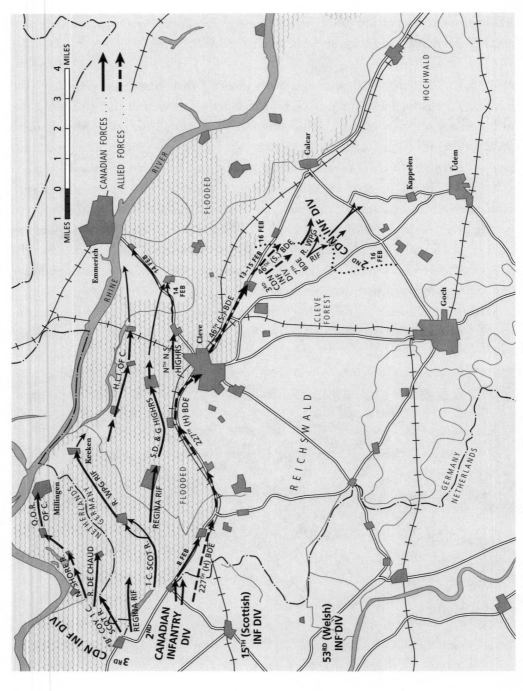

THE RHINELAND, FEBRUARY 8–21, 1945

opposite them.[37] The 84th Infantry Division, backed by over 136 artillery pieces and self-propelled guns, and the 2nd Paratroop Division, one of the best remaining enemy formations, and up to a strength of about 12,000, stood across No Man's Land. The paratroopers were expected to fight hard, and other divisions were in reserve—such as the 7th Parachute Division and the 15th Panzer Grenadier Division—although it was too late for the enemy high command to shift strategic reserves to meet the initial thrust.

The Canadian offensive—Operation Veritable—was unleashed on February 8, 1945. The First Canadian Army, under the command of General Harry Crerar, had thirteen national divisions, over 470,000 troops (albeit far fewer for combat), and was supported by 1,200 guns and 3,400 tanks. It was the largest force ever commanded by a Canadian. Veritable was Crerar's first major set-piece campaign, since he had left much of the planning of Tractable and Totalize in August to Simonds and he had been ill for the Scheldt campaign. Now, in early 1945, Crerar was re-exerting control over his army, and in an apparent snub to Simonds—who had been a difficult subordinate and, perhaps, as temporary army commander during the Scheldt campaign, had grown a little too big for his britches—he gave British lieutenant-general Brian Horrocks, the commander of XXX Corps, control of the first phase of the battle, and of Simonds's II Canadian Corps. Simonds was not happy. Of course, Horrocks was an experienced and respected general, comfortable with the men and eternally optimistic. Brigadier J.A. Roberts, commander of the 8th Canadian Infantry Brigade, had the pleasure of seeing first-hand his qualities of leadership, later bemoaning, "Why, I wondered, rather guiltily, were our senior officers not of the same personality; and we were supposed to be Canadian, less stiff and formal than the British."[38] In this, Roberts spoke for many Canadians who were unimpressed by the lack of charisma and warmth from Crerar and Simonds, and most of the other senior commanders.

Crerar hoped his juggernaut of an army would steamroll the enemy, although he anticipated a long, drawn-out battle. He advised his officers, "In spite of all the difficulties of weather and terrain we should continue to fight the enemy hard, wear down his strength at a greater rate than our own, and then, by securing an important military objective, wrest the initiative completely away from his possession."[39]

Crerar's army leapt forward at 10:30 A.M. on the 8th, with three British, Welsh, and Scottish divisions in the lead, along with elements of the 2nd and 3rd Canadian Infantry Division on the left flank, behind a 1,200-gun barrage that was thickened up with tanks, airpower, machine-gun fire, rockets, anti-aircraft guns, and anything else that could deliver hell upon the Germans. The Anglo-Canadian forces nick-named the brutal show of force a "pepper pot." Canadian Gunner J.P. Brady of the 50th Battery, 4th Medium Regiment, Royal Canadian Artillery, witnessed German prisoners stumbling around in the haze of smoke and fire: "Some reel drunkenly, others stare vacantly; some shamble along in tears, while others laugh hysterically."[40] None had ever experienced such annihilating shellfire. In addition to the pepper pot, over 850 bombers dropped their loads on the German-held towns of Cleve and Goch, and on the Reichswald forest. Afterwards, according to infantryman Donald Pearce, the former woodland "was simply a tangled mass of chewed and broken for-est trees, blasted trenches and smashed equipment."[41]

But even with the awe-inspiring firepower, the British advance was slow, as armour floundered and was confined to a few road systems, all of which were mined and defended by the Germans' 84th Infantry Division.[42] Horrocks later wrote that there was "no room for manoeuvre and no scope for cleverness."[43] The minefields were particularly effective in delaying the operation. As always, the Germans were ingen-ious in these activities: their mines were often fashioned in a checker-board pattern, with several visible to the eye while others were buried below the surface in the other squares; so the infantry, walking gingerly, thought they were avoiding the visible mines but actually stepped on the hidden ones. Trooper Al LaRose of the Sherbrooke Fusilier remembered, "I was glad for the security of my tank. In the Hochwald, in a minefield, there were a lot of wounded foot soldiers lying on the ground. Even with my earphones on I could hear them shouting, 'Stretcher-bearer! Stretcher-bearer!' These guys screaming."[44]

But neither mines nor guns could withstand the surge for long. The 84th Division was overrun along the front, although it was backed by paratroopers who threw themselves into the path of the Allies. Canadian sergeant Alex Troy of the 5th Field Regiment, Royal Canadian Artillery, recalled that the Germans were always good on the defence, but now they were "really tough because the enemy had always before been fighting in some other poor devil's country, [and] now he was defending his own land."[45] With the flooded terrain channelling the Allied soldiers towards the more solid roads, these became natural kill grounds and allowed the outnumbered German forces to concentrate their strength.

The veteran 3rd Canadian Infantry Division—known as the Water Rats after the Scheldt—mucked forward on the left flank. "The mud was unbelievable," reported one Canadian infantryman. "The ruts in the roads were up to three and four feet deep, and all of our armour was being continually bogged down."[46] Much of the front was submerged under water. Engineers threw down Bailey bridges to span impassable fields, and one of them, a pontoon bridge nicknamed Quebec, was 390 metres long. One hundred and fourteen Buffalos, the amphibious tracked vehicles, ferried the troops, but they were lightly armoured and vulnerable to enemy fire, which poured into the Canadian sector from the German-held side of the Rhine. Veterans of the Scheldt realized that there would be no rapid advance under such conditions, but by February 10 the Siegfried Line was broken.

With the 3rd Division guarding the left flank, it was Major-General Bruce Matthews's 2nd Division, fighting under Lieutenant-General Guy Simonds's now engaged II Canadian Corps, that was given the best roads to advance on enemy positions. The previous commander, Major-General Foulkes, had been unpopular and unimaginative, and he had been sent to replace the fired Burns in Italy, where he could do less harm to the Canadian war effort. Matthews had accrued a fine record in Italy, Normandy, and the Scheldt, and his experience in set-piece battles would assist the infantry as they punched forward. In the first few days of combat, his infantry and armour met little opposition and secured their objectives.

However, the American assault to the south, which was to have been launched within forty-eight hours of the First Canadian Army's offensive, was delayed when the Germans sabotaged dams over the Roer River. The Roer was transformed into a 1,000-metre wide raging torrent. With the Americans unable to advance, the Germans shifted their reserves—especially good units such as the 15th Panzer Grenadier and 116th Panzer Division—to the Anglo-Canadian front. Despite these new defenders, Crerar's army swept onward, capturing village after village, although all of them cost a toil in attackers' lives. Behind the lines, Nurse Harriet Sloan wrote of the terrible wreckage she witnessed: "It was just, again, like early France. Just end-less streams of wounded."[47] Resistance stiffened, and by February 13, the day the Reichswald was finally cleared, the Allied drive had stagnated.

AFTER A BRIEF PAUSE to bring forward guns, ammunition, and supplies, the offen-sive was renewed on February 15, with four British divisions and the 2nd and 3rd Canadian Divisions forming a formidable spearhead. The ground forces were ably assisted by the Second Tactical Air Force, which flew 1,500 sorties that day, shooting up anything along the enemy roads.[48] Canadian pilot Hedley Everard recalled that the Spitfires and Typhoons roamed all over the battlefield, like a "gathering of vul-tures at a carcass. Everything below was a war-legitimate target."[49]

Though some significant advances were made, especially through the placement of infantry in armoured Kangaroos, the enemy troops were resilient as they fought to defend against the invasion into Germany. The Canadian Scottish and the Regina Rifles, for instance, engaged in a fervent struggle at Moyland Wood, a forested hilly region. On February 16, the Canadians moved through the edge of the woods, step-ping over and around the unburied bodies of the 15th Scottish Division, who had assaulted unsuccessfully days earlier.

Throughout the forest were camouflaged paratroopers from the 6th German Parachute Division, who ambushed the Canadians. Artillery observers could locate few targets, and the tanks, unable to make progress in the woods, were forced to fire from the perimeter. The Germans, in turn, were backed by artillery from the east bank of the Rhine. The Reginas' war diary noted, "Coy [Company] Commanders agree that the shelling and fighting in these woods have been just as bad as anything encountered in NORMANDY."[50]

After trading fire over several days, the under-strength Reginas mounted an attack from the south on the 18th, supported by Wasps. With the Canadian Scottish sweep-ing in from the east, the paratroopers were overwhelmed in several clashes but always found ways to filter back to other positions. "Fighting in the Woods," remembered one gunner, "was extremely difficult for no sooner would the enemy be chased out of one sector than they would turn up in another."[51] The paratroopers showed, according to one Canadian report, "fanatical resistance."[52]

The worn-out 7th Brigade commander, Brigadier Jock Spragge, who had commanded the unit since August 1944, was relieved on the 20th. Lieutenant-Colonel A.S. Gregory, who had led the Reginas, took over the formation and a new phase of the operation was planned for the 21st, when the Royal Winnipeg Rifles, Sherbrooke tanks, and a number of Wasps would saturate the southern part of the woods in fire. The Little Black Devils from Winnipeg had captured a difficult position to the south at Louisendorf a few days earlier, and had taken a cage-bulging 240 prisoners. Following a concentrated barrage, the Devils stalked their way through the woods, defeating the Germans. The Royal Winnipeg Rifles took 105 casualties, adding to the 380 other Canadians lost during the six-day battle.[53] The Germans lost even more men, often in wild counterattacks, and the combat here added to their crippling casualties, which numbered, on the First Canadian Army's front, approximately 12,000 killed and another 12,000 made prisoner.[54]

There were other costly engagements. On the 19th, for instance, one of the most bitter struggles occurred on the 4th Canadian Infantry Brigade's sector, as the Royal

Infantrymen of the South Saskatchewan Regiment during mopping-up operations.

Hamilton Light Infantry and the Essex Scottish, moving forward in armoured Kangaroos in an attempt to open the road from Goch to Calcar, ran into a force of panzers. Canadian infantrymen dug in and, supported by Fort Garry Horse Shermans, held off two German battlegroups from Panzer Lehr and the 116th Panzer Division. Corpses littered the fields and forests. Lieutenant-Colonel Denis Whitaker of the Royal Hamilton Light Infantry, who would be awarded the Distinguished Service Order, described the fierce defence: "The Germans fought like hell—like demons. This was their last stand for their homeland, and they were not giving an inch."[55] Both sides were mauled over two days, but the Canadians held the ground. The Essex suffered 204 killed, wounded, and made prisoner; the Rileys lost 125; and the Royal Regiment, which had been rushed from reserve, had 64 casualties.[56]

Major-General Dan Spry, commander of the 3rd Division, agonized over the losses and the pressure from his superiors to keep sending his men through the German buzz saw: "They really didn't understand the sharp end of battle. They had a mental block; they'd never been there."[57] After serving in Italy and Northwest Europe, and having seen too much destruction, General Spry, deemed not aggressive enough, was relieved of his command on March 22nd. The view from the front was just as agonizing. Corporal Tom Didmon of the Rileys returned from leave to find most of his friends stacked like cordwood in piles, while the survivors waited for the ground to thaw before burying them. "I had spent all winter with these fellows and now half of them were dead—after I thought that the heaviest fighting was over."[58]

THE CANADIAN INFANTRY SHORTAGES of 1944 carried over into 1945. Private Donald Tansley of the Regina Rifles described the composition of his ever-shifting battalion in the final four months of the war: "In my platoon, which was always under strength—18 or 20, instead of 33–35—the most common age was 19 or 20.... Our NCOs (corporals, sergeants, and company sergeant major) might have been 22–26 years old. Our officers were not much older—23 and up. I recall how shocked I was to discover that one of my heroes, a captain, was only 23. I, at 19, always thought of him as a very senior adult." Of his comrades, Tansley said, "Many were farm boys, strong, tough, used to hard work and hardship, loyal to one another, with no high expectation of their life ahead." In his estimation, most had no more than grade four or five education. Tansley was impressed with his officers, noting "They were involved in the front lines of battle as were we. They led, they fought, they endured the same shit, mud, lack of sleep, danger, irregular food and casualties of the men they commanded."[59]

With all infantry units devastated in the fighting and at skeleton levels, new reinforcements trickled into the formations. Many of the old-timers knocked out during the Scheldt battles also returned around this time, adding an injection of experienced men. "To a battalion which had by now come to consider an 'old friend' one who had been with you for a week, this was a welcome change," remarked one chronicler of the infantry.[60] The conscripted NRMA soldiers also came on strength. There were many complaints about them, but as Lieutenant Donald Pearce of the North Novas observed, "for some reason they have made excellent soldiers."[61] Recent studies suggest that most of the new reinforcements, either NRMA or infantry converted from other arms, had received adequate basic training.[62] Few infantrymen carried a grudge against volunteers or conscripts; it only mattered if a man could carry his share of the load. Queen's Own Rifles officer John D. McLean noted of the reinforcements, "A lot were killed in their first action because they didn't know what to do. If a person survived his first action as a reinforcement then he could go on and be a good soldier."[63] Some 2,463 conscripts saw service in the battle zone; of these, 313 were wounded and 69 killed.[64] Such figures suggest that far fewer conscripts were lost in their first week of combat than is often stated. Yet even with conscripts added to the Canadian rifle companies, they were consistently under strength,

Privates Raoul Archambault and Albert Harvey of Le Régiment de Maisonneuve firing a 2-inch mortar in battle. Harvey was killed on February 26, 1945.

as were British and American forces, who combed through their rear echelon communication and logistical units to convert those soldiers into infantry. The Western Allies were feeling the sting of six months of combat.

But Hitler's armies were far worse off. Germany was being beaten on all fronts. And still the German people refused to lay down arms in a lost war. Some fought for the Führer, others for the Fatherland, while many knew that they had caused or supported mass atrocities that had been unleashed on numerous nations and their peoples, and now they had to hold out until some sort of negotiation might be made. It was a delusion of the damned, especially since the Allied high command's demand for unconditional surrender had not wavered. And even those Germans who wished for a cessation of hostilities found themselves conscripted. Hitler established the Volkssturm—"People's Storm"—in September 1944; it was a desperate attempt to alleviate the shortages of military personnel by drafting all males from the ages of sixteen to sixty. With almost no training, few uniforms, and cast-off weapons, this ragtag army was no match for the soldiers on the Eastern or Western Front, and no fewer than 175,000 were killed in the final months of the war.[65]

Having kicked in the rotten German door, the Allies expected the house to cave in. But the Germans again surprised all and continued on in their doomed cause. Crerar even lamented in an official report in the final months of the war how the enemy contested with dogged relentlessness: "Our infantry suffered heavy casualties from shelling, mortaring and rockets. This was consistent with the enemy's tactics throughout the whole of the operation. His firepower, particularly from machine-guns, mortars and cannons, had been more heavily and effectively applied than at any other time in the Army's fighting."[66] The enemy's refusal to surrender angered Allied soldiers, who were frustrated by the prolonged war that was killing off their friends, keeping them from home, and requiring that they continue to battle through cities and towns that were often ruined during liberation. Private Tom Didmon of the Rileys remembered talking to one enemy prisoner for several hours: "He told me that he was looking forward to being sent to Canada. Imagine that! A bloody German prisoner going to Canada and I was in his country with the prospect of getting killed. How is that for rotten?"[67]

This frustration was also occurring among the air crews, who flew through flak as thick as hail, bombed unremittingly, and watched as their comrades were shot out of the skies. Surely those on the ground would give up now that the aerial war had reached a crescendo of destruction. Yet even in the dead cities such as Hamburg, opinion surveys revealed that there was no indication of a pending insurrection or surrender.[68] This resistance, in its many forms, saw 1.4 million German soldiers and countless hundreds of thousands of civilians killed in the final five months of the war, by the advancing Soviet forces, the bomber attacks, and, to a far lesser extent, the steady march of the armies from the west.[69]

As they battled the German soldiers in the field, the Canadians maintained a remarkable ability in those difficult final months to offer humane treatment to the enemy. Canadians in uniform were taught to kill but also to exercise restraint, although all knew that the hard-core Nazis had a despicable history of giving no quarter or exerting uncommon brutality on those who fell into their clutches.[70] The relatively humane treatment by the Canadians of their prisoners enticed more wavering troops from the opposite side to decide that a prisoner-of-war camp was preferable to a shallow grave. Soldiers would usually fight to the last bullet if they knew that their fate, as soon as they downed their weapons, was death at the hands of the enemy. While adrenalin, fear, and even brief fury might lead to the killing of prisoners attempting to surrender on the chaotic battlefield, these cases were isolated in number. In fact, at this stage in the war, Corporal Bruce Evans of the 1st Hussars recounted that the Canadians felt pity on the adolescents and old men they encountered in combat. "The prisoners we took were boys of 16 and 17 ... they were not really old enough to have ever shaved properly."[71] The Allied soldiers harboured no great hatred of the enemy, save for the despicable Waffen SS troops.

The Germans executed at least 20,000 of their own soldiers—and most of them in the final year of the war, as a warning to other soldiers to not give up the fight.[72] One German prisoner noted that many of his comrades were willing to surrender but were too scared: "the Army had been infused with very young Nazi officers who were willing to die for their country and these Officers knew they must watch their men and shoot them if necessary to stop them from surrendering."[73] The Canadians executed none of their soldiers for desertion; the Americans, only one. This was the difference between democratic armies and ruthless totalitarian ones, but it meant that the Nazi forces would continue to fight in their doomed defence.

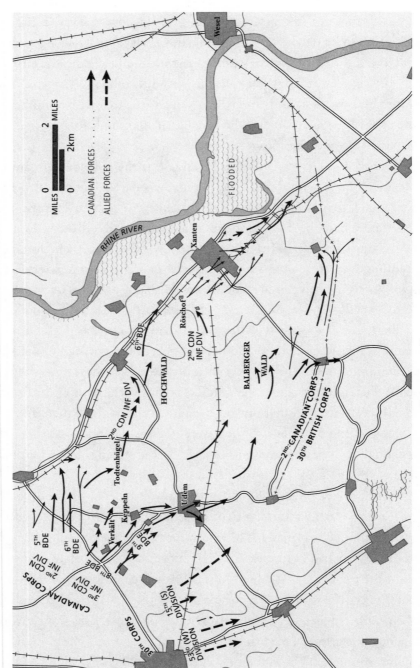

OPERATION BLOCKBUSTER

THE MESSY BATTLEFIELD and German resilience had slowed the Canadians in Operation Veritable, but the Anglo-American steamroller kept advancing. The U.S. Ninth Army to the south, twelve divisions strong, began its delayed offensive on February 23. Resistance was light because much of the enemy reserve had been moved north to counter Crerar's thrust. As the Americans made rapid inroads towards the Rhine, the next four days saw the Canadians manoeuvre forward, wipe out strongpoints, and prepare for a renewed offensive. On February 26, Crerar launched Operation Blockbuster against enemy units in the Hochwald forest, with the goal of eventually reaching Xanten, which lay on the Rhine. It would be one of the most costly Canadian campaigns of the entire war.

With the Americans advancing behind the Germans in late February, Montgomery might have called off Blockbuster, unless the Ninth Army planned to turn back and be the anvil for the Anglo-Canadian hammer—which they showed no intention of doing as they drove to the Rhine. But Montgomery was aching to see the Anglo-Canadian forces do their part in the war, as they were now vastly overshadowed by the Americans that were three times as large and finding success. Neither Crerar nor Simonds

Canadian infantrymen, worn and weary, slog through the mud in the final months of the war. The enemy was beaten but refused to surrender, and the war continued on with no end in sight.

questioned the orders that would see lead elements of the 2nd and 3rd Canadian Infantry Divisions punch forward to the southeast at 3:45 A.M. on the 26th.

The Canadians got off to a good start, with the two divisions' brigades rushing through the skeleton ruins of Udem. Opposition was overcome all along the front. One of the many German strongpoints was the hamlet of Mooshof. The Queen's Own Rifles, attacking as part of the first wave of seven infantry regiments, battled through the surrounding fields that were reduced to porridge. Preplanned enemy artillery, mortar, and Nebelwerfer fire pinned down the infantry, but a few tanks from the 1st Hussars broke through, as well as a handful of infantrymen from the Queen's Own Rifles. Led by Sergeant Aubrey Cosens of Porquis Junction, Ontario, who had enlisted in 1939 as an eighteen-year-old railway section hand, the Queen's Own destroyed a number of paratrooper positions, although more defenders remained in three fortified farms. When the enemy struck back, the junior officers were killed and Cosens assumed command of the remaining troops in his vicinity. At one point, the Queen's Own were down to five men, and Cosens ordered that the four provide covering fire while he raced across the open ground to direct one of the last Shermans towards the camouflaged Germans. Somehow Cosens survived the death charge, and the now alerted tank crashed through a farm. Cosens cleared the other two farms on his own, wiping out a number of paratroopers. He appeared protected by a divine hand, but later in the day he was shot through the head. His courage under fire earned him a posthumous Victoria Cross.

A 3rd Canadian Infantry Division official report observed that the Queen's Own Rifles advance, which suffered 101 casualties, "proved to be a slow costly business. The enemy, basing his defence on maximum fire and the minimum number of men, protested every gain. They supported these tactics with anti-tank and anti-personnel mines and unusually heavy concentrations of artillery and mortar fire. Every advance was counter attacked."[74] Dick Medland of the Queen's Own remembered, "The Germans contested every foot. They put up one hell of a fight. They threw everything at us. We did the same to them."[75] But more than 300 paratroopers were bagged by the regiment, revealing again that the best defence the Germans could offer was no longer good enough.

While the Canadian infantry and armour crashed through the 47 Panzer Corps and 2nd Parachute Corps, the Germans threw reinforcements into the breach and all were supported by a heavy concentration of artillery—over 1,000 guns and 700 mortars.[76] Even as the Ninth Army was penetrating deeply to the rear, the Germans continued to divert their reserves to block the Canadian advance. It was a clumsy way to fight, but Allied airpower always made it difficult for the Germans to shift forces to meet emerging threats. Nonetheless, the Germans almost cleared the path for the Americans as they turned to face the Canadian thrust.

The Canadians continued to take villages and make ground. On February 27, Lion Group—consisting of the South Alberta and Algonquin Regiments from the 4th Canadian Armoured Division—moved towards the Hochwald, a kidney-shaped forest. Infantry–tank cooperation had vastly improved, with the infantry sticking close to the armour to drive off enemy panzerfaust teams while the tanks provided raking machine-gun and shellfire from the mobile gun platform. The assault cast out the Germans from a series of crucial crests and ridges, and back-and-forth fighting failed to stop Lion Group. In the Hochwald forest, following an Allied barrage, an insane asylum was damaged, and hundreds of inmates were found wandering the shattered field. They must have been at home in the twisted wreckage that mirrored the scenes in their tortured minds.

The German units were buckling under the pressure, yet still the defenders fought on in smash-mouth battles. One First Canadian Army intelligence report noted incredulously on the fourth day of combat, "It is impossible to rationalize the present tactics of the enemy between the Rhine and the Maas. Not those of an Army planning to conserve its forces to fight another day, they are more of the cornered-rat variety."[77] The view from the front was no less perplexing. "The bastards are fighting maniacs," observed one long-service Canadian officer.[78]

The medieval town of Xanten, with its Roman amphitheatre, finally fell to the Canadians on March 8, and Operation Veritable came to an end. The Germans, having thrown ten divisions into the line to hold the First Canadian Army, had lost 22,239 soldiers who were made prisoners, and about that many again in killed and wounded. The Canadian casualties were 5,304 killed, wounded, and captured— slightly more than during the attritional battles of the Normandy campaign.[79] As the Canadian soldiers sang bitterly,

> If this war isn't over
> And pretty damn soon
> There'll be nobody left
> In this old platoon.[80]

AS THE CRERAR'S FORMATIONS clawed their way forward onto German soil, another group of Canadians was trying to escape. Allied prisoners behind barbed wire were in a desperate situation. By the last full year of the war, almost all the prisoners were suffering from systemic malnutrition. With the German economy crippled under the multi-front onslaught, prisoners' rations had been cut significantly, usually to less than 750 calories a day, about one quarter of the requirement for adult males. The Allied bombing of the transportation lines added to the struggle, as Red Cross package deliveries were disrupted. By early 1945, the German POW system collapsed, along with the rest of the economy. The hundreds of thousands of prisoners became a tremendous burden on the wavering state. With the Russians advancing in the east, the prison and death camps in Poland and eastern Germany would soon be overrun or evacuated. The order went out from Berlin to begin a forced march of prisoners to the west.[81]

To stay ahead of the Russians, wasted prisoners, almost all of them inadequately dressed, were hounded under threat of execution through snow drifts and freezing conditions. Often not fed for days on end, the long parade of lice-ridden and sore-plagued men was herded along by bayonet-wielding guards, allowed to stop only at night in barns. Fat melted away rapidly and then the body began to consume itself. It was not uncommon for gaunt prisoners during the unending march to drop 30 or 40 percent of their weight, leaving only shuffling skeletons with sunken faces and xylophone ribs.

Prisoners used the few goods or items they had left, especially cigarettes, to bribe their guards, and many of the prisoners quietly crept out from the barns at night to trade with or rob local farmers. The exhausted guards did little to stop them because there was no place for them to go. Even the Allied prisoners were wary of encountering the marauding Soviet troops. This exodus of prisoners westward added to the overcrowding on roads thronged with tens of thousands of refugees. Starving prisoners shared the road with starving civilians. Despite his misery, Pilot Officer Earle White shuddered with sadness as one young German mother with two little children tried to keep up with the straggling prisoners whose feet were tramping down the snow. A nearly physically broken White gave her his last pack of cigarettes, noting sadly that "One child had frozen to death and I hoped the mother would be able to barter the cigarettes to help save the other one."[82]

After three years of imprisonment, Roland Carlson, a wireless air gunner, recounted the march westward. "One day in a severe snow storm, we had just left the town Jena, when we passed a convoy of German soldiers moving westward. Their personal equipment was being hauled in larger wooden wagons pulled by Hungarian and Russian women. We tried to share with them some of the food we had, but one of the guards smashed his rifle into the face of one of the women who accepted a piece of bread. That stopped our philanthropy.... One woman, wearing sacking on her feet and wrapped in a ragged blanket, shouted to us as she passed—'Courage, Englander.'" During those fifty-one days of marching some 650 kilometres with little food, Carlson often thought of that brave woman who had offered him solace. He was determined "to be no less courageous."[83]

With bloodied and blistered feet, gnawing hunger, and diphtheria-riddled excrement running down their legs, the prisoners stumbled on. Frostbite ate into extremities. The death march pushed the already battered prisoners to the brink of survival. Alexander Molnar, a signaller with the Essex Scottish captured in July 1944, described the horror of seeing sickeningly thin Russian prisoners executed by the side of the road. The Canadians refused to let that happen to their comrades, banding together to aid the helpless. Those who could no longer walk were carried by mates or put on makeshift sleighs, even though this weakened the already emaciated men still upright. Despite the prisoners' despondence and weakness, the bonds of comradeship remained strong, although Molnar winced that "the stark cheapness of life was horribly depressing."[84] Clement Pearce of Toronto, who was shot down as an air gunner from No. 101 Squadron, RAF, nearly perished on the road. "I remember one point on this dreadful march, curling up in the snow, and just wanting to die. I was in agony and couldn't move and frankly didn't care what happened to me." But two army comrades—who had listened to his life story over and over again in the camps—came along and pulled him to his feet, scolding him that his mother had already buried one son. "And with that, they dragged me between them, slept with me one on each side, and generally hauled me along on this march, and so saved my life."[85]

With almost no food provided, grubs and bugs were eaten, as was grass or bark from trees after digging through the snow. Local German civilians sometimes offered what little they could through trades for cigarettes, but they too were often dangerously underfed and were packing up their own households, having caught word of what the Russians did to anyone in their path. There was little sympathy for the prisoners at the highest levels of the Nazi command. After the unyielding bombardment of German cities in early 1945, a raging Hitler considered executing thousands of Allied prisoners in retaliation.[86] He was talked out of it, but while the prisoners did not know of Hitler's rage, they understood that their lives were on the line in the final crumbling months of the 1,000-year Reich.

Flight Sergeant George Brown wrote that "During the last four months of our confinement we were kept alive only by the knowledge that the Americans were on their way."[87] During his two years of incarceration, but especially during the marches, Brown dropped 65 pounds, ending at a bone-rattling 117 pounds. Andrew Cox, imprisoned for five years, was an emaciated 80 pounds when he was finally freed. Most of the prisoners were in equally dire health, victims of disease, malnutrition, and starvation.

In the last weeks of April, the German guards overseeing the prisoners disappeared. They did not want to be around when the prisoners gained access to guns. Most of the Canadians were liberated in late April or early May. Had the war gone on a few more weeks, it is likely that large numbers of prisoners would have succumbed to starvation or disease.

In all theatres, 9,724 Canadians became prisoners of war. Flyers made up 2,475 of the prisoners, the navy claimed 98, and the rest were from the army.[88] Some men spent more of the war behind barbed wire than in combat, but they fought a battle of the flesh, mind, and spirit. Attesting to the inner strength required to survive, one Canadian airman inscribed in his secret prisoner log, "Tethered but not tamed."[89]

ON THE EASTERN FRONT, the 2.5 million Russians were now unstoppable. Understrength German divisions were fed into battle and consumed within days. At the

Führer's headquarters, Hitler was reduced to moving around now-destroyed armies on a map, planning counterattacks with non-existent forces, and raging impotently about how the German people had failed him. In London, Churchill worried that Stalin's armies would sweep over all of Germany and then refuse to relinquish the territory. With the Soviet Union having bled for its victory, Stalin was in no mood to negotiate over occupied territory. The Soviets were shifting from ally to rival in the final months of the war.

After the fighting of late February attrited much of the German combat capacity across the Rhine, the U.S. First Army crossed the Rhine Bridge at Remagen on March 7. A bridgehead was secured, but inroads were not made until the end of the month, as Eisenhower held back the Americans to allow Montgomery's forces to jump the Rhine and save some face. This they did, on March 23, after an overly long preparation and buildup of military might that was accompanied by a spectacular paratroop airdrop. Most of the Canadian units were in reserve at this point, but the 9th Canadian Infantry Brigade crossed the Rhine and the 1st Canadian Parachute Battalion dropped into a hot zone on the morning of March 24.

Though the Germans were vastly outnumbered and outgunned, they put up a fierce resistance, and both the 9th Brigade and the paratroopers fought for their lives. The Canadian paratroopers swarmed through German defences just north of Diersfordt Wood, clearing their object-ives. "Germans were killed by the hundreds," recounted the 1st Canadian Parachute Battalion's war diary. The Canadians twenty-three killed, includ-ing their inspiring commanding offi-cer, Lieutenant-Colonel J.A. Nicklin, a former Canadian Football League star with the Winnipeg Blue Bombers.[90] One of the battalion's orderlies, Corporal F.G. Topham, was awarded the Victoria Cross for treating a num-ber of wounded men, even though he

A Canadian on the road to Cleve, Germany.

had been shot through the nose and was bleeding badly. Topham carried one critically injured man off the battlefield on his back, and rescued three more comrades
from a burning carrier. He survived.

Once the Rhine was breeched, and Canadians stormed across it in late March,
most of them relished a long-planned urination on the Fatherland. Nineteen-year-
old driver Jim Guy, from Carp, Ontario, remembered coming across a large sign that
advised, "You are conquerors now, not liberators. Use the people as such. Do not
fraternize."[91] The soldiers-turned-occupiers were warned about terrorist activities
being perpetrated by hardcore Nazis, but in the villages they usually found only the
cowed and compliant. While one Canadian officer suggested it would be "safer to
shoot the lot," the civilians were not executed.[92] But nor were they treated gently. The
Canadians had witnessed the murders of French and Belgian resistance fighters and
those who aided them. They had heard the stories of tortured civilians—women,
children, and the elderly. "Memories of their own dead comrades were also fresh in
their minds," recalled Brigadier Richard Malone. "Now for the first time, the people
of Germany would in some measure see and experience what fearful horrors of the
war they had unleashed on the world."[93]

"We continued to 'live off the land,'" claimed Private Donald Tansley, "occupying
a new farmhouse every night or so, enjoying commandeered cattle, pigs, chick, pre-
serves out of the cellar, and fresh milk, occasionally sleeping in a house."[94] Any sign
of confrontation was dealt with coldly, and enemy snipers firing at troops often led
to the razing of houses and buildings.

The order not to fraternize was difficult to obey when Canadian soldiers were
billeted in German civilian houses, or when they were asked for chocolate by children who reminded them of cousins and younger siblings left behind, but many of
their attitudes hardened as labour camps were encountered. "I am not in the habit of
telling what I see over here but this is something that should be told to everyone,"
wrote a private with the 3rd Canadian Division, describing a ghastly scene he and his
comrades happened upon. "It is about ten Dutch civilians that were murdered right
close to where we are now in a concentration camp. One of them was buried alive.
The others were all battered to pieces either with rifles or sticks. Some had their heads
bashed in, some their ankles were broke or twisted, their chests bashed in. You should

see some of the things that were used for torture." Recounting a similar discovery, another corporal averred, "Never have I seen butchery or mutilated mankind of that sort before."[95] Elmer Bell witnessed one camp where Russian women were "starved to death." While the Canadians distinguished between the Nazi thugs and the German citizens, Bell noted perceptively that there was a "brutality" to the Germans who had allowed such horrors to occur in the name of their nation, concluding, "Here is a confusing picture of the people."[96]

The Canadians—packs stuffed with warm clothing, watches, and other loot—were uneasy occupiers as they continued to push into Germany in April. Ray Lane, now a sergeant in the Sherbrooke Fusilier, wearied of the countless small skirmishes, the never-ending stress, and the dreary sights of the dead, noting, "Everyone considered and feared the possibility of reaching a breaking point when he could no longer take the ordeal of being constantly in danger, constantly under fire and constantly witnessing someone blown to bloody pieces."[97] Captain Harold MacDonald of the New Brunswick Regiment shared his cumulative exhaustion with his wife: "Nine months of not knowing if the next 24 hours would be the last or not. Of living either in holes in the ground, damp cellars or broken down houses, of seeing bodies & parts of bodies of friends, of burying them, of killing & helping to kill.... Darling, I'm tired.... It's a tiredness that a week or a month or two months won't erase."[98]

AFTER A DREARY WINTER IN ITALY, I Canadian Corps was only too happy to exit the Mediterranean theatre. Shortages of everything—from shells to soldiers—had revealed what everyone already knew: the Italian front had long since become a stagnant strategic backwater. While the Canadians wept over leaving their thousands of comrades buried under white crosses, almost all were anxious to sail to Europe. In a turn of events typical of the sad-sack campaign, only days before the men embarked on ships, the chronically undersupplied Canadian headquarters received over 100,000 pairs of boots, 54,000 trousers, and 1.5 million razors.[99] Most of the kit was left behind.

The Canadians from Italy joined their comrades in Northwest Europe, arriving over the span of March and April 1945 to be reunited under Crerar's First Canadian Army. New and better equipment was issued, with the 5th Canadian Armoured Division and 1st Armoured Brigade receiving upgraded Shermans and Fireflys. There was more of everything, from food and supplies to armaments and air support. Sergeant Jack Shepherd of the Hastings and Prince Edward Regiment described France as "a totally different world" from Italy. "The most memorable [thing] was the mile after mile of wrecked German transport bumper to bumper, caught by rocket firing typhoon planes we'd only heard about. It felt good; perhaps this would all come to an end after all!"[100] It would, but not without further fighting.

The two Canadian corps were to liberate the northern Netherlands and occupy parts of Germany, where about 100,000 enemy troops remained. They had to move fast. The Dutch were walking skeletons. Their meagre rations had been cut repeatedly in the last year of the war by the Nazi occupiers, and now most were wasting away on less than 500 calories a day. "I had never seen anything that moved me like the hunger I saw in Holland," observed one shaken Canadian infantryman.[101] Many of the

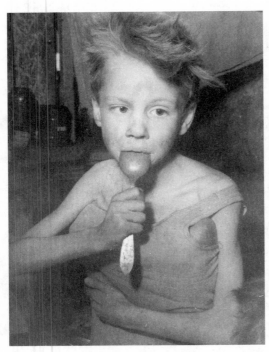

Dutch were forced to eat flower bulbs to survive. The elderly had begun to perish, and soon the young would follow. Gunner J.P. Brady, a Métis soldier from Wetaskiwin, Alberta, recounted saving his rations for the small children, "some of them so hungry they actually howl like little wolf whelps, while others whine weakly from starvation."[102] The Allies were now staving off a humanitarian disaster. Trucks that could be carrying shells were loaded with wheat; bombers dropped supplies rather than high explosives. Soldiers at the front chose to go hungry, giving away their food to the grateful civilians who greeted them not only as liberators but as saviours.

The liberation of the Netherlands by the Canadians was a desperate race against time as the Dutch people were on the verge of starvation.

The Canadians pushed aside their natural instincts for self-preservation and crashed forward against enemy positions to save the starving Dutch. Most of the Germans surrendered with little bloodshed, and soon the Dutch were liberated in Emden, Arnhem, and Apeldoorn. But there were also ugly cases such as the battle at Groningen on April 15. With Dutch SS troops dug into the sixth largest city in the Netherlands, a two-brigade Canadian assault, with the Essex Scottish and the Royal Hamilton Light Infantry in the lead, broke the enemy, but it cost 209 Canadian casualties. Harry Fox, one observer of the resistance, believed that the "Dutch SS troops knew there was no future for them but death. It was the very young ones, sixteen or seventeen years old, that were the most fanatical, however, and they would die before giving up."[103]

Lieutenant-General Charles Foulkes, commander of I Canadian Corps, met with German representatives to open up starving Dutch towns to food deliveries and to establish an agreed-upon temporary truce, but it was a slow process, and while much of the fighting had ended by April 19, there was no ceasefire until the 28th. The beaten enemy, far from Berlin, did not have a lot fight left in him and tended to follow the unofficial ceasefire from mid-month onward, but there remained fierce clashes, such as Major-General Bert Hoffmeister's 5th Armoured Division's attack on the Dutch port of Delfzijl.

To liberate Delfzijl, Hoffmeister began a series of probing skirmishes on April 21, with more intense ones set in motion four days later. The Canadians were trying not to use their artillery, in order to avoid killing Dutch civilians, but the result was akin to fighting with one hand tied behind their back. The Perth and Irish regiments, along with the Westminsters and British Columbia Dragoons, slowly reduced the German-held perimeter defence. The most ferocious part of the battle commenced on April 28 and raged for three days. Platoon commander Lieutenant Reg Roy of the Cape Breton Highlanders penned in his diary, "It was horrible to see our fellows cut up so.... I hope to never see another battle like it. It was murder."[104] Hoffmeister's men took 4,143 prisoners at the cost of 230 killed and wounded. The captives were added to the First Canadian Army's total count since July 23 of more than 190,000 prisoners.[105] The lopsided victory at Delfzijl was a marvel of combined arms fighting on the part of the Canadians, but the lives lost in the final days of the war were a testament to the continuing sacrifice required against an enemy who refused to surrender.

"'They' keep telling us the war is almost over," wrote nineteen-year-old Donald Tansley, who with three months at the front was considered a long-service veteran in the Regina Rifles. "But, we ask each other, why are the buggers still firing at us?... A new fear was beginning to take over—would we survive the remaining days or weeks?"[106] Most did, but not all. In the first week of May, from the 1st to the 5th, with fighting almost at an end, 114 Canadians died, including 12 on May 7, the last day of battle in Europe.[107]

Canadian soldiers fought until the last day of the war, May 7.
Everyone feared being killed as the end neared.

CHAPTER 15

VETERANS

"When you've seen your friends blown to bits around you," observed one Canadian soldier, "it makes you think that the post-war world ... better be good!"[1] The ghastly war limped towards its end in early May. Every day saw tens of thousands of combatants die, while Europeans held on in starvation conditions, scrambled for cover under the fall of bombs, or fed the stoves in the death camps. When Hitler put a bullet in his brain in a Berlin bunker on April 30, 1945, to avoid capture by the Soviet armies that were swarming through the city (a day after Mussolini was executed by Communist forces in Italy), the war was all but over for Germany.

On May 2, the German armies in Italy surrendered. Grand Admiral Karl Dönitz, an ardent Nazi who was handed the toxic leadership of the ruined Third Reich, delayed the surrender of his beaten armies to allow fleeing German civilians additional time to escape the vengeful Soviet army and reach Allied lines. The Germans in the Netherlands, northern Germany, and Denmark surrendered on the 5th, and negotiations for the total surrender of Germany came to a close in the early hours of May 7, with celebrations around the world set for the next day. The war in Europe was over.

The war with Germany ended on May 8, 1945. These Canadians hold a Nazi banner in victory.

The Canadian Army had suffered 44,339 casualties since D-Day; 961 officers and 10,375 other ranks had been killed.[2] Captain Jack Martin, an historical officer at the front, witnessed his comrades' reactions to the end of the war, remarking, "The effects of the cease fire order is difficult to explain. Many were almost incapable of realizing that the war was over for them. All were mindful of the many problems of the immediate, and more distant future."[3] Charlie Martin (no relation to Jack, above), who was in the first wave to land at Juno, declared, "That any of us had survived seemed like a miracle."[4] This sentiment would have been shared by most of the service personnel at the sharp end, be they in Sherman tanks, behind a 25-pounder, in a Halifax, or in the belly of a corvette. The news of the war's end brought little excitement to the exhausted Canadians in the field. Theirs was a long and costly war, with relentless combat sapping strength and claiming comrades. Most flyers in the bombers and in the infantry wrote off their lives to cope. Now, these dead men wondered what they would do with the rest of their lives.

IN CANADA, six years of pent-up fear and anxiety came to a boil. Across the Dominion, wild celebrations broke out in the streets, even though the war against Japan still raged in the Far East. But, as in Europe, not everyone embraced the wild release, and at least 44,000 families who had lost a loved one, as well as countless additional others related to the fallen, must have been unsure of how to mark the end of the nightmare. Lieutenant Barney Danson, who was blinded in one eye during the Normandy fighting, remembered his profound sadness on VE Day "when, with the memories of my dead friends still fresh in my mind, I could not bring myself to join the crowds rejoicing on Toronto's streets.... Since then, hardly a day has gone by that I haven't thought of one of my friends."[5] Kathleen Lynett, the youngest of three siblings, grieved for her eldest brother, Sergeant John Griffin, who was killed while flying a Stirling in July 1942. Three years later, on VE Day, she allowed herself a smile now that the war was finally over, but the cessation of hostilities also "brought it home that John wasn't coming back."[6]

The police and authorities turned a blind eye to some of the raucous behaviour across the country, but in Halifax the community leaders closed the bars and liquor stores. For the celebrating civilians and sailors, this would not do. Sailors already had an ambivalent relationship with the city and its inhabitants, feeling that Haligonians had exploited the servicemen with high prices throughout the war and had never welcomed them into the community. Halifax, remarked Lieutenant Fredrick Watt, commander of the Naval Boarding Service, the body that inspected the merchant ships' cargos and tried to sooth poor relations with ships' crews and their captains, was "an overcrowded hellhole."[7] On May 8, the joyous gatherings soon degenerated into out-of-control riots. When the government liquor stores were found closed, sailors "opened" them by kicking down doors. The alcohol-fuelled mayhem led to looting. The deliriously happy folk dancing around burning cars or kissing in front of shattered windows created, as one sailor described it, "an atmosphere of total chaos."[8] Some sailors were wearing dresses and some women were wearing nothing at all. In the riot's smoking aftermath, the navy was blamed for losing control of its sailors, although civilians and other service members had taken part in the destruction and the city officials had been extraordinarily inept in planning for war's end. Nonetheless, the navy received a black eye and its sailors were labelled hooligans.[9] Admiral Leonard Murray, Canada's only theatre commander of the war, became the scapegoat. It was an inglorious end to Murray's career as Canada's most distinguished flag officer, and after having spent the war fighting the U-boats, he was taken down by his own countrymen in victory. Unceremoniously removed from command a few days after the riot, Murray lived out his remaining days exiled in England, almost entirely forgotten by Canadians at the time of his death in 1971.

THE CHALLENGE OF DEMOBILIZING the million-man Allied armies was nightmarish in complexity. "I had done my job," recalled one Canadian. "I was looking forward to just getting back to my wife and child.... That was all I was interested in."[10] The overseas soldiers, sailors, and airmen had enlisted to fight a menace and they had prevailed. Now, impatient, angry, and lonely, these citizen-warriors wanted to get home. But the Allies needed their units in the field to ensure the German nation would abide by the surrender agreement and, even more worrisome, to ensure that the Soviet forces did not keep pushing westward to occupy all of Germany. Shortages of transport and shipping also ensured that the demobilization of several million men would not be timely.

Almost from the start of the war, the King government had planned for its finish. Committees were struck in late 1939 to prepare for demobilization and postwar economic recovery.[11] A system based on points, which took into account length of service and prioritized men, attempted to ensure that there was a "first in, first out" policy tempered by suitable exigencies for men with families. Yet, as individuals were sent to Canada, the overseas units were slowly denuded of their most experienced rank and file.[12] This also meant that individual service personnel were welcomed in their communities, but that the regiments, squadrons, or ships, for the most part, could not be celebrated or feted as a whole. The process of demobilization began shortly after Germany's surrender, but most Canadians realized that it would be a long wait.

The Canadian liberation of the Netherlands was a time of joy. The Dutch welcomed their liberators with tears of celebration, and the Canadians fully understood that the terrible sacrifice and suffering of the previous year of combat had saved lives and banished evil.

In the Netherlands, the Canadians' arrival was proof positive to the Dutch that the long war was over. Town after town was freed by the Canucks in the final weeks of the war, and the young Dominion soldiers had encountered near-hysterical crowds throwing flowers, waving flags, and passing out kisses. Captain T.J. Allen wrote of the pandemonium, "Whatever their routes, the convoys were greeted with the wildest enthusiasm by the hysterically happy crowds lining the roads.... To a liberated Dutchman that day it was a privilege even to touch the sleeve of a Canadian uniform. Each Canadian private was a Christ, a saviour."[13]

The nine million Dutch had passed through a cruel ordeal. The brutalized civilians were starved of food and fuel in the final winter of 1944–1945, and thousands of already weakened Dutch men, women, and children died from the wilful neglect of their Nazi overlords. Records would later show that 104,000 Jews had been murdered and another 150,000 or so Dutch had died during the occupation. Hundreds of thousands of others had been deported and forced to work as slave labourers. The Dutch had survived on about 500 "official" calories a day in the last winter, and anyone who remained strong had been forced to steal, trade on the black market, or find ways to augment their meagre rations. Much of the country's population was only months away from mass starvation.

There were also some 150,000 German soldiers in the Netherlands when the high command surrendered on May 5. What were the Canadians to do with them? Putting them in huge camps guarded by battalions of troops would have siphoned off resources, and so the Germans were disarmed but allowed to keep their own commanders, who exerted discipline, occasionally through firing squads.[14] The Canadians did not interfere with the sometimes brutal discipline. This handing of control to German officers was a necessary pill to swallow, but the Allies also hunted down senior Nazi officials to put them on trial for their wartime actions.[15] Remarkably few revenge killings occurred, of Germans by the Dutch, even though General Crerar warned his superiors that the Dutch underground was "eager to deal with the defeated enemy."[16] Retribution was, however, brought by the resistance and others against their own countrymen who had collaborated with the Nazis. Summary trials and executions were carried out; women who had taken up with German occupiers were publicly humiliated, usually by violently shearing their hair and dying their bloodied heads orange. Many Canadian soldiers were uncomfortable with this rough justice, but they rarely interfered.

Food was rushed into the cities. RAF and RCAF bombers carried out Operations Faust and Manna in late April and early May, which involved dropping thousands of tons of food to suffering Dutch communities. The relief flights brought pilot Colin Friesen enormous satisfaction as Dutch families raced out of their farms, waving and cheering as the bomber bay doors opened to drop essential supplies. "As the mission went on, we saw that every barn over which we flew had painted on its roof the words 'Thank-you, Canadians!'"[17]

As the new dawn pushed away the grim drabness of the last six years, a Canadian summer bloomed. The grateful Dutch and Dominion troops drank, danced, and enjoyed themselves. Canadian boys were taken into the Dutch homes, feted and celebrated, nurtured, and shown kindness, and they reciprocated with food, cigarettes, and even surplus army uniforms. Many soldiers subsided on half rations. "Whatever we were able to get our hands on we gave to the people," recounted Robert Sawdon of the Saskatoon Light Infantry, whose older brother did not survive the war. "I have never forgotten the sight of starving children."[18] Other Canadians adopted entire households, providing food, chocolate, and cigarettes, and handing over money, working around the house, and acting as adopted sons.

A Canadian enjoying himself among Dutch women. The Canadian liberators were heroes, as they shared food and bonhomie among the Dutch population ravaged by war.

But armies of occupation, even liberating ones, can wear out their welcome. For the Dutch—dispirited, humiliated, and starving—the Canucks were a breath of fresh air. Their passion, desire to celebrate, and access to money and goods made them an appealing group. But as infantryman Lester Sugarman remarked after the war, "The temptations for soldiers were fantastic."[19] Few Canadians were without girlfriends. Dutch campaigns were mounted that warned young women against cavorting with the Canadians, but they had little success. Dutch men took to pressuring women to avoid the liberators in uniform out of patriotism, but this transparent appeal by the shabbily dressed and church-mouse-poor nationals also had little impact. The young women made up their own minds and the Canadians continued to benefit from all aspects of the liberation. As one contemporary Dutch journalist commented wickedly, "Dutch men were beaten militarily in 1940; sexually in 1945."[20]

Most Canadians entered the war inexperienced and innocent; few remained so at the end. Despite the issuing of prophylactics, thousands of babies were born. Shotgun marriages of both love and convenience led to lifelong unions; in other cases, weddings joined unsuited individuals who were not ready for a life together. Some of these new families came back to Canada, but others were abandoned. Seventy years later, there is a group of elderly Dutch, born in late 1946 or early 1947, who are still searching for their Canadian fathers.

Even if every soldier had been a saint, friction between the Canadians and the local civilians would still have been palpable. Nonetheless, the Dutch have remained forever grateful to their liberators, and there were tearful farewells when most of the Canadians left before Christmas 1945. The saving of the Netherlands remains a crucial signpost in the Canadians' memory of the war, and the soldiers rightly took pride in the freeing and feeding of the Dutch. As signaller Norman Penner noted, "There was no doubt that we had been fighting a just war."[21]

IF THE LIBERATION revealed the necessity of having fought in the brutal war to save Europe, the stomach-churning revelation of concentration camps was further evidence of the evil Nazi regime. Even after the war ended, these sites of mass death still held the evidence of the millions murdered, in the form of carefully documented records, collections of personal effects, and open graves filled with thousands of emaciated corpses. The skeletal survivors and mounds of ash were horrific to contemplate.

Canadian private Gordon McLean was not a warrior. He was touring with an entertainment group, the Army Show, when he visited the death camp at Bergen-Belsen; he wrote, shaken, "what a horrible sight that was. Wholesale murder, efficient, and well planned."[22] When British troops arrived at Belsen they discovered 10,000 unburied bodies. Charlie Hancock had survived flying in a Halifax as a wireless operator with RCAF's No. 408 Squadron. At the end of the war, he was part of a crew that flew dignitaries to the Belsen death camp, and was witness to the sickening sights:

Victims of a Nazi death camp. The discovery of the death camps revealed for many the evil of Hitler's Third Reich and confirmed the justness of the war.

As my eyes surveyed this devastation—and as my mind came to realize the full scope of the wickedness explicit here—I wondered how this had been allowed to happen by a literate people, people who could build bridges and compose beautiful music, who loved their children, and who could pray to a God they recognized. The horror of seeing the victims, their nondescript bodies—or what was left of their bodies—entwined in lime pits with the bones of their friends, their parents, their children; of those dead eyes—if they had not yet rotted from the sockets—without a fire left in them; the horror of that remains with me to this day. The validity of the war could never again be denied, it seemed to me, insofar as that war was fought to prevent or avenge a human tragedy such as this one.[23]

The Nazis murdered six million Jews by lethal gas, bullet, and deliberate starvation. Hundreds of thousands of additional innocents, including Communists, homosexuals, and the mentally disabled, were also exterminated. Allied Supreme Commander Eisenhower ordered his commanders to march the local German civilian populations through the death camps so they could witness the disgusting actions to which they had lent support and turned a blind eye. It was not enough. The world had to see the atrocities. Photographers, cameramen, and artists created records offering irrefutable proof of the horror of what has come to be known as the Holocaust. While the United States, Britain, and Canada did not go to war to save the Jews, the death camps confirmed the truth that the war had been a struggle against a malevolent and evil regime.

Even as the true nature of the Nazi Third Reich was exposed, Canadians were almost immediately thrust into protecting Germans. An army of occupation marched into the Fatherland. Most soldiers went forward with hardened hearts, wanting to make the civilians pay, especially if there was a hint of resistance. They encountered quiet compliance. There were other dangers. Roving bands of now freed slave labourers and Russian prisoners of war were looting, inflicting serial sexual violence, and carrying out mass murder against civilians. John Bradley, a twenty-six-year-old Mohawk serving with the Royal Canadian Artillery, remembered that he and others were forced to offer protection as "the Russians were kicking the shit out of German civilians."[24] There was no such protection in eastern Germany, where a human tidal wave of over eight million German refugees was driven from their lands by the rampaging Soviet armies.[25] While few records were kept, historians believe that more than a million Germans were likely killed in the aftermath of the war, millions of women raped, and hundreds of thousands of the survivors left as Displaced Persons who eked out a grim existence in refugee camps for the better part of a decade.[26] Such was one aspect of the hard hand of war in the aftermath of the greatest conflict in human history.

THE DEMOBILIZATION DELAYS were long, and soldiers were restless. "I urged the commanders to see to it that their officers and men were kept mentally and physically active," noted General Crerar.[27] Yet a combination of military training and organized recreation only went so far. Some service personnel took advantage of education courses or trade instruction, but most were too unsettled to crack open the books. Sports and socializing remained popular, and there was generous leave. As during the war, Canadians converged on London, but many also visited relatives throughout England, Scotland, Wales, and Ireland.

Al Armstrong, a veteran of the Italian campaign, was granted leave and was on his way to visit a friend in Kent when he stopped into a pub while waiting for his train. An elderly couple were enjoying a pint when they saw him, turning white at his appearance. Armstrong tried to ignore them but noticed the woman sobbing quietly. They eventually bought him a beer and he joined them. The father told him quietly that he looked like their son, who had fought with the Eighth Army in North Africa. Not fully aware of the situation, Armstrong asked if their son had returned yet. "The man gave me a long look and said their lad wouldn't be coming back. I was at a complete loss for words." He gulped down his drink. The mother, who had uttered not a word but continued to cry softly, gave him a tight hug as he got up to leave. "For me the war was over, but for that English couple it would be a very long time before they would know peace. Damn this war."[28]

Amid the finality of loss there was also romantic love and an opportunity to start anew. The long garrison years in England had allowed relationships to flourish, and some 48,000 Canadians married during the course of the war, with about 94 percent of the brides being British.[29] Thousands of Canadians decided to make their life in Britain, but given the depressed state of the nation's economy, most opted to move their new families home to Canada. From August 1941 to January 1947, 41,251 wives and 19,737 children made the trip across the Atlantic.[30] Most of the women and children travelled separately from their husbands, who were still in uniform, and so English, French, Belgian, and Dutch war brides set off for the terrifying leap into the unknown.

Some of these women won the lottery and found themselves in large cities with all the modern amenities of culture and society, free from the rebuilding and rationing that would plague Britain for the next decade. Others sat day after day on trains that chugged across the impossibly large Dominion until they were deposited in small towns, picked up by strangers-in-law, and transported out into the wheat fields. The glamour of wartime love was tested by the reality of postwar living. Outhouses, hand pumps, and isolation were everyday aspects of lives on a farm. As one war bride lamented in Toronto's *Globe and Mail*: "Most British war brides who have traveled to Canada to begin the job of making new homes are received as warmly as they deserve ... [but] in far too many cases the reception ranges from polite hostility to studied rudeness. Particularly if she is setting up housekeeping in a small community the girl from abroad is likely, sooner or later, to meet the girl her husband left behind him, a thwarted mother-in-law, or simply a few third parties who have no legal standing in the discussion at all but feel that their duty to a jilted friend compels them to 'take sides.'"[31] These new Canadian wives waited for their husbands, marvelling at the differences in food and culture, and shuddering through winters so cold they could scarcely have imagined them. As Olga Rains, a nineteen-year-old war bride from the Netherlands, recounted, "I cried a lot

Canadian war brides and babies who are soon to travel to Canada.

the first few months.... It was a difficult period for everybody but I knew that it would work out all right in the end."[32] It did for Rains, and for most of the other war brides, who, with their new families, helped to build a postwar Canada.

AS CANADIANS OVERSEAS were preparing to return to a welcoming nation, the American war against Japan was entering its endgame. U.S. bombers smashed wooden cities in a unyielding campaign that fired the night skies. Japan was already soundly beaten by late 1944, but the Japanese army and people vowed to never surrender. An American invasion of the Japanese homeland would be a costly affair, and casualty projections were in the hundreds of thousands for the Allies, in addition to the millions of civilians who would be cut down. Women and small children were being trained to contest every foot of terrain, often armed only with sharpened sticks against American marines wielding automatic weapons.

The Canadian senior military command wished to be in at the final fight. While Prime Minister King did not want to send any troops to the Pacific theatre of war, he was pressured by his ministers and he eventually relented as long as the force was composed only of volunteers. Experienced service personnel in Britain and Europe were given the option of serving in the Pacific, and 20,000 had volunteered from Europe by mid-July, many enticed to do so because they would first be allowed to return home to their families for a brief visit.[33] Though the United States needed little assistance, the plan was for Major-General Bert Hoffmeister to command an infantry division structured and equipped like American formations and supported by RCAF squadrons and RCN warships. The RCN's cruiser, HMCS *Uganda*, was steaming towards the Pacific battles in late July when its crew heard that Canada would send only those who volunteered.[34] Much to the surprise and embarrassment of their officers, the crew voted against continuing the voyage to the war zone, and despite threats and offered prizes, the vessel turned around and returned to port. The navy's top brass was humiliated; *Uganda's* sailors shrugged and looked to reunite with their families.

All hope for Japan ended with the atomic bombing of Hiroshima on August 6 and of Nagasaki three days later. The initial blasts, fireballs, and radiation killed about 200,000 people from the first second to four months after the detonations, with tens of thousands more dying from radiation illness over the coming decades.[35] A terrifying new age had arrived. Nonetheless, the casualties from the two atomic bombs, despite their horror, were far fewer than if the Americans had fought their way through the Japanese towns and villages.[36] The atomic bombs were also a political tool—a significant and tested threat to use against Stalin to negotiate with reason in the war's aftermath.

A few hundred Canadians in Japanese prisoner-of-war camps witnessed the fireballs. Close to death from starvation and fearful that the camp guards would murder him and his friends after the American invasion, William Bell, who had served with and lost his younger brother Gordon during the Battle of Hong Kong four years earlier, believed, "If it weren't for the use of the atomic bomb, as horrible as it was, I would not have survived."[37] Even with the bombs threatening the annihilation of the Japanese people, it was not until the Allies signalled that Emperor Hirohito would not be held responsible for the actions of his war leaders that Japan agreed to the unconditional surrender. The Pacific War ended on August 14, and VJ Day led to new celebrations.

In Canada, there was little sympathy for the Japanese in the aftermath of the atomic bombs, and even less after news spread of how prisoners taken at Hong Kong had been beaten, starved, and executed. Of the 1,685 Canadians captured, 264 had died at the hands of the cruel Japanese prison guards through abuse, torture, malnourishment, and execution. When the prisoners were finally freed after Japan's surrender, American and British forces fed and cared for the scarecrow-thin men. One Canadian left Japan weighing 79 pounds; when he arrived in Winnipeg months later, he was up to 179 pounds.[38] The Hong Kong veterans set foot on Canadian soil in October 1945, and all had put on weight from the abundant

Captain Stanley Banfill, a Hong Kong prisoner, meets his son for the first time on returning to Montreal, October 13, 1945. Banfill had been in captivity for almost four years.

food laid before them. There was a sad irony in that few loved ones could readily identify the inhumane abuse the prisoners had endured.

Hong Kong veteran and prisoner of war Frank Christensen wrote, "The world, as I had known it, was no longer there. Everything around me had changed. I couldn't understand it, or adjust to it."[39] He eventually married and re-enlisted in the army. But as George MacDonell recounted of his four years of imprisonment, "No one escaped the emotional and physical trauma of Hong Kong and the starvation, malnutrition, and humiliation suffered in Japanese camps."[40] Medical studies conducted years later proved that most of the Hong Kong veterans endured lifelong illnesses, went blind at an early age, and died prematurely young, their malnourished and disease-ridden bodies never able to fully recover from the wartime ordeal.[41]

The Hong Kong survivors, along with their fellow prisoners in Europe, had to adjust to a very different life upon returning to their homeland. The overseas service personnel were greeted as conquering heroes. But what was it like to come home as a defeated warrior, one who had been ripped from his own service arm and made to be a Kriegie? If the fighting soldier's experience was difficult for civilians to understand, the prisoner-of-war's experience was entirely alien.[42] One postwar study revealed that 48 percent of Dieppe prisoners had psychological problems in adjusting to life back home, with most prisoners from other battles similarly traumatized.[43] However, only 5 percent of the former prisoners were allotted a pension, illustrating the challenge of the medical and military professionals in recognizing mental trauma as a wound. In 1976, after years of lobbying, the federal government provided the Hong Kong veterans with compensation for their wartime ordeal that had led to long-term disabilities.[44] Further pensions and payouts followed in 1998, but nothing could make up for almost five years of brutal incarceration.

BY MARCH 1946, close to 600,000 women and men were discharged from the Canadian forces. They arrived in Canada, mainly docking at Halifax, and then travelled on by rail to cities and towns across the Dominion. Jack Shepherd, who had served through Italy and Northwest Europe, was greeted by his mother on the train platform at Maple Creek. The normally reserved woman held him in a death grip for a long time, and Shepherd admitted, "I was ashamed that I hadn't written as often as

I might [have]."[45] Shepherd saw his mother more over the next year and a half, but her visits to him were in a sanatorium for tuberculosis at Fort Quappelle. Nora Cook, a battlefield nurse who would forever be shaken by the "unbearably tragic" sights she had witnessed, described her reunion with her parents, seven siblings, and extended family, remarking, "I was treated like a hero. But I didn't feel like any kind of hero."[46] The war weighed heavily on all the survivors.

Even after returning home, all of the overseas service personnel remained members of the armed services, but they were given thirty days leave during which time their papers were processed. Final medical and dental examinations were provided, with men and women given opportunities to receive counselling. Few warriors decided to talk to the psychologists for fear it would delay their return to civvy street. Upon their discharge, they were issued $100 for clothing and a war service gratuity of $7.50 for each thirty days of service, plus an additional 25 cents for each day overseas, with the average total payment being $488.[47] War-service buttons and release certificates were part of the final transition; the demobilized were allowed to retain their uniforms but were to hand in all weapons. Most did, but not all, as the instinct for mementoes was strong.

The country had changed. Those who had enlisted early in the war had left a destitute nation struggling in the grips of the Depression. But under the leadership of William Lyon Mackenzie King's efficient Liberal government, and supported by the patriotic and profitable work of Canadians, the Dominion had become a wealthier and more confident nation. Canada could afford to treat veterans with care and respect, and to find proper recompense for their service.

Few had expected the Liberals to win the June 1945 election. Mackenzie

Canadian veterans waiting to process papers in preparation for their return to civvy street.

King's cabinet was severely weakened during the war, and the party seemed vulnerable due to its handling of conscription. Complaints were heard from both those who thought King had not acted fast enough in implementing conscription and those who felt the government should have stood against the reckless decision and kept to its early promises of no conscription. But somehow the old warhorse held on. King's turn to the left in the previous year, with the introduction of family allowances (the "baby bonus," as it was known, offering monthly payments of six to nine dollars per child), as well as his skilful if unglamorous guidance of the nation through the war, left Canadians shaking their heads but deciding ultimately that he was better than the socialist Co-operative Commonwealth Federation (CCF) and the out-of-touch Conservatives who had run on a platform of conscription for the war against Japan. Not necessarily King, but King if necessary, was the weak battle cry of the Liberals. It was enough. Quebec again sided with the Liberals, and sufficient voters across the country were willing to give King a renewed mandate to lead the country into the years of peace and prosperity. Roosevelt was two months in his grave and Churchill would soon be thrown out of office; somehow, King had survived against the odds, as he had done through three decades of political dominance.

King could not have done it without the vote of the overseas forces. While the prime minister was the butt of many jokes among service personnel, a plurality of them voted for the Liberals. Why did they do so after suffering through the reinforcement shortages in late 1944? Perhaps because the King government had publicly announced that it would reward veterans for their service. No one wanted veterans to be lost to society. Public surveys in early 1945 revealed that Canadians were convinced that the government had planned efficiently and generously for the return of veterans.[48] King had been willing to sacrifice the soldiers overseas during the course of the war—by not enacting conscription in a timely manner to meet the need for reinforcements—but he sought to reward those same survivors in postwar Canada. The most important assistance to the re-establishment of returning service personnel was the Veterans Charter.

THE VETERANS CHARTER, a compendium of legislation and benefits, offered returning service personnel a university education, vocational training, land grants, dependants' benefits, and low-interest loans for businesses or houses.[49] The federal civil service was instructed to hire veterans: first, those who had war-related disabilities; second, those who had served overseas; and third, the widows of killed service personnel. The gratuities to veterans, when augmented by the new family allowance, allowed households to spend and to build new lives.[50] While some veterans slipped through the new social security net, and others, such as First Nations, were treated unequally, or, like the merchant sailors, even denied veterans status, there was a sense that Canadians were repaying some of the debt owed to those who had served their country. The Veterans Charter was one of the most significant groupings of legislation ever passed, and it allowed Canada to win the peace after having paid such a dear price during the war.

The Veterans Charter sent returned service personnel to university for free. Many of the veterans could not stomach returning to their prewar Depression jobs and took the opportunity to better themselves in the universities that were previously regarded as sites only for the elite. The educators, to accommodate the veterans, offered staggered start dates as service personnel came back throughout late 1945 and early 1946. Temporary buildings were thrown up to house the young and not-so-young warrior-scholars, and by February 1947 almost 35,000 veterans were enrolled across the country. That same year, at the University of Toronto, veterans accounted for 49 percent of the student body.[51] Gregory Biefer, an RCAF ground crew radar mechanic, enrolled in October 1945 at Sir George Williams College in Montreal. He was, in his words, "ahead of the flood from overseas, so there were only a few other war veterans among the hordes of chattering youngsters."[52] Although ill at ease in this new setting, Biefer was determined to see it through. And he did. New universities, such as Carleton in Ottawa, benefited from the rapid influx of students. All universities moved to accommodate the experienced, earnest, older, and often scarred scholars.

Though the three women's wartime formations were disbanded, some of the 50,000 who served in the Canadian Women's Army Corps (CWAC), the RCAF's Women's Division (WD), and the RCN's Women's Royal Canadian Naval Service also took advantage of the Veterans Charter. Many used their wartime experience as a springboard to enter the job market, while others benefited from access to veterans' education programs. Sergeant Norma Walmsley, who as a WD spent much of the war in the RCAF Records Station, attended McGill University, eventually teaching as a university professor in Brandon, Manitoba. Corinne Sevigny, who enlisted in Montreal as a CWAC, was fiercely proud of her accomplishments, remarking, "We were the pioneers. We were the ones who could show them that women could take on any serious assignment."[53]

Alex Colville, an infantryman turned official war artist, returned to teach at Dalhousie after the war and found that the veterans who attended the university were "hungry to learn."[54] Flight Lieutenant Douglas Humphreys of the RCAF worried, like many of his comrades, about the "nagging question of what one would do after the war." He was determined to make a new life for himself, and he did, at the University of Toronto. "At the age of twenty-five I, like many others, had a lot of catching up to do and a lot of hard work lay ahead. But it is difficult to put into words that thrill I felt when on a warm September day I first walked up the steps of Victoria College and realized that a dream was finally coming true. The future would take care of itself."[55]

Canada's Veterans Charter was far more effective than the mishmash of poorly conceived and even worse-funded British veterans' programs, and in terms of impact it ranks with the American GI Bill, which was highly instrumental in propelling forward the U.S. economy and people. The fair treatment of veterans in both Canada and the United States went some way towards forging the idea of the Second World War as being the last, and possibly only, "good war." Canada had committed to a fight to the finish, and beyond.

BUT THERE WAS NO EASY ROAD ahead for veterans. After years of fear and discipline, confessed Jim Brown of Fredericton, New Brunswick, who served on HMCS *Monnow*, his demobilization from the services left him feeling lost; it was "just like starting to live over again."[56] Gerald Bowen served three years in the Battle of the Atlantic, and noted, "It was a very, very tough life." He was only twenty when he was discharged, but he felt "old before [his] time."[57] Almost all veterans had to remake themselves. J.K. Chapman returned to his wife in Fredericton after two years of service overseas with Bomber Command. "I had left her as a boy and returned to her as a man and not a very nice one at that." He swore and drank, and visibly wore the strain of combat. In his final tour of operations, he had lost thirty pounds from six months of insomnia, and he was "nervous, travel-worn, and weary." Chapman was also a stranger to his wife. "She knew only that I had changed and I had difficulty explaining why I had." But after a few months, they learned to reconnect, and, as he was to write in his memoirs, "to draw closer together and to build a marriage which has endured more than forty years."[58]

While there was romance in reunion, many of the servicemen were surprised to find how their wives had coped and survived in their absence.[59] Not all had done it alone, and infidelity and sexual suspicion tormented many relationships. Children also struggled to know or reconnect with their fathers. Andre Bernard wept as his son, who knew him only from photographs, jumped into his arms and exclaimed, "Now, I have a real Daddy, instead of a cardboard Daddy."[60] Not all greetings were so touching. Egg-shell walking was the order of the day. Those on the home front had little understanding of the ex-serviceman's experience, but nor did the overseas warriors have much sympathy for the trials of those who had gone on in their absence.[61] War is death and destruction, but it is also infused with dislocation and distance. Some families were strengthened by the war; others disintegrated under the strain. The return to normalcy took time and patience, and often forgiveness.

THE WAR NEVER ENDED FOR THOUSANDS. Of the 54,000 Canadians wounded in battle, more than 29,000 were listed as seriously disabled from their wounds, and most required years of care, surgery, treatment, and rehabilitation.[62] Men who were once happy-go-lucky youths with full futures now faced a dark path. Many of the severely wounded never married, turned to alcohol, and found little stability outside of veterans' facilities. By 1946, the newly formed Department of Veterans Affairs was running more than thirty hospitals, many of them recently constructed, the largest being Sunnybrook in Toronto. Four facilities offered specialized treatment for paraplegics; new prosthetic limbs were manufactured and distributed; and veterans had skin peeled off and grafted onto other parts of their bodies in the hope of healing burn wounds.

Yet even service personnel with serious injuries rejoined the workforce in high numbers. They learned to operate machinery or work in an office environment in spite of missing limbs, blindness, or chronic pain. Private Bill Hennessey, who had enlisted at age sixteen and was hit through the spine with shrapnel at the end of 1944, entered the Christie Street Veterans' Hospital in Toronto as a paraplegic. He was discharged twenty months later, after painful physiotherapy and surgery; but he left under his own power. Ronald Shawcross, an infantry officer with the Regina Rifles, fought from D-Day to the end of the war. It took a lot to stop the hulking six-foot-three man of 220 pounds, and during the war he was hit several times by shell splinters. Years later, x-rays revealed that many pieces of jagged steel splinters were still embedded in his body.[63] It is chilling to think that among the ashes of the many veterans who were cremated after their deaths lay twisted steel. These men of war carried the metal of the battlefield in their bodies for decades.

Veterans also carried the weight of the war in their minds. Bernard Finestone, a tank officer from Montreal who fought through Italy with the British Columbia Dragoons, recalled the savagery of combat, and how the Germans fired on the wounded to further demoralize survivors or draw out more soldiers to be gunned down as they sought to help their vulnerable comrades. In his words, Canadian troops "started to behave the exact same way." Battle brutalized men. Finestone, like countless veterans, was haunted by the war, and he believed, "There isn't anybody who was in real battle who came out unmarked."[64] Archie Marsh survived the torpedoing of two ships on the Atlantic. His last ship to go down, the corvette HMCS *Regina*, left him badly shaken by the trauma, and throughout his long life he could not stand to hear an alarm clock ring.[65] The sound brought back devastating war memories, especially of the last Action Station alarm before *Regina* was hit and sunk. Private Ted Patrick of the Irish Regiment of Canada was affected by nightmares of being locked in hand-to-hand battle with Germans, and would awaken to find himself choking his wife. Patrick was plagued by his "war dreams" all his life and it took decades before he was formally diagnosed with post-traumatic stress disorder, for which he received a partial pension.[66] Many veterans suffered "recurrent, invasive memories" that built in force, leading to many suicide attempts. One such case was that of RCAF Rear Gunner Richard Pyves, who flew in the sortie against Dresden. Each time he read about the "occasional arguments in the media about the role of Bomber Command," Pyves slipped into a depression, and he eventually succeeded in taking his own life.[67] Ernest

Maller of the Carleton and York Regiment, who was shot in both legs and survived a bout of jaundice, revealed forty years after the war, and shortly before his death in 1988 at age sixty-eight, how war-inspired terror stalked him day and night: "It sometimes surprises me from behind, my skin crawls."[68]

Survivor's guilt plagued many veterans who mourned the comrades they lost, and unanswered questions plucked at the mind. Bomber Command veteran Howard Hewer survived his two tours and continued to serve in the postwar RCAF. Throughout his life he enjoyed the company of fellow veterans, often at the Toronto branch of the Aircrew Association of Great Britain. As former fighting mates came together over the years to reminiscence and share the joys of life, Hewer thought about his friends who never had a chance to grow old. Why was his life spared? "We are grateful, but there is a trace of guilt; we have no answers."[69] It would take most veterans years to let go of the painful, tightly held memories.

The war lingered on in the mind, replayed at the conscious and subconscious levels, but not all veterans were in turmoil. Most, in fact, were not. We must not make victims of everyone who served, and indeed, innumerable men took strength from the challenges they faced and overcame in the war. The stories of three must stand here for those of the many. Frank Curry harkened back to the battles in the Atlantic: "Those first few months of operations in the North Atlantic in winter were forever washed deep into my bones, my being, never to be lost or forgotten, even all these years later. They tested me in a way which shaped my life, and my future."[70] Curry had faced the sea and the enemy and he had won. Lancaster pilot Donald Cheney survived thirty-nine sorties, including the one on which his bird came down, and he was awarded a Distinguished Flying Cross. Cheney went to university and made a career in the civil service. In reflecting on his war experience, he understood that "it changed me tremendously. I had always been very shy. I was a little fellow.... I developed an awful lot of confidence that gave me tremendous amount of personal pride and I felt that I had really achieved something very important in my life to start with.... The confidence stayed with me although terrible memories have always been with me."[71] John O'Brien grew up poor, fighting and scrapping on the Halifax docks. He had dropped out of school in grade ten and was told by one teacher that he would never amount to more than a ditch digger. He served with the West Nova

Scotia Regiment, maturing, surviving, and emerging as a leader. Having passed the test of fire, O'Brien applied himself to school on his return to the Maritimes, as a twenty-seven-year-old veteran who entered grade eleven.[72] He eventually went on to receive a degree at Dalhousie University in 1951. A wife and ten children were in the cards, too, as well as running his own pharmacy for twenty-five years. There is no doubt that the war put O'Brien on a more determined path. Curry and Cheney walked with him along it, as did hundreds of thousands of their comrades.

"THE LEGION IS MY CLUB—a shared experience," described Bill Bettridge of the Queen's Own Rifles.[73] Though many wives and children caught a glimpse of the war that continued to rage in the minds of veterans, most ex-servicemen would not talk about the internal struggle. They came from a generation that was not given to sharing their emotions, and many, even if they were so inclined, could not find the words to capture the swirling stories and hurtful images. Who could understand? What was there to say about battle that encompassed the all-out chaos and carnage? Who wanted to tell their young children or wife about bombing cities or killing other men, or losing control of their bowels in combat or holding a bloodstained hand while waiting for a friend to die in agony?

Hundreds of thousands of veterans took solace by turning to one another. As the wartime history for the Governor General's Horse Guards of the 5th Canadian Armoured Division observed, "The war has been fought on an island, suspended in the time and space, that had little relation to the life we left or to the one which we were now returning. That, after all, is true of any war. Those who have taken part belong to a fraternity that is forever closed."[74] Most veterans stayed in touch with at least a handful of their former comrades, while others joined the Legion or attended the Legion halls that marked the small and large communities across the country. More than 300,000 veterans were members of the Legion in the late 1960s, although this number included those from the Great War and Korea. In the two decades after the Second World War, there was some tension between the veterans of the two world wars, as the 1914–1918 veterans held most of the key administrative positions, but this changed slowly over time, and harmony held sway more than discordance as the veterans found more to bind them together than chisel them apart.[75] "The Legion," remarked one veteran, "is an organization of survivors."[76]

Bruce Walker, who served as an infantryman in the 48th Highlanders of Canada, spoke of his satisfaction in attending the regimental club in Toronto: "Everybody would get together. Any night of the week, you'd go in, and there'd be forty or fifty guys in there. You could fight the war over again."[77] Veterans groups also produced postwar newspapers to link men across the country. At the same time, *The Legion* magazine has been published, under various names, since the early 1920s, and it brought together veterans and shared their stories. As the years marched on, men moved across or out of the country, raised their families, and took on new jobs. Many lost touch with former mates, although stray encounters on the street or at a church could renew long-lost relations. In the 1980s, RCAF veteran J.K. Chapman described his relationship with his wartime companions: "We remain friends despite the passage of forty years and despite following widely differing careers and living in different countries.... But when we do meet, the decades contract to weeks and it's as though we are still comrades in arms."[78]

Reunions were arranged for units, ships, or squadrons. Here the aging warriors would come together, lift a glass to the dead, and recount the outrageous fortunes of old. Most focused on the humorous or ironic events of the past, choosing to let the traumatic ones lie buried. Men discovered those they thought had died. B.G. McDonald survived thirty bomber operations during the war, and witnessed dozens of airmen disappear throughout his service. He was married in 1946, had three children, and rejoined a mining company, where he worked as an advertising manager. One of his great regrets was his inability to track down those he trained with after the war. "Information as to the postwar whereabouts of former RCAF aircrew comrades was extremely hard to come by after the war.... In many cases, it was not known whether or not the airman had survived." Reunions allowed him to re-engage with some old companions, but not all attended, as "veterans were busy settling into civilian life and bringing up their young families in these years, long before the advent of instant communication."[79] It was not until the 1992 publication of *They Shall Not Grow Old*, a compendium of those RCAF flyers killed during the war, that McDonald knew the fate of several chums: some had survived to grow into old age; others had remained the teenagers and young men he had once served with in a terrible war almost half a century in the past.

WHILE VETERANS FACED their own personal battles and tried to make meaning of their war experiences, not all who served during the war were recognized as veterans. The merchant seamen suffered proportionately higher casualties than any other Canadian military arm, yet because the mariners were not in uniform (save for a few isolated cases) or organized as a fighting arm, and because of a series of government and later veterans groups' decisions, it took almost fifty years for the merchant mariners to be recognized as veterans.[80]

Immediately following the war, the Liberal government set a policy of encouraging merchant mariners to stay in the peacetime trade. Ottawa did this in part by denying the mariners the same benefits as veterans, but it also promised them continued employment in a national merchant fleet. Most merchant seamen shrugged away the double standard of having served their country but being denied veteran status. Men who had lived through the Depression and the war were not going to give up good-paying jobs. And so while veterans were going back to school or setting up businesses, the mariners continued to move Canadian goods around the world. But in 1949 the Department of Transport radically cut the merchant fleet, casting thousands out of work.

The merchant seamen were cheated. The mariners had been lauded by politicians and the media during the war as the military's "fourth arm," but they remained small in comparison to the worldwide Allied fleet. And while the seaman casualties were heavy, the losses were not only on Canadian ships; as a result, they usually did not receive the same newspaper coverage as the wounded or killed uniformed personnel who served on identifiable Canadian ships.[81] Moreover, in the postwar years, the mariners had few champions, and fewer histories, to explain their role during the war. They may have been the fourth arm, but they were easily forgotten and, save for a few short-lived groups in the early 1950s, there was no merchant marines veterans' organization until 1982.[82] Slowly, throughout the 1980s, the Canadian Merchant Navy Association rallied support for the cause of recognition and recompense, but it had little impact in convincing Liberal and Conservative governments that mariners should receive veteran status. The fight for rights was made harder because the Legion and others veterans' organizations had long argued that the merchant mariners, while serving their country, had been civilians in the war zone.

In 1989, the Senate Subcommittee on Veterans Affairs was finally approached by a coalition of merchant navy groups and asked to rectify their status as non-combatants. The subcommittee's January 1991 report, *It's Almost Too Late*, recommended that veterans' benefits be extended to the mariners who had served in "dangerous waters." The Merchant Navy Book of Remembrance was soon compiled. In 1994, for Remembrance Day, the government was open to the idea that the merchant mariners be included in the wreath-laying ceremony. The Legion's high command had blocked this for years, but it relented on the grounds that the Book of Remembrance was being officially dedicated on November 11. However, the Legion insisted that the

act was not a precedent, even though two years earlier, the *Merchant Navy Veteran and Civilian War Related Benefits Act* had given merchant mariners limited veteran status.[83] But even with formal recognition, the act did not provide full veterans' benefits.

"We are the men that saved the world," claimed seventy-two-year-old Merchant Navy veteran Ossie MacLean in 1998.[84] Starting on October 1 of that year, he was one of several merchant mariners who staged a hunger strike on the steps of Parliament Hill. The strike embarrassed the government. And when the National Council of Veteran Associations in Canada finally backed the merchant mariners in their quest for full veteran status in 2000, fifty-five years after the end of

The Halifax Memorial in Nova Scotia's Point Pleasant Park, unveiled in November 1967, marks the sacrifice of the men and women of the Royal Canadian Navy and the Merchant Navy during the world wars. The Cross of Sacrifice stands over 12 metres high and contains the inscribed names of 3,257 Canadians buried at sea.

the war, the federal government announced a compensation package for the mariners, of up to $24,000 for each surviving veteran.[85] In a final act of recognition, in 2003, Parliament declared September 3 to be Merchant Navy Veterans' Day.

The demand for full rights was also taken up by Aboriginal veterans. Even as they were treated as wards of the state, some 4,300 First Nations and Métis served during the war—with several thousand more rejected because of medical reasons or racial restrictions in the navy and air force. More than 200 First Nations soldiers lost their lives on battlefields around the world. Those who served with their white comrades usually testified that they were treated with respect, something they had never experienced in Canada. Wilfred Westeste of the Bird Tail First Nation remembered after the war, "In the fighting zone ... we were all equals. The only time in my life I was equal to the white society or anybody else."[86] Nonetheless, these Canadians who served their country came home to an indifferent nation. Though the Veterans Charter applied to the First Nations soldiers who served, many veterans returning to their bands and reserves were isolated and not informed of the many options open to them. The Indian agents—the government-appointed civil servants on the reserves who controlled much of the resources and finances—also sometimes actively dissuaded them from following up with the Department of Veterans Affairs. First Nations warriors, who had liberated nations and oppressed people, continued to live in a country where they did not even receive the right to vote until 1960. "I don't expect the government to grant me a fancy living," asserted Russell Modeste. "But certainly treat me the same as you been treating the white guy that done the same service as I have."[87] In 2002, after decades of pressure and a series of Royal Commissions and Senate studies, and under the weight of academic

Three First Nations Second World War veterans. First Nations veterans had to fight for veterans' benefits in the aftermath of the war, and were granted them only grudgingly by successive federal governments.

scholarship and the persistence of aging veterans, the government finally agreed to pay qualifying veterans or their surviving spouses up to $20,000 each because of past failures to ensure that the Veterans Charter was made available to all veterans.[88] That this measure was so long in the waiting was another shameful legacy of Canada's treatment of its First Nations citizens.

NOW, MORE THAN SEVENTY-FIVE YEARS after the start of the Second World War, hundreds of veterans are dying every week across the country, with their obituaries filling the papers. One studies the lined faces and white hair, although sometimes there is a contemporary wartime photograph of a young man or woman in uniform. The "veteran" component of the individual's life is part of the obituary, but not often the central part. This is an indication of the full, rich lives these veterans led. While war service remains one of their greatest life contributions, at the same time they were men and women who worked, loved, and lived. But we in the twenty-first century look at these former servicemen and women with new eyes. We see how their personal experiences shaped the narrative of the nation at war, and how the Canadian contribution to that brutal conflict changed world history. In 2010, 163,000 Second World War Canadian veterans remained alive, with an average age of eighty-six.[89] Now, in 2015, fewer than 80,000 of the 1 million veterans who survived the war are still living, and they have an average age of over ninety. No covenant was struck in 1939, or any other year, between those who served and those who stayed at home, but there is a debt that must be repaid. At the very least, the nation must honour and remember both those who left and never returned, and those who left and returned forever changed.

CHAPTER 16

THE SECOND WORLD WAR AND MEMORY

The Second World War killed at least 60 million combatants and civilians. Between September 1939 and August 1945, there were, on average, 25,000 war-related deaths per day. It was a historic bloodletting. While battles were fought on continents and oceans around the world, the majority of dead were civilians rather than soldiers. The black stain of the Holocaust, with its six million murdered Jews and other deemed "undesirables," can never be erased from human history, but most of the world has long forgotten the more than fifteen million Chinese killed as Japanese soldiers, famine, and disease swept over their communities from 1937 to 1945.[1] The Soviet Union bore the brunt of fighting against Germany and paid the price with an estimated 27 million dead, but only 4.7 million of these were combatants, the rest being civilians caught in the war's maw. The aggressor, Germany, lost 6.9 million dead, of whom 5.3 million were combatants, illustrating how the nation's war was experienced mainly beyond its borders, save for the bombing campaign against the German homeland.[2] The defeated Poland lost more than 5 million dead, almost all civilians, showing the appalling cost of being occupied by the genocidal Nazis. By the war's end, few Jews remained in Poland. Italy, having bowed out of the war early and fought on the periphery, was left with some 455,000 dead. The United States and Britain lost 418,500 and 449,000 killed, almost all of them military personnel. Whether victor or vanquished, a heavy price was paid in lives, although the bald statistics reveal that defeat and occupation brought massive civilian deaths. It is unknown how many combatants and civilians were wounded during the Second World War, but the number is more than 100 million.

In the aftermath of the war, the worst of the Nazi leadership was rounded up and tried, although many committed suicide rather than face justice for their crimes. The Nuremberg trials were derided by some as victor's justice, and perhaps they were, but the judges showed restraint and, in the process, exposed the criminal Nazi regime. The trials also rendered visible the horror of the Holocaust, even if most Nazis directly involved in the crimes avoided punishment.[3] It was not until the 1960s that Jews and other victims of the Holocaust finally began to publicly share their experiences and thus begin the long process of coming to grips with what they had endured.

The Second World War was a death blow for Fascism, but Stalin's total victory in the east created new conditions for the spread of Communism, such as endemic poverty, war weariness, and a repressive internal security apparatus. The invasion of Poland was ostensibly Britain's impetus for going to war, but that nation was abandoned to a cruel fate behind Stalin's Iron Curtain as the helpless Allies could do nothing but heave a sigh of regret at their own impotence in relieving the Polish people's ongoing suffering. Stalin emerged stronger from the war, with the Soviet Union occupying new nations and claiming 90 million souls as war booty.[4] It could have been worse for the war-weakened democratic nations of Western Europe, and the threat of the atomic bomb kept Stalin's armed forces at bay. Stalin escaped the justice he was due for his alliance with Hitler and his murder of millions before the war. It was only after his death in 1953 that the Soviet dictator was revealed as the monster that he was.

Europe went from a hot war to a cold one. The threat of atomic weapons hung over all, and these—as the bomber war had shown—now extended the war from the fighting fronts and slit trenches to home and hearth. Yet unlike after the Great War, when the United States had retreated into isolation, the Americans, under the guidance of President Harry Truman and Secretary of State George Marshall, showed strategic foresight and generosity in rebuilding Europe by loaning and giving billions of dollars in capital and goods through the 1948 Marshall Plan. The United States's injection of capital saved many blighted nations from a generation of destitution and from succumbing to internal Soviet-directed Communist insurgents and Moscow-backed political parties. The ideological battlegrounds were already too firmly set for the U.S. to give aid to the Soviet Union, and the rapidly festering acrimony would set the foundation for the next five decades of wars, cold, hot, and by proxy—but not atomic.

THE CANADIAN HUMORIST and economist Stephen Leacock had captured the mentality of English Canadians in an article only a few months before the start of the Second World War: "If you were to ask any Canadian, 'Do you have to go to war if England does?' he'd answer at once, 'Oh, no.' If you then said, '*Would* you go to war if England does?' he'd answer, 'Oh yes.' And if you asked, 'Why?' he would say, reflectively, 'Well, you see, we'd *have* to.'"[5] Six years later, through war and anguish, the attitude had not evolved much. Canada would almost certainly have gone to war at Britain's side again in the late 1940s had the Cold War with the Soviets gone hot. But something had changed among Canadians. Many saw themselves differently as a result of the wartime exertions.

Dave McIntosh flew forty-one sorties as a navigator in a Mosquito with No. 418 Squadron, RCAF. As an intruder squadron that patrolled the skies over known enemy bases to shoot down fighters when they left or returned from their sorties, No. 418 was isolated from other RCAF squadrons, both fighters and bombers. McIntosh noted that in the shared messes with other squadrons or while on leave, he and his mates rarely proclaimed themselves to be Canadian, especially among the hordes of British or Americans, but they felt "different." As one surprised American in the squadron observed of McIntosh and his comrades, after spending time with them, "Why you bastards, you're not American at all."[6] Indeed they were not. Nor was the Royal Canadian Navy the same as the Royal Navy, or the soldiers in the Canadian Army the same as their British counterparts. While Canadians had long seen themselves as having a separate identity from the British, during and after the war it was asserted more fiercely. It is not easy to put into words, but symbols contributed to a growing sense of uniqueness. The maple leaf was important, as was the Canada badge worn by all. There were other intangible factors such as fighting together as a coherent national formation. Regimental, ship, and squadron traditions fostered unity and morale, and were intertwined with local communities across the

Dominion. Most Canadians chose survival over flag waving, but they did not like others lumping them in with the Americans. The BBC gave a 10 P.M. nightly report that was surprisingly frank in its descriptions of the previous day's aerial operations, the damage inflicted on the enemy, and the number of planes that failed to return. Douglas Harvey remarked that at his RCAF No. 408 Squadron mess there was always a "howl of protest from the enraged Canadians.... Never a mention of the RCAF; that we had taken part."[7] But sometimes a sense of national character flourished in the absence of recognition. Stretcher-bearer David Gordon described his fellow Canadians, from different regions, races, and religions, who formed the 24th Field Ambulance: "We learned to accept and respect our differences in background and enjoyed heated arguments over any subject you could name. The East taunted the West and the Maritimers the rest of us and the French Canadians held their own with all. There was Canadian unity and we were all proud to have that Canada badge on our shoulders and God help the Yank who called us Brits."[8] Norman Penner, a wartime signaller and later a professor of political science at York University, reflected upon the war's meaning: "When we went overseas, for the first time in our lives we felt that we represented Canada. In Europe the badge on our shoulder meant something. The nationalism of these Canadian boys was a direct result of their participation in the war.... It was widely recognized that we had taken our place among the soldiers of other nations and helped to win this great world struggle."[9]

Canada emerged from the war battered and weary, but also wealthier and more confident as a self-governing nation. The government had intervened in the lives of citizens at unprecedented levels, by rationing food, imposing wartime taxes, controlling wages for workers and the price of goods, and stimulating industry. The control lessened after the war, but the government never fully loosened its grip on society, and the Baby Bonus and the Veterans Charter were a firm foundation upon which to build what would become the welfare state. The Dominion had entered the war a broken nation, in debt and with a despondent people. The war effort pulled the country out of its yawning slough, even though the total cost of the war was calculated at $21,786,077,519 (which did not include medical expenses and payments to dependants, or the pensions for 122,077 veterans).[10] No one had fought Hitler to restore the economy, but through industrialization, the British Commonwealth Air Training

Program (BCATP), and the immense exertions on farms and in factories, a new Canada had emerged. At the same time, while Canada went into the war with Britain, motivated by ties of blood and belonging, it emerged financially linked to the United States.

Canada had stood with its allies, and though often taken for granted by Britain and the United States, it had done its part. But perpetually wary Prime Minister William Lyon Mackenzie King did not ache to stride onto the world stage. Instead, the seventy-five-year-old prime minister inched his way forward cautiously, terrified of being drawn into a war against the Communist Soviet Union, but aware that he had no choice but to back Britain and the United States at the dawn of the Cold War.

As Canada demobilized its military, its new wealth allowed it to send several billion dollars to Britain in the form of direct loans and favourable trade agreements. Canadians propped up the shell-shocked mother country even as they turned their gaze firmly to North America by seeking new financial markets to the south. Some felt that Canada squandered its chance to exert authority as a middle power, but King selected his well-trod path of caution and kept his eyes firmly on building up the Dominion. By the time King retired in 1948, he left a prouder and more prosperous nation than the one he had inherited. The unglamorous and stodgy Mackenzie King, who preferred the incremental over the monumental, was the father of modern Canada.

King's hand-picked political successor, Louis St. Laurent, took a different path on the world stage than that of his party's respected former leader. The new prime minister and his close advisor at external affairs, Lester Pearson, were energized by what Canada had done in the war and the evil it had prevented by emerging from its isolationist position in North America. Canada embraced more meaningful involvement in world affairs and was a founding member of NATO in 1949. Canadians were surprised to find that they liked to see themselves as helpful fixers, even if the nation's foreign policy was guided by its own interests rather than altruism, and by an understanding that a strong military defence of Western Europe might stave off another war. Appeasement in the 1930s had allowed Hitler to rise to power and unleash his terrible madness; now Canada, along with its allies, pursued a harder line with the Communists, while still working towards peace in multiple ways and through back channels. A wealthier and more confident Canada was one of the war's most profound legacies, although there were 44,000 fewer Canadians to experience it and the renewed nation was poorer for it.

CORPORAL JOSEPH NORTON enlisted in London, Ontario, with the Royal Canadian Regiment and was killed at age twenty-three in Sicily. The inscription on his headstone reads, "In the prime of life I left this world, my beloved wife and dear little girl."[11] His brother, John, was killed in action later the same year. The world's ghastly death toll far outnumbered Canada's 43,637 dead, but each of those fallen Canadians left behind a pool of anguish, starting with their families and seeping out through communities of neighbours, schoolmates, and church members. It is callous to tell devastated widows and orphans, as they look to an uncertain future without a loved

Grosbeek Canadian War Cemetery contains 2,610 Commonwealth burials, most of whom are Canadians who were killed in the winter battles of February and March 1945.

husband or father, that their nation got off easy in comparison to wartorn Europe. For the grief-stricken, the war would only—and could only—be viewed through the lens of loss and despair.

The Dominion of Canada, some 12 million strong, put 1,086,343 men and women into uniform. A total of 96,456 were killed or wounded, not including the merchant mariners. The total number of deaths remains somewhat uncertain due to the use of different methods of accounting, but Canada's 1970 official history, *Arms, Men and Governments*, notes that 2,343 were killed or wounded in the Royal Canadian Navy, 75,596 in the Canadian Army, and 18,517 in the Royal Canadian Air Force. Those who lost their lives numbered 2,024 in the RCN (a figure that has been modified to 1,990 in the most recent official history, *No Higher Purpose*), 22,917 in the army, and 17,101 in the air force. Since these calculations were made, in 1970, the Merchant Navy, in which some 1,629 Canadian and Newfoundland merchant mariners lost their lives, has been formally acknowledged as the fourth arm of the military.[12]

Twenty-one-year-old Flight Sergeant George King was killed on September 23, 1943, when his Stirling Mk III bomber was shot down over Hanover. His nephew later wrote that "the pall which my uncle's death cast over those who had known him was an all-encompassing one. In his small hometown of Summerberry, Saskatchewan, he left behind many grieving friends, and of course his family, including my aged grandparents whose poor health left them ill-prepared to cope with the death of their youngest child.... The grief which my family experienced after George's death has been a longstanding one, since for the next six decades it was not only shared by his immediate family, but also passed on to me and my siblings through my father's memories of a younger brother whose life was tragically cut short in 1943."[13] From time immemorial, one of war's greatest burdens has been the forcing of parents to bury their sons. Frank Périard, who served with the Stormont, Dundas and Glengarry Highlanders, recounted that his parents died in their fifties, unable to recover from the loss of their youngest son, Corporal Aimé Periard, who had been killed on April 4, 1945. "They were never the same again."[14]

Doug Craig was the grandson of Pilot Officer Walter Craig from Timmins, Ontario, who served with the RCAF in North Africa during the Sicily campaign and was listed as missing in action on August 13, 1943. Walter Craig's wife agonized over his "unknown" status—a purgatory between life and death—and she suffered through seventeen years of uncertainty until his body was finally discovered in 1960. A widow at twenty-four years old, and with a young child, she never remarried. Doug Craig treasured his grandfather's letters to his grandmother and he returned to them time and time again. "As you go through your life you understand, even with the three children I have, missing your grandfather is a constant reminder of war and what happens when tragedy like that strikes. It affects lives for a long time."[15] The bodies of the missing continue to be found to this day, disgorged from swamps, dug up from farmer's fields, or discovered in heavily wooded areas. There is something remarkably moving about Canada's dead from seventy-five years ago being given a proper burial. But there is also something infinitely sad about loved ones having to wait so long to know the fate of their family members.

CANADA DID NOT REPATRIATE ITS DEAD, except in the rarest of circumstances. Tens of thousands of Canadians were left overseas, buried near to where they fell in combat, and often alongside their comrades in arms from throughout the British Commonwealth. When the battle moved on, and at the end of the war, the bodies were disinterred from graves and gathered together in permanent Commonwealth War Graves Commission cemeteries, first established in 1917. Battlefields in Britain, France, Belgium, Italy, Germany, Burma, Japan, Hong Kong, and other sites contain Canadians. These silent cities, with their headstones of carved maple leafs, are testimony to the price of victory against Fascism.

The fallen are solemnly commemorated overseas, but grieving families also needed memorials closer to home. Almost every town, village, and hamlet across Canada has a memorial for the Great War, but the question raised in 1945 and after was whether new memorials should be erected.[16] The voice of veterans, *The Legionary*, carried a number of articles arguing that the Peace Tower and poppies, recognizable icons from the Great War, must now become symbols for veterans of the two world wars. Yet Canadians wanted to somehow mark the new war, even if there was little appetite for building several thousand new stone monoliths. Canadians instead embraced functional memorials that would enrich the living and provide contemplative spaces where they could reflect upon those who gave their lives in the war.[17] Gardens, libraries, and wooded areas were created, but also extended to the less sacred, such as hockey arenas, symphonies, and beaches—and then crept towards the absurd in including tennis courts and movie theatres. As early as 1946, *The Legionary* spoke to a "great controversy" over these new war memorials. Though some saw the monuments of stone and bronze as being "outmoded," the Legion opposed suggestions that sporting venues and places of popular entertainment might become part of the commemorative landscape. One editorial observed that these spaces would fail to "inspire remembrance and reverence."[18] While the debate continued, the Legion's insistence that existing Great War memorials in the towns, villages, and cities across the Dominion could be adapted to include those killed during the Second World War ultimately won out, and so the names of the dead from those communities were added to the sepulchres.

Some survivors of the war and their families felt there was a need for a new national memorial, even as most veterans looked towards a bright future instead of dwelling on the war's past.[19] The national memorial in Ottawa, *The Response*, unveiled near the Parliament Buildings by King George VI in May 1939, is so clearly a Great War memorial, with its multiple sculptured figures in period uniforms, that a Second World War memorial was thought to be required. There was little urgency to the process, but periodic discussions were held throughout the 1940s and 1950s, about what shape such a memorial would take. In 1955, for instance, *The Legionary* argued that the national memorial in Ottawa did not fully embrace the sacrifice of Canadians from the Second World War and the Korean War, and that family members of those who died in the country's recent wars had "expressed surprise and disappointment that the memory of their dead [had] not yet been commemorated visually by the nation."[20] By early 1963, the Conservative government of John Diefenbaker appeared ready to erect a national shrine of remembrance in Ottawa, at Nepean Point.[21] But the next year, the new Lester B. Pearson government, following through with the seemingly safe suggestion of a memorial to be unveiled in 1967, the year marking the country's 100th anniversary, found itself derided by letter-writing citizens who claimed the money could be better spent on veterans in need, or that it was simply not needed. What was the point of commemorating the last generation's war as Canada looked to a bright future? The Legion was unwilling to vigorously defend a new memorial, and the government slunk away from the project, eventually burying it.[22] The angry public reaction against a Second World War memorial was a surprising slap against veterans. It was not until 1982 that the Second World War dates were added to the existing national memorial.

The Second World War was not entirely forgotten, however, and it remained memorialized in other ways. Formal and informal naming programs occurred across the country, with the most prominent being an official federal program started in 1947 to designate geographical features such as mountains and lakes after killed servicemen. In 1960, the program was devolved to the provinces, and those in Saskatchewan and Manitoba were the most ambitious, with several thousand lakes in those provinces named after servicemen. For example, Flight Lieutenant Leslie McCaig, DFC, from Ormstown, Quebec, who was killed in January 1944 when his Lancaster was shot down, had a bay at Ananngiarjuk Point on the northeastern coast of Nunavut named in his honour. Thousands of other geographical places carry the names of service personnel, revealing another way that these Canadians have been honoured and, perhaps, have come to occupy the vast uninhabited parts of Canada. Naming commemorations also extended to veterans' offspring. Robert Skipper survived a tour with No. 424 Squadron, RCAF, and ended his service as a signals officer with No. 415 Squadron, RCAF. He made a pact to remember his dear chum, Jack Kerry. Skipper named his son, John Kerry Skipper, after his friend who is buried overseas and never had a chance to start his own family.[23]

AS SOON AS THE FIGHTING OVERSEAS STOPPED, the sniping began in the war of reputations. While some senior Allied generals, such as Eisenhower and Montgomery, produced memoirs to meet the demand of an adoring public, Canada's senior officers—Crerar, Simonds, McNaughton, Vokes, Foulkes, Nelles, Murray, and McEwen—were silent. The senior military high command showed little outward inclination to refight the war in print. That did not mean, though, that they wanted their reputations to be open to all comers. The army generals used the official army historian, Colonel Charles Stacey, in a historical war by proxy to ensure that their version of the past was the one presented in the official histories. Crerar and Simonds had grown to dislike one another during the stress of the war, and especially after Crerar had used his influence to deny Simonds the postwar chief of the general staff position, recommending instead the mediocre Charles Foulkes, who was revealed to be a surprisingly adept political general. In the war's aftermath, Simonds was particularly nasty and came at Crerar with dagger drawn, insisting repeatedly that he be blamed for the Dieppe raid.[24] Stacey walked a tightrope between the two warring generals, and his official histories remain enduring works, although largely non-judgmental studies of the high command.

In Canada, as in all nations, official history programs were developed, in which state historians in uniform started the laborious work of sifting through the millions of pages of official records to reconstruct the war. The Canadian Army was lucky to have Colonel Stacey, who led a team of narrators and historians. Unlike the Great War official history program, which had failed to produce more than a single volume after twenty years of work, Stacey delivered a series of brief histories during the war and immediately afterwards, and then published technically brilliant books in the 1950s. The navy was less well served by its historian, academic Gilbert Tucker, but he was starved of resources. Two administrative accounts were produced, although he refused to write the war-fighting story of the navy until the German archival documents were released. He was dumped by the government for his sensible stand, and a breezy and readable monograph, *The Far Distant Ships*, was penned in 1952 by the prolific playwright and author Joseph Schull.[25] The air force history crashed on takeoff, due to neglect from senior air marshals who were more focused on the future than the past. The Canadian Forces eventually recognized the value of its own history and funded a robust official history program from the late 1960s onward. Over the years, the military's Directorate of History and Heritage also encouraged the study of academic history in Canada and produced numerous critical works. These first generation of official histories laid the foundation for the study of the army during the Second World War, and a second generation of historians produced other works of synthesis and original research, with three volumes on the Royal Canadian Air Force and three volumes on the Royal Canadian Navy, histories covering the period from their origins to the end of the Second World War, with the last published in 2010.[26]

Most regiments and regimental associations were fast off the mark to codify their war efforts in commemorative history books, which were meant to glorify service rather than pass condemnation. The histories were usually enlivened by insights from survivors or the official records, and subsequent generations of historians have used the regimental and official histories as foundations upon which to build their narratives and analysis. The opening of the official archives in the 1960s also facilitated the writing of new books.

The official and regimental histories were mostly guarded in assigning blame, but other historians, veterans, and filmmakers felt no such constraints, and the Canadian war effort has been dissected almost from the first days of peace to this very day. The battles for memory were fought and refought, and since this book has explored the effectiveness of Canada's formations in combat, it is necessary to come to grips with some of the conclusions that have emerged over several decades.

"The only thing more melancholy than a battle won," wrote the Duke of Wellington after defeating Napoleon at Waterloo in 1815, "is a battle lost." Every single Second World War campaign, engagement, and battle has been contested and dissected over time. As part of this process, several key assessments of the fighting capabilities of Canadian units remain touchstones of controversy. The Dieppe raid is an open wound. Even though it took place on a single day in a long and costly war, the blunder weighed on the nation. Many of the raid's veterans shared a firm belief that they had been sacrificed by their own Canadian commanders and the British generals. While the planning was shoddy and there was more than enough blame to go around, concrete explanations informed the decision to execute the raid—from the need to open a Second Front to the desire to explore the viability of a large-scale multi-service operation against a fortified port—even if these reasons were difficult to understand or unsatisfying for the soldiers on the beaches. While the Dieppe plan was flawed in conception and the forces failed in its execution, few have ever questioned the fighting abilities and commitment of the soldiers.

The disaster at Hong Kong was different. The Canadian battalions in that theatre of war were accused of lacklustre morale by the senior British officer, Major-General Christopher Maltby. His official report was started in the prisoner-of-war camps but finished after his freedom. With a firm eye on his reputation and his place in history, Maltby divided the blame for defeat among many, but was particularly harsh in accusing the Canadians as suffering from poor training and combat skills. He was wrong, and the Canadians fought with enormous bravery and endurance. And so when advance news of the accusations reached the Mackenzie King government shortly after the war, senior ministers were rightly outraged and complained, first informally, through official historian C.P. Stacey, and then formally, threatening to cause a diplomatic row over the matter.[27] The report was released in an expurgated form in 1948, although it was still overly harsh towards the Canadians.

Some forty-five years later, in early 1993, Maltby's official dispatch was finally made public by the British government in its entirety.[28] Canadian veterans lashed out against the British for their own failures during the battle, and especially for Maltby's poor generalship. Nationalistic journalists, engaging in new skirmishes for honour, reminded their readers that the British military high command had also blamed the Australians for their own pitiful performance in the 1942 surrender of Singapore. At the same time, Mackenzie King and his government were excoriated for ordering their countrymen to their doom. The tenor of the debate was summed up by *Globe and Mail* columnist Michael Valpy, who opined that it was "a toss-up who posed the greater threat to [Canadian troops]—the British and Canadian generals and politicians who sent them, or the Japanese."[29]

Over the years, Hong Kong and Dieppe have been portrayed as senseless operations, and their orchestrators charged with incompetence and deceit. The clear-cut defeats over a short period made the memory of the battles even more painful to bear, and while the odds for the pilots of Fighter Command during the Battle of Britain or for the merchant mariners during the worst years of the Battle of the Atlantic, or for a rifleman in an infantry company in Italy or Northwest Europe, offered not much better chances of survival, these campaigns delivered or contributed to the victorious endgame, while Hong Kong and Dieppe are seen as sacrificial throwaways. But, of course, staving off war with Japan through an aggressive reinforcement of a forward base was thought to be a viable strategy at the time, and the need for large-scale raids to give the impression of a Second Front to appease Stalin was necessary in a war of uneasy alliances. This is not to say that Hong Kong and Dieppe should be viewed as victories—only that we must understand such events without imposing hindsight. We should attempt to place ourselves in the mindset of those commanders, military or political, who were fighting a colossal war over several continents and oceans, and were forced to make unimaginably difficult decisions concerning the lives of millions of civilians and military personnel. That said, I am aware that these admonitions, sensible words of caution and context, may be delivered easily by an arm-chair historian, even as they ring hollow to veterans and their families who still wear raw the memories of war.

THE RCN'S SUSTAINED EXERTIONS during the Battle of the Atlantic helped keep the lifeline to Britain open, and Canadian sailors, those in uniform and the Merchant Navy, made significant contributions to victory. But the RCN's massive expansion—thirty-three-fold in terms of manpower, and growing from a handful of ships to become the third largest navy in the world at war's end—brought growing pains. Equally damaging was Ottawa's eagerness to spread its forces thin in assisting the Royal Navy's combating of the U-boats. This strain was further exacerbated by the Americans, who steadily drew off strength to the Pacific War. That the Royal Navy was ungenerous in sharing the latest technological advances in radar in a timely manner may not come as a surprise, but perhaps, then, the British navy's accusation of the Canadians' not meeting their standards was more than a little unfair. Captain Donald Macintyre of the Royal Navy was one of the most vociferous critics of the RCN during and after the war, describing Canada's expanded wartime fleet as "travesties of warships."[30] Few would deny the challenges the RCN faced, but Macintyre's broad dismissal of the naval contribution did a grave disservice to the Canadian seamen during the Battle of the Atlantic. RCN veterans were miffed at the meanness, but it took decades before naval scholars came to grips with some of the reasons for the navy's overstretch, and despite newer scholarship that highlights the enormous success of the Canadians during the Battle of the Atlantic, the approach generally taken outside Canada is to either entirely downplay the RCN or dismiss it as the Royal Navy's ineffectual cousin.

All of this condemnation hinges on how victory in the North Atlantic is defined. For many sailors and scholars, it was framed by how many U-boats were killed, and in that deadly field, the RCN achieved fewer tangible results for its enormous efforts than the Royal Navy. But surely that was not the point of the Battle of the Atlantic, and the question of victory in fact turned on the number of merchant ships guided to safety. About 99 percent of merchant ships carrying war materiel arrived safely in the United Kingdom. For much of the war, the Canadian warships were involved in almost half of the convoy protection in the North Atlantic—and then, from mid-1944 onward, they assumed even greater responsibility for the protection of all convoys across the Atlantic. The RCN helped to win the Battle of the Atlantic, a victory it shared with the roving Cansos and other aircraft of the RCAF's Eastern Air Command.

The British and Canadian land forces have also not fared well over the years under historians' microscopes. The Mediterranean theatre of war has been portrayed by most of them as a sideshow theatre at best, and even as irrelevant, and so the success of the Canadian Corps there has gone largely unnoticed. At the same time, the Canadian land formations in Normandy have been condemned by chroniclers for their slow and tentative fighting against the outnumbered Wehrmacht.[31] With the Allies reinforced by a mass of industrial might from the United States and in absolute command of the air, it was widely believed for several decades after the war that they should have been able to break the German armies more rapidly and with fewer casualties. But as we have seen in the detailed analysis of warfighting in this book, the defenders enjoyed tremendous advantages when dug-in on terrain of their choosing, with good fields of fire for their machine guns, mortars, and anti-tank weapons. Allied firepower—from concentrated artillery barrages to high explosives deposited by bombers—almost never annihilated enemy positions, and even a few machine guns, tanks, or anti-tank guns could punish advancing troops. All had to be destroyed in frontal assaults.

Over the years, the Canadians were accused of relying too heavily on rigid set-piece battles. Others found fault with the junior officers leading the companies and platoons. For example, the respected official historian, Charles Stacey, in searching for answers to the seemingly long Normandy campaign (which was won in seventy-seven days, twenty-three short of the pre-battle planners' estimates), blamed the junior officers for not aggressively pressing home the plans of senior commanders. Stacey was wrong to assign blame at that level, but the accusation of carrying out safe and unimaginative operations continues to dog the Canadians. No plan survives contact with the enemy, as the old military adage goes, and rigid set-piece battles limited the ability of forces to manoeuvre and exploit the shifting nature of combat of Normandy. Yet these types of battle were part of the Anglo-Canadian approach to war, with their origins in the war-winning tactics of the latter half of the Great War. The Americans fought differently, albeit with an equally heavy emphasis on the application of fire in their quest for battles of annihilation. The Soviets are sometimes held up, especially in armoured warfare, as better than all, especially for their forces' ability to absorb blows and keep fighting, pushing the pace with deep operational thrusts. They learned this, of course, from the Germans on the Eastern Front. What is often left unsaid by the admirers of the Soviets is that their casualties were horrendous, with fast-moving units outpacing their supporting artillery and often finding themselves smashed by counterattacks.[32] Neither the British nor the Canadians could afford such a bloodletting, and it remains a truism that Fascist and Communist armies fight differently than democratic ones—with the Communists and Fascists less concerned about the welfare of their soldiers and more willing to accept losses.

It took a brave man to be a coward in the Russian Army, Stalin quipped ominously. Tens of thousands were executed on the spot with no trial; the same occurred in the German army, "pour encourager les autres." The Canadians were not willing to murder their own men in the pursuit of victory. The senior generals in the Anglo-Canadian armies were further aware of the need to ration lives as they suffered soldier shortages by the first month of battle in Normandy. Given that the Canadian Army did not have its junior officers shooting those who faltered, it is astonishing that its formations were able to fight for so long through Normandy, the Scheldt, and finally into the Netherlands and Germany. Canadians understood that they had a dirty job to finish and that they were not going home until Nazism was destroyed. Any analysis of battle reveals that in Normandy, and especially during the horrendous Scheldt campaign, and finally fighting into Germany, the Canadian contributions have been badly undersold. Crerar's fighting men paled in comparison to no national force, and in many campaigns often proved far more effective in delivering victory.

THE MOST SUSTAINED CRITIQUE of the Allied war effort has been directed against Bomber Command, and here the focus has been not on Canadian flyers but on the very morality and value of the bombing campaign. In this seventy-year debate, the Royal Canadian Air Force's bombing efforts have remained tied to those of the Royal Air Force, under whose operational command it served.

Churchill's post-Dresden order of curtailing city bombing was a visible walk back from the bomber-inflicted carnage, and he completed his distancing from the aerial campaign on May 13, 1945. In his victory speech to the nation, the prime minister went out of his way to highlight the work of the many who contributed to defeating Hitler: the navy, which kept the sea lanes open; the doggedly resilient merchant navy; and the "few" in Fighter Command who held off the Luftwaffe hordes. The hard-won victories by the army in North Africa, in the Mediterranean theatre, and in Europe were also underlined. Churchill spoke of the determination and resolve of the British people who withstood privation and direct attack. However, he slighted the costly service of the bomber crews by excluding them from his speech—a hurtful omission given that it was they who had struck back early in the war when no other service arm could. The survivors of the bomber war were bewildered by their exclusion from the verbal victory parade.

With the Labour Party's ascendance to power after the defeat of Churchill's coalition government in July 1945, no new gratitude was shown towards the aircrews. The bomber veterans found it especially hurtful that a unique campaign medal was not struck and awarded to them for their service, like the medals that commemorated those who served in the Battle of Britain, Africa, the Far East, France, and Germany. The aircrews received a Home Defence Medal, although Bomber Command airmen who served sixty hours or more with an operational squadron between September 3, 1939, and June 5, 1944, qualified for the Air Crew Europe Star, and those who served after D-Day were awarded the France and Germany Star. But without a unique medal, it appeared that the bomber veterans' Home Defence Medal was on par with those who had not participated in front-line service.[33] The lack of a specific medal—and all that it connoted—cast a deeper pall over the aircrews' service. Veterans took to calling their lack of formal recognition "The Great Ingratitude."[34]

What had gone wrong? While a handful of commentators have gone so far as to consider the bombing campaign against German civilians to be morally equivalent to the Holocaust, this idea of a mutual descent into barbarism is surely mistaken.[35] The bomber offensive was used to liberate an oppressed continent from the Nazi regime and its willing followers—a regime that started the war (in addition to commencing the direct aerial assault against civilians), but that also had as part of its strategic objectives a policy of genocide. The Allies took advantage of their growing technological and military superiority in the final two years, but such tactics are a far cry from the Nazis' wars of extermination. Even when posed from a historical distance from the war, any suggestion of a moral equivalency between the Allied and Axis powers, or that the bomber war was out of proportion to the endgame, is odious and wrong. Such claims misconstrue that Germany continued waging war up to the bitter end, withheld food from the starving Dutch, and went on murdering Jews and others in sickening numbers through the death camps.

Despite the postwar slights against Bomber Command, Sir Arthur Harris continued to brusquely defend the bombing strategy. Roaring that the bombers had been decisive, he was, at times, his worst enemy, as his defiant and dogmatic vision allowed others to scalpel away at Bomber Command's achievements. Bombing had not won the war, even as it had clearly contributed to victory, but critics used Harris's own bluster to further show that not only had bombing not achieved its goals, it had been a wasteful or ill-used resource in the Allied arsenal. Harris retired as an air marshal in 1946, moved to South Africa, and was made a baronet in 1953 when Churchill returned to power as prime minister. The "Bomber," as he was known to his largely respectful aircrew veterans, refused to be shamed by his wartime command, never recanted the strategy his military and political superiors implemented, and remained unrepentant about the necessity of city bombing. And on this last count he was surely backed by the vast majority of Bomber Command veterans. But the images of the dead cities continued to haunt. Over the years, as the stories of German civilians who survived the firestorms of Hamburg and Dresden came to light, Harris remained a convenient scapegoat for the actions of Bomber Command.[36] Air Marshal Portal—Harris's senior officer—escaped condemnation, perhaps because Harris was so impolitic in his demands of recognition for his boys and in his refusal to question his own wartime tactics.

The threat of nuclear weapons led, from the 1950s onward, to growing dread over strategic bombing. The new generation of long-range aircraft that would be unleashed when the Cold War flared hot were now carrying planet-destroying bombs. The vocal antiwar movement turned, not surprisingly, to the bomber war as evidence of the horror of conventional weapons, and expressed fear about what atomic ones could do to cities.[37] In some circles, especially academic and pacifist, the Second World War bombing campaign was conflated with the new nuclear threat, and this dread was stirred up in the antiwar, anti-authoritarian consciousness emerging in the mid-1960s.

Most of the Canadian bomber veterans did not contribute to this memory creation. Flyers were young men who had hardly expected to survive their wartime sorties, and now they were raising families, working, and living in the society they helped to make prosperous. The war began to recede and few felt the need to refight old battles. At the same time, no veteran could forget. With regard to the bomber war, RCAF navigator L. Ray Silver wrote of his experience: "Later-day revisionists have described us as callow kids duped to do the devil's work innocent of the humanity on target below us. Of course, we knew there were people down there. We did what we had to do and to do it we suppressed the human imagery.... We found no glory and we still taste the ashes."[38] Silver did not regret his part in the war, but his words reveal that he bore both physical and mental scars. Silver's generation carried the taste of ashes for years, as a result of what they had seen and what they had been forced to do, and this applied to not just bomber crews but to all those who fought. But the veterans of the bomber war seemed especially susceptible to second-guessing. Lancaster pilot Douglas Harvey was burdened by his service, the memories of which were stirred up after a return to Berlin in 1961. Within the rebuilt Berlin, Harvey mused, "I could not visualize the horrible deaths my bombs had caused here. I had no feeling of guilt. I had no feeling of accomplishment."[39] The trauma faded with time, but it would return in shocking blasts from a trigger memory.

We'll never know if most, many, or just a few Bomber Command veterans were troubled by their wartime deeds. Warrant Officer B.G. McDonald, who flew thirty operations on a Lancaster in 1944, recounted how, over the years, family and strangers asked him about his reaction to bombing German cities. "It may seem strange but I have to say that I hadn't thought much about the subject," he admitted. "In the intervals between raids I seldom thought about it and never discussed the subject with other RCAF/RAF aircrew. I felt confident that the bombing of enemy cities was winning the war against Germany. I considered it to be in retaliation for the fire-bombing of British cities in 1940–41.... My instinctive main concern was one of self preservation. Would I die or live to fight another day?"[40] As one RAF air gunner remarked, "Sometimes the only way to overcome a great evil is to resort to a lesser evil."[41] Such sentiments would have resonated with many who lived through the war years. Flight Lieutenant John Zinkhan observed, "In retrospect some of the saturation bombing attacks were deliberately and viciously planned with the thought of killing civilians." But these missions, in his mind, were a part of total war, and directed against civilians producing weapons, food, and supplies for the front-line forces. Noting his own limited view as one among millions, Zinkhan asserted provocatively, "Maybe you can figure out what is right and what is wrong in a 'total war.'"[42] Some have tried, but all with the benefit of hindsight and with the intellectual freedom to do so that traces directly to the wartime victory of the Allies over Nazi Germany.

The uncowed and still belligerent Sir Arthur Harris died in 1984. Throughout his postwar life, he had fought those who questioned the bombing campaign and had backed the bomber crews unfailingly. Over time, he was tarred as the leader of the "bloodthirsty bone-heads and blimps"—as one 1989 BBC production labelled the senior Bomber Command staff.[43] Harris's supporters fired back and his official biographer condemned his critics in words that might have been spoken by Harris himself about the war: "Memories faded and soon the horrors and fears of Nazism receded, to be replaced by a fanatical desire on the part of historians, sensation writers, some journalists, and television writers and producers to degrade and assassinate the character of the commander and the one Command to whom they owe their very liberty, and to pour out, unchallenged and unchecked, their scurrilous and, more frequently than not, inaccurate reports on the war which most of them never knew."[44]

How the bomber war would be remembered was shaped significantly in 1992, by two controversial events. In that year, Harris's old comrades banded together to erect a statue in his honour outside the RAF church of St. Clement Danes in the Strand, London. Unveiled on May 31, 1992, the memorial was established in the face of considerable anger. Several German mayors protested honouring the memory of a man they characterized as a war criminal. The British media fanned the flames, and many papers robustly defended Harris. The ongoing salvoes in the war of reputations were as much about fighting wars of old as they were about the economic and political uncertainty in the aftermath of the fall of the Soviet Union and the remaking of Europe. Yet it is telling that the Queen Mother, who lived through the dark days of the war, refused to listen to her advisors and would not be dissuaded from attending the event. She and many of her generation understood the debt owed to the aircrews and Harris. Not all agreed. Guards had to be placed around the eight-foot-tall statue as it was repeatedly defaced with red paint.

In Canada, an equally polarizing event occurred that year: the airing of *The Valour and the Horror*, a three-part documentary series on the CBC caused outrage among veterans. Lauded by much of the media and viewed by record-numbers of Canadians, it was excoriated by the majority of veterans. The most contentious episode, "Death by Moonlight: Bomber Command," argued not only that the Allied bombing of Germany was a strategic failure but that it was a secret campaign to indiscriminately murder innocent civilians. Directors Terence and Brian McKenna cited a moral equivalency between the Nazis and the Allies, as both sides resorted to targeting civilians, but they refused to go so far as to condemn the flyers as baby killers. Instead, the aircrews were depicted as innocent dupes who did not understand what they were doing. The film suggested there was an active cover-up, with government-issued propaganda and compliant newspapers claiming the bombs hit only industrial and military targets. "Few Canadians," the film emphasized, "would ever learn of that plan," which was blamed almost solely on the monster Sir Arthur Harris.[45] The film's claims were ham-fisted and erroneous on almost every front, and its argument was unmistakably presentist— a 1990s perception of the moral reprehensibility of bombing civilians projected backwards onto the total war of 1939 to 1945. Historians lined up to condemn the series, highlighting error after error, both of commission and omission.[46] The historical drubbing did not calm veterans, who convinced the Senate to hold hearings and even attempted to sue for $500 million in a defamation of character suit. The veterans' lawsuit failed. The anger festered.

A 1944 Royal Air Force poster.
The bombing of German cities was no secret.

Veterans commissioned their own film, *No Higher Purpose*, which was far better historically (if watched by far fewer viewers) than *The Valour and the Horror*, and they increasingly wished for more control over how their history was to be interpreted. A further row over how Bomber Command was presented to the public occurred at the Canadian War Museum. Upon its opening of a new building in 2005, the museum received accolades by visitors, the media, and veterans, but a public disagreement rapidly developed over a sixty-eight-word text panel (in a museum of thousands of artifacts and tens of thousands of words of text) that referred to—but did not take a position on—the enduring controversy over the value and morality of the bomber campaign. The single panel led to a two-year-long battle between several veterans' organizations and the museum.[47] After a Senate committee hearing all but insisted on a change, the CWM and the veterans eventually reached a compromise to rewrite the panel. The anger exhibited over the historical wording in the museum, and even the seemingly harmless act of drawing attention to past controversies, was just one more chapter in a longer narrative.

In June 2012, the Canadian government announced that Bomber Command veterans would receive a special bar to be worn on their Canadian Volunteer Service Medal, which all service personnel had been issued at war's end. This recognition came just as a new Bomber Command memorial to the 55,573 killed flyers was dedicated in London's Green Park. The memorial's neoclassical pavilion houses oversized bronze figurative statues of a seven-man bomber crew, and the roof above the memorial is constructed from parts of a recovered Halifax III downed over Belgium in May 1944. Unveiled by the Queen, with hundreds of Bomber Command veterans in attendance, the pavilion was not universally appreciated, with one critic lamenting its "architectural crassness" that was "like the nervously loud voice of someone trying to shout down opposition."[48] Yet the memorial is inscribed to both the fallen and the victims of the bombs. Surely that is more of a quiet gesture towards the horror of war than a vigorous defence of old accusations. Jack Watts, then a ninety-one-year-old Canadian veteran, noted, "It's just sad as hell that it came this late, and there are so few of us now to see it."[49]

While the bravery and endurance of the bomber crews has never been in doubt, the battle over the memory of the bomber campaign continues on—rife with broad-brush attacks or unbelievable denials mixed with heated rhetoric and political posturing, and including few attempts by anyone other than historians to understand the bombing campaign within the context of the time. The veterans finally received their memorial, medal, and respect, but these just recognitions will not end the debate around the bombing campaign.

IF HISTORIANS HAVE QUESTIONED almost all aspects of the war, and especially the effectiveness of the Canadian fighting services and their place in the war's constructed memory, veterans have also struggled over their own personal histories of the war. Gordon Cameron, writing in *The Legionary* in the war's immediate aftermath, shed light on the place of memory in ex-service personnel: "One minute he wants above all to forget what he has been through, the pals he has lost and all the miseries of war. The next moment he knows that he can never forget. He won't ever forget, and something within him cries out that the people here at home must be made aware of the ghastly, bloody price paid by the 'few' for the freedom of the 'many.'"[50]

Queen Elizabeth II at the Bomber Command memorial to the 55,573 killed flyers in London's Green Park.

Gordon Francis Cook, a Canadian veteran who served in RAF Bomber Command, is perhaps instructive in providing a window into one veteran's engagement with personal memory and war. Cook had graduated from high school in Lethbridge, Alberta, in 1933, during the worst of the Depression, and he kicked around in a semi-skilled job in a hardware store while keeping active offering instruction at the YMCA and winning Alberta-wide track-and-field events. Fit and sporty, with a mop of curly dark hair, he was also a dead-eye shot, earning the Dominion Marksman crest. Cook saw war coming in 1939. He visited his English cousins that summer and enlisted in the RAF at age twenty-five on June 21, 1939. After training as a navigator, he flew 200 operational hours with No. 601 Squadron on Blenheim two-seater fighters, including sorties over France before it was conquered. After his long tour, in mid-1940 he was sent to Canada to act as an instructor with the BCATP. The instructor became a student, however, and he was retrained as a pilot. He also married his childhood sweetheart, Olive Roper, who had been waiting for him. Her wait would extend three more years. Cook was commissioned as a flight lieutenant in November 1943 and he piloted Hudsons—usually his bird, "Dominion Castle"—in the Mediterranean theatre with No. 608 Squadron, RAF. He flew anti-submarine patrols and bombing missions from early 1944 for six months before serving with the South African Air Force from July to November 1944. In that capacity, he survived fifty-six bombing sorties in Venturas over Yugoslavia and southern Germany, before ending his war flying VIP officials. He survived one serious crash into a mountainside in Yugoslavia on a bombing run and had numerous close calls with flak. For pension, health care, and administrative convenience, he was transferred from RAF to RCAF before discharge.

Like most veterans, Gordon Cook did not know what to do upon his return to Canada, but his exit interview records suggest that he thought he might like to pursue civil aviation or work with the civil service. He was described as "mature, co-operative and a pleasing personality."[51] When he was discharged in September 1945, Cook did not take advantage of the Veterans Charter and go to university, or borrow money for a house, or start a business, although he took his wartime gratuity for service and purchased a small house in Vancouver. He was soon hired by Imperial Oil as a low-level white-collar manager, where he worked his entire postwar life. His wartime service had resulted in the job. His brother, Allan, a veteran of the RCN, did go to university courtesy of the government and became an architect.

While Cook remained proud of his service, he did not talk much about the war to his family, which he started with two sons born in 1947 and 1953. But the war's presence was rarely far from him. Throughout his house, he displayed souvenirs, including his flying scarf, leather pilot's helmet and headset, a book of aerial photographs, tourist paintings, carvings, and woodcuts, and a shell splinter that during a sortie had lodged in his cockpit inches from his head. Service, camaraderie, and even death, in the form of the shell splinter, were with him daily. But these were not sacred objects, and his two sons, Terry and Barry, frequently wore his flying helmet in make-believe games or thumbed through the photographs. He kept his medals in a cardboard box in a dresser drawer, though he placed enough value on them—and the memories they evoked of service and friendships—to pursue a ten-year correspondence with the RAF-RCAF to obtain a missing medal. He had an RAF uniform that he wore for several years on Remembrance Day, but he grew out of it as he aged and never had it replaced. He did wear his RAF peaked pilot's cap to the Vancouver Cenotaph every November 11, the one day a year the medals emerged from the drawer. Closest to his heart was an official logbook documenting his six years of flying, which, to judge from its crumbling pages, broken binding, and many later-added notes and explanations, was evidently a living record. It was his memory talisman, his war service, his proof he'd been there.

Two symbols of Cook's service included a tattoo on his left forearm of the No. 608 Squadron crest, and his moustache, which he grew during the war, RAF-style, and never shaved off. There were other permanent reminders. While he did not receive a pension for wounds, Cook suffered from a debilitating neck injury from his wartime crash. He had to endure a few times a week sitting for an hour in the basement with a medieval-looking rehabilitative collar brace, attached by ropes and pulleys to a weighty bag of sand, which he used to stretch his neck, a bit like a man slowly hanging himself. As the years wore on, he talked occasionally to his oldest son, Terry, about his service, but he had very little interest in studying the war, and rarely picked up history books. He did make model planes of the aircraft he'd flown, painting them meticulously, almost as if to recapture a vanished world. He very occasionally went to the local Legion hall to have a few drinks there in the company of fellow veterans and away from the prying eyes of his wife, a devout teetotaller, but he never formally joined the Legion. When he got together with his brother, Allan, the two often talked about the war, and while Gordon was a gentle man—soft-spoken and deferential, eager to please—he reserved a bit of vitriol for his sister's husband, who had chosen not to serve during the war and instead made a significant amount of money as a businessman in Montreal. He did not bear ill feelings towards his wife's brothers, who were conscientious objectors, apparently because they had stood their ground and shown their own moral courage. In Gordon and Allan's minds, their sister's husband had not done his duty in the war against Fascism, perhaps because he had profited from the war.

Gordon retired at age fifty-eight in 1972 and passed away two years later. He never regretted his service and remarked more than once that it had been the "peak of his life." His overseas flying symbolized in his memory that interlude between prewar Depression and postwar office work, the only time in his life when he saw castles and palaces in England, Roman antiquities across Italy, the pyramids near Cairo, the always romanticized Isle of Capri. These were the subjects of the paintings and woodcuts he brought back from the war, and they became the images central to his memory of the best times of his life, of excitement and adventure and travel, a momentary escape in time from a life otherwise ordinary.

Like my grandfather, Gordon Cook, all of Canada's million veterans had their own war legacy. Each veteran shared commonalities of experiences as well as having his own unique narrative. Few of the stories follow the traditional trajectory of what we might think equates with veteran's status: the Veterans Charter, the Legion, and an abiding interest in the war. Yet nor were many Canadian veterans unaffected by the war or unable to escape its long reach over the many years of their remaining lives. Donald Pearce, who served in Northwest Europe, believed, "No one has really been in the same places as anyone else; and I refuse to play the game of comparing experiences. The whole war seems to me a quite private experience."[52] Tragedy, hardship, and loss were mixed equally with camaraderie, profound experiences, and the need to mature in a hurry. Every Canadian found a different war, and then, as veterans, experienced it differently again in memory. For some, it was the defining moment of their lives, while for others it was just a brief interlude. In almost all veterans, however, the war was also something that resurfaced over time, and often unexpectedly. And it tended to gather in strength as age brought the natural tendency to regret, celebrate, and reflect on a life lived.

AS THESE ONCE-YOUNG WARRIORS AGED, they looked upon their lives. Many chose to draw out their personal narratives of war. Gerald Bowen, more than fifty-five years after the war ended, felt, "A lot of the horror that you witnessed or you experienced gets locked away in the back of your head.... It's very hard to get it out.... For years and years and years, the boys never spoke out because, you know, people had families and people had mortgages and that was the concern. Reestablishment and going to school and getting jobs. It has only been in the last couple of years that the guys have really started talking."[53] Over time, most veterans shared their war experiences and some put pen to paper, seeking to exorcise the war that prowled through the corners of their minds.

Using wartime letters, regimental histories, and diaries to augment their memories, many veterans at the end of their lives left a legacy for their children or grandchildren. Others wrote to set the record straight, feeling that historians had ignored their war experiences by focusing on senior commanders or the actions of divisions and brigades. For some it was a more personal journey. "The process has been a catharsis," observed Hal Lawrence in capturing his five and a half years on the Atlantic in a corvette. "Setting down at last the inchoate thoughts and daydreams, the nostalgia, fear, hope and despair, that the period arouses."[54] Revisiting the ghosts of the past put some of them to rest. "Writing this memoir has been like looking at a diorama in a department store window," penned Robert Crozier, a veteran of the Irish Regiment of Canada. "The figures and events are familiar, but this time you are standing outside looking in—detached, observant, but no longer involved. It's a nice, safe feeling."[55] In writing about the war, many veterans found it was the first time that they truly understood what they had taken part in, and how their service had fit into a national or international Allied war effort. Arthur Bridge, a private in the Argyll and Sutherland Highlanders, recalled in 2000, "We low rankers seldom knew what was going on, where we were, where we were going, or what to expect when we got there. It has only been since the war, and with the help of history books, that I have been able to retrace my steps through the campaign and to put names to the places that had no particular meaning at the time—just another place to run in, dig in and prepare for the counterattack."[56] William Victor Williamson, a sergeant in the Algonquin Regiment, was taken prisoner at the Leopold Canal in September 1944. As he penned in the preface to his unpublished memoirs, "As most POWs know, … there is a certain amount of private conflict as one struggles with the memories of such tragic events. Freedom from captivity did not end my suffering. I've struggled with it for the last forty-seven years. Without sounding too melodramatic, my personal freedom would not have been achieved had I not embarked upon the telling of this story." The reforming of traumatic experiences into words was summed up in the title of his memoir: "My Final Freedom."[57]

THE SECOND WORLD WAR stirs the imagination for many Canadians, and it has been used as fodder for novels, plays, films, documentaries, and all manner of cultural products. Despite this fascination with the war, Canadian writers have produced few exceptional novels or plays on the subject. The Great War spawned Timothy Findley's *The Wars*, Jane Urquhart's *The Stone Carvers*, and Joseph Boyden's *Three Day Road*; and John Gray's *Billy Bishop Goes to War* and Kevin Major's Newfoundland play *No Man's Land* are staged time and time again. In contrast, the most compelling of the Second World War literary products are by those who served or who were deeply affected by the war. Infantry officer Colin McDougall's *Execution* is a little remembered classic that won the 1958 Governor General's Award. In the long tradition of finding dark humour in war, Earle Birney, a major during the war and one of Canada's most respected poets, penned *Turvey*, which won the 1950 Stephen Leacock Award for Humour. Joan Walker's wickedly funny book on her experiences as an English war bride in Canada, *Pardon My Parka*, received the same award four years later. In Quebec, Gratien Gélinas's *Tit-Coq*, about a French-Canadian soldier who loses his girl to another suitor during the war while he is serving overseas, has been staged countless times since 1947, and was made into a movie in 1953. Gélinas did not serve during the war, but the story of disillusionment was one that resonated throughout Quebec. Other than these early classics—none of which appear to be taught anymore in university literature classes—there are no touchstone cultural products from the "good war."

If the panoramic sweep of the Second World War experience has been a challenge to capture in novels or plays, it has, however, been an influential impetus for video games. Critics may scoff at one-man armies wiping out German divisions in countless first-person shooter games, but the creators of these products often go to great lengths to achieve historical accuracy in weapons and uniforms, and even devote time to including the contextualizing history. These entertaining games have, somewhat surprisingly, become an impetus for younger generations to engage in the war. There are online reference guides for gamers to better understand the history they are enacting, and surveys suggest that almost all students in North America, male and female, have played video games by the time they reach college or university.[58] Interest and knowledge are sparked in different ways, and the sales of video games dwarf those of history books.

While a slew of Second World War films have been made, Canadians have never produced one of any stature. This is a shame, as stories like the Great Escape of 1944, which so many Canadian prisoners planned, orchestrated, and took part in, and in which six lost their lives, have been co-opted by Hollywood. *The Great Escape* (1963), starring Steve McQueen, will always be an American tale no matter how often Canadian historians remind an amnesiac public that their countrymen were there and held crucial roles, and all the groaning shelves of history books will never have the same impact as a single blockbuster like *The Longest Day* (1962) or *Saving Private Ryan* (1998). Of the latter film, it could be said that Spielberg stole D-Day from the British and Canadians in his powerful if focused telling of the American landing at Omaha Beach. Canadians watching that film might be excused for being unaware that a Canadian division landed on the D-Day beaches. There was a brief surge in interest in Canada's Second World War history in the film's aftermath, but *Saving Private Ryan* did not strike deep into the nation's consciousness and no Canadian film or CBC production has ever been able to build upon Spielberg's success. Perhaps this is because, as one *Globe and Mail* critic sniped, "A quick survey of Canadian film and TV treatments of the Second World War suggests that if we'd made *Saving Private Ryan*, the Allies never would have gotten off the beach."[59] It is not Hollywood's job to portray a balanced account of the war, but if Canadians do not take the time or put in the resources to tell their own stories, we can rest assured that the Americans or British will not do it for us; and they may even seize Canadian history as their own.

IF FEW CULTURAL PRODUCTS inspired by or grounded in the Second World War have resonated over time with Canadians, a few recognizable symbols do remain. Vimy has become a national icon. The four-day battle of April 1917 emerged over several decades to be woven into the very fabric of Canadian history, identity, and society during the second half of the twentieth century, with some claiming it marked the birth of the nation. Such lofty ideas are ascribing too much to Vimy, but when we talk about this battle, we are in fact talking about the traumatic and nation-shaping Great War writ large, and about Canada's slow maturation to full nationhood. But nations can't be born twice. So what is the touchstone of the Second World War? Judging by the history books, documentaries, and national discourse, at least up to the mid-1990s, this appeared to be the Battle of Dieppe, an unqualified defeat, or the tragedy of Hong Kong, or even the evacuation of Japanese Canadians from the west coast to the interior because of the misplaced fear that they were fifth columnists who would aid a Japanese invasion of Canada. In Quebec, the war was seen differently, as all wars are, and the celebrated fighting units—including the Royal 22e Regiment, Le Régiment de la Chaudière, No. 425 "Alouette" Squadron, or HMCS *Dunver* (supported by the people of Verdun, a suburb of Montreal)—are often devalued for political reasons, in favour of the debate over conscription and its limited implementation in late 1944. It says something about the Canadian psyche that we focus on defeats and injustice rather than the victories at Ortona, the Scheldt campaign, or the Battle of the Atlantic—or munitions production at home, massive patriotic war work, the BCATP, or the host of other ways that Canadians banded together behind their armed forces overseas. What do these other battles, programs, or events lack, in contrast to Vimy, so that they have not been moulded into a nation-making and nation-building myth? While such mythical status perhaps should not be the ultimate destiny of any historical event, the Second World War, from the 1960s to the mid-1990s, in our classrooms and in national discourse, was portrayed as little more than a series of disasters and disgraces. In 1996, veteran Doug Fisher raged in *The Legion* about the lopsided, even twisted, memory that Canadians had of the war, and he wondered why so many of his countrymen and women took "such little pride in the mighty achievements of WW II."[60]

Perhaps some of the impact of the Second World War is lost because so many of the symbols of remembrance remain intricately linked to the Great War. The community memorials, first erected to honour the Great War's dead, contain the names of Second World War fallen almost as an afterthought, especially on memorials that include inscribed lists of battle names from 1914 to 1918, which is often the case. The poppy, Remembrance Day, the Books of Remembrance, and even the national memorial are all deeply associated with the First World War. There are some new ceremonies and symbols that were born of the Second World War, such as the Battle of the Atlantic Sunday (the first Sunday in May) and Ottawa's Tulip Festival (which originated when the grateful Dutch people sent tulips to their liberators), but the absence of recognizable and stand-alone monuments, symbols, and icons remains remarkable.[61] Moreover, while the Vimy memorial in France is a towering site of remembrance, no Second World War overseas equivalent exists. There are numerous regimental plaques and modest markers, as well as a memorial garden in Caen, but these all pale in comparison to Vimy.[62] Even the Juno Beach Centre, opened June 6, 2003, and the closest thing we have to a window for Europeans into Canadian Second World War history, is clearly a site of education rather than reverence. Perhaps this centre will take on a greater presence over time, but at the moment it falls short.

THOSE WHO HAD FOUGHT, served, and sacrificed during the Second World War knew that it was a necessary conflict. The ultimate triumph over evil had been worth the loss of comrades, dislocation from family, and the wounds to bodies and minds. But this generation of veterans and their families did not dwell on the war. Almost all were too young to retire, and save for a small minority that remained in the armed forces, the civilian-warriors returned to civvy street to build up the newly revitalized nation. Canada, too, was young and changing, and looking forward instead of backward. Ted Barris, a journalist and author, remembered of his education in Canada in the early 1960s, "By edict or accident … the school curriculum virtually eliminated war as a subject worth studying.… I never heard of the words 'war hero' or 'Canada' in the same sentence. It just wasn't done. Those weren't names or facts worth acknowledging, much less celebrating."[63] Young Canadians coming of age in the 1960s chose a different path from their parents, and one that pushed back, perhaps not surprisingly, against some of the things that the older generation held dear. A greater voice in politics, an embracing of change, a valuing of new symbols like the Canadian flag, multiculturalism, reforms in gender and sexual relations, and a host of other issues became the standard bearers of the new generation. Prominent in the 1960s, and indeed throughout the length of the Vietnam War, was a strong revulsion towards all war. While large parts of Canada supported U.S. military involvement in Southeast Asia, there was much questioning of American foreign policy by intellectuals, students, and indeed all Canadians. Intensifying protest in Canada against the war saw the nation welcome more than 30,000 draft-dodgers coming north and even more body bags going home to American families.

Against this societal backdrop, the slow shunting of Canada's Second World War history to the irrelevant periphery or the dusty past was amplified in the latter part of the 1960s, and there is ample evidence that Canadians' disillusionment and anger over the Vietnam War was directed against all soldiers and veterans.[64] Moreover, with the Cold War following on the heels of the Second World War, turning the former Soviet ally into an enemy, the Second World War—like the Great War—had its own futile narrative thread. The war was fought against a heinously evil regime, but it had been replaced, according to Cold War propagandists, by an equally malicious one. What had been the point of the Second World War? What was the point of any war?

Lester B. Pearson's Nobel Peace Prize for his deft work during the 1956 Suez Crisis, in averting a worse rift between the principal Western allies—the United States, Britain, France, and Israel—ushered in a new era. Many Canadians took pride in Pearson's award, particularly as they saw their one-time impoverished, colonial, and ignored country finding a role on the world stage.[65] Peacekeeping became an important symbol. It was also much cheaper than preparing for conventional or nuclear warfare. Over decades, the defence budgets were cut and Canada's military role abroad shifted in public perception from protecting Europe or North America against Soviet attack to worldwide peacekeeping, even though the latter remained a small commitment for the Canadian Forces, with the vast majority of resources put towards Canadian military contributions in NATO and NORAD. Yet there was scarcely a peacekeeping mission from the second half of the twentieth century to which Canada did not contribute service personnel. A new peacekeeping image was embraced by Canadians, and traditional warfighting fell out of favour in the public eye. In the

1970s, it was not uncommon for members of the Canadian Forces to avoid wearing their uniforms while travelling on Canada's city streets for fear of being the target of verbal assaults; by the 1990s, the members of the Canadian Forces were so few in number that they appeared entirely absent from the streets of almost every major city or town across Canada, save for those few that had military bases. Veterans took to publicly pleading that Remembrance Day was not a day to celebrate war but to mark sacrifice. It was sad that they even had to say such things in the face of misplaced antiwar sentiments that had given rise to a questioning of the need for commemoration. Major A.J. Hamilton, who served with the Stormont, Dundas and Glengarry Highlanders, wrote at the beginning of the 1990s, "Our ranks are thinning fast. The veterans will never forget, but at times we worry whether our children are taught the price for the freedom they take for granted."[66]

BY THE EARLY 1990S, the Canadian Forces was at its nadir. Years of cuts to the defence budgets had rendered the military a hollow shell. While peacekeeping was esteemed by Canadians and the media, the Canadian Forces was losing its military capability. Its lowest ranks were paid starvation wages. There were few resources for those military personnel who served on traumatic missions to receive any counselling. Among the officer corps, obtaining a graduate degree was not only anathema but was damaging to one's career in the anti-intellectual armed forces. The rot was deep. The disintegration of the Soviet Union from 1989 to 1991 hastened in a new age of Western power, which was then used by politicians to justify further cutbacks to the military. But soon the new world order slipped into chaotic disorder. Peacekeeping missions in Somalia, Rwanda, and the Balkans during the early 1990s went disastrously wrong, and despite the Canadian Forces' saving of lives through protecting the helpless and rebuilding shattered societies, the message as reported in the media was one of incompetence, loss, and futility. In Somalia, a handful of rogue soldiers murdered a Somali teenager, after which their unit, and then senior defence officials, perpetrated a cover-up. The subsequent investigation badly damaged the image of the Canadian military.

In the mid-1990s, even as the Canadian Forces were being openly splayed in the media as a relentless freak-show of cover-ups, hazings, scandals, and embarrassments,

Canadians paradoxically—or perhaps in opposition to their armed forces' scraping barrel bottom—returned to their aged veterans. The years 1994 and 1995 marked the fiftieth anniversary of the Second World War. Anniversaries focused the attention of the media. Widespread celebrations in Britain, France, Belgium, and especially the Netherlands honoured veterans. The Canadian warriors of old, some 15,000 strong, were welcomed to the lands they liberated. Everywhere, signs and banners flew, bearing the message "Bless You, Boys." To wear a Maple Leaf flag was to be greeted with hugs of thanks and tears of joy. Day after day, CBC and CTV, under the steady hands of anchors Peter Mansbridge and Lloyd Robertson, offered coverage of events from the old battlegrounds. The stories of Canadian veterans, their courage, and their history were broadcast into millions of living rooms. The nation's leading historian, J.L. Granatstein, who participated as a television commentator on the events, described the moving scenes at Apeldoorn, Netherlands: "I shall never forget the

Canadian veterans were honoured in 1995 in the Netherlands,
the nation they liberated fifty years earlier.

sight of young mothers in their twenties, weeping and cheering simultaneously while holding their babies up to get a sobbing veteran's kiss. Nor will I forget the Dutch mothers telling astonished and typically blasé Canadian reporters that they were doing this because they wanted their children to be able to say that they had been touched by one of the men who liberated the Netherlands a half-century before."[67] Canadians woke up abruptly to find much of Europe thanking their veterans for their service and sacrifice, though they themselves had been ambivalent to these same veterans for decades.

Something changed in Canadian society as nationalism mixed with nostalgia. And since the fiftieth anniversary of the Second World War, Canadians' have shown a greater appreciation for veterans. This change was also spurred on by the near dissolution of the country in 1995, with the Quebec referendum on whether to separate from Confederation provoking an existential gut-check for many Canadians who realized that they had for too long drifted from the anchors of the past, and who recognized the power of history to provide shared stories.

The public buildup and commemoration of the return home of Canada's Unknown Soldier in May 2000 raised the profile of all veterans, even though Canada's fallen soldier came from the Great War. Questions surrounding the commemoration of the Second World War were heightened again three years later when there was a furor over funding for the Juno Beach Centre and the embarrassing revelation that the museum in France had only opened because the American mega-company Walmart had donated $1.8 million to its completion.[68] Even normally complacent Canadians averted their eyes a little at the shame of having to go palm out to the Americans in matters of national history and heritage. The federal government was more generous in providing funds for a new Canadian War Museum that opened in 2005, and it has attracted about half a million visitors a year to learn about the nation's military history. This new interest was in keeping with increased participation in Remembrance Day ceremonies across the country; these events had been heavily attended for at least a decade before the museum's opening and have continued to be so to the present. As grandfathers and grandmothers passed away, their surviving family members often paid homage to them and their service to the country on November 11. This renewed desire to honour has only increased as a new generation of Afghanistan service personnel, numbering 40,000, were added to the ranks of veterans after Canada's long war in that fractured country from 2001 to 2011.[69] Red Shirt days of appreciation, the naming of the Highway of Heroes in Ontario, moving ramp ceremonies, and public displays of support all revealed how millions of Canadians were moved to honour Afghanistan service personnel and veterans.

For much of the second half of the twentieth century, the nation that prided itself on peacekeeping had forgotten much of its pre-Confederation history, a period of open warfare, low-level conflict, and careful negotiation with friends and foes. Through neglect, ignorance, and wishful thinking, Canadians had downplayed the impact of fighting six wars in the twentieth century and the withstanding of some fifty years of the Cold War. Now, after the Afghanistan war, and with perhaps a greater appreciation of how war, in all its complexity, has shaped Canada, the ever-shifting Canadian identity is again redefining and reinventing itself, as it has always done and always will.

SEVENTY FIVE YEARS ON, and as veterans pass away in significant numbers, more Canadians have come to grips with the fundamental role their country played in the war against Nazi Germany. New school curriculums, university courses, histories and documentaries, as well as citizenship guides, museums, and memorials give Canadians an opportunity to understand the Second World War while veterans are still among us.

Canadians have moved through the ebb and flow of memory and commemoration, through neglect and respect, and through sadness for the passing of a generation and the understanding that we can never forget them and their sacrifice. Not all Canadians share these sentiments, but enough do, and the nation and its changing people shall continue to mark, honour, shudder, and shed a tear for those who fought for us, and for all of humanity.

ENDNOTES

INTRODUCTION

1. See Philip Longworth, *The Unending Vigil: A History of the Commonwealth War Graves Commission, 1917–1984* (London: Leo Cooper, 1985).

2. For these powerful stories, see Eric McGeer, *Words of Valediction and Remembrance: Canadian Epitaphs of the Second World War* (St. Catharines: Vanwell, 2008) 12–14.

3. At least 420 Jewish Canadians were killed serving in the forces during the Second World War. Peter J. Usher, "Jews in the Royal Canadian Air Force, 1940–1945," *Canadian Jewish Studies* 20 (2012) 93,109.

4. Jean Portugal (ed.), *We Were There: The Navy, the Army and the RCAF: A Record for Canada*, volume III (Shelburne, ON: Battered Silicon Dispatch Box, 1998) xii.

5. Richard Overy, *The Bombing War: Europe 1939–1945* (London: Allen Lane, 2013) 113–14.

6. David Bashow, *No Prouder Place: Canadians and the Bomber Command Experience, 1939–1945* (St. Catharines: Vanwell, 2005) 456–7.

7. Portugal (ed.), *We Were There*, volume II, 654.

CHAPTER 1: AIR WAR

1. Canadian War Museum (hereafter CWM), 20060191-003, Leslie McCaig diaries, 25 August 1943.

2. Overy, *The Bombing War*, 294.

3. John Terraine, *The Right of the Line: The Royal Air Force in the European War, 1939–1945* (London: Hodder and Stoughton, 1985) 425.

4. Andrew Roberts, *Storm of War: A New History of the Second World War* (London: Penguin Books, 2010) 433.

5. Phillips P. O'Brien, "East versus West in the Defeat of Nazi Germany," *Journal of Strategic Studies* 23.2 (2000) 101.

6. Tim Cook, *The Necessary War: Canadians Fighting the Second World War, Volume I: 1939–1943* (Toronto: Allan Lane, 2014) 319.

7. Brereton Greenhous, Stephen J. Harris, William C. Johnston, William G.P. Rawling, *The Crucible of War, 1939–1945: The Official History of the Royal Canadian Air Force, volume III* (Toronto: University of Toronto Press, 1994) 701.

8. Greenhous et al., *The Crucible of War*, 701.

9. John Cornwell, *Hitler's Scientists: Science, War and the Devil's Pact* (London: Viking, 2003) 343–4.

10. Greenhous et al., *The Crucible of War*, 731.

11. Sir Arthur T. Harris, *Despatch on War Operations, 23rd February, 1942, to 8th May, 1945* (London: Frank Cass, 1995) xviii.

12. Gebhard Aders, *History of the German Night Fighter Force* (London: Janes, 1979) 104.

13. Terraine, *The Right of the Line*, 550.

14. Spencer Dunmore, *Above and Beyond: The Canadians' War in the Air, 1939–45* (Toronto: McClelland & Stewart, 1996) 271.

15. Martin Middlebrook, *The Berlin Raids* (London: Viking, 1988) 148–9.

16. W.A.B. Douglas and Brereton Greenhous, *Out of the Shadows: Canada in the Second World War* (Toronto: Dundurn Press, 1995) 189.

17. CWM, 20060191-003, Leslie McCaig diaries, 21 December 1943.

18. Ken Wright, "One of the Moosemen: Vernon (Doug) Hawkes," *CAHS Journal* (Spring 2010) 23; Leslie Nuttal, "Canadianizaton and the No. 6 Bomber Group RCAF," (PhD: University of Calgary, 1990) 214–15.

19. Christopher Shelley, "Bomber Command and 6 Royal Canadian Air Force Group in the Battle of Berlin," in W.A. March, *Big Sky, Little Air Force* (Ottawa: National Defence, 2011) 47.

20. Spencer Dunmore and William Carter, *Reap the Whirlwind* (Toronto: McClelland & Stewart, 1991) 107–109, 176–177.

21. J. Douglas Harvey, *Boys, Bombs, and Brussels Sprouts: A Knees-up, Wheels-up Chronicle of World War II* (Toronto: McClelland & Stewart, 1981) 155.

22. Bernie Wyatt, *Maximum Effort: The Big Bomber Raids* (Erin: The Boston Mills Press, 1986) 15.

23. Richard Evans, *The Third Reich at War* (New York: Penguin Press, 2009) 460.

24. Directorate of History and Heritage (DHH), 181.003 (D4223), 6 Group Operational Research Section, 13 January 1944.

25. Bernie Wyatt, *Two Wings and a Prayer* (Erin: Boston Mills Press, 1984) 65.

26. Norman Emmott, *One Foot on the Ground* (Toronto: Lugus Publications, 1992) 122.

27. Georgina Matthews (ed.), *Wartime Letters of Flt. Lieut. D.J. Matthews* (self-published, 2003) 172.

28. Serge Durflinger, "'I Regret to Inform You': Next-Of-Kin Notification and Official Condolences: The Case of Flight Lieutenant George J. Chequer, RCAF," *Canadian Military History* 9.4 (2000) 44–55.

29. Canadian Letters and Images Project (hereafter CLIP), James Baker, letter, 10 December 1942.

30. Howard Hewer, *In for a Penny, in for a Pound: The Adventures and Misadventures of a Wireless Operator in Bomber Command* (Toronto: Anchor Canada, 2004) 79.

31. B. Graham McDonald, *Have No Fear: "B.G." Is Here* (Belleville: B.G. McDonald, 2007) 124.

32. Les Perkins, *Flight into Yesterday: A Memory or Two from Members of the Wartime Aircrew Club of Kelowna* (Victoria: Trafford, 2002) 227.

33. CWM, 20030316-001, G. Stuart Brown, *My Life in the R.C.A.F.*, 10.

34. Hewer, *In for a Penny, in for a Pound*, 100.

35. CWM, 20070044-008, Warren Alvin Duffy, letters, July 1st, 1943.

36. Walter Thompson, *Lancaster to Berlin* (Guernsey: The Guernsey Press Company, 1997 [original 1985]) 103.

37. Wyatt, *Two Wings and a Prayer*, 65.

38. Jack Singer (ed.), *Grampa's War in Bomber Command* (self-published, 1998) 70.

39. Allan English, "Leadership and Lack of Moral Fibre in Bomber Command, 1939–1945: Lessons for Today and Tomorrow," in Howard G. Coombs (ed.), *The Insubordinate and the Noncompliant: Case Studies of Canadian Mutiny and Disobedience, 1920 to the Present* (Kingston: Canadian Defence Academy Press, 2007) 114.

40. Larry Milberry, *Canada's Air Force at War and Peace, volume II* (Toronto: CANAV Books, 2000) 27.

41. CWM, MHRC, Walter A. Irwin, *World War II Memoirs of Walter A. Irwin* (self-published, 1998) 24.

42. Hewer, *In for a Penny, in for a Pound*, 98.

43. A.G. Sherwood, *Flying 40 Missions with Red: Memoirs of WWII* (Penticton: Durango Publishing Corp, 2005) 127.

44. Murray Peden, *A Thousand Shall Fall* (Stittsville: Canada's Wings, 1979) 426–7.

45. Max Hastings, *Bomber Command* (New York: Dial Press, 1979) 214.

46. Mark K. Wells, *Courage and Air Warfare: The Allied Aircrew Experience in the Second World War* (London: Frank Cass, 1995) 71.

47. Harvey, *Boys, Bombs, and Brussels Sprouts*, 159.

48. John Harding, *The Dancin' Navigator* (Guelph: Asterisk Communications, 1988) 38.

49. John Patterson, *World War II: An Airman Remembers* (Burnstown: General Store, 2000) 65.

50. Queen's University, Chubby Powers papers, box 64, file D1086, Morale Survey, by Parks and Vlastos, [1942].

51. CWM, oral history interview, 31D 4 CHANCE, page 20.

52. Allan English, *Cream of the Crop: Canadian Aircrew, 1939–1945* (Kingston: McGill-Queen's University Press, 1996) 128; Patrick Bishop, *Bomber Boys: Fighting Back, 1940–1945* (London: Harper, 2007) 249.

53. Leslie Roberts, *Let There Be Wings* (London: George Harrap, 1960) 194.

54. Brereton Greenhous and Hugh A. Halliday, *Canada's Air Forces, 1914–1999* (Montreal: Art Global, 1999) 114.

55. Harvey, *Boys, Bombs, and Brussels Sprouts*, 154–5.

CHAPTER 2: EVADERS AND PRISONERS

1. Flt. Lt. John E. Mahoney, "Stalag Luft III, part I," *The Roundel* 1.12 (October 1949) 11.

2. Wells, *Courage and Air Warfare*, 54.

3. Randall T. Wakelam, *The Science of Bombing: Operational Research in RAF Bomber Command* (Toronto: University of Toronto Press, 2009) 150.

4. Hugh Halliday, *Valour Reconsidered: Inquiries into the Victoria Cross and other Awards for Extreme Bravery* (Toronto: Robin Brass studio, 2006) 83.

5. Stan Coldridge, *Recollections of Stan Coldridge (Halifax Pilot)* (self-published, 2008) 2.

6. Allan S. Walker, *Australia in the War of 1939–1945: Volume IV—Medical Services of the Royal Australian Navy and Royal Australian Air Force with a section on women in the Army Medical Services* (1st edition, 1961) 377–8.

7. DHH, Bio file, Lieutenant Commander R.E. Bartlett, interview, 12 April 1981, 13.

8. CLIP, Jo Foreman, memoirs, no page references.

9. Blake Heathcote, *Testaments of Honour: Personal Histories from Canada's War Veterans* (Toronto: Doubleday, 2002) 172.

10. Emerson Lavender and Norman Sheffe, *The Evaders: True Stories of Downed Canadian Airmen and Their Helpers in World War II* (Toronto: McGraw-Hill Ryerson, 1992) 25–6.

11. Larry Milberry and Hugh Halliday, *The Royal Canadian Air Force at War, 1939–1945* (Toronto: Canav Books, 1990) 437.

12. Flt. Lt. John E. Mahoney, "Stalag Luft III, part I," *The Roundel* 1.12 (October 1949) 12.

13. Dave McIntosh, *Terror in the Starboard Seat* (Don Mills: General Publishing, 1980) 104.

14. Jorg Arnold, *The Allied Air War and Urban Memory: The Legacy of Strategic Bombing in Germany* (Cambridge University Press, 2011) 31–2.

15. Bishop, *Bomber Boys*, 177.

16. [no author], *Memories on Parade: Aircrew Recollections of World War II* (Winnipeg: Wartime Pilots' and Observations' Association, 1995) 216–17.

17. See S.P. Mackenzie, "The Treatment of Prisoners of War in World War II," *Journal of Modern History* 66 (1994) 487–520.

18. For interrogation methods, see S.P. Mackenzie, *The Colditz Myth: The Real Story of POW Life in Nazi Germany* (Oxford: Oxford University Press, 2006) 35–63.

19. Joyce Hibbert, *Fragments of War: Stories from Survivors of World War II* (Toronto: Dundurn, 1985) 242.

20. Gwilym Jones (ed.), *Living History Chronicles* (Burnstown: General Store Pub. House, 2001) 152.

21. Joan Beaumont, "Rank, Privilege and Prisoners of War," *War and Society* 1.1 (1983) 67–94.

22. John Dreiford, "Anything but Ordinary: POW Sports in a Barbed Wire World," *Journal of Sports History* (Fall 2007) 419.

23. CLIP, John Taylor, memoir, n.p.

24. CWM, 20030316–002, Alexander Molnar, Gluck Auf Mel: Memoir—WW2, 9.

25. See Vasilis Vourkoutiotis, "The German Armed Forces Supreme Command and British and American Prisoners-of-War, 1939–1945: Policy and Practice," (Ph.D. thesis: McGill University, 2000) 194.

26. CWM, 20030316–001, G. Stuart Brown, *My Life in the R.C.A.F.*, 27.

27. CWM, 20090029, 58A 1.232.4, George Hill collection, Casey Smyth to Mrs George Hill, n.d. [summer 1944].

28. Jonathan F. Vance, "Men in Manacles: The Shackling of Prisoners of War, 1942–1943," *Journal of Military History* 59.3 (July 1995) 483–504.

29. Andrew Cox, "Five Years as a Prisoner of War," *Canadian Military History* 2.1 (1993) 118.

30. L. Ray Silver, *Last of the Gladiators: A World War II Bomber Navigator's Story* (Shrewsbury, England: Airlife Pub., 1995) 139.

31. Hibbert, *Fragments of War*, 242.

32. CLIP, John Taylor, memoir, n.p.

33. Hibbert, *Fragments of War*, 243.

34. CWM, Oral history interview, 31D 1 FINNIE, page 14 and 16.

35. CWM, 20030316–001, G. Stuart Brown, *My Life in the R.C.A.F.*, 29.

36. Flt. Lt. John Mahoney, "Stalag Luft III: Part 5," *The Roundel* 2 (March 1950) 6.

37. James Crandell, *Thomas Merlin Crandell, Time Line* (self-published, n.d.) 34. In author's possession.

38. Daniel Dancocks, *In Enemy Hands: Canadian Prisoners of War, 1939–45* (Edmonton: Hurtig, 1983) 88.

39. Emily Gann, "Correspondence, Camaraderie, and Community: The Second World War for a Mother and Son" (Master's thesis: Carleton University, 2012); Erle Sinclair Miller, POW Journal, March 31st, 1942.

40. Jonathan Vance (ed.), *Encyclopedia of Prisoners of War and Internment* (Santa Barbara: ABC-CLIO, Inc., 2000) 20.

41. Hong Kong Veterans Commemorative Association (at www.hkvca.ca), Gleanings from the Diary of A Winnipeg Grenadier, H6737 Private Tom Forsyth, ex. P.O.W., 9 January 1941.

42. Heathcote, *Testaments of Honour*, 113.

43. CWM, 20030316-001, G. Stuart Brown, *My Life in the R.C.A.F.*, 28.

44. CLIP, John Taylor, memoir, n.p.

45. CWM, 20030316–001, G. Stuart Brown, *My Life in the R.C.A.F.*, 28.

46. James Hale, *Branching Out: The Story of The Royal Canadian Legion* (Ottawa: Royal Canadian Legion, 1995) 67; David Rolf, "The Education of British Prisoners of War in German Captivity, 1939–1945," *History of Education* 18.3 (1989) 257–65.

47. Murray Winston Bishop and Arthur Adelbert Bishop, *The Bishop Brothers of New Minas in World War Two* (self-published, 2003) 92.

48. Flt. Lt. John E. Mahoney, "Stalag Luft III, part I," *The Roundel* 1.12 (October 1949) 15.

49. Silver, *Last of the Gladiators*, 140.

50. Dancocks, *In Enemy Hands*, 50.

51. George A. Reid, *Speed's War: A Canadian Soldier's Memoir of World War II* (Madrona Books and Publishing, 2007) 53.

52. [no author], *Memories on Parade: Aircrew Recollections of World War II* (Winnipeg: Wartime Pilots' and Observations' Association, 1995) 247.

53. Hibbert, *Fragments of War*, 242.

54. Dancocks, *In Enemy Hands*, 100.

55. Letters in the collection of Adele Fry. John Fry to Prue Evans, 20 May 1944.

56. CWM, 20080029-002, 58A 1 232.3, George Hill collection, Wartime log, 92–94.

57. Dancocks, *In Enemy Hands*, 86.

58. CWM, 20030316-001, G. Stuart Brown, *My Life in the R.C.A.F.*, 27.

59. CWM, 20030316-001, G. Stuart Brown, *My Life in the R.C.A.F.*, 29–30.

60. DHH, Bio file, Joseph E.T. Asselin, Questionnaire for Service Personnel, 10–12.

61. Aidan Crawley, *Escape from Germany: The Methods of Escape Used by RAF Airmen During the Second World War* (London: HMSO, 1985) 3–6.

62. Dominion Institute, The Memory Project, John Anderson.

63. Andrew Cox, "Five Years as a Prisoner of War," *Canadian Military History* 2.1 (1993) 117.

64. For Flood and the tunnels, see Ted Barris, *The Great Escape: A Canadian Story* (Toronto: Dundurn Press, 2013).

65. Jonathan Vance, "Their Duty Twice Over: Canadians in the Great Escape," *Canadian Military History* 3.1 (1994) 116.

66. DHH, Bio file, Lieutenant Commander R.E. Bartlett, interview, 12 April 1981, 37.

67. Philip La Grandeur, *We Flew We Fell We Lived: Stories from RCAF Prisoners of War and Evaders, 1939–1945* (St. Catharines: Vanwell, 2006) 147.

CHAPTER 3: THE HITLER LINE

1. MacGregor Knox, *Hitler's Italian Allies: Royal Armed Forces, Fascist Regime, and the War of 1940–1943* (Cambridge: Cambridge University Press, 2000) 21.

2. For reinforcement challenges, see DHH, Historical Report 166, Administrative Aspects of the Operations of 1 Cdn Inf Div in Italy, December 1943.

3. CWM, MHRC, Jack Shepherd, *March to Fear* (self-published, 2003) 25.

4. John O'Brien, *Through the Gates of Hell and Back: The Private War of a Footslogger from "The Avenue"* (Halifax: New World Publishing, 2010) 103.

5. See Brereton Greenhous, "Would it not have been better to bypass Ortona completely...?" *Canadian Defence Quarterly* (April 1989) 51–5.

6. DHH, Historical Report No. 18, "The Campaign in Southern Italy, Sep–Dec 1943, Information from German Military Documents," 59–60, and 69; Daniel Dancocks, *The D-Day Dodgers*, 187.

7. Robert Thexton, *Times to Remember: Some Recollections of Four and a Half Years Service with the West Nova Scotia Regiment during 1940–1944* (Wolfville, NS: R. Thexton, 2008) 47.

8. Farley Mowat, *The Regiment* (Toronto: McClelland & Stewart, 1973) 67.

9. DHH, CMHQ Report 179, 2.

10. G.W.L. Nicholson, *The Canadians in Italy, 1943–1945* (Ottawa: Queen's Printer, 1955) 678.

11. Norman Gelb, *Ike & Monty: Generals at War* (New York: William Morrow and Company, 1994) 337.

12. Strome Galloway, *The General Who Never Was* (Belleville: Mika Pub., 1981) 193.

13. Colonel Bernd Horn, *Establishing a Legacy: The History of the Royal Canadian Regiment, 1884–1953* (Toronto: Dundurn Press, 2008) 171.

14. Laurence Wilmot, *Through the Hitler Line: Memoirs of an Infantry Chaplain* (Waterloo: Wilfrid Laurier University Press, 2003) 34.

15. See Brandey Barton, "Public Opinion and National Prestige: The Politics of Canadian Army Participation in the Invasion of Sicily, 1942–1943," *Canadian Military History* 15.2 (Spring 2006) 23–34.

16. Christine Leppard, "Politics by Other Means: Canadian 'Strategy' and the Italian Campaign, 1943," *Journal of Military and Strategic Studies* 13.4 (Summer 2011) 1–22.

17. Stephen Brooks, *Montgomery and the Battle of Normandy* (England: The Army Records Society, 2008) 200.

18. LAC, RG 24, v.10,788, 224.C1.2.6013 (D1), RCASC, 5th Canadian Armoured Division, 1943–1944.

19. Rowland Ryder, *Oliver Leese* (London: Hamish, 1987) 155–6.

20. Strome Galloway, *Bravely into Battle* (Don Mills: Stoddart, 1988) 175.

21. Chris Vokes, *Vokes: My Story* (Ottawa: Gallery Books, 1985) 152–3. Also see Mowat, *The Regiment*, 174.

22. Nicholson, *The Canadians in Italy*, 364.

23. Galloway, *The General Who Never Was*, 187.

24. Stanley Scislowski, *Not All of Us Were Brave* (Toronto: Dundurn Press, 1997) 103.

25. George Kitching, *Mud and Green Fields: The Memoirs of Major General George Kitching* (Langley: Battleline Books, 1986) 186–7.

26. Scislowski, *Not All of Us Were Brave*, 117.

27. LAC, RG 24, v. 10780, 224.C1.013 (D14), 1 Cdn Inf Bde Battle, 17 January 1944 [report by the historical officer, interview with Lt. Col. W.S. Rutherford, OC Perth Regiment].

28. LAC, RG 24, v. 15136, War Diary, Perth Regiment, 17 January 1944.

29. Stafford Johnston, *The Fighting Perths* (Stratford: Perth Regiment Veterans' Association, 1964).

30. Fred Cederberg, *The Long Road Home: The Autobiography of a Canadian Soldier in World War II* (Toronto: General Pub., 1984) 87.

31. LAC, RG 24, v. 10450, file 212C1.011 (D1), Battle Experience Questionnaire, No. 27, Major Herbert Fulleston.

32. Nicholson, *The Canadians in Italy*, 370–1.

33. Alex Morrison and Ted Slaney, *The Breed of Manly Men: The History of the Cape Breton Highlanders* (Toronto: Canadian Institute of Strategic Studies, 1994) 147–8.

34. DHH, CMHQ Report 178, 9.

35. E.L.M. Burns, *General Mud: Memoirs of Two World Wars* (Toronto: Clarke, Irwin, 1970) 130.

36. Johnston, *The Fighting Perths*, 70.

37. W.R. Feasby, *Official History of the Canadian Medical Services, 1939–1945, volume I* (Ottawa: E. Cloutier, Queen's Printer, 1953) 172.

38. Scislowski, *Not All of Us Were Brave*, 107.

39. Bill McNeil, *Voices of a War Remembered: An Oral History of Canadians in World War Two* (Toronto: Doubleday Canada, 1991) 238.

40. C.S. Frost, *Once a Patricia* (St. Catharines: Vanwell, 1988) 134.

41. CWM oral history interview, 31D 4 WALKER, page 19–20.

42. Churchill, *Closing the Ring*, 488.

43. See James A. Wood, *We Move Only Forward: Canada, the United States, and the First Special Service Force, 1942–1944* (St. Catharines: Vanwell, 2006).

44. Heathcote, *Testament of Honour*, 231–2.

45. Robert D. Burhams, *The First Special Service Force: A War History of the North Americans, 1942–1944* (Washington: Infantry Journal Press, 1947) 124.

46. Matthew Parker, *Monte Cassino: The Hardest Fought Battle of World War II* (Toronto: Knopf Publishing Group, 2005).

47. Flint Whitlock, *The Rock of Anzio: From Sicily to Dachau, a History of the U.S. 45th Infantry Division* (2005) 265.

48. C.J.C. Molony, *The Mediterranean and Middle East, volume VI* (London: HMSO, 1984) 29.

49. DHH, CMHQ Report 179, 14.

50. J.L. Granatstein, *The Generals: The Canadian Army's Senior Commanders in the Second World War* (Toronto: Stoddart, 1993) 127.

51. DHH, CMHQ Report 179, 8; LAC, RG 24, v. 10881, file 234.C1.012(D3), GOC 1 Cdn Division, Confidential report [issued by Vokes, GOC, 1st] n.d. [March–April 1943].

52. Albert Kesselring, *The Memoirs of Field Marshal Kesselring* (London: William Kimber and Co. Ltd, 1953) 191; F.H. Hinsley, *British Intelligence in the Second World War, Volume III: Its Influence on Strategy and Operations, Part I* (London: Her Majesty's Stationary Office, 1984) 199.

53. CWM oral history, 31D1 Troy, 10.

54. DHH, 141.4A14011(D1), Report of Operations ... in breaking of Gustav and Hitler Line, 1. [no editor], *The Calgary Regiment* (published by the unit in Hilversum, Holland in 1945; reprinted, Vancouver, 1989) chapter 3, page 3.

55. LAC, RG 24, v. 18207, War Diary, 12th Canadian Armored Regiment, 17 May 1944.

56. DHH, CMHQ Report 179, 34.

57. LAC, RG 24, v. 15051, War Diary, Carleton and York Regiment, May 1944, Appendix 16.

58. Kim Beattie, *Dileas: History of the 48th Highlanders of Canada 1929–1956* (Toronto: The 48th Highlanders of Canada, 1957) 525.

59. Charles Allan Eddy, "Before They Were the D-Day Dodgers: 1st Canadian Infantry Division and Operation CHESTERFIELD" (Masters thesis: University of New Brunswick, 2009) 95.

60. Douglas E. Delaney, *The Soldiers' General: Bert Hoffmeister at War* (Vancouver: UBC Press, 2005) 137.

61. RG 24, v. 15239, War Diary, Royal 22e Regiment, 19 May 1944.

62. Jean Allard and Serge Bernier, *The Memoirs of General Jean V. Allard* (Vancouver: University of British Columbia Press) 76–7.

63. Scislowski, *Not All of Us Were Brave*, 185.

64. Gwilym Jones, *To the Green Fields Beyond: A Soldier's Story* (Burnstown: General Store Publishing House, 1993) 93.

65. DHH, 143.121013(D2), History of the Royal Canadian Engineers, 1 Canadian Corps, Operations in Italy, 7.

66. Vokes, *My Story*, 158.

67. LAC, RG 24, v. 10841, 230.C1.(D16), Report on the Hitler Line Defences, [June 1944], 2.

68. DHH, 142.5.M009 (D9), Artillery lessons learned from the Sicilian and Italian Campaigns, 1944–1945, Artillery Lessons, first year of the Italian campaign, n.d., 1.

69. Burns, *General Mud*, 149–50.

70. Doug Delaney, *Corps Commanders: Five British and Canadian Generals at War, 1939–1945* (Vancouver: UBC Press, 2011) 88–95.

71. LAC, RG 24, v. 17505, War Diary, 1 Cdn Fd Hist Section, 23 May 1944.

72. LAC, RG 24, v. 10881, File 224.C1.2013 (D1), Operations of Canadian Artillery in Italy, May to June 1944, 26.

73. LAC, RG 24, v. 10881, File 224.C1.2013 (D1), Operations of Canadian Artillery in Italy, May to June 1944, 16.

74. LAC, RG 24, v.10787, 224.C1.093 (D2), Report of Air Operations in Support of 1 Cdn Corps, 11 May–6 June 44.

75. Farley Mowat, *And No Birds Sang* (Toronto: McClelland & Stewart, 1979) 138.

76. Cederberg, *The Long Road Home*, 121.

77. G.R. Stevens, *Princess Patricia's Canadian Light Infantry, 1919–1957* (Griesbach: Hamilton Gault Barracks, Historical Committee, 1958) 160–1.

78. LAC, RG 24, vol. 12748, 24/DIARIES/8/2, "Report, Hitler Line Defences, by G.S. 1 Cdn Inf Div," Extracts from War Diaries and Memoranda (Series 25), June 1944.

79. John Marteinson (ed.), *We Stand on Guard: An Illustrated History of the Canadian Army* (Montreal: Ovale Publications, 1992) 276.

80. LAC, RG 24, v. 15256, War Diary, Seaforth Highlanders of Canada, 23 May 1944.

81. Bill McAndrew, *Canadians and the Italian Campaign, 1943–1945* (Montreal: Art Global, 1996) 100.

82. Robert L. McDougall, *A Narrative of War: From the Beaches of Sicily to the Hitler Line with the Seaforth Highlanders of Canada, 10 July, 1943–8 June 1944* (Kemptville: Golden Dog Press, 1996) 195.

83. LAC, RG 24, v. 10841, 230C1 (D16), 1 Cdn Inf Div in the Liri Valley, 15–28 May 1944, Appendix VI, 8–9.

84. Ronald Cormier (ed.), *The Forgotten Soldiers: Stories from Acadian Veterans of the Second World War* (Fredericton, N.B.: New Ireland Press, 1992) 31.

85. RG 24, v. 17505, War Diary, 1 Cdn Fd Hist Section, Personal account by Captain R.T. Currelly, 25 May 1944.

86. Frost, *Once a Patricia*, preface.

87. Robert Crozier, *Looking Backward: A Memoir* (self-published, 1998) ix.

88. DHH, CMHQ Report 179, 58.

89. G.W.L. Nicholson, *The Italian Campaign, 1943–1945* (Ottawa: Queen's Printer, 1955) 425.

90. Howard Mitchell, *My War* (self-published, n.d.) 103.

91. McDougall, *A Narrative of War*, 194.

92. John Ellis, Cassino: *The Hollow Victory* (London: Andre Deutsch, 1984) 408–10.

93. LAC, RG 24, v.10927, 244.C5.013(D19) Summary of Operations, 5th Cdn Armoured Division, [Hitler Line] 4 July 1944.

94. LAC, RG 24, v. 10779, file 224.C1.011 (D2), letter to Nicholson, 3 April 1951, diary entry for 25 May 1944.

95. DHH, 141.4A9 (D1), personal stories of members of 9th Cdn Armoured Brigade concerning the Battle of Melfa River, Recollections of the Battle of the Melfa River, n.d [by G.T.D.].

96. DHH, 145.2W 1011 (D3), The Melfa Crossing (by Mahony, VC) 4.

97. LAC, RG 24, 10927, no file number, 5 Cdn Armd Div Reports of Operations, 25 to 31 May 1944, Appendix D(1), Report on operations, Lord Strathcona's Horse.

98. DHH, 141.4A 2011 (D1), Interview with Major Watsford, 16 September 1944.

99. Roy J. Whitsed, *Canadians: A Battalion at War* (Mississauga: Burlington Books, 1996) 144.

100. Peter Stursberg, *The Sound of War: Memoirs of a CBC Correspondent* (Toronto: University of Toronto Press, 1993) 173–4.

101. DHH, 145.2W 1011 (D3), The Melfa Crossing (by Mahony, VC) 10.

102. DHH, 141.4A 2011 (D1), Account of Action by Lt. E.J. Perkins, 9.

103. Eldon S. Davis, *An Awesome Silence: A Gunner Padre's Journey through the Valley of the Shadow* (Wilfrid Laurier Press, 2003) 62.

104. LAC, RG 24, v. 15283, War Diary, The Westminster Regiment, 24 May 1944.

105. Robert Gordon Sawdon, *Another River to Cross* (self-published, 2000) 56–7.

106. Stevens, *Princess Patricia's Canadian Light Infantry*, 154.

107. Michael Pearson Cessford, "Hard in the Attack: The Canadian Army in Sicily and Italy, July 1943–June 1944" (Ph.D. dissertation, Carleton University, 1996) 376–7.

108. Douglas Porch, *The Path to Victory: The Mediterranean Theater in World War II* (New York: Farrar, Straus and Giroux, 2004) 514.

109. See, for example, DHH, 141.4A5011 (D1), Report on Operations from Hitler Line to Ceccano, 24–31 May 1944, for the 5th Armoured Regiment (8th NB Hussars).

110. Scislowski, *Not All of Us Were Brave*, 205.

111. CWM, 20060029–001, letter, Broomhall to Darling, 26 May 1944.

112. Antony Beevor, *The Second World War* (New York: Little, Brown and Co., 2012) 536, 569, 571.

113. LAC, RG 24, v. 17505, War Diary, 1 Cdn Fd Hist Section, Personal account by Captain R.T. Currelly, 25 May 1944.

114. Ronald Gendall Shawcross, *What Was It Like??: A Rifleman Remembers* (Victoria: Trafford, 2004) 155.

115. G.D. Mitchell, *RCHA—Right of the Line: An Anecdotal History of the Royal Canadian Horse Artillery from 1871* (Ottawa: RCHA History Committee, 1986) 129.

116. Kenneth B. Smith, *Duffy's Regiment* (Don Mills: T.H. Best, 1983) 11–12.

117. Ian Gooderson, *A Hard Way to Make War: The Italian Campaign in the Second World War* (London: Conway, 2008) 279–80.

118. J.L. Granatstein, *The Generals: The Canadian Army's Senior Commanders in the Second World War* (Toronto: Stoddart, 1993) 133–4; LAC, RG 24, v. 11005, file WO 214/55, Alexander to Brooke, 29 June 1944.

119. Galloway, *Bravely into Battle*, 196.

CHAPTER 4: PLANNING THE INVASION

1. Forrest C. Pogue, *The Supreme Command* (Washington: Office of the Chief of Military History, Dept. of the Army, 1967) 545.

2. Norman Gelb, *Ike & Monty: Generals at War* (New York: William Morrow and Company, 1994) 12.

3. David M. Glantz and Jonathan M. House, *When Titans Clashed: How the Red Army Stopped Hitler* (Lawrence: University Press of Kansas, 1995) 283.

4. Michael Howeard, *Strategic Deception* (London: Cambridge University Press, 1990) 71–83; also see Ben Macintyre, *Double Cross: The True Story of the D-Day Spies* (New York: Crown, 2012.)

5. Dwight D. Eisenhower, *Crusade in Europe* (Garden City: Doubleday, 1948) 244.

6. On control, see Russell F. Weigley, *Eisenhower's Lieutenants: The Campaign of France and Germany, 1944–1945* (Bloomington: Indiana University Press, 1981) 61; on Harris's appreciation, see Randall Wakelam, "Bomber Harris and Precision Bombing—No Oxymoron Here," *Journal of Military and Strategic Studies* 14.1 (Fall 2011) 12.

7. See Richard J. Overy, "Air Power in the Second World War: Historical Themes and Theories," in Horst Boog (ed.), *The Conduct of the Air War in the Second World War: An International Comparison* (New York: Berg, 1992) 23; Alfred C. Mierzejewski, *The Collapse of the German War Economy, 1944–1945* (Chapel Hill: University of North Carolina Press, 1988) xii–xiii.

8. See Paul A. Ludwig, *P-51 Mustang: Development of the Long-Range Escort Fighter* (Surrey: Ian Allen, 2003).

9. Hayword S. Hanswell Jr., *The Air Plan that Defeated Hitler* (Atlanta: Higgins, 1972) 281–2; Williamson Murray, *Strategy for Defeat: The Luftwaffe, 1933–1945* (Maxwell Air Force Base: Air University Press, 1983) 182; Adam Tooze, *The Wages of Destruction: The Making and Breaking of the Nazi Economy* (London: Allen Lane, 2006) 626–7.

10. Greenhouse, et al., *The Crucible of War*, 292.

11. Paul Kennedy, *Engineers of Victory: The Problem Solvers Who Turned the Tide in the Second World War* (Toronto: HarperCollins, 2013) 131.

12. Richard Davis, *Carl A. Spaatz and the Air War in Europe* (Washington: Centre for Air Force History, 1993) 413–14; D'Este, *Eisenhower*, 514.

13. W.A.B. Douglas, et al., *A Blue Water Navy: The Official Operational History of the Royal Canadian Navy in the Second World War, 1939–1945, volume II, part II* (St. Catharines: Vanwell Publishing, 2007) 231.

14. Douglas, et al. *A Blue Water Navy*, 159.

15. Marc Milner, *Canada's Navy: The First Century* (Toronto: University of Toronto Press, 2010) 138.

16. Milner, *Canada's Navy*, 143.

17. C.P. Nixon, *A River in September: HMCS* Chaudière *1943–1945* (self-published, 1995) 14–15.

18. LAC, RG 24, v. 6797, "Employment of Tribal Destroyers," 7 December 1942.

19. Latham B. Jenson, *Tin Hats, Oilshins & Seaboots: A Naval Journey, 1938–1945* (Toronto: Robin Brass Studio, 2000) 213.

20. Douglas, et al. *A Blue Water Navy*, 194.

21. John Gardam (ed.), *Fifty Years After* (Burnstown: General Store Pub. House, 1990) 28.

22. Michael Whitby, "'Fooling' around the French Coast: RCN Tribal–Class Destroyers in Action, April 1944," *Canadian Defence Quarterly* 19.3 (December 1989) 55.

23. Michael Whitby, "The Case of the Phantom MTB and the Loss of the HMCS *Athabaskan*," *Canadian Military History* 11.3 (Summer 2002) 5–14.

24. CWM oral history, 31D 1 Audet, pages 20–1.

25. Dancocks, *In Enemy Hands*, 146.

26. See LAC, RG 24, v. 6890, file NSS 8870—355/3, Account of the loss of *Athabaskan*, 3 May 1945; and Len Burrows and Émile Beaudoin, *Unlucky Lady: The Life and Death of HMCS Athabaskan* (Stittsville: Canada's Wings, 1992).

27. Carlo D'Este, *Decision in Normandy: The Unwritten Story of Montgomery and the Allied Campaign* (London: Collins, 1994) 58.

28. RG 24, v.10907, file 235.C3.013(D8), Comments on Op Overlord by Maj Gen RFL Keller, as told to Historical Officer, 21 June 1944

29. Terry Copp, *Fields of Fire: The Canadians in Normandy* (Toronto: University of Toronto Press, 2003) 15; also see Geoffrey Hayes, "The Development of the Canadian Army Officer Corps, 1939–1945," (Ph.D. dissertation, University of Western Ontario, 1992).

30. See Andrew Iarocci, "Equipment of the Canadian Infantryman, 1939–1982: A Material/Historical Assessment," *Canadian Military History* 9.4 (2000) 35–43; Jean Bouchery, *The Canadian Soldier in North-West Europe* (Paris: Histoire & Collections, 2003).

31. Mowat, *And No Birds Sang*, 195.

32. Robert C. Engen, *Canadians Under Fire: Infantry Effectiveness in the Second World War* (Montreal: McGill-Queen's University Press, 2009) 121–6, 167–9.

33. Marc Milner, *Stopping the Panzers: The Untold Story of D-Day* (Kansas, University of Kansas Press, 2014) 58–9.

34. Portugal (ed.), *We Were There*, volume II, 648.

CHAPTER 5: D-DAY

1. CWM, 20110078–018, F.H. Baldwin, "The whole horizon exploded: D-Day 36 years later," 1.

2. Alex Souchen, "Beyond D-Day: Maintaining Morale in the 3rd Canadian Infantry Division, June–July 1944," (Master's thesis, University of Ottawa, 2010) 23.

3. RG 24, v. 15270, War Diary, Stormont, Dundas, and Glengarry Highlanders, 1 June 1944; Rollie Bourassa (ed.), *One Family's War: The Wartime Letters of Clarence Bourassa, 1940–1944* (Regina: Canadian Plains Research Centre, 2010) 548.

4. Portugal (ed.), *We Were There*, volume II, 609–10.

5. Reader's Digest, *The Canadians at War, 1939/45* (Redfern, Que.: Reader's Digest, 1986) 316.

6. Ben Mackereth, *To Do or Die* (self-published, 1993) 40.

7. Donald Graves, "'Stepping Forward and Upward': The Royal Canadian Navy and Overseas Operations, 1939–1945," in Richard H. Gimblett (ed.) *The Naval Service of Canada: 1910–2010* (Toronto: Dundurn Press, 2010) 71.

8. Portugal (ed.), *We Were There*, volume I, 14.

9. Michael Whitby, "There Must Be No Holes in Our Sweeping": The 31st Canadian Minesweeping Flotilla on D-Day," *Canadian Military History* 3.1 (1994) 63.

10. Gordon Gross, "A Trip to Remember: An Airman's view of D-Day," *Canadian Military History* 10.2 (Sprint 2001) 77–8.

11. Olivier Wieviorka, *Normandy: The Landings to the Liberation of Paris* (Cambridge: The Belknap Press of Harvard University Press, 2008) 179.

12. Harry Butcher, *My Three Years with Eisenhower* (New York: Simon & Schuster, 1946) 538.

13. Portugal (ed.), *We Were There*, volume VI, 2875.

14. Douglas, et al., *A Blue Water Navy*, 236.

15. Ben Mackereth, *To Do or Die* (self-published, 1993) 49.

16. Daniel P. Malone, "Breaking Down the Wall: Bombarding FORCE E and Naval Fire Support on JUNO Beach," (Master's thesis, University of New Brunswick, 2005) 44–5.

17. Charles Cromwell Martin, *Battle Diary: From D-Day and Normandy to the Zuider Zee and VE* (Toronto: Dundurn Press, 1994) 4.

18. Portugal (ed.), *We Were There*, volume II, 636.

19. "The Technique of the Assault: The Canadian Army on D-Day After-action reports by commanders," *Canadian Military History* 14.3 (2005) 59.

20. Portugal (ed.), *We Were There*, volume II, 648.

21. RG 24, v. 15233, War Diary, Royal Winnipeg Rifles, 6 June 1944.

22. Bruce Tascona, *Little Black Devils: A History of the Royal Winnipeg Rifles* (Canada: Frye Publishing, 1983) 145–6.

23. Portugal (ed.), *We Were There*, volume VI, 2896.

24. Lt. F. Stark, *A History of the First Hussar Regiment, 1856–1945* (published by the regiment, 1951) 56.

25. C.P. Stacey, *The Victory Campaign: The Operations in North-West Europe, 1944–1945, Official History of the Canadian Army in the Second World War* (Ottawa: Queen's Own Printer, 1960) 104.

26. Terry Copp and Gordon Brown, *Look to your Front ... Regina Rifles, a Regiment at War: 1944–45* (Waterloo: Laurier Centre for Military, Strategic and Disarmament Studies, 2001) 34

27. Ronald Gendall Shawcross, *What Was It Like??*, 136.

28. Brown and Copp, *Look to your Front*, 27.

29. Captain Eric Luxton (ed.), *The 1st Battalion: The Regina Rifle Regiment, 1939–1945* (published by the regiment, 1946) 34.

30. Blake Heathcote, *Testaments of Honour*, 284

31. Portugal (ed.), *We Were There*, volume III, 1106.

32. Gordon Bell (ed.), *We Went Where They Sent Us ... and Did as We Were Told (Most of the Time)* (Lantzville, British Columbia: Oolichan Books, 2000) 179.

33. Martin, *Battle Diary*, 7.

34. Stacey, *The Victory Campaign*, appendix B, 650; Portugal (ed.), *We Were There*, volume II, 680.

35. Ben Mackereth, *To Do or Die* (self-published, 1993) 52.

36. Portugal (ed.), *We Were There*, volume II, 554–5.

37. Will R. Bird, *North Shore (New Brunswick) Regiment* (Fredericton: Brunswick Press, 1963) 201–2.

38. No author listed, *Vanguard: The Fort Garry Horse in the Second World War* (Doetinchem, Netherlands: Printed by the Uitgevers-Maatschappij "C. Nisset," 1945) 16.

39. Bird, *North Shore (New Brunswick) Regiment*, 205.

40. Portugal (ed.), *We Were There*, volume IV, 2009.

41. Portugal (ed.), *We Were There*, volume V, 2320.

42. Martin, *Battle Diary*, 14–15.

43. RG 24, v.10913, 235.C3.056 (D1), Operation Overlord, Administrative Plan, 11 May 1944.

44. Portugal (ed.), *We Were There*, volume II, 682.

45. RG 24, v.10986, 265.C7.011 (D1) Interview with Brig H.W. Foster, Commander 7th Brigade, 22 June 1944.

46. Patrick Delaforce, *Churchill's Secret Weapons: The Story of Hobart's Funnies* (London: Pen & Sword, 2008).

47. A.E. Powley, *Broadcast from the Front: Canadian Radio Overseas in the Second World War* (Toronto: Hakkert, 1975) 87.

48. Portugal (ed.), *We Were There*, volume VII, 3404.

49. Sarah Klotz, "Shooting the War: The Canadian Army Film Unit in the Second World War," *Canadian Military History 14*.3 (2005) 32.

50. Stan Biggs, *As Luck Would Have It in War and Peace: Memoirs, 1913 to 2007* (self-published, 2007) 43–4.

51. Portugal (ed.) *We Were There*, volume V, 2545.

52. RG 24, v.10986, 265.C8.013 (D1), Interview with Brig K.G. Blackader, commander of 8th Brigade, 24 June 1944.

53. Williamson Murray and Allan R. Millett, *A War to Be Won: Fighting the Second World War* (Cambridge: Harvard University Press, 2000) 423.

54. Copp, *Fields of Fire*, 55.

55. Walter Warlimont, *Inside Hitler's Headquarters, 1939–1945* (London: Weidenfeld & Nicholson, 1964) 425; Wieviorka, *Normandy*, 204.

56. Stacey, *The Victory Campaign*, 650.

CHAPTER 6: A BATTLE FOR SURVIVAL

1. CWM, 20110078–018, F.H. Baldwin, "The whole horizon exploded: D-Day 36 years later," 3.

2. Whitsed, *Canadians: A Battalion at War*, 3–5.

3. H. Clifford Chadderton, *Excuse Us! Herr Schicklgruber: A Memoir of an Officer who Commanded an Infantry Company of the Royal Winnipeg Rifles (Canadian Army) in Normandy* (Ottawa: War Amputations of Canada, 2004) 30–1.

4. Greenhous et al., *The Crucible of War*, 294.

5. Lieutenant-Colonel Richard M. Ross, *The History of the 1st Battalion Cameron Highlanders of Ottawa (MG)* (Ottawa: published by the regiment, 1948) 43.

6. Louis Lazarus Trenton, *My Eyes Have Seen* (self-published, 2008) 109.

7. Portugal (ed.), *We Were There*, volume V, 2457.

8. CLIP, Leslie Abram Neufeld, letter to parents, 4 June 1944.

9. Bernd Horn and Michel Wyczynski, "A Most Irrevocable Step: Canadian Paratroopers on D-Day, The first 24 hours, 5–6 June 1944," *Canadian Military History* 13.3 (Summer 2004) 20.

10. Don Learment, "Soldier, POW, Partisan: My Experience during the Battle of France, June–September 1944," *Canadian Military History* 9.2 (Spring 2000) 94.

11. See Hubert Meyer, *The 12th SS: The History of the Hitler Youth Panzer Division* (Mechanicburg: Stackpole, 2005); Niklas Zetterling, *Normandy 1944: Germany Military Organization, Combat Power, and Organizational Effectiveness* (Winnipeg: J.J. Fedorowicz, 2000); Roman Jarymowycz, *Tank Tactics: From Normandy to Lorraine* (Boulder: Lynne Rienner, 2001) 97–100, 104–5.

12. Michel Reynolds, *Steel Inferno: 1 SS Panzer Corps in Normandy* (New York: Sarpedon, 1997) 60.

13. "The Technique of the Assault: The Canadian Army on D-Day After-action reports by commanders," *Canadian Military History* 14.3 (2005) 69.

14. Milner, *Stopping the Panzers*, 153, 178–9.

15. John Marteinson and Michael McNorgan, *The Royal Canadian Armoured Corps: An Illustrated History* (Toronto: Robin Brass Studio, 2000) 243.

16. Portugal (ed.), *We Were There*, volume V, 2468.

17. "Analysis of 75 mm Sherman Tank Casualties Suffered Between 6th June and 10th July 1944," *Canadian Military History* 7.1 (Winter 1998) 73.

18. Ray W. Lane, *In Chariots of Iron* (self-published, 2009) 94; Portugal (ed.), *We Were There*, volume 5, 2533.

19. Portugal (ed.), *We Were There*, volume V, 2421.

20. George G. Blackburn, *The Guns of Normandy: A Soldier's Eye View, France 1944* (Toronto: McClelland & Stewart, 1995) 128–9.

21. John English, *Surrender Invites Death: Fighting the Waffen SS in Normandy* (Mechanicsburg: Stackpole Books, 2011) 55.

22. Bill McAndrew, Donald E. Graves, Michael Whitby, *Normandy 1944: The Canadian Summer* (Montreal: Art Global, 1994) 52.

23. Marc Milner, "No Ambush, No Defeat: The Advance on the Vanguard of the 9th Infantry Brigade, 7 June 1944," in Geoffrey Hayes, Mike Bechthold, and Matt Symes, *Canada and the Second World War: Essays in Honour of Terry Copp* (Waterloo: Wilfrid Laurier University Press, 2012) 359.

24. For two opposing views, see Russel A. Hart, *Clash of Arms: How the Allies Won in Normandy* (Boulder: Lynne Rienner, 2001) 248.

25. CWM, MHRC, *1st Battalion, The Regina Rifle Regiment, 1939–1946* (no publisher, 1946) 38.

26. John Macfie, *Sons of the Pioneers: Memories of Veterans of the Algonquin Regiment* (Parry Sound: The Hay Press, 2001) 103.

27. Brian A. Reid, *Named by the Enemy: A History of the Royal Winnipeg Rifles* (Toronto: Robin Brass Studio, 2010) 172–3.

28. CWM, MHRC, Harry Roberts, *A Memoir of a Lad Serving in a Battalion at War*, (unpublished, 2011) unpaginated.

29. Portugal (ed.), *We Were There*, volume IV, 1949.

30. Portugal (ed.), *We Were There*, volume V, 2553.

31. Tony Foulds, "In Support of the Canadians: A British Anti-Tank Regiment's first five weeks in Normandy," *Canadian Military History* 7.2 (Spring 1998) 74.

32. Oliver Haller, "The Defeat of the 12th SS, 7–10 June 1944," *Canadian Military History* 3.1 (1994) 18.

33. *1st Battalion, The Regina Rifle Regiment, 1939–1946* (no publisher, 1946) 40.

34. LAC RG 24, v. 20348, 952.013 (D71), "Report on Experiences of a Panzer Division," 26 August 1944.

35. Frank Proctor, *I Was There: An Autobiography* (self-published, 1999) 308–9.

36. LAC, RG 24, v. 15198, War Diary, Regina Rifles, 15 June 1944.

37. RG 24, v.10986, 265.C7.011 (D1) Interview with Brig H.W. Foster, Commander 7th Brigade, 22 June 1944.

38. Hubert Meyer, *The History of the 12SS Panzer Division Hitlerjugend* (Winnipeg: J.J. Fedorowicz, 1992) 57.

39. Shawcross, *What Was It Like??*, 161.

40. Brown and Copp, *Look to Your Front ... Regina Rifles*, 83.

41. LAC, RG 24, v. 10450, file 212C1.011 (D1), Battle Experience Questionnaire, No. 15, Captain Donald Findlay.

42. LAC, RG 24, v. 10450, file 212C1.011 (D1), Battle Experience Questionnaire, No. 31, Acting Major J.P.G. Kemp.

43. LAC, RG 24, v. 10450, file 212C1.011 (D1), Battle Experience Questionnaire, No. 30, Acting Captain Yuile.

44. Milner, "Stopping the Panzer," 491.

45. Stephen Hart, *Sherman Firefly vs. Tiger: Normandy 1944* (Oxford: Ospery, 2007) 4; David Edgerton, *Britain's War Machine: Weapons, Resources, and Experts in the Second World War* (London: Allan Lane, 2011) 224.

46. Milner, *Stopping the Panzers*, 517–20.

47. Reynolds, *Steel Inferno*, 81.

48. Lieutenant-Colonel W.T. Barnard, *The Queen's Own Rifles of Canada, 1860–1960* (Don Mills: The Ontario Publishing Company, 1960) 201.

49. Portugal (ed.), *We Were There*, volume III, 1047.

50. Alexander McKee, *Caen: Anvil of Victory* (London: Souvenir Press, 1964) 95.

51. Martin, *Battle Diary*, 20.

52. Portugal (ed.), *We Were There*, volume II, 658.

53. On the casualties, see Michael R. McNorgan, "Black Sabbath for the First Hussars: Action at Le Mesnil–Patry," in Donald Graves (ed.), *Fighting for Canada: Seven Battles, 1758–1945* (Toronto: Robin Brass Studio, 2000) 311; Barnard, *The Queen's Own Rifles of Canada, 1860–1960,* 202.

54. Ian J. Campbell, *Murder at the Abbaye: The Story of Twenty Canadian Soldiers Murdered at the Abbaye d'Ardenne* (Ottawa: Golden Dog, 1996) and Howard Margolian, *Conduct Unbecoming: The Story of the Murder of Canadian Prisoners of War in Normandy* (Toronto: University of Toronto Press, 1998) 57–74; Reid, *Named by the Enemy*, 174–9.

55. LAC, Harry Crerar papers, MG 30 E157, v. 5, 958.C.009 (D132), First Canadian Army in the Field to all commanders, 1 August 1944.

56. See Michael E. Sullivan, "Combat Motivation and the Roots of Fanaticism: The 12th SS Panzer Division Hitlerjugend in Normandy," *Canadian Military History* 10.3 (Summer 2001) 43–56, Craig H.W. Luther, *Blood and Honor: The 12th SS Panzer Division "Hitler Youth," 1939–1945* (San Jose: R James Bender Publishing, 1998). For the brutality of the regular

German army, see Sonke Neitzel and Harald Welzer, *Soldaten: On Fighting, Killing and Dying, The Secret World War II Transcripts of German POWs* (Toronto: McClelland and Stewart, 2011) and S.G. Fritz, *Frontsoldaten: The German Soldier in World War Two* (Lexington: University Press of Kentucky, 1995).

57. Martin, *Battle Diary*, 23.

58. Portugal (ed.), *We Were There*, volume II, 683.

59. English, *Surrender Invites Death*, 91–3.

60. LAC, RG 24, v. 13766, War Diary, 3rd Division, Comments on Operation Overlord, 21 June 1944.

61. Beevor, *The Second World War*, 595.

62. Copp, *Fields of Fire*, 86–7.

63. RG 24, v. 15198, War Diary, Regina Rifles, 22 June 1944.

64. LAC, RG 24, v. 12745, Extracts, 2nd Cdn Corps, DDME Branch, War Diary, 2 July 1944.

65. Barnard, *The Queen's Own Rifles of Canada*, 205.

66. CWM, oral history interview, 31D1 Harper 3, pages 4–5.

67. Andrew Iarocci, "Dangerous Curves: Canadian Drivers and Mechanical Transport in Two World Wars," in Geoffrey Hayes, et al. (eds.) *Canada and the Second World War* (Waterloo: WLU Press, 2012) 130.

68. Bird, *North Shore (New Brunswick) Regiment*, 300.

69. Souchen, "Beyond D-Day," 62.

70. Tom Didmon, *Lucky Guy: Memoirs of a World War II Canadian Soldier* (Victoria: Trafford, 2000) 52.

71. CWM, oral history interview, 31D1 Harper 3, page 5.

72. Bird, *North Shore (New Brunswick) Regiment*, 278.

73. For quote see, RG 24, v. 10986, 265.C7.013 (D1) Combat Lessons, 7th Brigade (n.d.). See S. P. Mackenzie, "Vox Populi: British Army Newspapers in the Second World War," *Journal of Contemporary History*, 24. 4 (1989): 665–81.

74. Harold MacDonald and M. A. MacDonald, "In the Heat of Battle: Letters from the Normandy Campaign," *Canadian Military History* 11.2 (2002) 37.

75. Souchen, "Beyond D-Day," 69.

76. Barnard, *The Queen's Own Rifles of Canada*, 205.

77. See Alex Souchen, "The Culture of Morale: Battalion Newspapers in the 3rd Canadian Infantry Division, June–August 1944," *Journal of Military History* 77 (April 2013) 523–56; Barry Rowland and J. Douglas MacFarlane, *The Maple Leaf Forever: The Story of Canada's Foremost Armed Forces Newspaper* (Toronto: Natural Heritage, 1987).

78. LAC, RG 24, v. 15037, War Diary, Canadian Scottish Regiment, *The Tommy Cooker* 1.19 [n.d.].

CHAPTER 7: FIGHTING ON ALL FRONTS

1. See Alan Wilt, *The Atlantic Wall: Rommel's Plan to Stop the Allied Invasion* (New York: Enigma Books, 2004); Murray and Millett, *A War to be Won*, 425.

2. Greenhous et al., *The Crucible of War*, 272.

3. Christopher Evans, "The Fighter-Bomber in the Normandy Campaign," *Canadian Military History* 8.1 (Winter 1999) 30.

4. Robert Bracken, *Spitfire: The Canadians* (Erin: The Boston Mills Press, 1995) 17.

5. Gordon Harrison, *Cross-Channel Attack* (Washington: US Government Printing Office, 1951) 265–6.

6. Greenhouse, et al., *The Crucible of War*, 304–5, 321.

7. Robert Vogel, "Tactical Air Power in Normandy: Some Thoughts on the Interdiction Plan," *Canadian Military History* 3.1 (1994) 40.

8. Milberry and Halliday, *The Royal Canadian Air Force at War, 1939–1945*, 178.

9. Wayne Ralph, *Aces, Warriors & Wingmen: Firsthand Accounts of Canada's Fighter Pilots in the Second World War* (Mississuga: John Wiley & Sons Canada, 2005) 178.

10. CWM oral history interview, 31D 6 FRIEDLANDER, page 13.

11. Paul Johnston, "Tactical Air Power Controversies in Normandy: A Question of Doctrine," *Canadian Military History* 9.2 (Spring 2000) 63; Michael Bechthold, "A Question of Success: Tactical Air Doctrine and Practice in North Africa, 1942–43," *Journal of Military History* 68 (July 2004) 821–51.

12. Bill McRae, "Bed and Breakfast: a Canadian Airman Reflects on Food and Quarters during the Second World War," *Canadian Military History* 9.1 (2000) 69. Also see HDI, Memory Project, Interview, Norman Dawber.

13. RG 24, v. 10553, 215.A21.093 (D2), No. 2 Operational Research Section, 21st Army Group and Operational Research Section, 2nd Tactical Air Force, Joint Report No. 3, "Rocket-Firing Typhoons in Close Support of Military Operations"; "Tactics Employed by Fighter-Bombers Operating Against Special Targets," *Canadian Military History* 15.2 (Spring 2006) 71; Terry Copp (ed.) *Montgomery's Scientists: Operational Research in Northwest Europe: The Work of No.2 Operational Research Section with 21 Army Group June 1944 to July 1945* (Waterloo: Laurier Centre for Military Strategic and Disarmament Studies, 2000) 219–239, 399–406; Evans, "The Fighter-Bomber in the Normandy Campaign," 21–30; and Perry Moore, *Operation Goodwood, July 1944: A Corridor of Death* (Solihull: Helion & Company Ltd, 2007) 171.

14. Vogel, "Tactical Air Power in Normandy," 44–6.

15. RG 24, v.10676, 215.C1.2.013 (D2), Notes on Recent Ops, [RCA], 28 June 1944.

16. MacDonald and MacDonald, "In the Heat of Battle," 37.

17. McAndrew, *Normandy 1944*, 74.

18. D'Este, *Eisenhower*, 498; Tami Davis Biddle, *Rhetoric and Reality in Air Warfare: The Evolution of British and American Ideas about Strategic Bombing, 1914–1945* (Princeton University Press, 2002) 235.

19. See Lindsay Dodd and Andrew Knapp, "'How Many Frenchmen Did You Kill?' British Bombing Policy Towards France (1940–1945)," *Society for the Study of French History* 22.4 (2008) 469–92; William Hitchcock, "The Price of Liberation," MHQ: The Quarterly Journal of Military History 21.3 (Spring 2009) 20–9.

20. Biddle, *Rhetoric and Reality in Air Warfare*, 275.

21. For Montgomery's claims, see Bernard Law Montgomery, *The Memoirs of Field-Marshal the Viscount Montgomery of Alamein* (London: Collins, 1958) 228; for a firm refuting, see D'Este, *Decision in Normandy*.

22. Martin Blumenson, *The Battle of the Generals* (New York: Morrow, 1994) 121.

23. Geoffrey Hayes, *The Lincs: A History of the Lincoln and Welland Regiment at War*, second edition (Waterloo: Wilfred Laurier University, 2007) 20.

24. Bird, *North Shore (New Brunswick) Regiment*, 248.

25. Martin, *Battle Diary*, 33.

26. For the place of the battle in the larger British strategy, see David Patterson, "Outside the Box: A New Perspective on Operation Windsor—The Rationale behind the Attack on Carpiquet, 4 July 1944," *Canadian Military History* 17.2 (Spring 2008) 66–74.

27. G.W.L. Nicholson, *The Gunners of Canada: The History of the Royal Regiment of Canadian Artillery, volume II* (Toronto: McClelland & Stewart, 1967) 285.

28. RG 24, v. 10799, 225.C2.012 (D8), Lessons Learned from Ops during War, by Lt-General G.G. Simonds, 1 July 1944.

29. Bird, *North Shore (New Brunswick) Regiment*, 266.

30. RG 24, v. 10912, 235.C3.035 (D4), Headquarters, 3 Canadian Infantry Division, 12 July 1944.

31. RG 24, v. 10986, 265.C8.013 (D3), Battle Lessons, 3 August 1944, 2.

32. Portugal (ed.), *We Were There*, volume V, 2325.

33. Capt. Bernard-Georg Meitzell, "Part 2," *Canadian Army Journal* (May 1950) 67.

34. Reader's Digest, *The Canadians at War, 1939/45* (Redfern: Reader's Digest, 1986) 362.

35. Reid, *Named by the Enemy*, 186.

36. *We Were There*, volume IV, 1675.

37. Bird, *North Shore (New Brunswick) Regiment*, 284.

38. Captain T.J. Bell, *Into Action with the 12th Field* (Utrecht: J. van Boekhoven, 1945) 58.

39. Portugal (ed.), *We Were There*, volume III, 1101.

40. Bird, *North Shore (New Brunswick) Regiment*, 277.

41. Michael Doubler, *Closing with the Enemy: How GIs Fought the War in Europe, 1944–1945* (Lawrence: University Press of Kansas, 1994) 285.

42. Bird, *North Shore (New Brunswick) Regiment*, 287.

43. Stacey, *The Victory Campaign*, 155.

44. Wilfrid Laurier, Terry Copp Archives, Normandy War Diaries, Montgomery to Crerar, 8 July 1944 and Crerar to Simonds, 10 July 1944; Granatstein, *The Generals*, 167.

45. Stephen Brooks, *Montgomery and the Battle of Normandy* (England: The Army Records Society, 2008)185.

46. MHRC, [no author], *1st Battalion The Regina Rifle Regiment, 1939–1945* (official publication, 1946) 43.

47. On tank and infantry doctrine, see David A. Wilson, "The Canadian Role in Operation 'Charnwood,' 8 July 1944: A Case Study in Tank/Infantry Doctrine and Practice," *Canadian Military History* 8.3 (Summer 1999) 7–21.

48. Lt. Col. Doug Barrie (ed.), *Buron Remembered* (self-published, 2007) no pagination [Donald to Mom and Dad, 19 July 1944].

49. J.A. Snowie, *Bloody Buron* (Erin: Boston Mills Press, 1984) 71–2.

50. Copp, *Fields of Fire*, 104–5.

51. RG 24, v. 12745, 24/AEF/1, Extracts from First Canadian Army Intelligence, No. 28, 27 July 1944.

52. Terry Copp (ed.), *Montgomery's Scientists: Operational Research in Northwest Europe* (Waterloo: LCMSDS, 2000) 436–7; John Ellis, *The Sharp End of War: The Fighting Man in World War II* (Newton Abbot: David & Charles, 1980) 89.

53. Lt. Col. Doug Barrie (ed.) *Buron Remembered* (self–published, 2007) no pagination [Memories of the Padre].

54. Barrie (ed.), *Buron Remembered*, no pagination [Operation Charnwood, Battle of Buron, 8 July 44]; Copp, *Fields of Fire*, 103–4.

55. Portugal (ed.), *We Were There*, volume V, 2560.

56. Gordon Brown, "The Capture of the Abbaye D'Ardenne by the Regina Rifles, 8 July 1944," *Canadian Military History* 4.1 (1995) 91, 93.

57. Terry Copp and Michelle Fowler, "Heavy Bombers and Civil Affairs: First Canadian Army in France, July–September 1944," *Canadian Military History* 22.2 (Spring 2013) 8; Lt. Col. C.D. Stewart Leef, *A Short History of the Fifteenth Canadian Field Ambulance* (self-published, 1998) 23.

58. RG 24, v.15206, War Diary, Cameron Highlanders of Ottawa, diary of Honorable Major John Forth, 10 June 1944.

59. MacDonald and MacDonald, "In the Heat of Battle," 31.

60. Stacey, *The Victory Campaign*, 163–4.

61. Barry M. Gough and James A. Wood, "'One more for Luck': The Destruction of U971 by HMCS *Haida* and HMS *Eskimo*, 24 June 1944," *Canadian Military History* 10.3 (Summer 2001) 10.

62. McAndrew et al., *Normandy 1944*, 101.

63. Marc Milner, *The U–boat Hunters: The Royal Canadian Navy and the Offensive against Germany's Submarines* (Toronto: University of Toronto Press, 1994) 137.

64. Anthony Law, *White Plumes Astern: The Short, Daring Life of Canada's MTB Flotilla* (Halifax: Nimbus Publishing, 1989) 14–15.

65. McNeil, *Voices of a War Remembered*, 298.

66. Law, *White Plumes Astern*, 42.

67. Michael Whitby, "Masters of the Channel Night: The 10th Destroyer Flotilla's Victory off Ile De Batz, 9 June 1944," *Canadian Military History* 2.1 (1993) 4–21; Douglas, et al., *A Blue Water Navy*, 276–9.

68. Jenson, *Tin Hats*, 190.

69. A.G.W. Lamont, *Guns Above, Steam Below in Canada's Navy of WW II: In Canada's Navy of W.W. II* (self-published, 2002) 133.

70. Mark Lynch (ed.), *Salty Dips*, volume II (Ottawa: Ottawa Branch, Naval Officers' Associations of Canada, 1984) 20.

71. Douglas M. McLean, "Confronting Technological and Tactical Change: Allied Anti-Submarine Warfare in the Last Year of the Battle of the Atlantic," *Canadian Military History* 7.3 (1998) 31.

72. Portugal (ed.), *We Were There*, volume I, 198.

73. Cy Torontow (ed.), *There I Was: A Collection of Reminiscences by Members of the Ottawa Jewish Community Who Served in World War II* (Ottawa: Jewish War Veterans and the Ottawa Jewish Historical Society, 1999) 19–20.

74. Douglas, *No Higher Purpose*, 169.

75. Ministry of Defence (Navy), *The U–boat War in the Atlantic, 1939–1945* (London: Her Majesty's Stationery Office, 1984) 83–6.

76. Timothy P. Mulligan, *Neither Sharks Nor Wolves: The Men of Nazi Germany's U-boat Arm, 1949–1945* (Annapolis: US Naval Institute Press, 1999) 251–6.

77. Marc Milner, "Fighting the U–boats, 1939–45," in Richard H. Gimblett (ed.), *The Naval Service of Canada: 1910–2010* (Toronto: Dundurn Press, 2010) 104.

78. Clay Blair, *Hitler's U-boat War: The Hunted, 1942–1945* (New York: Random House, 1998) 707.

79. Douglas, *No Higher Purpose*, 634.

80. Dominion Institute Oral History, John Kilpatrick.

81. Frank Curry, *War at Sea: A Canadian Seaman on the North Atlantic* (Toronto: Lugus, 1990) 43.

CHAPTER 8: OPERATION SPRING

1. Alta R. Wilkinson (ed.), *Ottawa to Caen: Letters from Arthur Campbell Wilkinson* (Ottawa: Tower Books, 1947) 119.

2. Copp, *Fields of Fire*, 117.

3. CWM, 20030316-002, Alexander Molnar, Gluck Auf Mel: Memoir—WW2, 2.

4. Historica-Dominion Institute, *We Were Freedom: Canadian Stories of the Second World War* (Toronto: Key Porter, 2010), 150.

5. Didmon, *Lucky Guy*, 54.

6. Rod Mickleburgh with Rudyard Griffiths, *Rare Courage: Veterans of the Second World War Remember* (Toronto: McClelland & Stewart, 2005) 164.

7. John Buckley, *Monty's Men: The British Army and the Liberation of Europe* (New Haven: Yale University Press, 2013) 4.

8. DHH, 81/289, *Morale in Battle: Analysis*, foreword.

9. For the letters, see LAC, RG 24, v 10784, Censorship Reports, 21 Army Group, Canadian Mail.

10. Geoffrey Hayes, *The Lincs: A History of the Lincoln and Welland Regiment at War* (Alma: Maple Leaf Route, 1986) 122.

11. See Anthony Kellett, *Combat Motivation* (Ottawa: Dept. of National Defence, Operational Research and Analysis Establishment, 1980).

12. Hayes, *The Lincs*, 4.

13. On battle drill, see Timothy Harrison Place, *Military Training in the British Army, 1940–1944* (London: Frank Cass, 2000).

14. LAC, RG 24, v. 10450, file 212C1.011 (D1), Battle Experience Questionnaire, No. 16, Lieutenant Thomas McCoy.

15. Historica-Dominion Institute, *We Were Freedom*, 40.

16. MacDonald and MacDonald, "In the Heat of Battle," 34.

17. Shawcross, *What Was It Like??*, 156.

18. H.G. Gee, *Battle Wastage Rates, British Army, 1940–45* (Waterloo: Laurier Centre for Military Strategic and Disarmament Studies, 2010) 17.

19. Portugal (ed.), *We Were There*, volume III, 1247.

20. Portugal (ed.), *We Were There*, volume III, 1019.

21. LAC, RG 24, v. 15706, War Diary, Hamilton Light Infantry, 25 June 1944.

22. Trenton, *My Eyes Have Seen*, 111.

23. Torontow (ed.), *There I Was*, 39.

24. Macfie, *Sons of the Pioneers*, 69.

25. RG 24, v. 10669, 215.C1.063 (D2), First Canadian Army Report on Honours and Awards.

26. RG 24, v. 10669, 215.C1.063 (D2), First Canadian Army Report on Honours and Awards.

27. William Horrocks, *In Their Own Words* (Ottawa: Rideau Veterans Home Residents Council, 1993) 189.

28. See Joanne Benham Rennick, *Religion in the Ranks: Belief and Religious Experience in the Canadian Forces* (Toronto: University of Toronto Press, 2011).

29. DHH, 145.2C4 (D4), "Battle Narrative Putot-en-Bessin Counter Attack—June 8th, 1944," Lt-Col C. M. Wightman, 7.

30. Barney Danson, *Not Bad for a Sergeant: The Memoirs of Barney Danson* (Toronto: Dundurn Press, 2002) 57.

31. Scislowski, *Not All of Us Were Brave*, 152.

32. Morrison and Slaney, *The Breed of Manly Men,* 140.

33. Charles D. Kipp, *Because We Are Canadians: A Battlefield Memoir* (Vancouver: Douglas & McIntyre, 2003) 139.

34. Macfie (ed.), *Sons of the Pioneers*, 51.

35. CWM, oral history interview, 31D1 Harper 3, page 7–8. On the Canloan officers, Wilfrid Smith, *Code Word: Canloan* (Toronto: Dundurn Press, 1992).

36. Copp, *Fields of Fire*, 109.

37. Steven J. Zaloga, *Bagration 1944: the Destruction of Army Group Centre* (Oxford: Osperey Press, 1996)

38. "General Simonds Speaks: Canadian Battle Doctrine in Normandy," *Canadian Military History* 8.2 (Spring 1999) 71.

39. Portugal (ed.), *We Were There*, volume III, 1255.

40. D'Este, *Decision in Normandy*, 255. On tank repair, see Doug Knight (ed.), *A Collection of RCEME Individual Unit Histories in North-West Europe in World War II* (special report for Canadian War Museum, 2006).

41. John Burwell Hillsman, *Eleven Men and a Scalpel* (Winnipeg: Columbia Press, 1948) 89.

42. Murray and Millett, *A War to Be Won*, 428.

43. Bell, *Into Action with the 12th Field,* 64.

44. Copp, *Fields of Fire*, 159.

45. MacDonald and MacDonald, "In the Heat of Battle," 33.

46. Barnard, *The Queen's Own Rifles of Canada*, 211.

47. Portugal (ed.), *We Were There*, volume V, 2444.

48. LAC, RG 24, v. 10797, file 225.C2.008 (D8), Lt. Gen. Simonds, GOC's Activities, 18–20 July 1944.

49. For the full speech see, "General Simonds Speaks: Canadian Battle Doctrine in Normandy," *Canadian Military History* 8.2 (Spring 1999) 64–76.

50. Greenhous, et al., *The Crucible of War*, 312–13.

51. John S. Edmondson, "The Pawns of War: Personal Account and Study of Aspects of the Attack on Verrières Ridges by the South Saskatchewan Regiment on 20 July 1944 by Lt. Col. John S. Edmondson," (self-published, 2003) 9.

52. John Maker, "The Essex Scottish Regiment in Operation Atlantic: What Went Wrong?" *Canadian Military History* 18.1 (Winter 2009) 13–16, 19.

53. RG 24, v. 12745, 24/AEF/1, Canadian Operations—North West Europe, War Diary, The Essex Scottish Regiment, 21 July 1944.

54. Nicholson, *The Gunners of Canada*, 299.

55. Brian A. Reid, *No Holding Back: Operation Totalize : Normandy, August 1944* (Toronto: Robin Brass Studio, 2005) 48.

56. Delaney, *Corps Commanders*, 226.

57. Stacey, *The Victory Campaign*, 176; RG 24, 215.C1.065 (D10), Battle Casualties, NWE, from D-Day to 22 July 1944, 25 Sept 1958.

58. Copp, *Fields of Fire*, 153, 157–8.

59. Stacey, *The Victory Campaign*, 183–5; Wilmot, *Struggle for Europe*, 447–9.

60. Norman Gelb, *Ike & Monty: Generals at War* (New York: William Morrow and Company, 1994) 322.

61. David R. O'Keefe, "Fortune's Fate: The Question of Intelligence for Operation Spring, Normandy, 25 July 1944," *Canadian Defence Quarterly* 24.3 (March 1995) 20–1.

62. English, *Surrender Invites Death*, 137.

63. RG 24, v. 10911, 235.C3.016 (D9), 3rd Cdn Div Operational Order, No. 6, Operation Spring.

64. RG 24, v. 10912, 3·CD 1–8, Artificial Moonlight, 5 August 1944.

65. No author listed, *Vanguard: The Fort Garry Horse in the Second World War* (Doetinchem, Netherlands: Printed by the Uitgevers-Maatschappij 'C. Nisset", 1945) 46.

66. J.L. Granatstein, *Canada's Army: Waging War and Keeping the Peace* (Toronto: University of Toronto Press, 2003) 268.

67. Stacey, *The Victory Campaign*, 190.

68. Didmon, *Lucky Guy*, 57.

69. Roman Jarymowycz, "German Counterattacks during Operation 'Spring': 25–26 July 1944," *Canadian Military History* 2.1 (1993) 79.

70. Marteinson and McNorgan, *The Royal Canadian Armoured Corps*, 257.

71. Didmon, *Lucky Guy*, 61.

72. J.M. Rockingham, "The Royal Hamilton Light Infantry at Verrières," *Canadian Military History* 2.1 (1993) 90–2.

73. Hayes, *The Lincs*, 122.

74. RG 24, v. 12745, 24/AEF/1, Canadian Operations—North West Europe, Extracts, 5 September 1944, 12.

75. Terry Copp, "Operation Spring: An Historian's View," *Canadian Military History* 12.1–2 (2003) 64–5.

76. Terry Copp, "Fifth Brigade: Verrières Ridge," *Canadian Military History* 1.1–2 (1992) 62.

77. Jones (ed.) *Living History Chronicles*, 167.

78. Alexander Fitzgerald-Black, "Investigating the Memory of Operation Spring: The Inquiry into the Black Watch and the Battle of St. André-sur-Orne, 1944–46," *Canadian Military History* 21.2 (Spring 2012) 29.

79. McAndrew, *Normandy, 1944*, 126.

80. Stacey, *The Victory Campaign*, 194.

81. Copp, "Fifth Brigade: Verrières Ridge," 61.

82. Dominick Graham, *The Price of Command: A Biography of General Guy Simonds* (Toronto: Stoddart, 1993) 279–80.

83. C.P. Stacey, *A Date with History: Memoirs of a Canadian Historian* (Ottawa: Deneau Publishers, 1983) 177.

84. Copp, *Fields of Fire*, 180.

CHAPTER 9: WAR AND MEDICINE

1. Hillsman, *Eleven Men and a Scalpel*, 34–5.

2. Desmond Morton, *When Your Number's Up: The Canadian Soldier in the First World War* (Toronto: Random House, 1993) 181.

3. Bill Rawling, "To the Sound of the Guns: Canadians and Combat Surgery, 1938–1953," *Canadian Military History* 6.1 (Spring 1997) 60.

4. Colonel S.W. Thompson, "Wounded in Sicily, 12 July 1943," *Canadian Military History* 2.2 (1993) 109.

5. John O'Brien, *Through the Gates of Hell and Back: The Private War of a Footslogger from "The Avenue"* (Halifax: New World Publishing, 2010) 72.

6. *We Were There*, volume IV, 1743.

7. *We Were There*, volume IV, 1740.

8. Dominion Institute, The Memory Project, George Couture.

9. Ben Mackereth, *To Do or Die* (self-published, 1993) 55.

10. Mackereth, *To Do or Die*, 58.

11. RG 24, v. 12745, Extracts, RCAMC No. 11 Canadian Field Ambulance, July 1944, Appendix 9.

12. G.W.L. Nicholson, *Seventy Years of Service: A History of the Royal Canadian Army Medical Corps* (Ottawa: Borealis Press, 1977) 146; Heathcote, *Testament of Honour*, 149.

13. Bill Rawling, *Death Their Enemy: Canadian Medical Practitioners and War* (self-published, 2001) 192.

14. "Joe Boy," 16–17 August 1944, unpublished manuscript based on war diaries; courtesy of Dr. Alec Douglas.

15. Portugal (ed.), *We Were There*, volume V, 2231.

16. Historica-Dominion Institute, *We Were Freedom*, 119.

17. J.L. Granatstein and Dean Oliver, *The Oxford Companion to Canadian Military History* (Don Mills: Oxford University Press, 2010) 267.

18. McNeil, *Voices of a War Remembered*, 254.

19. Horrocks, *In Their Own Words*, 190.

20. Portugal (ed.), *We Were There*, volume II, 534.

21. Angus Campbell Derby, *Not Least in the Crusade: Memoirs of a Military Surgeon* (self-published, 2005) no pagination.

22. Frost, *Once a Patricia*, 134.

23. Terry Copp, *No Price Too High: Canadians and the Second World War* (Toronto: McGraw-Hill Ryerson, 1996) 194.

24. See Ryan Flavelle, "Help or Harm: Battle Exhaustion and the RCAMC during the Second World War," *Journal of Military and Strategic Studies* 9.4 (Summer 2007) 1–22.

25. Mathew Halton, "Losing Your Nerve," CBC Radio archives, December 4, 1944.

26. J.W.B. Barr, *From Barnyard to Battlefield and Beyond: The Story of a Military Medical Officer* (Ottawa: Borealis Press, 2005) 136.

27. Martin Blumenson, *Breakout and Pursuit* (Washington: Office of the Chief of Military History, 1961) 175.

28. Terry Copp and Bill McAndrew, *Battle Exhaustion: Soldiers and Psychiatrists in the Canadian Army, 1939–1945* (Montreal: McGill-Queen's University Press, 1990) 187.

29. T.E. Dancey and B.H. McNeel, "The Personality of the Successful Soldier," *American Journal of Psychiatry* 11.5 (November 1945) 337.

30. Terry Copp and Mark Humphries, *Combat Stress in the 20th Century: The Commonwealth Perspective* (Kingston: Canadian Defence Academy Press, 2010), 245; Copp, *No Price Too High*, 170; Copp, *Fields of Fire*, 123.

31. Mary Jo Leddy, *Memories of War, Promise of Peace* (Toronto: Lester & Orpen Dennys, 1989) 107.

32. Chadderton, *Excuse Us!*, 86.

33. Copp and McAndrew, *Battle Exhaustion*, 178.

34. W.J. McAndrew, "Recording the War: Uncommon Canadian Perspectives of the Italian Campaign," *Canadian Defence Quarterly* 18.3 (Winter 1988), 48.

35. A.M. Jack Hyatt and Nancy Geddes Poole, *Battle for Life: The History of No. 10 Canadian Stationary Hospital and No. 10 Canadian General Hospital in Two World Wars* (Waterloo: Laurier Centre for Military, Strategic and Disarmament Studies, 2004) 129–30.

36. CWM, oral history interview, 31D 5 SLOAN, 8.

37. Mickleburgh with Griffiths, *Rare Courage*, 134.

38. Portugal (ed.), *We Were There*, volume V, 2238.

39. McNeil, *Voices of a War Remembered*, 89.

40. Kevin Brown, *Fighting Fit: Health, Medicine and War in the Twentieth Century* (London: The History Press, 2008) 136.

41. Biggs, *As Luck Would Have It*, 69.

42. *The Canadians at War 1939/45* (Montreal: Reader's Digest, 1969) 99.

43. Portugal (ed.), *We Were There*, volume V, 2518.

44. See E.R. Mayhew, *The Reconstruction of Warriors: Archibald McIndoe, the Royal Air Force and the Guinea Pig Club* (London: Greenhill Books, 2004).

45. *The Canadians at War 1939/45*, 98.

46. George Duncan Mitchell, *RCHA—Right of the Line: An Anecdotal History of the Royal Canadian Horse Artillery from 1871* (Ottawa: RCHA History Committee, 1986) 284.

CHAPTER 10: THE DRIVE TO FALAISE

1. Chester Wilmot, *The Struggle for Europe* (London: Collins, 1954) 313.

2. Ralph, *Aces, Warriors & Wingmen*, 111.

3. CWM oral history interview, 31D 6 McKAY, page 20.

4. Steve Pitt, *Day of the Flying Fox: The True Story of World War II Pilot Charley Fox* (Toronto: Dundurn, 2008).

5. Shawcross, *What Was It Like??*, 166.

6. Bird, *North Shore (New Brunswick) Regiment*, 354. Also see RG 24, v. 10913, 235. C3.093 (D1), Air Support, report by historical officer, 29 August 1944.

7. CLIP, John Fitzgerald, letter, 17 August 1944. Also see, RG 24, v. 10671, 215. C1.091 (D1), Lecture to the Canadian Staff Coruse, 25 July 1946, by Major-General C.C. Mann.

8. John Morgan Gray, *Fun Tomorrow: Learning to Be a Publisher and Much Else* (Toronto: Macmillan of Canada, 1978) 282.

9. Buckley, *Monty's Men*, 166–9.

10. LAC, MG 30 E157, v. 2, H. D. G. Crerar Papers, 21 Army Group M516, 4 August 1944.

11. Paul Dickson, *A Thoroughly Canadian General: A Biography of General H.D.G. Crerar* (Toronto: University of Toronto Press, 2007) 270.

12. See Crerar Papers, v. 8, D181, Crerar to Montgomery, 24 July 1944; RG 24, v. 10637, 215.C1.013 (D22), Memo on the Circumstances of the planning of operations Rawlingson and Byng.... [n.d.].

13. Richard Lamb, *Montgomery in Europe, 1943–1945* (London: Buchan and Enright, 1983) 253.

14. Granatstein, *The Generals*, 110–11.

15. LAC, RG 24, v. 11001, 215C1.011 (D1), First Canadian Army Report, 7 August to 23 August 1944, by Gen H.D.G. Crerar.

16. Crerar Papers, v. 2, Outline plan for Operation "Totalize"; on challenges of coordination, see Ian Gooderson, "Heavy and Medium Bombers: How Successful Were They in the Tactical Close Air Support Role During World War II?," *Journal of Strategic Studies* 15.3 (1992) 395–6.

17. Delaney, *Corps Commanders*, 228.

18. RG 24, v. 10669, 1 Cdn Armoured Personnel Carrier Sqn, 23 Oct 1944; John R. Grodzinski, "Kangaroos at War: The History of the 1st Canadian Armoured Personnel Carrier Regiment," *Canadian Military History* 4.2 (Autumn 1995) 44–5.

19. McAndrew, *Normandy 1944*, 130.

20. Granatstein, *Canada's Army*, 271.

21. Crerar papers, v. 2, Appreciation of probable enemy reaction to Operation Totalize prepared by Lt.-Col. P.E.R. Wright, 7 August 1944.

22. Major D.W. Grant, *Carry On: The History of the Toronto Scottish Regiment (M.G.), 1939–1945* (1949) 86.

23. Special Interrogation Report, "Brigadefiihrer Kurt Meyer, Commander 12th SS Panzer Division 'Hitler Jugend' (6 June–25 August 1944), *Canadian Military History* 11.4 (Autumn 2002) 64.

24. RG 24, v. 10649, 215.C1.016 (D15), Operation Totalize, 1 August 1944.

25. No author listed, *Vanguard*, 51.

26. Copp, *Fields of Fire*, 200.

27. Terry Copp, *Cinderella Army: The Canadians in Northwest Europe, 1944–1945* (Toronto: University of Toronto Press, 2006) 291.

28. Macfie (ed.), *Sons of the Pioneers*, 48.

29. Portugal (ed.), *We Were There*, volume III, 1075.

30. Reid, *No Holding Back*, 221.

31. RG 24, v. 11001, 215C1.011 (D1), First Canadian Army Report, 7 August to 23 August 1944, by Gen H.D.G. Crerar, 2. Also see, Special Interrogation Report, "Brigadefiihrer Kurt Meyer, Commander 12th SS Panzer Division 'Hitler Jugend' (6 June–25 August 1944), *Canadian Military History* 11.4 (Autumn 2002) 66.

32. McAndrew, *Normandy 1944*, 138.

33. Wieviorka, *Normandy*, 245.

34. Hubert Meyer, *The History of the 12. SS-Panzerdivision "Hitlerjugend,"* trans. H. Harri Henschler (Winnipeg: J.J. Fedorowicz, 1994) 172–6; Roman Johnn Jarymowycz, "Canadian Armour in Normandy: Operation 'Totalize' and the Quest for Operational Maneuver," *Canadian Military History* 7.2 (Spring 1998) 19–40.

35. Reid, *No Holding Back*, 242–3 and 410–30.

36. Chadderton, *Excuse Me!*, 111.

37. Crerar papers, v. 5, 958C.009 (D118) Crerar to 2nd Cnd Corps, 10 August 1944; Jody Perrun, "Best-Laid Plans: Guy Simonds and Operation Totalize, 7–10 August 1944," *Journal of Military History* 67.1 (January 2003) 167–8.

38. MacDonald and MacDonald, "In the Heat of Battle," 39.

39. Jones (ed.), *Living History Chronicles*, 54–5.

40. CWM, 20030008–004, Into Battle with the 26th Canadian Field Battery (unpublished, 1946) 9.

41. Ray W. Lane, *In Chariots of Iron* (self-published, 2009) 74.

42. For the failure in communication, see Mike Bechthold, "Lost in Normandy: The Odyssey of Worthington Force, 9 August 1944," *Canadian Military History* 19.2 (Spring 2010) 5–24.

43. Capt. Bernard-Georg Meitzell, "Part 2," *Canadian Army Journal* (May 1950) 71.

44. Macfie (ed.), *Sons of the Pioneers*, 25.

45. Ibid.

46. RG 24, v. 15000, War Diary, Algonquin Regiment, Appendix, "The Algonquins First Battle Inoculation by Lt. Ken Gartley."

47. RG 24, v. 14049, War Diary, 4 Canadian Armoured Brigade, 9 August 1944; Bechthold, "Lost in Normandy," 21.

48. Reid, *No Holding Back*, 333.

49. Angelo N. Caravaggio, "Commanding the Green Centre Line in Normandy: A Case Study of Division Command in the Second World War," (Ph.D. dissertation, Wilfrid Laurier University, 2009) 214–16.

50. Copp, *Fields of Fire*, 211.

51. Blumenson, *The Battle of the Generals*, 273–4; Murray and Millett, *A War to Be Won*, 432.

52. Dickson, *A Thoroughly Canadian General*, 313.

53. Donald Graves, *Century of Service: The History of the South Alberta Light Horse* (Toronto: Published for the South Alberta Light Horse Regiment Foundation by Robin Brass Studio, 2005) 120; Graham, *Simonds*, 154.

54. DHH, 314.009(D324) Report on Flame Throwers in Attacks ... 8 August 1944.

55. *Vanguard*, 55–7.

56. RG 24, v. 10671, 215.C1.093 (D2), Operation Tractable, report, 8 October 1946.

57. Portugal (ed.), *We Were There*, volume II, 694–5.

58. Bill Rawling, "To the Sound of the Guns: Canadians and Combat Surgery, 1938–1953," *Canadian Military History* 6.1 (Spring 1997) 63.

59. Stacey, *The Victory Campaign*, 243.

60. Bell, *Into Action with the 12th Field*, 73–4.

61. RG 24, v. 10913, 235.C3.093 (D1), Air Support, report by historical officer, 29 August 1944

62. Ian Gooderson, *Air Power at the Battlefront: Allied Close Air Support in Europe 1943–45* (London: Frank Cass, 1998) 33.

63. RG 24, v. 10685, 215C1.98 (D137), Interrogation report of 12th SS prisoners of war, 17 August 1944.

64. Stephen Brooks, *Montgomery and the Battle of Normandy* (England: The Army Records Society, 2008) 185, 192, 200, 206.

65. RG 24, v. 10912, 235.C3.035 (D4) Headquarters, 3 Canadian Infantry Division, 12 July 1944.

66. RG 24, v. 11001, 215C1.011 (D1), First Canadian Army Report, 7 August to 23 August 1944, by Gen H.D. G. Crerar, 3.

67. Evans, "The Fighter-Bomber in the Normandy Campaign," 28.

68. Max Hastings, *Overlord: D-Day and the Battle for Normandy* (London: Michael Joseph, 1984) 247.

69. Capt. Bernard-Georg Meitzell, "Part 2," *Canadian Army Journal* (May 1950) 73.

70. Portugal (ed.), *We Were There*, volume V, 2424.

71. Russell A. Hart, *Clash of Arms: How the Allies Won in Normandy* (London: Lynne Rienner Publishers, 2001) 357.

72. Paul Fussell, *Wartime: Understanding and Behaviour in the Second World War* (Oxford: Oxford University Press, 1989) 131.

73. See Leonard V. Smith, *Between Mutiny and Obedience* (Princeton: Princeton University Press, 1994).

74. Arthur Bridge, "In the Eye of the Storm, A Recollection of Three Days in the Falaise Gap, 19–21 August 1944," *Canadian Military History* 9.3 (2000) 64.

75. See Donald Graves, *South Albertans: A Canadian Regiment at War* (Toronto: Robin Brass, 1999) 146–7.

76. Copp, *No Price Too High*, 177.

77. Bridge, "In the Eye of the Storm," 68.

78. Lane, *In Chariots of Iron*, 98.

79. David Bercuson, *Maple Leaf Against the Axis: Canada's Second World War* (Toronto: Stoddart, 1995) 232.

80. Eisenhower, *Crusade in Europe*, 279.

81. Sullivan, "Combat Motivation and the Roots of Fanaticism," 42. See P. Whitney Lackenbauer and C.W. Madsen, *Kurt Meyer on Trial: A Documentary Record* (Kingston: Canadian Forces Leadership Institute, 2007).

82. Murray and Millett, *A War to Be Won*, 445.

83. Rick Atkinson, *The Guns at Last Light: The War in Western Europe, 1944–1945* (New York: Henry Holt, 2013) 182.

84. On Canadian casualties, see Terry Copp, "To the Last Canadian? Casualties in 21st Army Group," *Canadian Military History* 18.1 (Winter 2009) 3–6, Table 1; Bernard Law Montgomery, *The Memoirs of Field Marshal Montgomery* (New York: Signet, 1959) 277.

85. Gee, *Battle Wastage Rates,* 14–15.

86. Ellis, *The Sharp End of War*, 158; Stacey, *The Victory Campaign*, 284.

87. Stacey, *The Victory Campaign*, 306.

88. For a brief recounting of the historiographical debates over Normandy, see John Buckley, "Introduction," in John Buckley (ed.), *The Normandy Campaign: Sixty Years On* (London: Routledge, 2006) 1–11.

89. On the manpower issue, see David French, *Raising Churchill's Army* (Oxford: Oxford University Press, 2000) 244–9.

90. Granatstein, *The Generals*, 146.

91. Blackburn, *The Guns of Normandy*, xiii–xiv.

CHAPTER 11: THE GOTHIC LINE

1. Alexander of Tunis, *The Alexander Memoirs* (London: Cassell, 1962) 127.

2. Granatstein, *The Generals*, 107.

3. Nicholson, *The Canadians in Italy*, 452.

4. RG 24, v. 10788, 224.C1.2.013 (D23), Canadian operations in the Mediterranean Area, May–June 1944, Series 24, [with Burns's hand-written notes]. Also see Burns, *General Mud*, 164–8.

5. McAndrew, *The Canadians in Italy*, 112.

6. Burns, *General Mud*, 168.

7. Imperial War Museum (IWM), Papers of General Sir Oliver Leese, Box 4, Leese to Sir John Kennedy, 1 August 1944. I thank Dr. Doug Delaney for sharing this research.

8. E.L.M. Burns, *Manpower in the Canadian Army, 1939–1945* (Toronto: Clarke, Irwin, 1956) 175–6.

9. Dancocks, *D-Day Dodgers*, 293.

10. Gordie Bannerman, *Memoirs of Gordie Bannerman—World War II*, unpublished memoir, Chapter 84, http://gordiebannerman.com. Also see, Laurel Halladay, "'It Made Them Forget About the War for a Minute': Canadian Army, Navy, and Air Force Entertainment Units During the Second World War," *Canadian Military History* 11.4 (Autumn 2002) 21–35.

11. Jeffrey Keshen, *Saints, Sinners, and Soldiers: Canada's Second World War* (Vancouver: University of British Columbia Press, 2004) 248.

12. Scislowski, *Not All of Us Were Brave*, 101.

13. Kathryn Rose, "Frontlines and Headlines: The 'Maple Leaf' Newspaper and Army Culture during the Second World War," *Canadian Army Journal* 9.3 (Winter 2006) 82.

14. Dick Malone, *Missing From the Record* (Toronto: Collins, 1946) 80–2.

15. Davis, *An Awesome Silence*, 54.

16. Barry D. Rowland, *Herbie and Friends: Cartoons in Wartime* (Toronto: Natural Heritage/Natural History Inc., 1990). On the quote, see Colonel Edward William Cutbill, *A Brown Job's War* (self-published, 2007) 97.

17. Craig B. Cameron, *Born Lucky: RSM Harry Fox, MBE, One D-Day Dodger's Story* (St. Catharines: Vanwell, 2005) 79.

18. William F. Rannie (ed.), *To the Thunderer His Arms: The Royal Canadian Ordnance Corps* (Lincoln: W.F. Rannie, 1984), 144.

19. Lee Windsor, "Anatomy of Victory: 1st Canadian Corps, Allied Containment Strategy and the Battle for the Gothic Line," (Ph.D. dissertation, University of New Brunswick, 2006) 11–12; Matthew Jones, *Britain, The United States and the Mediterranean War, 1942–1944* (London: MacMillan, 1996) 150.

20. Army Headquarters Report No. 21, pages 4–5; McAndrew, *Canadians and the Italian Campaign*, 116.

21. Army Headquarters Report No. 21, pages 13–14.

22. Atkinson, *The Guns at Last Light*, 96.

23. William McAndrew, "Eighth Army at the Gothic Line: Commanders and Plans," *RUSI* (March 1986) 55.

24. McAndrew, *Canadians and the Italian Campaign*, 117.

25. Christine Leppard, "Documenting the D-Day Dodgers: Canadian Field Historians in the Italian Campaign, 1943–1945," *Canadian Military History* 18.3 (2009) 14.

26. Bannerman, *Memoirs of Gordie Bannerman*, Chapter 100.

27. RG 24, v.10982, 264.C2.013 (D3), Interview with Brigadier T.G. Gibson, 1.

28. Army Headquarters Report No. 21, pages 22, quote from 23.

29. RG 24, v.15115, War Diary, Loyal Edmonton Regiment, After Action Report, 26–28 August 1944.

30. Dancocks, *The D-Day Dodgers*, 310.

31. Mitchell, *My War*, 101.

32. RG 24, v. 10779, 224.C1.013 (D4), Olive, The Battle for the Gothic Line, 1 Canadian Corps Narrative of Events, 4.

33. Burns, *General Mud*, 185.

34. David A. Gordon, *The Stretcher Bearers* (Stroud: Pacesetter Press, 1995) 73.

35. Wilmot, *Through the Hitler Line*, 81.

36. Wilmot, *Through the Hitler Line*, 78.

37. Nicholson, *The Canadians in Italy*, 515.

38. G.R. Stevens, *Princess Patricia's Canadian Light Infantry, 1919–1957* (Griesbach: Hamilton Gault Barracks, Historical Committee, 1958) 185.

39. Cutbill, *A Brown Job's War*, 81.

40. Alex Morrison, *The Breed of Manly Men: the History of the Cape Breton Highlanders* (Toronto: Canadian Institute of Strategic Studies, 1994) 228–9.

41. Scislowski, *Not All of Us Were Brave*, 251–2.

42. Stafford Johnston, *The Fighting Perths: The Story of the First Century in the Life of a Canadian County Regiment* (Stratford: Perth Regiment Veterans' Association, 1964) 88–90.

43. Hunter Dunn, *Memoirs of a WW II Armoured Officer* (self-published, 2005) 72.

44. RG 24, v. 10982, 264.C11.013 (D6), 11th Brigade and the Smashing of the Gothic Line, n.d. [2 September 1944]; Nicholson, *The Canadians in Italy*, 516.

45. RG 24, v. 10989, 270.C5 (D5) Lessons Learned, HQ, 5th Cdn Armd Division, Report by Captain R.T. Currelly, 15 Sept 1944.

46. R.H. Roy, *Sinews of Steel: The History of the British Columbia Dragoons* (Kelowna: British Columbia Dragoons, 1965) 302–3.

47. RG 24, v. 10982, 264.C11.013 (D6), 11th Brigade and the Smashing of the Gothic Line, n.d. [2 September 1944].

48. Nicholson, *The Canadians in Italy*, 521.

49. Nicholson, *The Canadians in Italy*, 524.

50. McAndrew, *Canadians and the Italian Campaign*, 126.

51. Windsor, "Anatomy of Victory," 310, note 649.

52. RG 24, v. 10779, 224.C1.013(D13), Summary of Operations, 3 September 1944.

53. RG 24, v. 10787, 224.C1.093 (D3), Results of Allied Bombing Attacks in Italy, period 8 July to 3 Oct. 1944.

54. Cederberg, *The Long Road Home*, 157.

55. RG 24, v. 10927, 244.C5.013 (D19) Summary of Operations, 5th Cdn Armoured Division, 15 Sept 1944.

56. Robert Crozier, *Looking Backward: A Memoir* (self-published, 1998) 66.

57. RG 24, v. 10989, 270.C5 (D5) Lessons Learned, HQ, 5th Cdn Armd Division, Report by Captain R.T. Currelly, 15 Sept 1944.

58. Ron and Merla Lawruck, *For Love and Country: A Canadian Soldier's Story, A Biography of Ted Patrick* (self-published, 2011) 117.

59. Crozier, *Looking Backward*, 67.

60. Nicholson, *The Canadians in Italy*, 535–7.

61. McAndrew, *The Canadians in Italy*, 128; Nicholson, *The Canadians in Italy*, 536.

62. Serge Bernier, *The Royal 22e Regiment, 1914–1999* (Montreal: Art Global, 2000) 157.

63. Thomas Raddall, *West Novas: A History of the West Nova Scotia Regiment* (Liverpool: no publisher listed; second printing, 1986) 226.

64. RG 24, v. 10982, 264.C2.013 (D3), Interview with Brigadier T.G. Gibson, 6.

65. Frost, *Once a Patricia*, 278.

66. RG 24, v. 10787, 224.C1.093 (D3), Report of Air Operations, 24 August to 22 September 1944.

67. Greenhous et al., *The Crucible of War*, 310. The DAF had supplied crucial aerial support: "Between 24 August and 22 Sept 1944, a total of 11,510 sorties of all types were flown." RG 24, v. 10787, 224.C1.093 (D3), Report of Air Operations, 24 August to 22 September 1944.

68. RG 24, v. 10982, 264.C2.013 (D3), Interview with Brigadier T.G. Gibson, 7.

69. Nicholson, *The Canadians in Italy*, 562.

70. Vokes, *Vokes: My Story*, 183–4.

71. RG 24, v. 10927, 240.C5 (D2), Quarterly Reports of Medical Services for 5 Cdn Armd Division, 3.

72. Mowat, *The Regiment*, 244.

73. Rob Engen, "The Canadian Soldier: Combat Motivation in the Second World War, 1943–1945," (Ph.D. dissertation, Queen's University, 2014) 200–3; British Historical Section Central Mediterranean, Administrative Monographs 1946, "The Problem of Desertion," LCMSDS Archives. I thank Professor Terry Copp for sharing his research with me.

74. Wilmot, *Through the Hitler Line*, 121.

75. Delaney, *Corps Commanders*, 119.

76. DHH, Charles Foulkes Papers, 73/1223, series 6, box 225, McCrerry to Alexander, 24 October 1944.

77. Burns, *General Mud*, 220.

78. Gooderson, *A Hard Way to Make War*, 327.

79. Nicholson, *The Canadians in Italy*, 678.

80. Porch, *The Path to Victory*, 656.

81. Dominic Graham and Shelford Bidwell, *Tug of War: The Battle for Italy, 1943–1945* (London: Hodder & Stoughton, 1986) 402.

Chapter 12: The Long Left Flank

1. Alex Danchev and Dan Todman, *War Diaries, 1939–1945: Field Marshal Lord Alanbrooke* (University of California Press, 2003) 585

2. RG 24, v. 10636, 215.C1.013 (D3), The Battle of the Scheldt by Major General C.C. Mann, 21 Oct 1946, 2.

3. Carlo D'Este, *Eisenhower: A Soldiers' Life* (New York: Holt, 2003) 585.

4. CWM, MHRC, Reginald Richard Dixon, *I was Forged on the Anvil of War* (self-published, 1998) chapter 4, page 1; LAC, RG 24, v. 10985, 265.C.011 (D2), Account of 6 Brigade in the Advance to the River Seine.

5. Doug W. McIntyre, "Pursuit to the Seine: The Essex Scottish Regiment and the Foret de la Londe, August 1944," *Canadian Military History* 7.1 (Winter 1998) 59.

6. Kipp, *Because We Are Canadians*, 119.

7. CWM, MHRC, Reginald Richard Dixon, *I Was Forged on the Anvil of War* (self-published, 1998) chapter 4, page 3.

8. RG 24, v. 10911, 235.C3.016 (D15), 3 Cdn Inf Div OO No. 2, 28 August 1944.

9. RG 24, v. 10651, 215.C1.019 (D7), Notes re: Situation, 2/3 September 1944.

10. Portugal (ed.), *We Were There*, volume 5, 2537.

11. Granatstein, *Canada's Army*, 285; Copp, *A Nation at War*, 134.

12. RG 24, v. 15020, War Diary, Calgary Highlanders, 29 August 1944.

13. Stacey, *The Victory Campaign*, 292.

14. D'Este, *Eisenhower*, 589.

15. Copp, *Cinderella Army*, 151.

16. Nicholson, *The Gunners of Canada*, volume II, 331.

17. Grant, *Carry On,* 93.

18. Terry Copp, "Return to Dieppe, September 1944," *Canadian Military History* 1.1–2 (1992) 71.

19. Dickson, *A Thoroughly Canadian General*, 337.

20. Nigel Hamilton, *Monty: Final Years of the Field-Marshal, 1944–1976* (London: Hamish Hamilton, 1986) 126.

21. RG 24, v. 10638, 215.C1.013 (D31) Capture of Boulogne, 5.

22. *We Were There*, volume IV, 1821.

23. RG 24, v. 10907, 235.C3.013 (2), Capture of Boulogne, Operation Wellhit, 17–22 September 1944, 7.

24. John Macfie, *Sons of the Pioneers: Memories of Veterans of the Algonquin Regiment* (Parry Sound, 2001) 14–15.

25. RG 24, v. 10,638, 215.C1.013 (D31) Capture of Boulogne, 7.

26. Martin Middlebrook and Chris Everitt, *The Bomber Command War Diaries* (Harmondsworth: Penguin Books, 1985) 585.

27. Donald Pearce, *Journal of a War* (Toronto: Macmillan, 1965) 65.

28. RG 24, v. 10669, Use of Kangaroos, 22 October 1944.

29. CWM, MHRC, Reginald Richard Dixon, *I was Forged on the Anvil of War* (self-published, 1998) chapter 5, page 9.

30. Bird, *North Shore (New Brunswick) Regiment*, 414.

31. Stacey, *The Victory Campaign*, 343.

32. Major W.H.V. Matthews, "Assault on Calais," *Canadian Military History* 3.2 (1994) 89; Bell, *Into Action with the 12th Field*, 84.

33. RG 24, v. 10636, 215.C1.013 (D1), Crerar to McNaughton, 8 November 1944.

34. Reid, *Named by the Enemy*, 201.

35. Stacey, *The Victory Campaign*, 352.

36. Atkinson, *The Day of Battle*, 180.

37. Brian Horrocks, *A Full Life* (London: Collins, 1960) 204.

38. For a discussion, see Buckley, *Monty's Men*, 200–2.

39. Horrocks, *Corps Commander*, 98–9; Buckley, *Monty's Men*, 218,

40. Sebastian Ritchie, *Arnhem: Myth and Reality* (London: Robert Hale, 2010) 132–3.

CHAPTER 13: BATTLE OF THE SCHELDT

1. *The Canadians at War, 1939/45*, volume II, 547.

2. War Diary, 5th Canadian Infantry Brigade, 11–12 September 1944.

3. Atkinson, *The Guns at Last Light*, 110.

4. James Alan Roberts, *The Canadian Summer: The Memoirs of James Alan Roberts* (Toronto: University of Toronto Bookroom, 1981), 82.

5. LAC, Harry Crerar papers, MG 30 E157, v. 5, 958C.009 (D107),The Campaign in North West Europe from the "Break Out" South of Caen to 31 December 1944, 7.

6. Portugal (ed.), *We Were There*, volume IV, 1721.

7. Hayes, *The Lincs*, 378–80.

8. RG 24, v. 10907, 235C3.013 (D3), Report on Operation Switchback by historical officer, 3rd Division, n.d. [ca. January 1945]

9. Portugal (ed.), *We Were There*, volume IV, 1605.

10. RG 24, v. 10911, 235.C3.021 (D1), Interrogation of Maj–Gen Eberding, 64th Division, 1 November 1944.

11. R. Daniel Pellerin, "'You Have Shut Up the Jerries': Canadian Counter-Battery Work in the Clearing of the Breskens Pocket, October–November 1944," *Canadian Military History* 21.3 (Summer 2012) 24.

12. RG 24, v. 10907, 235.C3.013 (D3), Report on operation Switchback, 3rd Division, 5.

13. Engen, "*The Canadian Soldier,*" 298.

14. Terry Copp, "Crossing the Leopold Canal," *Legion Magazine* (January 2001) online.

15. Stacey, *The Victory Campaign*, 395.

16. RG 24, v. 10682, 215.C1.98 (D60), Interrogation report of Lt. Col. Siegried Erfurth, 1038 Grenadier Regiment.

17. Stacey, *The Victory Campaign*, 395.

18. Copp, *Cinderella Army*, 102.

19. RG 24, v. 10907, 235.C3.013 (D3), Report on Operation Switchback, 3rd Division, 8.

20. Portugal (ed.), *We Were There*, volume IV, 1765.

21. RG 24, v. 10911, 235.C3.021 (D1), Interrogation of Maj-Gen Eberding, 64th Division, 1 November 1944.

22. Pearce, *Journal of a War*, 85–6.

23. Portugal (ed.), *We Were There*, volume VI, 2841.

24. RG 24, v. 10907, 235.C3.013 (D3), Report on Operation Switchback by historical officer, 3rd Division, n.d. [ca. January 1945].

25. RG 24, v. 10912, 235.C3,023 (D1), Intelligence Summary No 48, 14 October 1944.

26. Copp, *Cinderella Army*, 110.

27. RG 24, v. 10912, Operation Switchback, Study Period, Dyke and Polder Fighting, 20 November 1944.

28. RG 24, v. 10907, 235.C3.013 (D3), Report on Operation Switchback, 3rd Division, 19.

29. Dixon, *I Was Forged on the Anvil of War*, chapter 6, page 6.

30. RG 24, v. 10636, 215.C1.013 (D1), Simonds to Crerar, 22 November 1944, 2.

31. Martin, *Battle Diary*, 89.

32. Pearce, *Journal of a War*, 88. For civilians, also see RG 24, v. 10912, Operation Switchback, Study Period, Dyke and Polder Fighting, 20 November 1944.

33. See W.W. Barrett, *The History of the 13th Canadian Field Regiment* (Holland: 13th Canadian Field Regiment, 1945) 83–5.

34. RG 24, v. 10907, 235.C3.013(D3), Report on Operation Switchback by historical officer, Appendix B—Account by Brigadier PAS Todd, CCRA 2 Cdn Corps (formerly CRA 3rd Div).

35. Bird, *North Shore (New Brunswick) Regiment*, 468.

36. Cameron Pulsifer (ed.), "Striking into Germany: From the Scheldt to the German Surrender," *Canadian Military History* 12.3 (Summer 2003) 42.

37. See Michael Bechthold, "Air Support in the Breskens Pocket: The Case of First Canadian Army and 84 Group RAF." *Canadian Military History 4.2* (Autumn 1994) 57.

38. WD, RG 24, v. 15169, Queen's Own Rifles of Canada, 28 October 1944.

39. RG 24, v. 10913, 235.C2.093 (D2), Air Support in Operation Switchback, 20 November 1944.

40. RG 24, v. 10911, 235.C3.021 (D1), Interrogation of Maj-Gen Eberding, 64th Division, 1 November 1944.

41. RG 24, v. 10913, 235.C2.093 (D2), Air Support in Operation Switchback, 20 November 1944.

42. Portugal (ed.) *We Were There*, volume V, 2534.

43. Barnard, *The Queen's Own Rifles of Canada*, 237.

44. RG 24, v. 10912, Operation Switchback, Study Period, Part II, Adm Notes, 20 November 1944.

45. RG 24, v. 10907, 235.C3.013 (D3), Report on Operation Switchback, 3rd Division, 19.

46. Stacey, *The Victory Campaign*, 400.

47. Portugal (ed.), *We Were There*, volume IV, 1730.

48. David Bercuson, *Battalion of Heroes: The Calgary Highlanders in World War II* (Toronto: Penguin, 1994) 159; Terry Copp and Robert Vogel, *Maple Leaf Route: Scheldt* (Alma: Maple Leaf Route, 1985) 28–32.

49. WD, Calgary Highlanders, 11 October 1944.

50. Copp, *A Nation at War*, 166.

51. RG 24, v. 10669, 215.C1.065 (D4), Extract from a report on the action at Woensdrecht, 8–14 Oct 1944, Account by Lt. W.J. Shea, RHC given to historical officer, 15 October 1944.

52. RG 24, v. 10669, 215.C1.065 (D4), Extract from a report on the action at Woensdrecht, 8–14 Oct 1944, Account by Lt. W.J. Shea, RHC given to historical officer, 15 October 1944.

53. Stacey, *The Victory Campaign*, 384.

54. George Blackburn, *The Guns of Victory: A Soldier's Eye View, Belgium, Holland, and Germany, 1944–1945* (Toronto, 1996) 100.

55. Nicholson, *Gunners of Canada*, 358.

56. WD, 5th Canadian Infantry Brigade, 16 October 1944.

57. For liberation and the challenges, see Geoffrey Hayes, "'Where Are Our Liberators?' The Canadian Liberation of West Brabant, 1944," *Canadian Military History* 4.1 (1995) 7–19.

58. Hayes, *Lincs*, 46.

59. Portugal (ed.), *We Were There*, volume II, 645.

60. Gordon, *The Stretcher Bearers*, 91.

61. Copp and McAndrew, *Battle Exhaustion*, 143–4.

62. Portugal (ed.), *We Were There*, volume II, 624.

63. John Morgan Gray, *Fun Tomorrow: Learning to Be a Publisher and Much Else* (Toronto: Macmillan of Canada, 1978) 292.

64. Cy Torontow (ed.), *There I Was: A Collection of Reminiscences by Members of the Ottawa Jewish Community Who Served in World War II* (Ottawa: Jewish War Veterans and the Ottawa Jewish Historical Society, 1999) 39–40.

65. Copp, *No Price Too High*, 170.

66. LAC, Harry Crerar papers, MG 30 E157, v.4, 958.009 (D110), Crerar to Simonds, 15 July 1944.

67. LAC, Harry Crerar papers, MG 30 E157, v.4, 958.009 (D110), 2nd Cdn Corps headquarters to divisions, 29 August 1944.

68. Portugal (ed.), *We Were There*, volume 5, 2559.

69. LAC, Crerar papers, MG 30 E157, v.4, Absentees Reported by Cdn Sec 2 Ech HQ 21 A Gp, period 1 Sep 44 to 20 Jan 1945, date 26 Jan 1945.

70. Kipp, *Because We Are Canadians*, 163.

71. Barr, *From Barnyard to Battlefield and Beyond*, 134.

72. LAC, Harry Crerar papers, MG 30 E157, v. 5, 958C.009 (D116), SIW: Summary of Position of SIW cases as at 6 Oct 1944.

73. LAC, RG 24, v. 12745, Extracts, RCAMC No. 11 Canadian Field Ambulance, July 1944, Appendix 9.

74. Portugal (ed.), *We Were There*, volume II, 687.

75. RG 24, v. 10637, 215.C1.013 (D22), Operation Infatuate, 17–1–9/Ops, 26 September 1944.

76. Lord Tedder, *With Prejudice* (London: Cassell, 1966) 606.

77. Bercuson, *Battalion of Heroes*, 185.

78. LAC, RG 24, v. 10985, 265.C5.011 (D1), The Capture of Zuid Beveland, 5th Brigade operations, interview with Brigadier W.J. Megill, [ca. December 1944].

79. Terry Copp, "Taking Walcheren Island: Army, Part 38, Legion Magazine (November 2001) online.

80. Shawcross, *What Was It Like??*, 176

81. RG 24, v.10669, 215.C1.065 (D4) Report on Infantry Reinforcements, 10 December 1957.

82. Stacey, *Six Years of War*, 427–31.

83. Stacey, *The Victory Campaign*, 284.

84. Granatstein, *Canada's Army*, 293.

85. Gray, *Fun Tomorrow,* 254–6.

86. See Graham Broad, *A Small Price to Pay: Consumer Culture on the Canadian Home Front, 1939–45* (Vancouver: UBC Press, 2013)

87. See Tim Cook, *Warlords: Borden, Mackenzie King, and Canada's World Wars* (Toronto: Allan Lane, 2012) 318–35.

88. Dean Oliver and Laura Brandon, *Canvas of War: Painting the Canadian Experience, 1914 to 1945* (Vancouver: Douglas & McIntyre, 2001) 134.

89. RG 24, v. 10636, 215.C1.013 (D1), Simonds to Crerar, 22 Nov 1944.

90. Granatstein, *Canada's Army*, 291.

91. LAC, Harry Crerar papers, MG 30 E157, v. 5, 958C.009 (D107),The Campaign in North West Europe from the 'Break Out' South of Caen to 31 December 1944, 8.

92. Bernard Montgomery, *The Memoirs of Field Marshal Montgomery* (London: Collins, 1958) 297.

CHAPTER 14: BATTERING GERMANY

1. Henry Probert, *Bomber Harris: His Life and Times: The Biography of Marshal of the Royal Air Force Sir Arthur Harris, the Wartime Chief of Bomber Command* (Mechanicsburg: Stackpole Books, 2001) 306.

2. Max Hastings, *Bomber Command* (London: M. Joseph, 1980) 328–36; for a re-evaluation of Harris and the oil plan, see Sebastian Cox, Introduction to Sir Arthur T. Harris, *Despatch on War Operations: 23rd February to 8th May 1945* (London: Frank Cass, 1995) xxii. Also see Peloquin, "Area Bombing by Day," 40 and Overy, *Bomber Command, 1939–1945*, 131.

3. Greenhous and Halliday, *Canada's Air Forces, 62*.

4. See Roy Irons, *The Relentless Offensive: War and Bomber Command, 1939–1945* (Barnsley: Pen & Sword Aviation, 2009) 190–2.

5. CWM, 19770102–006, Miller Gore Brittain, letters, November 8th, 1944.

6. Overy, *Bomber Command 1939–1945*, 200; David L. Bashow, "The Balance Sheet: The Costs and Gains of the Bombing Campaign," *Canadian Military History* 15.3&4 (Summer–Autumn, 2006) 43.

7. See, for example, the use of slave labour in the aircraft industry: Daniel Uziel, *Arming the Luftwaffe: The German Aviation Industry in World War II* (Jefferson: McFarland, 2012).

8. See Gerhard Weinberg, *A World at Arms: A Global History of World War II* (Cambridge: Cambridge University Press, 1994) 773–4; Bashow, *None but the Brave*, 121–61; Richard Overy, *Why the Allies Won the War*, 130–3; R.J. Overy, "Rationalization and the 'Production Miracle' in Germany during the Second World War," in R.J. Overy (ed.) *War and Economy in the Third Reich* (New York: Oxford University Press, 1994) 343–75; Tooze, *The Wages of Destruction*, 606.

9. Overy, *Bomber Command, 1939–1945*, 214.

10. Greenhous et al., *The Crucible of War*, 867.

11. Phillips P. O'Brien, "East versus West in the Defeat of Nazi Germany," *Journal of Strategic Studies* 23.2 (2000) 101.

12. Evans, *The Third Reich at War*, 465.

13. Bercuson, *Maple Leaf Against the Axis*, 258.

14. Peloquin, "Area Bombing by Day," 27.

15. Irwin, *World War II Memoirs*, 25.

16. David Bashow, "Four Gallant Airmen," in Colonel Bernd Horn (ed.) *Intrepid Warriors: Perspectives on Canadian Military Leaders* (Toronto: The Dundurn Group, 2007) 160–1.

17. Patterson, *World War II: An Airman Remembers*, 133.

18. Patterson, *World War II: An Airman Remembers*, 137.

19. Charles Webster and Noble Frankland, *The Strategic Air Offensive Against Germany, 1939–1945*, volume III (London: H.M.S.O., 1961) 103.

20. Atkinson, *The Guns at Last Light*, 125.

21. Richard Overy, "Introduction," in Claudia Baldoli, Andrew Knapp and Richard Overy (eds.), *Bombing, States and Peoples in Western Europe 1940–1945* (London: Continuum, 2011) 3.

22. Tami Davis Biddle, "Bombing the Square Yard: Sir Arthur Harris at War, 1942–45," *International History Review* 21 (1999) 626–64.

23. Paul Addison and Jeremy A. Crang (eds.), *Firestorm: The Bombing of Dresden* (London: Pimlico, 2006) 194; Frederick Taylor, *Dresden: Tuesday 13 February 1945* (London: Bloomsbury, 2004).

24. See the CBC report, "The Bombing of Dresden." www.cbc.ca/archives/categories/war-conflict/second-world-war/general-22/the-bombing-of-dresden.html

25. Henry Pelling, *Winston Churchill* (London: Macmillan, 1974) 589. Also see, Sebastian Cox, "The Dresden Raids: Why and How," in Paul Addison and Jeremy Crang (eds.), *Firestorm: The Bombing of Dresden, 1945* (London: Pimlico, 2006) 18–61.

26. See Oliver Haller, "Destroying Hitler's Berghof: The Bomber Command Raid of 25 April 1945," *Canadian Military History* 20.1 (Winter 2011) 6; Peter Lee, "Return from the Wilderness: An Assessment of Arthur Harris' Moral Responsibility for the German City

Bombings," *Air Power Review* 16.1 (2013) 84–6; David Reynolds, *In Command of History: Churchill Fighting and Writing the Second World War* (London: Penguin, 2005) 281.

27. Statistics at www.bombercommandmuseum.ca

28. David Hall, "Black, White and Grey: Wartime Arguments for and against the Strategic Bombing Offensive," *Canadian Military History* 7.1 (Winter 1998) 7–19.

29. Richard Overy, *Bomber Command, 1939–1945: Reaping the Whirlwind* (London: Harper Collins, 1997) 200.

30. Greenhous et al., *The Crucible of War*, 864.

31. For statistics, see Halliday and Greenhous, *Canada's Air Force*, 120.

32. David Bashow, *None but the Brave: The Essential Contributions of RAF Bomber Command to Allied Victory during the Second World War* (Kingston: Canadian Defence Academy Press, 2009) 148.

33. RG 24, v. 10947, 249.C5 (D63), Extracts from Directive GOC 4-2 of 6 January 1945.

34. RG 24, v. 10636, 215.C1.013 (D1), Crerar to McNaughton, 31 January 1945.

35. RG 24, v. 10947, 249.C5 (D54), See numerous documents on intelligence reports in this file.

36. Beevor, *The Second World War*, 671.

37. RG 24, v. 10637, 215.C1.013 (D22), Operation Veritable, Note on Enemy, 6 February 1944.

38. Roberts, *The Canadian Summer*, 108.

39. RG 24, v. 10636, 215.C1.013 (D1), Crerar to McNaughton, 5 April 1945, 3.

40. Portugal (ed.), *We Were There*, volume IV, 1628.

41. Pearce, *Journal of a War*, 138.

42. RG 24, v. 10907, 235.C3.011 (D4), Operation Veritable, Report by Historical Officer, Captain R.F. Gray, 17 March 1945.

43. Stacey, *The Victory Campaign*, 464.

44. Copp, *No Price Too High*, 213.

45. CWM, oral history interview, 31D1 Troy, 10.

46. McNeil, *Voices of a War Remembered*, 257.

47. CWM, oral history interview, 31D 5 SLOAN, 11.

48. Bill McAndrew, Bill Rawling, and Michael Whitby, *Liberation: The Canadians in Europe* (Montreal: Art Global, 1995) 132.

49. Hedley Everard, *A Mouse in My Pocket* (Picton: Valley Floatplane Services, 1988) 380.

50. WD, South Saskatchewan Regiment, Message Logs, 18 February 1945.

51. Bell, *Into Action with the 12th Field*, 116.

52. RG 24, v. 10986, 265.C7.011 (D3) The Clearing of Moyland Wood, historical report.

53. Reid, *Named by the Enemy*, 221.

54. Copp, *A Nation at War*, 212.

55. McNeil, *Voices of a War Remembered*, 257.

56. Granatstein, *Canada's Army*, 299.

57. W. Denis Whitaker & Shelagh Whitaker, *Rhineland: The Battle to Win the War* (Toronto: Stoddard, 1989) 145.

58. Didmon, *Lucky Guy*, 140.

59. Donald D. Tansley, *Growing Up and Going to War: 1925–1945* (Waterloo: Laurier Centre for Military Strategic and Disarmament Studies, Wilfrid Laurier University, 2005) 73–4.

60. G.L. Cassidy, *Warpath: The Story of the Algonquin Regiment, 1939–1945* (Cobalt: Highway Book Shop, 1990) 202.

61. Pearce, *Journal of a War*, 160.

62. Andrew Brown, "New Men in the Line: An Assessment of Reinforcements to the 48th Highlanders in Italy, January–October 1944," *Canadian Military History* 21.3 (2012) 35–47; Caroline D'Amours, "Reassessment of a Crisis: Canadian Infantry Reinforcements during the Second World War," *Canadian Army Journal* 14.2 (2012) 73–89.

63. Portugal (ed.), *We Were There*, volume II, 625–6.

64. Oliver and Brandon, *Canvas of War*, 138. Also see, Mélanie Morin-Pelletier, «J'ai combattu le bon combat, j'ai achevé ma course, j'ai gardé la foi» : Récit de guerre d'un conscript néo-brunswickois, 1943–1945,» *Canadian Military History* 22.4 (2013) 45–58.

65. Evans, *The Third Reich at War*, 676.

66. RG 24, v. 10636, 215.C1.013 (D1), Crerar to McNaughton, 5 April 1945, 10.

67. Didmon, *Lucky Guy*, 143.

68. See Robert Gellately, *Backing Hitler: Consent and Coercion in Nazi Germany* (New York: Oxford University Press, 2001) 224.

69. Tooze, *The Wages of Destruction*, 653.

70. See David French, "'You Cannot Hate the Bastard Who is Trying to Kill You ...': Combat and Ideology in the British Army in the War against Germany, 1939–45," in Gordon Martel (ed.), *The World War Two Reader* (New York: Routledge, 2004) 188–92; S.P. Mackenzie, "The Treatment of POWs in World War Two," *Journal of Modern History* 66 (1994) 490.

71. Portugal (ed.), *We Were There*, volume III, 1079.

72. Denis Showalter, "The U.S. War Effort and its Consequences," in Chickering et al., *A World at Total War*, 120.

73. Didmon, *Lucky Guy*, 144.

74. RG 24, v. 10907, file 235.C3.013(D5), Monthly Consolidated Summary of Cdn Ops and Activities, 3 Cdn Inf Div, 1–31 March 1945.

75. Whitsed, *Canadians: A Battalion at War*, 149, 140–1

76. Dickson, *A Thoroughly Canadian General*, 395.

77. RG 24, v. 10912, 235.C3.023 (D2); Intelligence Summary, No. 76, Based on Infm received up to 2000 hrs 1 March 1945.

78. Cameron Pulsifer (ed.), "Striking into Germany: From the Scheldt to the German Surrender," *Canadian Military History* 12.3 (Summer 2003) 46.

79. Granatstein, *Canada's Army*, 302.

80. Terry Copp, "'If this war isn't over, And pretty damn soon, There'll be nobody left, In this old platoon...' First Canadian Army, February–March 1945," in Paul Addison and Angus Calder (eds.), *Time to Kill: The Soldier's Experience of War in the West, 1939–1945* (London: Pimlico, 1997) 147.

81. See John Nichol and Tony Rennell, *The Last Escape: The Untold Story of Allied Prisoners of War in Europe, 1944–45* (London: Viking, 2002).

82. Hibbert, *Fragments of War*, 245.

83. [no author], *Memories on Parade: Aircrew Recollections of World War II* (Winnipeg: Wartime Pilots' and Observations' Association, 1995) 26.

84. CWM, 20030316–002, Alexander Molnar, Gluck Auf Mel: Memoir—WW2, 10.

85. Heathcote, *Testaments of Honour*, 141–2.

86. H. Trevor Roper (ed.), *The Goebbels Diaries: The Last Days* (London: Book Club Associates, 1978) 78.

87. CWM, 20030316–001, G. Stuart Brown, *My Life in the R.C.A.F.*, 31.

88. Dancocks, *In Enemy Hands*, ix.

89. CWM, 20080029–002, 58A 1 232.3, George Hill collection, Wartime log.

90. Stacey, *The Victory Campaign*, 537.

91. CWM oral history interview, 31D 1 GUY, 18.

92. Sean Longden, *To the Victors the Spoils: D-Day to VE Day, The Reality Behind the Heroism* (Moreton: Arris Books, 2005) 82.

93. Richard Malone, *A World in Flames 1944–1945: A Portrait of War* (Toronto: Collins, 1984) 190.

94. Tansley, *Growing Up and Going to War*, 79. For a wider discussion of looting, see Seth A. Givens, "Liberating the Germans: The US Army and Looting in Germany during the Second World War," *War in History* 21.1 (2013) 33–54.

95. Engen, "The Canadian Soldier," 322.

96. CLIP, Elmer Bell collection, letter, 7 April 1945.

97. Lane, *In Chariots of Iron*, 136.

98. Cameron Pulsifer (ed.), "Striking into Germany: From the Scheldt to the German Surrender," *Canadian Military History* 12.3 (Summer 2003) 48.

99. Rannie (ed.), *To the Thunderer His Arms*, 146.

100. CWM, Jack Shepherd, *A March to Fear: WWII* (self-published, 2003).

101. Frank Proctor, *I Was There: An Autobiography* (self-published, 1999) 257.

102. Portugal (ed.), *We Were There*, volume IV, 1627.

103. Cameron, *Born Lucky*, 193.

104. Morrison and Slaney, *The Breed of Manly Men*, 321; Daniel Byers, "Operation "Canada": 5th Canadian Armoured Division's Attack on Delfzijl, 23 April to 2 May 1945," *Canadian Military History* 7.3 (1998) 35–46.

105. RG 24, v. 10636, 215.C1.013 (D1), Crerar to McNaughton, 29 May 1945.

106. Tansley, *Growing Up and Going to War*, 98.

107. Copp, *No Price Too High*, 218.

CHAPTER 15: VETERANS

1. Jeff Keshen, "Getting it Right the Second Time Around: The Reintegration of Canadian Veterans of World War II," in Peter Neary and J.L. Granatstein (eds.), *The Veterans Charter and Post-World War II Canada* (Montreal: McGill-Queen's University Press, 1998) 67.

2. Stacey, *The Victory Campaign*, 611. For a slightly different breakdown of casualties—killed, wounded, and prisoners—see RG 24, 215.C1.065 (D10), Casualties—6 June 1944 to end of War, 27 April 1966.

3. RG 24, v.10907, 235.C3.013 (D5), Weekly Summary of Cdn Ops, 29 April 45–5 May 1945, 3rd Cdn Inf Div.

4. Martin, *Battle Diary*, 16.

5. Danson, *Not Bad for a Sergeant*, 11.

6. Dominion Institute interview, Kathleen Lynett, online.

7. Watt, *In All Respects Ready*, 2.

8. Graves, *In Peril on the Sea*, 218.

9. R.H. Caldwell, "The VE Day Riots in Halifax, 7–8 May 1945," *The Northern Mariner* 10.1 (January 2000) 3–20.

10. Dean Oliver, "Awaiting Return: Life in the Canadian Army's Overseas Repatriation Depots, 1945–1946," in Peter Neary and J.L. Granatstein (eds.), *The Veterans Charter and Post–World War II Canada* (McGill-Queen's University Press, 1998) 35–6.

11. Dean Oliver, "Canadian Military Demobilization in World War II," in Granatstein and Neary (eds.), *The Good Fight: Canadians and World War II* (Toronto: Copp Clark, 1995) 368.

12. For the plans, see RG 24, v. 10649, 215.C1.016 (D27), Operation Eclipse, 2 April 1945.

13. RG 24, v. 10895, 1st Divisional weekly report, week ending 12 May 1945.

14. RG 24, v. 10649, 215.C1.016 (D27), First Cdn Army OP Eclipse, Instr Number 4, 13 May 1945; and Ibid., Use of German Manpower, 22 May 1945; Chris Madsen, "Victims of Circumstance: The Execution of German Deserters by Surrendered German Troops Under Canadian Control in Amsterdam, May 1945," *Canadian Military History* 2.1 (1993) 93–113.

15. See RG 24, v. 10895, Captain T.J. Allen, "The Concentration, Disarming and Evacuation of Germans in Western Holland," 7 June 1945; Gray, *Fun Tomorrow*, 315–20; Wady Lehmann, "Recollections Concerning Canadian War Crimes Investigations and Prosecutions," *Canadian Military History* 11.4 (Autumn 2002) 71–80.

16. RG 24, v. 10636, 215.C1.013 (D1), Crerar to McNaughton, 1 August 1945, 2.

17. David Kaufman and Michael Horn, *A Liberation Album: Canadians in the Netherlands, 1944–1945* (Toronto: McGraw-Hill, 1980) 104–5.

18. Robert Gordon Sawdon, *Another River to Cross* (self-published, 2000) 99–100.

19. Kaufman and Horn, *A Liberation Album*, 154.

20. Michael Horn, "More than Cigarettes, Sex and Chocolate: The Canadian Army in the Netherlands, 1944–1945," *Journal of Canadian Studies* 16. 3&4 (1981) 166.

21. Kaufman and Horn, *A Liberation Album*, 164.

22. CWM, 20050178-009, McLean to Stennett, 13 October 1945.

23. Glen Hancock, *Charley Goes to War* (Kentville: Gaspereau Press, 2004) 282.

24. Kirk Du Guid, *Soldiers' Stories* (self-published, 2009) 43. Also see Longden, *To the Victor the Spoils*, 86–8.

25. Timothy Snyder, *Bloodlands: Europe between Hitler and Stalin* (New York : Basic Books, 2010) 316–17.

26. Ben Shephard, *The Long Road Home: The Aftermath of the Second World War* (London: The Bodley Head, 2010) 59.

27. RG 24, v. 10636, 215.C1.013 (D1), Crerar to McNaughton, 1 August 1945, 7.

28. Jones (ed.), *Living History Chronicles*, 13.

29. Melynda Jarratt, *War Brides: The Stories of The Women Who Left Everything behind to Follow the Men They Loved* (Toronto: Dundurn, 2009) 15.

30. Copp, *No Price Too High*, 229.

31. Jarratt, *War Brides*, 17.

32. McNeil, *Voices of a War Remembered*, 333.

33. RG 24, v. 10636, 215.C1.013 (D1), Crerar to McNaughton, 1 August 1945, 6.

34. See Bill Rawling "A Lonely Ambassador: HMCS *Uganda* and the War in the Pacific," *The Northern Mariner* VIII.1 (January, 1998).

35. John Dower, *Cultures of War: Pearl Harbor, Hiroshima, 9/11, Iraq* (New York: W.W. Norton, 2010) 199.

36. D.M. Giangreco, *Hell to Pay: Operation DOWNFALL and the Invasion of Japan, 1945–1947* (Naval Institute Press, 2009).

37. "William Bell," *Maclean's* (22 April 2013) 82. Also see Heathcote, *Testaments of Honour*, 73.

38. Carl Christie, *No Reason Why: The Canadian Hong Kong Tragedy—An Examination* (Stittsville: Canada's Wings, 1981) 238.

39. Hong Kong Veterans Commemorative Association, Frank Christensen's story.

40. George S. MacDonell, *One Soldier's Story (1939–1945) From the Fall of Hong Kong to the Defeat of Japan* (Toronto: Dundurn, 2002) 46.

41. Dave McInosh, *Hell on Earth: Aging Faster, Dying Sooner. Canadian Prisoners of the Japanese during World War Two* (Toronto: McGraw-Hill Ryerson, 1997).

42. Joan Beaumont, "Prisoners of War in Australian National Memory', in Bob Moore and Barbara Hately-Broad (ed.), *Prisoners of War, Prisoners of Peace: Captivity, homecoming and memory in World War II* (New York: Berg Publishers, 2005) 185–94.

43. Terry Copp, "From Neurasthenia to Post-Traumatic Stress Disorder: Canadian Veterans and the Problem of Persistent Emotional Disabilities," in Neary and Granatstein (eds.), *The Veterans Charter*, 155.

44. Christie, *No Reason Why*, 246.

45. CWM, Jack Shepherd, *A March to Fear: WWII* (2003) 65.

46. Heathcote, *Testament of Honour*, 152.

47. R. Scott Sheffield, *A Search for Equity: A Study of the Treatment Accorded to First Nations Veterans and Dependents of the Second World War and Korea* (Ottawa: Final Report o the National Round Table on First Nations Veterans' Issues, 2000) 11; Peter Neary, "Introduction," in Neary and Granatstein, *The Veterans Charter and Post-World War II Canada*, 10.

48. Oliver, "Canadian Military Demobilization in World War II," in Granatstein and Neary (eds.), *The Good Fight*, 373.

49. See Peter Neary, *On to Civvy Street: Canada's Rehabilitation Program for Veterans of the Second World War* (Montreal: McGill-Queen's University Press, 2011).

50. Doug Owram, *Born at the Right Time: A History of the Baby Boom Generation* (Toronto: University of Toronto Press, 1996) 3–53.

51. Jeff Keshen, "Getting It Right the Second Time Around: The Reintegration of Canadian Veterans of World War II," in Neary and Granatstein (eds.), *The Veterans Charter*, 74; Peter Neary, "Canadian Universities and Canadian Veterans of World War II," in Neary and Granatstein (eds.), *The Veterans Charter*, 122.

52. DHH, Gregory Biefer, "The Air War from the Ground," unpublished mss, [1992] 65.

53. Historica-Dominion Institute, *We Were Freedom*, 192.

54. Heathcote, *Testaments of Honour*, 263, 265.

55. CWM, 20020026–003, D.J.R. Humphreys, A Personal Memoir, 1939–1945 (self-published, 2000) 63.

56. Historica-Dominion Institute, *We Were Freedom* 53.

57. CWM oral history interview, 31D 1 BOWEN, G, page 17.

58. J.K. Chapman, *River Boy at War* (Fredericton: Goose Lane Publications, 1985) 86.

59. For an analysis of one community, see Magda Fahrni, *Household Politics: Montreal Families and Postwar Reconstruction* (Toronto: University of Toronto Press, 2005) and Magda

Fahrni, "The Romance of Reunion: Montreal War Veterans Return to family Life, 1944–49," *Journal of the Canadian Historical Association* 1998 (9): 187–208.

60. Horrocks, *In Their Own Words*, 225–6.

61. Alan Allport, *Demobbed: Coming Home after World War Two* (New Haven Yale University Press, 2009) 125.

62. Mary Tremblay, "Going Back to Main Street: The Development and Impact of Casualty Rehabilitation for Veterans with Disabilities, 1945–1948," in Neary and Granatstein (eds.), *The Veterans Charter*, 161. Also see Serge Marc Durflinger, *Veterans with a Vision: Canada's War Blinded in Peace and War* (Vancouver: UBC Press, 2010).

63. Shawcross, *What Was It Like??*, 141.

64. Historica-Dominion Institute, *We Were Freedom*, 187.

65. Portugal (ed.), *We Were There*, volume 1, 208.

66. Ron and Merla Lawruk, *For Love and Country: A Biography of Private Ted Patrick* (self-published, 2011) 15–162.

67. Richard Pyves, *Night Madness: A Rear Gunner's Story of Love, Courage, and Hope in World War II* (Markam: Red Deer Press, 2012)248.

68. Cormier, *The Forgotten Soldiers*, 33.

69. Hewer, *In for a Penny, in for a Pound*, 254.

70. Curry, *War at Sea*, 43.

71. CWM oral history interview, 31D 1 CHENEY 2, no pagination.

72. O'Brien, *Through the Gates of Hell and Back*, viii.

73. Portugal (ed.), *We Were There*, volume III, 1100.

74. Quoted in John Marteinson, *The Governor General's Horse Guards: Second to None* (Toronto: Robin Brass Studio, 2002) 250.

75. "The Legion Log," *The Legionary* XXI.1, 37, 42.

76. McNeil, *Voices of a War Remembered*, 223–4.

77. CWM oral history interview, 31D 4 WALKER, page 19.

78. Chapman, *River Boy at War*, 101.

79. McDonald, *Have No Fear*, 185. Les Allison and Harry Hayward, *They Shall Not Grow Old: A Book of Remembrance* (Brandon: Commonwealth Air Training Plan Museum Inc., 1992).

80. Robert G. Halford, *The Unknown Navy: Canada's World War Two Merchant Navy.* (St. Catharines: Vanwell Pub., 1995) 40.

81. Jay White, "Hardly Heroes: Canadian Merchant Seamen and the International Convoy System," *The Northern Mariner* 5.4 (1995) 19–20.

82. Halford, *The Unknown Navy*, 250.

83. Doug Fraser, *Postwar Casualty: Canada's Merchant Navy* (Nova Scotia: Pottersfield Press, 1997) 25.

84. CBC Television broadcast, 1 October 1998.

85. For the history of veterans' benefits, see Peter Neary, *The Origins and Evolution of Veterans Benefits in Canada, 1914–2004* (Ottawa: Veterans Affairs Canada, 2004) 40–1.

86. R. Scott Sheffield, *A Search for Equity: A Study of the Treatment Accorded to First Nations Veterans and Dependents of the Second World War and Korea* (Ottawa: Final Report o the National Round Table on First Nations Veterans' Issues, 2000) 49.

87. Sheffield, *A Search for Equity*, 52.

88. See R. Scott Sheffield, "Canadian Aboriginal Veterans and the Veterans Charter after the Second World War," in P. Whitney Lackenbauer et al. (eds.) *Aboriginal Peoples and Military Participation: Canadian & International Perspectives* (Winnipeg: Canadian Defence Academy Press, 2007) 77–98.

89. Granatstein and Oliver, *The Oxford Companion to Canadian Military History*, 433.

Chapter 16: The Second World War and Memory

1. Rana Mitter, *Forgotten Ally: China's World War II, 1937–1945* (New York: Houghton Mifflin Harcourt, 2013) 378.

2. Hastings, *All Hell Let Loose*, 669; Jurgen Forster, "From 'Blitzkrieg' to 'Total War': Germany's War in Europe," in Chickering, et al., *A World at Total War*, 102.

3. David Reynolds, *The Long Shadow: The Legacies of the Great War in the Twentieth Century* (New York: W.W. Norton, 2014) 277–309; and Tony Kushner, *The Holocaust and the Liberal Imagination* (Oxford: Oxford University Press, 1994).

4. Anne Applebaum, *Iron Curtain: The Crushing of Eastern Europe, 1944–1956* (New York: Doubleday, 2012).

5. Stephen Leacock, "Canada and Monarchy," *Atlantic Monthly* (June 1939) 735.

6. Dave McIntosh, *Terror in the Starboard Seat* (Don Mills: General Publishing, 1980) 108.

7. Harvey, *Boys, Bombs, and Brussels Sprouts*, 156.

8. Gordon, *The Stretcher Bearers* [no page, "Reflections."]

9. Kaufman and Horn, *A Liberation Album*, 164.

10. C.P. Stacey, *Arms, Men and Governments: The War Policies of Canada, 1939–1945* (Ottawa: Queen's Printer, 1970) 66.

11. Eric McGeer, Terry Copp, with Matt Symes: *The Canadian Battlefields in Italy: Sicily and Southern Italy* (Waterloo: Canadian Battlefields Foundation, 2008).

12. Douglas, *No Higher Purpose*, 634; Stacey, *Arms, Men and Governments*, 66.

13. Stephen L.V. King (ed.), *Your Loving Son: Letters of an RCAF Navigator* (Regina: Canadian Plains Research Centre, 2002) 2.

14. Henk Dykman, "Leesten, 50 Years Later," *Canadian Military History* 4.2 (Autumn 1995) 96.

15. Dominion Institute interview, Doug Craig, interview, online.

16. See Jonathan Vance, "An Open Door to a Better Future: The Memory of Canada's Second World War," in Geoffrey Hayes et al. (eds.), *Canada and the Second World War* (Waterloo: Wilfred Laurier University Press, 2012).

17. See Alex King, *Memorials of the Great War in Britain: The Symbolism and Politics of Remembrance* (Oxford: Berg, 1998), 65–6; Jonathan Vance, *Death So Noble: Memory, Meaning, and the First World War* (Vancouver: UBC Press, 1997) 204–5.

18. "Editorial Views," *The Legionary* XXI.4, 11.

19. "Editorial Views," *The Legionary* XX.8, 27.

20. "A National Cenotaph," *The Legionary* (December 1955) 12.

21. John Hundevad, "Plans for National Memorial to All Canada's Fallen are Announced," *The Legionary* (April 1963) 13–14.

22. Malcolm Ferguson, "Canada's Response: The Making and Remaking of the National War Memorial," (Master's thesis, Carleton University, 2012).

23. Robert Skipper, *I Never Got to Be a Teenager. Volume II: On a Wing and a Prayer—"Until Our Last Bombing Mission"* (self-published, 1996) 100–1.

24. Crerar, *A Thoroughly Canadian General*, 254 and 461–3.

25. Joseph Schull, *The Far Distant Ships:* An Official Account of Canadian Naval Operations in the Second World War (Ottawa: King's Printer, 1952).

26. S.F. Wise, *The Official History of the Royal Canadian Air Force:* Canadian Airmen and the First World War, volume 1 (Toronto: University of Toronto Press, 1980); W.A.B. Douglas, *The Creation of a National Air Force: The Official History of the Royal Canadian Air Force Volume II* (Toronto: University of Toronto Press and the Department of National Defence, 1986); Brereton Greenhous, et al., *The Crucible of War, 1939-1945: The Official History of the Royal Canadian Air Force, volume III* (Toronto: University of Toronto Press, 1994); W.A.B. Douglas, et al., *No Higher Purpose: The Official Operational History of the Royal Canadian Navy in the Second World War, 1939–1943, volume II, part 1* (St. Catharines: Vanwell Pub., 2002); W.A.B. Douglas, W.A.B., et al., *A Blue Water Navy: The Official Operational History of the Royal Canadian Navy in the Second World War, 1943–1945, volume II, part 2* (St. Catharines: Vanwell Pub., 2007); Michael Whitby, et al., *The Seabound Coast: The Official History of the Royal Canadian Navy, 1867–1939, Volume I* (Toronto: Dundurn Press, 2010).

27. C.P. Stacey, *A Date with History: Memoirs of a Canadian History* (Ottawa: Deneau Publishers, 1983) 240.

28. Kent Fedorowich, "'Cocked Hats and Swords and Small, Little Garrisons': Britain, Canada and the Fall of Hong Kong, 1941," *Modern Asian Studies* 37 (February 2003) 153.

29. Michael Valpy, "Why the Canadians Were in Hong Kong in 1941," in *The Globe and Mail*, 3 February 1993, quoted in Galen Perras, "Defeat Still Cries Aloud for Explanation: Explaining C Force's Dispatch to Hong Kong," *Canadian Military Journal* 11.4 (Autumn 2011).

30. Milner, *Canada's Navy*, 96.

31. See Copp, *Fields of Fire*, 5–31.

32. See Roman Jarymowycz, *Tank Tactics from Normandy to Lorraine* (Boulder: Luymme Rienner, 2001).

33. See Peter Gray, "A Culture of Official Squeamishness? Britain's Air Ministry and the Strategic Air Offensive Against Germany," *Journal of Military History* 77.4 (October 2013) 1349–78.

34. Gray, "A Culture of Official Squeamishness?" 1353.

35. See, for example, A.C. Grayling, *Among the Dead Cities: Is the Targeting of Civilians in War Ever Justified?*, Paperback Edition (London: Bloomsbury, 2007); E. Markusen and D. Kopf, *The Holocaust and Strategic Bombing: Genocide and Total War in the Twentieth Century* (Boulder: Westview Press, 1995).

36. Peter Lee, "Return from the Wilderness: An Assessment of Arthur Harris' Moral Responsibility for the German City Bombings," *Air Power Review* 16.1 (2013) 85–6.

37. Bishop, *Bomber Boys*, 372–3; Gerald J. DeGroot, *The Bomb: A Life* (Cambridge: Harvard University Press, 2005) 281–2.

38. Silver, *Last of the Gladiators*, 14–15.

39. Harvey, *Boys, Bombs, and Brussels Sprouts*, 210.

40. McDonald, *Have No Fear*, 166.

41. Historica-Dominion Institute, *We Were Freedom*, 27.

42. Wyatt, *Maximum Effort*, 150–1.

43. Hall, "Black, White and Grey," 7.

44. Dudley Saward, *"Bomber" Harris: The Story of Marshal of the Royal Air Force, Sir Arthur Harris, Bt, GCB, OBE, AFC, LLD, Air Officer Commanding-in-Chief, Bomber Command, 1942–1945* (London: Cassell, 1984) 333.

45. Brian McKenna, *Death by Moonlight: Bomber Command* (Post Production Script, 1992), 4.

46. See David J. Bercuson and S.F. Wise (eds.), *The Valour and the Horror Revisited* (Montreal: McGill-Queen's University Press, 1994); Graham Carr, "Rules of Engagement: Public History and the Drama of Legitimation," *Canadian Historical Review* 86.2 (June 2005): 317–54.

47. See David Dean, "Museums as Contact Zones: The Canadian War Museum and Bomber Command," *Museum and Society* 7.1 (March 2009) 1–15; Norman Hillmer, "The Canadian War Museum and the Military Identity of an Unmilitary People," *Canadian Military History* 19.3 (Summer 2010) 19–26.

48. Jonathan Jones, "The Artistic Jingoism of the Bomber Command Memorial," *The Guardian*, 29 June 2012.

49. Elizabeth Renzetti, "A Memorial for Bomber Command—Too Late for Many," *The Globe and Mail*, 20 June 2012.

50. Gordon Cameron, "Understanding the Veteran," *The Legionary* XXI.10, 13.

51. Gordon Cook personnel file, in possession of Tim Cook. Interview with Terry Cook, 12 February 2014. Gordon Cook personal archives, including log book, photographs, and documentation.

52. Pearce, *Journal of a War*, 179.

53. CWM oral history interview, 31D 1 BOWEN, G, pages 17–18.

54. Hal Lawrence, *A Bloody War: One Man's Memories of the Canadian Navy, 1939–45* (Toronto: Macmillan of Canada, 1979) vii.

55. Robert Crozier, *Looking Backward: A Memoir* (self-published, 1998) ix.

56. Arthur Bridge, "In the Eye of the Storm: A Recollection of Three Days in the Falaise Gap, 19–21 August 1944," *Canadian Military History* 9.3 (Summer 2000) 61.

57. CWM, 20100129–001, William Victor Williamson, "My Final Freedom," preface.

58. See "Teens, Video Games and Civics," *Pew Research*, 16 September 2008. Accessed at www.pewinternet.org/2008/09/16/teens-video-games-and-civics.

59. *Globe and Mail*, 24 August 1998.

60. Douglas Fisher, "editorial, *Legion Magazine* (May 1996) online.

61. Michael L. Hadley, "The Popular Image of the Canadian Navy," in Michael Hadley, et al. (eds.), *A Nation's Navy: In Quest of Canadian Naval Identity* (Montreal: McGill–Queen's University Press, 1996) 54.

62. Matt Symes, "The Personality of Memory: The Process of Informed Commemoration in Normandy," in Geoffrey Hayes (eds.), *Canada and the Second World War* (Waterloo: Wilfird Laurier University Press, 2012). See Paul Gough, "A Difficult Path to Tread: The New Memorial Garden at Caen, Normandy," *Canadian Military History* 8.1 (Winter 1999) 78–80.

63. Ted Barris, *Breaking the Silence: Veterans' Untold Stories* (Toronto: Thomas Allen, 2009) 9.

64. See Brian Bond, *The Unquiet Western Front: Britain's Role in Literature and History* (Cambridge: Cambridge University Press, 2002).

65. On peacekeeping, see Norman Hillmer, "Peacekeeping: The Inevitability of Canada's Role," in Michael A. Hennessy and B.J.C. McKercher (eds.) *War in the Twentieth Century: Reflections at Century's End* (Wesport: Praeger, 2003) 145–65; J.L. Granatstein, "Peacekeeping: Did Canada Make a Difference? And What Difference Did Canada Make to Peacekeeping," in John English and Norman Hillmer (eds.), *Making a Difference? Canada's Foreign Policy in a Changing World Order* (Toronto: Lester, 1992).

66. Portugal (ed.), *We Were There*, volume II, vi.

67. J.L. Granatstein, "A Half-Century On: The Veterans' Experience," in Neary and Granatstein, *The Veterans Charter*, 226.

68. Terry Copp, "Canada's D-Day: Politics, Media, and the Fluidity of Memory," in Michael Dolski (eds.), *D-Day in History and Memory: The Normandy Landings in International Remembrance and Commemoration* (University of North Texas Press, 2014) 148–9.

69. Ian McKay and Jamie Swift, *Warrior Nation: Rebranding Canada in an Age of Anxiety* (Toronto: Between the Lines, 2012) and Noah Richler, *What We Talk About When We Talk About War* (Fredericton: Goose Lane, 2012).

ACKNOWLEDGMENTS

Writing books is usually like attritional warfare: fraught with heavy casualties and yielding few breakthroughs. This book was different. I wrote it alongside volume I, *The Necessary War*, and like it, *Fight to the Finish* was an anchor in the storm for me. During the long process of putting words to paper, I was battling a serious illness and these books offered a coping mechanism for my own personal war. I took solace and strength from the writings of Canadian soldiers, sailors, and airmen, even as I marvelled at how men, usually half my age, dealt with their own fear, anxiety, and strain. Most faced death with a grim but resilient attitude.

As in my previous seven books, I have benefited from the generosity of fellow historians who took time from their busy schedules to read the manuscript. Their comments have saved me from errors of commission and omission, and have helped to sharpen and shape key parts of the argument and text. I am indebted to Dr. Mike Bechthold, Eric Brown, Dr. Terry Cook, Dr. Doug Delaney, Dr. Serge Durflinger, Dr. John Maker, Dr. J.L. Granatstein, Dr. Stephen Harris, Dr. Peter MacLeod, Mike McNorgan, Chris Chance, and Dr. Roger Sarty.

I would like to thank Lara Andrews, Carol Reid, Jane Naisbitt, and Maggie Arbour Doucette at the Canadian War Museum's Military History Research Centre, and Sonia Doyon from the Ottawa Public Library, for their supply of books and access to archival material. My colleagues at the CWM have offered ongoing scholarly comradery, especially James Whitham, Peter MacLeod, and Andrew Burtch.

I would like to thank Sarah Cook and Matthew Walthert for researching into the Canadian Images and Letters Project and the Dominion Institute's Memorial Project. For the better part of a decade, Diane Turbide has been my champion at Penguin and I am grateful for her ongoing support and friendship. Diane and the large team at Penguin work tirelessly on behalf of authors. They are an inspiration. I would especially like to thank Mary Ann Blair for her professional management of the book in production. My friend and agent, Rick Broadhead, is generous, talented, and has been an ongoing source of support. In our sixth book together, Tara Tovell offered her usual brilliant line and copy editing with skill, cheerfulness, and patience.

The oncologists and nurses at the Ottawa General Hospital have been unfailingly professional and supportive in treating me over three years. Norman and Serge have been supporters in our walks and talks, sharing wisdom and positive thoughts. The Trent University crowd of Rachel, John, Lucy, Rick, Staci, Brien, and Gesa have been there through thick and thin. Friends in Manor Park, throughout Ottawa, and around the world have provided kind words and welcome aid.

My mother, Dr. Sharon Cook, has been a rock during exceedingly difficult times. As scholar, educator, mother, and grandmother, she remains optimistic, strong, and relentless in reminding everyone there is a light at the end of the tunnel. My brother, Graham, has offered continuous good humour and advice. Graham, Sam, Calla, and Redden Shantz, as well as Jennifer Klotz, have been there for us.

Sarah has proved stronger than anyone could have imagined. The fight would not be possible without her. She is my partner and love, and this book is as much hers as mine. Our three delightful girls, Chloe, Emma, and Paige, bring a thousand smiles and surprises, reminding us of the joy of youth and the promise of a future.

During the writing of this book, my father, Dr. Terry Cook, passed away. He was the most important figure in my life in training me as a historian. He was a good dad. As a world-reknowned archivist, he has been missed by the international community of scholars, librarians, and archivists. We miss him even more.

Bibliography

Canadian War Museum, Ottawa

20030008-004, 26th Canadian Field Battery collection
20110078-018, F.H. Baldwin collection
19770102-006, Miller Gore Brittain collection
20060029-001, Broomhall collection
20030316-001, G. Stuart Brown collection
19910181-043, George Joseph Chequer collection
20040074-004, Harold Edison DeMone collection
20070044-008, Warren Alvin Duffy collection
20080086-001, Raymond Elliot collection
19830038-001, Donald Geraghty collection
20080118-007, Joseph Harrison collection
20080029-002, George Hill collection
20110062-014, Geoffrey Hughson collection
20020026-003, D.J.R. Humphreys collection
19910163-014, Ben Malkin collection
20050097-001, Kenneth MacNeil collection
20060191-003, Leslie McCaig collection
20050178-009, McLean collection
20030316-002, Alexander Molnar collection
19950077-001, John Oliver Payne collection
20010200-002, Thomas Reid collection
20050094-002, A. Ray Squire collection
19810684-004, D.L. Welsh collection
20100129-001, William Victor Williamson collection
MHRC, *1st Battalion, The Regina Rifle Regiment, 1939–1946*. No publisher, 1946.

MHRC, Reginald Richard Dixon, *I was Forged on the Anvil of War*. Self-published, 1998.

MHRC, Herbert Hoskin, *Sometimes with Laughter: Recollections 1929–1964*. Self-published, 1982.

CWM, MHRC, Walter A. Irwin, *World War II Memoirs of Walter A. Irwin*. Self-published, 1998.

MHRC, Richard C. Pearce, "Recollections." Self-published, n.d.

MHRC, Harry Roberts, *A Memoir of a Lad Serving in a Battalion at War*, n.d.

MHRC, Jack Shepherd, *March to Fear*. Self-published, 2003.

MHRC, Roy Spackman, *A Hell of a Crew*. Self-published, n.d.

MHRC, Robert Thexton, *Times to Remember: Some Recollections of four and a half years service with the West Nova Scotia Regiment during 1940–1944*. Self-published, 2008.

Canadian War Museum Oral History Program

31D 1 AUDET
31D 1 BOWEN, G.
31D 4 CHANCE
31D 1 CHENEY
31D 1 FINNIE
31D 6 FRIEDLANDER
31D 1 GUY
31D1 HARPER
31D 1 MEDD
31D 6 McKAY
31D 5 SLOAN
31D1 TROY
31D 4 WALKER

Library and Archives Canada, Ottawa

H.D.G. Crerar
A.G. L. McNaughton
Guy Simonds
William Lyon Mackenzie King
Library and Archives Canada, William Lyon Mackenzie King personal diary, digitized and online

PRIVATE COLLECTIONS

John Fry letters, courtesy of Adele Fry.

"Joe Boy," unpublished manuscript based on war diaries; courtesy of Dr. Alec Douglas.

Angus Campbell Derby, *Not Least in the Crusade*: *Memoirs of a Military Surgeon.* Self-published, 2005.

DIRECTORATE OF HISTORY AND HERITAGE, OTTAWA

Bio file, Lieutenant Commander R.E. Bartlett

DHH, 141.4A 2011 (D1), Interview with Major Watsford

DHH, Charles Foulkes papers

DHH, Gregory Biefer, "The Air War from the Ground." Unpublished manuscript, 1992.

CANADIAN IMAGES AND LETTERS PROJECT

James Baker, Jo Foreman, John Taylor, Leslie Abram Neufeld, John Kilpatrick, John Fitzgerald, Elmer Bell.

DOMINION INSTITUTE ORAL HISTORY PROGRAM

Kathleen Lynett, John Anderson, Norman Dawber, George Couture, Doug Craig.

QUEEN'S UNIVERSITY

Charles Power papers.

HONG KONG VETERANS COMMEMORATIVE ASSOCIATION:

Frank Christensen's story, Gleanings from the Diary of A Winnipeg Grenadier, H6737 Private Tom Forsyth, ex. P.O.W., 9 January 1941.

ARTICLES

Armstrong, John G. "RCAF Identity in Bomber Command: Squadron Names and Sponsors." *Canadian Military History* 8.2 (Spring 1999) 43–52.

Barton, Brandey. "Public Opinion and National Prestige: The Politics of Canadian Army Participation in the Invasion of Sicily, 1942–1943." *Canadian Military History* 15.2 (Spring 2006) 23–34.

Bashow, David L. "The Balance Sheet: The Costs and Gains of the Bombing Campaign." *Canadian Military History* 15.3&4 (Summer–Autumn, 2006) 43–70.

Beaumont, Joan. "Prisoners of War in Australian National Memory," in Bob Moore and Barbara Hately-Broad (eds.), *Prisoners of War, Prisoners of Peace: Captivity, Homecoming and Memory in World War II* (New York: Berg, 2005) 185–94.

Beaumont, Joan. "Rank, Privilege and Prisoners of War." *War and Society* 1.1 (1983) 67–94.

Bechthold, Michael. "Air Support in the Breskens Pocket: The Case of First Canadian Army and 84 Group RAF." *Canadian Military History* 4.2 (Autumn 1994) 53–62.

Bechthold, Michael. "Lost in Normandy: The Odyssey of Worthington Force, 9 August 1944." *Canadian Military History* 19.2 (Spring 2010) 5–24.

Bechthold, Michael. "A Question of Success: Tactical Air Doctrine and Practice in North Africa, 1942–43." *Journal of Military History* 68 (July 2004) 821–51.

Biddle, Tami Davis. "Bombing the Square Yard: Sir Arthur Harris at War, 1942–45." *International History Review* 21 (1999) 626–64.

Bridge, Arthur. "In the Eye of the Storm: A Recollection of Three Days in the Falaise Gap, 19–21 August 1944."" *Canadian Military History* 9.3 (2000) 61–8.

Brown, Andrew. "New Men in the Line: An Assessment of Reinforcements to the 48th Highlanders in Italy, January–October 1944." *Canadian Military History* 21.3 (2012) 35–47.

Brown, Gordon. "The Capture of the Abbaye D'Ardenne by the Regina Rifles, 8 July 1944." *Canadian Military History* 4.1 (1995) 91–9.

Byers, Daniel. "Mobilising Canada: The National Resources Mobilization Act, the Department of National Defence, and Compulsory Military Service in Canada, 1940–1945." *Journal of the Canadian Historical Association* 7.1 (1996) 184–92.

Byers, Daniel. "Operation 'Canada': 5th Canadian Armoured Division's Attack on Delfzijl, 23 April to 2 May 1945." *Canadian Military History* 7.3 (1998) 35–45.

Caldwell, R.H. "The VE Day Riots in Halifax, 7–8 May 1945." *The Northern Mariner* 10.1 (January 2000) 3–20.

Carr, Graham. "Rules of Engagement: Public History and the Drama of Legitimation." *Canadian Historical Review* 86.2 (June 2005) 317–54.

Copp, Terry. "Canada's D-Day: Politics, Media, and the Fluidity of Memory," in Michael Dolski (ed.) *D-Day in History and Memory: The Normandy Landings in International Remembrance and Commemoration* (University of North Texas Press, 2014) 131–58.

Copp, Terry. "Fifth Brigade: Verrières Ridge." *Canadian Military History* 1.1–2 (1992) 45–63.

Copp, Terry. "'If this war isn't over, And pretty damn soon, There'll be nobody left, In this old platoon....' First Canadian Army, February–March 1945," in Paul Addison and Angus

Calder (eds.) *Time to Kill: The Soldier's Experience of War in the West, 1939–1945* (London: Pimlico, 1997) 147–58.

Copp, Terry. "Operation Spring: An Historian's View." *Canadian Military History* 12.1–2 (2003) 63–70.

Copp, Terry. "Return to Dieppe, September 1944." *Canadian Military History* 1.1–2 (1992) 71–8.

Copp, Terry. "To the Last Canadian? Casualties in 21st Army Group." *Canadian Military History* 18.1 (Winter 2009) 3–6.

Copp, Terry and Michelle Fowler. "Heavy Bombers and Civil Affairs: First Canadian Army in France, July–September 1944." *Canadian Military History* 22.2 (Spring 2013) 4–18.

Cox, Andrew. "Five Years as a Prisoner of War." *Canadian Military History* 2.1 (1993) 115–22.

D'Amours, Caroline. "Reassessment of a Crisis: Canadian Infantry Reinforcements during the Second World War." *Canadian Army Journal* 14.2 (2012) 73–89.

Dean, David. "Museums as Contact Zones: the Canadian War Museum and Bomber Command." *Museum and Society* 7.1 (March 2009) 1–15.

Delaney, Douglas. "When Leadership Really Mattered: Bert Hoffmeister and Morale During the Battle of Ortona, December 1943," in Bernd Horn (ed.) *Intrepid Warriors: Perspectives on Canadian Military Leaders* (Toronto: Dundurn, 2007)139–54.

Dickson, Paul. "Harry Crerar and an Army for Strategic Effect." *Canadian Military History* 17.1 (Winter 2008) 37–48.

Dodd, Lindsay and Andrew Knapp, "'How Many Frenchmen Did You Kill?' British Bombing Policy Towards France (1940–1945)." *Society for the Study of French History* 22.4 (2008) 469–92.

Durflinger, Serge. "'I Regret to Inform You': Next-of-Kin Notification and Official Condolences: The Case of Flight Lieutenant George J. Chequer, RCAF." *Canadian Military History* 9.4 (2000) 44–55.

Durflinger, Serge. "'Nothing Would Be Too Much Trouble': Hometown Support for H.M.C.S. *Dunver*, 1943–1945." *The Northern Mariner* 12.4 (October 2002) 1–12.

English, Alan. "Leadership and Lack of Moral Fibre in Bomber Command, 1939–1945: Lessons for Today and Tomorrow," in Howard G. Coombs (ed.) *The Insubordinate and the Noncompliant: Case Studies of Canadian Mutiny and Disobedience, 1920 to the Present* (Kingston: Canadian Defence Academy Press, 2007) 101–24.

Evans, Christopher. "The Fighter-Bomber in the Normandy Campaign." *Canadian Military History* 8.1 (Winter 1999) 21–31.

Fedorowich, Kent. "'Cocked Hats and Swords and Small, Little Garrisons': Britain, Canada and the Fall of Hong Kong, 1941." *Modern Asian Studies* 37 (February 2003) 111–57.

Fisher, Robert. "Canadian Merchant Ship Losses, 1939–1945." *The Northern Mariner* 5.3 (1995) 57–73.

Fisher, Robert C. "Tactics, Training, Technology: The RCN's Summer of Success, July–September 1942." *Canadian Military History* 6.2 (Autumn 1997) 7–20.

Fitzgerald-Black, Alexander. "Investigating the Memory of Operation Spring: The Inquiry into the Black Watch and the Battle of St. André-sur-Orne, 1944–46." *Canadian Military History* 21.2 (Spring 2012) 21–32.

Flavelle, Ryan. "Help or Harm: Battle Exhaustion and the RCAMC during the Second World War." *Journal of Military and Strategic Studies* 9.4 (Summer 2007) 1–22.

Foulds, Tony. "In Support of the Canadians: A British Anti-Tank Regiment's First Five Weeks in Normandy." *Canadian Military History* 7.2 (Spring 1998) 71–8.

Givens, Seth A. "Liberating the Germans: The US Army and Looting in Germany during the Second World War." *War in History* 21.1 (2013) 33–54.

Glover, William. "The RCN: Royal Colonial or Royal Canadian Navy," in Michael Hadley et al. (eds.) *A Nation's Navy: In Quest of Canadian Naval Identity* (Montreal: McGill-Queen's University Press, 1996) 71–90.

Goette, Richard. "Britain and the Delay in Closing the Mid-Atlantic 'Air Gap' during the Battle of the Atlantic." *The Northern Mariner* 15.4 (October 2005) 19–41.

Gooderson, Ian. "Heavy and Medium Bombers: How Successful Were They in the Tactical Close Air Support Role During World War II?" *Journal of Strategic Studies* 15.3 (1992) 367–99.

Gough, Barry M., and James A. Wood, "'One more for luck': The Destruction of *U971* by HMCS *Haida* and HMS *Eskimo*, 24 June 1944." *Canadian Military History* 10.3 (Summer 2001) 7–22.

Gough, Paul. "A Difficult Path to Tread: The New Memorial Garden at Caen, Normandy." *Canadian Military History* 8.1 (Winter 1999) 78–80.

Gray, Peter. "A Culture of Official Squeamishness? Britain's Air Ministry and the Strategic Air Offensive Against Germany." *Journal of Military History* 77.4 (October 2013) 1349–77.

Greenhous, Brereton. "Would it not have been better to bypass Ortona completely ...?" *Canadian Defence Quarterly* (April 1989) 51–5.

Gross, Gordon. "A Trip to Remember: An Airman's View of D–Day." *Canadian Military History* 10.2 (Sprint 2001) 75–9.

Harris, Stephen J. "The Halifax and Lancaster in Canadian Service." *Canadian Military History* 15.3&4 (Summer–Autumn, 2006) 5–26.

Hall, David. "Black, White and Grey: Wartime Arguments for and against the Strategic Bombing Offensive." *Canadian Military History* 7.1 (Winter 1998) 7–19.

Haller, Oliver. "The Defeat of the 12th SS, 7–10 June 1944." *Canadian Military History* 3.1 (1994) 8–25.

Haller, Oliver. "Destroying Hitler's Berghof: The Bomber Command Raid of 25 April 1945." *Canadian Military History* 20.1 (Winter 2011) 5–20.

Halladay, Laurel. "'It Made Them Forget About the War For a Minute': Canadian Army, Navy, and Air Force Entertainment Units During the Second World War." *Canadian Military History* 11.4 (Autumn 2002) 21–35.

Hayes, Geoffrey. "'Where Are Our Liberators?' The Canadian Liberation of West Brabant, 1944." *Canadian Military History* 4.1 (1995) 7–19.

Hillmer, Norman. "The Canadian War Museum and the Military Identity of an Unmilitary People." *Canadian Military History* 19.3 (Summer 2010) 19–26.

Hitchcock, William. "The Price of Liberation," *MHQ: The Quarterly Journal of Military History* 21.3 (Spring 2009) 20–9.

Horn, Bernd and Michel Wyczynski. "A Most Irrevocable Step: Canadian Paratroopers on D-Day, The First 24 Hours, 5–6 June 1944." *Canadian Military History* 13.3 (Summer 2004) 14–32.

Horn, Michael. "More than Cigarettes, Sex and Chocolate: The Canadian Army in the Netherlands, 1944–1945." *Journal of Canadian Studies* 16. 3&4 (1981) 156–73.

Iarocci, Andrew. "Equipment of the Canadian Infantryman, 1939–1982: A Material/Historical Assessment." *Canadian Military History* 9.4 (2000) 35–43.

Jarymowycz, Roman. "Canadian Armour in Normandy: Operation 'Totalize' and the Quest for Operational Maneuver." *Canadian Military History* 7.2 (Spring 1998) 19–40.

Jarymowycz, Roman. "German Counterattacks during Operation 'Spring': 25–26 July 1944." *Canadian Military History* 2.1 (1993) 74–89.

Johnston, Paul. "Tactical Air Power Controversies in Normandy: A Question of Doctrine." *Canadian Military History* 9.2 (Spring 2000) 59–71.

Keshen, Jeff. "Getting It Right the Second Time Around: The Reintegration of Canadian Veterans of World War II," in Peter Neary and J.L. Granatstein (eds.) *The Veterans Charter and Post–World War II Canada* (Montreal: McGill-Queen's University Press, 1998) 62–84.

Klotz, Sarah. "*Shooting* the War: The *Canadian* Army Film Unit in the Second World War." *Canadian Military History* 14.3 (2005) 21–38.

Lackenbauer, Whitney. "'A Hell of a Warrior': Remembering Sergeant Thomas George Prince." *Journal of Historical Biography* 1 (Spring 2007) 26–79.

Learment, Don. "Soldier, POW, Partisan: My Experience During the Battle of France, June–September 1944." *Canadian Military History* 9.2 (Spring 2000) 91–104.

Lee, Peter. "Return from the Wilderness: An Assessment of Arthur Harris' Moral Responsibility for the German City Bombings." *Air Power Review* 16.1 (2013) 70–90.

Lehmann, Wady. "Recollections Concerning Canadian War Crimes Investigations and Prosecutions." *Canadian Military History* 11.4 (Autumn 2002) 71–80.

Leppard, Christine. "Documenting the D-Day Dodgers: Canadian Field Historians in the Italian Campaign, 1943–1945." *Canadian Military History* 18.3 (2009) 7–18.

Leppard, Christine, "Politics by Other Means: Canadian 'Strategy' and the Italian Campaign, 1943," *Journal of Military and Strategic Studies* 13.4 (Summer 2011) 1–22.

Madsen, Chris. "Victims of Circumstance: The Execution of German Deserters by Surrendered German Troops Under Canadian Control in Amsterdam, May 1945." *Canadian Military History* 2.1 (1993) 93–113.

Mahoney, Flt. Lt. John E. "Stalag Luft III, part I." *The Roundel* 1.12 (October 1949).

Maker, John. "The Essex Scottish Regiment in Operation Atlantic: What Went Wrong?" *Canadian Military History* 18.1 (Winter 2009) 7–20.

McAndrew, William. "Eighth Army at the Gothic Line: Commanders and Plans." *RUSI* (March 1986) 50–7.

McAndrew, W.J. "Recording the War: Uncommon Canadian Perspectives of the Italian Campaign." *Canadian Defence Quarterly* 18.3 (Winter 1988) 43–50.

McLean, Douglas M. "Confronting Technological and Tactical Change: Allied Anti-Submarine Warfare in the Last Year of the Battle of the Atlantic." *Canadian Military History* 7.3 (1998) 23–34.

McRae, Bill. "Bed and Breakfast: A Canadian Airman Reflects on Food and Quarters during the Second World War." *Canadian Military History* 9.1 (2000) 60–70.

MacDonald, Harold and M.A. MacDonald, "In the Heat of Battle: Letters from the Normandy Campaign." *Canadian Military History* 11.2 (2002) 29–43.

Mackenzie, S.P. "The Treatment of Prisoners of War in World War II." *Journal of Modern History* 66 (1994) 487–520.

Mackenzie, S.P. "Vox Populi: British Army Newspapers in the Second World War." *Journal of Contemporary History*, 24.4 (1989): 665–81.

McIntyre, Doug W. "Pursuit to the Seine: The Essex Scottish Regiment and the Forêt de la Londe, August 1944." *Canadian Military History* 7.1 (Winter 1998) 59–72.

McWilliams, Caitlin. "Camaraderie, Morale and Material Culture: Reflections on the Nose Art of No. 6 Group Royal Canadian Air Force." *Canadian Military History* 19.4 (Autumn 2010) 21–30.

Meitzell, Capt. Bernard-Georg, "Part 2." *Canadian Army Journal* (May 1950) 47–50.

Milner, Marc. "The Implications of Technological Backwardness: The Royal Canadian Navy, 1939–1945." *Canadian Defence Quarterly* 19.3 (Winter 1989) 46–52.

Morin-Pelletier, Mélanie. « ‹ J'ai combattu le bon combat, j'ai achevé ma course, j'ai gardé la foi › : Récit de guerre d'un conscript néo–brunswickois, 1943–1945. » *Canadian Military History* 22.4 (2013) 45–58.

O'Brien, Phillips. "East Versus West in the Defeat of Nazi Germany." *Journal of Strategic Studies* 23.2 (2000) 89–113.

O'Keefe, David R. "Fortune's Fate: The Question of Intelligence for Operation Spring, Normandy, 25 July 1944." *Canadian Defence Quarterly* 24.3 (March 1995) 17–21.

Oliver, Dean. "Awaiting Return: Life in the Canadian Army's Overseas Repatriation Depots, 1945–1946," in Peter Neary and J.L. Granatstein (eds.) *The Veterans Charter and Post-World War II Canada* (McGill-Queen's University Press, 1998) 32–61.

Oliver, Dean. "Canadian Military Demobilization in World War II," in J.L. Granatstein and Peter Neary (eds.). *The Good Fight: Canadians and World War II* (Toronto: Copp Clark, 1995) 367–86.

Parks, W. Hays. "'Precision' and 'Area' Bombing: Who Did Which and When?" *Journal of Strategic Studies* 18.1 (1995) 145–74.

Patterson, David. "Outside the Box: A New Perspective on Operation Windsor—The Rationale behind the Attack on Carpiquet, 4 July 1944." *Canadian Military History* 17.2 (Spring 2008) 66–74.

Pellerin, R. Daniel. "'You Have Shut Up the Jerries': Canadian Counter–Battery Work in the Clearing of the Breskens Pocket, October–November 1944." *Canadian Military History* 21.3 (Summer 2012) 17–34.

Peloquin, Laurie. "Area Bombing by Day: Bombing Command and the Daylight Offensive, 1944–1945." *Canadian Military History* 15.3&4 (Summer–Autumn, 2006) 27–42.

Peloquin, Laurie. "A Conspiracy of Silence? The Popular Press and the Strategic Bombing Campaign in Europe." *Canadian Military History* 3.2 (1994) 23–30.

Perras, Galen. "Defeat Still Cries Aloud for Explanation: Explaining C Force's Dispatch to Hong Kong." *Canadian Military Journal* 11.4 (Autumn 2011) 37–47.

Perrun, Jody. "Best-Laid Plans: Guy Simonds and Operation Totalize, 7–10 August 1944." *Journal of Military History 67.1* (January 2003) 137–73.

Pulsifer, Cameron. "Striking into Germany: From the Scheldt to the German Surrender." *Canadian Military History* 12.3 (Summer 2003) 35–56.

Rawling, Bill. "A Lonely Ambassador: HMCS *Uganda* and the War in the Pacific." *The Northern Mariner* VIII.1 (January, 1998) 39–63.

Rawling, Bill. "To the Sound of the Guns: Canadians and Combat Surgery, 1938–1953." *Canadian Military History* 6.1 (Spring 1997) 57–68.

Redford, Duncan. "Inter and Intra-Service Rivalries in the Battle of the Atlantic." *Journal of Strategic Studies* 32.6 (2009) 899–928.

Rockingham, J.M. "The Royal Hamilton Light Infantry at Verrières." *Canadian Military History* 2.1 (1993) 90–2.

Rolf, David. "The Education of British Prisoners of War in German Captivity, 1939–1945." *History of Education* 18.3 (1989) 257–65.

Russell, Harold. "24th Canadian Field Ambulance: Royal Canadian Army Medical Corps." *Canadian Military History* 8.1 (Winter 1999) 65–74.

Sheffield, R. Scott. "Canadian Aboriginal Veterans and the Veterans Charter after the Second World War," in P. Whitney Lackenbauer et al. (eds.) *Aboriginal Peoples and Military*

Participation: Canadian & International Perspectives (Winnipeg: Canadian Defence Academy Press, 2007) 77–98.

Sheffield, Scott. "Fighting a White Man's War?: First Nations Participation in the Canadian War Effort, 1939–1945," in Geoffrey Hayes et al. (eds.) *Canada and the Second World War: Essays in Honour of Terry Copp* (Waterloo: Wilfrid Laurier University Press, 2012) 67–91.

Souchen, Alex. "The Culture of Morale: Battalion Newspapers in the 3rd Canadian Infantry Division, June–August 1944." *Journal of Military History* 77 (April 2013) 523–56.

Sullivan, Michael. "Combat Motivation and the Roots of Fanaticism: The 12th SS Panzer Division Hitlerjugend in Normandy." *Canadian Military History* 10.3 (Summer 2001) 43–56.

"The Technique of the Assault: The Canadian Army on D-Day After-Action Reports by Commanders," *Canadian Military History* 14.3 (2005) 57–61.

Usher, Peter J. "Jews in the Royal Canadian Air Force, 1940–1945." *Canadian Jewish Studies* 20 (2012) 93–114.

Vance, Jonathan, "Men in Manacles: The Shackling of Prisoners of War, 1942–1943." *The Journal of Military History* 59.3 (July 1995) 483–504.

Vance, Jonathan. "An Open Door to a Better Future: The Memory of Canada's Second World War," in Geoffrey Hayes et al. (eds.) *Canada and the Second World War* (Waterloo: Wilfred Laurier University Press, 2012) 461–77.

Vance, Jonathan, "Their Duty Twice Over: Canadians in the Great Escape." *Canadian Military History* 3.1 (1994) 111–16.

Vogel, Robert. "Tactical Air Power in Normandy: Some Thoughts on the Interdiction Plan." *Canadian Military History* 3.1 (1994) 37–47.

Wakelam, Randall. "Bomber Harris and Precision Bombing—No Oxymoron Here." *Journal of Military and Strategic Studies* 14.1 (Fall 2011) 1–15.

Whitby, Michael. "'Fooling' Around the French Coast: RCN Tribal-Class Destroyers in Action, April 1944." *Canadian Defence Quarterly* 19.3 (December 1989) 54–61.

Whitby, Michael. "The Case of the Phantom MTB and the Loss of the HMCS *Athabaskan*." *Canadian Military History* 11.3 (Summer 2002) 5–14.

Whitby, Michael. "Masters of the Channel Night: The 10th Destroyer Flotilla's Victory off Île De Batz, 9 June 1944." *Canadian Military History* 2.1 (1993) 4–21.

Whitby, Michael. "'There must be no Holes in our Sweeping'": The 31st Canadian Minesweeping Flotilla on D-Day." *Canadian Military History* 3.1 (1994) 61–6.

White, Jay. "Hardly Heroes: Canadian Merchant Seamen and the International Convoy System." *The Northern Mariner* 5.4 (1995) 19–36.

Wilson, David A. "The Canadian Role in Operation 'Charnwood,' 8 July 1944: A Case Study in Tank/Infantry Doctrine and Practice." *Canadian Military History* 8.3 (Summer 1999) 7–21.

Zimmerman, David. "The Social Background of the Wartime Navy: Some Statistical Data," in Michael Hadley (eds.) *A Nation's Navy: In Quest of Canadian Naval Identity* (McGill-Queen's University Press, 1996) 256–79.

BOOKS

Addison, Paul and Jeremy A. Crang (eds.). *Fire-Storm: The Bombing of Dresden*. London: Pimlico, 2006.

Aders, Gebhard. *History of the German Night Fighter Force*. London: Janes, 1979.

Alexander of Tunis. *The Alexander Memoirs*. London: Cassell, 1962.

Allard, Jean and Serge Bernier, *The Memoirs of General Jean V. Allard*. Vancouver: UBC Press, 1988.

Allison, Les and Harry Hayward. *They Shall Not Grow Old, a Book of Remembrance*. Brandon: The Commonwealth Air Training Plan Museum, 1991.

Allport, Alan. *Demobbed: Coming Home after World War Two*. New Haven: Yale University Press, 2009

Antal, Sandy and Kevin Shackleton. *Duty Nobly Done: The Official History of the Essx and Kent Scottish Regiment*. Windsor: Walkerville, 2006.

Applebaum, Anne. *Iron Curtain: The Crushing of Eastern Europe, 1944–1956*. New York: Doubleday, 2012.

Arnold, Jorg. *The Allied Air War and Urban Memory: The Legacy of Strategic Bombing in Germany*. Cambridge: Cambridge University Press, 2011.

Atkinson, Rick. *The Guns at Last Light: The War in Western Europe, 1944–1945*. New York: Henry Holt, 2013.

Baldoli, Claudia, Andrew Knapp and Richard Overy (eds.). *Bombing, States and Peoples in Western Europe 1940–1945*. London: Continuum, 2011.

Barrett, W.W. *The History of the 13th Canadian Field Regiment*. Netherlands: Published by the regiment, 1945.

Barnard, Lieutenant-Colonel W.T. *The Queen's Own Rifles of Canada, 1860–1960*. Don Mills: Ontario Publishing, 1960.

Barrie, Lt. Col. Doug (ed.). *Buron Remembered*. Self-published, 2007.

Barris, Ted. *Breaking the Silence: Veterans' Untold Stories*. Toronto: Thomas Allen, 2009.

Barris, Ted. *The Great Escape: A Canadian Story*. Toronto: Dundurn, 2013.

Bartov, Omar. *The Eastern Front 1941–1945: German Troops and the Barbarisation of Warfare*. Basingstoke: Palgrave Macmillan, 2001.

Bashow, David. *All the Fine Young Eagles: In the Cockpit with Canada's Second World War Fighter Pilots*. Toronto: Stoddart, 1997.

Bashow, David. *None but the Brave: The Essential Contributions of RAF Bomber Command to*

Allied Victory during the Second World War. Kingston: Canadian Forces Defence Academy, 2009.

Bashow, David. *No Prouder Place: Canadians and the Bomber Command Experience, 1939 to 1945*. St. Catharines: Vanwell, 2005.

Beattie, Kim. *Dileas: History of The 48th Highlanders of Canada, 1929–1956*. Toronto: Published by the regiment, 1957.

Beevor, Anthony. *The Second World War*. New York: Little, Brown and Co., 2012.

Bercuson, David. *Battalion of Heroes: The Calgary Highlanders in World War II*. Toronto: Penguin, 1994.

Bercuson, David. *Maple Leaf against the Axis: Canada's Second World War*. Toronto: Stoddart, 1995.

Bercuson, David J. *The Patricias: The Proud History of a Fighting Regiment*. Toronto: Stoddart, 2001.

Bercuson, David J. and S.F. Wise (eds.). *The Valour and the Horror Revisited*. Montreal: McGill-Queen's University Press, 1994.

Bell, Captain T.J. *Into Action with the 12th Field*. Utrecht: J. van Boekhoven, 1945.

Bernier, Serge. *The Royal 22e Regiment, 1914–1999*. Montreal: Art Global, 2000.

Biddle, Tami Davis. *Rhetoric and Reality in Air Warfare: The Evolution of British and American Ideas about Strategic Bombing, 1914–1945*. Princeton: Princeton University Press, 2002.

Bird, Will R. *North Shore (New Brunswick) Regiment*. Fredericton: Brunswick, 1963.

Bishop, Patrick. *Bomber Boys: Fighting Back, 1940–1945*. London: Harper, 2007.

Blair, Clay. *Hitler's U-boat War: The Hunted, 1942–1944*. New York: Random House, 1996.

Blumenson, Martin. *The Battle of the Generals*. New York: Morrow, 1994.

Blumenson, Martin. *Breakout and Pursuit*. Washington: Office of the Chief of Military History, 1961.

Blumenson, Martin. *Patton: The Man behind the Legend, 1885–1945*. New York: William Morrow, 1985.

Boog, Horst (ed.). *The Conduct of the Air War in the Second World War: An International Comparison*. New York: Berg, 1992.

Bothwell, Robert and William Kilbourn. *C.D. Howe: A Biography*. Toronto: McClelland & Stewart, 1979.

Bouchery, Jean. *The Canadian Soldier in North-West Europe*. Paris: Histoire & Collections, 2003.

Boutilier, James A. (ed). *The RCN in Retrospect, 1910–1968*. Vancouver: UBC Press, 1982.

Bracken, Robert. *Spitfire: The Canadians*. Erin: Boston Mills, 1995.

Bradley, Omar N. *A Soldier's Story*. New York: Modern Library, 1999.

Broad, Graham. *A Small Price to Pay: Consumer Culture on the Canadian Home Front, 1939–45*. Vancouver: UBC Press, 2013.

Brode, Patrick. *Casual Slaughter and Accidental Judgements: Canadian War Crime Prosecutions, 1944–1948*. Toronto: Osgoode Hall, 1997.

Brooks, Stephen. *Montgomery and the Battle of Normandy*. England: Army Records Society, 2008.

Brown, Gordon and Terry Copp. *Look to the Your Front ... Regina Rifles: A Regiment at War, 1944–1945*. Waterloo: Laurier Centre for Military Strategic and Disarmament Studies, 2001.

Buckley, John. *Monty's Men: The British Army and the Liberation of Europe*. New Haven: Yale University Press, 2013.

Buckley, John (ed.). *The Normandy Campaign: Sixty Years On*. London: Routledge, 2006.

Burhams, Robert D. *The First Special Service Force: a War History of the North Americans, 1942–1944*. Washington: Infantry Journal Press, 1947.

Burns, E.L.M. *Manpower in the Canadian Army, 1939–1945*. Toronto: Clarke, Irwin, 1956.

Burrow, Len and Beaudoin, Emile. *Unlucky Lady: The Life & Death of HMCS Athabaskan, 1940–44*. Toronto: McClelland & Stewart, 1987.

The Calgary Regiment. Hilversum, Netherlands: Published by the unit, 1945; reprinted in Vancouver, 1989.

Campbell, Ian J. *Murder at the Abbaye: The Story of Twenty Canadian Soldiers Murdered at the Abbaye d'Ardenne*. Ottawa: Golden Dog, 1996.

Cassidy, G.L. *Warpath: The Story of the Algonquin Regiment, 1939–1945*. Cobalt: Highway Book Shop, 1990.

Chickering, Roger, Stig Förster, and Bernd Greiner (eds.). *A World at Total War: Global Conflict and the Politics of Destruction, 1937–1945*. Cambridge: Cambridge University Press, 2005.

Christie, Carl. *No Reason Why: The Canadian Hong Kong Tragedy—an Examination*. Stittsville: Canada's Wings, 1981.

Citino, Robert. *The Wehrmacht Retreats: Fighting a Lost War, 1943*. Lawrence: University Press of Kansas, 2012.

Cook, Tim. *Clio's Warriors: Canadian Historians and the Writing of the World Wars*. Vancouver: UBC Press, 2006.

Cook, Tim. *The Necessary War: Canadians Fighting the Second World War, Volume I: 1939–1943*. Toronto: Allan Lane, 2014.

Cook, Tim. *Shock Troops: Canadians Fighting the Great War, Volume II: 1917–1918*. Toronto: Viking, 2008.

Cook, Tim. *Warlords: Borden, Mackenzie King, and Canada's World Wars*. Toronto: Allen Lane, 2012.

Copp, Terry. *Cinderella Army: The Canadians in Northwest Europe, 1944–1945*. Toronto: University of Toronto Press, 2006.

Copp, Terry. *Fields of Fire: The Canadians in Normandy*. Toronto: University of Toronto Press, 2003.

Copp, Terry (ed.). *Montgomery's Scientists: Operational Research in Northwest Europe: The Work of No.2 Operational Research Section with 21 Army Group June 1944 to July 1945*. Waterloo: Laurier Centre for Military Strategic and Disarmament Studies, 2000.

Copp, Terry. *No Price Too High: Canadians and the Second World War*. Toronto: McGraw-Hill Ryerson, 1996.

Copp, Terry and Mark Humphries. *Combat Stress in the 20th Century: The Commonwealth Perspective*. Kingston: Canadian Defence Academy Press, 2010.

Copp, Terry and Bill McAndrew. *Battle Exhaustion: Soldiers and Psychiatrists in the Canadian Army, 1939–1945*. Montreal: McGill-Queen's University Press, 1990.

Copp, Terry and Robert Vogel. *Maple Leaf Route: Scheldt*. Alma: Maple Leaf Route, 1985.

Cormier, Ronald (ed.). *The Forgotten Soldiers: Stories from Acadian Veterans of the Second World War*. Fredericton: New Ireland, 1992.

Crawley, Aidan. *Escape from Germany: The Methods of Escape Used by RAF Airmen during the Second World War*. London: HMSO, 1985.

D'Este, Carlo. *Decision in Normandy: The Unwritten Story of Montgomery and the Allied Campaign*. London: Collins, 1994.

D'Este, Carlo. *Eisenhower: A Soldier's Life*. New York: Henry Holt and Company, 2002.

D'Este, Carlo. *Patton: A Genius for War*. New York: Harper, 1995.

Danchev, Alex and Dan Todman. *War Diaries, 1939–1945: Field Marshal Lord Alanbrooke*. Berkeley: University of California Press, 2003.

Dancocks, Daniel. *The D-Day Dodgers: The Canadians in Italy, 1943–1945*. Toronto: McClelland & Stewart, 1991.

Dancocks, Daniel. *In Enemy Hands: Canadian Prisoners of War, 1939–45*. Edmonton: Hurtig, 1983.

Davis, Richard. *Carl A. Spaatz and the Air War in Europe*. Washington: Centre for Air Force History, 1993.

Delaforce, Patrick. *Churchill's Secret Weapons: The Story of Hobart's Funnies*. London: Pen & Sword, 2008.

Delaney, Doug. *Corps Commanders: Five British and Canadian Generals at War, 1939–1945*. Vancouver: UBC Press, 2011.

Delaney, Doug. *The Soldiers' General: Bert Hoffmeister at War*. Vancouver: UBC Press, 2005.

Dickson, Paul. *A Thoroughly Canadian General: A Biography of General H.D.G. Crerar*. Toronto: University of Toronto Press, 2007.

Doubler, Michael. *Closing with the Enemy: How GIs Fought the War in Europe, 1944–1945*. Lawrence: University Press of Kansas, 1994.

Douglas, W.A.B. et al. *A Blue Water Navy: The Official Operational History of the Royal Canadian Navy in the Second World War, 1943–1945, volume II, part 2*. St. Catharines: Vanwell, 2007.

Douglas, W.A.B. *The Creation of a National Air Force: The Official History of the Royal Canadian Air Force Volume II.* Toronto: University of Toronto Press and the Department of National Defence, 1986.

Douglas, W.A.B. et al. *No Higher Purpose: The Official Operational History of the Royal Canadian Navy in the Second World War, 1939–1943, volume II, part 1.* St. Catharines: Vanwell., 2002.

Douglas, W.A.B. *The RCN in Transition, 1910–1985.* Vancouver: UBC Press, 1988.

Dower, John. *Cultures of War: Pearl Harbor, Hiroshima, 9/11, Iraq.* New York: W.W. Norton, 2010.

Dower, John. *War without Mercy: Race and Power in the Pacific War.* London: Faber, 1986.

Du Guid, Kirk. *Soldiers' Stories.* Self-published, 2009.

Dundas, Barbara. *A History of Women in the Canadian Military.* Montreal: Art Global, 2000.

Dunmore, Spencer. *Above and Beyond: The Canadians' War in the Air, 1939–45.* Toronto: McClelland & Stewart, 1996.

Dunmore, Spencer and William Carter. *Reap the Whirlwind.* Toronto: McClelland & Stewart, 1991.

Durflinger, Serge Marc. *Veterans with a Vision: Canada's War Blinded in Peace and War.* Vancouver: UBC Press, 2010.

Edgerton, David. *Britain's War Machine: Weapons, Resources, and Experts in the Second World War.* London: Allen Lane, 2011.

Ellis, John. *Cassino: The Hollow Victory.* London: Andre Deutsch, 1984.

Ellis, John. *The Sharp End of War: The Fighting Man in World War II.* Newton Abbot: David & Charles, 1980.

Engen, Robert C. *Canadians under Fire: Infantry Effectiveness in the Second World War.* Montreal: McGill-Queen's University Press, 2009.

English, Allan. *Cream of the Crop: Canadian Aircrew, 1939–1945.* Kingston: McGill-Queen's University Press, 1996.

English, John A. *Failure in High Command: The Canadian Army and the Normandy Campaign.* Ottawa: Golden Dog, 1995.

English, John A. *Surrender Invites Death: Fighting the Waffen SS in Normandy.* Mechanicsburg: Stackpole Books, 2011.

Evans, Richard J. *The Third Reich at War.* New York: Penguin, 2009.

Fahrni, Magda. *Household Politics: Montreal Families and Postwar Reconstruction.* Toronto: University of Toronto Press, 2005.

Feasby, W.R. *Official History of the Canadian Medical Services, 1939–1945, volume I.* Ottawa: E. Cloutier, Queen's Printer, 1953.

1st Battalion, The Regina Rifle Regiment, 1939–1946. No publisher, 1946.

Francis, Martin. *The Flyer: British Culture and the Royal Air Force, 1939–1945.* Oxford: Oxford University Press, 2008.

Fraser, Doug. *Postwar Casualty: Canada's Merchant Navy.* Nova Scotia: Pottersfield Press, 1997.

Fritz, Stephen G. *Frontsoldaten: The German Soldier in World War Two*. Lexington: University Press of Kentucky, 1995.

Fritz, Stephen G. *Ostkrieg: Hitler's War of Extermination in the East*. Lexington: University Press of Kentucky, 2011.

Fussell, Paul. *Wartime: Understanding and Behaviour in the Second World War*. Oxford: Oxford University Press, 1989.

Gelb, Norman. *Ike & Monty: Generals at War*. New York: William Morrow, 1994.

Gellately, Robert. *Backing Hitler: Consent and Coercion in Nazi Germany*. New York: Oxford University Press, 2001.

Gee, H.G. *Battle Wastage Rates, British Army, 1940–45*. Waterloo: Laurier Centre for Military Strategic and Disarmament Studies, 2010.

German, Tony. *The Sea Is at Our Gates: A History of the Canadian Navy*. Toronto: McClelland & Stewart, 1990.

Giangreco, D.M. *Hell to Pay: Operation DOWNFALL and the Invasion of Japan, 1945–1947*. Annapolis: Naval Institute Press, 2009.

Gimblett, Richard H. (ed.). *The Naval Service of Canada, 1910–2010: The Centennial Story*. Toronto: Dundurn, 2009.

Gimblett, Richard H., Haydon, Peter T., and Whitby, Michael J. (eds.). *The Admirals: Canada's Senior Naval Leadership in The Twentieth Century*. Toronto: Dundurn, 2008.

Glantz, D.M. and J.M. House. *When Titans Clashed: How the Red Army Stopped Hitler*. Lawrence: University of Kansas Press, 1995.

Gooderson, Ian. *Air Power at the Battlefront: Allied Close Air Support in Europe 1943–45*. Westport: Routledge, 1998.

Gooderson, Ian. *A Hard Way to Make War: The Italian Campaign in the Second World* War. London: Conway, 2008.

Granatstein, J.L. *Canada's Army: Waging War and Keeping the Peace*. Toronto: University of Toronto Press, 2002.

Granatstein, J.L. *Canada's War: The Politics of the Mackenzie King Government, 1939–1945*. Toronto: Oxford University Press, 1975.

Granatstein, J.L. *The Generals: The Canadian Army's Senior Commanders in the Second World War*. Toronto: Stoddart, 1993.

Granatstein, J.L. *The Last Good War: An Illustrated History of Canada in the Second World War, 1939–1945*. Vancouver: Douglas & McIntyre, 2005.

Granatstein, J.L. and J.M. Hitsman, *Broken Promises: A History of Conscription in Canada*. Toronto: Oxford University Press, 1977.

Granatstein, J.L. and Dean F. Oliver, *The Oxford Companion to Canadian Military History*. Toronto: Oxford University Press, 2011.

Graham, Dominick. *The Price of Command: A Biography of General Guy Simonds*. Toronto: Stoddart, 1993.

Graham, Dominick and Shelford Bidwell. *Tug of War: The Battle for Italy, 1943–1945*. London: Hodder & Stoughton, 1986.

Grant, Major D.W. *Carry On: The History of the Toronto Scottish Regiment (M.G.), 1939–1945*. Published by the regiment,1949.

Graves, Donald. *Century of Service: The History of the South Alberta Light Horse*. Toronto: Published for the South Alberta Light Horse Regiment Foundation by Robin Brass Studio, 2005.

Graves, Donald (ed.). *Fighting for Canada: Seven Battles, 1758–1945*. Toronto: Robin Brass Studio, 2000.

Graves, Donald. *South Albertans: A Canadian Regiment at War*. Toronto: Robin Brass, 1999.

Graves, Donald E., and Jenson, L.B. *In Peril on the Sea: the Royal Canadian Navy and the Battle of the Atlantic*. Toronto: Published for the Canadian Naval Memorial Trust by Robin Brass Studio, 2003.

Greenfield, Nathan. *The Forgotten: Canadian POWs, Escapers and Evaders in Europe, 1939–45*. Toronto: HarperCollins, 2013.

Greenhous, Brereton. *"C" Force to Hong Kong: A Canadian Catastrophe, 1941–1945*. Toronto: Dundurn, 1997.

Greenhous, Brereton. *Dieppe, Dieppe*. Montreal: Art Global, 1992.

Greenhous, Brereton and W.A.B. Douglas. *Out of the Shadows: Canada in the Second World War*. Toronto: Dundurn, 1995.

Greenhous, Brereton and Hugh A. Halliday. *Canada's Air Forces, 1914–1999*. Montreal: Art Global, 1999.

Greenhous, Brereton, Stephen J. Harris, William C. Johnston, William G.P. Rawling, *The Crucible of War, 1939–1945: The Official history of the Royal Canadian Air Force, volume III*. Toronto: University of Toronto Press, 1994.

Hadley, Michael L. *U-boats Against Canada: German Submarines in Canadian Waters*. Kingston: McGill-Queen's University Press, 1985.

Hale, James. *Branching Out: The Story of The Royal Canadian Legion*. Ottawa: The Royal Canadian Legion, 1995.

Halford, Robert G. *The Unknown Navy: Canada's World War Two Merchant Navy*. St. Catharines: Vanwell, 1995.

Hall, David Ian. *Strategy for Victory: The Development of British Tactical Air Power, 1919–1943*. Westport: Praeger Security International, 2008.

Halliday, Hugh and Brereton Greenhous. *Canada's Air Forces, 1914–1999*. Montreal: Art Global, 1999.

Hamilton, Nigel. *Monty: Final Years of the Field-Marshal, 1944–1976*. London: Hamish Hamilton, 1986.

Hansen, Randall. *Fire and Fury: The Allied Bombing of Germany 1942–1945*. Toronto: Doubleday Canada, 2008.

Harris, Sir Arthur T. *Despatch on War Operations, 23rd February, 1942, to 8th May, 1945*. London: Frank Cass, 1995.

Harris, Stephen J. *Canadian Brass: The Making of a Professional Army, 1860–1939*. Toronto: University of Toronto Press, 1998.

Harrison, Gordon. *Cross-Channel Attack*. Washington: US Government Printing Office, 1951.

Hart, Russel A. *Clash of Arms: How the Allies Won in Normandy*. Boulder: Lynne Rienner, 2001.

Hart, Stephen. *Sherman Firefly vs. Tiger: Normandy 1944*. Oxford: Ospery, 2007.

Hastings, Max. *All Hell Let Loose: The World at War (1939–45)*. London: HarperCollins, 2012.

Hastings, Max. *Overlord: D-Day and the Battle for Normandy*. London: Michael Joseph, 1984.

Hayes, Geoffrey. *The Lincs: A History of the Lincoln and Welland Regiment at War*, 2nd ed. Waterloo: Wilfrid Laurier University, 2007.

Hayes, Geoffrey, Mike Bechthold, and Matt Symes. *Canada and the Second World War: Essays in Honour of Terry Copp*. Waterloo: Wilfrid Laurier University Press, 2012.

Heathcote, Blake. *Testaments of Honour: Personal Histories from Canada's War Veterans*. Toronto: Doubleday, 2002.

Hibbert, Joyce. *Fragments of War: Stories from Survivors of World War II*. Toronto: Dundurn, 1985.

Historica-Dominion Institute. *We Were Freedom: Canadian Stories of the Second World War*. Toronto: Key Porter, 2010.

Horn, Colonel Bernd. *Establishing a Legacy: The History of the Royal Canadian Regiment, 1884–1953*. Toronto: Dundurn, 2008.

Horn, Colonel Bernd (ed.). *Intrepid Warriors: Perspectives on Canadian Military Leaders*. Toronto: Dundurn, 2007.

Horrocks, Brian. *A Full Life*. London: Collins, 1960.

Horrocks, William (ed.). *In Their Own Words*. Ottawa: Rideau Veterans Home Residents Council, 1993.

Hyatt, A.M. Jack and Nancy Geddes Poole. *Battle for Life: The History of No. 10 Canadian Stationary Hospital and No. 10 Canadian General Hospital in Two World Wars*. Waterloo: Laurier Centre for Military, Strategic and Disarmament Studies, 2004.

Irons, Roy. *The Relentless Offensive: War and Bomber Command, 1939–1945*. Barnsley: Pen & Sword Aviation, 2009.

Jarratt, Melynda. *War Brides: The Stories of the Women Who Left Everything behind to Follow the Men They Loved*. Toronto: Dundurn, 2009.

Jarymowycz, Roman. *Tank Tactics: From Normandy to Lorraine*. Boulder: Lynne Rienner, 2001.

Johnston, Mac. *Corvettes Canada: Convoy Veterans of WWII Tell Their True Stories*. Toronto: McGraw-Hill Ryerson, 1994.

Johnston, Stafford. *The Fighting Perths*. Stratford: Perth Regiment Veterans' Association, 1964.

Jones, Matthew. *Britain, the United States and the Mediterranean War, 1942–1944*. London: Macmillan, 1996.

Kaufman, David and Michael Horn. *A Liberation Album: Canadians in the Netherlands, 1944–1945.* Toronto: McGraw-Hill, 1980.

Kellett, Anthony. *Combat Motivation.* Ottawa: Dept. of National Defence, Operational Research and Analysis Establishment, 1980.

Kennedy, Paul. *Engineers of Victory: The Problem Solvers Who Turned the Tide in the Second World War.* Toronto: HarperCollins, 2013.

Kerry, A.J. and W.A. McDill. *The History of the Corps of the Royal Canadian Engineer, Volume 2: 1936–1946.* Ottawa: Military Engineers Association of Canada, 1966.

Kershaw, Ian. *Hitler: A Biography.* New York: W.W. Norton, 2010.

Keshen, Jeffrey. *Saints, Sinners, Soldiers: Canada's Second World War.* Vancouver: UBC Press, 2004.

Kesselring, Albert. *Kesselring: A Soldier's Record.* New York: William Morrow, 1954.

Knight, Doug (ed.). *A Collection of RCEME Individual Unit Histories in North-West Europe in World War II.* Special report for Canadian War Museum, 2006.

Knox, MacGregor. *Hitler's Italian Allies: Royal Armed Forces, Fascist Regime, and the War of 1940–1943.* Cambridge: Cambridge University Press, 2000.

Kushner, Tony. *The Holocaust and the Liberal Imagination.* Oxford: Oxford University Press, 1994.

Lackenbauer, P. Whitney and C.W. Madsen. *Kurt Meyer on Trial: A Documentary Record.* Kingston: Canadian Forces Leadership Institute, 2007.

La Grandeur, Philip. *We Flew We Fell We Lived: Stories from RCAF Prisoners of War and Evaders, 1939–1945.* St. Catharines: Vanwell, 2006.

Lamb, James. *The Corvette Navy: True Stories from Canada's Atlantic War.* Toronto: Macmillan of Canada, 1977.

Lamb, Richard. *Montgomery in Europe, 1943–1945.* London: Buchan and Enright, 1983.

Lavender, Emerson and Norman Sheffe. *The Evaders: True Stories of Downed Canadian Airmen and Their Helpers in World War II.* Toronto: McGraw-Hill Ryerson, 1992.

Lawruk, Ron and Merla Lawruk. *For Love and Country: A Biography of Private Ted Patrick.* Self-published, 2011.

Leef, Lt. Col. C.D. Stewart. *A Short History of the Fifteenth Canadian Field Ambulance.* Self-published, 1998.

Linderman, Gerald F. *The World within War: American's Combat Experience in World War II.* Cambridge: Harvard University Press, 1997.

Longden, Sean. *To the Victors the Spoils: D-Day to VE Day, The Reality Behind the Heroism.* Moreton: Arris Books, 2005.

Longworth, Philip. *The Unending Vigil: A History of the Commonwealth War Graves Commission, 1917–1984.* London: Leo Cooper, 1985.

Lowe, Keith. *Inferno: The Fiery Destruction of Hamburg, 1943.* New York: Scribner, 2007.

Ludwig, Paul A. *P-51 Mustang: Development of the Long-Range Escort Fighter*. Surrey: Ian Allen, 2003.

Luther, Craig H.W. *Blood and Honor: The 12th SS Panzer Division "Hitler Youth," 1939–1945*. San Jose: R. James Bender, 1998.

Luxton, Captain Eric (ed.). *The 1st Battalion: The Regina Rifle Regiment, 1939–1945*. Published by the regiment, 1946.

Lynch, Thomas J. (ed.). *Fading Memories: Canadian Sailors and the Battle of the Atlantic*. Halifax: Atlantic Chief and Petty Officers Association, 1993.

Macri, David. *Clash of Empires in South China: The Allied Nations' Proxy War with Japan, 1935–1941*. Kansas: University Press of Kansas, 2012.

Malone, Dick. *Missing from the Record*. Toronto: William Collins, 1946.

Malone, Richard. *A World in Flames, 1944–1945: A Portrait of War*. Toronto: Collins, 1984.

Martel, Gordon (ed.). *The World War Two Reader*. New York: Routledge, 2004.

Mayhew, E.R. *The Reconstruction of Warriors: Archibald McIndoe, the Royal Air Force and the Guinea Pig Club*. London: Greenhill, 2004.

Margolian, Howard. *Conduct Unbecoming: The Story of the Murder of Canadian Prisoners of War in Normandy*. Toronto: University of Toronto Press, 1998.

Marteinson, John (ed.). *We Stand on Guard: An Illustrated History of the Canadian Army*. Montreal: Ovale, 1992.

Marteinson, John and Michael McNorgan. *The Royal Canadian Armoured Corps: An Illustrated History*. Toronto: Robin Brass Studio, 2000.

Macfie, John. *Sons of the Pioneers: Memories of Veterans of the Algonquin Regiment*. Parry Sound: Hay, 2001.

Mackenzie, S.P. *The Colditz Myth: The Real Story of POW Life in Nazi Germany*. Oxford: Oxford University Press, 2006.

Mayne, Richard O. *Betrayed: Scandal, Politics, and Canadian Naval Leadership*. Vancouver: UBC Press, 2006.

McAndrew, Bill. *Canadians and the Italian Campaign, 1943–1945*. Montreal: Art Global, 1996.

McAndrew, Bill, Donald E. Graves and Michael Whitby. *Normandy 1944: The Canadian Summer*. Montreal: Art Global, 1994.

McGeer, Eric. *Words of Valediction and Remembrance: Canadian Epitaphs of the Second World War*. St. Catharines: Vanwell, 2008.

McGeer, Eric and Terry Copp, with Matt Symes. *The Canadian Battlefields in Italy: Sicily and Southern Italy*. Waterloo: Laurier Centre for Military Strategic and Disarmament Studies, 2008.

McIntosh, Dave. *Hell on Earth: Aging Faster, Dying Sooner. Canadian Prisoners of the Japanese during World War Two*. Toronto: McGraw-Hill Ryerson, 1997.

McKay, Ian and Jamie Swift. *Warrior Nation: Rebranding Canada in an Age of Anxiety*. Toronto: Between the Lines, 2012.

McKee, Alexander. *Caen: Anvil of Victory*. London: Souvenir Press, 1964.

McNeil, Bill. *Voices of a War Remembered: An Oral History of Canadians in World War Two*. Toronto: Doubleday, 1991.

Memories on Parade: Aircrew Recollections of World War II. Winnipeg: Wartime Pilots' and Observations' Association, 1995.

Meyer, Hubert. *The 12th SS: The History of the Hitler Youth Panzer Division*. Mechanicburg: Stackpole, 2005.

Mickleburgh, Rod, with Rudyard Griffiths. *Rare Courage: Veterans of the Second World War Remember*. Toronto: McClelland & Stewart, 2005.

Middlebrook, Martin. *The Berlin Raids*. London: Viking, 1988

Middlebrook, Martin and Chris Everitt. *The Bomber Command War Diaries*. Harmondsworth: Penguin, 1985.

Mierzejewski, Alfred C. *The Collapse of the German War Economy, 1944–1945*. Chapel Hill: University of North Carolina Press, 1988.

Milberry, Larry. *Canada's Air Force at War and Peace*, volume II. Toronto: Canav, 2000.

Millberry, Larry and Hugh Halliday, *The Royal Canadian Air Force at War, 1939–1945*. Toronto: Canav, 1990.

Milner, Marc. *Battle of the Atlantic*. St. Catharine's: Vanwell, 2003.

Milner, Marc. *Canada's Navy: The First Century*. Toronto: University of Toronto Press, 1999. 2nd ed., 2010.

Milner, Marc. *North Atlantic Run: The Royal Canadian Navy and the Battle for the Convoys*. Toronto: University of Toronto Press, 1985.

Milner, Marc. *Stopping the Panzers: The Untold Story of D-Day*. Lawrence: University of Kansas Press, 2014.

Milner, Marc. *The U-boat Hunters: The Royal Canadian Navy and the Offensive Against Germany's Submarines*. Toronto: University of Toronto Press, 1994.

Mitchell, George Duncan. *RCHA—Right of the Line: An Anecdotal History of the Royal Canadian Horse Artillery from 1871*. Ottawa: RCHA History Committee, 1986.

Mitter, Rana. *Forgotten Ally: China's World War II, 1937–1945*. New York: Houghton Mifflin Harcourt, 2013.

Molony, Brigadier C.J.C. *The Mediterranean and the Middle East*, volume V. London: HMSO, 1973.

Montgomery, Bernard Law. *The Memoirs of Field-Marshal the Viscount Montgomery of Alamein*. London: Collins, 1958.

Moore, Perry. *Operation Goodwood, July 1944: A Corridor of Death*. Solihull: Helion & Company, 2007.

Morrison, Alex and Ted Slaney. *The Breed of Manly Men: The History of the Cape Breton Highlanders*. Toronto: Canadian Institute of Strategic Studies, 1994.

Mulligan, Timothy P. *Neither Sharks Nor Wolves: The Men of Nazi Germany's U-boat Arm, 1949–1945*. Annapolis: U.S. Naval Institute Press, 1999.

Munro, Ross. *Gauntlet to Overlord*. Toronto: Macmillan, 1945.

Murray, G.E. Patrick. *Eisenhower vs. Montgomery: The Continuing Debate*. Westport: Praeger, 1996.

Murray, Williamson. *Strategy for Defeat: The Luftwaffe, 1933–1945*. Maxwell Air Force Base, AL: Air University Press, 1983.

Murray, Williamson and Allan R. Millett. *A War to Be Won: Fighting the Second World War*. Cambridge: Harvard University Press, 2000.

Neary, Peter. *On to Civvy Street: Canada's Rehabilitation Program for Veterans of the Second World War*. Montreal: McGill-Queen's University Press, 2011.

Neitzel, Sonke and Harald Welzer. *Soldaten: On Fighting, Killing and Dying, The Secret World War II Transcripts of German POWs*. Toronto: McClelland & Stewart, 2011.

Nichol, John and Tony Rennell. *The Last Escape: The Untold Story of Allied Prisoners of War in Europe, 1944–45*. London: Viking, 2002

Nicholson, G.W.L. *Canada's Nursing Sisters*. Toronto: A.M. Hakkert, 1975.

Nicholson, G.W.L. *The Canadians in Italy, 1943–1945*. Ottawa: Queen's Printer, 1955.

Nicholson, G.W.L. *The Gunners of Canada: The History of the Royal Regiment of Canadian Artillery*, volume II. Toronto: McClelland & Stewart, 1967.

Nicholson, G.W.L. *Seventy Years of Service: A History of the Royal Canadian Army Medical Corps*. Ottawa: Borealis, 1977.

O'Connor, Edward. *The Corvette Years: The Lower Deck Story*. Vancouver: Cordillera, 1995.

O'Keefe, David. *One Day in August: The Untold Story behind Canada's Tragedy at Dieppe*. Toronto: Knopf Canada, 2013.

Oliver, Dean F. and Laura Brandon, *Canvas of War: Painting the Canadian Experience, 1914 to 1945*. Vancouver: Douglas & McIntyre, 2000.

Overy, Richard J. *Bomber Command, 1939–1945*. London: HarperCollins, 1997.

Overy, Richard J. *The Bombing War: Europe, 1939–1945*. Penguin: Allen Lane, 2013.

Overy, Richard J. *Russia's War: A History of the Soviet War Effort, 1941–1945*. London: Penguin, 1997.

Overy, R.J. (ed.). *War and Economy in the Third Reich*. New York: Oxford University Press, 1994.

Overy, Richard J. *Why the Allies Won*. London: Pimlico, 1995.

Owram, Doug. *Born at the Right Time: A History of the Baby Boom Generation*. Toronto: University of Toronto Press, 1996.

Parker, Matthew. *Monte Cassino: The Hardest Fought Battle of World War II*. Toronto: Knopf, 2005.

Parker, Mike. *Running the Gauntlet: An Oral History of Canadian Merchant Seamen in World War II*. Halifax: Nimbus, 2003.

Pelling, Henry. *Winston Churchill*. London: Macmillan, 1974.

Perkins, Les. *Flight into Yesterday: A Memory or Two from Members of the Wartime Aircrew Club of Kelowna*. Victoria: Trafford, 2002.

Perry, Mark. *Partners in Command: George Marshall and Dwight Eisenhower in War and Peace*. New York: Penguin, 2007.

Pierson, Ruth Roach. *They're Still Women after All: Canadian Women and the Second World War*. Toronto: McClelland & Stewart, 1986.

Pitt, Steve. *Day of the Flying Fox: The True Story of World War II Pilot Charley Fox*. Toronto: Dundurn, 2008.

Place, Timothy Harrison. *Military Training in the British Army, 1940–1944: From Dunkirk to D-Day*. London: Frank Cass, 2000.

Porch, Douglas. *The Path to Victory: The Mediterranean Theatre in World War II*. New York: Farrar, Straus and Giroux, 2004.

Portugal, Jean (ed.). *We Were There: A Record for Canada*. Toronto: Royal Canadian Military Institute Heritage Society, 1998.

Powley, A.E. *Broadcast from the Front: Canadian Radio Overseas in the Second World War*. Toronto: Hakkert, 1975.

Probert, Henry. *Bomber Harris: His Life and Times*. London: Greenhill, 2003.

Pyves, Richard. *Night Madness: A Rear Gunner's Story of Love, Courage, and Hope in World War II*. Markam: Red Deer, 2012.

Raddall, Thomas. *West Novas: A History of the West Nova Scotia Regiment*. Liverpool, NS: No publisher, 1947.

Ralph, Wayne. *Aces, Warriors & Wingmen: Firsthand Accounts of Canada's Fighter Pilots in the Second World War*. Mississauga: John Wiley & Sons Canada, 2005.

Rannie, William F. (ed.). *To the Thunderer His Arms: The Royal Canadian Ordnance Corps*. Lincoln: W.F. Rannie, 1984.

Rawling, Bill. *Death Their Enemy: Canadian Medical Practitioners and War*. Self-published, 2001.

Reader's Digest. *The Canadians at War, 1939/45*. Montreal: Reader's Digest, 1986.

Reid, Brian A. *Named by the Enemy: A History of the Royal Winnipeg Rifles*. Toronto: Robin Brass Studio, 2010.

Reid, Brian A. *No Holding Back: Operation Totalize: Normandy, August 1944*. Toronto: Robin Brass Studio, 2005.

Rennick, Joanne Benham. *Religion in the Ranks: Belief and Religious Experience in the Canadian Forces*. Toronto: University of Toronto Press, 2011.

Reynolds, David. *In Command of History: Churchill Fighting and Writing the Second World War*. London: Penguin, 2005.

Reynolds, David. *The Long Shadow: The Legacies of the Great War in the Twentieth Century*. New York: W.W. Norton, 2014.

Reynolds, Michel. *Steel Inferno: 1 SS Panzer Corps in Normandy*. New York: Sarpedon, 1997.

Richler, Noah. *What We Talk About When We Talk About War*. Fredericton: Goose Lane, 2012.

Rickard, John. *The Politics of Command: Lieutenant-General A.G.L. McNaughton and the Canadian Army 1939–1943*. Toronto: University of Toronto Press, 2010.

Ritchie, Sebastian. *Arnhem: Myth and Reality*. London: Robert Hale, 2010.

Roberts, Andrew. *Storm of War: A New History of the Second World War*. New York: Allen Lane, 2010.

Roberts, Leslie. *Let There Be Wings*. London: George Harrap, 1960.

Roper, Trevor H. (ed.). *The Goebbels Diaries: The Last Days*. London: Book Club Associates, 1978.

Ross, Lieutenant-Colonel Richard M. *The History of the 1st Battalion Cameron Highlanders of Ottawa (MG)*. Ottawa: Published by the regiment, 1948.

Ross, Richard M. *The History of the 1st Battalion Cameron Highlanders of Ottawa (MG)*. Ottawa: Published by the regiment, 1948.

Rowland, Barry. *Herbie and Friends: Cartoons in Wartime*. Toronto: Natural Heritage/Natural History, 1990.

Rowland, Barry and J. Douglas MacFarlane. *The Maple Leaf Forever: The Story of Canada's Foremost Armed Forces Newspaper*. Toronto: Natural Heritage, 1987.

Roy, R.H. *The Seaforth Highlanders of Canada, 1919–1965*. Vancouver: Published by the regiment, 1969.

Roy, R.H. *Sinews of Steel: The History of the British Columbia Dragoons*. Kelowna: Published by the regiment, 1965.

Ryder, Rowland. *Oliver Leese*. London: Hamish, 1987.

Sarty, Roger. *Canada and the Battle of the Atlantic*. Montreal: Art Global, 1998.

Saward, Dudley. *"Bomber" Harris: The Story of Marshal of the Royal Air Force, Sir Arthur Harris, Bt, GCB, OBE, AFC, LLD, Air Officer Commanding-in-Chief, Bomber Command, 1942–1945*. London: Cassell, 1984.

Schull, John Joseph. *The Far Distant Ships: An Official Account of Canadian Naval Operations in the Second World War*. Ottawa: King's Printer, 1950.

Sheffield, R. Scott. *A Search for Equity: A Study of the Treatment Accorded to First Nations Veterans and Dependents of the Second World War and Korea*. Ottawa: Final Report of the National Round Table on First Nations Veterans' Issues, 2000.

Shephard, Ben. *The Long Road Home: The Aftermath of the Second World War*. London: Bodley Head, 2010.

Smith, Kenneth B. *Duffy's Regiment*. Don Mills: T.H. Best, 1983.

Smith, Leonard V. *Between Mutiny and Obedience*. Princeton: Princeton University Press, 1994.

Smith, Wilfred I. *Code Word: Canloan*. Toronto: Dundurn, 1992.

Snowie, J.A. *Bloody Buron*. Erin: Boston Mills, 1984.

Snyder, Timothy. *Bloodlands: Europe between Hitler and Stalin*. New York: Basic, 2010.

Stacey, C.P. *Arms, Men and Governments: The War Policies of Canada, 1939–1945*. Ottawa: Queen's Printer, 1970.

Stacey, C.P. *A Date with History: Memoirs of a Canadian Historian*. Ottawa: Deneau, 1983.

Stacey, C.P. *Six Years of War: The Army in Canada, Britain and the Pacific*. Ottawa: Queen's Printer, 1955.

Stacey, C.P. and Barbara Wilson. *The Half Million: The Canadians in Britain, 1939–1946*. Toronto: University of Toronto Press, 1987.

Stark, Lt. F. *A History of the First Hussar Regiment, 1856–1945*. Published by the regiment, 1951.

Stevens, G.R. *Princess Patricia's Canadian Light Infantry, 1919–1957*. Griesbach: Hamilton Gault Barracks, Historical Committee, 1958.

Stevens, G.R. *The Royal Canadian Regiment, volume II (1933–1966)*. London: London Printing, 1967.

Stursberg, Peter. *The Sound of War: Memoirs of a CBC Correspondent*. Toronto: University of Toronto Press, 1993.

Tascona, Bruce. *Little Black Devils: A History of the Royal Winnipeg Rifles*. Canada: Frye, 1983.

Taylor, Frederick. *Dresden: Tuesday 13 February 1945*. London: Bloomsbury, 2004.

Tedder, Lord. *With Prejudice*. London: Cassell, 1966.

Terraine, John. *The Right of the Line: The Royal Air Force in the European War, 1939–1945*. London: Hodder & Stoughton, 1985.

Tooze, Adam. *The Wages of Destruction: The Making and Breaking of the Nazi Economy*. London: Allen Lane, 2006.

Torontow, Cy (ed.). *There I Was: A Collection of Reminiscences by Members of the Ottawa Jewish Community Who Served in World War II*. Ottawa: Jewish War Veterans and the Ottawa Jewish Historical Society, 1999.

Tucker, Gilbert Norman. *The Naval Service of Canada: Its Official History. Volume 2: Activities on Shore during the Second World War*. Ottawa: King's Printer, 1952.

Uziel, Daniel. *Arming the Luftwaffe: The German Aviation Industry in World War II*. Jefferson: McFarland, 2012.

Vance, Jonathan. *Death So Noble: Memory, Meaning, and the First World War*. Vancouver: UBC Press, 1997.

Vance, Jonathan (ed.). *Encyclopedia of Prisoners of War and Internment*. Santa Barbara: ABC-CLIO, Inc., 2000.

Vanguard: The Fort Garry Horse in the Second World War. Doetinchem, Netherlands: Uitgevers-Maatschappij "C. Nisset," 1945.

Wakelam, Randall T. *The Science of Bombing: Operational Research in RAF Bomber Command*. Toronto: University of Toronto Press, 2009.

Watt, Frederic B. *In All Respects Ready: The Merchant Navy and the Battle of the Atlantic, 1940–1945.* Scarborough: Prentice-Hall Canada, 1985.

Webster, Sir Charles and Noble Frankland, *The Strategic Air Offensive against Germany*, volume I. London: HMSO, 1961.

Weigley, Russell F. *Eisenhower's Lieutenants: The Campaign of France and Germany, 1944–1945.* Bloomington: Indiana University Press, 1981.

Weinberg, Gerhard. *A World at Arms: A Global History of World War II.* Cambridge: Cambridge University Press, 1994.

Wells, Mark K. *Courage and Air Warfare: The Allied Aircrew Experience in the Second World War.* London: Frank Cass, 1995.

Wheeler, William J. *Flying Under Fire: Canadian Fliers Recall the Second World War.* Calgary: Fifth House, 2001.

Whitaker, W. Denis and Shelagh Whitaker. *Rhineland: The Battle to Win the War.* Toronto: Stoddart, 1989.

Whitby, Michael (ed.). *The Admirals: Canada's Senior Naval Leadership in the Twentieth Century.* Toronto: Dundurn, 2006.

Whitsed, Roy J. *Canadians: A Battalion at War.* Mississauga: Burlington Books, 1996.

Wieviorka, Olivier. *Normandy: The Landings to the Liberation of Paris.* Cambridge: Belknap Press of Harvard University Press, 2008.

Wilmot, Chester. *The Struggle for Europe.* London: Collins, 1954.

Wilt, Alan. *The Atlantic Wall: Rommel's Plan to Stop the Allied Invasion.* New York: Enigma, 2004.

Wood, James A. *We Move Only Forward: Canada, the United States, and the First Special Service Force, 1942–1944.* St. Catharines: Vanwell, 2006.

Wyatt, Bernie. *Maximum Effort: The Big Bombing Raids.* Erin: Boston Mills, 1986.

Wyatt, Bernie. *Two Wings and a Prayer.* Erin: Boston Mills, 1984.

Zaloga, Steven J. *Bagration 1944: The Destruction of Army Group Centre.* Oxford: Osperey, 1996.

Zetterling, Niklas. *Normandy 1944: Germany Military Organization, Combat Power, and Organizational Effectiveness.* Winnipeg: J.J. Fedorowicz, 2000.

DISSERTATIONS AND THESES

Caravaggio, Angelo N. "Commanding the Green Centre Line in Normandy: A Case Study of Division Command in the Second World War." Ph.D. dissertation: Wilfrid Laurier University, 2009.

Cessford, Michael Pearson. "*Hard in the Attack*: The Canadian Army in Sicily and Italy, July 1943–June 1944." Ph.D. dissertation: Carleton University, 1996.

Eddy, Charles Allan. "Before They Were the D-Day Dodgers: 1st Canadian Infantry Division and Operation CHESTERFIELD." Master's thesis: University of New Brunswick, 2009.

Engen, Rob. "The Canadian Soldier: Combat Motivation in the Second World War, 1943–1945." Ph.D. dissertation: Queen's University, 2014.

Ferguson, Malcolm. "Canada's Response: The Making and Remaking of the National War Memorial." Master's thesis: Carleton University, 2012.

Field, Vincenzo. "Explaining Armageddon: Popular Perceptions of Air Power in Canada and Britain and the Destruction of Germany, 1939–45." Master's thesis: University of New Brunswick, 2003.

Gann, Emily. "Correspondence, Camaraderie, and Community: The Second World War for a Mother and Son." Master's thesis: Carleton University, 2012.

Hayes, Geoffrey. "The Development of the Canadian Army Officer Corps, 1939–1945." Ph.D. dissertation: University of Western Ontario, 1992.

Malone, Daniel P. "Breaking Down the Wall: Bombarding FORCE E and Naval Fire Support on JUNO Beach." Master's thesis: University of New Brunswick, 2005.

Nuttal, Leslie. "Canadianization and the No. 6 Bomber Group RCAF." Ph.D. dissertation: University of Calgary, 1990.

Souchen, Alex. "Beyond D-Day: Maintaining Morale in the 3rd Canadian Infantry Division, June–July 1944." Master's thesis: University of Ottawa, 2010.

Windsor, Lee. "Anatomy of Victory: Allied Containment Strategy and the Battle for the Gothic Line." Ph.D. dissertation: University of New Brunswick, 2006.

Vourkoutiotis, Vasilis. "The German Armed Forces Supreme Command and British and American Prisoners-of-War, 1939–1945: Policy and Practice." Ph.D. dissertation: McGill University, 2000.

CANADIAN SERVICE PERSONNEL MEMOIRS, PUBLISHED AND SELF-PUBLISHED

Bannerman, Gordie. *Memoirs of Gordie Bannerman—World War II*. Unpublished memoir.

Barr, J.W.B. *From Barnyard to Battlefield and Beyond: The Story of a Military Medical Officer*. Ottawa: Borealis, 2005.

Bell, Gordon (ed.). *We went where they sent us ... and did as we were told (most of the time)*. Lantzville, BC: Oolichan, 2000.

Biggs, Stan. *As Luck Would Have It in War and Peace: Memoirs, 1913 to 2007*. Self-published, 2007.

Bishop, Murray Winston and Arthur Adelbert Bishop. *The Bishop Brothers of New Minas in World War Two*. Self-published, 2003.

Blackburn, George G. *The Guns of Normandy: A Soldier's Eye View, France 1944*. Toronto: McClelland & Stewart, 1995.

Bourassa, Rollie (ed.). *One Family's War: The Wartime Letters of Clarence Bourassa, 1940–1944.* Regina: Canadian Plains Research Centre, 2010.

Burns, E.L.M. *General Mud: Memoirs of Two World Wars.* Toronto: Clarke, Irwin, 1970.

Butcher, Harry. *My Three Years with Eisenhower.* New York: Simon & Schuster, 1946.

Cameron, Craig B. *Born Lucky: RSM Harry Fox, MBE: One D-Day Dodger's Story.* St. Catharines: Vanwell, 2005.

Cederberg, Fred. *The Long Road Home: The Autobiography of a Canadian Soldier in World War II.* Toronto: General, 1984.

Chadderton, H. Clifford. *Excuse Us! Herr Schicklgruber: A Memoir of an Officer who Commanded an Infantry Company of the Royal Winnipeg Rifles (Canadian Army) in Normandy.* Ottawa: War Amputations of Canada, 2004.

Chapman, J.K. *River Boy at War.* Fredericton: Goose Lane, 1985.

Clark, John Irwin. *My Memoirs of the War Years.* Self-published, 2005.

Coldridge, Stan. *Recollections of Stan Coldridge (Halifax Pilot).* Self-published, 2008.

Crandell, John. *Thomas Merlin Crandell, Time Line.* Self-published, n.d.

Crozier, Robert. *Looking Backward: A Memoir.* Self-published, 1998.

Culley, Ray. *His Memories Can Survive.* Self-published, 2003.

Curry, Frank. *War at Sea: A Canadian Seaman on the North Atlantic.* Toronto: Lugus, 1990.

Cutbill, Colonel Edward William. *A Brown Job's War.* Self-published, 2007.

Danson, Barney. *Not Bad for a Sergeant: The Memoirs of Barney Danson.* Toronto: Dundurn, 2002.

Davis, Eldon S. *An Awesome Silence: A Gunner Padre's Journey through the Valley of the Shadow.* Carp: Creative Bound, 1991.

Didmon, Tom. *Lucky Guy: Memoirs of a World War II Canadian Soldier.* Victoria: Trafford, 2000.

Dunn, Hunter. *Memoirs of a WW II Armoured Officer.* Self-published, 2005.

Edmondson, John S. *The Pawns of War: Personal Account and Study of Aspects of the Attack on Verrières Ridges by the South Saskatchewan Regiment on 20 July 1944 by Lt. Col. John S. Edmondson.* Self-published, 2003.

Eisenhower, Dwight D. *Crusade in Europe.* Garden City: Doubleday, 1948.

Emmott, Norman. *One Foot on the Ground.* Toronto: Lugus Publications, 1992.

Everard, Hedley. *A Mouse in My Pocket.* Picton: Valley Floatplane Services, 1988.

Frost, C. Sydney. *Once a Patricia.* St. Catharines: Vanwell, 1988.

Galloway, Strome. *Bravely into Battle.* Don Mills: Stoddart, 1988.

Galloway, Srome. *The General Who Never Was.* Belleville: Mika, 1981.

Gardam, John (ed.). *Fifty Years After* (Burnstown: General Store, 1990.

Gordon, David A. *The Stretcher Bearers.* Stroud: Pacesetter, 1995.

Gray, John Morgan. *Fun Tomorrow: Learning to Be a Publisher and Much Else.* Toronto: Macmillan of Canada, 1978.

Hancock, Glen. *Charley Goes to War: A Memoir*. Kentville: Gaspereau, 2004.

Harding, John. *The Dancin' Navigator*. Guelph: Asterisk, 1988.

Harvey, J. Douglas. *Boys, Bombs, and Brussels Sprouts: A Knees-up, Wheels-up Chronicle of World War II*. Toronto: McClelland & Stewart, 1981.

Hewer, Howard. *In for a Penny, in for a Pound: The Adventures and Misadventures of a Wireless Operator in Bomber Command*. Toronto: Anchor Canada, 2004.

Hillsman, John Burwell. *Eleven Men and a Scalpel*. Winnipeg: Columbia Press, 1948.

Irwin, Walter. *World War II Memoirs*. Self-published, 1998.

Jackson, W.G.F. *Alexander of Tunis as Military Commander*. London: Batsford, 1971.

Jenson, Latham B. *Tin Hats, Oilskins & Seaboots: A Naval Journey, 1938–1945*. Toronto: Robin Brass Studio, 2000.

Jones, Gwilym (ed.). *Living History Chronicles*. Burnstown: General Store, 2001.

Jones, Gwilym. *To the Green Fields Beyond: A Soldier's Story*. Burnstown: General Store, 1993.

Jones, Harlo. *Bomber Pilot: A Canadian Youth's War*. St. Catharines: Vanwell, 2001.

Kensett, Robert C. *A Walk in the Valley*. Burnstown: General Store, 2002.

King, Stephen L.V. (ed.). *Your Loving Son: Letters of an RCAF Navigator*. Regina: Canadian Plains Research Centre, 2002.

Kipp, Charles D. *Because We Are Canadians: A Battlefield Memoir*. Vancouver: Douglas & McIntyre, 2003.

Kitching, George. *Mud and Green Fields: The Memoirs of Major General George Kitching*. Langley: Battleline, 1986.

Lamont, A.G.W. *Guns Above, Steam below in Canada's Navy of WW II: In Canada's Navy of W.W.II*. Self-published, 2002.

Lane, Ray W. *In Chariots of Iron*. Self-published, 2009.

Law, C. Anthony. *White Plumes Astern: The Short, Daring Life of Canada's MTB Flotilla*. Halifax, NS: Nimbus, 1989.

Lawrence, Hal. *A Bloody War: One Man's Memories of the Canadian Navy, 1939–45*. Toronto: Macmillan of Canada, 1979.

Lawruck, Ron and Merla Lawruck. *For Love and Country: A Canadian Soldier's Story, A Biography of Ted Patrick*. Self-published, 2011.

Leddy, Mary Jo. *Memories of War, Promise of Peace*. Toronto: Lester & Orpen Dennys, 1989.

MacDonell, George S. *One Soldier's Story (1939–1945): From the Fall of Hong Kong to the Defeat of Japan*. Toronto: Dundurn, 2002.

Mackereth, Ben. *To Do or Die*. Self-published, 1993.

Margison, John. *H.M.C.S. Sackville, 1942–1943: Memoirs of a Gunnery Officer*. Cobalt: Highway Book Shop, 1998.

Martin, Charles Cromwell. *Battle Diary: From D-Day and Normandy to the Zuider Zee and VE*. Toronto: Dundurn, 1994.

Matthews, Georgina (ed.). *Wartime Letters of Flt. Lieut. D.J. Matthews to his wife 1943–1945*. Guelph: Georgina H. Matthews, 2003.

McDonald, B. Graham. *Have No Fear: "B.G." Is Here*. Belleville: Self-published, 2007.

McDougall, Robert L. *A Narrative of War: From the Beaches of Sicily to the Hitler Line with the Seaforth Highlanders of Canada, 10 July 1943–8 June 1944*. Kemptville: Golden Dog, 1996.

McIntosh, Dave. *Terror in the Starboard Seat*. Don Mills: General, 1980.

Memories on Parade: Aircrew Recollections of World War II. Winnipeg: Wartime Pilots' and Observations' Association, 1995.

Miseferi, Frank. *I Never Forget: Memoirs of Frank Miseferi, World War 2 Heavy Bomber Air Gunner*. Self-published, 2006.

Mitchell, Howard. *My War*. Self-published, n.d.

Morrison, Les. *Of Luck and War: From Squeegee Kid to Bomber Pilot in World War II*. Burnstown: General Store, 1999.

Mowat, Farley. *And No Birds Sang*. Toronto: McClelland & Stewart, 1979.

Nixon, Charles Patrick. *A River in September: HMCS Chaudière, 1943–1945*. Montreal: John Mappin, 1995.

O'Brien, John. *Through the Gates of Hell and Back: The Private War of a Footslogger from "The Avenue."* Halifax: New World, 2010.

Patterson, John. *World War II: An Airman Remembers*. Burnstown: General Store, 2000.

Pearce, Donald. *Journal of a War*. Toronto: Macmillan, 1965.

Peden, Murray. *A Thousand Shall Fall*. Stittsville: Canada's Wings, 1979.

Peel, Ron. *My Time at War ... and a little bit more*. Self-published, 2004.

Proctor, Frank. *I Was There: An Autobiography*. Self-published, 1999.

Reid, George A. *Speed's War: A Canadian Soldier's Memoir of World War II*. Royston: Madrona, 2007.

Roberts, James Alan. *The Canadian Summer: The Memoirs of James Alan Roberts*. Toronto: University of Toronto Bookroom, 1981.

Sawdon, Robert Gordon. *Another River to Cross*. Self-published, 2000.

Scislowski, Stanley. *Not All of Us Were Brave*. Toronto: Dundurn, 1997.

Shawcross, Ronald Gendall. *What Was it Like??: A Rifleman Remembers*. Victoria: Trafford, 2004.

Sherwood, A.G. *Flying 40 Missions with Red: Memoirs of WWII*. Penticton: Durango, 2005.

Silver, L. Ray. *Last of the Gladiators: A World War II Bomber Navigator's Story*. Shrewsbury: Airlife, 1995.

Skipper, Robert. *On a Wing and a Prayer until Our Last Bombing Mission*. Self-published, 1996.

Smith, Sydney Percival with David Scott Smith. *Lifting the Silence: A World War II RCAF Bomber Pilot Reunites with his Past*. Toronto: Dundurn, 2010.

Tansley, Donald D. *Growing Up and Going to War: 1925–1945*. Waterloo: Laurier Centre for Military Strategic and Disarmament Studies, 2005.

Thompson, Walter R. *Lancaster to Berlin*. London: Goodall, 1985.

Trenton, Louis Lazarus. *My Eyes Have Seen*. Self-published, 2008.

Turnbull, Fred. *The Invasion Diaries*. Kemptville: Veterans Publications, 2007.

Wilkinson, Alta R. (ed.). *Ottawa to Caen: Letters from Arthur Campbell Wilkinson*. Ottawa: Tower, 1947.

Wilmot, Laurence. *Through the Hitler Line: Memoirs of an Infantry Chaplain*. Waterloo: Wilfrid Laurier University Press, 2003.

Vokes, Chris. *Vokes: My Story*. Ottawa: Gallery, 1985.

INDEX

CREDITS

Unless otherwise stated, images are from the author's collection. Permission to reproduce the following copyrighted works is gratefully acknowledged.

Page 15: Department of National Defence, PL-144256

Page 18: Department of National Defence, PL-29474

Page 20: Department of National Defence, PL-42536

Page 32: Department of National Defence, PL-144281

Page 41: Library Archives Canada, C-014171

Page 56: Library Archives Canada, 188911

Page 65: Library Archives Canada, PA-129764

Page 69: Library Archives Canada, 128986

Page 77: Library Archives Canada, PA-130353

Page 84: Library Archives Canada, PA-115198

Page 86: Department of National Defence, 29249-N

Page 100: Department of National Defence, PL-144257

Page 102: Library Archives Canada, PA-131800

Page 103: Library Archives Canada, 116838

Page 105: Department of National Defence, PL-61357

Page 111: Library Archives Canada, PA-132456

Page 122: Department of National Defence, PL-42818

Page 142: Laurier Centre for Military Strategic and Disarmament Studies

Page 146: Laurier Centre for Military Strategic and Disarmament Studies

Page 187: Library Archives Canada, PA-131405

Page 189: Library Archives Canada, 204655

Page 191: Library Archives Canada, 151743

Page 203: Department of National Defence, 758
Page 228: Library Archives Canada, 10869428
Page 231: Library Archives Canada, PA-196285
Page 234: Library Archives Canada, PA-196287
Page 236: Department of National Defence, 33872
Page 245: Laurier Centre for Military Strategic and Disarmament Studies
Page 273: Laurier Centre for Military Strategic and Disarmament Studies
Page 280: Library Archives Canada, PA-129763
Page 282: Library Archives Canada, PA-189888
Page 298: Library Archives Canada, PA-160454
Page 299: Department of National Defence, ZK-544
Page 345: Library Archives Canada, 319668
Page 368: Laurier Centre for Military Strategic and Disarmament Studies
Page 379: Department of National Defence, PA-168908
Page 385: Library Archives Canada, 113908
Page 406: Department of National Defence, PA-131376
Page 415: Department of National Defence, PA-115236
Page 417: Library Archives Canada, C-049434